Wissenschaftliche Untersuchungen
zum Neuen Testament

Begründet von Joachim Jeremias und Otto Michel
Herausgegeben von
Martin Hengel und Otfried Hofius

36

The Name of God
and the Angel of the Lord

Samaritan and Jewish Concepts of Intermediation
and the Origin of Gnosticism

by

Jarl E. Fossum

J. C. B. Mohr (Paul Siebeck) Tübingen 1985

CIP-Kurztitelaufnahme der Deutschen Bibliothek

Fossum, Jarl E.:
The name of God and the Angel of the Lord: Samaritan and Jewish concepts of intermediation and the origin of gnosticism / by Jarl E. Fossum. –
Tübingen: Mohr, 1985.
  (Wissenschaftliche Untersuchungen zum Neuen Testament; 36)
  ISBN 3-16-144789-1
  ISSN 0512-1604

NE: GT

Printed in Germany. – Typeset by Sam Boyd Enterprise, Singapore; printed by Gulde-Druck GmbH, Tübingen; bound by Heinrich Koch KG, Tübingen.

Foreword

This book has been some time in coming. It is a revised version (essentially an abridgement) of my doctoral dissertation submitted to the Faculty of Theology at the University of Utrecht in 1982, but already at the International Conference on Gnosticism at Yale, March 28-31, 1978, I presented the principal material and argument in a research paper, "The Origin of the Concept of the Demiurge", read in the section on Judaism and Gnosticism.

The main objective of the work is to develop and bear out the theory of Professor Gilles Quispel that the concept of the Gnostic demiurge was forerun by Jewish ideas about the creative agency of the hypostasized divine Name and of the Angel of the Lord, who was the possessor of the Tetragrammaton. For the first time in a treatise on Gnostic origins, the Samaritans and their traditions have been made the focal point. Since non-specialists often misconstrue the identity and religion of the Samaritans, I have felt it necessary to preface the central Chapters with a fairly comprehensive introduction to what has been termed "the Samaritan problem". After having dealt with the main aspects of that question, the introductory Chapter broaches the view that Dositheism, the lay-movement among the Samaritans, was a forcing-bed for Gnosticism.

Since no Samaritan source pre-dates the rise of Gnosticism, my thesis might seem to amount to a mistake like that of the *religionsgeschichtliche Schule*, which read nearly every religious text of the Hellenistic world through Manichean glasses and postulated the existence of a pre-Christian Iranian and/or Babylonian Gnosticism. However, we do not have to postulate the existence of Samaritanism in the first century C.E.; by that time, the Samaritan community had been in existence for more than 200 years. And even those who do not accept the reports of the Church Fathers that the author of Gnosticism was Simon Magus — who is associated with Dositheus, the arch-heretic among the Samaritans — will have to admit that the account in *Acts* ch. viii evidences a peculiar form of Samaritanism.

Furthermore, while the history of religions school only has been able to make assumptions in the realm of the history of ideas (one may think of the notion of the ascent of the soul to heaven), a discussion of the Samaritan evidence will reveal a historical-genetic connection between Samaritan tradition and Gnosticism. This, of course, does not mean that each and every form of Gnosticism is derived from Samaritanism, and I have supplemented the picture in Part II with details from Judaism, within the wider phenomenon of which Samaritanism has to be considered. Finally, as is shown in the two Chapters which I have added to the central part of the work, Jewish material, which is in part pre-Christian, corroborates the thesis that Gnosticism developed traditions from Israelite-Jewish religion.

Several people contributed to the production of the dissertation. My obligation to Professor Quispel, my *Doktorvater*, is obvious. I have cited his works when specifically relevant, but his advice and encouragement underlie the whole thesis.

For help in questions about Samaritan religion and exegesis, I am indebted to the quick answers of Professors John Bowman, Melbourne, and Simeon Lowy, Leeds. I am also grateful to my friends, Dr. Alan D. Crown and Father Dr. Paul Stenhouse, both of Sydney, for their willingness to aid me in my enquiries into the Samaritan problem. It is also my agreeable duty to thank Professor Hans Gerhard Kippenberg, Groningen, for having read Part I and II and offered critical comments and suggestions for improvement. (At that time, Part I even included a lengthy survey of the research on Gnosticism which eventually had to be left out in the interest of not overburdening the reader.)

Last but far from least, I express my gratitude to Professor Alan F. Segal, Barnard College, Columbia University. His doctoral dissertation was just completed when I began to work on mine, and his research and personal communications have been of great support and inspiration in the formulation of my view that there were proto-Gnostic heretics believing in "two powers in heaven" among the Samaritans as well as in the community with which the rabbis were immediately concerned.

In the period after the completion of the dissertation, Professors Ugo Bianchi, Rome, and Roel van den Broek, Utrecht, have shown themselves helpful. I am of course also very grateful to the editors of WUNT for the acceptance of this work for publication in their series. Professor Martin Hengel must be thanked in particular for his encouragement during the revision of the work. I would also like to thank Mr. Ulrich Gaebler at J.C.B. Mohr (Paul Siebeck) for his care in shepherding the book through the press. Dr. Pieter W. van der Horst, Utrecht, wonderfully volunteered to read the proofs with me and tracked down several errors which had evaded my notice; naturally I appreciate his helpful work very much.

There is yet one person to be acknowledged, *viz.*, my daughter, Maria Fossum Johns. During formative years, she has shown a remarkable forbearance with an often preoccupied or unavailable father.

Finally, I would like to express my thankfulness to the Norwegian Research Council for Science and the Humanities for the provision of the *Druckkostenzuschuss* required by the publisher as well as for a grant which made the typing and offset-printing of my dissertation possible.

Bilthoven, The Netherlands   *Jarl E. Fossum*
Ascension Day, 1985

Contents

Foreword. iii
Contents v
Abbreviations. vii

Part One: Introduction 1
Chapter One: The Problem 3

Part Two: The Samaritan Mould of Gnosticism. 25
Chapter Two: Introduction: The Samaritans and their Religion 27
    The Origin of Samaritanism. 27
    The Origin and Development of Dositheism 45
    The Influence of Dositheism 55

Chapter Three: The Name of God 76
    The Samaritan Logos Doctrine: The Creation through the Name 76
    The Concept of the Divine Name 84
    The Investiture with the Name I: The Samaritan Evidence. 87
    The Investiture with the Name II: Non-Samaritan Evidence. 95
    The Hypostasized Name 106
    Simon Magus as the Eschatological Prophet like Moses 112
    The Ascension of the Prophet like Moses 129
    The Apostle of God. 144
    Samaritanism and "Iranian" Gnosticism. 156
    Simon Magus as "the Great Power (of God)" 162

Chapter Four: The Angel of the Lord 192
    Angel Cult and Polemics against Demiurgic Notions 192
    The Evidence of Philo 197
    Rabbinic Evidence. 204
    Extraneous Evidence for Angelic Assistance in Creation 211
    The Development of Gnostic Dualism 213
    The Angel of the Lord in Samaritanism 220

Part Three: The Jewish Evidence 239
Chapter Five: The Name of God. 241
    The Golem Legend and the Demiurgic Rôle of the Alphabet 241
    The "Sealing" of the Creation with the Divine Name 245
    The Creation through the Name 253

Chapter Six: The Angel of the Lord 257
    The Demiurgic Oath and Name of Michael 257
    The Angel and Apostle Gabriel. 259
    The Heavenly Man. 266
    The Ascension to Heaven and Reception of the Name 292
    Gnostic Intermediaries 301
    The Angel of the Lord 307
    Ariel and Michael in Gnosticism 321
    The Magharians. 329
    Wider Scope and Conclusion 332

Bibliography. 339

Indexes 365

Abbreviations

Anthologies frequently cited, Encyclopediae, Periodicals, and Series

AAA	R.A. Lipsius, ed., *Acta Apostolorum Apocrypha*, I, Leipzig, 1891, reprinted Hildesheim, 1959; M. Bonnet, ed., II/1-II/2, Leipzig, 1898/1903, reprinted Hildesheim, 1959
AB	Analecta Biblica (Rome)
AB	Anchor Bible (New York)
ADAIK	Abhandlungen des Deutschen Archäologischen Instituts, Kairo
AET	Arbeiten zur Evangelischen Theologie
AEWK	*Allgemeine Encyklopädie der Wissenschaften und Künste,* Leipzig
AGB	Association Guillaume Budé
AGJU	Arbeiten zur Geschichte des Antiken Judentums und des Urchristentums
AGSU	Arbeiten zur Geschichte des späteren Judentums und des Urchristentums
AHL: TS	Academy of the Hebrew Language: Texts and Studies
AJT	*American Journal of Theology*
AKBAW	Abhandlungen der königlich bayerischen Akademie der Wissenschaften
AKGWG	Abhandlungen der königlichen Gesellschaft der Wissenschaften zu Göttingen
AKM	Abhandlungen für die Kunde des Morgenlandes
ALC-RDS	Ayer Lectures of the Colgate-Rochester Divinity School
ALUOS	*Annual of Leeds University Oriental Society,* Leiden
A-NF	A. Roberts & J. Donaldson, translation ed., *The Ante-Nicene Fathers*, revised American edition by A. Cleveland Coxe, Buffalo, 1884 ff., reprinted Grand Rapids
ANRW	*Aufstieg und Niedergang der römischen Welt,* Berlin & New York
AO	Anecdota Oxoniensia
APAT	E. Kautzsch, translation ed., *Die Apokryphen und Pseudepigraphen des Alten Testaments,* I (Die Apokryphen)-II (Die Pseudepigraphen), Tübingen, 1900, reprinted 1921
APOT	R.H. Charles, translation ed., *The Apocrypha and Pseudepigrapha of the Old Testament,* I (Apocrypha)-II (Pseudepigrapha), Oxford, 1913 and reprints
ASNU	Acta Seminarii Neotestamentici Upsaliensis
ATA	Alttestamentliche Abhandlugen
AT	Arbeiten zur Theologie
AT-F-G	K.W. Tröger, ed., *Altes Testament-Frühjudentum-Gnosis,* Berlin, 1980
ATR	*Anglican Theological Review*
BA	*Biblical Archeologist*

BASOR	*Bulletin of the American Schools of Oriental Research*
BC	The Beginnings of Christianity, ed. by F.J. Foakes Jackson & K. Lake
BCNH	Bibliothèque copte de Nag Hammadi
BETL	Bibliotheca Ephemeridum Theologicarum Lovaniensium
BGBE	Beiträge zur Geschichte der biblischen Exegese
BH	A. Jellinek, ed., בית המדרש, I-IV, Leipzig, 1853-57, and V-VI, Vienna, 1873/77; reprinted in a two-volume edition (vol. I: I-III; vol.II: IV-VI), with the pagination of the original, Jerusalem, 1938, re-issued 1967
BJRL	*Bulletin of John Ryland's Library*
BKV	Bibliothek der Kirchenväter
BL	Bohlen Lectures
BM	S.A. Wertheimer, ed., בתי מדרשות, I-II, 2nd enlarged and amended edition by A.J. Wertheimer, Jerusalem, 1954
BNTC	Black's New Testament Commentaries
BO	Biblica et Orientalia
BO	*Bibliotheca Orientalis*
BOS	Bonner orientalistische Studien
BS	Bollingen Series
BSR	Biblioteca di Scienze Religiose
BWANT	Beiträge zur Wissenschaft vom Alten und Neuen Testament
BZ	*Biblische Zeitschrift*
BZAW	Beihefte zur Zeitschrift für die alttestamentliche Wissenschaft
BZNW	Beihefte zur Zeitschrift für die neutestamentliche Wissenschaft
CB	Coniectanea Biblica
CBQ	*Catholic Biblical Quarterly*
CGTC	Cambridge Greek Testament Commentaries
CH	*Corpus Haereseologicum*
CLL	Classical Life and Letters
CRAI	*Comptes-Rendus de l'Académie des Inscriptions et Belles-Lettres*, Paris
CRB	Cahiers Revue Biblique
CSEL	Corpus Scriptorum Ecclesiasticorum Latinorum
CUF	Collection des Universités de France
EC	*Enciclopedia Cattolica*, The Vatican
EFERE	Édition de la Fondation Égyptologique Reine Elisabeth
EHPR	Études d'histoire et de philosophie religieuses publiées par la faculté de théologie protestante de l'université de Strasbourg
EI	*Eretz Israel*
EJ	*Encyclopaedia Judaica*, Jerusalem, 1971
E-J	*Eranos-Jahrbuch*, –XXXVII, Zürich; XXXVIII–, Leiden
EKK	Evangelisch-katholischer Kommentar zum Neuen Testament
EL	*Ephemerides Liturgicae*
EPRO	Études préliminaires aux religions orientales dans l'Empire Romain
ExT	*Expository Times*

ET	*Evangelische Theologie*
ETL	*Ephemerides Theologicae Lovanienses*
FDV	Franz Delitzsch-Vorlesungen
FRLANT	Forschungen zur Religion und Literatur des Alten und Neuen Testaments
GCS	Griechischen christlichen Schriftsteller der ersten (drei) Jahrhunderte
GG	K. Rudolph, ed., *Gnosis und Gnostizismus* (WF, CCLXII), Darmstadt, 1975
GGA	*Göttingische Gelehrte Anzeigen*
Gnosis, I-II	W. Foerster, translation ed., *Gnosis,* I (Patristic Evidence)-II (Coptic and Mandean Sources), English Translation ed. by R. McL. Wilson, Oxford, 1972/74
Gnosis	B. Aland, *et al.,* ed., *Gnosis* (Festschrift für Hans Jonas), Göttingen, 1978
GNT	K.-W. Tröger, ed., *Gnosis und Neues Testament,* Berlin, 1973
GPT	Growing Points in Theology
GTA	Göttinger Theologische Arbeiten
HNT	Handbuch zum Neuen Testament
HO	*Handbuch der Orientalistik,* Leiden
HR	G. Widengren & C.J. Bleeker, ed., *Historia Religionum,* I (Religions of the Past)-II (Religions of the Present), Leiden, 1969
HS	Horae Soederblomianae
HSM	Harvard Semitic Monographs
HTKNT	Herders Theologischer Kommentar zum Neuen Testament
HTR	*Harvard Theological Review*
HTR: HDR	Harvard Theological Review: Harvard Dissertations in Religion
HTS	Harvard Theological Studies
HUCA	*Hebrew Union College Annual*
ICC	International Critical Commentary
IEJ	*Israel Exploration Journal*
IJMES	*International Journal of Middle East Studies*
JA	*Journal Asiatique*
JBL	*Journal of Biblical Literature*
JE	*The Jewish Encyclopedia,* New York
JJS	*Journal of Jewish Studies*
JPSA	Jewish Publication Society of America
JQR	*Jewish Quarterly Review*
JSF	Jahresbericht des jüdisch-theologischen Seminars "Fraenkel'scher Stiftung"
JSJ	*Journal for the Study of Judaism*
JSOR	*Journal of the Society of Oriental Research*
JTS	*Journal of Theological Studies*
JTSA	Jewish Theological Seminary of America

KKSANT	Kurzgefasster Kommentar zu den heiligen Schriften Alten und Neuen Testamentes
KNT	Kommentar zum Neuen Testament
KVHAH	Kungliga Vitterhets Historie och Antikvitets Akademiens Handlingar
LBS	Library of Biblical Studies
LCL	Loeb Classical Library
LJK	Library of Jewish Knowledge
LJL	Library of Jewish Literature
LL	Lutterworth Library
LUOS	Leeds University Oriental Society
M-D	*Maison-Dieu*
MG	Musée Guimet
MGWJ	*Monatsschrift für Geschichte und Wissenschaft des Judentums*
MHSChB	Manichäische Handschriften der Sammlung A. Chester Beatty
MHSMB	Manichäische Handschriften der Staatlichen Museen Berlin
MKKNT	Meyers kritisch-exegetischer Kommentar über das Neue Testament
MP	*Mélanges d'histoire des religions offerts à Henri-Charles Puech*, Paris, 1974
MR	Mythes et Religions
MS	Maitres Spirituels
MS	J.R. Hinnels, ed., *Mithraic Studies* (Proceedings of the First International Congress of Mithraic Studies), two volumes paginated as one, Manchester, 1975
MTS	Marburger Theologische Studien
NCB	New Century Bible
NEMBR	*Notices et extraits des manuscrits de la Bibliothèque du Roi*, Paris
NHS	Nag Hammadi Studies
NIC	New International Commentary on the New Testament
NT	*Novum Testamentum*
NTA	Neutestamentliche Abhandlungen
NTA	E. Hennecke, translation ed., *New Testament Apocrypha*, 3rd ed. by W. Schneemelcher, I (Gospels and Related Writings)-II (Writings relating to the Apostles, Apocalypses and Related Subjects), English Translation ed. by R. McL. Wilson, Oxford, 1963 (2nd impression 1973)/1965 (reprinted 1974)
NTD	Das Neue Testament Deutsch
NTT	*Nederlands Theologisch Tijdschrift*
NTL	New Testament Library
NTS	*New Testament Studies*
OG	U. Bianchi, ed., *Le Origini dello Gnosticismo* (Colloquio di Messina 13-18 Aprile 1966) (SHR: Suppl. *Numen*, XII), Leiden, 1967
OLZ	*Orientalische Literaturzeitung*

OrChr	*Oriens Christianus*
OrChrA	*Orientalia Christiana Analecta*
OS	*Oudtestamentische Studien,* Leiden
OTL	Old Testament Library
PAAJR	*Proceedings of the American Academy for Jewish Research*
PAW	Preussische Akademie der Wissenschaften zu Berlin
PBS	Programm des Breslauers Seminars
PELOV	Publications de l'École des Langues Orientales Vivantes
PEQ	*Palestine Exploration Quarterly*
PGM	K. Preisendanz, ed. & trans., *Papyri Graecae Magicae*, I-II, Berlin & Leipzig, 1928/31
PIASH	Proceedings of the Israel Academy of Sciences and Humanities
PL	Preacher's Library
PNTC	Pelican New Testament Commentaries
POT&TS	Pittsburgh Original Texts and Translation Series
PPF	Publications of the Perry Foundation
PSBA	*Proceedings of the Society for Biblical Archaeology*
PTMS	Pittsburgh Theological Monograph Series
PTS	Patristische Texte und Studien
PW	*Paulys Real-Encyclopädie der classischen Altertumswissenschaft*, new edition commenced by G. Wissowa, Stuttgart
QFAGG	Quellen und Forschungen zur alten Geschichte und Geographie
RA	J. Neusner, ed., *Religions in Antiquity* (Essays in Memory of Erwin Ramsdell Goodenough) (SHR: Suppl. *Numen*, XIV), Leiden, 1968
RAC	*Reallexikon für Antike und Christentum*, Stuttgart
RAS: OTF	Royal Asiatic Society: Oriental Translation Fund
RB	Recherches Bibliques
RB	*Revue Biblique*
RE	*Realencyklopädie für protestantische Theologie und Kirche*, Leipzig
REJ	*Revue des Etudes Juives*
RGG	*Die Religion in Geschichte und Gegenwart,* Tübingen
RGVV	Religionsgeschichtliche Versuche und Vorarbeiten
RHR	*Revue de l'Histoire des Religions*
RM	*Rheinisches Museum für Philologie*
RoB	*Religion och Bibel* (Nathan Söderblom-sällskapets Årsbok), Uppsala
RQ	*Revue de Qumrân*
RSR	*Recherches de Science Religieuse*
SBE	*Semana Bíblica Española*, Madrid
SBL: SCS	Society of Biblical Literature: Septuagint and Cognate Studies
SBL: TT	Society of Biblical Literature: Texts and Translations

SBT	Studies in Biblical Theology
SCGJ-I	Studien aus dem Carl Gustav Jung-Institut
SChr	Sources Chretiennes
SCL	Sather Classical Lectures
SGKA	Studien zur Geschichte und Kultur des Altertums
SGTK	Studien zur Geschichte der Theologie und der Kirche
SHAW	Sitzungsberichte der Heidelberger Akademie der Wissenschaften
SHR:Suppl. *Numen*	Studies in the History of Religion: Supplements to *Numen*
SIFIL	Studien aus dem Institut zur Förderung Israelitischer Literatur
SJ	Studia Judaica
SJLA	Studies in Judaism in Late Antiquity
SJT	*Scottish Journal of Theology*
SL	Schweich Lectures
SLJC	Schiff Library of Jewish Classics
SMR	*Studia Montis Regii*
SNTS	Society for New Testament Studies
SOAS: JL	School of Oriental and African Studies, University of London: Jordan Lectures in Comparative Religion
SP-B	Studia Post-Biblica
SPh	*Studia Philonica*
ST	Studi e Testi
STL	Sammlung theologischer Lehrbücher
Str.-Bill.	H.L. Strack & P. Billerbeck, *Kommentar zum Neuen Testament aus Talmud und Midrasch,* Munich
Studies	R. van den Broek & M.J. Vermaseren, ed., *Studies in Gnosticism and Hellenistic Religions* (Presented to Gilles Quispel on the Occasion of his 65th Birthday) (EPRO, 91), Leiden, 1981
Suppl. *NT*	Supplements to *Novum Testamentum*
Suppl. *VT*	Supplements to *Vetus Testamentum*
TB	Temple Books
TE	Textos y Estudios
TED	Translations of Early Documents
TGUOS	*Transactions. Glasgow University Oriental Society*
TB	Theologische Bücherei
TDNT	G. Kittel, ed., *Theological Dictionary of the New Testament,* I-IV, trans. by G.W. Bromiley, Grand Rapids, 1964-67 and reprints; G. Friedrich, ed., V-IX, trans. by G.W. Bromiley, Grand Rapids, 1968-74 and reprints
THNT	Theologischer Handkommentar zum Neuen Testament
TLZ	*Theologische Literaturzeitung*
TR	*Theologische Rundschau*
TS	*Theological Studies*
TSK	*Theologische Studien und Kritiken*
TW	Theologie und Wirklichkeit

TIES	Textes publiés par l'Institut d'Études Slaves
TS	Texts and Studies
TU	Texte und Untersuchungen
UMS	University of Michigan Studies
UNH-AII	Uitgaven van het Nederlands Historisch-Archaeologisch Instituut te Istanbul
UNT	Untersuchungen zum Neuen Testament
UUÅ	Uppsala Universitets Årsskrift
VD	*Verbum Domini*
VFVRUL	Veröffentlichungen des Forschungsinstituts für vergleichende Religionsgeschichte an der Universität Leipzig
VigChr	*Vigiliae Christianae*
VKAWA	Verhandelingen der Koninklijke Akademie van Wetenschappen te Amsterdam
VLÅ	*Vetenskapssocieteten i Lund, Årsbok,* Lund
VT	*Vetus Testamentum*
VoxTheol	*Vox Theologica*
WF	Wege der Forschung
WMANT	Wissenschaftliche Monographien zum Alten und Neuen Testament
WUNT	Wissenschaftliche Untersuchungen zum Neuen Testament
WW	*Wort und Wahrheit*
WZKM	*Wiener Zeitschrift für die Kunde des Morgenlandes*
WZUH	*Wissenschaftliche Zeitschrift der Martin-Luther-Universität Halle-Wittenberg*
YJS	Yale Judaica Series
ZDMG	*Zeitschrift der Deutschen Morgenländischen Gesellschaft*
ZDPV	*Zeitschrift des Deutschen Palästina-Vereins*
ZNW	*Zeitschrift für die neutestamentliche Wissenschaft*
ZPE	*Zeitschrift für Papyrologie und Epigraphik*
ZRGG	*Zeitschrift für Religion und Geistesgeschichte*
ZTK	*Zeitschrift für Theologie und Kirche*
ZWT	*Zeitschrift für wissenschaftliche Theologie*

Part One

Introduction

CHAPTER ONE

The Problem

After World War II, the theory of the Jewish origin of Gnosticism has been reasserted with reference to the Nag Hammadi texts[1]. But the theory is not undisputed. H. Jonas, who still adheres to the view of the *religionsgeschichtliche Schule*, which found the essence and origin of Gnosticism in a pre-Christian *Erlösungsmysterium* of Babylonian and/or Iranian derivation[2], maintains that Gnosticism shows an "antagonism to the Jewish people as a whole, a kind of metaphysical antisemitism, which precisely the sources most lavish in the use of Jewish motifs (at the same time the most archaic ones) evince."[3] If this is correct, it would be hard to explain how Gnosticism could have developed from Judaism.

Jonas cites the figure of the demiurge as a prime testimony to his thesis, since the demiurge "often is a clearly recognizable caricature of the Old Testament God," "a parody of the Biblical Creator"[4]. Jonas is right that the demiurge "is a gnostic symbol of the first order. In his general conception he reflects the gnostic contempt for the world... ."[5] The opposition between the highest God and the demiurge is the theological-metaphysical correlate to the ontological and anti-cosmic dualism of Gnosticism[6]. The demiurge's "place

---

1 Before the publication of the Nag Hammadi texts, the only scholar who thought that Gnosticism was of Jewish origin was E. Peterson; see, *e.g.*, Art. "Gnosi", in *EC*, VI, 1951, cols. 876 ff., especially cols. 880 f.

2 For Jonas' adherence to the history of religions school, see his declaration in *Gnosis und spätantiker Geist*, I (Die mythologische Gnosis) (FRLANT, 51), 3rd ed. with *Ergänzungsheft*, Göttingen, 1964, p. 24, n. 1.

3 "Delimitation of the Gnostic Phenomenon – Typological and Historical", in *OG*, p. 102 (=*GG*, p. 642). On the basis of the different texts, K.-W. Tröger wants to distinguish between "anti-Jewish attitude", "anti-Jewish conception", "anti-Jewish topos", *etc.* ("Gnosis und Judentum", in *AT-F-G*, p. 163). He rightly reminds us that "anti-Jewish" *topoi* must not automatically be seen as anti-Jewish polemics, since these *topoi* early became traditional material in Gnosticism. See also below, p. 17, for an interesting theory of E.H. Pagels. Tröger, p. 164, nn. 41 f., gives further references to Gnostic use of polemical mythology against the catholic Church.

4 "Delimitation", p. 96 and p. 97 (= *GG*, p. 634 and p. 635).

5 *Ibid.*, p. 96 (= *GG*, p. 634).

6 The anti-cosmic dualism is the fundamental characteristic of Gnosticism; see now

may be taken by a plurality of powers (e.g., the collective 'Seven'); but the complete absence of any such symbol for an inferior or degraded cause of the world, or of its particular order, or of its matter, would make one greatly hesitate to accept a doctrine as gnostic."[7]

The figure of the demiurge thus presents the greatest obstacle to the theory of the Jewish origin of Gnosticism. This is acknowledged by G. Quispel, a prime champion of this theory in our time: "It seems to me that the real issue is this: most Gnostics were against the Jewish God who created the world and gave the Law. Is it possible that this doctrine is of Jewish origin? This problem has not been discussed until now. Even those who do accept that many Gnostic views are to be derived from Judaism, seem to have avoided this theme."[8] The main objective of the present work is to demonstrate that the concept of the demiurge derives from Judaism.

The assertion that Gnosticism shows an "antisemitism" or an "antagonism to the Jewish people" is not veracious. The erring and blind in Gnostic literature are not the Jews, and there is relatively little polemic against the Jewish people in Gnostic texts as compared to what we find in Christian literature[9].

K. Rudolph, *Die Gnosis*, Göttingen, 1978, pp. 65, 67 f. This description of Gnosticism, of course, does not fit the teaching of all who called themselves "Gnostics" – *e.g.*, the orthodox or catholic Clement of Alexandria. The modern usage of the term "Gnostic" as a label for the somewhat amorphous group of religious systems refuted by the ancient Christian heresiologists and found in certain indigenous writings has a certain basis in Irenaeus, who ironically referred to the heretics and their teachings by this name, although actually only very few of the sects used the term to describe themselves. Still, this usage of the term need not be misleading, for these heretical groups (anti-dualists such as the Ebionites being excluded) do seem to have a common *genus*.

In attempting to give a definition of Gnosticism, however, it is easy to overlook differences between the various groups intended to be covered by the definition; see, of late, M. Smith, "The History of the Term Gnostikos", in B. Layton, ed., *The Rediscovery of Gnosticism* (Proceedings of the International Conference on Gnosticism at Yale, March 28-31, 1978) (SHR: Suppl. *Numen*, XLI), II, Leiden, 1981, pp. 806 ff., being a contribution to a discussion with Professor Ugo Bianchi which began with Smith's criticism of the definition of Gnosticism proposed by the Messina Colloquium. Moreover, the elaborate definition of the Messina Colloquium takes as its focal point "certain groups of systems of the Second Century A.D." (*OG*, p. XXVI) and thus leaves out teachings of the first century C.E. which definitely belong to the Gnostic movement. Smith's concern had been anticipated by R.P. Casey, who, however, considered it unwise to discontinue the established usage of the term "Gnosticism", because "behind it lies a definite historical reality" ("The Study of Gnosticism". *JTS*, 36, 1935, p. 60 (= *GG*, p. 373).

7 Jonas, "Delimitation", p. 96 (= *GG*, p. 634).

8 "The Origins of the Gnostic Demiurge", in P. Granfield & J.A. Jungmann, ed., *Kyriakon* (Festschrift Johannes Quasten), Münster Westf., 1970, p. 271.

9 Cp. W.C. van Unnik, "Gnosis und Judentum", in *Gnosis*, p. 85.

Still, Christianity began as a Jewish sect, so criticism of Judaism and the Jews does not rule out a Jewish origin. Furthermore, Christians also had the Jewish Bible as a holy book and worshipped the same God as the Jews; but there certainly were Christian Gnostics, and, by analogy, the possibility of the existence of a Jewish Gnosticism hostile to the ancestral traditions cannot be ruled out[10]. G. Scholem has suggested that Gnosticism, "or at least certain of its basic impulses, was a revolt, partly perhaps of Jewish origin, against anti-mythical Judaism, a late eruption of subterranean forces, which were all the more pregnant with myth for being cloaked in philosophy. In the second century of our era, classical Rabbinical Judaism banished this form of heresy... ."[11]

This was the time when the so-called anti-Jewish elements developed in Gnosticism, obviously provoked by the reaction of the orthodox. Thus Jonas, H.J.W. Drijvers, and others give a distorted picture of the Jewish heritage in Gnosticism when saying that "all" the Jewish motifs, which were taken especially from the first chapters of *Genesis,* are given an inverse meaning of the original import by means of a "protest-exegesis"[12]. In the "Book of Baruch" by Justin the Gnostic, for instance, the basic meaning of the Biblical narrative is preserved; the "protest-exegesis" obviously is a secondary phenomenon[13].

W.C. van Unnik is wrong that Gnostics did not treasure the Law or venerate Moses[14]. According to one account, Simon Magus, the alleged fountain-head of Gnosticism, venerated the Torah; and even Irenaeus, the first to give us any substantial knowledge about Simon's teaching, does not relate that the heretic

---

10 Tröger cites Mandeism as an example of the anti-Jewish sentiment of "entire Gnostic movements" (p. 163), and this shows how insignificant the presence of anti-Jewish elements is in the discussion of whether or not there was a Jewish Gnosticism, for Mandean literature contains even more polemic against the Christians than against the Jews.

11 *On the Kabbalah and Its Symbolism*, trans. by R. Manheim, New York, 1965, Schocken paperback edition, 1969 and reprints, p. 98. In the discussion following the paper of Professor Robert M. Grant at the Messina Colloquium, Jean Cardinal Daniélou voiced the opinion that the anti-cosmic attitude of Gnosticism was a result of an inner-Jewish revolt; see *OG*, p. 157.

12 See Drijvers, "The Origins of Gnosticism as a Religious and Historical Problem", *NTT*, 22, 1967/68, p. 347 (= *GG*, pp. 831 f.), referring to Jonas, "Response to G. Quispel's "Gnosticism and the New Testament"", in J.P. Hyatt, ed., *The Bible in Modern Scholarship* (Papers Read at the 100th Meeting of the Society of Biblical Literature, December 28-30, 1964), New York & Nashville, 1965, p. 288. The expression "protest-exegesis" is taken from K. Rudolph, "Randerscheinungen des Judentums und das Problem der Entstehung des Gnostizismus", *Kairos*, 9, 1967, p. 117 (= *GG*, p. 789).

13 See below, pp. 216, 305.

14 See *op. cit.*, pp. 80, 82.

made any detraction of the Law of *Moses*[15]. Cerinthus, another Gnostic of the first century C.E., enjoined the practice of circumcision and the keeping of the Sabbath, both of which are prescribed in the Torah[16].

In some of the writings from the Nag Hammadi library, it is spoken with denunciation of "lawless" people (see *Gospel of Truth* 33.24 ff.; *Hyp. Arch.* 93.12; *Apoc. Jac.* 40.19 ff.; *Apoc. Paul* 20.18 ff.). The *Apocalypse of Adam* (83.11 ff.; 84.4 ff.) even identifies the Law with *gnōsis*[17].

Van Unnik takes Ptolemaeus' distinction between important and insignificant parts of the Law to belong to the discussion going on in orthodox Christianity, but it must not be forgotten that this discussion – in which the great pupil of Valentinus partook – had antecedents in Jewish Christianity and even in Judaism and Samaritanism. Moreover, the history of the Jews and the Samaritans, a branch of the Jewish people, knows eruptions of a real antinomianism which is not behind that of the radical Gnostics[18].

According to the "Book of Baruch", summarized for us by Hippolytus, the angel Baruch was sent with the revelation to Moses, but the evil powers managed to twist the latter's commands (see Hipp., V. xxvi.24 f.). But other Gnostics taught that Moses brought the divine revelation to men. The Sethians had books named after him (see Epiphan., *Pan.* XXXIX.v.1; cp. Hipp., V. xx.1). Monoimus the Arabian found deep mysteries in the works and words of Moses (see Hipp., VIII.xiv.1 ff.). The Peratae viewed Moses as a hierophant having shown the way to salvation in *Num.* ch. xxi (see *ibid.*, V. xvi.7 ff.). According to the Naassenes, Moses was a type of "the undominated race" that ascends to heaven (see *ibid.*, V.viii.2).

The Gnostics did not only preserve the belief in Moses being a revealer of God; they also continued the pseudepigraphic tradition that the Adamites and the ante- and postdeluvian patriarchs were conveyors of divine mysteries. A. Böhlig and others have pointed out that the apocrypha and pseudepigrapha of the Old Testament furnished the Gnostics with many themes[19], and so did apparently other kinds of Jewish sources. Thus, Hekaloth or Merkaba mysticism, describing the world of the throne of the chariot first seen by Ezekiel, is one of the ingredients which has been used to make up the myth in the *Hypo-*

---

15 See below, pp. 60 f.

16 See below, p. 16.

17 H.-F. Weiss, "Das Gesetz in der Gnosis", in *AT-F-G*, pp. 71 ff., has now given a balanced account of the estimation of the Law in various Gnostic quarters.

18 See below, pp. 62 ff.

19 See Böhlig, "Religionsgeschichtliche Probleme aus der Schrift ohne Titel des Codex II von Nag Hammadi", *WZUH*, Ges.-Sprachw. Reihe, X, 1961, pp. 1325 ff. (= *Mysterion und Wahrheit* (AGSU, VI), Leiden, 1968, pp. 119 ff.); "Der jüdische und judenchristliche Hintergrund in gnostischen Texten von Nag Hammadi", in *OG*, pp. 109 ff.; cp. B. Gärtner, *Die rätselhaften Termini Nazoräer und Iskariot* (HS, IV), Uppsala, 1957, pp. 31 ff. (about the Mandeans).

stasis of the Archons and *On the Origin of the World*, both from Codex II of the Nag Hammadi library[20]. The most recondite part of this mysticism or esotericism was the vision of the Kabod, having "a likeness as the appearance of man" (*Ez.* i.26), and already M. Gaster saw that Marcus, one of Valentinus' pupils, when giving a fantastic description of "the Body of Truth" (see Iren., I.xiv.3), was dependent upon Jewish traditions about שעור קומה, the "Measurement of the Body", *viz.*, the enormous body of the Kabod, the Glory of God[21]. In recent works, G. Quispel has argued that the Glory is the model of the Gnostic Anthropos, the heavenly Man[22].

These adoptions and adaptations by the Gnostics have not been put to a ridiculous use, and the same can be said for other Gnostic appropriations from Jewish traditions. O. Betz and others, who object to the derivation of the Gnostic Sophia from the Jewish figure of Wisdom, known from *Proverbs* and apocryphal literature, overlook the fact that not every Gnostic form of Sophia is negative (and that the ambivalent character of Wisdom is not absent in Jewish sapiential tradition)[23]. As Jonas himself has to admit, even the demiurge is not always portrayed as a wholly evil being[24]. According to some of the Gnostics, the demiurge is in strife with Satan[25]. Cerinthus and Justin

---

20 Cp. below, pp. 303 f. J. Maier, who tries to deny any kind of Jewish contribution to Gnostic origins, says that "the material from Ez 1 ff. suffices as an antecedent" of the description of the divine chariot in these works ("Jüdische Faktoren bei der Entstehung der Gnosis?", in *AT-F-G*, p. 252, n. 64). This is an example of his superficial knowledge of the sources. I. Gruenwald, "Jewish Merkavah Mysticism and Gnosticism", in J. Dan & F. Talmage, ed., *Studies in Jewish Mysticism* (Proceedings of the Regional Conferences held at the University of California, Los Angeles, and McGill University in April, 1978), Cambridge, Mass., 1982, pp. 41 ff., has shown that there is a close agreement between the description of the Merkaba in these works and in Jewish mysticism.

21 See "Das Shiur Komah", in his *Studies and Texts*, II, London, 1927, pp. 1330 ff., especially p. 1344.

22 See "Hermetism and the New Testament, especially Paul", in W. Haase, ed., *ANRW*, II.22 (Religion: Gnostizismus und Verwandtes), forthcoming; "Ezekiel 1:26 in Jewish Mysticism and Gnosis", *VigChr*, 34, 1980, pp. 1 ff.

23 See Betz, "Was am Anfang geschah (Das jüdische Erbe in den neugefundenen koptisch-gnostischen Schriften)", in O. Betz, *et al.*, ed., *Abraham unser Vater* (Festschrift für O. Michel) (AGSU, V), Leiden, 1963, p. 40. About Sophia, see the forthcoming article on Helena in *RAC* by Professor Gilles Quispel and the present author.

24 "... we deal with a principle not outright evil, but rather inferior and degenerate, as the cause and essence of creation" (*The Gnostic Religion*, 2nd ed., Boston, 1963, reprinted 1967, p. 132); "... over the whole range of gnostic mythologizing, his image varies, and there are milder versions in which he is more misguided than evil, thus open to correction and remorse, even to final redemption" ("Delimitation", p. 96 (= *GG*, p. 634)).

25 See below, pp. 217, 303, 326. R. Haardt is not unreservedly right that "Gnosticism distinguishes ... in its systems the highest deity ... as sharp as possible from the inferior world creator" ("Schöpfer und Schöpfung in der Gnosis", in *AT-F-G*, p. 44).

the Gnostic do not teach that there is any animosity between God and the demiurge. According to Justin, the demiurge even is the *factotum* for the salvation of men. The definition of Gnosticism by J. Doresse, who avails himself
of the title of ch. ix of Plotinus' second *Ennead*, "Against the Gnostics, or
against those who say that the creator of this world is evil and that the world
is bad", is only partially correct[26]. The Gnostics would agree that the world
was more or less bad, but they did not all teach that the creator was evil. Nor is
the demiurge always a "caricature of the Old Testament God"; we shall see
that "the most archaic" systems do *not* represent the demiurge as "a parody
of the Biblical Creator".

J.A.W. Neander, who appears to have been the first to assert that Gnosticism originated from the Jewish fold[27], tried to derive all the important
Gnostic *topoi* from Alexandrian Jewish philosophy, and would explain the
demiurge as a derivative from Philo's Logos concept[28]. Philo may have media-
ted Greek philosophical terminology to the great Gnostic systems of the 2nd
century, but there is no warrant for regarding him as a proto-Gnostic[29], which
is seen clearly when we consider him in relation to the more primitive systems.
The Logos in Philo is – in spite of all personifications – a philosophical concept, and it is out of the question that it was the antecedent of the figure of
the Gnostic demiurge, who is a mythological individual of considerable
vividness. Any similarity between the two is due to the fact that one of the
facets of Philo's Logos is a philosophical adaptation of the antecedent of the
Gnostic demiurge[30].

F. Chr. Baur, who also saw Alexandrian philosophy of religion as the
cradle of Gnosticism, asserted that the Gnostic concept of the demiurge
derived from Platonism, which was the mother of Alexandrian Jewish philosophy of religion[31]. The identification of the demiurge with the God of the

---

26 See "Gnosticism", in *HR*, I, pp. 536 f.

27 "The schools and sects of philosophy of religion already in existence among the Jews
   were the first source of those Gnostic sects which we see appearing in the second
   century Church" (*Genetische Entwickelung der vornehmsten gnostischen Systeme*,
   Berlin, 1818, p. 1). In the century before, scholars had thought that there were pre-
   Christian Jewish Gnostics; see J.F. Buddeus, *Introductio ad historiam philosophiae
   Hebraeorum*, Halle, 1702/21; J.L. von Mosheim, *Geschichte der Schlangenbrüder*
   (Versuch einer unpartheiischen und gründlichen Ketzergeschichte, I), Helmstädt,
   1746. But they did not regard Jewish teachings as "the *first* source" of Gnosticism.

28 See *op. cit.*, p. 19.

29 See now Chr. Elsas, "Das Judentum als philosophische Religion bei Philo von Alexan-
   drien", in *AT-F-G*, pp. 195 ff., especially his conclusion, pp. 218 ff., where he also
   cites previous literature on the relationship between Philo and Gnosticism.

30 See below, pp. 109, 110, 200, 203, 227, 268 ff., 287, 291, 315, 332 f., 335 f.

31 *Das Christentum und die christliche Kirche der drei ersten Jahrhunderte*, 2nd ed.,
   Tübingen, 1860, p. 185 (= *GG*, p. 13). Baur, p. 183 (= *GG*, p. 9), speaks expressly

Jews expressed the Gnostics' low estimation of the religion of the Old Testament with its unsophisticated way of presenting ideas.

But the first Gnostics did not identify the demiurge with the God of the Old Testament; they ascribed the creation to one or more of the angels. The first Gnostics were not philosophers, though they tried to contrive a theodicee and guard the transcendence of God. They did this by ascribing the creation of the imperfect world and the anthropomorphic features of its author and ruler to a lesser deity, an angel. That the Platonic demiurge was an important model for this construction is not to be denied[32], but the first Gnostics —

---

about *Christian* Gnosticism as having developed from Alexandrian philosophy of religion. In his earlier *Die christliche Gnosis*, Tübingen, 1835, reprinted Osnabrück, 1967, p. 37, Baur admits that educated Jews in dialectic with "pagan religion and philosophy" developed Gnostic ideas in an attempt to transcend the nationalistic borders. In this book, he also stresses the Oriental heritage in Gnosticism. H. Graetz, *Gnosticismus und Judenthum*, Krotoschin, 1846, thought that Gnosticism was Hellenistic speculative metaphysics which also penetrated Judaism. Cp. M. Joël, *Blicke in die Religionsgeschichte zu Anfang des zweiten christlichen Jahrhunderts*, I, Breslau, 1880, pp. 103 ff.

M. Friedländer, who often is given the honour of being the first to maintain that Gnosticism originated in Judaism, found the first Gnostics in antinomian Jews of Alexandria; see especially *Der vorchristliche jüdische Gnosticismus*, Göttingen, 1898. Cp. now the attempt at rehabilitating Friedländer's thesis by B. Pearson, "Friedländer Revisited. Alexandrian Judaism and Gnostic Origins", *SPh*, 2, 1973, pp. 23 ff. Pearson, however, thinks that it is more probable that Gnosticism arose in Palestine; see p. 35. He rightly points out that it is impossible to distinguish between "Hellenistic" and "Palestinian" Judaism, since "Hellenization" was a strong factor in Palestine itself. This also weakens the theory of R. McL. Wilson, *The Gnostic Problem*, 2nd ed., London, 1964, pp. 173 ff., who thinks that Diaspora Judaism was the channel through which Greek philosophy and other elements entered into Gnosticism, or even that Judaism and these other elements in combination gave rise to Gnosticism. He thus says that the source of Gnosticism is a "Jewish speculation of a more or less unorthodox character" ("Gnostic Origins", *VigChr*, 9, 1955, p. 211); cp. *Problem*, pp. 176, 216. But Wilson would seem to have to call this phenomenon "pre-Gnosticism" or "proto-Gnosticism", since he defines Gnosticism as an assimilation "of Christianity and Hellenistic thought" ("Gnostic Origins", p. 199), "an assimilation of Christianity and contemporary thought" (*Problem*, p. VII), and "the accommodation of Christianity and Hellenistic culture" (*ibid.*, p. 265); see also *Problem*, pp. 97 f. This is similar to Baur's view in *Christentum*. In other places, however, Wilson speaks of Gnosticism as an element in Hellenism, presumably excluding Christianity; see *Problem*, pp. 103, 118, 151, 172. He thus can view Gnosticism and Christianity as parallel phenomena; see *ibid.*, pp. 64 ff., 261 ff. He even says that "Gnosticism is not Christian, but a phase of heathenism" (*ibid.*, p. 265).

An iteration of Baur's view in *Gnosis* is made by P. Pokorný, "Der Ursprung der Gnosis", *Kairos*, 9, 1967, pp. 94 ff. (= *GG*, 749 ff.), who thinks that Gnosticism originated when Alexandrian Judaism met with a spiritual and syncretistic current which made use of the allegorical way of interpreting the sacred texts. See also J. Ménard, "Les origines de la gnose", *RSR*, 43, 1968, pp. 24 ff., especially pp. 36 ff.

32 See below, pp. 332 ff.

who were Jews and did not disparage their Bible[33] — had a model of their own in the figure of the Angel of the Lord. In many Biblical texts, the concept of the Angel of the Lord has been introduced in order to detach God from the world and tone down the anthropomorphisms of the older source.

A. Hilgenfeld, who accepted the testimony of the Church Fathers that Simon Magus from Samaria was the first Gnostic, asserted that Simon in order to outdo the universal message of Christianity "separated the national God, who was the creator of the world and giver of the Law, from the highest God, who was revealed from the time of Christ."[34] Hilgenfeld can find support in some passages in the *Pseudo-Clementines*, where Simon argues that the god making himself known in the Old Testament cannot be the one of whom Jesus speaks when saying that "no man knows the Father but the Son," but it is well known that "Simon" in the *Clementina* does not stand for the same person throughout, and the Jewish Christian group behind the Clementine romance could here be imputing a Christian Gnostic or ultra-Pauline view to the arch-heretic. In any case, when Simon speaks about the creation and the giving of the Law, he states that God commissioned angels for these works[35]. This squares with the account of Simon's teaching given by Irenaeus, who tells that Simon taught that the world was made by angels. This doctrine cannot be said to denigrate nationalism and underscore universalism. Simon himself was a manifestation of "the Great Power", which was a Samaritan substitute for the name of YHWH, "the national God".

Hilgenfeld cites the fact that there were also Jews who held that the Law had been given by angels. However, the angels did not act on their own, but as God's agents. Thus, it is only logical to assume that the Gnostic notion of the angel(s) who created the world and man as well as conveyed the Law derives from Judaism and Samaritanism.

That the first Gnostics belonged to the history of Jewish religion and conceived of the demiurge as God's agent, an angel, was seen by R.A. Lipsius, but he did not try to derive the concept of the demiurge from Judaism. Lipsius found the source of Gnosticism in the mingling of Judaism and other Near Eastern religions in Syria[36], but he reckoned that the first historical Gnostics were Jewish Christians, whose forerunners were "Christianized Essenes", and that they endeavoured to present Christianity as "the true and perfected Judaism"[37]. But the figure of the demiurge cannot be said to serve this pur-

---

33 See below, pp. 17 ff., 213 ff.

34 "Der Gnostizismus", *ZWT*, 33, 1890, p. 6 (= *GG*, p. 178); see already *Das Urchristenthum in den Hauptwendepuncten seines Entwickelungsganges*, Jena, 1855, pp. 90 ff.; *Die Ketzergeschichte des Urchristentums*, Leipzig, 1884, pp. 163 ff.

35 See below, p. 215.

36 See Art. "Gnosticismus", in *AEWK*, I/71, 1860, p. 270 (= *GG*, p. 92).

37 *Ibid.*, p. 287 (= *GG*, p. 94).

pose. Although Cerinthus and Justin probably were Jewish Christians, our Jewish Christian sources and the patristic evidence for Jewish Christian sects do not know the concept of the demiurge.

A. von Harnack, who coined the famous phrase that Gnosticism was "the acute Hellenization of Christianity", did not miss the fact that Christian Gnosticism had forerunners: these were products of the syncretism of the age. This syncretism caused Jews to doubt the authority of their Bible and the identity of "the national God" with the God of all men[38]. According to Harnack, the concept of the demiurge was "proof of a syncretism with dualistic tendency"[39]. But Simon and Cerinthus, who are Harnack's first known representatives of this syncretism with a universal prospect, did not distinguish between the highest God and "the national God" or concoct a universal religion.

A. Hönig, in a book that unfortunately has remained unknown in the discussion about Gnosticism,[40] argued that the first Gnostics were Jews and designed the concept of the demiurge in order to answer the question: *unde malum*? Their conception of God prevented them from ascribing the creation of the imperfect and even evil world to him, and they posited a demiurge mediating between the good God and the defective or evil creation[41]. However, the Gnostic demiurge could not be regarded as the agent of God, since the creation then would have to be considered faultless[42]. Hönig follows J.L. von Mosheim in taking the Ophites to be a pre-Christian Jewish sect[43], and identifies the Ophites with the Naassenes, saying that Hippolytus (V.vi.4) reports that these people were the ancestors of the other Gnostic heresies[44]. The demiurge of the Ophites was born from chaos, and Hönig takes this to mean that he was a personification of the material world[45].

But Hippolytus does *not* say that the Naassenes were the first Gnostics; he

---

38 See *Lehrbuch der Dogmengeschichte*, I (Die Entstehung des kirchlichen Dogmas) (STL, I), Freiburg, 1886, pp. 170 ff. (= *GG*, pp. 157 ff.).

39 *Ibid.*, p. 180 (= *GG*, p. 167).

40 Hönig's work seems to have passed unnoticed until G. Quispel, in his review of *GG*, cited it; see *VigChr*, 29, 1975, p. 236.

41 See *Die Ophiten*, Berlin, 1889, pp. 12, 15 ff., 27 f., 36 ff.

42 See *ibid.*, p. 34.

43 See Mosheim, p. 12, *et passim.*

44 See *op. cit.*, pp. 28 f.

45 See *ibid.*, pp. 7, 36. Hönig maintains that the name of the demiurge, Jaldabaoth, comes from ילדא בהות and means "child of chaos", an interpretation first offered by A.J. Matter, *Histoire critique du gnosticisme*, II, Paris, 1828, p. 198. The etymology has been strongly opposed by G. Scholem, "Jaldabaoth Reconsidered", in *MP*, pp. 405 ff., who suggests that the name was an invention by a Jew who joined the Gnostic camp and designated the demiurge, the procreator of the archons, as the "Begetter", ילד, of the archons, Sabaoth, a plural word. Since the name obviously is not original in Gnosticism, we do not have to enter into this discussion.

only states: "Many have split off from them and divided the heresy into many factions [...]."[46] Moreover, Jaldabaoth, the demiurge of the Ophites, is identified explicitly with the God of the Old Testament; we find a veritable protest-exegesis which twists the intentions behind the divine words and acts to the extent that there emerges a grotesque travesty of the Biblical God as a foolish and malicious being. This picture is not easy to conceive of as a Jewish production, although Ophitism shows a solid Jewish groundwork and apparently existed in anti-Christian forms (see Orig., *Contra Cels.* III.13; VI.28). Finally, the idea of an imperfect creation does not have to lead to the idea that its maker is anti-divine. The Platonists posited a demiurge, who was no evil being, as mediator between the transcendent and good God and the imperfect material creation. So did some Jews, the direct ancestors of the Gnostics.

Since Origen (*Contra Cels.* IV.30 f.) tells that the demiurge of the Ophians (Ophites) was lion-faced and connected with Saturn, W. Bousset theorized that the model of Jaldabaoth was the syncretistic god Baal-Kronos, whose symbol was the lion and whose planet was Saturn. This god could also be welded with Zurvan-Chronos of the Mithraic mysteries who had the head of a lion.[47] John of Damascus (*De princ.* 270) actually says that the Phoenicians held Kronos to be a kind of demiurge[48]. Because the Sabbath, which had been sanctified by YHWH, was the day of Saturn, the demiurge was welded with the God of the Old Testament.

Even if it could be established that Bousset's construction is right, Baal-Kronos cannot be regarded as the antecedent of the Gnostic demiurge, for the lion-faced Jaldabaoth was not the original form of the Gnostic demiurge. Moreover, as we shall see, even the lion-faced demiurge has been incorporated into a Jewish system of reference[49]. In Ophitism, Jaldabaoth and the six archons are connected with the seven planets, and Bousset would derive this notion from the Babylonian teaching about the planetary gods, who had become evil powers under the influence of Hellenistic dualism, but we shall see that the background is to be found in the Jewish doctrine of the seven archangels.

H. Jonas, in his influential work on Gnosticism and the spirit of late anti-

---

46 Philaster of Brescia, however, begins his heresiography by mentioning the Ophites as a pre-Christian heresy; cp. Hönig, p. 12.

47 See *Hauptprobleme der Gnosis* (FRLANT, 10), Göttingen, 1907, reprinted Darmstadt, 1973, pp. 351 ff.

48 G. Quispel, "Gnosticism and the New Testament", in Hyatt, *Bible*, pp. 261 f., has followed Bousset's lead and drawn attention to the statement by Plutarch (*De Is.* 44) that Kronos as Chronos, "Time", is the creator, since time in its course produces everything.

49 See below, pp. 321 ff.

quity, repeated the old view that the Gnostic demiurge had his roots in Platonic and Jewish teachings of the creation[50]. He did not take account of the
fact that the Gnostic demiurge was an angel and is not to be equated instan-
taneously with the creator in the Biblical narrative.

R.M. Grant, who has offered the thesis that Gnosticism was founded by
Jews of the apocalyptic wing becoming disillusioned by the fall of Jerusalem,
asserts that the Gnostic demiurge came into being through an identification
of the Biblical God with Satan, the ruler of the present aeon. Grant, K.
Schubert, and K. Rudolph have suggested many starting-points for Gnostic
speculation in Jewish apocalypticism[51], but the doctrine of the demiurge is
not taken from this tradition. In support of his thesis, Grant cites the statement of the *Apocryphon of John* (*BG* 37.21) that the demiurge has the
appearance of a serpent and a lion, for this connects him with the horrific
statues of a man with the head of a lion and a huge serpent winded around
his body which have been recovered in Mithraic temples and are taken by
some scholars to represent Ahriman, the devil in Iranian religion[52]. However,
neither the Iranian Ahriman nor the Jewish Satan is a demiurge.

G. Quispel now has argued that the Gnostic image of the demiurge with
the face of a lion and the body of a serpent who originates from the chaos is
moulded after the Orphic representation of the demiurge, Phanes or Eros,
who, in Hellenistic times, became the new Aion, who was born again
every year[53]. The orientation towards Orphicism would seem right. The
Orphic demiurge, however, is *not* said to be a serpent or to have the head of
a lion, though he is told to have a serpent upon his head and to roar like a
lion as well as like a bull, and is depicted on a relief with his body entwined
by a serpent and a mask of a lion's head on the chest[54]. The Orphic all-god
Chronos, on the other hand, is said to be a serpent with the heads of a bull, a
god, and a lion. No statue of the Mithraic leontocephaline figure has been

---

50 See *Gnosis*, p. 167.
51 See Grant, *Gnosticism and Early Christianity*, New York, 1959; Schubert, *Die
  Gemeinde vom Toten Meer*, Munich, 1958, pp. 66 ff.; "Jüdischer Hellenismus und
  jüdische Gnosis", *WW*, 18, 1963, pp. 455 ff.; Rudolph, "Randerscheinungen des
  Judentums und das Problem der Entstehung des Gnostizismus", *Kairos*, 9, 1967, pp.
  115 f. (= *GG*, pp. 788 f.); *Die Gnosis*, pp. 294 ff., with further references in the notes
  on p. 410, col. b. M. Hengel says that "Jewish apocalypticism, especially in its Essene
  form, has influenced the development of the later Jewish Christian Gnosticism"
  (*Judentum und Hellenismus* (WUNT, 10), Tübingen, 1969, p. 417).
52 See *op. cit.*, pp. 48 ff.; cp. pp. 56 ff.
53 See "The Demiurge in the Apocryphon of John", in R. McL. Wilson, ed., *Nag Hammadi and Gnosis* (Papers Read at the First International Congress of Coptology
  (Cairo, December 1976)) (NHS, XIV), Leiden, 1978, pp. 6 ff. For Phanes as the new
  Aion, see also Quispel, "Herman Hesse and Gnosis", in *Gnosis*, pp. 504 ff.
54 See Kern, Fragment 54; 79; cp. Quispel, "Demiurge", pp. 15 f.

found in Iran, and the Orphic description of Chronos is probably the model of the horrific statues[55]; thus, they may picture the Iranian all-god Zurvan or Aion, apparently in his gloomy aspect of finite Time and Fate — perhaps even as Ahriman, since Time allows Ahriman to work and brings dissolution and death — and not as Infinite Zurvan, Eternity, as thought by F. Cumont[56].

It is true that the Gnostic picture of the demiurge rising from chaos to ascendancy over the cosmos can find a precedent in the Orphic myth of Phanes, but it must not be forgotten that Chronos, too, was born from the primordial water and earth. Moreover, as noted above, there were Hellenistic traditions knowing that he was the creator.

Admittedly, the real nature of the connections between the Mithraic statues, the Orphic fragments, and the Gnostic texts is complex; here, it suffices to note that the Gnostic demiurge was not originally identical with Satan. The Samaritan Gnostics, Simon and Menander, ascribed the creation to a plurality of angels; they did not speak about the devil. Cerinthus, another Gnostic of the first century, allotted the creation to an angel "far separated and remote from that supreme Principality which is over the universe" (Iren., I.xxvi.1); this is no description of the devil. Satornil, who came from the school of Simon, and Carpocrates, his contemporary, both spoke about Satan, but they clearly set him apart from the band of the angelic world-creators. Apelles and Severus, who were associates of Marcion, both distinguished between the demiurge and Satan[57]. The latter taught that the devil was the son of the demiurge, and so did the Ophites and the Archontics; like Satornil, these Gnostics taught that there was enmity between the creator and the devil[58].

Grant himself admits that YHWH *before* he was regarded as one with

---

55 See S. Wikander, "Études sur les mystères de Mithras I", in *VLÅ*, 1950, pp. 33 ff. Recently R.L. Gordon has laid down that there are "many grounds for rejecting any theory which assumes that it is valid to look to Iranian religion, Zoroastrian or not, in order to explain the significance and function of symbols in the Western mystery religion of Mithras" ("Franz Cumont and the Doctrines of Mithraism", in *MS*, p. 242). But Gordon is sceptical about the possibility of ascertaining the origin and significance of the leontocephaline figure.

56 See *Textes et monuments figurés relatifs aux mystères de Mithra*, I, Bruxelles, 1899, pp. 74 ff. For the identification of the leontocephaline figure with Ahriman, see J. Legge, "The Lion-Headed God of the Mithraic Mysteries", *PSBA*, 34, 1912, pp. 125 ff.; J. Duchesne-Guillemin, *Ormazd et Ahriman* (MR, 31), Paris, 1953, pp. 126 ff.; "Ahriman et le dieu suprême dans les mystères de Mithra", *Numen*, 2, 1955, pp. 190 ff.; R.C. Zaehner, *Zurvan*, Oxford, 1955, pp. viii f.; *The Dawn and Twilight of Zoroastrianism*, London, 1961, pp. 175 ff.

57 See below, p. 303.

58 See below, p. 326. Haardt, pp. 40 f., is thus not unconditionally right that the figure who is responsible for the creation also is responsible for the existence of evil.

Satan was identified as "an unfriendly angel"[59], which certainly would be a simple identification from reading *Gen.* chs. xviii f. and other parts of the Bible. Furthermore, in another connection, Grant points out that both Marcionitism and Valentinianism at first did not teach that the demiurge was evil; the idea of the evil demiurge was the result of a development in these theologies[60]. We may thus infer that more primitive systems could hold the demiurge to be a more or less ambiguous angel designated by the Tetragrammaton.

G. Widengren, who discerns that the Gnostic demiurge is not identical with the devil, subscribes to the old view that he simply is a coalescence of the Platonic demiurge and the creator in the Old Testament. Furthermore, since he seeks the origin of Gnosticism in a radical Iranian dualism where the powers of darkness are pre-existent and independent of God, Widengren has to regard the demiurge as not belonging to original Gnosticism, because the demiurge derives from the divine realm. According to Widengren, the demiurge has absorbed the planetary rulers, the malefic powers of Eastern Gnosticism[61].

Whether the concept of a plurality of world-creating angels preceded that of a single demiurgic angel or *vice versa* need not occupy us, but we must lay down that the theory that primitive Gnosticism was characterized by an extreme dualism is entirely unsupported. Simon, Menander, and Satornil, who taught that the world and man were created by seven angels, held that the angels were generated by Wisdom or even made by God himself. In the Gnostic system of *Poimandres*, the first tract of *Corpus Hermeticum*, the demiurge – who is an agent of God – creates the planetary rulers; the one concept is not a substitute for the other.

S. Pétrement – who sees Gnosticism as an extreme anti-Jewish form of Christianity, a radicalization of the Christian *theologia crucis* over against the Jewish *theologia creationis* – asserts that the idea of the seven world-creating angels is to be understood as anti-Jewish polemic developed from the Pauline conception of "the powers and principalities" of this world[62]. But the Christians who disputed with the Jews did not denounce the creation and the Old Testament, and did not identify the fiendish powers with the God of the Jews and his angels[63]. The idea that the world was ruled by sinister powers actually

59 *Op. cit.*, p. 59.
60 See *ibid.*, pp. 136 f.
61 See "Les origines du gnosticisme et l'histoire des religions", in *OG*, p. 40 (= *GG* p. 682).
62 See "Le mythe des sept archontes créateurs peut-il s'expliquer à partir du christianisme?", in *OG*, pp. 460 ff.
63 Cp. the criticism by U. Bianchi, "Perspectives de la recherche sur les origines du gnosticisme", in *OG*, pp. 731 ff. (= *GG*, pp. 727 ff.).

came from Judaism itself and continued in Jewish Christianity without being turned against the Jews[64]. Finally, the early Gnostics were not Christians or anti-Jewish. The small recognition of Christianity in Simon's system is certainly not original[65], and Menander had no need for Christ[66], the figure of whom would seem essential to Gnosticism if it were an original Christian heresy[67].

Satornil and Carpocrates, however, both gave Jesus a place in their systems, but an anti-Jewish bias is completely lacking in the latter's teaching and is not very pronounced in that of the former. There is no evidence that Carpocrates identified the world-creating angels, whose band did not include the devil, with the God of the Old Testament and his angels; Carpocrates really was a Jewish Christian who continued the Ebionite Christology and saw Jesus as "no more than a prophet and a model"[68]. Satornil taught· that "Christ came for the destruction of the god of the Jews" (Iren., I.xxiv.2), but he put Satan below the god of the Jews and the other angels who created the world, and said that marriage and procreation are from Satan. Moreover, Satornil did not expressly equate the god of the Jews with the God of the Old Testament, and we should perhaps take "god" as synonymous with "angel"; the "god" of the Jews is said explicitly to be one of the seven angels, and the words in *Gen.* i.26, which are spoken by Elohim, a plural often taken to indicate the angels, actually are ascribed to all the angels[69].

Pétrement thinks that the concept of a single demiurge is secondary to that of the seven creating angels; we therefore should note that the demiurge in Cerinthus' system, which is prior to that of Satornil, is not identified with the God of the Jews and set off in opposition to the highest God. There is no reason to believe that Cerinthus was anti-Jewish; on the contrary, he continued the adoptionist Christology of the Jewish Christians (see Iren., I.xxvi.1), was a partisan of the idea of an earthly millennium in Jerusalem (see Euseb., *Hist. eccl.* III.xxviii.4), and enjoined the practice of circumcision and the keeping of the Sabbath (see Epiphan., *Pan.* XXVIII.v.1 ff.).

U. Bianchi has suggested to study the figure of the Gnostic demiurge within a world-wide field, citing the Greek hero Prometheus, various "trickster" figures of primitive peoples, *etc.*[70]. From the perspective of a scholar of com-

---

64 See J. Daniélou, *The Theology of Jewish Christianity* (The Development of Christian Doctrine before the Council of Nicaea, I), trans. by J.A. Baker, London, 1964, pp. 187 ff.

65 See below, p. 129.

66 See below, pp. 142 ff., 153 ff.

67 See Drijvers, pp. 345 f. (= *GG*, pp. 822 f.).

68 Daniélou, p. 85.

69 See below, pp. 216 f.

70 See "Le problème des origines du gnosticisme et l'histoire des religions", *Numen*, 12, 1965, pp. 170 ff. (= *GG*, pp. 608 ff.).

parative religion or even of the history of ideas, this is legitimate, but Bianchi's broad orientation is of little help in the search for the immediate antecedent of the Gnostic demiurge.

E. Pagels has criticized the scholars who follow Irenaeus and define the Gnostics as people who distinguished between God and the creator, the latter an inferior being[71]. Pagels does not see the Gnostics being refuted by Irenaeus as dualists but as modifiers of the monotheistic doctrine. But it is of course not befitting to characterize the system of the Cainites or the Barbelo-Gnostics as "a modification of monotheistic doctrine"[72]. Pagels unfortunately does not define what she means by dualism, but it probably must be something like the Manichean religion. It is true that the Valentinians confessed one God the Father, but so did the Manicheans, radical Gnostics.

Pagel's thesis is that the demiurge is the mythological counterpart to the ecclesiastical bishop, whose authority was challenged by the Gnostics. The Valentinians took the idea of the people of Israel in the Old Testament to denote the church of the psychics, and Pagels argues that the God of Israel, who is the creator of the world, signifies the catholic bishop. We do not have to discuss this thesis, for there were Gnostics inculcating a lower demiurge long before the Valentinians. Moreover, their demiurge was not the God of the Old Testament, but his angel. These Gnostics had no reinterpretation of the Old Testament imagery similar to that of the Valentinians.

A.F. Segal sees the origin of Gnosticism in a battle between the rabbis and the heretics who believed that there were "two powers in heaven". The second power was enthroned in heaven, had a human shape, and — according to some traditions — carried the Name of God. Segal points out that the Gnostic demiurge, being ignorant of the highest God, utters the divine words which the rabbis adduced against the heretics (*e.g., Deut.* xxxii.39; *Is.* xlvi.9), and argues that "two powers" heretics replied to the rabbinic attack by splitting up the angelic agent into a good saviour and an evil demiurge, identifying the latter with the God of the Old Testament, the God of their opponents[73].

This is an ingenious explanation of the presence of the anti-Jewish sentiment in Gnosticism, but I repeat that not all Gnostic systems were anti-Jewish and identified the God of the Old Testament with the inferior and evil demiurge. Already "two powers" heretics accredited the second figure, who was God's angel, with the demiurgic office. In his chapter of conclusions, Segal says: "Phenomenologically and historically the gnostic demiurge is the second deity of the earlier "two powers" theology. Usually he has appro-

---

71 See "The Demiurge and His Archons — A Gnostic View of the Bishop and Presbyters?", *HTR*, 69, 1976, pp. 301 ff.

72 *Ibid.*, p. 303.

73 See *Two Powers in Heaven* (SJLA, XXV), Leiden, 1977.

priated half of the traditions about the second power, yielding the honorable traditions to the gnostic saviour."[74] But Segal does not present evidence that the second power was seen to be the demiurge[75]; once this is realized, it becomes easier to see why the heretics could identify the debased version of the second figure with their opponents' god, the God of the Old Testament, the creator and ruler of this world.

It was G. Quispel who first tried to allocate the origin of the Gnostic concept of the demiurge in a heterodox Jewish doctrine according to which the world is the creation of an angel of God. He cites the evidence of al-Qirqisani's account of the Jewish sects: "It tells us that the pre-Christian Jewish sect of the Magharians in Palestine distinguished between God, who is beyond anthropomorphism, and one of his angels, who is responsible for all the anthropomorphic features contained in the Old Testament, and who is the creator of the world... .

"This report is of late date (Qirqisānī lived in the 10th century). ... [But] the views expounded are so remarkable and unique, that it is difficult to consider them a medieval hoax. Therefore, I think we must suppose that such a group did exist before the Christian era in Palestine. It is possible that the angel referred to is the so-called "Angel of the Lord". In that case the views of the Magharians could be the outcome of an inner Jewish process. Already in the Old Testament we find several passages, in which the anthropomorphism of the source has been toned down and the name of the Lord has been replaced by the more cautious expression, "The Angel of the Lord". ... towards the beginning of our era the Jewish concept of God became more and more transcendent... Jewish scholars explained away anthropomorphisms in Holy Scripture. These sectarians seem to have gone so far as to attribute even the creation of the world to the Angel of the Lord, because this is described in the Bible as a creation by the word or by handicraft, both anthropomorphisms."[76]

Quispel cites that H. Wolfson has suggested that the Gnostics derived their concept of the demiurge from the teaching of the Magharians[77]. The present work will support the orientation of Wolfson and Quispel. It will be seen that the reason for positing the Angel of the Lord as the demiurge not only was to explain the anthropomorphisms of Scripture, but also to avoid bringing God into contact with the material world and making him respon-

---

74 *Ibid.*, p. 266.

75 R. van den Broek is wrong that the second power in Segal's evidence "shared in or was wholly responsible for the creation of the world and man" ("The Present State of Gnostic Studies", *VigChr*, 37, 1983, p. 60).

76 "Origins", pp. 272 f.

77 See Wolfson, "The Pre-Existent Angel of the Magharians and Al-Nahawandi", *JQR*, 11, 1960, p. 97.

sible for the imperfect and even evil creation. For this motive, the Jewish Gnostics would seem to have been dependent upon Platonism.

According to Quispel's knowledge, al-Qirqisani's account of the Magharians is the only "Jewish text which attests that there were Jews who taught a highest God and an inferior creator of the world."[78] Moreover, al-Qirqisani alleges that this teaching was proffered by a sect which had expired long ago. However, there do exist other Jewish texts which propound the same doctrine. So far, these texts, which belong to the literature of the Samaritan branch of Judaism, have not been adduced in the discussion about the origin of Gnosticism.

This evidence will satisfy the first of the two tests to which Jonas will submit the theory of the Jewish root of Gnosticism: "Are there *Hebrew* writings ... which are Gnostic in the sense here specified?"[79] Jonas has just described the malicious demiurge in the *Apocryphon of John* as an illustration of Gnostic dualism, and he goes on to cite G. Scholem, who says that "Jewish Gnosticism" always was striving "hard to maintain a strictly monotheistic character."[80] W.C. van Unnik, P. Pokorný, H.J.W. Drijvers, and others have also denied that Jews would teach that there had occurred a split in the godhead which had to be restored, and use this as the main argument in support of their contention that Gnosticism cannot be derived directly from Judaism[81]. But Scholem himself has posed the rhetorical question whether "Jewish Gnosticism", by which he means Merkaba mysticism, cherished the "belief in a fundamental distinction between the appearance of God the Creator, the Demiurge, i.e. one of His aspects, and His indefinable essence"[82]. There is no denying the fact that the Jewish mystics or Gnostics called the Kabod, the enormous man-like being upon the heavenly throne, יוצר בראשית, the "Creator in the Beginning". Scholem speculates whether this notion was an attempt to soften the antagonism between God and the demiurge in classical Gnosticism. But why should Jews feel it necessary to adapt this dualism at all? It is more plausible to reckon that the radical dualism is secondary to the Jewish dualism of subordination. As shall be seen in Chapter VI, there were Jewish teachings about the heavenly Man being the demiurge already in pre-Christian times. There is corresponding Samaritan evidence showing that the

---

78 "Origins", p. 272.
79 "Response", p. 290.
80 *Jewish Gnosticism, Merkabah Mysticism, and Talmudic Tradition* (JTSA), New York, 1960, p. 42.
81 See van Unnik, "Die jüdische Komponente in der Entstehung der Gnosis", *VigChr*, 15, 1961, pp. 74 f. (= *GG*, p. 485); "Gnosis", p. 77; Pokorny, "Der Ursprung der Gnosis", *Kairos*, 9, 1967, p. 98 (= *GG*, p. 760); Drijvers, p. 348 (= *GG*, pp. 834 f.).
82 *Major Trends in Jewish Mysticism*, 3rd ed., New York, 1954, Schocken paperback edition, New York, 1961 and reprints, p. 65.

dualism of the *Apocryphon of John* was preceded by a dualism where the demiurge was God's agent.

Jonas' second test, namely, whether any of the Gnostics had Jewish names, is satisfied — as Jonas himself must admit — by the interesting personage of Simon Magus. Simon is both a Samaritan and allegedly the first individual Gnostic of whom we have any record, and his teaching will engage us considerably in this book. As a matter of fact, the prime testimony to the Jewish derivation of the Gnostic heresies gives Samaritan sectarianism great importance. This testimony comes from Hegesippus, who was a Jewish Christian living in the 2nd century and thus should know what he was talking about. The original of Hegesippus' work on the growth of the Church is lost, but fragments of it are quoted by Eusebius, another historian of the Church who wrote a little later. Eusebius reports:

> The same writer [*viz.*, Hegesippus] also describes the beginning of the heresies of his time in the following way: "After James the Just had suffered martyrdom for the same reason as the Lord, Simeon, his cousin, the son of Clopas, was appointed bishop, whom they all proposed because he was another cousin of the Lord. For this cause, they called the Church a virgin; for it had not yet been corrupted by vain messages. But Thebuthis, because he had not been made bishop, began its corruption by means of the seven sects existing among the people and to which he also belonged. From these [came] Simon, whence the Simonians, and Cleobius, whence the Cleobians, and Dositheus, whence the Dositheans, and Gorthaeus, whence the Gorathenians and the Masbotheans. From these came the Menandrianists, Marcianists, Carpocratians, Valentinians, Basilidians, and Saturnilians. Each of these puts forward in its own peculiar way its own opinion [...] ." The same writer also described the sects which once existed among the Jews as follows: "Now, there were various opinions among the circumcision, among the children of Israel, against the tribe of Judah and the Messiah, as follows: Essenes, Galileans, Hemerobaptists, Masbotheans, Samaritans, Sadducees, and Pharisees."

> (*Hist. eccl.* IV. xxii. 4 ff.)

It is probable that Hegesippus' picture of the emergence of Gnosticism out of Jewish sectarianism is somewhat elaborated, but this does not have to mean that his information is unreliable in its general outline. Obviously, Judaism about the beginning of our era was a heterogeneous movement[83].

---

83 *Apost. Const.* VI, ch. vi, lists the following bodies as the sects of the Jews: the Sadducees, Pharisees, Masbotheans, Hemerobaptists, Ebionites, and the Essenes. In ch. vii, Simon is described. If Simon is taken to be a representative of the Samaritans, we have essentially the same list as that given by Hegesippus. But Simon actually is represented as a heretic arising from the formerly mentioned sects; he is thus a Jewish heretic, as is also Hegesippus' view of him. The Ebionites are substituted for the Galileans of Hegesippus; this perhaps was done because the Jewish sect of the Galileans was absorbed by the Jewish Christian Ebionites. Note that James the Just, a Galilean, was the head of the first Jewish Christian community in Jerusalem. In a postscript to the Armenian translation of Ephrem the Syrian's commentary on Tat-

Origen (*Contra Cels*. III.12 f.) says that different interpretations of Scripture gave rise to different sects in Judaism. According to the Palestinian Talmud (*Sanh*. x.5), there were as many as twenty-four kinds of *minim*, "heretics" or "sectarians", at the time of the destruction of the temple. Although the numbers of seven and twenty-four are conventional, they illustrate the complexity of the situation within Palestinian Judaism.

It would seem that Hegesippus does not regard "the seven sects among the people", that is, the Jewish people, as heterodox factions but as groups within the Jewish fold. The real schisms occurred with the emergence of the derivative sects. From these sects, the Gnostic heresies took their rise.

The Masbotheans appear both in the list of the seven earlier sects and in the list of the five sects derived from them. Their occurrence at the end of the listing of the derivative sects may be due to a gloss, or it may be that the enumeration of the Masbothean sect between the Hemerobaptists and the Samaritans is an interpolation caused by the fact that the Masbotheans were known to be a Samaritan sect of baptizers. As a matter of fact, all of the five derivative sects from which the Gnostic heresies originated appear to have Samaritan connections, a circumstance which has not been emphasized sufficiently until now. Epiphanius, bishop of Salamis in the island of Cyprus in the 4th century, in his disquisition on the sects of the Samaritans lists the Gorothenians after the Sebueans ($\Sigma\epsilon\beta o\nu a \hat{i}o\iota$), apparently צבועייא or צבואייא, and the Masbotheans and the Sebueans may be identical, both names being derived from the root צבע, to "baptize", and denoting the people who belong to the community of those who are מצבע or צבו, "baptized"[84].

---

ians's *Diatessaron*, the Ebionites are substitutes for the Hemerobaptists in the record of Hegesippus.

Like Hegesippus, Justin (*Dial*. lxxx.3 f.) also has seven Jewish sects, namely, the Sadducees, Genistae, Meristae, Galileans, Hellenians, Pharisees, and the Baptists. Epiphanius (*Pan*. chs. XIV-XX) has the following seven Jewish sects: the Sadducees, Scribes, Pharisees, Hemerobaptists, Nasareans, Ossenes (sic!), and the Herodians. In addition, Epiphanius (*ibid*. chs. X-XIII) has four special Samaritan sects, *viz*., the Essenes (*sic!*), Sebueans, Gorothenians, and the Dositheans. Philaster of Brescia (*De haer*. chs. 4 ff.), being a little later than Epiphanius, has the following Jewish sects: the Dositheans, Sadducees, Pharisees, Samaritans, Nazoreans, Essenes, various Canaanite groups, and the Herodians. Both Epiphanius and Philaster, whose lists are in pretty close agreement, must be based in one way or another upon the list of the heresies in the lost *Syntagma* of Hippolytus, for they both seem to be more complete versions of the record of the four sects of the Dositheans (defined as Samaritans), Sadducees, Pharisees, and the Herodians which is given by Pseudo-Tertullian (that is, Tert., *De praescript. haer*. chs. XLVII-LIII), commonly believed to be a summary of Hippolytus' *Syntagma*.

84 See below, p. 69. Several of the Gnostic sects apparently preserved baptismal rites going back to a Palestinian *baptismus*; see K. Rudolph, *Die Mandäer*, II (Der Kult) (FRLANT, 75), Göttingen, 1961, pp. 380 ff. Parallels between the Qumran texts

Cleobius appears in the company of Simon Magus, the Samaritan here-siarch, in the apocryphal epistolary intercourse between Paul and the Corin-thians found in the *Acts of Paul* and composed in the 2nd century (see ch. VIII). The same pairing is found in the 3rd century Syrian source called the *Didascalia Apostolorum* (vi.8). In the 4th century expansion of this work known as the *Apostolic Constitutions*, Cleobius and Simon are described as pupils of Dositheus, whom they had ousted from his position (see VI.viii.1). Dositheus was the well-known Samaritan heretic who is associated with Simon and, according to earlier tradition, is even said to have been dispossess-ed by the latter[85].

W.C. van Unnik asserts that the Samaritans in the first century C.E. did not belong to the Jewish fold; he says that "the breach was complete."[86] He seems to argue that the Samaritans were not Jews in a "historical sense", since they were not regarded as such by the Jews in Judea. With the same right it could be said that the Jews did not belong to the people of Israel, because they were not regarded as true Israelites by the Samaritans. It all depends on the angle from where the problem is viewed. The truth is, of course, that the Jews and the Samaritans have the same historical root and are two branches of the Hebrew nation. Moreover, though the relationship be-tween Jews and Samaritans was strained in the first century, there was no complete breach before around 300 C.E. Thus, in the 2nd century, R. Aqiba granted the Samaritans status as belonging to Israel in the endeavour to raise a strong insurrection against the Romans[87].

Simon Magus, who was a Samaritan and thus belonged to the northern branch of the people of Israel, conceived of the hypostasized figure of Wisdom as having been split off from God, just like the later Kabbalists actually taught that Shekina, the feminine part of God and the vehicle of the power of punishment and stern judgment, had been exiled from God[88]. Of course, it

---

and the Mandean texts have been noted; see Gärtner, pp. 26 ff.; K. Rudolph, *Die Mandäer*, I (Prolegomena: Das Mandäerproblem) (FRLANT, 74), Göttingen, 1960, 223 ff. Rudolph, "War der Verfasser der Oden Salomos ein Qumran-Christ? Ein Beitrag zur Diskussion um die Anfänge der Gnosis", *RQ*, 4, 1964, pp. 523 ff., argues for a line of tradition from the *Thanksgiving Hymns* of Qumran to both the *Odes of Solomon* and the Mandean hymns. See now also the summary by Rudolph, *Die Gnosis*, pp. 296 f.

85 See below, pp. 114 ff.

86 "Gnosis und Judentum", p. 78.

87 See below, pp. 36 ff., for the discussion about the relations between the Jews and the Samaritans.

88 See Scholem, *On the Kabbalah*, pp. 105 ff. Some scholars think that the Jewish wis-dom schools, where a pessimism had asserted itself, were hotbeds for the growth of Gnosticism; see, for instance, A. Adam, "Neuere Literatur zur Gnosis", *GGA*, 215, 1963, pp. 31 ff.; "Ist die Gnosis in aramäischen Weisheitsschulen entstanden?", in

can be said that Simon (and the Kabbalists) then no longer belonged to the
Samaritan (or Jewish) people. This issue is illustrated by the respective articles
of G. Kretschmar and H.J. Schoeps on the origin of Gnosticism. Both follow
the Fathers of the Church and think that it is probable that Simon was the
author of the Gnostic religion; Kretschmar takes this to mean that Gnosticism
originated in "a syncretistic Judaism"[89], whereas Schoeps maintains that
there cannot be a transition from Jewish religion to Gnosticism and ascribes the origin of Gnosticism to "the syncretistic circles of Samaria"[90]. K.
Rudolph retorts against Schoeps that it is a "terminological question"
whether "an extreme heresy" should be reckoned as belonging to the "religious mother soil"[91], but to me there seems to be found a gauge for making a
judgment in this case. Is there a Jewish potential of the idea of a split within
the deity — the theological correlate to the ontological anti-cosmic dualism —
which was developed by the Gnostics? H.J.W. Drijvers says that the idea of a
"crisis in the divine world" would be shocking "even in Samaria"[92], and this
statement is typical of the common attitude to think of Gnosticism as a
phenomenon which was born like Athena, who sprang out of her father's

---

OG, pp. 291 ff. (= *Sprache und Dogma*, Gütersloh, 1969, pp. 101 ff.); *Lehrbuch
der Dogmengeschichte*, I (Die Zeit der alten Kirche), Gütersloh, 1965, pp. 49 ff.,
especially pp. 55 f.; Rudolph, "Randerscheinungen", pp. 109 ff., 118 ff. (= *GG*,
pp. 774 ff., 790 ff.); cp. *Die Gnosis*, pp. 298 f. For the relationship between Jewish
Wisdom teachings and Gnosticism, see now K. Rudolph, "Sophia und Gnosis", in
AT-F-G, pp. 221 ff.

89 "Zur religionsgeschichtlichen Einordnung der Gnosis", *ET*, 13, 1953, p. 357 (= *GG*,
p. 432).

90 "Zur Standortbestimmung der Gnosis", *TLZ*, 81, 1956, col. 418 (= *Urgemeinde –
Judenchristentum – Gnosis*, Tübingen, 1956, p. 35; *GG*, p. 470). A concomitant of
the idea that Jews would not abandon the doctrine of the *monarchia* of God is that it
is anachronistic to speak about a "heretical" Judaism at the beginning of our era; see
van Unnik, "Komponente", pp. 74 f. (= *GG*, pp. 484 f.); "Gnosis", p. 78; Drijvers,
p. 348 (= *GG*, p. 833; cp. the appendix from 1971, *ibid.*, p. 839); H.-F. Weiss, "Einige
Bemerkungen zum Problem des Verhältnisses von "Judentum" und "Gnosis"",
OLZ, 64, 1969, cols. 540 ff. But there were obviously Jews who did not maintain the
belief in God and practise life according to the Law to the satisfication of the rabbis,
who actually had several terms designating a "heretic". Thus, positions which qualified for being labelled a מין included the denial of God's unity, the idea that God
was a cruel jester, and the belief in an independent deity (see *Sanh*. 38b-39a). The
כופר בעיקר is said to be one who denies his Creator and the Giver of the Law (see
Tos. Shab. iii.7). That Jews could be considered heretics is also shown by the rabbinic
discussions about whether or not a heretic may offer sacrifice (see *Hull*. 13a; *Gitt*.
45b; *Ab. Zar.* 32b). See also Scholem, *Major Trends*, p. 359, n. 24. The most famous
heretic was Elisha ben Abuya, who was not a Gnostic, but whose views apparently
contained the germ of Gnosticism; see below, pp. 308 ff.

91 "Randerscheinungen", p. 111 (= *GG*, p. 781).

92 *Op. cit.*, p. 349 (= *GG*, p. 835).

head in full accoutrements. The truth of the matter is, of course, that Gnosticism, like every religion, *grew*. The sharp dualism found in the *Apocryphon of John* has developed from a dualism of subordination, according to which the demiurge was God's angel. There is evidence showing that Samaritans took the Angel of the Lord, who is said already by the Bible (*Ex.* xxiii. 20 f.) to possess God's Name, which denotes God's own nature or mode of being, to be a real hypostasis acting in the creation. Furthermore, we shall see that Simon Magus availed himself of certain traditions about this figure. Simon actually was the possessor of the Name of God.

The importance of the notion of the Divine Name in the discussion of Gnostic origins has not been unnoticed. When the *Gospel of Truth* became known, G. Quispel at once asserted that the elaborate Christology of the Name found in this Valentinian source goes back "ultimately to more, or less hererodox Jewish conceptions which were taken over into Gnosis as early as the beginning of the second century."[93] He cites apocalyptical and mystical texts where the principal angel is described as the possessor of the Divine Name or even as the hypostasized Name. But, like the Son in the *Gospel of Truth*, this angel is never described as the demiurge. Quispel also adduces Jewish texts presenting the Name as the instrument through which the world came into being and by which it is sustained, but this cosmogonic and cosmological force is no personal being. It is the Samaritan material which is of prime importance in this work, for here we find firm evidence that the principal angel, even the Angel of the Lord, who is the possessor of the Name of God or even the hypostasized Name, is the demiurge.

---

93 "The Jung Codex and Its Significance", in H.-Ch. Puech, G. Quispel & W.C. van Unnik, *The Jung Codex*, trans. by F. Cross, London, 1955, p. 72. See also "De Joodse achtergrond van de Logos-Christologie", *VoxTheol*, 25,1954,pp.48 ff.; "Christliche Gnosis und jüdische Heterodoxie", *ET*, 14, 1954, pp. 481 ff.; "Het Johannesevangelie en de Gnosis", *NTT*, 11, 1957, pp. 173 ff.; "L'Évangile de Jean et la Gnose", in F.M. Braun, ed., *L'Évangile de Jean* (RB, III), Bruges, 1958, pp. 197 ff.; "Jewish Gnosis and Mandaean Gnosticism", in J.-E. Ménard, ed., *Les Textes de Nag Hammadi* (Colloque du Centre d'Histoire des Religions, Strasbourg, 23-25 octobre 1974) (NHS, VII), Leiden, 1975, pp. 117 ff.; "Demiurge", pp. 23 ff.

Part Two

The Samaritan Mould of Gnosticism

CHAPTER TWO

Introduction: The Samaritans and their Religion

The Origin of Samaritanism

In 1970, 430 Samaritans were counted in Palestine[1]. Most of these people live in Nablus, Samaria's greatest urban centre, founded by Vespasian in 72 C.E. as Flavia Neapolis on the site of the village Mabartha, probably meaning "the passage", *viz.*, between Mt. Ebal in the north and Mt. Gerizim in the south (cp. Joseph., *Bell.* IV.449). Nablus is situated about two kilometres west of the village Balatha, which is the site of Biblical Shechem, the holy city of the Samaritans which was destroyed by John Hyrcanus (cp. Joseph., *Ant.* XIII.254 ff.; *Bell.* I.63)[2]. The Samaritans, claiming to be the descendants of Ephraim and Manasseh, did not leave the territory in the highlands of central Palestine which had been allotted to the two Joseph tribes by Joshua, for they believed — and still do — that Mt. Gerizim had been sanctified by God. According to the Samaritans, the great schism in the history of Israel did not occur when the Kingdom was divided, but when Eli, a descendant of Aaron's son Ithamar, disrupted the cult of YHWH on Mt. Gerizim and instituted worship in Shiloh, attracting some of the people to the cult there. This event put an end to the era of divine favour. God caused the tabernacle, which had been erected on Mt. Gerizim, to disappear into a cave, and withdrew his face. Still, according to Samaritan annals, worship directed by a high priest descended from the genuine Aaronite line through Eleazar and his son Phinehas continued on Mt. Gerizim, where already Joshua had sited the sanctuary[3].

---

1 See B. Tsedaka, par. "Statistics", in Art. "Samaritans", in *EJ*, 14, col. 738.

2 Shechem was hallowed by the memory of the patriarchs and was the first shrine for the confederation of the Hebrew tribes, but was eclipsed by other sanctuaries already in the period of Judges; see below, p. 40. However, it no doubt survived as a holy ground, at least in memory; cp. below, p. 37, n. 28. For the date of its resuscitation as the Samaritan sanctum in late Persian or early Hellenistic times, see below, pp. 36 f., 40 f. For Shechem in general, see the „traditio–historical investigation" by E. Nielsen, *Shechem*, Copenhagen, 1955, and the "biography" by G.E. Wright, *Shechem*, London, 1965.

3 See J. Macdonald, ed. & trans., *The Samaritan Chronicle No. II* (BZAW, 107), Berlin, 1969, pp. 47 ff. in the text and pp. 123 ff. in the translation. Chronicle II is late, but

The conventional view of the Samaritans and their religion is very different. It was assumed for a long time – and still is in some conservative circles – that *II Kings* ch. xvii gives the correct picture of the origin of the Samaritan community. The Biblical account tells that, after the Assyrian conquest of the Northern Kingdom of Israel, in 722/21 B.C.E., the inhabitants of the land were deported never to return. In the place of the people who came to be known as "the ten lost tribes", the Assyrian king, who was actually Sargon II and not Shalmaneser V, repopulated the land with people from "Babylon, Cuthah, Avva, Hamath, and Sepharvaim". These people brought their religious beliefs and practices to Samaria. However, since the colonists were plagued by lions (perhaps because of a drought bringing wild beasts into the land looking for food), they took to the religion of Israel in order to appease "the god of the country" (*v.* 26). The Assyrian king sent back one of the Israelite priests, and a YHWH worship was established in Bethel. The immigrants, then, "worshipped YHWH and served their own gods at the same time, with rites of the countries from which they had been deported" (*v.* 33), and their descendants persisted in this way (see *v.* 41). According to the "Deuteronomistic History", then, the people in the North are a heathen people of mixed origin, having grafted a superficial Yahwism upon their original worship. The customary view has been to accept this account and see the forefathers of the Samaritans as the pagans described in *II Kings* ch. xvii.

The Samaritans, however, know of a return (even two returns) to the Holy Land. Whether or not this has some basis in fact need not occupy us; the important point to remember is that the representation of *II Kings* ch. xvii now has been abandoned as a strong polemical description of the people and the religion in the North, especially at the religious centre of Bethel. According to Sargon's own annals, he exiled only 27,290 people[4]. If we

---

based on an old source or a source containing old elements; see now J.M. Cohen, ed. & trans., *A Samaritan Chronicle* (SP-B, XXX), Leiden, 1981, pp. 174 ff., 184 ff. References to the Eli schism in other Samaritan chronicles, which on the whole are less reliable, are given by J.D. Purvis, *The Samaritan Pentateuch and the Origin of the Samaritan Sect* (HSM, 2), Cambridge, Mass., 1968, p. 88, n. 1.

4 The Assyrian inscriptions are quoted by J.A. Montgomery, *The Samaritans* (BL, 1906), Philadelphia, 1907, reprinted New York, 1968, p. 50. See also H.G. Kippenberg, *Garizim und Synagoge* (RGVV, XXX), Berlin & New York, 1971, p. 35; R.J. Coggins, *Samaritans and Jews* (GPT), Oxford, 1975, p. 117.

Chronicle II (Macdonald, p. 89 in the text and p. 186 in the translation) says that the Samaritans under the high priest Seriah returned from the Assyrian exile after 47 years. J. Macdonald, *The Theology of the Samaritans* (NTL), London, 1964, pp. 20 f., states that this chronicle says that 300,000 men with their families returned, but we do not read about any number in this work. The *Book of Joshua* (ch. 45), however, says that 300,000 Samaritans returned, but this chronicle, which stems

compare this figure to the information in *II Kings* xv.19 f., from which we can deduce that there were 60,000 "men of rank" in the Northern Kingdom about 740, it is to be concluded that but a small part of the population was carried away. It has been estimated that no more than five per cent of the population was deported[5]. The colonists, who apparently arrived in successive waves (see *Ezra* iv.2, 8 ff.; cp. *Is.* vii.8), must have been in a minority and undoubtedly were engulfed by the autochthonous inhabitants in the course of time.

That the people and religion in the North were essentially Yahwistic also after 720 is evidenced by several Biblical passages. Since the time of Hezekiah, Northerners were accepted as worshippers in Jerusalem and supporters of the cult there (see *II Chron.* ch. xxx; xxxiv.9; xxxv.18). During the exile, offerings still were presented at Sion by people from Shechem and Shiloh (see *Jer.* xli.5). *Jeremiah* and *Ezekiel* contain many passages voicing the hope of a future restoration and reunion of the two Kingdoms, and there cannot be found allusions to the existence of an impure population and a syncretistic religion in the North in these prophecies (see *Jer.* xxiii.5 f.; xxx.3; xxxi.5, 17 ff.; *Ez.* xxxvii.15 ff.; cp. *Is.* xi.12, which is post-Isaiahnic; *Zech.* ix.13; x.6 f.).

It was undoubtedly during the time of the restoration of the Jerusalem

---

from the 13th century, but includes earlier sources, maintains that the exile in question was one which Nebuchadnezzar had imposed upon Samaritans and Judaeans alike. The occasion for the return is given in a story strongly reminiscent of that in *II Kings* xvii.25 ff., which Macdonald erroneously connects with the return from the captivity under an "Assyrian king (name not specified)" (*Theology*, p. 20). In par. "History, Until 1300", in Art. "Samaritans", in *EJ*, 14, col. 728, Macdonald says that it is related by Chronicle II, and that the leader during the return, which took place in Cyrus' time, was a high priest by the name of Abdel. Macdonald does not tell us that Chronicle II actually knows of a second exile, but the part relating this unfortunately is still unpublished; in a later summary statement (Cohen, §10,7), it is said that this was in the Greek period and that Abdel was the leader when the people returned.

The Chronicle *Tolida*, which stems from the 12th century, also speaks of two exiles, one under Nebuchadnezzar and one under a certain "king of the Greeks" (Neubauer, p. 401; Bowman, *Tolidah*, p. 14); Seriah led the people back from the first exile, and Abdel shepherded 300,000 men back from the latter. Abu'l Fath's chronicle from the 14th century knows only of the exile under Nebuchadnezzar (see Vilmar, pp. 55 ff.), as does the *Book of Joshua*, but Abu'l Fath (Vilmar, pp. 79 ff.) does relate a voluntary exile of some of the people in the Persian period due to Darius' support of the Jews against the Samaritans. Abu'l Fath (p. 61) says that Abdel led the people back from the Babylonian exile. The Chronicle Adler, which extends to the end of the 19th century, agrees with Chronicle II as to the Assyrian exile and the return thence, but knows also of a deportation under Nebuchadnezzar and a return of 300,000 men under Abdel after 55 years of this exile.

5 See H.G. May, "The Ten Lost Tribes", *BA*, 6, 1943, p. 58; cp. R. de Vaux, *Ancient Israel*, 1, trans. from the French, London & New York, 1961, reprinted as McGraw-

temple and the reorganization of the Judaean community after the exile that
the first material effects of the Deuteronomistic history-work's view of the
people in the North came to pass. Even if it may be true that the reference to
the foreign rootstock of the "adversaries of Judah and Benjamin" in *Ezra*
iv.1 ff. is an invention of the Chronicler and the people in question thus cannot be identified as inhabitants of Samaria[6], it is obvious that the denial of
Zerubbabel and his confidants to let others than Judaeans help to rebuild
the temple implied that the people of Samaria as well as the population of the
other neighbouring provinces were regarded as cultically unclean[7]. It is also
reasonable to assume that the measures of Nehemiah and Ezra against the
marriages of the Judaeans with the "peoples of the land(s)" must have struck
at relations between Judaeans and inhabitants of Samaria; this may account
for the strong Samaritan malice against "the cursed Ezra", as the great cultic
reformer often is called in the Samaritan chronicles[8].

However, we are not justified in reckoning with the existence of the Samaritan community at this time. The name of the Samaritans is derived from
the name of their land. When the Northern Kingdom was turned into an
Assyrian province, the name of the capital, שמרון, Shomron, erected by
Omri about 880 on the hill belonging to a certain Shemer (see *I Kings* xvi.24),
was extended to the whole province, which is known as *Samerina* in the
Assyrian records (see *II Kings* xvii.24, 26; *et al.*). Consonantly, the LXX
renders the name of the province as well as that of the city as Σαμάρεια.
When Herod the Great in 27 B.C.E. gave the city the new name of Σεβαστή
(*Augusta*), the name of Samaria continued in use for the territory alone, as
constantly in the New Testament. Jewish sources from pre-Christian times
refer to the people worshipping God on Mt. Gerizim by characterizing them
as the people living in Shechem or at Mt. Gerizim (see *Sir.* 1.26; *II Macc.*
v.22 f.; cp. Joseph., *Ant.* XI.340 ff.), but Josephus calls them Σαμαρεῖς or,

---

Hill paperback, New York, 1965, pp. 65 f.; H.H. Rowley, "The Samaritan Schism in
Legend and History", in B.W. Anderson & W. Harrelson, ed., *Israel's Prophetic Heritage* (Essays in Honor of James Muilenburg) (PL), New York, 1962, p. 209.

6 It seems incomprehensible that Coggins, accepting the hypothesis that the reference
is an invention, can assert that the present text is "remarkably allusive" and does not
intend "to decry any specific rival" (p. 66).

7 Although the unclean people in *Hag.* ii. 10 ff. is not to be identified as that of Samaria or any other neighbouring province, this oracle – deriving from the time of the
rebuilding of the temple and addressing the whole *ecclesia* – shows that ritual purity
was absolutely mandatory for those associated with the cult in Jerusalem. The
reason for denying non-Judaeans access to the place of worship apparently was that
the people of the neighbouring provinces – in contrast to the people in Judah – had
suffered the imposition of foreign upper classes and thereby been made cultically
unclean.

8 For possible post-exilic reference to the people in the North in other Biblical passages,
see Coggins, pp. 37 ff.; cp. Kippenberg, pp. 49 f.

preferably, Σαμαρεῖται, and the New Testament knows the people of Samaria by the latter name.

The name Σαμαρεῖται is taken from LXX *II Kings* xvii.29, the only place in the Old Testament where the people of Samaria is given a name of their own. The Bible here tells us that the Assyrian colonists put their idols on the high places that had been made by the שמרנים: Σαμαρεῖται. Thus, the name has a strong connotation of paganism and idolatry, and Josephus (*Ant.* IX. 290) says that the Greek Σαμαρεῖται corresponds to the Hebrew Χουθαῖοι, which translates the rabbinic כותים, a contemptuous name pointing to the city of Cuthah in northern Mesopotamia, the place of origin of one of the groups of people introduced into the land of the vanquished Kingdom of Israel by the Assyrians. But when we learn to know the Samaritan religion through the Samaritans' own literature and cult, Samaritanism appears to be no idolatrous religion but a true Yahwism in dogmas, modes of worship and law. Rather than associating the term "Samaritan" with what is heathen, it would seem appropriate to follow the Samaritans' own rendering of the name applied to them as meaning שמרים, Shamerim, their form of the Hebrew Shomerim, *i.e.*, "keepers" or "observers", *viz.*, of the Law. Anyway, we must distinguish between the Samaritans, meaning the people who worshipped YHWH on Mt. Gerizim, and the Samarians, meaning the inhabitants of Samaria. We obviously must understand *II Kings* xvii.29 to speak of Samarians. Whatever is the truth in the Samaritans' own traditions, there is no historical evidence that the community of the Samaritans existed in the Assyrian epoch.

This brings us to the critical questioning of the origin of the Samaritan community. J.A. Montgomery, who, in the beginning of this century, published a comprehensive book on the Samaritans making use of all the material that was available at that time, saw them as a "Jewish sect", "content to draw its teaching and stimulus from the Jews, even long after the rupture was final." At the same time, Montgomery passed the judgment that Samaritanism "possessed a certain patriotic hardiness which enabled it to preserve its own characteristic, and in many cases to maintain the elder and more conservative position as against progressive Pharisaism."[9] Montgomery saw the conservative priestly party of the Sadducees in Jerusalem as the supplier of the doctrines of Samaritan theology[10]. The theory of the Sadducean substructure of Samaritanism goes back to A. Geiger, who asserted that the Sadducees were the descendants of the Sadoqites, the priestly dynasty of Jerusalem in Old Testament times, and that these people at one time also had

---

9 *Op. cit.*, p. 205.
10 See *ibid.*, pp. 46, 71 f., 186 ff. See also J.W. Nutt, ed. & trans., *Fragments of a Samaritan Targum*, London, 1874, pp. 29, 41 f., 64, 79 f.

supplied the priesthood of Shechem. When the Pharisees came into power and the Sadducean theology was repressed, according to Geiger, the Samaritans kept to the old ways[11].

Montgomery claimed to know the occasion of the origination of Samaritanism. This took place, he asserted, by Nehemiah's expulsion of Jerusalem priests married to women from the upper classes in Samaria. Nehemiah relates that he expelled one of the grandsons of the high priest because he was married to the daughter of "Sanballat the Horonite" (*Neh.* xiii.28 f.; cp. xii.10 f., 22). It is not stated explicitly in the Biblical record who Sanballat was, but it seems to be implied in the account of Nehemiah's dealings with him that he was the governor of Samaria, now being a Persian province; and this impression actually is corroborated by the evidence of the Elephantine papyri, mentioning Sanballat as being the name of the Persian governor of Samaria shortly before 400 B.C.E.[12] The *Book of Nehemiah* does not say that the expelled priest went to Samaria and founded a temple on Mt. Gerizim, and this has to be inferred by the help of a relation by Josephus (*Ant.* XI.302 ff.). According to Josephus, a certain Manasseh, a brother of the high priest, married the daughter of Sanballat, "who was of Cuthean race," and was expelled from Jerusalem on this account. Josephus goes on to tell that Sanballat promised Manasseh that a temple should be built for him on Mt. Gerizim, and that many others having contracted similar marriages joined Manasseh.

However, a great discrepancy between *Nehemiah* and Josephus is found in dating, for Josephus says that the incident took place in the year that Alexander the Great came to Palestine, and that Sanballat transferred his allegiance to him. Further, while Nehemiah relates that the expelled priest, who is unnamed in his book, was the son of Yehoyada and the grandson of Elyashib, the high priest, Josephus has it that the priest, Manasseh by name, was the brother of Yaddua, the high priest, who is known from *Neh.* xii.11 to have been the grandson of Yehoyada and the great-grandson of Elyashib. Still, the two accounts have been taken to describe the same event. Montgomery dismissed the dating by Josephus, deemed to be "absolutely irresponsible in Persian history and chronology" and drawing the Samaritan schism "into the great vortex of the Alexander Legend"[13]. Others, however, have accepted the

---

11 See "Zur Theologie und Schrifterklärung der Samaritaner", *ZDMG*, 12, 1858, pp. 132 ff. (= *Nachgelassene Schriften*, ed. by L. Geiger, III, Breslau, 1876, pp. 255 ff.); cp. *Urschrift und Übersetzungen der Bibel*, Breslau, 1857, pp. 56, 99 ff., 146, 172 ff., 493. That the high priesthoods in Shechem and Jerusalem guarded the same family traditions was a theory accepted by Montgomery, p. 72.

12 See A.E. Cowley, ed. & trans., *Aramaic Papyri of the Fifth Century B.C.*, Oxford, 1923, reprinted Osnabrück, 1967, No. 30, line 29 (text on p. 113; translation on p. 114).

13 *Op. cit.*, p. 68. There was a tendency among previous scholars to suppose that the

date given by Josephus and thought that he incorrectly connected Sanballat with the Samaritan temple[14]. Some have also argued that the Sanballat of the Josephus narrative was a direct descendant of Nehemiah's contemporary who, on the principle of papponymy, bore the same name[15]. This hypothesis has gained favour recently owing to the discovery of Samaritan legal and administrative papyri in a cave in Wadi Daliyeh, about 14 kilometres north of Jericho. These documents witness the existence of a Persian governor of Samaria by the name of Sanballat born about 435[16]. This Sanballat could have been the grandson of Nehemiah's opponent, and he could have had a grandson with the same name who would qualify for the Sanballat of Josephus[17].

Archeological evidence too supports the theory that the Samaritan temple was built at the end of the 4th century, for excavations have shown that there was in fact a resettlement of Shechem at this time[18]. But this does not have to mean that the Josephus story is all true. The resettlement of Shechem can in fact be explained from events taking place in the province of Samaria exclusively. Literary sources from the beginning of the Christian era narrate that Alexander the Great (or one of his generals) turned the city of Samaria

---

Sanballat mentioned by Josephus was Nehemiah's contemporary; see H.H. Rowley, "Sanballat and the Samaritan Temple", *BJRL*, 38, 1955, pp. 183 f. (= *Men of God*, London, 1963, pp. 263 f.). An enumeration is also given by Purvis, p. 11, n. 17. J. Bowman also thinks that *Nehemiah* describes the origin of the Samaritan schism; see now *The Samaritan Problem*, trans. by A.M. Johnson, Jr. (PTMS, 4), Pittsburgh, 1975, pp. xii f. But see also next note.

14 See the citations by Rowley, "Sanballat", pp. 179 f. (= *Men of God*, pp. 259 f.); cp. Purvis, p. 11, n. 18. J. Bowman, trans., *Samaritan Documents* (POT&TS, 2), Pittsburgh, 1977, p. 119, now would seem to mean that Josephus is right that the temple was built in Alexander's time.

15 See the references by Rowley, "Sanballat", p. 171 (= *Men of God*, p. 251), tracing the theory back to I. Vossius in the 18th century. Cp. Purvis, p. 103, n. 33. The theory was reiterated in modern times by G.E. Wright, "The Samaritans at Shechem", *HTR*, 55, 1962, pp. 357 ff. This article is found in an expanded version in Wright's *Shechem*, pp. 170 ff.

16 See F.M. Cross, Jr., "The Discovery of the Samaritan Papyri", *BA*, 26, 1963, pp. 110 ff.; cp. "Aspects of Samaritan and Jewish History in Late Persian and Hellenistic Times", *HTR*, 59, 1966, pp. 201 ff. See also Wright, *Shechem*, pp. 180 f.

17 For subscriptions to this theory, see Wright, *loc. cit.*; Cross, Jr., *loc. cit.*; Purvis, pp. 103 ff.; Kippenberg, pp. 44, 50 ff. I.H. Eybers, "Relations between Jews and Samaritans in the Persian Period", in *Biblical Essays 1966* (Proceedings of the Ninth Meeting of the Oud-Testamentiese Werkgemeenskap in Suid-Afrika), Potchefstroom, 1967, p. 80, thinks that the Sanballat referred to in the papyri from Wadi Daliyeh is the one said by Josephus to have built the temple. B. Reicke, *The New Testament Era*, London, 1969, pp. 28 f., thinks that the *Book of Nehemiah* and Josephus refer to the same event, which really took place in the time of the governor mentioned in the Samaritan papyri.

18 See Wright, *Shechem*, pp. 167 ff.; cp. O.R. Sellers, "Coins of the 1960 Excavation at Shechem", *BA*, 25, 1962, pp. 87 ff. For the preliminary reports on the archeolo-

into a colony for his Macedonian troops[19], and it has been suggested that Samarians expelled from the city on this occasion planted themselves in Shechem and thus gave rise to the Samaritan community[20]. As will be suggested below, it is also possible that people, even priests, from Bethel migrated to Shechem at about this time or even before[21].

There is no need to follow F.M. Cross, Jr., G.E. Wright, and J.D. Purvis, and balance the archeological evidence with the story by Josephus. In fact, there are good reasons to dismiss the Josephus account. To begin with, the existence of a Sanballat III, living at Alexander's time, has never been demonstrated; it is only conjectured. It is also merely a conjecture that intermarriage between the ruling family in Samaria and the high priestly family in Jerusalem took place on more than one occasion. Further, a high priest by the name of Manasseh is lacking in the Samaritan lists of high priests for the period in question. Lastly, Josephus implies that the Samaritan temple was erected during the period that Alexander stayed in Palestine, but this was less than a year and thus a time much too brief for the building of the temple[22].

In *Ant.* XI.342, however, it is implied that the Samaritan temple already was in existence when Alexander traversed Palestine, and this account seems to have been taken from an older source. This paragraph belongs to a block of material which refers to the Samaritans as "Shechemites", which is the older Jewish designation of the people living at Shechem and not used by Josephus elsewhere. H.G. Kippenberg, who has tried to enisle the "Shechemite source", does not observe the difference between this block of material and that in §§ 302 ff., these two sections being split by §§ 325 ff., which relate that Alexander greeted the high priest in Jerusalem reverently[23]. In §§ 316ff.,

---

gical work at Shechem, see the articles cited by Purvis, p. 106, n. 42 (continued from the previous page).

19 For the relevant sources, coming from Quintus Curtius, Eusebius, Jerome, and Syncellus, see Appendix C, entitled "Alexander the Great and the Jews", by R. Marcus, ed. & trans., *Josephus* (LCL), VI, London & Cambridge, Mass., 1951, pp. 523 ff.; cp. Kippenberg, pp. 45 ff.

20 See E. Bickerman, "The Historical Foundations of Postbiblical Judaism", in his *From Ezra to the Last of the Maccabees*, New York, 1962, pp. 41 ff. Cp. already L. Haefeli, *Geschichte der Landschaft Samaria von 722 vor Chr. bis 67 nach Chr.* (ATA, VIII/1-2), Münster, 1922, p. 68. Wright, Cross, Jr., and Purvis think that the Jerusalem priests said by Josephus to have come to Shechem became the spiritual leaders of these "Samaritan Yahwists of mixed ethnic descent" (Purvis, p. 108).

21 See pp. 40 f.

22 For criticism of the Josephus story, see Rowley, "Sanballat", pp. 166 ff. (= *Men of God*, pp. 246 ff.); cp. V. Tcherikover, *Hellenistic Civilization and the Jews*, Philadelphia, 1961, pp. 42 ff. See further Coggins, pp. 95 ff. Already G. Hölscher dismissed Josephus' narrative as a "false exegesis of the Nehemiah passage" (*Palästina in der persischen und hellenistischen Zeit* (QFAGG), Berlin, 1903, p. 39).

23 Kippenberg says that the account of Manasseh being followed by many priests

Alexander — on his way south — meets Sanballat and consents to the project of the building of the temple on Mt. Gerizim, and Manasseh is made high priest. In §§ 342 ff., Alexander — on his way to Egypt from Jerusalem — is met by the "Shechemites"and *does not know who they are*. Furthermore, the latter — calling themselves "Hebrews" (which is actually a name that the Samaritans apply to themselves) — deny that they are Jews and *already have* their temple. Josephus' account thus has inner inconsistencies.

The Samaritan chronicles narrate that the temple was built after the return from the exile and thus agree with the "Shechemite source" that the temple on Mt. Gerizim existed before Alexander came to Palestine. We cannot trust the chronicles in this respect, however, because Samaritan hagiography obviously has adapted the Jewish tradition that the Jerusalem temple was rebuilt after the Babylonian exile[24]. What seems certain is that the erection of

---

and lay men does not harmonize with Josephus' chronic view of the Samaritans as "Cutheans". H.G.M. Williamson, *Israel in the Book of Chronicles*, Cambridge, 1977, p. 137, n. 4, justly asks why Kippenberg leaves out §§ 302 f. and 306 f., which also summarize the Manasseh story and thus cannot be separated from the postulated source. In § 302, however, we find the terms "Cuthean" and "Samaritans". The only criterion for isolating the "Shechemite source" is the use of the term "Shechemites". Thus, § 340, which Williamson as well as Kippenberg wants to reckon to the source, must be eliminated, since it uses "Samaritans" and not "Shechemites". Furthermore, this paragraph and its continuation, which cannot be treated separately, show the same confusion with regard to the Samaritans as the previous material, for it is said that Shechem "was inhabited by apostates from the Jewish nation," but also that these people, who professed themselves Jews when they thought they could gain anything by it, in reality were not Jews. In §§ 342 ff., however, we hear that the "Shechemites" denied that they were Jews, though this could have ensured Alexander's favour to them, and that people in Jerusalem violating the Law used to flee to the "Shechemites". However, Williamson may be right that the last assertion is "a generalizing statement of the situation by Josephus on the basis of other material" (p. 138). The context shows that the founding of the Samaritan temple is the leitmotif ("As for the temple on Mt. Gerizim, it remained. And whenever anyone was accused by the people in Jerusalem..."), and this is not dealt with at all by the "Shechemite source".

24 The *Tolida* (Neubauer, p. 401; Bowman, *Tolidah*, p. 14) says that Abdel, upon returning from the second exile in the Greek period, built an altar on Mt. Gerizim; then the account introduces Alexander. The *Book of Joshua* (ch. 45) tells about the building of the temple after the Babylonian exile, and then it passes on to the time of Alexander. The chronicle contains an adaptation of the story in Joseph., *Ant.* XI.325 ff., with the Samaritans substituted for the Jews, and the Samaritan high priest replacing Yaddua, the Jewish high priest. Abu'l Fath (Vilmar, p. 61) says that Abdel, returning from the Babylonian captivity, built a temple. The Chronicle Adler omits this report. Abu'l Fath (p. 80) says that the temple was destroyed by Simon the Maccabee, who, however, is placed in the *Persian* period. Bowman, *Documents*, pp. 118 ff., argues that Abu'l Fath knew the Josephus story and dated the destruction of the temple *before* Alexander's time in order to make pointed that the Macedonian king had

the temple on Mt. Gerizim was a consequence of the exclusion of Northerners
from the cult in the restored temple in Jerusalem. Since Bethel at this time
had lost its importance, the attempt at a religious consolidation in the North
would naturally reach back to the ancient religious centre at Shechem. That
this would have waited until the latter part of the 4th century is improbable,
and even if Josephus' story may contain a grain of truth in that the temple
was not finished before Alexander's time or that the permission to build it
was given by Greek authorities, Northerners must have gathered in Shechem
long before this time. The circumstances related by Josephus certainly are
unhistorical and based upon *Neh*. xiii.28.

The first source to mention the Samaritans' temple on Mt. Gerizim is
II Maccabees (vi.1 ff.), which was written by the end of the 2nd century
B.C.E. But, already in the *Book of Sirach*, from about 180 B.C.E., we hear
about "the foolish people that dwell in Shechem" (i.26). This is the first
clear reference to the community of the Samaritans, and it would seem that
the *terminus ante quem* of the erection of the temple on Mt. Gerizim is about
200 B.C.E. As for the determination of the *terminus post quem*, a letter from
the Elephantine Jews to the governor in Judah may be of some help. The
colonists, writing in 407, state that they have written an earlier letter to the
governor and the high priest in Jerusalem asking for assistance to rebuild their
temple, destroyed at the instigation of Egyptian priests, and they announce
further in all simplicity that they also have approached the sons of Sanballat,
the Persian governor in Samaria, on the same matter[25]. The Elephantine colonists betray no awareness of a break between the Jews and the people in the
North, but this in itself does not have to be of particular relevance to the question regarding the time of the building of the Samaritan temple[26]. More important, however, is the fact that the letter implies no knowledge of the existence
of a Samaritan priesthood, which it would have been natural for the colonists

---

nothing to do with it. This may very well be the explanation of the anachronism of
Abu'l Fath, but it does not follow that Josephus is right. However, Macdonald, par.
"History, Until 1300", col. 729, says that Chronicle II actually narrates that the tem-
ple was built under Alexander.

   The Samaritan chronicles are on the whole friendly towards Alexander. A. Büchler thought that the Sanballat story as given by Josephus is of Samaritan origin and
that its aim is to trace the origin of the temple on Mt. Gerizim "to this great king"
("La relation de Josèphe concernant Alexandre le Grand", *REJ*, 36, 1898, p. 10).
See now also Purvis, p. 105, n. 39. If this were to be granted, however, the apparent
elaborations upon *Neh*. xiii.28 would have to be excised as not belonging to the
postulated Samaritan source. But without the personage of Manasseh, the story of
the founding of the Samaritan temple seems too incomplete, and nothing like it is
found in Samaritan sources.

25 See Cowley, *Aramaic Papyri*, No. 30, line 29 (text on p. 113; translation on p. 114).
26 See the next note.

to address when writing to the authorities in Samaria. Thus, if it is allowed to use this *argumentum ex silentio*, it would seem that the Samaritan temple was built at some time between 400 and 200 B.C.E.

Probably we shall never know the exact time of the erection of the Samaritan temple, the existence of which — although perhaps not occasioning an immediate breach with the Jews[27] — soon became the main point of divergence between the Jews and the Samaritans[28]. The Samaritans have a creed confessing faith in God, the Law, Moses, Mt. Gerizim, and the Last Day and the Resurrection[29]; and, except the fourth article of faith — which is also made the Tenth Commandment of the Samaritan Decalogue (counting the ten Masoretic commandments as nine and joining a composition of *Deut.* xi.29 f. and xxvii.2-7 to *Ex.* xx.17 and to *Deut.* v.18) — the Samaritan creed contains only tenets which are cardinal to all Jews (although the Samaritans exalt Moses to a position far superior to the place allotted to him in Judaism). The post-Talmudic tractate *Masseketh Kuthim*, that is, the "Tract on the

---

27 It has become increasingly clear that the Deuteronomic requirement that God should be worshipped in only one place was not recognized at once and by all. There were post-Deuteronomic temples of Jews in Egypt, both in Elephantine and Leontopolis, and possibly also in Transjordan and Babylonia. For the possible existence of a Jewish temple at the Transjordanian centre of the Tobiads, see A. Spiro, "Samaritans, Tobiads, and Judahites in Pseudo-Philo", *PAAJR*, 20, 1951, pp. 314 f.; cp. P.W. Lapp, "The Second and Third Campaigns at ʿArâq el-ʾEmîr", *BASOR*, 171, 1963, pp. 8 ff. For the possible existence of a Jewish temple in Babylonia, see L.E. Browne, "A Jewish Sanctuary in Babylonia", *JTS*, 17, 1916, pp. 400 ff.; cp. *Early Judaism*, Cambridge, 1929, pp. 53 ff. See also Cross, Jr., "Aspects", p. 208; Coggins, pp. 101 f., 112 f. Regarding the Elephantine colonists, the epistolary intercourse between these immigrants and the authorities in Jerusalem shows that the former were not regarded as schismatics. Rowley, "Sanballat", p. 188 (= *Men of God*, p. 268), does not think that the Jerusalem authorities would have found the building of the Samaritan temple so unacceptable, since they would not like to have Northerners worshipping in Jerusalem.

28 Since it is highly probable that *Deuteronomy* originated in the Northern Kingdom, "the place which YHWH has chosen for His Name to dwell there" (if belonging to the original compilation of Levitical traditions forming the backbone of the book) perhaps originally referred to Shechem. There is something to be said for the Samaritan reading of *Deut.* xxvii.4 f. that, as soon as the Israelites had crossed the Jordan, they should erect an altar and set up large stones with the Law written upon them on Mt. Gerizim, for the continuation says that blessings and curses are to be pronounced on Mt. Gerizim and Mt. Ebal respectively (cp. xi.26 ff.; *Josh.* viii.30). There is obviously some connection between this story and that of *Josh.* xxiv.25 ff., which relates how the inter-tribal pact was sealed at Shechem. The prescription of *Deut.* xxxi.10 ff. that the Law should be read periodically, during a feast, could have been enacted just at Shechem. But a strong case may also be made out for Bethel as "the place which YHWH has chosen"; see below, pp. 40 f.

29 For the Samaritan creed, see Montgomery, pp. 207 ff.; Macdonald, *Theology*, pp. 49 ff.

Samaritans", ends with the following statement: "When shall we take them back? When they renounce Mt. Gerizim and confess Jerusalem and the resurrection of the dead. From that time on, he who robs a Samaritan shall be as he who robs an Israelite" (61b). Jewish and Christian authorities of the first centuries of our era agree that the Samaritans do not believe in the resurrection of the dead, and also the Samaritan literature would seem to evidence that this doctrine was not adopted by the Samaritans before at a rather late date[30]; but also the Jewish party of the Sadducees denied the resurrection of the body, and it was really the belief in the holiness of Mt. Gerizim that separated the Samaritans from all other Jewish groups in the centuries immediately preceding and succeeding the turn of our era (cp. *John* iv.20; Joseph., *Ant.* XII.10; XIII.74 ff.).

As was mentioned in Chapter I, the Jews' attitude towards the Samaritans was variable[31], and the phrase "take them back" in *Masseketh Kuthim* implies the recognition that the Samaritans are not of foreign breed, but simply constitute a schismatic group within the Jewish fold. If it is true that the Gerizim cult was instituted by priests expelled from Jerusalem, this view would seem warranted in part at least. But if the Samaritans' version of the early Israelite history is correct, then the schismatics are really the Jews, being the descendants of the followers of Eli, who moved from Shechem and established a priesthood descended from Ithamar in place of the legitimate priesthood of the line of Eleazar. In any case, both groups maintain that the split is bound up with dissensions within the priesthood. An attempt to throw more light on the Samaritans' renunciation of the Jews and their priesthood is the theory — worked out especially by J. Bowman — that the Samaritan priesthood was Sadoqite, a requisite for Israelite priests after the time of *Ezekiel* (see chs. xl ff.), and anxious to be separated from the priesthood in Jerusalem, where battles over the right to the high priestly office were going on[32]. There was a conflict between the "sons of Sadoq", the priest of David and Solomon, and the descendants of Eli persevering in Jerusalem[33], and,

---

30 There are some references to the event of the resurrection in the great 4th century Samaritan midrashic work known as *Memar Marqa*, which is among the oldest literary monuments of the Samaritans (excluding their Pentateuch), but when citing the creed, the author does not include the tenet of the resurrection; see Macdonald, *Theology*, pp. 50 f.; cp. Montgomery, pp. 207, 239, 240, 250 f. Furthermore, every reference to the resurrection is lacking in the oldest ms.; see D. Rettig, ed. & trans., *Memar Marqa* (BOS, 8), Stuttgart, 1934, p. 31; Z. Ben-Hayyim, in his review of J. Macdonald's edition and translation, in *BO*, 23, 1966, pp. 185 ff. See now the discussion by S.J. Isser, *The Dositheans* (SJLA, XVII), Leiden, 1976, pp. 143 ff.

31 See p. 22.

32 See "Ezekiel and the Zadokite Priesthood", *TGUOS*, 16, 1955/56, pp. 1 ff.; cp. "Is the Samaritan Calendar the Old Zadokite One?", *PEQ*, 91, 1959, pp. 23 ff.

33 See R. de Vaux, *Ancient Israel*, 2, trans. from the French, London & New York,

after the death of Onias III, the last legitimate Sadoqite, the high priesthood became a price in the troubled politics of the time. It is possible that the origin of the Essene sect is to be sought in the migration of Sadoqite priests and their supporters following the elimination of Onias III under Antiochus IV Ephiphanes[34], and we should here also mention the hypothesis of Bowman that the oft-noted similarities between Essenism and the Samaritan sectarian movement of the Dositheans are due to the fact that both bodies consisted of Sadoqite priests expelled from Jerusalem[35]. According to Bowman, then, the formation of both Samaritan orthodoxy and Samaritan sectarianism is a result of the dissensions in the priesthood in Jerusalem.

The name of Sadoq does occur in the Samaritan list of high priests found in the Samaritan chronicle *Tolida* (Chronicle III)[36], but this priest (being the thirteenth after Uzzi, during whose time Eli hailed himself as high priest) is at least a century younger than David's and Solomon's priest by the same name (being the fifth after Uzzi in the genealogy in *I Chron.* vi.5 ff.). Furthermore, it is never stated in the Samaritan chronicles that Sadoq, the priest of David and Solomon, re-established the genuine line from Aaron through Eleazar: rather, the Samaritans insist that the genuine succession from Eleazar and Phinehas continued uninterrupted in the North — and there alone! — after Eli moved to Shiloh[37]. There is no record in the texts of the Samaritans that their preisthood was Sadoqite and contravening the priesthood of the Jews by the fact that it was remaining Sadoqite even after the last Sadoqite was removed in Jerusalem. This, however, is exactly what would be expected if the Samaritan priesthood had its origin in the settlement of Jerusalem priests at Shechem before Seleucide times. It must be concluded that the similarities between the Sadducees, often thought to have a relationship to the old Sadoqites (although the nature of this relationship is far from clear!)[38], and the Samaritans are due to the circumstance that both groups were "in an analogous relationship to what came to be orthodox Judaism.

1961, reprinted as McGraw-Hill paperback, New York, 1965, pp. 372 ff., 394 ff.

34 See E. Stauffer, "Probleme der Priestertradition", *TLZ*, 81, 1956, cols. 138 f.; P. Kahle, "Zu den Handschriftrollen in Höhlen beim Toten Meer", *Das Altertum*, 3, 1957, pp. 34 ff.

35 See "Pilgrimage to Mt. Gerizim", *EI*, 7, 1964, pp. 21[+]b-22[+]a; *Problem*, pp. 40, 91 ff.; cp. "The Importance of Samaritan Researches", in J. Macdonald, ed., *ALUOS*, I, 1958/59, pp. 47, 54. Bowman was more careful in his "Contact between Samaritan Sects and Qumran?", *VT*, 7, 1957, pp. 184 ff.

36 Neubauer, p. 400, actually reads צדיק, while Bowman, *Tolidah*, p. 13, has צדוק.

37 For criticism of Bowman, see Rowley, "Sanballat", pp. 184 f. (= *Men of God*, pp. 264 f.); Kippenberg, pp. 65 f.; Coggins, pp. 143 f.; S. Lowy, *The Principles of Samaritan Bible Exegesis* (SP-B, XXVIII), Leiden, 1977, pp. 25 f., 224.

38 On this relationship, see R. Meyer, Art. Σαδδουκαῖος, in *TDNT*, VII, 1971, reprinted 1975, pp. 35 ff., especially pp. 41, 43 f.

It is not necessarily a case of direct influence or borrowing, but both groups display similar tendencies within the total picture of Judaism."[39]

It is in fact probable that the priesthood descended from Eleazar and Phinehas is a Northern institution. Eleazar is said to have been buried in the mountains of Ephraim, south of Shechem, at the hill given to his son Phinehas (see *Josh.* xxiv.33). "Phinehas, son of Eleazar and the grandson of Aaron", is said to have been ministering as Israel's high priest in Bethel, which seems to have replaced Shechem as the main sanctuary in the period of Judges (see *Judg.* xx.18, 26 ff.; xxi.2 ff.). Bethel was a town possessed by "the house of Joseph" (*Judg.* i.22 ff.), from which the Samaritans claim descendance.

When the Ark was moved from Bethel (see *ibid.* xx.27) to Shiloh (see *I Sam.* iii.3; iv.1 ff.)[40], Bethel was no longer in the limelight, but it no doubt remained as a sanctuary (see *ibid.* vii.16; x.3). Jeroboam, when establishing the Northern Kingdom, chose Bethel as one of his two main sanctuaries — the other being Dan — and officiated there at the Sukkoth festival (see *I Kings* xii.32). The sanctuary at Bethel survived the Assyrian destruction of the Kingdom of Israel, for one of the deported priests was sent home in order to instruct the people of the land in the worship of YHWH at Bethel (see *II Kings* xvii.28). The temple at Bethel became a serious rival to the temple on Sion; and, in Josiah's scheme of reform, which extended to the cities of Samaria (see *II Chron.* xxxiv.6), being part of the Assyrian empire, particular prominence is given to the Judaean king's dismantling of the altar and high place of Bethel (see *II Kings* xxiii.15). The evidence of archeology, however, shows that Bethel was revived and occupied down into the latter part of the 6th century B.C.E., when it was destroyed by a great conflagration, and then resettled once more and remained inhabited down into the 3rd century B.C.E.[41] The account of the census made in the time of Nehemiah tells that people from Bethel, which was considered more or less as a part of Judah after the time of Josiah, had returned to their city (see *Neh.* vii.32; *Ezra* ii.28). Actually, since Bethel, situated north of the pre-exilic border, was not destroyed by the Babylonians, it is possible that the people never did leave[42]. At some time during the period in which Bethel was depopulated, it would seem

---

39 Coggins, p. 157.
40 What prompted this shift to Shiloh (probably via Gilgal) is uncertain, for Shiloh clearly was not hallowed by such memories as were Shechem and Bethel; see M. Noth, *The History of Israel*, 2nd ed., translation revised by P.R. Ackroyd, London, 1959 and reprints, pp. 95 f.; de Vaux, 2, p. 304.
41 See W.F. Albright, *Archaeology and the Religion of Israel* (ALC-RDS, 1941), 2nd ed., Baltimore, 1946, pp.172 f.; *The Biblical Period from Abraham to Ezra*, Harper Torchbook, New York, 1963, p. 93.
42 According to one reading of *Zech.* vii.2 f., there were cult practices going on in Bethel when the Judaeans returned. But the text is utterly obscure.

that the temple on Mt. Gerizim was built; and Bethel traditions could then have been transferred to Shechem.

The Samaritans call Mt. Gerizim, their holy place, "Bethel" (בית אל), using the latter name both as a mere place name and as a term with a theophanic meaning[43]. It is strange that J.A. Montgomery, who knew this[44], could state that he could not detect Northern traditions in Samaritanism[45], for no *Southerner* would call the place of worship by the name of Bethel, the central sanctuary of the Northern Kingdom where pagan practices were flourishing according to the historical books and the prophets[46]. The designation of the Samaritan shrine as "Bethel" could very well derive from priests coming to Shechem from the old sanctuary at Bethel during the desolation of the latter place; these priests could have called their new shrine with the name of their former sanctuary. Thus, rather than being Sadoqites disjoined from the priesthood in Jerusalem, the Samaritan priests would appear to have carried on the priestly institution of Bethel[47].

In his studies of Samaritan texts, J. Macdonald has discerned that the

---

43 See Kippenberg, pp. 188 ff.

44 See *op. cit.*, p. 236.

45 See *ibid.*, p. 46.

46 *Jub.* xxxii.1 ff. and *Test. Levi* ix.1 ff. (cp. cols. 9 ff. of the Aramaic fragments) relate that Levi was installed as priest at Bethel and received tithes from Jacob, his father. Jacob wanted to build a sanctuary at Bethel (see *Jub.* xxxii.16; cp. *Gen.* xxviii.20 ff.), but was told by God not to do so (see *v.* 22); the place where God is going to make his Name dwell (see *v.* 10) obviously is Jerusalem (see i.29; iv.26; viii.19; *Test. Levi*, Aram. Frag. col. 10). According to this tradition, Bethel was the former sanctuary. The usual Jewish position, however, is that the shrine which was precursory of Jerusalem was Shiloh, and the rabbis maintained this against the Samaritans; see A.S. Halkin, "Samaritan Polemics against the Jews", *PAAJR*, 7, 1935/36, p. 37, nn. 102 f. It has often been noted that *Jubilees* and the Samaritans share some traditions – *e.g.*, in chronological matters – which stand in opposition to the usual Jewish position; see already L. Wreschner, *Samaritanische Traditionen*, Halle, 1888, *passim*. This may be taken to indicate that both the Samaritans and the group responsible for *Jubilees* preserve traditions stemming from the same centre, even Bethel.

47 G. Widengren, "Till det sakrala kungadömets historia i Israel", in *Melangés Johs. Pedersen* (HS, I), 3, Uppsala, 1947, pp. 12 ff., argues that the Samaritan Sukkoth ritual (Cowley, pp. 782 ff.) represents an ancient tradition from the Northern Kingdom, for the ritual says that the "king of Israel" shall present tithes to the priest "at Bethel". In the Samaritan liturgy, however, "Bethel" of course is understood to be Mt. Gerizim, but Widengren may still be right, for the text is clearly related to that in *Jub.* ch. xxxii. According to *Jubilees*, Jacob paid his tithes at the last day of the Sukkoth festival, and this date is the same as the one given in the Samaritan Sukkoth ritual. Thus it appears that the king in the Samaritan liturgy is acting as the representative of his people, as is Jacob, the ancestor of the Israel (see *Gen.* xxviii.10 ff.; xxxv.1 ff., 14 f.), for it is obvious that the story that Jacob went on pilgrimage from Shechem to Bethel and paid tithes serves as the paradigm of later practices: the pilgrimage is attested by *I Sam.* x.30, the tithe by *Am.* iv.4.

midrashic literature of the Samaritans continues some traditions found in the
Elohist document, a Pentateuchal source commonly believed to have originated in the North[48]. It is true that the sacred Scripture of the Samaritans is
not E but the Pentateuch in its entirety, but the Samaritan theologians apparently fancy Northern traditions[49].

Since the Pentateuch "is essentially a Judaean work,"[50] J.D. Purvis asserts
that this is an argument which repudiates the position of the Samaritans as
being Northerners. But the Pentateuch, the canonization of which took place
about 400 B.C.E., was obviously adopted by the proto(?)-Samaritans before
the rupture with the Judaeans was final[51]. The people in the North need not
have had any scruples about doing this, for they undoubtedly shared the legal
and historical traditions recurring throughout all the sources of the Pentateuch. In fact, "it has even been suggested that these themes constituted a
kind of national credo that was recited periodically in the sacred cities of
ancient Israel, especially in Shechem, the northern religious center... ."[52] The
Pentateuch also bears witness to the sanctity of Mt. Gerizim and Shechem[53],
while it does not mention Jerusalem as a Hebrew sanctuary.

Purvis' other argument for the Judaean and non-Northern origin of the
Samaritans is that "if Samaritanism is the surviving remnant of a religious

---

48 See Macdonald, ed. & trans., *Memar Marqah: The Teaching of Marqah* (BZAW, 84),
   I (The Text), Berlin, 1963, pp. XLI f.; *Theology*, p. 42, p. 88, n. 1, pp. 182, 188,
   196 f., 286, p. 299, n. 2, p. 302, n. 1, pp. 307, 319, 397, 447.
49 Already K. Lincke, *Samaria und seine Propheten*, Tübingen, 1903, tried to show
   that the Samaritans were the heirs of the religious traditions in the North; but,
   since his thesis was that they were the successors of Elijah, Elisha, and Hosea, he was
   bound to be unsuccessful. Although the Samaritan chronicles show no sympathy to
   the Northern Kingdom as such, asserting that only eight of the tribes and not Ephraim
   and Manasseh comprised it, we search in vain for a sympathetic attitude towards the
   prophets mentioned, who were bitterly opposed to the northern kings of their days.
   In fact, the northern prophets are described in very hostile terms; see G. Fohrer, "Die
   israelitischen Propheten in der samaritanischen Chronik II", in M. Black & G. Fohrer,
   ed., *In Memoriam Paul Kahle* (BZAW, 103), Berlin, 1968, pp. 129 ff.
50 Purvis, p. 93.
51 "Most authorities agree that the Samaritan Pentateuch ... existed in the third century
   B.C.E. ..." (J. Macdonald, par. "Dating", in Art. "Pentateuch, Samaritan", in *EJ*,
   13, col. 267).
52 M. Weinfeld, par. "The Tradition Underlying the Sources – Form Criticism", in
   Art. "Pentateuch", in *EJ*, 13, col. 258. That the Samaritans were deeply conservative
   folks who did not alter anything in their religion reaching back to ancient Shechemite
   traditions was the view of M. Gaster, *The Samaritans* (SL, 1923), London, 1925,
   pp. 45 f., *et passim.* More recently, Macdonald has affirmed that "the Samaritans did
   not borrow from Judaism, but rather derived ideas from common sources" (*Theology*, p. 14; cp. his statements on p. 53 and p. 452). On the conservatism of the
   Samaritans, see also Lowy, pp. 220 ff., *et passim.*
53 See above, p. 37, n. 28.

movement whose essential character had already been formed in pre-exilic times, one would expect to find within it those characteristic elements of northern Israelite religion known from biblical and archaeological sources, that is, the syncretistic practices of the cult of Bethel and the open air sanctuaries, the curious type of Yahwism represented in the Elephantine literature, and the admixture of Yahwism and paganism reported in II Kings 17:24-41."[54] Purvis is right that the absence of such elements cannot be explained by adopting the Samaritans' own view of their community "as a self-contained and hermetically sealed entity during the period of Israelite apostasy and syncretism,"[55] but the representation in *II Kings* ch. xvii undoubtedly is exaggerated, and the religion in the North would obviously undergo refinement in the course of time. No one will doubt that the religion in Judah in pre-exilic times contained syncretistic elements, but it is still uncontestable that Judaism is "the surviving remnant" of pre-exilic Hebrew religion. There may have been more syncretism in Israel than in Judah, but neither in the North nor in the South was the "essential character" of Hebrew religion distinguishable as syncretism.

However, since the Samaritans claim to be the descendants of Ephraim and Manasseh — a claim permeating all of their literature and witnessed already in the first century C.E. (see Joseph, *Ant.* XI.341) — and distinguish sharply between their ancestors and the other eight tribes of the old Kingdom of Israel, it is far from uncomplicated to maintain that the Samaritans were and are "the North" *tout court*[56]. I, for one, can see no reason why the Samaritans' own claim regarding their origin cannot be based on generally correct memory. After all, "the house of Joseph" was the most vigorous among the central Palestinian tribes, that were historically the most important of the tribes from the beginning; Ephraim and Manasseh possessed a more extensive area than any of the other tribes[57]. We have seen that it is plausible that Bethel as well as Samaria furnished the resettlers of Shechem, and both these towns lie in Ephraimite territory. Why would the Samaritans identify themselves as the two Joseph tribes over against the Judeans if they really had come from Jerusalem and preserved a Sadoqite priesthood long after the latter had lost theirs and mourned because of it?

Admittedly, the problem of the original identity of the Samaritans is complicated, but a final solution is really of no great importance for our

---

54 *Op. cit.*, p. 92. Purvis appears to accept the account of *II Kings* ch. xvii as a fairly true picture of the facts; see pp. 94, 96.

55 *Ibid.*, p. 92.

56 For the Samaritans' view of the relation between themselves and the other groups within the Chosen People in the time of the divided Kingdom, see Macdonald, *Theology*, pp. 18 ff.; Coggins, pp. 122 ff.

57 See Noth, *History*, pp. 58 ff.

study. The important point to bear in mind is that the Samaritans are a branch of the Jewish people. We are thus faced with a terminological problem because of the wide connotation of the term "Jew". If the word is restricted to mean a Judean, an inhabitant of Judea, the old Southern Kingdom (encompassing the territory of the tribe of Benjamin as well as the territory of the tribe of Judah), or a member of the tribe of Judah (or Benjamin), the Samaritans cannot be considered Jews[58]. If one insists on such a usage of the term "Jew", the name "Israelite" would have to be revived in order to characterize the Samaritans, for it is now clear that the people of the old Kingdom of Israel did not vanish completely, and that the Samaritans must be considered their descendants and the brethren of the Judeans, their neighbours in the south, and even of all Jews, members of the tribe of Judah (and Benjamin), wherever they live. However, since the name of Israel is used both in Biblical books written after the fall of the Northern Kingdom and in later customary course to denote the Jewish people as a whole, it would only be confusing to begin to make a distinction between the Jewish people and the people of Israel (all the more so because the modern state of Israel above all is the home of Jews). The only sensible view is to regard the Samaritans as a branch of the Jewish people and Samaritanism as belonging within the wider phenomenon of Judaism[59]. That the Samaritans are Jews in terms of religion as well as ethnic origin is made plain if we substitute the modern term "Mosaism" for "Judaism", for the religion of the Samaritans, recognizing only the five books of Moses as canonical and extolling Moses to a place far exceeding the position allotted to him by the Jews coming from Judea, is in truth a Mosaism. Some ambiguity, then, will be unavoidable because the word "Jew" is used of those to whom and by whom the Samaritans were opposed, while at the same time it is assumed that the Samaritans are a branch of the Jewish people. In order to make it pointed that the Samaritans

---

58 If it were granted that the founders of the Gerizim cult were priests from Jerusalem, this narrow circumscription would make it impossible to maintain even that only the descendants of the first Samaritan priests were Jews, for, since the priests are said to have contracted marriages with non-Jewish women, the Jewish status of their children is ruled out on the halakhic definition that "Your son by a heathen woman is not called your son" (*Qidd.* 68b). Cp. R. Posner, par. "Halakhic Definitions", in Art. "Jew", in *EJ*, 10, cols. 23 ff. It is true that the halakhic canon was not yet in operation by the time that the Samaritan community emerged, but both *Nehemiah* and Josephus make it clear that the marriages were regarded as illegal.

59 This is in fact the modern Jewish view of the Samaritans and Samaritanism. In 1949, the Samaritans were recognized as citizens under the Law of Return, and this actually allows that they are Jews, for the Law of Return declares that every Jew has the right to settle in Israel as an *oleh*, being defined as "a Jew immigrating to Israel for settlement". Since the Law of Return does not apply to Jews having embraced another religion, it is clear that Samaritanism is considered a kind of Judaism.

are Jews within the wider meaning of the name, the term "Samaritan Jew" will often be used[60].

The Origin and Development of Dositheism

The above-mentioned theory of J. Bowman that the Dositheans were Sadoqites having fled from Jerusalem cannot be established on the basis of the sources. The Samaritan chronicler Abu'l Fatḥ of the 14th century, who gives us the most extensive information on the Dositheans, actually reports on *two* Dosithean sects, namely, the Dustan (דסתאן) movement, which originated in the time of Simeon Maccabeus' son 'Arḳiya, *i.e.*, Hyrcanus, and the movement inaugurated by Dusis (דוסיס), *i.e.*, Dositheus, who came from Judea in the time right after the death of Baba Rabba, the great Samaritan revivalist of the 4th century C.E.[61] Bowman considers these two movements

---

The civil definition of who is a Jew clashes with that of the religious law, according to which a person must be considered a Jew – that is, a person having a Jewish mother or being a convert to Judaism – even if he or she has lapsed from Judaism. By regarding the Samaritans as proselytes, both Israeli civil law and religious law could agree that the Samaritans are Jews and at the same time maintain that they are of alien blood. Already the rabbis of the first centuries of our era discussed whether the Samaritans were "true" or "righteous", that is, genuine, proselytes or "lion-proselytes", that is, converts to the religion of Israel because of having been plagued by lions (cp. *II Kings* xvii.25 ff.); see Montgomery, pp. 176 f., citing the discussion in *Qidd*. 75a-76a (cp. Jer. *Gitt*. ch. i,43c; *Tos. Ter*. iv.14). But, as we have seen, the traditional view that the Samaritans come from the east is not historically founded. Moreover, it is difficult to conceive of how the Samaritans could be fitted into the formal category of proselyte. A forced mass conversion of the Samaritan people – resembling the forced conversion of the Edomites by John Hyrcanus – is not attested. It appears that the more sensible of the Jewish religious authorities regard the Samaritans as Jews of ethnic origin as well as in terms of religion. Thus, already in the middle of the 19th century, the chief rabbi in Jerusalem laid down that "the Samaritan people is a branch of the Jewish people that confesses the truth of the Torah" (as quoted by B. Tsedaka, par. "History, 1300-1970", in Art. "Samaritans", in *EJ*, 14, col. 734.)

60 Cp. Coggins, p. 8.
61 See Vilmar, pp. 82 f. (about the Dustan sect), 151 ff. (on Dusis and his followers). Chronicle II mentions only Dusis; see the summary by Kippenberg, pp. 133 f., which is based on a transliteration given him by Professor John Macdonald. The story is similar to that of Abu'l Fatḥ. The *Tolida*, too, has only "Dusethis or Dustis" (Neubauer, p. 405; Bowman, *Tolidah*, p. 18). The Chronicle Adler, however, has the Dustan sect, which it places a bit later than does Abu'l Fatḥ (see *REJ*, 45, pp. 72 f.), as well as Dositheus (see *ibid*., pp. 225 ff.). The *Book of Joshua* does not report on sectarianism. All previous scholarly literature is now superseded by Isser, who includes a translation of Abu'l Fatḥ's text made by Mr. Lee Scanlon and corrected and commented upon by Professor Leon Nemoy. Isser also appends Vilmar's text. Bowman, *Documents*, pp. 124 ff., 162 ff., has also afforded a translation of Abu'l Fatḥ's two accounts furnished with copious notes.

to be the same and having originated during Hyrcanus' time; he says that a Jewish teacher (he calls him both Dustan and Dusis) founded the Samaritan sect at this time[62]. But Abu'l Fatḥ does *not* say that the Dustan sectaries came from Judah: he imparts that they were Samaritans who "abolished the true holidays and everything that had been handed down to them by their fathers and grandfathers."[63] Although there is no reason to place Dositheus in a pre-Christian period, the time of Hyrcanus certainly seems to be the most appropriate for the emergence of Samaritan sectarianism. Bowman quotes Yūsuf b. Salāmā, a Samaritan theologian of the 11th century, as saying: "When the Temple was destroyed, some people did not see the need to make

---

62 See "Importance", p. 47; "Pilgrimage", pp. 21⁺a-22⁺a; *Problem*, pp. 38, 39 f. This is the reversal of the thesis of K. Kohler, "Dositheus, the Samaritan Heresiarch and His Relations to Jewish and Christian Doctrines and Sects", *AJT*, 15, 1911, pp. 404 ff., who argued that the Jewish sect of the Sadoqites was founded by the Samaritan heretic Dositheus. This hypothesis is of course untenable, since the Sadoqite Fragments (published by Solomon Schechter in 1910) as well as the Qumran library (discovered in 1947) quote extensively from the Prophets, while Dositheus, like his fellow Samaritans, is told to have rejected the prophetical canon of the Jews.

M. Black, *The Scrolls and Christian Origins*, London, 1961, pp. 60 ff., 65 f., would seem to argue that Dositheism originated already in the time of the restoration of the Jerusalem temple as a result of the immigration of estranged Judaean priests in pursuit of a habitat where the old Israelite traditions had a stronghold. Further, according to Black, a southward remigration of such people gave rise to the Essene sect. But none of the sources assign such an early date to Dositheism or warrant the theory that it cultivated ancient traditions. Moreover, the theory would make the estranged priests allies of the traditionalists in the North, and this runs counter to the Samaritan chronicles, according to which Dositheism was a revolutionary sect opposing the authority of the priesthood.

63 Vilmar, p. 82. Abu'l Fatḥ says that they were called "Dustan" just because of this. A.I.S. de Sacy, ed. & trans., *Chrestomathie arabe*, I, Paris, 1826, p. 335, thought that the name really was *Darastān*, from the Arabic *darasa*, to "efface". Disregarding Abu'l Fatḥ's explanation, other scholars offer other etymologies; see Bowman, *Problem*, p. 38; *Documents*, p. 179, n. 24; A.D. Crown, "Dositheans, Ressurection and a Messianic Joshua", *Antichton*, 1, 1967, p. 77; Isser, p. 88, n. 130. Lowy, p. 262, n. 821, and pp. 264 f., cites de Sacy. For my view, see below, p. 53 with n. 81.

Since Epiphanius (*Pan.* chs. X ff.) reports that calendaric disputes split the Samaritan community and that the Dositheans adopted the Jewish calendar, Crown begs the question that priests from Jerusalem came to Samaria and postulates that they introduced a calendar which caused divergences and eventually hatched "the Dosithean movement in the early third century B.C." (*loc. cit.*). This is also a construction which makes the Dositheans confederates of the priests. Moreover, although Epiphanius apparently believes that the time immediately after the North-South schism was the period when the Samaritan sectarian pattern emerged, his account is clearly anachronistic; see below, pp. 71 f. At this point, we can note that the Jewish calendar which is assumed by Epiphanius is the Pharisaic one, which belongs to a much later time.

a pilgrimage to the Mountain or to worship there; they said that to worship in a synagogue was enough."[64] The crisis caused by the destruction of the Gerizim temple by John Hyrcanus was obviously a crucial turning-point in the history of the Samaritans, who then began to split up into several factions, giving divergent answers to the problem of how to re-establish religion.

As for the sect founded by Dositheus, it is clear that the Samaritans have post-dated its origin by three centuries, for the story about Dositheus and the movement started by him is followed by a strange account of Simon Magus, who is even said to have visited Philo[65]. Thus, we find ourselves in the first century C.E. This tallies with the time assigned to Dositheus in early Christian sources. Hegesippus, a 2nd century author of Jewish origin, states: "From these [*viz.*, "the seven sects" among the Jews at the time of Jesus], [came] Simon, whence the Simonians; and Cleobius, whence the Cleobians; and Dositheus, whence the Dositheans; and Gorthaeus, whence the Gorathenians and the Masbotheans" (*apud* Euseb., *Hist. eccl.* IV.xxii.5)[66]. Although Hegesippus speaks of *Jewish* sects, one cannot deduce that he denies Dositheus' Samaritan origin, for Simon — who is most definitely a Samaritan — heads the list of heresiarchs deriving from the seven sects among the people. Furthermore, as was pointed out in Chapter I, the Gorathenians and the Masbotheans appear to be Samaritan sects. Apparently, Hegesippus regards the Samaritans, whom he actually lists as one of the seven sects, as a branch of the Jewish people.

Origen also associates Simon and Dositheus, saying that they both were Samaritans appearing "after the time of Jesus" (*Contra Cels.* I.57) or "in the time of the Apostles" (*Comm. in Matt.* 33, *ad* xxiv.4 f.), and securing a following for themselves (see further *Contra Cels.* VI.11; *Comm. in Joh.* XIII.27, *ad* iv.25; *Hom. in Luc.* 25). The account in *Contra Cels.* I.57 is probably reflected by Eusebius in *Theoph.* IV.35, where Origen's assertion that Dositheus "wanted to persuade the Samaritans that he was the Christ prophesied by Moses" is amended to "the very prophet whom Moses predicted" (see *Deut.* xviii.15, 18).

In the *Pseudo-Clementines* (*Hom.* II.23 f.; *Rec.* II.8 ff.), Simon and Dositheus are represented as rivals to the office left vacant by John the Baptist. In the *Apostolic Constitutions* from the 4th century, Cleobius and Simon are described as pupils of Dositheus, whom they are said to have ousted from his position (see VI.viii.1). The *Bibliotheca* of Photius, a 9th century patriarch

---

64 *Kitab al-Kafi* ch. 18; quoted by Bowman, "Importance", p. 46.
65 Montgomery, p. 256, n. 16, says that the account of Simon precedes that of Dositheus, but the former begins on p. 157. For translation, see Bowman, *Documents*, pp. 168 f.
66 The passage is quoted in context and discussed above, pp. 20 ff.

of Constantinople, quotes from a book by Eulogius, patriarch of Alexandria at the end of the 6th century, that a party of Samaritans living in the city in his day proclaimed "Dosthes or Dositheus, himself also a Samaritan by race, who flourished at the same time as Simon Magus," as the Prophet like Moses (285a)[67].

The episode in the Clementine romance in which Simon and Dositheus are rivals admits Simon's Samaritan origin, but has nothing to say about the cradle of Dositheus. A short tale found in *Ps.-Clem. Rec.* I.54, however, says that Dositheus was the author of the teaching of the Sadducees, who denied the resurrection of the flesh and were the first schismatics among the Jews. This report, then, seems to make Dositheus a pre-Christian Jew, for the Sadducees were a Jewish party emerging in pre-Christian times. However, the tale says that the schism caused by Dositheus took place in the time of John the Baptist, and that Dositheus was followed by Simon Magus. So, after all, we can maintain a first century C.E. date for Dositheus. Further, Dositheus' Samaritan affiliation is recognizable in the continuation of the narrative, saying that "another schism" was constituted by the Samaritans, who also denied the resurrection of the body and were prevented by Dositheus from believing that Jesus was the Prophet foretold by Moses. The implication of the last communication is no doubt that Dositheus reserved this claim for himself; in addition to Origen (and Eusebius) and Photius, Shahrastani, the 12th century Muslim historian of religion, asserts this[68].

Th. Caldwell and S.J. Isser, both of whom have made a source-critical analysis of Dositheism, agree that the Pseudo-Clementine representation of Dositheus as a proto-Sadducee is a mistake derived from the so-called *Syntagma* tradition[69]. Pseudo-Tertullian's *Adversus omnes haereses*, held by many to be a translation or at least a summary of the lost *Syntagma* of Hippolytus, describes the Sadducees as the first to deny the doctrine of the resurrection of the body and as having originated from the heresy of Dositheus, who is said to have been a Samaritan and the "first" to reject the prophets (ch. 1). The last annotation seems strange, since the Samaritans *in toto* rejected the prophetical canon. Pseudo-Tertullian's aim is to present Dositheus as the first of "the heretics of Judaism" (*ibid.*), and it appears as if he deems Samaritanism prior to the defection of Dositheus as being equal to orthodox Judaism. However, he does not state expressly that Dositheus himself was an anti-resurrectionist.

---

67 Crown, p. 79, says that Eulogius also met a Dosithean sect which identified the Prophet like Moses as Joshua, but — as remarked by Isser, p. 124 — it is not stated that the Samaritans who made this identification were Dositheans.

68 Shahrastani is quoted below, p. 52, n. 80.

69 See Caldwell, "Dositheus Samaritanus", *Kairos*, 4, 1962, p. 109; Isser, p. 56; cp. Kippenberg, p. 131.

Philaster of Brescia, writing at the end of the 4th century C.E., affirms that Dositheus — allegedly the teacher of a certain Saddoc — was the first dissenter of the pro-resurrectionist community and the fountain-head of the sect of the Sadducees, "who strengthened this heresy" (*De haer*. ch.5). That Philaster is dependent upon the *Syntagma* tradition is shown by the fact that his listing of sects sticks closely to the list of Pseudo-Tertullian[70]. Philaster (*De haer*. ch. 7) agrees with Pseudo-Tertullian in viewing the Samaritans as a Jewish sect, and this may account for his describing Dositheus as "a Jew by race" (*ibid.* ch. 4). However, Philaster's firm opinion that Dositheus as well as the Samaritans denied the resurrection of the flesh is not matched by Pseudo-Tertullian and would seem to come from another source, perhaps directly from the *Syntagma,* of which Pseudo-Tertullian is an abridgment. On this matter, *Ps.-Clem. Rec.* I.54 is nearer to Philaster than to Pseudo-Tertullian.

Epiphanius (*Pan.* chs. XIII f.), writing a short time before Philaster, holds Dositheus to be the fountain-head of Sadduceism. This obviously derives from the *Syntagma* tradition, because the bishop of Salamis is in close accord with the list of Jewish sects given by Pseudo-Tertullian and Philaster[71]. But Epiphanius' outspoken conviction that the Dositheans believed in the resurrection and his somewhat strained description of Dositheus as a renegade Jew who went to Samaria and founded a Samaritan sect, which, in its turn, gave rise to the *Jewish* sect of the Sadducees, indicate that he also used other sources. Isser convincingly shows that the Christian bishop also relied on a tradition very similar to the one adopted by Abu'l Fath[72]: the Samaritan chronicler says that the Dositheans were pro-resurrectionists, and that Dositheus was a Jew who "committed adultery with the wife of a man who was one of the chiefs of the Jews,"[73] who, instead of killing him, allowed Dositheus to go to Samaria in order to create a schism in the Samaritan community. As Isser remarks, this "sounds more like a propagandistic literary motif than history."[74] As a matter of fact, neither the *Tolida* nor the Chronicle Adler knows about the adventures of Dositheus in Judea before his arrival in Nablus, and it is clear that we cannot seize upon this tradition in order to evince that Dositheism is of Jewish origin.

Regarding the lumping together of Dositheus, Sadduceism, and Samaritanism, Isser wants to explain this as deriving from Hippolytus' *Philosophumena* (IX.xxix.4), stating that Sadducean beliefs, which included the denial of the resurrection, were prevalent in Samaria. Isser speculates whether this view also was professed in the *Syntagma,* thus making it easier for the users of the

---

70 See Isser, pp. 165 f.
71 Cp. Caldwell, p. 111; Isser, pp. 45 f.
72 See *op. cit.*, pp. 46 f., 60, 95 ff., 107 f.
73 Vilmar, p. 151.
74 *Ibid.*, p. 96.

Syntagma tradition to understand why Dositheus, the well-known Samaritan heretic, was described as the forerunner of the Sadducees[75]. Anyway, the reason of Hippolytus for connecting Sadduceism and Samaritanism is probably due to the fact that the Samaritans in the 2nd century C.E. still did not believe in the resurrection. If it is corrrect to assume that the *Syntagma* not only saw Dositheus as the first schismatic but also Samaritanism prior to Dositheus as being equal to orthodox Judaism, then it is only logical that Dositheus should be portrayed as the fountain-head of the heretical anti-resurrectional belief maintained by the Samaritans as well as the Jewish party of the Sadducees, known to have originated in pre-Christian times.

It will be realized, then, that there is no historical reason for holding Dositheus to be a Jew and a pre-Christian sectarian. Dositheus was a Samaritan schismatic of the first century C.E. There is no indication in any of our sources that Dositheus was a priest or of priestly orientation, and this is in effect a disproval of the theory that the Dosithean sect was Sadoqite or Sadducean. Actually, as shall be described below, the Dosithean movement had a bent for reform and even abolition of the religious duties, and this is not congruent with a movement assumed to have had its origin in priestly circles[76]. It appears odd that J. Bowman, who has taught us that Samaritanism developed through an interaction between the old priestly party and the Dosithean lay movement, alleges that the latter as well had a priestly origin. Moreover, the traditon of main line Samaritanism — described by Epiphanius as well as the Samaritan chronicles — pictures Dositheus and his followers as pro-resurrectionists, and this casts further doubts on the presumed link between Dositheus and the Sadducees as found in the *Syntagma* tradition[77].

---

75 See *ibid.*, pp. 36 f., developing a speculation by M. Smith, "The Description of the Essenes in Josephus and the Philosophumena", *HUCA*, 29, 1958, pp. 273 ff.

76 See pp. 53 ff., 63 ff.

77 However, Epiphanius is the only one who makes the plain statement that the Dositheans differ from the other Samaritan sects in that "they admit the resurrection" (*Pan.* ch. XIII). Abu'l Fath does say that the followers of Dositheus taught that "the dead would rise soon," but he also adds somewhat confusingly that "they believed that, as soon as a dead man is buried, he arises from the grave and goes to Paradise" (Vilmar, p. 157). Although Pseudo-Tertullian is ambiguous, the assumption of the *Syntagma* tradition seems to be that Dositheus rejected the belief in the resurrection. This is at least what is stated outright by Philaster and the *Pseudo-Clementine Recognitions*. Hegesippus (as quoted by Eusebius), the *Apostolic Constitutions*, and Origen (and Eusebius) have no reference to Dositheus' view on the resurrection, *pro* or *con.* Photius, however, reports that Eulogius, after having proved to the Samaritans that Jesus was the Prophet like Moses, strove "to demonstrate the resurrection [...], thus refuting from Holy Scripture Dositheus' impious teaching about the resurrection" (286a). This implies that Dositheus was an anti-resurrectionist. Judah Hadassi — a 12th century Karaite author who has been overlooked by Isser — states in his *Eshkol ha-Kofer*, published in Eupatoria, in 1836, that the Samaritans were divided into two

The Dustan sect, however, is said to have had priests of its own, and nothing is told about its views on the resurrection[78]. This poses the problem of the relationship between the two sectarian movements. While Bowman holds the Dustan group and the sect of Dositheus to be one and the same and having originated when the temple was destroyed, the old theory that there were two separate sects named after two men called Dositheus has been

---

factions, the Kushan and the Dustan, and that the latter denied the resurrection (see 41b). Shahrastani narrates that, whereas the orthodox Samaritans believed in "a life beyond, and reward and punishment, the Dusitaniya held the opinion that reward and punishment take place in this world" (Cureton, p. 170; Haarbrücker, p. 258).

To assume that this tradition merely is dependent upon the *Syntagma* tradition is complicated by the fact that the authors who are saying that the Dositheans were anti-resurrectionists ·do not connect them with the Sadducees, which is the salient feature of the *Syntagma* tradition. Now it is a fact that at least some of the Dosithean sub-sects were deniers of the doctrine of the bodily resurrection; see below, pp. 53f. Thus, Eulogius and the Karaite-Muslim tradition may reflect the situation in the post-4th century Samaritan community, when the tenet of the resurrection had been adopted by the main body of the Samaritans but relinquished by the Dositheans in exchange for the concept of a spiritual resurrection and/or realized eschatology. Was the association of Dositheus and the Sadducees also partly due to the fact that some of the Dosithean groups had disavowed the belief in the resurrection of the body?

78 M. Appel, *Quaestiones de rebus Samaritanorum*, Breslau, 1874, p. 92, n. 4, and pp. 96 f., asserted that the Dustan sect was pro-resurrectionistic because of the fact that it is reported to have rejected the formula ברוך אלהינו לעולם (see Vilmar, p. 82), since *Ber.* ix.5 says that the conclusion of every benediction in the temple was changed from לעולם to לעולם ולעולם in order to counteract some *Minim*, apparently Sadducees, who took the old form of the benediction to imply that there was only one world and no resurrection. (Crown, p. 82, mistakenly says that the *old* form of the benediction was directed against anti-resurrective arguments; thus he erroneously concludes that the banning of it amounted to a *denial* of the resurrection.) Bowman, *Problem*, p. 47, offers the same interpretation as Appel, and Isser, pp. 89 f., endorses Appel's explanation. Abu'l Fath goes on to say that the Dustan sectaries also "prohibited [the reading of] YHWH according to the tradition of the people, [insisting upon] reading it "Elohim"," and Lowy, pp. 267 ff., has shown that this refers to the substitution of שמה for the Tetragrammaton and that the controversy must have centered upon the frequent cultic refrain "Blessed be our God לעולם and blessed be His Name לעולם." If this ancient cultic formula ever was used as anti-resurrectional proof, it is strange that it was kept unchanged when the Samaritans accepted the doctrine of the resurrection. Shaliḥ, the head of one of the Dosithean splinter groups, is told to have "changed the reading of the Great Name by saying: "One should recite only: בריך הוא" " (Vilmar, p. 162). It is hard to see how this could amount to a pro-resurrectional benediction, which, on the analogy of the Mishnaic story, is what should be expected if the old form of the benediction was seen as an argument to the effect that there was no resurrection. Moreover, Shaliḥ is reported to have *denied* the resurrection of the body. The evidence simply does not allow us to infer why the Dositheans opposed the ancient cultic refrain.

reiterated by Th. Caldwell[79]. But, inasmuch as the association of Dositheus and the Sadducees obviously is an anachronism, there is no reason to maintain that there was a Samaritan separatist by the name of Dositheus in a pre-Christian age[80]. As already mentioned, Abu'l Fath has nothing to say about a founder of the Dustan movement, although he does impart that the son of the high priest – not a Sadoqite from Judea! – became the leader of the sect. On the other hand, it cannot be denied that the Dustan move-

---

79 S. Krauss, "Dosithée et les Dosithéens", *REJ*, 42, 1901, pp. 27 ff., sorted out an early Samaritan sect-leader, whose teaching is reflected in the Dustan account and who is described as a proto-Sadducee, a Christian heretic associated with Simon Magus, and even a Cilician encratite, who is described by Macarius Magnes (*Apocritus* II.43; IV.15) and has been fused with the second Dositheus in Epiphanius' account. Cp. already Nutt, p. 78. (As for the encratite, Isser, pp. 47 f., rightly points out that there is no reason to think that this person was assimilated into Epiphanius' portrait of Dositheus.) Montgomery, pp. 261 ff., reduced the number of persons to two, both of whom he saw as Samaritans. Revising the theory that Dositheus founded Essenism, R. McL. Wilson, "Simon, Dositheus and the Dead Sea Scrolls", *ZRGG*, 9, 1957, pp. 21 ff., argues that the "Sadducees" with whom Dositheus is associated in reality are the "Sons of Sadoq", *i.e.*, the Essenes, but he agrees with Montgomery that there were two persons called Dositheus, one at the beginning of the schism and one at the time of Simon. Cp. J. Daniélou, "L'étoile de Jacob et la mission chrétienne à Damas", *VigChr*, 11, 1957, pp. 121 ff.; G.R. Driver, *The Judaean Scrolls*, Oxford, 1965, pp. 78 ff. But it is unlikely that the Qumran folk should have been mistaken for the Sadducees, for the former held the doctrine of the resurrection and stood aloof from the Hellenized Sadducees who were associated with the management of the temple.

80 Shahrastani says that the sect of the Dusitaniya was founded by a certain al-Ilfan about 100 B.C.E. He goes on to relate that this person gave himself out to be "the one Moses had foretold," and that his sect differed from the other Samaritans in questions over the Law (*loc. cit.*). We cannot assign importance to this dating, for Shahrastani seems to be dependent on late evidence. Thus, al-Ilfan is said to have claimed to be "the star shining with the light of the moon", and this apparently is an allusion to "the star out of Jacob" in *Num.* xxiv.17, which was an important text in later Samaritan soteriology, but does not figure in the other reports on Dositheus. For the etymology of "al-Ilfan", see the discussion by Isser, p. 73, n. 114 (continued on the next page).

Josephus (*Ant.* XIII.74 f.) says that Theodosius, *i.e.*, Dositheus, was one out of two Samaritan representatives arguing before Ptolemy Philometor (181-145) that the Law said that the temple should be built on Mt. Gerizim, and Medieval Jewish sources (*Midrash Tanh., Wayesheb* 2; *Pirke de R. Eliezer* ch. 38) speak about Dostai or Dosethai as one out of two teachers of the Law sent back to the Assyrian colonists. Krauss and Montgomery, pp. 254, 260 ff., argued that the names represent eponymous or real founders of Samaritan *sects*, but, even if this is to be granted, the use of the names must be considered anachronistic; see Isser, pp. 5 ff. Crown is wrong when stating that the Hebrew sources "regard the *founding* of the sect [*prb l* sects] as having taken place with the help of two men, Sabbai and Dostai ..." (p. 77; italics original).

ment and the sect founded by Dositheus have many traits in common, for instance, strict sabbatarianism and the possession of books of their own where the ritual law and the calendar were altered. A.D. Crown has submitted that the "Dosithean" sect arose in a pre-Christian period (but he pushes the date of its origin too far back), though not as the result of the activity of one Dositheus; later, it developed a schismatical sub-sect believing in the resurrection and in a certain Dositheus as the saviour. Similarly, S.J. Isser has suggested that Dositheus appeared as an eschatological prophet in the Dustan movement. But then is must be Dositheus (Dusethis or Dustis, as the *Tolida* calls him) who has given the whole movement its name, and "Dustan" must be anachronistic[81]. This theory also explains the differences between the two groups: the eschatological orientation and the belief in the resurrection, for instance, were not part of the doctrinal manufacture of the sect which originated at the end of the 2nd pre-Christian century, but were adopted by Dositheus in the first century C.E.

From Abu'l Fath's account of the Dosithean splinter groups[82], which are described, characteristically, after the excursus on Simon Magus, we see how the leaven continues to work and causes further transmutations within Samaritan sectarianism. To keep to the sample of the resurrection: some of the Dosithean sub-sects are said to have denied the resurrection of the flesh, and a couple of them at least are told to have substituted a spiritual resurrection

---

81 Vilmar, pp. LXXII f., thought that the Dusis sect had appropriated the name of its predecessor, but the form "Dustan" obviously must be explained as the responsibility of Abu'l Fath, who apparently changed the name in order to give it what would seem to him to be an intelligible meaning; see above, p. 46, n.63. There is also the possibility that the whole Dustan sect is fictitious; see Isser, pp. 109 f., 160 ff. Actually, Bowman, *Documents*, pp. 178 f., note continued from p. 177, and p. 206, n. 251, now contemplates this possibility. He also suggests a first century C.E. date for Dusis; see p. 210, n. 282; cp. p. 116. This is in reality a reversion to a position he once held; see "Contact", pp. 185 f. According to the view of Bowman set forth in these two places, Abu'l Fath antedated the Dustan sect in order to meet the Jewish charge that Dositheus was a teacher of the Assyrian colonists; the intention of the Samaritan chronicler was to make clear that Dosithean teachings were branded for what they were. As mentioned above, p. 29, n. 4, and p. 35, n. 24, Abu'l Fath knows only the Babylonian exile and places the destruction of the temple and the emergence of the Dustan sect in the Persian period. Moreover, as has also been pointed out, p. 45, n. 61, the *Tolida,* being older than Abu'l Fath, mentions only the Dusethis or Dustis sect. On the other hand, Yusuf ben Salama of the 11 th century corroborates Abu'l Fath's date of the rise of sectarianism in the time after the destruction of the temple; see above, pp. 46 f. Moreover, Abu'l Fath himself shows awareness of the connection between the two movements: in describing the splinter groups of the Dusis sect, he refers to them as "Dustan" (see Vilmar, p. 162).

82 See Vilmar, pp. 159 ff. Isser includes a translation and discussion of this text too. For another translation, with notes, see Bowman, *Documents*, pp. 169 ff.

doctrine and/or a realized eschatology for the doctrine of the bodily resurrection. Thus, the group that "pretended to be Saduqay"[83] said that "people will be resurrected because Dusis had died a disgraceful death and Levi was stoned; for [−as they said−] if Dusis [really] had died, then all the righteous people of the world have died".[84] The text appears to say that the departed righteous were not really dead, just as Dositheus was thought not to have died but to have been translated[85]. Isser, however, speculates that "all the righteous people of the world" might not refer exclusively to the righteous of previous generations but also include living believers, and that we have an example of a radical realized eschatology according to which the resurrection is thought to be experienced in full in this life[86]. In any case, the doctrine of a realized eschatology was espoused by the followers of Aulianah, a Dosithean enthusiast who said that the epoch of divine mercy was about to dawn. Those who followed his religion "thought that they [*already*] lived in the period of the divine favour".[87]

The followers of Abiyyah and Dosah and the Fasqutay are said to have believed that there was no "salvation or period of divine favour" and "neither paradise nor resurrection"; and, while this seems to indicate a step back to the old Samaritan ways, it can also be understood as a vivid emphasizing of a position of radical eschatology. The salvation and the period of the divine favour are not future events; paradise and resurrection are to be found here and now. It is worthy of note that the Fasqutay had a sort of trial (although a rather peculiar one!)[88] to which one had to submit; this might have been their means of marking the difference between those who were redeemed and those who were not.

A man called Shaliḥ, who appears to have secured quite a retinue, is said to have declared: "How evil is the teaching of those who say that the dead will rise soon!"[89] This does not have to mean that Shaliḥ denied all forms of resurrection doctrine, but can imply that he held that the pious would experi-

---

83 Is it possible that some Samaritans' self-designation "the Righteous Ones" to some extent is responsible for the linking of Dositheus and the Sadducees?

84 Vilmar, p. 160. Bowman, however, understands the text to say "that the world shall endure because Dusis died his shameful death, and Levi was stoned because Dusis had died and all the righteousness of the world had died" (*Documents*, p. 170; cp. *Problem*, p. 49). This does not make much sense. Why would the world have been dissolved if Dositheus had not died the way he did? The sect did believe in the resurrection; see below, p. 74.

85 See below, pp. 129f., 136.

86 See *op. cit.*, p. 104.

87 Vilmar, p. 164.

88 See Isser, p. 82; Bowman, *Documents*, p. 173.

89 Vilmar, p. 161.

ence the resurrection as the release of the soul after death, or that the resurrection of the true believer already had taken place as a mystical and spiritual event. Paul blames some of the Corinthians for saying that "there is no resurrection of the dead" (*I Cor.* xv.12), but it is generally agreed that the people in question held *some* form of resurrection or immortality doctrine. Considering that Dositheus believed in some kind of resurrection, it would be strange if the sub-sects taking their resort to him emphatically denied all sorts of resurrection tenets.

That the resurrection to immortal life is not a visible ecumenical event taking place at the coming of the universal Kingdom of God, but occurs as an individual experience, was also the classical Gnostic position. In fact, it was already in the teachings of the first Gnostics, Simon and his successor, Menander. These people were Samaritans, and they evidently derived their spiritual resurrection doctrine from Dositheism[90].

The Influence of Dositheism

In Simonianism, the status of possessing immortal life was expressed by the designation "the Standing One", which, in fact, also is found in Samaritan texts as a name of God and the angels. M. Heidenheim, who published Samaritan texts in the latter half of the previous century, took this to mean that Simonianism had influenced Samaritan religion[91]. More recently, J. Macdonald has asserted that there are traces of Gnostic influence in Samaritan literature, but he thinks that the Samaritans adopted only the terminology of Gnosticism and not its theological implications[92]. In a short monograph,

---

90 For the resurrection doctrine of the Samaritan Gnostics, see below, pp. 139ff., 155.
91 See *Die samaritanische Liturgie* (Bibliotheca samaritana, II), Leipzig, 1885, pp. XXXV ff.
92 Macdonald sees terminological borrowing from Gnosticism especially in the Samaritan usage of forms as "the Truth", "the Goodness", and "the (Great) Power", *etc.*; see *Memar Marqah*, I, p. XXXVIII; *Theology*, pp. 32, 72, 453. While these designations are used of the emanations of the godhead in Gnosticism, they appear as names of God in Samaritanism, and Macdonald translates "the True One", "the Good One", "the (Mighty) Powerful One", *etc.*, in order to convey the impression that they denote a personal being. C. Colpe, in his review of Macdonald's *Memar Marqah*, in *ZDMG*, 115, 1965, p. 203, criticizes Macdonald and says that these abstract nomina denote "hypostatizations". But this is wrong; the terms in question are paraphrases of the proper Name of God. However, there is no ground for believing that they have been taken from Gnostic emanation theology and therefore not translating the terms in a literal way. The employment of the names of the divine attributes as circumlocutions for the proper Name of God is found also in Judaism; see A. Marmorstein, *The Old Rabbinic Doctrine of God*, I (The Names and Attributes of God), London, 1927, pp. 54 ff. (also in *The Doctrine of Merits in Old Rabbinical Literature and the Old Rabbinic Doctrine of God*, with a prolegomenon by R.J. Zwi Werblowsky, New York, 1968, retaining separate and original pagination of the individual volumes).

R.J.F. Trotter has tried to distinguish polemics against Gnosticism as well as Gnostic influence in the great midrashic work of the Samaritan theologian Marqa, who wrote in the period of revival under Baba Rabba in the 4th century C.E.[93]

Others, however, have denied Simonian influence upon Samaritanism as well as the Samaritan derivation of Simonianism. Already J.A. Montgomery turned against Heidenheim. Maintaining his view of the Samaritans as being totally dependent upon Judaism, Montgomery asserted that the "traces of an incipient Gnostic speculation" which could be found in Samaritan texts actually were nothing but "a faint reflex" of "incipient Jewish Kabbalism"[94]. Besides, he argued, the view of the Christian heresiologists that the Gnostic heresies took their rise with Samaritans could find no support in the sources of the Samaritans: "... there is little or no proof for the hypothesis that the Samaritan religion was responsible for these processes of amalgamation, or became the mother of Gnosticism. So far as we have been able to sound the obscure ages of Samaritan religion, even according to the hostile Jewish evidence, we can find no syncretistic features therein, no native tendency to Gnosticism. Simon Magus appears not as a type of Samaritanism, but only as an incident... . Samaritanism cannot be held responsible for Simon Magus, or for the Gnostic developments of which the Christian heresiologues have made him the archetype."[95] As for the epithet קעים, the "Standing One", in Samaritanism, Montgomery explained this as a derivative from Hellenistic Judaism, since ὁ ἑστώς, "the Standing One", also occurs as a divine epithet in Philo's corpus[96].

Recently, S. Lowy, another writer on Samaritanism, has reiterated Montgomery's position[97]. He argues that, although the same term can be found in Samaritanism and Gnosticism, the Gnostics probably picked it from one of the many contemporary syncretistic currents and used it in a way not at all like that found in Samaritanism[98]. Lowy states that if קעים in Samaritanism is to be identified with ὁ ἑστώς in Simonianism, "it would indicate that the so-called 'Samaritan Gnosticism' is of a philosophical type presumably imbued with a Philonic type of theories." He obviously derives the Samaritan term from Philo. He goes on: "... this theory diametrically opposes the equally categorical claim that Samaritanism is the source of the mythological type of Gnosticism."[99]

---

93 See *Gnosticism and Memar Marqah* (LUOS, Monograph Series, 4), Leeds, 1964.
94 *Op. cit.*, pp. 268 f. with n. 42.
95 *Ibid.*, pp. 267 f. and p. 269.
96 See *op. cit.*, p. 215, inset; cp. p. 269, n. 42.
97 See *op. cit.*, pp. 244 ff., quoting Montgomery, p. 268, on p. 253.
98 See *op. cit.*, pp. 244 f., 246, 248, 249 ff.
99 *Ibid.*, p. 252. Lowy quite erroneously says that the ground for accepting the deriva-

Actually, already H. Waitz realized that the term as found in the cycle of Simon Magus legends in the *Pseudo-Clementines* had a different meaning than in Alexandrian philosophy, but he was still able to maintain the theory of an Alexandrian derivation by asserting that the Christian author had misunderstood the import of the concept[100]. L. Cerfaux did not think that the Simonians derived the term directly from philosophy; according to Cerfaux, "the

---

tion of the Gnostic ἐστώς concept from the Samaritan קעים is supplied by evidence "from Mandaic (not Samaritan) sources" (*ibid.*). In substantiating this allegation, he refers to an essay by G. Widengren (cited below, p. 58, n. 104); but, although the epithet does occur in Mandeism, Widengren does not adduce any Mandean evidence at all concerning "the Standing One" and in fact mentions the Simonian term only in passing.

Another distortion in Lowy's discussion of the theory of the relationship between Samaritanism and Gnosticism is found in the following statement: "One may find in Samaritan literature a parallel to the Simonean ἡ μεγάλη ἀπόφασις but this is hardly proof that the sect possesses "a clear Samaritan background". The term may rather exemplify in the above-mentioned way the distorted employment of Christian terms and a deeply syncretistic tendency ... " (p. 246). As every student of Simonianism knows, ἡ μεγάλη ἀπόφασις is *not* a technical "term" but the name of a book put into circulation under the protection of the name of Simon. The words put within quotation marks by Lowy are appended a foot-note referring to the above-mentioned article by Widengren, and this shows that Lowy in reality means ἡ μεγάλη δύναμις, the occurrence of which in Gnostic sects is dealt with by Widengren, although he does little in the way of establishing a Samaritan derivation. All the same, it would be difficult to prove that the occurrence of the term "the Great Power" in Simonianism is an instance of borrowing of "Christian terms". As far as I know, the only Christian source where we can find "the Great Power" as a name of God is Hegesippus' relation of the martyrdom of James, the brother of Jesus (as quoted by Euseb., *Hist. eccl.* II.xxiii.13); see below, p. 167.

Instead of going on enumerating all the confused remarks by Lowy in discussing the theory of the relationship between Samaritanism and Gnosticism, the following passage will suffice as evidence of his lack of knowledge of the study of Gnostic origins: "Despite the rich finds contained in the recent Coptic codices of Nag Hammadi, no further evidence has come to the light which might cogently indicate the existence of additional and previously unknown Jewish and Samaritan features [in Gnosticism]" (p. 249). It is characteristic that Lowy substantiates this statement by a footnote referring to a more than ten years old book on the Dead Sea scrolls (*sic!*), *viz.*, Driver, *op. cit.*, p. 562.

100 See "Simon Magus in der altchristlichen Literatur", *ZNW*, 5, 1904, pp. 138 ff. Other scholars postulate a Simonian dependence on the philosophical usage without noting the dissimilarity between the meaning of the term in contemporary philosophy and Simonian Gnosticism; see H. Leisegang, *Die Gnosis*, 2nd ed., Leipzig, 1936, reprinted 1941 and, as Kröner Taschenbuch, Stuttgart, 1955, pp. 62 f.; H.-F. Weiss, *Untersuchungen zur Kosmologie des hellenistischen und palästinischen Judentums* (TU, 97), Berlin, 1966, p. 136; K. Beyschlag, *Simon Magus und die christliche Gnosis* (WUNT, 16), Tübingen, 1974, pp. 45 ff., especially p. 47. Cp. already Heidenheim, *Liturgie*, p. XXXIX, n. 6.

term was in the air," but his suggestions as to the connotation of the Simonian usage were fantastic[101].

Now it is a fact that the Samaritans do not use the concept in the same way as it is used in Philo's works, where it denotes the immutability of God. On the other hand, there is a concurrence between the Samaritan and Simonian meaning of the concept[102]. This cannot have been due to the adaptation and transmittance of a philosophical term by the Simonians, for Judaism uses the participle קים in the same way as קעים is used in Samaritanism[103]. Thus, the concept of the Standing One in Simonianism would seem to reveal the existence of a genuinely Jewish-Samaritan foundation.

More than thirty years ago, G. Widengren was willing to recognize the Samaritan substructure of Simonianism, the first Gnostic heresy: "Now the Samaritan background of Simon ought to be accentuated in quite another way than has seemingly been the case. And especially the comparison between the doctrines of Simon and those of the Samaritan liturgies — preferably the hymns composed by Marqa — that invites itself, has been altogether neglected."[104] However, Widengren's own essay in this field, presented in a chapter entitled "Samaritan, Jewish- and Samaritan-Gnostic, and Jewish-Rabbinic Evidence", is remarkably unproductive. He quotes a passage from a hymn of Marqa to the effect that "God's own descent to Sinai is said to be that of the "Great Power","[105] and compares this passage to Syrian Christian and Mandean texts speaking of the descent of the divine "power" (iden-

---

101 See "La gnose simonienne", *RSR*, 16, 1926, pp. 492 ff. (= *Recueil Lucien Cerfaux* (BETL, VI-VII), I, Gembloux, 1954, pp. 249 ff.), where it is suggested a derivation from the Egyptian ritual of the raising of the *Djed* pillar, symbolizing Osiris' resurrection, or — alternatively — from some Gnostic teaching about the Primordial Man.

102 For full discussion see below, pp. 119ff.

103 See J. Levy, *Chaldäisches Wörterbuch über die Targumim und einen grossen Teil des rabbinischen Schrifttums*, II, 3rd ed., Leipzig, 1888, reprinted Köln, 1959, p. 358.

104 *The Ascension of the Apostle and the Heavenly Book* (King and Saviour, III) (UUÅ, 1950:7), Uppsala & Leipzig, 1950, p. 48. Already A. Merx, *Die vier kanonischen Evangelien*, II/2 (Das Evangelium des Johannes), Berlin, 1911, pp. 221 ff., had presented an "excursus on Samaritan Gnosticism". This essay, however, does little in the way of establishing a line of connection between Samaritan religion and Simonian Gnosticism. Merx does little more than reproduce Abu'l Fath's account of Dositheism and give an outline of Simon's teachings based on Irenaeus. The only Simonian *topos* which Merx tries to derive from Samaritanism is the concept of "the Great Power", which he takes to be a designation of the highest angel; see p. 231. This explanation is also given by W.F. Albright, "Simon Magus as "the Great Power of God"", Appendix VII in J. Munck, *The Acts of the Apostles* (AB, 31), revised by W.F. Albright & C.S. Mann, New York, 1967, p. 305, but without reference to Merx. Neither Merx nor Albright cites any evidence for this explanation.

105 *Ascension*, p. 55.

tified as the Holy Spirit in the Christian texts) upon the baptismal water, linking this *topos* to "the idea of the Great Power as being incarnated in Simon."[106] Furthermore, Widengren points out that the Samaritan saviour epithet "the True Prophet" has its equal in the "Samaritan-Jewish Gnosis" of the *Pseudo-Clementines*[107], and that the Samaritan religious terms "true" and "life" are occurring in expressions having correspondences in Mandean literature: thus, while we find "the True Prophet" in Samaritanism (and Ebionism), we meet with "the True Apostle(s)" and "the Apostle(s)" of Truth" in Mandeism, and, in both religions, we come across terms as "the Word of Life" and "the Treasure of Life"[108].

More recently, H.G. Kippenberg has demonstrated that the Simonian concept of $\dot{\eta}$ $\mu\epsilon\gamma\dot{\alpha}\lambda\eta$ $\delta\dot{\upsilon}\nu\alpha\mu\iota\varsigma$ is rooted in Samaritan theology[109]. The fact that

---

106 *Ibid.*, p. 48. For Simon as "the Great Power", see below, pp. 162ff.
107 See *ibid.*, pp. 55 f. The *Clementina*, however, are opposed to any kind of dualism and are not Gnostic.
108 See *ibid.*, pp. 56f. For a continuation of this essay, see below, pp. 156ff.
109 See *op. cit.*, pp. 328ff. Cp. already Black, pp. 64f. Rudolph, *Mandäer*, I, p. 173, n. 4 (continued on the next page), endorses Widengren's attempt to demonstrate a "connection between that part of Samaritan literature that belongs to the oldest stratification ..., Samaritan-Jewish Gnosticism, and Mandaean religion" (*Ascension*, p. 57). In the article "Randerscheinungen des Judentums und das Problem der Entstehung des Gnostizismus", *Kairos*, 9, 1967, pp. 116 f. (= *GG*, pp. 789 f.), Rudolph is sensible to the fact that a lot of Samaritan terms recurs in Gnosticism, especially in Mandeism. Since it is unthinkable that Simonianism or Mandeism has influenced Samaritanism, Rudolph assumes that the Samaritan religion reveals the common ground. Rudolph, "Gnosis und Gnostizismus, ein Forschungsbericht", *TR*, 37, 1972, pp. 344 f., speculates whether the teaching of the "Sethian" Gnostics that the pneumatics are the descendants of Seth is to be connected with the Samaritan doctrine that Seth is a special transmitter of the Light Image from Adam being manifested fully in Moses. For this Samaritan concept, see below, p. 94, n. 48. W. Beltz, "Samaritanertum und Gnosis", in *GNT*, pp. 89ff., says that Seth occurs neither in *Memar Marqa* nor in the Jewish Aggada, and that he therefore must represent the Dositheans, who were opposed by both the conservative Samaritans and the Jews. But Seth does not appear merely in late Samaritan writings allegedly showing Dosithean influence; he is reckoned as Adam's successor in a list of the illuminators of mankind in an early hymn (see Cowley, 42.10 ff.). Furthermore, that the Jewish Aggada does not mention Seth is also wrong; in *Pirke de R. Eliezer* ch. 22, the righteous are even regarded as the descendants of Seth. Philo (*De post. Caini* 42) seems to know this tradition. Both Rudolph and Beltz refer to J. Bowman, *Samaritanische Probleme* (FDV, 1959), Stuttgart, 1967, p. 51; but there is really no evidence to support Bowman's statement that the *Asatir, Molad Moshe*, and the *Malef* contain a Dosithean teaching to the effect that all Samaritans are potential "children of light" and thus Seth's descendants who only need to be awakened. Combining Bowman's assertion with a Samaritan tradition in the *Asatir* saying that Seth built the city of Damascus, Beltz is even misled to think that "the sons of Seth" who are associated with "Damascus" in the Qumran texts (see *CD* vii.18 ff.) indicate Dositheans.

Simon Magus also appears in Samaritan heresiography is taken by K. Rudolph as license to draw upon Samaritan traditions when unfolding Simonian Gnosticism[110]. As a matter of fact, the reports seem justified in associating Simon with Dositheus, the arch-heresiarch in the Samaritan sources. Kippenberg, who has distinguished different associations (those of the priests, chieftains, judges, and scribes) within the Samaritan community[111], reckons that Dositheus belonged to the association of scribes, whose provenience was the social and religious constellation which was formed around the institution of the synagogue and naturally attracted people from the lay movement. Dositheus "was at least no priest. His struggle for wisdom is mentioned. Writings were also ascribed to him."[112] Kippenberg wonders whether Simon, too, came from the class of scholars. It would seem so. If we are to believe the Clementine romance, Simon had written books. Peter is asking Simon to prove his opinion about the character of God:

> This God whom you assert to be incomprehensible and unknown to all – can you prove His existence from the Scriptures of the Jews, which are held to be of authority, or from some others of which we are ignorant, or from the Greek authors, or from your own writings (*an ex tuis scriptis propriis*)?
>
> (*Ps. -Clem. Rec.* II.38).

Since the *Megale Apophasis* was put into circulation under the protection of the name of Simon, it is apparent that the later Simonians thought of their leader as having been an author. The "Great Exposition" is a philosophical tractate basing its assertions on allegorical interpretations of the Bible – especially its first chapters – and Homer's works. As can be seen from Simon's answer to Peter's question in the *Clementina*, he did treasure the Law of Moses:

> I shall make use of assertions from the Law of the Jews only, for it is manifest to

---

For criticism, see also R. Bergmeier, "Zur Frühdatierung samaritanischer Theologoumena", *JSJ*, 5, 1974, p. 152, n. 235 (continued on the next page).

Recently, G. Quispel has acknowledged the presence of a Samaritan heritage in Simonianism; see review of R.M. Grant, *Gnosticism and Early Christianity*, 2nd ed., London, 1966, in *BO*, 26, 1969, p. 277, col. a; "From Mythos to Logos", *E-J*, XXXIX (1970), 1973, pp. 329 f.; review of Beyschlag, *op. cit.*, in *BO*, 32, 1975, p. 421, cols. a-b.

110 See "Simon – Magus oder Gnosticus?", *TR*, 42, 1978, p. 351. Lowy p. 248, asserts that the figure of Simon in Samaritan literature has been taken over from Christian sources, but already Montogomery had noted that the Samaritan version of the Simon legend contains "some independent details drawn probably from a Palestinian form of the story" (p. 267). For this legend, see below, p. 170. Bowman, *Documents*, pp. 116 f., says that the whole section on Dusis, Simon, and the Dosithean sub-sects has the appearance of having been translated from a Hebrew source and simply inserted where Abu'l Fath thought it belonged.

111 See *op. cit.*, pp. 175 ff.

112 *Ibid.*, p. 187. Cp. p. 162. See also Isser, p. 84.

all who take interest in religion that this Law is of universal authority, yet that everyone receives understanding of this Law according to his own judgment; for it has
been written by Him who created the world that the faith of things is made to depend upon it. Whence, whether anyone wishes to bring forward truth, or anyone
wishes to bring falsehood, no assertions will be received without this Law. Inasmuch,
therefore, as my knowledge is most fully in accordance with this Law [...].[113]

(*Ibid.* II.39)

Thus, Simon accepts the authority of the Law and claims that he knows
how to interpret it. In another Pseudo-Clementine passage, it is asserted
about Simon: "He allegorizes the things of the Law by his own presumption"
(*Ps.-Clem. Hom.* II.22). Simon is described as an expositor of the Law, a
scribe, although a rather unorthodox one.

According to Irenaeus, however, Simon was antinomian, but the heresiologist curiously says that the arch-heresiarch ascribed the invalid precepts of
Scripture to the *prophets*, and not to Moses:

The prophets [according to Simon] spoke their prophecies inspired by the angels
who created the world; hence, those who have their hope in him [*i.e.,* Simon] and
Helena[114] pay no further attention to them, but do as they wish as free men. For
men are saved through his grace and not by righteous works. Works are not good by
nature, but by convention, as the angels who made the world ordained in order to
lead men into slavery through such precepts.

(I.xxiii.3)

Thus, if we are to believe Irenaeus, Simon did not repudiate Moses and his
Law, but the prophets and *their* precepts. That Simon, who was a Samaritan,
disclaimed the "prophecies" of the Israelite-Jewish prophets is only natural,
but it seems strange that this repudiation is said to amount to an antinomianism. However, when we look at the addition made to the decalogue in the
Samaritan Pentateuch, it becomes understandable that the Israelite-Jewish
prophets are seen as law-givers. After *Ex.* xx.18 (in the Samaritan version,
v. 21a), the Samaritans read:

I [—it is God who is speaking—] have heard the voice of this people, which they
have spoken to you [*i.e.,* Moses]; they have spoken well in all that they said. Would
that they have a heart such as this to fear Me and observe My commandments all the
days, so that it might go well with them and their children forever. (*Deut.* v.28b-29;
in the Samaritan version, *vv.* 25b-26.) I shall raise up a prophet like you from among
their brothers for them, and I shall put My words into his mouth, and he shall speak
to them all that I shall command him. And it shall be that whoever does not listen to
his words which he shall speak in My name, I shall hold that person responsible. But
the prophet who shall presume to speak in My name that which I have not commanded him to speak, or who shall speak in the name of other gods, — that prophet shall

---

113 Simon proceeds to prove from the Pentateuch that there are several gods; see below,
p. 213.
114 For Helena, Simon's companion, see the forthcoming article in *RAC* by Professor
Gilles Quispel and the present author.

die. And if you say to yourself: "How will we recognize the word which YHWH has spoken?" – [then you should know:] When a prophet speaks in the name of YHWH, if the thing does not happen or come to pass, that is the thing which YHWH has not spoken to him; the prophet has spoken it in arrogance. You shall not be afraid of him. (*Deut*. xviii.18-22.) Go and.say to them: "Go back to your tents!" And as for you, stand here by Me, and I shall tell you all the commandments, statutes, and laws which you shall teach them, and they shall observe them in the land which I give them as possession. (*Deut*. v.30 f.; in the Samaritan version, *vv*. 27 f.)

Deut. xviii.18-22, which contains the prediction of the coming of a prophet like Moses and a warning against false prophets, by whom the Samaritans obviously understood the Israelite-Jewish prophets, splits *Deut*. v.28b-31: it follows *Deut*. v.28b-29 and precedes *Deut*. v.30 f. In this way, the words of the true prophet, the Prophet like Moses, are identified as "all the commandments, statutes, and laws" which God told Moses[115]; the Samaritans could then infer that also the false prophets spoke laws, although these had another origin. Moreover, the rabbis insisted that the prophets spoke only what was already contained in the Law[116]. Since congruity with the content of the Law was the criterion to both the Samaritans and the Jews when evaluating the message of the prophets, it is no wonder that Simon, who was a Samaritan, could repudiate the prophets in terms of denouncing their "precepts". Irenaeus would then interpret this as an antinomianism in the vein of a radical Pauline antagonism of Grace and Law like that of Marcion, but it is noteworthy that he does not go as far as accusing Simon of teaching libertinism.

It is interesting to note that Simon warrants the repudiation of the prophets and the encouragement of "antinomianism" by reference to his own rôle as a saviour (in the beginning of the paragraph, it is said that "to men he accorded redemption through the recognition of him"); we may ask whether Simon, like Dositheus, not only was a scribe but claimed to be the Prophet like Moses, who was a "messianic" figure in different quarters of Judaism, *e.g.*, Qumranism, but was *the* eschatological personage in the lay movement in Samaritanism[117]. Then, paradoxically, the allegation that Simon was antino-

---

115 See Kippenberg, p. 312.
116 See R. Meyer, par. C, "Prophecy and Prophets in the Judaism of the Hellenistic Roman Period", in Art. προφήτης κτλ., in *TDNT*, VI, 1968 and reprints, pp. 817 f.
117 For a discussion of Samaritan "messianic" figures, see Kippenberg, pp. 234 ff., 255 ff., 276 ff., 306 ff.; cp. the summary of his conclusions by Isser, pp. 128 ff. In reaction to the exploitation of the Prophet like Moses theme by the Dositheans, the priestly Samaritans referred *Deut*. xviii.15, 18 to Joshua; cp. below, p. 122. In the 4th century hymn cycle known as the *Durran*, the Taheb appears to be a *typus* of the community repenting and turning back to God; his name (תאבה/תהבה, obviously an active participle of תוב, the Aramaic equivalent of the Hebrew שוב) apparently signifies just this, although it later might have been understood as meaning the

mian need not be totally unfounded. W.D. Davies has discussed Jewish texts which show that there were expectations to the effect that the messianic age and/or age to come would bring not only the full explanation of the obscure demands of the Law or its final interpretation, but also a *new* Torah or a change or even cessation of some of the present laws – and possibly even the abrogation of the *whole* Torah[118]. As a matter of fact, the history of Jewish messianism knows several examples of the outburst of antinomianism. Writes G. Scholem: "There seems to be an intrinsic connection between active messianism and the courage for religious innovation. Messianic movements would often produce individuals with sufficient charismatic authority to challenge the established authority of rabbinic Judaism. ...there were always some individuals who realized the truth and who were attracted by the revolutionary aspects of the notion of a "renewed Torah" in the messianic age."[119]

It would seem that both Dositheus and Simon were "individuals with sufficient charismatic authority to challenge the established authority" of the Samaritan priesthood. Being the Prophet like Moses, Dositheus made alterations in the text of the Pentateuch and composed books of his own dealing with questions about the Law. We do not have to rest content with the Samaritan chronicles' assertion to this effect[120]. Eulogius says that Dositheus "adulterated the Mosaic octateuch [*sic!*] with myriads of spurious changes of all kinds, and he also left behind with his believers certain other works which he had composed" (*apud* Phot., 285a), and already Origen in a non-polemical context reports that the Dositheans of his day "preserve books of Dositheus" (*Comm. in Joh.* xiii.27, *ad* iv.28).

Abu'l Fatḥ says that that the Dositheans did not keep any festival except the Sabbath, but this is obviously not true, since he also relates that the followers of Dositheus accused the priestly Samaritans of having disordered the feasts. Reporting on the Dustan sect, the Samaritan chronicler – as has been seen – states that it abolished the holidays, but he goes on to say that the

---

One Turning Back (or even, causatively, the One Who Brings Back, the Restorer, *viz.*, of the Golden Age and the tabernacle), *i.e.*, Moses *redivivus*. The latter identification seems to be present in *Memar Marqa*, but the figure of the Taheb is here always associated with the resurrection and does not appear in the oldest ms.; see above, p. 38, n. 30. See also the review of A. Merx, *Der Messias oder Ta'eb der Samaritaner* (BZAW, 17), Giessen, 1909, by P. Kahle, in *TLZ*, 36, 1911, cols. 198 ff. Whatever be the age of the idea of the Moses *redivivus* and its original relationship to the figure of the Prophet like Moses in priestly Samaritanism (were they welded?), there is no indication that the Dositheans reckoned with a second eschatological figure.

118 See *Torah in the Messianic Age and/or Age to Come* (JBL, Monograph Series, 7), Philadelphia, 1952; *The Setting of the Sermon on the Mount*, Cambridge, 1964, Ch. II, *passim*.

119 *Sabbatai Ṣevi*, trans. by R.J. Zwi Werblowski (BS, 93), Princeton, 1973, p. 10.

120 See Vilmar, p. 154; Chronicle Adler, in *REJ*, 45, p. 227.

sect celebrated Passover at another time than the orthodox. The truth would
seem to be that the Dosithean sect deviated in festive matters[121].

According to Abu'l Fath, Shalih, the head of one of the Dosithean splinter
groups, is reported to have changed the calendar and introduced many novel-
ties in the precepts of the Pentateuch. It is probable that Shalih, too, cast
himself in the rôle as the Prophet like Moses. Abu'l Fath relates that his followers, whom he actually calls "Dustan", called him "our Father"[122], and
this is perhaps to be connected with the name "children of the Apostle",
which the Dustan sectaries are said to have applied to themselves; "the Apostle", however, was a frequent Samaritan title of Moses, and it thus would
seem that Shalih regarded himself as a new "Apostle", a new Moses.

Shalih promised that the tabernacle soon would reappear, and this connects him with the enthusiast who gathered quite a following of Samaritans
by promising to reveal the sacred contents of the tabernacle hidden on Mt.
Gerizim (see Joseph., *Ant.* XVIII.85). This man, whose group was crushed by
Pilate even before the mounting of Mt. Gerizim started, no doubt designed
himself as a new Moses, and probably so did Shalih. Abu'l Fath relates that
Shalih's followers made a large tent for him, and that he began to preach in
it, and it might be wondered whether this tent or hut was modelled upon the
tabernacle, in the doorway of which Moses stood speaking to the people. In
any case, the tent does not seem to have had more than transitory significance for Shalih, for he is reported to have said: "From this tent, let us go up
to Mt. Gerizim!"[123]   Shalih probably was designating himself as the eschatological Prophet like Moses, a kind of a new Moses, or even as Moses *redivivus*.
It would be on this authority that he introduced changes in the Law.

Shalih's sect seems to have developed in an antinomian direction. According to Abu'l Fath, Shalih at first preached an asceticism and honoured Mt.
Gerizim, but then changed the calendar, introduced innovations of a lenient
character in the regulations of purity, and spoke derogatorily about the rolled
up scroll in the ark in the synagogue and even about the holy mountain, the
ascension of which he forbade. We must also mention that one of the predecessors of Shalih, Ansami by name, is said to have abolished the feast days[124].
Did he, too, claim to be the Prophet like Moses?

If we are to believe Abu'l Fath, some of the Dosithean splinter groups
were thoroughly antinomian. The Qiltāy (or Qatitāy) are reported to have
said: "Do not perform any religious duty, for all religious duties have been

---

121 See Bowman, *Documents*, p. 181, n. 34 (continued on the next page), p. 205, n. 246
    (continued on the next page), p. 206, n. 247.
122 Vilmar, p. 162.
123 *Ibid.*, p. 161.
124 See *ibid.*, p. 159.

abolished!"[125] Waiting for God to reveal the tabernacle, these people gathered on Mt. Gerizim and announced that they had abrogated all the religious duties, just as "Dusis, Your Prophet, had said." This is possibly an exaggerated account, but it emerges clearly that the abolishment or change of the demands of the Laws is connected with "messianic" expectations, for the Qiltāy awaited the recovery of the tabernacle and warranted their antinomianism with reference to the command of Dositheus, the eschatological Prophet like Moses, whose return they apparently expected.

The sect formed by the two men named Abiyyah and Dosah also claimed that "all religious duties have been abolished,"[126] and went across the Jordan and far into the desert. Abu'l Fath says that this happened on a Sabbath, and that they even went past a cemetery; this notice obviously is meant to illustrate their disregard for the Sabbath laws and the purity regulations.

The motif of the journey across the Jordan and into the desert calls for especial notice, for we learn from Josephus' account of the Jewish messianic-revolutionary movements of the first century C.E. that all their leaders followed "the example of Moses by calling for an exodus into the wilderness and promising signs and wonders, and also deliverance."[127] Thus, we may discern a Moses pattern and an eschatological strain also in the sect of Abiyyah and Dosah. Furthermore, we may ask whether the Jewish "messiahs" actually were influenced by Samaritan ideas of the awaited redeemer, who was conceived of as the Prophet like Moses.

That also the antinomianism and soteriology of Simon Magus were tied to eschatological ideas is shown by the continuation of the account that he granted freedom in legal matters to those who put their trust in him:

> Hence he promised that the world would be dissolved, and that those who are his would be liberated from the dominion of those who made the world.
>
> (Iren., I.xxiii.3)

Thus, Simon fits into the history of Samaritan sectarianism, where people arose claiming to be the eschatological Prophet like Moses and introduced the "messianic" Law.

Simon Magus can be compared to the person of Elchasai, who is said to have arisen in the third year of Trajan's reign, *i.e.*, in 101 C.E. (see Hipp., IX.xiii.3), and to have swept a great following among the sects which had settled in Transjordanian country (see Epiphan., *Pan.* XIX.ii.10 ff.; LIII.i.

---

125 *Ibid.*, p. 160.
126 The text of Abu'l Fath (Vilmar, p. 160) actually reads that "all religious duties have *not* been abolished," but this does not make sense in view of the continuation; see the comment by Nemoy, in Isser, p. 83, n. f.
127 J. Jeremias, Art. Μωυσῆς, in *TDNT*, IV, 1967, reprinted 1975, p. 862. For John the Baptist, see below, pp. 115f.

1 ff.). Epiphanius says that Elchasai "rejected the Books of Moses, like the Nasareans" (ibid. XIX.v.1)[128]. This account, however, evidently is exag-

---

128 For the sect of the Nasareans, see ibid. ch. XVIII, where Epiphanius actually writes Ναξαραῖοι, whereas he has Νασαραῖοι in XIX.v.1, 4 and XXIX.vi.1, and Νασαρηνοί in XX.iii.2. Black, pp. 66 ff., convincingly argues against the old view that Epiphanius' account is a doublet of some description of a Jewish Christian sect, and plausibly suggests a Samaritan identity of the Nasareans, who said that the Jewish version of the Pentateuch was not that which was given to Moses, and venerated the ante- and post-deluvian patriarchs. Their name, from the root נָצַר, to "guard", "observe", is equivalent to שׁמרים, which the Samaritans substitute for שׁמרונים. However, since the Nasareans are said to have rejected the sacrificial system, they cannot have been orthodox Samaritans, but would rather have to be connected with the Dosithean movement, which was opposed to the cult on Mt. Gerizim.

Black, pp. 70 ff., obviously is wrong when he goes on to connect the Nasareans with "the ancient Israelite institution of the life-long Nazirate" (p. 83 and p. 167), which he sees as the common denominator of Palestinian sectarianism. Philaster in his heresiography has the Nazorei at a place which corresponds to where Epiphanius has his Nasareans, and Black argues that Philaster's report that this heresy "affirms that one should live carnally (carnaliter uiuendum adfirmat)" (ch. 8) is a misunderstanding of the Nazirite asceticism in the heresiologists' common source, which Epiphanius corrected by the statement that the Nasareans abstained from the eating of meat. However, since Philaster goes on to say that the sect "believes that all justification depends on carnal observance (omnemque iustificationem in carnali obseruantia consistere suspicatur)," it is clear that the phrase refers to the observance of the "carnal" Law of the old dispensation, as does the phrase that the Sadducees "preach that one should live according to the flesh, be circumcised [...]" (ch. 5); cp. F. Oehler, ed., Corpus Haereseologicum, I, Berlin, 1856, p. 8, n. b. Furthermore, neither Epiphanius nor Philaster depicts the sect in question with any of the specific Nazirite traits, i.e., the taboos of cutting the hair, drinking alcoholic beverages, and coming near a corpse. Finally, Epiphanius (XXIX.vi.1) distinguishes very carefully between the Nasareans and the Ναξιραῖοι (the meaning of whose name he correctly gives as "consecrated", that is, deriving it from נזר, to "separate", "dedicate oneself") as well as the Jewish Christian Ναζωραῖοι.

Emphasizing the importance of the Samaritan Nazirate (which lasted one solar year plus seven days and thus was no continuation of "the life-long Nazirate"), Bowman, Problem, p. 104, thinks that Abu'l Fath's account that Dositheus disclaimed the eating of meat for two years and then "ate and drank, and got drunk" (Vilmar, p. 151) implies that he also did not drink wine for two years and practised a double Nazirate. But the reason for not eating meat is said to be that the blood of the first-born was no longer sprinkled on the altar (cp. Num. xviii.17). After the destruction of the Jerusalem temple, many Jews are said to have refrained from eating meat and drinking wine on the account that there were no more tamid and wine offerings (see Tos. Sota xv.11; Baba Bathra 60b).

Since Abu'l Fath says that the followers of Dositheus "cut their hair" (Vilmar, p. 157), Isser, pp. 100 f., thinks that this hints at the Nazirite religious duty, but it is inconceivable that a characteristic trait of the Nazirs should be indicated by the mention of the act which marked the end (and, in Samaritanism, also the beginning) of the Nazirite term. The Dosithean practice of cutting the hair was probably done "in opposition to the Samaritan priests who as a general rule did not cut their hair"

gerated. Like the Nasareans, Elchasai did not reject the Law in its entirety, but only certain parts of it; Epiphanius reports that Elchasai "did not live according to the Law; he substituted some things for others and formed his own heresy" (XIX.i.5). Epiphanius also has to admit that Elchasai enjoined the circumcision and the observance of the Sabbath (see XIX.iii.5; cp. Hipp., IX.xiv.3). If we ask what was excised by Elchasai, we learn that he repudiated the sacrifices and the eating of meat (see Epiphan., *Pan*. XIX.iii.6). In this, then, he agreed with the Nasareans[129].

Like Simon and other Samaritan sect-leaders, Elchasai believed that he was living at the eve of the new aeon, for he predicted that a great eschatological battle involving the cosmic powers was to blaze up three years after the Parthian war, *i.e.*, in 119 C.E. (see Hipp., IX.xvi.2 ff.). Like the Samaritan heretics, this could have led him to introduce the Law in what he thought was its order and earned him the reputation of having rejected the Law. As is implied by Epiphanius, Elchasai's changes in the precepts of the Law would seem to have been made on his own authority, and this prompts us to ask whether he actually was influenced by Samaritan "messianology" and regarded himself as the eschatological Prophet like Moses[130]. His very name, the meaning of which is the "Hidden Power", connects him with Simon Magus, who was hailed as the "Great Power"[131]. Furthermore, Elchasai's apparent

---

(Bowman, *Problem*, p. 48). A disruption in the connection with the cult and the priesthood is the attendant of the emergence of sectarianism.

129 The anti-sacrificial and ascetic tendency emerges again in the Jewish Christian sect of the Ebionites. These people taught that Christ had said: "I have come into the world in order to destroy sacrifices" (Epiphan., *Pan*. XXX.xvi.5). They rejected the eating of meat (see *ibid*. XXX.xviii.7). Epiphanius could therefore say that the Ebionites "do not accept the whole of the Pentateuch of Moses, but suppress certain passages" (*ibid*.). The Ebionites themselves, however, taught that the task of the "True Prophet", who had manifested himself since the beginning of the world in a series of changing characters (see *Ps.-Clem. Hom*. III.20), the last of whom being Jesus, was to point out the false pericopes of the Law (see *ibid*. II.38; III.47; 49). The knowledge communicated by the True Prophet is thus identical with the Law which was given to Moses but later forged (see *ibid*. II.38; 52; III.48 ff.).

130 The True Prophet of the Ebionites is also the Prophet like Moses, for *Deut*. xviii.15, 18 is referred to Jesus (see *Ps.-Clem. Hom*. III.53; cp. *Rec*. I.43; 54). Furthermore, it is noteworthy that Moses is the last of the "seven pillars of the world" preceding Jesus (see *Hom*. XVIII.14), as can be seen by collating the list of the names of the six "pillars" in *Hom*. XVIII.13 (where Moses is not mentioned) with that of the five saints in II.52 (where Moses does occur, whereas Enoch and Isaac are lacking). The exclusion of the Israelite-Jewish prophets from the list of the manifestations of the True Prophet is suggestive of Samaritan influence. As a matter of fact, the "True Prophet" is a Samaritan title of Moses; see below, p. 150.

131 The "Power" was a name of the Glory of the Lord, the man-like manifestation of God, in both Jewish mysticism and Samaritanism; see below, pp. 179ff. The Jewish Christians took over this tradition and identified this figure as Christ, and Elchasai –

claim to be the final manifestation of Christ has a correspondence in the teaching of the Simonians that their hero had been present in Jesus and then returned before the dissolution of the world[132].

The description of Elchasai's sect corroborates the theory of a Samaritan connection. Epiphanius says that the Elchasaites are "neither Christians, nor Jews, nor Greeks; keeping to the middle way, they are actually nothing" (*Pan.* LIII.i.3). This may mean that they are Samaritans. This is possibly to be concluded also from the following statement: "They do not accept the Prophets or Apostles [...]" (LIII.i.7). Here, Epiphanius may be reflecting the fact that the Elchasaites accepted neither the prophetical canon nor the New Testament. This was also the Samaritan stand[133].

The bishop of Salamis goes on: "Water, however, is honoured by them; and they consider it to be God, saying: "I believe that life was derived from water" " (*ibid.*). This is probably an exaggerated account, but Hippolytus supports the relation that the Elchasaites placed great emphasis on the element of water, for he says that they offered a second baptism for the remission of grievous sins and enjoined the use of therapeutic bathings (see IX.xv.3 ff.)[134]. There were, of course, several pre- and non-Christian groups which had some type of ritual immersion or washing, but − in view of Epiphanius' assertion of the Jewish Christian homage to the very element of water − the nearest parallel seems to be found in the sect of the Dositheans, about whom Abu'l Fath says: "[...] they performed all their prayers in water. Because of their veneration of water, they would cover their bodies before entering it."[135]

According to the Christian heresiologists, the Jewish Christians immersed themselves fully clothed, like the Dositheans[136]. Hippolytus says that Elchasai

---

who agreed with the Ebionites in teaching the continuous appearances of the saviour (see Hipp., IX.xiv.1; X.xxix.2; Epiphan., *Pan.* LIII.i.8) − apparently claimed to be the eschatological manifestation of the Son; see J. Fossum, "Jewish-Christian Christology and Jewish Mysticism", *VigChr*, 37, 1983, pp. 273 ff.

132 See below, pp. 128f.

133 Origen, however, reports that the sect made selective use of the entire Old Testament and the Gospels (see Euseb., *Hist. eccl.* VI.38). But the New Testament did not exist at Elchasai's time, and the report can only hold good for the later Elchasaites.

134 The Ebionites recommended purificatory washings in addition to the initiation rite of baptism (see *Ps.-Clem. Hom.* XI.28 ff.).

135 Vilmar, p. 157. Abu'l Fath (Vilmar, p. 82) tells that the Dustan sectaries differed from the main body of the Samaritans by regarding a fountain in which there was a creeping thing as impure. Isser, pp. 85 f., notes that *Tosafot Mikwaoth* (vi.1) declares that the Samaritan pools for ritual immersion are clean, and concludes that the Samaritans observed the laws of cleanliness regarding the *mikwaoth* very strictly, and that the Dositheans would seem to have been even more strict than the main stream Samaritans.

136 Josephus says that the Essenes, "after girding their loins with linen cloths, bathe

admonished his followers to undergo the second baptism "with all your clothing" (IX.xv.3). If anyone had been bitten or even touched by a mad dog, he should "baptize himself with all he wears"(*ibid*. IX.xv.4). Concerning the Ebionites — allegedly being like the Elchasaites (see Epiphan., *Pan.* XXX.ii.1) and holding water to be θεοῦ (*Anaceph.* II.xxx.3) — Epiphanius has, *inter alia*, this to say: "If one meets somebody upon coming up from immersion in water and washing, one returns to wash oneself in the same way again, several times and fully clothed" (*Pan.* XXX.ii.5). It is significant that the bishop of Salamis notes that the Jewish Christians do "things more in the same way as the Samaritans than as the Jews" (*ibid*. XXX.ii.3), and assert that this is also true of their immersion practice: "They often baptize themselves in water, summer and winter, for sanctification, like the Samaritans" (*Anaceph.* II.xxx.4)[137].

Epiphanius relates that Elchasai became the head of the sect of the Σαμψαῖοι, and this name would seem to be related to the name of Σοβιαί, a certain person to whom Elchasai transmitted his book of revelation if we are to believe Hippolytus (IX.xiii.2). Many scholars, however, do not think this to have been the name of a person but the name of certain people who called themselves or were known by some passive participial form of the verb צבע or צבא, to "wash", "immerse"[138]. The name of the Sampseans may then be a false rendering of Σαβαῖοι, which has the same derivation[139]. Furthermore, Epiphanius (*Pan.* chs. X ff.) actually speaks about the Samaritan sect of the Σεβουαῖοι, a word which apparently transcribes an Aramaic form such as צבועייא. Finally, the Samaritan chronicles actually mention a sect by the name of the Subuai or Sabuai as opposing Baba Rabba[140].

---

their bodies in cold water" (*Bell.* II.129; cp. 161). This is no parallel to the Jewish Christian custom. The Mandeans immerse themselves in their cultic dress, but E. Segelberg, *Maṣbūtā*, Uppsala, 1958, pp. 122 ff., has shown that the investiture with the *rasta* originally followed the ascension from the water.

137 Whereas the Dositheans said all their prayers while standing in water, prayer followed immediately upon the purificatory washings in Ebionitism (see *Ps.-Clem. Hom.* X.1; XI.1; XIV.3). However, the *Contestatio*, an introductory writing handed down in the Greek recension of the Clementine romance, enjoins the candidate for a teaching position to speak his vow while standing in water (see i.1). Elchasai admonished anyone who had been bitten by a mad dog to "baptize himself with all he wears and pray to the great and most high God with a faithful heart" (Hipp., IX.xv.4). But, admittedly, there apparently were other sectaries than the Dositheans who prayed while being in water (see *Sib. Or.* IV.165 ff.).

138 See already W. Brandt, *Elchasai*, Leipzig, 1912, p. 42. However, since Greek transliterations of Semitic forms are made at random, we must refrain from seeking the exact original.

139 See already D. Chwolsohn, *Die Ssabier und der Ssabismus*, I, Petersburg, 1856, pp. 120 f.

140 Abu'l Fatḥ (Vilmar, p. 131) has this form, whereas Chronicle II denotes the oppon-

J. Bowman, however, argues that Baba Rabba had become a Dosithean, and that the people who opposed him must have been the priestly Samaritans. This is not the place to give a survey of Baba's work; suffice it to say that Baba Rabba cannot be seen as a Dosithean himself, although he did want to curtail the dominance of the priestly party and integrate the lay movement into the larger Samaritan society[141]. Bowman's reference to the two-division pattern in the accounts of the Samaritans in the Arabic sources is of no consequence, for these late reports speak of the Dositheans and the Kushan people[142]. As has been seen above, the Dosithean movement was split into several sects, and the Subuai (Sabuai) or Sebueans appear to have been one of them. They are said to have had priests of their own, that this is also what Abu'l Fatḥ relates of the Dustan sectaries.

In support of his contention that the Subuai (Sabuai) or Sebueans were the priestly Samaritans, Bowman also cites the Jewish sources where Dositheus and Sabbaeus or סבייא, or סבאי, appear as certain Samaritan protagonists[143]. But, granted that the names represent sects, the latter cannot stand for the priestly party, for the sources describe the two characters as confederates and representatives of the Samaritan community *en bloc*.

On Epiphanius' evidence, the Sebueans cannot have been the conservative priestly party, since they are said to have changed the calendar and celebrated the spring festivals in the autumn and *vice versa* (see *Pan.* ch. XI). That they actually made such a rabid alteration is extremely improbable, but

---

ents of Baba Rabba as משפחת השבעים (Cohen, § 7), which Cohen translates as "The Family of the Seventy" and thinks "underscores their claim to descent from the seventy Elders of the classical Era of Favour" (pp. 228 f.). However, Cohen does identify these people as the Dositheans.

141 For a discussion of Baba's work, see now Cohen, pp. 224 ff. Lowy, pp. 228 f., 259 f., goes too far when he seems to deny any Dosithean affiliation of Baba Rabba. In view of the Dosithean practice of praying while being in water, it is certainly interesting – as noted by Cohen, p. 233 – that Chronicle II relates that Baba had a purification cistern built at the foot of Mt. Gerizim in order that everyone who "wished to pray upon this mountain should immerse himself at the very moment of every prayer (לעת עתות כל צלות)" (Cohen, § 8, 4).

142 See "Contact", pp. 186 f.; *Problem*, pp. 27, 43. In the former place, Bowman faultily says that Masudi in the 10th century called the anti-Dositheans "Sabbaeans". There are several other witnesses in addition to Masudi and Shahrastani, who are the ones adduced by Bowman; see Isser, pp. 69 ff., and supplement his survey of the sources with the citation of Judah Hadassi, as quoted above, p. 50, n. 77. Shahrastani explains the Kushaniya as the "truthful community" (*loc. cit.*), and T.G.J. Juynboll, ed. & trans. (Latin), *Chronicon Samaritanum*, Leiden, 1848, p. 112, plausibly derived the name from קשט, an Aramaic word meaning "truth". As a matter of fact, *Qushta* is a frequent designation of God in Samaritan sources.

143 See "Contact", p. 186; "Pilgrimage", pp. 21⁺a, 22⁺a; *Problem*, pp. 27, 43. For the sources, see above, p. 52, n. 80. *Pirke de R. Eliezer* has ms. variants (Zechariah, Micaiah) for Dositheus' companion.

they apparently made *some* changes in the calendar. As has been seen above, calendaric peculiarities are a recurring trait in Abu'l Fatḥ's description of the Samaritan sects. If the bishop of Salamis had been of the opinion that the calendar governing the cult on Mt. Gerizim was identical with the Sebuean one, he obviously would have told us — either in ch. IX on the Samaritans or in the following chapters dealing with the Samaritan sects[144].

Epiphanius gives a somewhat confused account of the circumstances of the Sebuean schism. He first says that its occasion was that the Jews and the Samaritans, often celebrating their festivals at the same time, came in conflict with each other because of the transition of pilgrims through Samaria. After having added that the first conflict between the Jews and "the Samaritans" occurred over the fortification of Jerusalem, he states that the Sebueans set up their own calendar "first out of anger at Ezra, secondly for the aforementioned reason" (ch. XI). Whether or not the Sebueans really changed the calendar in an attempt to secure themselves associates need not concern us; the impor-

---

144 This is not considered by Bowman, *Problem*, pp. 26, 44, who thinks that the name of the Sebueans is derived from שבוע and refers to the seven feasts celebrated by the priestly Samaritans over against the Dositheans, who allegedly abolished all festivals. In *Documents*, p. 197, n. 171, however, Bowman accepts the old theory by Juynboll, *loc. cit.*, that the name alludes to the Sebueans' celebration of the Passover in the seventh month. Crown involves himself in great confusion when espousing the view that the Sebueans were the opponents of the Dositheans and "comprised the main stream of Samaritanism" (p. 75), for he argues that the Dositheans adopted the calendar of the priesthood; see above, p. 46, n. 63.

An interesting etymology of the name of the Sampseans is forthcoming in Epiphanius' explanation of the name as meaning ἡλιακοί, "sunny", obviously deriving it from שמש, "sun". Since Elchasai is said to have prohibited the custom of praying facing the east (see Epiphan., *Pan.* XIX.i.5), it would seem that the Sampseans previously had prayed facing the sun rising. This was also the custom of the Essenes known to Josephus (*Bell.* II.128 f.). Furthermore, Josephus' Essenes had an individual and spiritual ressurection doctrine which was not unlike that of some of the Dosithean splinter groups (see *ibid.* II.154). Epiphanius (*Pan.* chs. X ff.) in fact maintains that the Essenes were a Samaritan sect and that they shared the calendar of the Sebueans. Moreover, when dealing with the Sampseans-Elchasaites, he says that their sect had absorbed the "Ossenes" (see XIX.i.1 ff.; XX.iii.2, 4), a unique sect name which apparently is to be explained from the fact that Epiphanius asserts that the Essenes were Samaritans. Finally, it must be mentioned that Abu'l Fatḥ states that, of the three Jewish sects — the Pharisees, the Sadducees, and the חסידים — the last "is the one which is nearest to the Samaritans, and [...] they dwell in the villages which are in the neighbourhood of the Blessed Mountain in order to devote themselves to worship" (Vilmar, p. 102). The oft-noted similarities between the Qumran-Essenes and the Dositheans may be due to the fact that there was a communication between the various Palestinian sects with their splinter groups; cp. J. Massingberd Ford, "Can We Exclude Samaritan Influence from Qumran?", *RQ*, 6, 1967, pp. 109 ff. Furthermore, the name "Hasidim", which probably is the derivation of the "Essenes", perhaps was shared by Judean and Samaritan groups.

tant point is that the association of the emergence of Samaritan sectarianism with the North-South schism obviously is anachronistic. The Jewish-Samaritan strifes over pilgrims belong to the Roman period (see Joseph., *Ant.* XX.118; *Bell.* II.232 f.), and this was the bloom of Samaritan sectarianism.

On all this evidence, it would not seem unreasonable to conclude that Elchasai became the head of a Samaritan sect of baptizers, or at least that there were considerable Samaritan elements in Elchasaitism. In view of the thesis that Samaritanism contributed to the rise of Gnosticism, it may be asked whether Elchasaitism shows a Gnostic strain. Ibn al-Nadim, who wrote his *Fihrist al-'Ulum* in the 10th century, actually says that the Elchasaites – among whom Mani, the most extreme of the Gnostics, grew up[145] – "agreed with the Manicheans about the two elemental principles, but later their sect became separate" (IX.1)[146]. The two principles of Manicheism are the upper world of light or spirit and the lower world of darkness or matter, both of which have existed from eternity. If the Elchasaites cherished this doctrine, we must revise the judgment of G. Strecker that a cosmological dualism is only "suggestively" present in Elchasai's teaching of the antagonism of water and fire (see Epiphan., *Pan.* XIX.iii.7)[147]. We have seen that water was regarded as a divine element in Elchasaitism, and it might be tempting to connect the disavowal of fire with the estimation of fire in Gnosticism, where an anti-cosmic spirit brought about a revaluation of the Stoic idea of fire as the force permeating all the other elements of the material universe, and an identification of the demiurge as the "god of the fire"[148]. However, Epiphanius connects the Elchasaite repudiation of fire with the rejection of "sacrifices and priestly rites" (*Pan.* XIX.iii.6). Thus, the antagonism of water and fire does not refer to cosmology but to cult; in place of sacrifices, the performance of which required fire, Elchasai put baptism for the remission of sins[149]. If al-Nadim's report is generally correct, the Elchasaites must have espoused their dualism at a later stage[150].

---

145 See below, p. 159.
146 Text and translation are conveniently presented in G. Flügel, *Mani*, Leipzig, 1862, reprinted Osnabrück, 1969, pp. 133 f. Al-Nadim calls this Elchasaite sect *al-Mughtasilâ*, "the self-immersers", and *Sâbiʾat al-Baṭâʾih,* "the Sabeans of the marshes". We are led back to the Aramaic root צבע. Cp. already Chwolsohn, pp. 112 ff.
147 "Judenchristentum und Gnosis", in *AT-F-G*, p. 281; cp. Art. "Elkesai", in *RAC*, IV, 1959, col. 1184.
148 See Jonas, *Gnostic Religion*, pp. 167 f.
149 Epiphanius scoffs at Elchasai because the latter condemned sacrifices and cultic acts while at the same time admonished his followers to pray facing Jerusalem; but it is a question whether Elchasai would condemn a cult that had ceased to exist some thirty years ago. Brandt, *Elchasai*, pp. 23, 42, thinks that Elchasai tried to convert pagans adhering to his sect from their habit of bringing offerings to their former priests. But it is also possible that this is another example of Elchasai's Samaritan back-

As a matter of fact, it does not seem that Gnostic dualism had unfolded before the time of Elchasai. However, there is at hand an early account of Elchasai's teaching which appears to have bearing on the development of Gnosticism. According to Hippolytus, Elchasai prophesied that —

> [...] when three years of the emperor Trajan are completed from the time when he subjected the Parthians to his own rule — when these three years are fulfilled, the war between the godless angels of the north (τῶν ἀγγέλων τῆς ἀσεβείας τῶν ἄρκτων) will blaze up. Because of this, all the kingdoms of godlessness are going to be shuddered.
>
> (IX.xvi.4)

This passage presupposes the teaching that every nation has a heavenly representative, and that the disorders — wars and the like — between the peoples reflect conflicts between their angels[151]. Elchasai predicts that even the eschatological battle, which will overthrow the Roman empire[152], is going to break out on account of a war between the angels who are to be found in the northern region of the sky[153].

Furthermore, these angels are hostile towards men as well as towards God. They are the "evil, godless stars" (ἀστέρες πονηροὶ τῆς ἀσεβείας) that rule over those days on which it is forbidden to start a new work or baptize (see Hipp., IX.xvi.2 f.)[154]. Thus, Elchasai's universe is certainly under the sway of evil powers, who are able to destroy the works of men and even leading the history of the world to its end.

There is nothing in this which transcends the apocalyptic teaching of the

---

ground, for offerings were continued to be brought on Mt. Gerizim even after the destruction of the temple. Moreover, the Dosithean branch of the Samaritans substituted immersion rites and prayer for the old sacrificial cult. W. Bousset, *Hauptprobleme der Gnosis* (FRLANT, 10), Göttingen 1907, reprinted Darmstadt, 1973, pp. 156 f., thinks that Elchasai opposed a fire cult. Now it is a fact that there are some faint traces of fire rituals and the idea of fire purification in Samaritanism; see Montgomery, pp. 112, 319; Cohen, pp. 205 ff.

150 Before asserting that the Elchasaites agreed with the Manicheans regarding the two principles, al-Nadim says that they affirmed that there are two existences or natures, one male and one female, and that they divided the vegetation accordingly. The male-female dualism is reminiscent of the syzygies doctrine of the Ebionites, but there is no indication in the older sources that the Elchasaites shared this idea. The division of the plants into good (male) and evil (female) species seems to reveal an assimilation of some Persian doctrine; see Bousset, p. 153; Brandt, p. 136.

151 For this idea, see H. Bietenhard, *Die himmlische Welt im Urchristentum und Spätjudentum* (WUNT, 2), Tübingen, 1951, pp. 109 ff.

152 See Bousset, p. 156; Brandt, p. 13; Strecker, "Elkesai", col. 1182.

153 That the angels presided over the various stars and even were identified with them was a widely entertained notion; see J. Michl, Art. "Engel II (jüdisch)", in *RAC*, V, 1962, col. 71.

154 That the angels ruled over months and days was also a common idea; see *ibid.*

time, but – if we again can view Simon Magus as a parent of Gnosticism –
it would seem that it was this apocalyptic spirit which bred Gnostic dualism.
In Simon's system, there is no teaching to the effect that *matter* in and of
itself is evil. It is true that the angels not only rule the world but even have
created it, but this was not an anti-divine act; on the contrary, it was the will
of God that the angels should create the world. The dualism is determined by
the event that the angels *afterwards* turned against the divine world and
misconducted their government of the world of men[155]. In order to remedy
the situation arising from their bad rule, God had to descend in Simon:

> For since the angels were governing the world badly, because each one of them
> desired the supremacy for himself, he came in order to amend matters.
>
> (Iren., I.xxiii.3)

After having told about Simon's descent and docetic appearance among
men[156], Irenaeus relates his antinomianism, promise of deliverance, and prediction of the imminent dissolution of the world[157]. There is no teaching to
the effect that Simon descended in order to reveal the true nature of men's
spirit-selves and thus effect their awakening[158]. Like Elchasai, Simon stood
forth as the eschatological Prophet like Moses, bringing the final revelation
and offering deliverance from a chaotic world brought to the brink of destruction through the misconduct of the angels.

That the lot of the world was in the hand of evil powers was an idea which
Simon could have derived from his Dosithean provenance as well as from
Jewish apocalypticism, for Abu'l Fath reports that the Dosithean sub-sect of
the Saduqay "believed that the serpent will govern the lives of creatures until
the day of Resurrection."[159] The serpent undoubtedly is the serpent of
Genesis ch. iii, which was identified with the devil (see *Wisd.* ii.24; *Rev.*

---

155 See below, p. 215.
156 See below, pp. 128f.
157 See above, p. 61, and p. 65.
158 G. Lüdemann, *Untersuchungen zur simonianischen Gnosis* (GTA, 1), Göttingen,
    1975, p. 79, criticizes W. Foerster's translation of the sentence immediately preced-
    ing the passage quoted above: "... but to men he accorded redemption through the
    recognition of him" (*Gnosis*, I, p. 30). According to Lüdemann, the pronoun in
    per suam agnitionem does not refer to Simon but to men's *own* knowledge (cp.
    Hipp., VI.xix.5, διὰ τῆς ἰδίας ἐπιγνώσεως). This may be correct, but it does not
    follow that Lüdemann is right that this means "through *gnōsis* about the Self",
    for the Simonian myth does not tell that man has a Self of divine origin which must
    be rediscovered. If it is right to refer *suam* to men, the correct sense would be con-
    veyed by the translation of E. Klebba: "... *den Menschen durch die eigene Erkenntis
    das Heil zu bringen*" (p. 70). Thus, it is possible that the text should be understood
    to say that Simon accorded redemption to those who by themselves recognized God
    in him.
159 Vilmar, p. 160.

xii.9; xx.3)[160]. In Judaism, too, the devil could be called "lord of this world" and seen as the chief of the national angels, the angel of Rome[161]. However, men are not *eo ipso* under his rule, but have to be led astray[162], and Simon would rather seem to have developed some Dosithean view of the *kosmokrator* and his angels. When the world and the body of man are regarded as the wrongful products of this *kosmokrator* and his angels, it is evident that the anti-cosmic and anthropological dualism being the characteristic of Gnosticism is present. But before the world and man's natural existence were seen as totally infernal, the office of being the "ruler of this world" and even the demiurge could be attributed to a *positive* angel[163]. By ascribing the creation to this angel and referring the theophanies in Scripture to him, it was possible to exempt God from the responsibility of the imperfectness of the world and guard his transcendence. We now turn to the probe of the traditions concentering about this figure, who was transmuted into the Gnostic image of the demiurge.

---

160 Isser also refers to the teaching of the Gnostic Naassenes, "for whom the Serpent was the Cosmocrator" (p. 104). But in the Naassene as well as in the Ophite Gnosis, the serpent is the conveyor of *gnōsis* and is opposed to the evil rulers of this world. Other Gnostics, however, retained the apocalyptic idea of the serpent as the ruler of this world; thus, Epiphanius knew some people who said that "the ruler who possesses this world has the form of a serpent" (*Pan.* XXVI.x.8).

161 See Bietenhard, pp. 113 ff.; Michl, cols. 82, 89. For the idea that Samael/Satan and his angels were envious of each other and warred in heaven, see *Asc. Is.* vii.9 ff.

162 The "ruler of this world" has greater power according to New Testament ideology (see *John* xii.31; xiv.30; xvi.11; *II Cor.* iv.4; *Eph.* ii.2; vi.12; *I John* v.19; cp. *Luke* iv.6; *et al.*). Men *need* to be saved from his grip, as is the case in Simon's system. This dualistic strain in Christianity shows that it has developed in parallelism to Gnosticism; cp. above, pp. 4f., and pp. 15f.

163 I.P. Culianu, "The Angels of the Nations and the Origins of Gnostic Dualism", in *Studies*, p. 84, asserts that even the *title* "prince of the world" originally belonged to God's principal angel, but the evidence for this is late. A.F. Segal, "Ruler of This World", in E.P. Sanders, ed., *Jewish and Christian Self-Definition*, II (Aspects of Judaism in the Greco-Roman Period), London, 1981, pp. 246 ff., rightly points out that the establishment of the priority of either representation of the "ruler of this world" is not important, for the positive portrait of an angel with this *function* was certainly as old as the negative picture. Segal says that "the complete identification of the Lord of the World with the creator demiurge (who is at the same time God of the Jews and Prince of the Demons) must be from a later, more desperate time" (p. 263), but it would seem that already the positive form of the "ruler of this world" was ascribed with demiurgic functions. However, it is no doubt right that the identification of the negative version of the "ruler of the world", even the demiurge, with the God of the Old Testament must stem from the situation when the rabbis vehemently opposed the (proto-)Gnostics. See also above, pp. 17f. For the development of Gnostic dualism, see below, pp. 213ff.

CHAPTER THREE

The Name of God

The Samaritan Logos Doctrine: The Creation through the Name

Throughout all parts of the Samaritan literature, it is emphasized that God created by his word. To choose two late passages from the Liturgy:

> He spoke a word (מלה), and it was accomplished; through it, created things came into being.

(Cowley, 746.16)[1]

> He is the Great God, Creator and Sustainer of the world; He created everything out of nothing through a word (במלה) out of fullness.

(*ibid*. 770.33 f.)

The doctrine of the creation by means of the divine command is, of course, also a Jewish and Christian property; it is implied already in the creation narrative of the first verses of the first book in the Bible: God spoke and the creation ensued[2]. The Pentateuch was the Bible of the Samaritans, and it is not necessary to assume that they borrowed their Logos doctrine from the Jews or the Christians. Actually, the idea of the creation through the word seems to be a very primitive thought of man. "If there weren't any words, it would be very bad," said a boy of six and a half, "you couldn't make anything. How could things have been made?"[3] "What has been termed "creation from nothing," and celebrated by theologians as an extremely elevated

---

1 The mode of reference to texts from the Samaritan Liturgy denotes page and line(s).

2 The doctrine is spoken out explicitly in *Ps.* xxxiii.6, 9. It is also found in the apocrypha (see *Sir.* xlii.15; *Wisd.* ix.1) and pseudepigrapha (see *Jub.* ii.5). For the doctrine in rabbinism, see the references in Str.-Bill., III (Die Briefe des Neuen Testaments und die Offenbarung Johannis), 1926 and reprints, p. 671; cp. II (Das Evangelium nach Markus, Lukas und Johannes und die Apostelgeschichte), 1924 and reprints, pp. 304 f., 310 f. In ancient Christian literature, we find it in the New Testament (see *John* i.1 ff.; *Heb.* xi.3), the pseudepigrapha (see *Od. Sol* xvi.19), and the Apostolic Fathers (see *I Clem.* xxvii 4).

3 J. Piaget, *The Child's Conception of the World,* trans. by J. & A. Tomlinson, New York, 1929, reprinted London, 1971, p. 72; quoted by J. Campbell, *The Masks of God*, I (Primitive Mythology), 2nd ed., New York, 1969, reprinted London, 1973, p. 86.

notion, is actually — at least in the text in which the notion is supposed to be documented — a creation from the word, through the naming of the name, which is one of the primary notions of creation entertained by the human infant."[4] The suggestion of this very idea in the first chapter of *Genesis* apparently was reason more than enough for the Samaritans to develop their Logos doctrine.

Epitomes of God's creative work containing the so-called "Ten Words of Creation", that is, the ten short sentences from *Gen.* ch. i where the different works of the creation are actuated by God's naming of the phenomena to come into being, abound in the various forms of the Samaritan literary monuments[5]. The liturgical text last quoted continues:

> At the moment of creation, He brought forth words (מליך); and creatures arose before Him.
>
> (771.3)

But already "by Roman times they [*i.e.*, the Samaritans] had distinguished between 'the word' (Logos, Aramaic *milla*) and the (ten) words (*fiat*, Aramaic *millin*)."[6] Amram Dara, a liturgist writing in the period of the revival under Baba Rabba, apparently hints at the Ten Words of Creation in one of his hymns contained in the *Defter* (from Greek διφθέρα, "book"), where we find the oldest parts of the Liturgy[7]:

---

4 Campbell, *loc. cit.*

5 *Genesis* has "And God said" only nine times. In Judaism, the prevalent explanation seems to be that the first of the Ten Words was contained in the introductory statement of *Genesis*. The Ten Words of Creation are referred to already in the Mishna: "By ten words, the world was created" (*Aboth* v.1). For additional rabbinic material, see Str.-Bill., III, p. 371; L. Ginzberg, *The Legends of the Jews,* V (Notes to Volumes I and II), Philadelphia, 1925 and reprints, p. 63, n. 1. The Samaritans added *Ex.* iii.6 to the nine commands in *Gen.* ch. i. For the Samaritan material, see Montgomery, p. 274 and Pl. 2; Bowman, *Documents*, pp. 1 ff.

6 Macdonald, *Theology*, p. 176.

7 The *Defter* is contained in Cowley, pp. 1-92. From the 10th century onwards, there were made additions to the *Corpus Liturgicum* of the Samaritans, but the backbone of the *Defter* is made up of the hymns of Amram Dara and Marqa. (There is also a hymn by the latter's son; see Cowley, p. 16.) H.G. Kippenberg, "Ein Gebetbuch für den samaritanischen Synagogengottesdienst aus dem 2. Jh. n. Chr.", *ZDPV*, 85, 1969, pp. 76 ff., has tried to establish a higher age for the so-called *Durran* hymns (Cowley, pp. 38-48), which traditionally are ascribed to Amram Dara. There is now a new edition of the *Defter* by Z. Ben-Hayyim, *The Literary and Oral Tradition of Hebrew and Aramaic amongst the Samaritans*, III/2 (The Recitation of Prayers and Hymns) (AHL, VI), Jerusalem, 1967, pp. 41 ff., but his text does not contain variations which make it necessary to depose Cowley's well-established edition as reference source. However, Ben-Hayyim has a valuable English-phonetic transcription, and his copious notes (in modern Hebrew) are indispensable for a philological study of the texts.

Without a mouth, You [*i.e.,* God] called out words (מליך); and a world came into being. Swiftly, Your creation submitted to Your words (למליך).

(*Ibid.* 29.7)

But, just like the author of the late hymn who distinguishes between the (ten) words and *the* word, Amram Dara knows of a single word responsible for the creation:

While Your wisdom determines that You will create, Your power brings everything together by Your word (במלתך).

(*Ibid.* 28.7)

You have created all the hosts [*viz.*, the hosts of heaven] with a word (בדבר).

(*Ibid.* 492.2)[8]

Which word was *the* creative word? It would seem plausible to think of the divine command יהי, "Let there be," spoken by God in three of his Ten (actually, only nine) Words of Creation (*viz., Gen.* i.3, 6, 14), including the creation of the light (see *vv.* 3, 14), the first and essential element of the whole creation. That the Samaritans made this conclusion is evident. In a late hymn, the divine command *yehî* is connected with the concept of creation in the following way:

This is the new creation: ויהי, and He had no helper![9]

(Cowley, 801.22)

In a like vein, we read in another late hymn, a composition from the 14th century:

It was created by a word, [namely, by] יהי; and, in a flash, it was made new.

(*Ibid.* 445.2)

This extract is taken from the morning service for the festival of the seventh month and appears to pertain to the Sabbath, the seventh day. In another — but still later — passage from the same service, it is said:

S. Brown, trans., *A Critical Edition and Translation of the Ancient Samaritan Defter (i.e. Liturgy)*, Diss., Leeds, 1955, on the basis of data supplied by a modern ms. (the Jaffa ms., obtained by Professor John Bowman), has arranged the hymns as an order of service for the Samaritan Sabbath and weekday services, which had not been established previously. His translation, which comprises the whole *Defter*, is based upon Cowley's text, and alternate readings of other mss. are given in the notes. An appendix of nine pages contains texts not used by Cowley. For reference to other translations of the oldest *Defter* hymns, see Kahle, Kippenberg, Macdonald, and Szuster, as cited in the bibliography of primary sources.

8 The hymn in Cowley, pp. 491-93, is attributed to Amram Dara.

9 This quotation and the subsequent three are given in translation and transcription by J. Macdonald, "The Tetragrammaton in Samaritan Liturgical Compositions", *TGUOS* 17, 1959, pp. 43 f.

The most special of all days is the Sabbath which YHWH appointed by Ten Words; by His Name (בשמו) they were brought together.

(*Ibid.* 458.13)

I have followed the punctuation of J. Macdonald, though it is not certain that this is right. But it is certain that the Name has a demiurgic rôle. As a matter of fact, "that some Samaritan poets connected the Tetragrammaton with the divine command at creation is clear from several passages."[10] The Name of God is the real constituent part of God's creative command. In a 14th century hymn used in the service for the Day of Atonement, we read:

So, [the letters] *Yod* [and] *He* (י.ה·) are a sign, [namely of] "Let there be (יהי) light! And there was (ריהי) light" (*Gen.* i.3).

(*Ibid.* 505.15 f.)

The letters *Yod* and *He*, of course, are the two first letters of the Tetragrammaton and were often used — either together or apart — to signify the complete proper Name of God[11]. The meaning here may be that each letter is regarded as an equivalent of the Divine Name and, at the same time, as a sign of the creative command *yehî*, quoted twice as being indicated by י·ה·, for the separation of the letters would seem to have an import. Macdonald, however, asserts that this passage witnesses the peculiar Samaritan practice where "the Tetragrammaton is divided into two and each half is regarded as a divine name in itself."[12]

Whatever is the right explanation, it is certain that the Samaritans associated יהי, the divine command spoken at the creation, with יהוה, the proper Name of God. As a matter of fact, this was done also by the Jews. The evidence is found in a couple of Targumic passages to *Ex.* iii.14. The Bible tells that Moses asked God what he should be saying to the Israelites when they asked him by whom he was sent. *Ex.* iii.14 f. in the Bible reads:

And God said to Moses: "I am who I am (אהיה אשר אהיה)." And He said: "Thus you shall say to the people of Israel: "I am (אהיה) has sent me to you."" God also said to Moses: "Say this to the people of Israel: "YHWH (יהוה), the God of your fathers, the God of Abraham, the God of Isaac, and the God of Jacob has sent me to you." This is My Name for ever, and thus I am to be remembered throughout all generations."

In this text, "I am who I am" is given as an etymology of YHWH, which is treated as a verbal form derived from "to be" and formulated in the first person because God is the speaker. In the Targums, the explanation of the

---

10 *Ibid.*, p. 43; cp. p. 38, at the top.
11 See below, pp. 82 f., 253 ff.
12 Macdonald, "Tetragrammaton", p. 43. See *ibid.*, for a possible instance, in "the Leeds MS BK for the Day of Atonement Liturgy", of רה "as in some way a mysterious synonym (?) for YHWH and indeed for YH ..." (p. 44).

Tetragrammaton in *v.* 14 is interpreted through a citing of יהי, "Let there be!," God's creative command in *Gen.* ch. i. Thus, the Palestinian Targum contained in Codex Neofyti I of the Vatican Library retains the formula "I am who I am" and expounds the following utterance of God:

> He who spoke, and the world was there from the beginning, and is to say to it: יהי, and it will be there, – He it is who has sent me to you.

Here, the אהיה in the second of God's utterings is interpreted in the light of the repeated אהיה in the first uttering, אהיה אשר אהיה. The Targumists take the first occurrence of אהיה to refer to the creation of the world and the second to the future creation, and predicate them of God who said יהי and will say יהי. Thus, אהיה, "I am", the meaning of God's name, יהוה, is taken to intend the presence of God in the past and future acts of creation through the word יהי.

The Fragmentary Targum has the same basic interpretation, except that it expounds "I am who I am" and refers the exegesis to the final "I am":

> "He who said to the world from the beginning: יהי, and it was there, and is to say to it: יהי, and it will be there." And He said: "Thus you shall say to the Israelites: "He has sent me to you." "

Again, we note that the Targumists associate the divine command יהי with אהיה, "I am", the exposition of God's Name, יהוה. In view of the similarity between יהי and יהוה (as well as אהיה), it is not at all strange that the Samaritans and the Jews connected the Tetragrammaton with the divine command spoken at the creation, for both children and primitive people witness the idea that a similarity between two words is not meaningless: "they consistently assume that if two things are called by similar-sounding names this must imply the existence of some deep-lying point of agreement between them."[13]

These preliminaries have prepared the way for the citation of evidence that the Samaritans identified the creative word as the Tetragrammaton. Thus, we read in the Liturgy:

> O You whose Name is YHWH, let this Name be magnified, that creates what it will!
> (Cowley, 754.8 f.)

This text is culled from a late part of the Liturgy, but we ought to bear in mind the words of J. Macdonald that a study of the book on the Samaritans by M. Gaster "will convince most readers of the truth of the statement that the Samaritan liturgy certainly enshrines ancient material."[14] As a matter of

---

13 S. Freud, *Totem and Taboo*, trans. by J. Strachey, London, 1950, reprinted as Routledge paperback, 1960 and subsequently, p. 56.

14 "Tetragrammaton", p. 38. (Macdonald gives the name of the author of the Schweich

fact, there are scholars who maintain that "the liturgy is the best place in any religious system to discover vestiges of ancient belief and doctrinal traditions of the remote past."[15]

But we do not have to rest content with evidence from the younger part of the Liturgy, for the notion that the Name of God is the cosmogonic and —logical principle is found in the very oldest part of the Samaritan literature. Marqa, a prominent theologian and hymn composer who worked within Baba Rabba's scheme of revival, witnesses this idea at several places in his great midrashic work known as *Memar Marqa*. In the first book of Marqa's *Memar*, God promises Moses that he will deliver the people out of Egypt, and then goes on:

> I will reveal to you My Great Name YHWH. I did not reveal it to the righteous of the world. El-Shaddai was the name by which I revealed Myself to Abraham, Isaac, and Jacob; but this Great Name I did not reveal to them. It is a Glorious Name that fills the whole of creation (שם יקיר מלי כל בריתה). By it, the world is bound together (מצטעד); and all the covenants with the righteous are bound by it for ever. I shall not forget it as long as the world exists. Since you are found to be in the hands of the Most High of the whole world, I have revealed to you My Great Name.[16]
>
> (I.4)

God's Name, YHWH, that was revealed to Moses in the burning bush (see *Ex.* iii.13 ff.), is an immense force, filling the universe and holding it together. This idea is also known from Jewish and Christian literature. In the *Shepherd of Hermas*, written at the beginning of the 2nd century, we read: "The Name of the Son of God is great and infinite (ἀχώρητον), and sustains (βαστάζει) the whole world" (*Sim.* IX.xiv.5). "It is hard to resist the impression that what lies behind the present text is a train of thought in which not the 'Name of the Son of God', but the 'Name of God' sustained the Creation, and was equated with the 'Son of God', ... and that later this hypostatic use of the phrase 'the Name of God' was not understood, and the words 'Name of the Son of God' were substituted... ."[17] In Chapter VI, we shall see that a long passage in *I En.* ch. lxix describes the Divine Name as the means by which the universe is both created and stabilized[18]. The idea was obviously pre-Christian.

Lectures for 1923 as T. Gaster, but the author is, of course, Moses Gaster, the father of Theodor H. Gaster.)

15 *Ibid.*, p. 46.

16 If there is no statement to the contrary, my quotations from *Memar Marqa* do not deviate significantly from the translation of Macdonald.

17 J. Daniélou, *The Theology of Jewish Christianity* (The Development of Christian Doctrine before the Council of Nicaea, I), trans. by J.A. Baker, London, 1964, p. 152. For Christ as the possessor and even personification of the Name of God, see below, pp. 106 ff.

18 See pp. 257 f. Philo ascribes the function of sustaining the world to the Logos (see *De somn.* I.241; *De migr. Abr.* 6; *De spec. leg.* I.81; *De plant.* 8). In the *Epistle to the*

As in the Jewish pseudepigraphon, the Divine Name is described as the cosmogonic agent as well as a cosmological brace in *Memar Marqa*. In a midrash upon *Deut.* xxxii.3b, "and ascribe (והבו) greatness to God," Marqa professes:

> The great prophet Moses made it the gateway to all praises. In it is contained בראשית as well as what is like it. *Waw* represents the six days and everything created in them. *He* is the Name by which all creatures arose (דקם). *Beth* is the two worlds, the first and the second. *Waw* is the end.
>
> (*Memar Marqa* IV.2)

This is an ascription of a special meaning to each of the letters of the word והבו. The first *Waw* is said to represent the six days of the creation and the different creative works, since *Waw* is the sixth letter of the alphabet. The second *Waw*, the last letter of the word, is "the end", since it is "regarded as the tailpiece."[19] *Beth*, being the second letter of the alphabet, is thought of as representing the two worlds, this world and the future one, created by God. We are left with the letter *He*. This letter is said to represent the creative "Name"; and, since – as has been pointed out – this letter was a frequent abbreviation of the Tetragrammaton, there cannot be any doubt that the "Name" in question is the proper Name of God.

In ch. 7 of the same book of *Memar Marqa*, we find the following midrash upon another passage in *Deut.* ch. xxxii:

> He [*viz.*, Moses] instructed Israel in a great secret: *He* for the creation (ה' לבראשית); *Aleph* for the Day of Vengeance. *He* began and *Aleph* ended. So he said: "For the Lord will judge" (*Deut.* xxxii.36).

This midrash upon *Deut.* xxxii.36 seems incomprehensible at first, for the Scriptural passage contains neither *He* nor *Aleph*. But a clue is found in the preceding midrash which deals with *Deut.* xxxii.6, "Is He [*i.e.*, God] not your father and owner?" Marqa states: "He [*i.e.*, Moses] started with the word הלוא – a great word all of it. At all times and occasions, he began with it and ended with it." Then the passage on *v.* 36 follows. הלוא, the adverb of negation prefixed by the interrogative pronoun, apparently is taken by Marqa as an indication that everything proceeds from God (the "father") and returns to him (the "owner"). Since *He* is used as an abbreviation of the Tetragrammaton, we cannot doubt that we here have a reference to the Name of God: the Tetragrammaton "for the creation"; the Tetragrammaton "began". The Divine Name is here represented as a cosmogonic principle, as it also is described in the *First Epistle of Clement to the Corinthians:* "[...] Your

---

Hebrews, the Son is "bearing" ($\varphi\acute{\epsilon}\rho\omega\nu$) the world "by the word ($\tau\tilde{\omega}$ $\dot{\rho}\acute{\eta}\mu\alpha\tau\iota$) of his power" (i.3). Rabbinic texts speak about God "carrying" the world by his word; see Str.-Bill., III, p. 673.

19 Macdonald, *Memar Marqah*, II, p. 140, n. 33.

Name, which is the primal source (ἀρχέγονον) of all creation" (lix.2)[20]. The idea of the cosmogonic and -logical function of the Name of God in Christianity obviously had Samaritan as well as Jewish antecedents.

Later on in *Memar Marqa* IV.7, we find a midrash on the last phrase of *Deut.* xxxii.6, "He made you and established you (הוא עשך ויכוננך)." Marqa expounds this in the following way:

> He [*viz.,* Moses] put *Waw* first and then *Yod*; this time, he taught the world that it was a divine word (מלת אלהו). He who understands it knows that all was made by it and renewed by it, and that all returns to its origin by it.[21]

Possibly ו and י, both component letters of the Tetragrammaton, are used as an abbreviation of the proper Name, for there can be no doubt that it is the Name of God which is denoted by the word through which everything is created, renewed, and returning to its origin. All combinations of the letters of the Tetragrammaton evidently could be regarded as representing the proper Name. However, it is also possible that *Waw* has retained its meaning of a mere copula, and that the Tetragrammaton is suggested by *Yod* alone.

Memar Marqa contains also some passages where the divine name "Elohim" appears as the creative agent. In IV.2, we find the following passage: "Look at Bereshith and number the letters: [there are] six, like the six days, for each one resembles the other; and the Name which brought all created things into being sealed the whole. Therefore he said: "God finished" (*Gen.* ii.2)." בראשית, "In the beginning", symbolizes the six days of creation, since it contains six letters. "The Name which brought all created things into being" must be the "Elohim" which follows בראשית ברא in *Gen.* i.1, for Marqa says that the Name "sealed the whole" and quotes *Gen.* ii.2, "Elohim finished," the end of the creation narrative. The Samaritan Pentateuch actually reads: "On the *sixth* day, Elohim finished." Marqa obviously takes *Gen.* i.1 as a summary of the following account of the six days of creation.

In IV.7, the following sentences occur in a praise of God by Moses: "[...] vested me with Your Name by which You created the world (שמך דבראת בה עלמה), and revealed to me Your Great Name [...]." It would seem that this text distinguishes between the demiurgic Name with which Moses was "vested" and the "Great Name", which is a common designation of the Tetragrammaton. The former may be that of Elohim. In VI.11, the letter *He* speaks: "My number was made the number of the Name by which the world was created."

---

20 J. Ponthot judges that the idea of the cosmogonic function of the Divine Name in the Apostolic Fathers is indebted to the Jewish theme of the "cosmogonic rôle of the Name" (*Le "Nom" dans la théologie des Péres Apostoliques*, Diss., Louvain, 1950, p. 89).

21 Macdonald's translation, "He put BA first and YUD" (*Memar Marqah*, II, p. 160), must contain a slip of the pen.

This would also appear to be a reference to אלהים, which is made up of five letters, the same number as the numerical value of the letter ה.

Memar Marqa VI.11 contains also another passage where the name of Elohim is the cosmogonic agent. In this passage, the letter *Aleph* speaks: "I was made the first [of the letters] of the Great Name by which our Lord brought the world into being." This is apparently a reference to the divine name אלהים in *Gen.* i.1. But the "Great Name" — as has been pointed out above — is a frequent term for the Tetragrammaton, and here it "is undoubtedly employed in a freer sense."[22] We have seen that, in a passage from *Memar Marqa* I.4, Moses was revealed the "Great Name" by which the universe was filled and sustained, and that several other passages in Marqa's midrashic work represent the Tetragrammaton as the cosmogonic agent. Apparently, designations of the proper Name of God as well as offices delegated to it could be transferred to *all* the appellations of God. The Tetragrammaton, the "Great Name", is the original creative agent. In order to understand the implications of this idea, the significance of the concept of the name and of the Name of God in particular must be comprehended.

The Concept of the Divine Name

The very young child does not remember when or under which circumstances he first heard the name of things and persons whose names he knows; he believes that he came to know them by looking at them, and that the name came into being with the object. The name therefore expresses the object; it actually is a quality of the object, situated within it as it were. "Where is the name of the sun?" "Inside the sun," a child of seven said[23]. In regard to personal beings, "the name is an indispensable part of the personality."[24] W. Brede Kristensen compares the name to the image: Whereas the image is the material representation of the spirit or essence of a human or a god, the name is the "immaterial image"[25]. The name expresses the living essence, the vital energy, the power of the human person or the deity. Origen (*Contra Cels.* V.45 f.) therefore strongly opposes Celsus who asserted that it does not matter whether we call God by the name of Zeus or by the name of any other high god; according to Origen, names are not *thesei* but *physei*, bringing about the immaterial presence and power of their carrier when pronounced correctly.

Since the name is taken to express and represent the person, the Old

---

22 Lowy, p. 277.

23 Piaget, p. 72; quoted by Campell, p. 86.

24 H. Bietenhard, Art. ὄνομα, in *TDNT*, V, 1968 and reprints, p. 243.

25 *The Meaning of Religion*, trans. by J.B. Carman, The Hague, 1960 and reprints, p. 412.

Testament contains many passages where (יהוה) שם stands in parallelism to the Tetragrammaton or even has been substituted for it. The first usage is found especially throughout the *Book of Psalms*. Thus, the Psalmist says: "YHWH hear you in the day of trouble, and the Name of the God of Jacob defend you!" (xx.1). As for the second usage, we often find references to the desecration of God's "Name" (see, *e.g., Lev.* xviii.6; *et al.; Am.* ii.7).

The use of שם יהוה as an alternative for YHWH offered a solution to the problem of how the transcendent God could be with his people on earth. In the sphere of human communication, to speak or act "in (or, "with") the name of" someone implied the claim of being regarded as an extension of the person whose name was referred to. Thus, Nabal's insulting response to David's servants, who approached him "in the name of David" (*I Sam.* xxv.9), was in actual fact an insult to David himself. Similarly, by means of his "Name", God could benefact his people. In some passages, the Name has an instrumental suggestion. *Ps.* liv.3 reads: "O God, help me by Your Name and save me by Your power! " Here, the Name seems to be a power which God has available for action. In like manner, the Name appears as the means wherewith God assures David's prosperity (see *Ps.* lxxxix.5) and the instrument by which Israel conquers its enemies (see *Ps.* xliv.6; cxviii.10 f.).

In other passages, the Divine Name even appears as the acting subject without standing in parallelism to the Tetragrammaton; thus the Name of God acquires a certain independence of God himself. The Psalmist wants to praise the Name of YHWH, "because it is good; it saves me out of all distress, and I look upon my enemies with delight" (liv.6 f.). Similarly, in *Joel* ii.26, "YHWH's, your God's, Name" is the saving power. The Name of God is to be praised, because "His Name alone is exalted" (*Ps.* cxlviii.13). In *Prov.* xviii.10, it is said: "A strong tower is the Name of YHWH; the righteous flees into it and is safe." In *Mal.* i.11, God says that his Name will become great and receive offerings from the gentiles. In these passages, the concept of the Name appears to be used as a hypostasis[26], being defined as "an often only partly independent, divine entity, which represents a more or less complete personification of a characteristic, a function, or some attribute of a higher god."[27]

Especially illustrative is *Is.* xxx.27: "Behold! The Name of God is coming from far: burning is his anger, his lips are full of indignation, and his tongue is like a devouring flame!" What is normally said of YHWH is here said of his Name, which seems to be conceived of as an entity of its own at work in the world. The Name must here be understood as a divine hypostasis.

---

26 Cp. O. Grether, *Name und Wort Gottes im Alten Testament* (BZAW, 64), Giessen, 1934, pp. 44 ff.

27 H. Ringgren, Art. "Hypostasen", in *RGG*, III, 3rd ed., 1959, col. 504.

At a later time, the Word of God was portrayed in a similar manner: "Your all-powerful Word from heaven, from the royal thrones, leaped into the midst of the doomed land [*i.e.*, Egypt], bearing as a sharp sword Your irrevocable command, and, standing there, it filled all things with death. Its head touched the sky, though it stood firmly on the earth" (*Wisd.* xviii.15 f.). This depiction is modelled upon the description of the angel (the "Destroyer") who killed the firstborn of the Egyptians, and upon that of the Angel of the Lord in *I Chron.* xxi.16, who is "standing between earth and heaven, a drawn sword in his hand." The welding of the Word of God with the Angel of the Lord bears out the statement that the hypostasis formation "cannot conceive of the abstract concepts without a concrete basis or carrier and thus not without individualization and personification."[28] The following text, which is fundamental for the present work, shows the individualization and personification of the Name of God in the figure of the Angel of the Lord:

> Behold! I send My angel before you in order to keep you on the way and to bring you to the place which I have prepared. Give heed to him and hearken to his voice, and do not rebel against him, since he will not pardon your transgression, for My Name is in him (כי שמי בקרבו).
>
> (*Ex.* xxiii.20 f.)

When God promises to send his angel carrying his own Name in order to guide Israel to the land he has appointed for them, this means that he has put his power into the angel and thus will be with his people through the agency of the angel. The Angel of the Lord is an extension of YHWH's personality, because the proper Name of God signifies the divine nature. Thus, the Angel of the Lord has full divine authority by virtue of possessing God's Name: he has the power to withhold the absolution of sins.

The Angel of the Lord is only a temporary manifestation of God; when the exodus is over, he disappears until such times as God has use for him again. But there developed also a notion of the permanent existence of the hypostasis of the Divine Name. In *Ps.* viii, which deals with God's manifestations in nature, it is said that God's Name is glorious "over" (ב) the whole earth (see *vv.* 2, 10); hereby, it is implied that God in his essence does not work in nature. The same gist is to be discerned in the passage from *Memar Marqa* I.4 which has been quoted above; here, God says that his Name fills the creation and binds the world together. God himself, of course, cannot be said to fill the creation. In this train of thought, the Name has not only temporary existence, but is a lasting cosmological force.

Deuteronomy even localizes the Name. It teaches that, whereas God himself dwells in heaven (see iv.36; xxvi.36), he has chosen a place on earth as the abode for his Name (see xii.5, 11; xiv.23 f.; xvi.11; *et al.*); this dwelling-

---

28 *Ibid.*

place of the Divine Name is the sanctuary, which was sited on Mt. Sion by the Jews (see *II Sam.* vii.13; *I Kings* iii.2; v.7; viii.12ff.;ix.3, 7; *II Kings* xxi.7; *II Chron.* xx.8; *Ps.* lxxiv.7), but on Mt. Gerizim by the Samaritans. Thus, YHWH certainly inhabits the earthly temple, but not in person; he is present through the agency of his Name[29].

To be true, in the Bible, the Divine Name which is localized permanently in the temple has no personal carrier, but both Jews and Samaritans came to conceive of this hypostasis as an angel, even the Angel of the Lord. The association or even identification of the Name of God with a personal being is the main point in the subsequent sections.

The Investiture with the Name I: *The Samaritan Evidence*

First, the thread that Moses was "vested" with the Name which was the demiurgic agent will be taken up. This idea is not only found in the passage from *Memar Marqa* IV.7 which has been quoted above; it is recurring throughout the literature of the Samaritans. Marqa says that, among the announcements which God made to Moses in the Burning Bush, there was also the promise that he would be vested with the Divine Name:

> He said: "Moses, Moses," revealing that he would be vested with prophethood and the Divine Name (לבוש נביותה ושם אלהותה).

> *(Memar Marqa* I.1)

In a later revelation, made just before the exodus, God reminds his prophet that he has been vested with the Name:

> I have vested you with My Name (אלבשתך שמי) [...].

> *(Ibid.* I.9)

One of the chapters in *Memar Marqa* II which is devoted to the extolment of Moses opens in the following manner:

> Exalted is the great prophet Moses whom his Lord vested with His Name (דלבשה מרה שמה)!

> (ch. 12)

In the last book of Marqa's great midrashic work, we come across the following praise of Moses:

> O faithful one, who expounded the Law; O you to whom God gave the gift of prophethood and whom He vested with His Name (ואלבשה שמה)!

> *(Ibid.* VI.6)

---

29 Recently, T.N. Mettinger, *The Dethronement of Sabaoth* (CB, Old Testament Series, 18), Lund, 1982, has sought the origin of the Name and Glory theologies in a situation where the old idea of the presence of YHWH Sabaoth on Sion was confronted with the brutal facts of national disaster. Unfortunately, this book was not available to me before mine went to press. For the Glory, see below, pp. 177ff.

In the *Defter,* we find the following prasies of Moses being vested with the Name of God:

> Glory to the prophet who vested himself with Your Divine Name
> (דלבש בשם אלהותך)!

(Cowley, 33.7)

> Mighty is the great prophet Moses, who clad himself in the Name of the Godhead
> (דלבש שם אלהותה)!

(*Ibid.* 54.32)

In addition to the passages saying that Moses was vested with the Name of God, there is the statement that he had been "given" the Name. In a revelation to Aaron, God speaks the following concerning Moses:

> I have given him My Name (יהבת לה שמי), so that he need not fear.
> (*Memar Marqa* I.3)

J. Macdonald wants to explain the idea that Moses possessed the Name of God in light of the fact that many Samaritan writers stress the relation of Moses' name to the Name of God, the Tetragrammaton: Moses' name in Hebrew, משה, contains the same radicals as those of the substitute used for the proper Name of God, *viz.,* שמה, "the Name"[30]. The comtemplation upon the resemblance between the name of Moses and שמה is found in the earliest Samaritan sources (when the Pentateuch is excluded). Marqa says that God, on the seventh day, when he was resting from the work of creation, "established" Moses' name and made it "one" with his own Name, and that Moses was "crowned" with it; God speaks to Moses:

> I established your name then also — My Name and yours therein as one
> (ואשכנת שמך חורי תמן שמי ושמך לגוה כחדה); I established it, and you are crowned with it.

(*Memar Marqa* I.9)

In an eulogy of Moses in a later book of Marqa's *Memar,* Moses' name is said to have been "made" the Name of God:

> Where is there a prophet like Moses, and who can compare with Moses, whose name was made the Name of his Lord (דאתעבד שם מרה שמה)?

(*Ibid.* IV.1)

In a hymn by Amram Dara, we read that God combined his own Name with the name of Moses:

> He conjoined the Name [*viz.,* of Himself] to the name [*viz.,* of Moses] mightily
> (שמה לשמה אקפה ברבו).

(Cowley, 32.18)

---

30 See *Theology*, pp. 184 f.; cp. *Memar Marqah*, II, p. 31, n. 94, p. 137, n. 24; "The Theological Hymns of Amram Darah", in J. Macdonald, ed., *ALUOS*, II, 1961, p. 29. The two passages from *Memar Marqa* and the one from Amram Dara's hymns which are annotated by Macdonald on this score are quoted forthwith.

W.A. Meeks, however, objects to Macdonald's explanation. Having noted that Moses often is said to have been "vested" or "crowned" with light, Meeks states: "... several passages are found in which Moses' coronation or investiture is said to be "with God's name" rather than "with a crown" or "with light." Twice the phrase "vested with [God's] name" occurs in the same passage with and parallel to the phrase "crowned with the light." The "name" which is meant *in all these passages* is אלהים... ."[31] In substantiation of this statement, Meeks quotes one passage from *Memar Marqa* II.12 and one from V.1. The first passage runs: "The first name, with which *Genesis* opens, was that with which he was vested and made strong. "See, I make you a god (Elohim) to Pharaoh" (*Ex.* vii.1)." As the Scriptural references evince, the name in question undeniably is the name of Elohim. The second passage speaks about "the name with which he was vested at the top of Mt. Horeb," and the following acrostic on אלהים makes it perfectly clear that it is this name which is intended. Meeks could have strengthened his argument further by citing the passage from IV.7 which has been quoted above[32].

Yet, Meek's conclusion is precipitate. A midrash by Marqa on the words השירה הזאת, "this song", in *Deut.* xxxi.30 has been overlooked by Meeks. The Samaritan theologian finds deep mysteries in these two words:

> Observe the importance of the two. He [*viz.*, Moses] was increased in knowledge, in which there was no specification except the carrying out of it; for his Lord commanded him to expound truthfully. Moses expounded the five books. Thus, he said: השירה הזאת. *He* represents the five books; *Shin* and *Resh* the Great Name; *Yod* the Ten Words; and *He* is the seal. And הזאת: *He* is the Name with which he was vested (ה' שמה דלבשה); *Zayin* the Sabbath and the holy; *Aleph* the divinity; and *Taw* the preparing of the truth.
>
> (*Memar Marqa* IV.1)

The first word, השירה, is expounded as follows: the first letter, *He*, represents the five books of Moses, since *He* is the fifth letter of the alphabet; *Shin* and *Resh* represent the term שמה רבה, because one and the other come first in the two words respectively; *Yod* represents the Ten Words (*viz.*, of the Creation and/or of the Commandments), because it is the tenth letter of the alphabet; and the last letter, *He*, is called "the seal", probably because it forms the end of the word. As for the next word, הזאת, we start with the last letter. *Taw* is תעתיד קשטה, "the preparing of the truth", a phrase which begins with this letter. *Aleph* indicates אלהותה, "divinity", since this word begins with *Aleph*. *Zayin* represents the Sabbath, since it is the seventh letter of the alphabet and thus has the same number in the alphabet as the day of the Sabbath in the week.

---

31 *The Prophet-King* (Suppl. *NT*, XIV), Leiden, 1967, p. 235. (Italics mine.)
32 The name with which Moses is said to have been vested in the beginning of *Memar Marqa* IV.2 is probably also that of Elohim.

We are left with the first letter of the second word. This is a *He* and said to be the Name with which Moses was vested. We cannot doubt that it is a divine name which is indicated, for the continuation of the midrash reads: "Exalted is the great prophet Moses, whose every word is life and blessing, and who revealed in this expression the Name of his Lord, the holiness, and the five books which he received." The Name of the Lord is said to be found in the expression השירה הזאת; it is obviously to be found in the letter *He*, signifying the "Name" with which Moses was vested. As has been pointed out above, *He* often was employed as an abbreviation of the Tetragrammaton, and it is obviously with this Name that Moses was vested. We have seen that the name of Elohim could be assigned with functions being the property of the proper Name of God as well as designated with appellations originally referring to the latter[33], and when Moses is said to have been vested with the name of Elohim, this is obviously a secondary notion, derived from the original idea of his investiture with the Tetragrammaton.

Meeks states: "... the tradition is univocal that it was "on the top of Mt. Horeb" that Moses was thus named."[34] If this is right, it must be the proper Name of God with which Moses is said to have been vested in *Memar Marqa* I.9, since this passage deals with the events preceding the exodus. Furthermore, the quotation from *Memar Marqa* I.3, saying that Moses had been "given" the Name, must also refer to the Tetragrammaton, for the continuation reads: "I have provided a rod for him out of the fire. I have shown him My signs, so that his heart may not be weakened. Despite that, he said: "I am inexpert in speaking" [cp. *Ex.* iv.10]." This obviously refers to the episode of the Burning Bush (see *Ex.* iii.1- iv.17), where Moses was revealed the proper Name of God, explained as אהיה אשר אהיה. An outright statement to the effect that Moses was "vested" and "crowned" with this Name is found in a text which was cited already by A. Merx:

> On the day when Adam vested himself with the image (יום דלבש אדם הצלם),
> Moses vested himself (לבש משה) with the splendour of the first light and the crown
> (כלילה) on the four sides of which is written אהיה אשר אהיה.[35]

(Cowley, 822.19 ff.)

This does not mean that Moses was a contemporary of Adam, but is an example of the typological connection of the events of the exodus and the Sinai theophany with Bereshith[36]. In *Memar Marqa*, there is to be found a

---

33 See above, pp. 83 f.

34 "Moses as God and King", in *RA*, p. 360. This statement is preceded by the assertion that the "name with which Moses was "crowned" or "clothed" is always Elohim, as distinguished from YHWH, "the name which God revealed to him.""

35 Codex Gothanus No. 963, cited by Merx, *Evangelien*, p. 182.

36 On this subject, see J. Bowman, "The Exegesis of the Pentateuch among the Samari-

point-by-point correspondence between the creation of Adam and the giving
of the Law to Moses where it is said: "The two of them were vested with two
crowns of great light (הלבשו תריון תרי כילין מן אורה רבה)" (VI.3)[37].
The text which describes Moses' crown as being inscribed with אשר אהיה
אהיה clearly is related to the passage from *Memar Marqa* I.9 which says that,
on the first Sabbath, God "established" Moses' "name" and made it "one"

---

tans and among the Rabbis", in P.A.H. de Boer, ed., *OS*, VIII, 1950, pp. 24 f. However, it is true that the younger Samaritan literature identifies Moses with the primordial light and regards him as God's spokesman at the creation, the speaker of
the divine *fiat*; see Macdonald, *Theology*, pp. 135 f., 158 f., 162 ff., 173 ff., 423 f.,
et passim. Macdonald wants to find the idea of Moses' pre-existence also in the
oldest literature, but this would not seem possible. The following test, "Your
[*i.e.*, Moses'] speech is the speech of God, and He is the actual doer of all that you
have made" (*Memar Marqa* VI.4), does not refer to the creation, as is thought by
Macdonald, *Memar Marqah*, II, p. 226, n. 50. Just above, it is said: "From your
understanding, the whole world's understanding comes." This "understanding"
communicated to the world by Moses alludes to the understanding which derives
from the Law, and what was "made" by Moses apparently is the Torah, the "actual"
author of which is God. The comment on this text by Macdonald in *Theology*,
p. 182, actually is congruent with this interpretation.

  The only other text from the oldest literature which Macdonald finds to hint
at a demiurgic rôle of Moses is the following one: "O great prophet Moses, the
light of whose heart shines more brightly than the sun! The sun greatly supplies the
needs of living beings, but you are the one who brought into being that by which
living beings live" (*Memar Marqa* VI.8). I seriously doubt the interpretation that
"the reference in the latter half of the quotation is to the creative function of the
pre-existent Moses" (*Theology*, p. 168), for the context does not speak about the
creation but about the spiritual needs of man that are satisfied by the words of
the Law. The text goes on to say: "You are the one who supplied the world with
the light of life in order to make men great who believe in Him." The "light of life"
supplied by Moses obviously is the Law, and it must be the Law which is said to
have been "brought into being" by Moses in order that men might "live".

  In "Theological Hymns", p. 182, Macdonald actually expresses doubt as to whether the Samaritans had a developed Logos doctrine in Roman times. However, he
also argues that Amram Dara in one of his hymns sets out "the functions of the
pre-existent" Moses (p. 69). But the passage obviously speaks about the function
of the *historical* Moses; see below, p. 111 with n. 112. Moreover, if בריתה really
should be translated "creation", the passage would only speak about the pre-existent
function or office of Moses.

37 The idea that Adam was a king – a well-known notion from Jewish sources – is
found in the later parts of the Samaritan Liturgy, but is not significantly developed.
In *Memar Marqa* II.12 and IV.7, it is said that Moses was "crowned" with light, and,
at the latter place, the great prophet declares that he was crowned with "*Your*
[*i.e.*, God's] light". In VI.2, we read that "the Goodness", *i.e.*, God, "vested him
with His holy crown (אלבשה כליל קדשה)." (Macdonald renders "the crown of
holiness".) For the divine crown inscribed with the Name in Jewish mysticism, see
G.G. Scholem, *Jewish Gnosticism, Merkabah Mysticism, and Talmudic Tradition*
(JTSA), New York, 1960, pp. 54f. See also below, p. 300.

with his own, and that Moses was "crowned" with this special Name. The Name of God which was made "one" with the "name" of Moses (משה) can only be שמה, the circumlocution for the Tetragrammaton, which was explained as אהיה אשר אהיה[38].

The expression that Moses was "vested" or "crowned" with light or the Divine Name often is found in contexts revealing aspects of a disintegrated enthronement pattern where Moses' ascent to God on Mt. Sinai is depicted as an ascension to heaven and an installation as God's viceroy[39]. Considering the planetary and sidereal symbolism of the royal robe in old Near Eastern and later Hellenistic kingship[40], the frequent phrase that Moses was "vested with light" would seem to reflect the image of the investiture with the kingly garment. Since the "Name" appears to be used interchangeably with "light" in the expression "vested with ..." as well as in "crowned with ... ," it would seem that the idea that Moses was "vested with the Name" is a mutation of the notion that he was clad in the royal garb. Similarly, since the crown of the Name appears as an alternate for the crown of light, it obviously is a transformation of the astral or solar crown of Near Eastern kingship.

That the Samaritans used the term לבש also for the *coronation* of Moses exemplifies "the idea that clothing expresses the specific status by which a

---

38 That the crown was provided on the seventh day is perhaps to be connected with *Ex.* xxiv.15 f., which relates that, when Moses went up to God on Mt. Sinai, the cloud covered the mountain for six days, and God called Moses out of the cloud on the seventh day. Marqa says: "[...] when he went up to him and the cloud covered him for six days, his body was holy, and his holiness increased. He ascended from human status to the status of the angels (אל מיתרבית מלאכיה). [...] He was called on the seventh day from the midst of the cloud and saw the ranks of the angels in their array. He descended from the mountain with great might" (*Memar Marqa* V.3).

    However, if we press the parallel between Adam's investiture with the divine image and Moses' investiture with the light and the crown, it would seem that Moses was vested on the sixth day. On the other hand, there do exist Samaritan texts which put the creation of Adam on the Sabbath; see Bowman, *Documents*, p. 322 and p. 326, n. 6. This is not necessarily a late tradition, for already Philo could maintain that the creation of man took place on the seventh day (see *Quaest. in Gen.* II.56).

39 Widengren, *Ascension*, pp. 40 ff., has viewed the Samaritan picture of Moses' ascension and reception of the Law from the hand of God against the background of the mythical enthronement texts, which relate that the king ascended to heaven and received the tablets of destiny when being installed in his office. Meeks, *Prophet-King*, pp. 232 ff., has treated with attention that the Samaritan texts relate that Moses was crowned, received a royal robe, and sat on a throne on Mt. Sinai; but he seeks the immediate background in the "mystical ascent in traditions like the Enoch-literature and the *Merkabah* and *Hekalot* texts" (pp. 241 f.). See also "Moses", pp. 365 ff. In a preliminary and unpublished paper, "Reminisenser av det "konglige mönstret" i samaritanismen", I have scrutinized the oldest Samaritan literature for aspects of a disintegrated "royal pattern" used in the description of Moses.

40 See R. Eisler, *Weltenmantel und Himmelszelt*, I, Munich, 1910, pp. 39 ff.

man's existence is stamped at a given time. All the things which Yahweh has given man, which are about him and which shape his being, are as it were the raiment with which Yahweh clothes him (לבש), e.g., רוח, צדקה or צדק, הוד והדר etc."[41] Because Moses' crown was inscribed with the Name of God, the idea of his coronation as well as that of his investiture with the Name denotes his "clothing", his endowment, with divine nature. Since the celestial symbolism of the king's habiliments expressed that he was in some sense a divine being, the substitution of the "Name" for the garment and the crown merely gave a new turn to the old royal ideology.

The typological connection of Adam and Moses which has been noted above apparently reflects the idea that the king was the descendant and representative of the first man[42]. The Samaritans gave a peculiar twist to this idea. In *Memar Marqa* V.4, we read that Moses "was vested with the image which Adam cast off in the Garden of Eden (לבוש צלמה דאשלעה אדם בגן עדן.)." A ms. variant reads "beam of light and radiance" instead of "the image which Adam cast off in the Garden of Eden,"[43] but this makes really no difference, for – as we have seen – the light and the crown with which Moses "vested" himself can appear in parallelism to the image with which Adam "vested" himself. As a matter of fact, *Memar Marqa* bears witness to the well-known idea that Adam had a luminous body (before the fall)[44]. In II.1, we find the following declaration: "Glorious is the form in the likeness of Elohim (יקירה היא הצורה אשר על דמות האלהים)!" That this refers to the body of Adam, who was made in the "image and likeness" of God, becomes clear by the collation of the following text: "The form of Adam is glorified all over (קרתה צורתה דאדם תתיקר בכלה)" (IV.2)[45]. That Marqa

---

41 U. Wilckens, Art. στολή, in *TDNT*, VII, 1971, reprinted 1975, p. 689. Further, Wilckens makes the following observation which has bearing upon our subject: "Cf. the use of the prep. ב, e.g., in בשם־יהוה, where the idea of an enveloping and determining sphere undoubtedly stands in the background, so that ב has local as well as instrumental significance" (p. 689, n. 23, continued on the next page).

42 For the connection between the ruler and the primal man, see G. Widengren, "Early Hebrew Myths and their Interpretation", in S.H. Hooke, ed., *Myth, Ritual and Kingship*, Oxford, 1958, pp. 168 f., 175, *et passim*. Moses often is described as a new Adam in Samaritanism; see Macdonald, *Theology*, pp. 221, 437 f.; Meeks, *Prophet-King*, pp. 222 f. Meeks, pp. 255 f., wonders whether Moses' title "the Man (of God)" reflects the idea that he is the second Adam.

43 This is the Kahle ms., which actually in several aspects seems to be rather primitive; cp. above, p. 38, n. 30, and p. 63, n. 117.

44 In Jewish tradition, however, the glory lost by the fall does not seem to be unequivocally identified with the divine image after which Adam had been created; see G. Kittel, par. E, "The Divine Likeness in Judaism", in Art. εἰκών, in *TDNT*, II, 1964 and reprints, pp. 392 f.

45 That the "form" of Adam is the material body is seen clearly from *Memar Marqa* II.10. Here, we first read that "the form of Adam" (צורתה דאדם) was created

thinks that Moses was endowed with the identical glorious body as Adam is shown by his expression "the *glory* with which his [*i.e.*, Moses'] Lord vested him (איקרה דלבשה מרה)" (*ibid.*).

In a description of Moses as he descended from Mt. Sinai, Marqa says: "His image (צלמה) dwelt on him. How terrifying to anyone who beholds, and no one is able to stand before it!" (VI.3) This is obviously an allusion to *Ex.* xxxiv.29 ff., which relates that the skin of Moses' face shone when he descended from Mt. Sinai, and that he had to cover it because everyone was afraid to come near him. From Jewish sources, we know that the image of God was reflected especially in the radiance of Adam's *face*[46], and the Samaritans apparently interpreted the shining countenance which Moses received when he was on Mt. Sinai as the image of God which had been possessed by Adam. When Moses is said to have been "vested with light," this apparently refers to his endowment with the image of God.

Since the crown of light was the counterpart to the vestment of light, it would seem that the crown, too, could be viewed as a symbol of the divine image, and this is in fact a notion which can be corroborated by Jewish sources[47]. Thus, we can conclude that Moses' investiture and coronation, which usually were connected with his ascension of Mt. Sinai, were seen "not only as a heavenly enthronement, but also as a restoration of the glory lost by Adam."[48] The possession of this glory was conceived of as a sharing of God's own Name, *i.e.*, the divine nature[49].

"from the dust (עפר) of the goodly mount", and – a few lines below – it is said: "Therefore, the body of Adam (גויתה דאדם) was taken from a holy place."

In the quotation from II.1, "Elohim" – which is not a common word for God in Samaritanism – probably denotes the angels, for, in the Samaritan Targum *Gen.* ix.6, God asks: "Have I not created man after the image of the angels?" In the *Malef*, it is denied that Adam's image was "as the image of his children now", since "his image (צלמו) was as the image of the angels (כצלם המלאכים)" (5a). That the angels had a luminous bodily appearance is well known. According to the Samaritans, the penitent will receive the angelic image in the future paradise: "[...] after the likeness (כדמות) of the angels, they shall be clothed in light [...]" (*ibid.* 68b).

46 See J. Jervell, *Imago Dei* (FRLANT, 76), Göttingen, 1960, p. 45. This can be corroborated by Samaritan sources; see, *e.g.*, the quotation from the *Pitron* given below, n. 48.

47 See M. Smith, "Imago Dei", *BJRL*, 40, 1958, pp. 500 f.

48 Meeks, "Moses", p. 365. Moses' restoration of the glorious image of Adam was later developed into the idea that the primordial light was a kind of pre-existent Moses which was incarnated in Adam and then transmitted to Seth and so on from righteous to righteous in every generation until it reached perfection in the historical Moses; see Montgomery, p. 228; Macdonald, *Theology*, pp. 118 ff., 162 ff., 165 ff., 314 ff. Thus, the *Pitron*, a commentary on the *Asatir*, says: "And he (Adam) saw the image (lighting up) his [*i.e.*, Seth's] face [...] and this image is the luminous image of Moses – peace of God be upon him – and it was transmitted from man to man". (Gaster, pp. 191 f.; cp. *Malef* 13a).

49 This idea may be corroborated by Jewish sources. There was an exegesis of *Is.* xliii.7

The Investiture with the Name II: *Non-Samaritan Evidence*

G. Quispel has compared the Samaritan notion that Moses was vested with the Name of God to the teaching of the *Gospel of Philip* from Codex II of the Nag Hammadi Library that the Son "vested" himself with the Name of the Father[50]. In the Gnostic "gospel", this doctrine is set forth in a discussion on the nature of names which begins thus: "The names given to worldly things are very deceptive, for they turn our thoughts away from what is right to what is not right" (53.23 ff.). Every earthly thing has a *secret* name which reveals its true nature, and so it is with Jesus:

> One single Name is not pronounced in the world, [namely] the Name which the Father gave to the Son. It is exalted above all [cp. *Phil.* ii.9]; it is the Name of the Father. For the Son would not become Father unless he put on himself (ⲁϥ ⲣ ⲁⲓⲱⲱϥ) the Name of the Father. Those who have this Name know it, but they do not speak it, whereas those who do not have it do not know it [but nevertheless speak about it(?)].
>
> (54.5 ff.)

The secret Name which was given to Jesus and is identical with the Name of the Father obviously is the proper Name of God. In *Phil.* ii.9 ff., τὸ ὄνομα τὸ ὑπὲρ πᾶν ὄνομα, which is given to the exalted Jesus, is explained as κύριος, which is the Greek substitute for the Tetragrammaton[51]. In the Gnostic "gospel", the Son is said to have "vested" himself with this Name, and the similarity of this idea to that set forth in the Samaritan texts quoted above is conspicuous.

Quispel thinks that Jesus' investiture with the Name of God took place at the time of his baptism into the Jordan, "for the Valentinians thought that at that moment the Name of God descended upon Jesus ... ."[52] He points to a fragment in a collection made by Clement of Alexandria where Paul's words in *I Cor.* xv.29, "What are they doing who are baptized for the dead?," are interpreted to signify the baptism of the angels for the believers on earth in

---

which read: "Everyone who is called by My Name, him I have created, formed, and made that he should also share My glory" (*Baba Bathra* 75b). The Talmudic tradition infers that the righteous at the end of days are worshipped by angels in the same way as Adam before the fall, and Smith, pp. 478 ff., argues that the naming with God's Name here implies the restoration of the divine glory, which Adam had lost at the fall. In the future world, the Messiah and the righteous will be named with God's Name and partake in the divine *kabod*; see Str.-Bill., III, pp. 795 f.; G. Kittel, par. E, " כבוד and יקרא in Palestinian Judaism", in Art. δόξα, in *TDNT*, II, pp. 246 f.

50 See "Gnosticism and the New Testament", in J.P. Hyatt, ed., *The Bible in Modern Scholarship*, Nashville & New York, 1965, pp. 266 ff.; "John, Qumran and Jewish Christianity", in J. Charlesworth, ed., *John and Qumran*, London, 1972, p. 152.

51 For the hymn in *Phil.* ii.6 ff., see below, pp. 293 ff.

52 "Gnosticism and the New Testament", p. 267; cp. "John", p. 154.

order that the latter may be restored to the former. On earth, the believer is
"baptized in the same Name as that in which his angel was baptized before
him" (*Exc. ex Theod.* xxii.5). The fragment continues:

> In the beginning, the angels were baptized in the redemption of the Name which
> came down upon Jesus in the dove and redeemed him. For redemption was necessary
> even for Jesus [...].
>
> (xxii.6)

This is apparently an allusion to the Synoptic account of Jesus' baptism,
for it is told that, when Jesus came out of the Jordan, the Spirit descended
upon him "as a dove" (*Mark* i.10). The substitution of the Name for the
Spirit is reminiscent of the two epicleses addressed to the Divine Name in the
Acts of Thomas (ch. 27; 49 f.), where it is clear that the Name is equated
with the Spirit, even called the "holy dove" in the latter place (cp. also chs.
132 f.).[53] The Gnostics, however, went on to identify the Spirit-Name with
the pre-existent Son: Jesus' "invisible part was the Name, which is the only-
begotten Son" (*Exc. ex Theod.* xxvi.1). The Old Testament declares that the
Spirit of God "vests" (לבש) man (see *Judg.* vi.34; *I Chron.* xii.18; *II Chron.*
xxiv.20), and Paul says that the believers have "put on" (ἐνεδύσασθε) Christ
in baptism (see *Gal.* iii.27; cp. *Rom.* xiii.14)[54]; but it would be foolhardy to
argue that these ideas were the single sources of the Valentinian notion that
Jesus vested himself with the Divine Name — which appears to be an archaic
and thoroughly Semitic identification of Christ — and that the Samaritan idea
that Moses vested himself with the Name of God was dependent upon this
Gnostic development.

The Gnostic who was "baptized in the same Name as that in which his
angel was baptized before him" had beforehand "received the redemption
(ἀπολύτρωσις)" (*Exc. ex Theod.* xxii.5). This was a special Gnostic sacrament which could be connected with different ritual acts[55]. According to
the *Excerpta ex Theodoto*, the "redemption" seems to be connected with a
laying-on of hands, for it is said: "Hence also at the laying-on of hands they
say at the end: "For the angelic redemption", that is, the one which the
angels also have, in order that he who has received the redemption may be
baptized in the same Name as that in which his angel was baptized before
him." Since the redemption formula ends with the words "for the angelic
redemption", it is tempting to identify it with a Valentinian redemption
formula which is transmitted by Irenaeus:

---

53 Cp. below, p. 102.

54 Old Christian texts could continue this tradition and describe the baptized as being
   "clothed" with Christ or the Spirit; see G.H.W. Lampe, *The Seal of the Spirit*, London, 1951, pp. 112 f.

55 See H.-G. Gaffron, *Studien zum koptischen Philippusevangelium*, Diss., Bonn, 1969,
   p. 198.

Others refer to the redemption as follows: "The Name which is hidden (τὸ ὄνομα τὸ ἀποκεκρυμμένον) from every deity, dominion, and power, which Jesus the Nazarene put on (ὃ ἐνεδύσατο) in the spheres of light, [the Name] of Christ, the Christ who lives through the Holy Spirit for the angelic redemption."

(I.xxi.3)

The Name into which the believer was baptized apparently was invoked at the laying-on of hands in the redemption ritual immediately before the immersion. As we have seen, the Name into which the believer and his angel before him were baptized was the same Name as that which descended upon Jesus in the dove, and the redemption formula invokes the Name which Jesus "put on" and thus sustains the conclusion that Jesus clothed himself with the Name at his baptism into the Jordan.

However, the redemption formula appears to diverge from the *Excerpta* in that it says that Jesus put on the Name in the "spheres of light", which would seem to denote a heavenly region. This perplexity seems to me to be best solved by the scholarly distinction between texts describing the king's mythical enthronement in heaven and his ritual coronation in the earthly temple[56], for Jesus' baptism justly has been seen as his installation as the messianic king[57]. Admittedly, the distinction between mythical enthronement texts and ritual coronation texts is rather academic, for often the perspective in the ritual texts is expanded to cosmic proportions through, *e.g.*, the introduction of divine personages administering the royal ritual[58]. In like vein, already in the Synoptics, the description of Jesus' baptism contains mythical or legendary elements (the opening of heaven, the descent of the Spirit in the dove, and the voice from heaven), and other writings develop this perspective; thus, the *Gospel of the Ebionites* says that, after the voice from heaven had spoken, "[...] there shone about (περιέλαμψε) the place a great light" (*apud* Epiphan., *Pan.* XXX.xiii.7).

The Name which Jesus "put on in the spheres of light" obviously is identical with the Name of the Father with which he is said to have clothed himself according to the *Gospel of Philip*. In the *Acts of Thomas*, the Name summoned at the unction immediately prior to baptism in a way recalling the invocation of the Valentinian redemption formula is presented as the Divine Name: "Come, Holy Name of Christ that is above every Name!" (ch. 27, Greek version; cp. ch. 132; 157). Like the *Gospel of Philip*, this epiclesis defines the Name of Christ as the Divine Name with a reference to *Phil.* ii.9.

---

56 See G. Widengren, "Den himmelska intronisationen och dopet", in *RoB*, V, 1946, pp. 28 ff.

57 See E.O. James, *Christian Myth and Ritual*, London, 1933, pp. 100 ff.

58 Thus, for instance, it is said in the ritual *bit rimki* texts that the king is cleansed by the gods; see, *e.g.*, the text in A. Schollmeyer, ed. & trans., *Sumerisch-babylonische Hymnen und Gebete an Šamaš*, Paderborn, 1912, pp. 34 f. and p. 40.

Furthermore, we may note that the *Acts of Thomas* in another chapter say: "You are not able to hear his [*i.e.*, Christ's] true Name (τὸ ἀληθινὸν ὄνομα) at this time, but the name given to him is "Jesus Christ"" (ch. 163)[59]. That the true Name of Jesus must be kept secret squares with the assertion in the *Gospel of Philip* that the Name must not be uttered. We thus understand that the Valentinian redemption formula calls it the "Hidden Name". This secret Name of the Son obviously is the Jewish המפרש שם, the separated, special Name peculiar to God, which was generally ineffable and had become the *Hidden* Name.

The Gnostic, too, obtained the Divine Name which was invoked upon him and into which he was baptized. Clement quotes a statement saying that the angels were "baptized for us in order that we, too, possessing the Name, may not be held back [...] from entering into the Pleroma" (*Exc. ex Theod.* xxii.4). It appears that the possession of this Name was symbolized by some sort of mark on the body, for it is said that "the faithful bear through Christ the Name of God as if it were an inscription. Even dumb animals show by the seal (σφραγίς) they bear whose property they are" (lxxxvi.2). That the reception of this "seal" could be seen as an investiture would seem to be a natural conclusion in view of Paul's statement that the believers in baptism had "put on" Christ, for – as we have seen – the Name is identified with the "only-begotten Son" in the *Excerpta*.

There is in fact a text which says that the believer vests himself with the Name; in the *Odes of Solomon*, we read:

> Put on (ܐ), therefore, the Name of the Most High and know Him, and you shall cross without danger while the rivers shall be obedient to you.
>
> (xxxix.8)

While it is probably right that "the Odes, taken *en bloc*, are not baptismal hymns,"[60] this text at least seems to reveal the well-known image of baptism

---

59 In ch. 47, Thomas says that Jesus set him apart from his companions and spoke "three words" which he could not reveal to others. In the *Gospel of Thomas* (35.7 ff.), Jesus – in response to the disciples' assertions of what he is like – takes Thomas aside and whispers three things into his ear. B. Gärtner, *The Theology of the Gospel of Thomas*, trans. by E. Sharpe, London, 1961, pp. 122 f., interprets this in the light of the passage from *Act. Thom.* ch.163 and thinks that the name אהיה אשר אהיה is hinted at. Thomas says that the disciples would throw stones at him if he told them what Jesus said, and stoning was the penalty for blasphemy, which required mention of God's Name. Cp. below, p. 126, n. 151. H.-Ch. Puech, "Une collection de paroles de Jésus retrouvée", *CRAI*, 1957, p. 156, suggests that the Three-Fold Name is hinted at. For other interpretations, see R. McL. Wilson, *Studies in the Gospel of Thomas*, London, 1960, p. 112.

60 J. Rendel Harris & A. Mingana, ed. & trans., *The Odes and Psalms of Solomon*, II, Manchester, 1920, p. 197.

as a dangerous sea journey[61]. In order to make the journey safely, the baptizand has to "put on" (ـٮـﻠ) the Name of God.

J.H. Bernard, the great champion of the baptismal setting of the *Odes*, argued for an allusion to the investiture with baptismal garments in several of the *Odes*[62]. But this cannot be the signification of *lbš* in xxxix.8, for the investiture apparently takes place *before* the immersion[63]. Furthermore, this fact also excludes that it is the immersion into water which is seen as the investiture, which is a view propounded in some Christian and Mandean texts[64]. The verse immediately preceding the quotation above reads: "Because the sign ( )ﻠ{) on them is the Lord (ﻣـ), and the sign is the way for those who cross in the Name of the Lord." This "sign"(*'t'*) which is the "lord" (*mr*) probably is identical with the "Name of the Most High" in the next verse. Like the Valentinians, the group behind the *Odes of Solomon* seems to have bestowed some "sign" or "seal" of the Name on the initiand.

The seal or sign of the Name occurs also in Mandeism. Here, רושומא, an alternate term for which actually is אתא, sometimes seems to be identical with baptism itself (מאצבותא)[65], but in reality it refers to the "sealing" of

---

61 For this image, see P. Lundberg, *La typologie baptismale dans l'ancienne église* (ASNU, X), Uppsala, 1942; pp. 73 ff.

62 See *The Odes of Solomon* (TS, VIII/3), Cambridge, 1912, pp. 72, 78, 90, 167. Cp. Lampe, pp. 111 f.; Segelberg, p. 166. The *Odes* declare that the elect "puts on" (*lbš*) God's "love" (iii.1b; xxiii.3), his "grace" (iv.6; xx.7), the saviour himself (see vii.4; cp. *Gal.* iii.27), "holiness" (xiii.3), "incorruptibility through His Name" (مـلـٮ ـﻣـ , xv.8), "light" (xxi.3), "joy" (xxiii.1), and the "Perfect Virgin" (xxxiii.12), as well as the "Name".

63 The Mandeans put on their ritual dress before descending into the water, but Segelberg, pp. 122 ff., persuasively argues that the *vestitio* originally followed upon the ascent. The practice of the Dositheans and the Jewish Christians of immersing themselves fully clothed is of no relevance in this connection, for we are not informed that they put on a special garment.

64 For Christian evidence that baptism itself is called a "garment" (ἔνδυμα), see J. Daniélou, "Catéchèse pascale et retour au Paradis", *M-D*, 45, 1956, p. 115. For the Mandean notion that the immersion is an investiture with light garments, see K. Rudolph, *Die Mandäer*, II (Der Kult) (FRLANT, 75), Göttingen, 1961, p. 186; cp. pp. 183 f. As Rudolph, pp. 184, 186 f., points out, this idea is a corollary of the notion that the baptismal water, "Jordan" by name, is the heavenly element. In the *Gospel of Philip*, it is said: "The living water is a body (σῶμα); it is necessary that we put on (ΕΤ ΡΝ̄† ⳇⲓⲱⲱ Ν)the Living Man" (75.21 f.). But the idea of the baptismal water as a vestment apparently is secondary; see Lampe, p. 112; Segelberg, pp. 122f.

65 According to W. Brandt, *Die mandäische Religion*, Leipzig, 1889, p. 104, the "seal" or "sign" denotes baptism in the oldest texts. Baptism is explicitly called a "seal" in some Christian works, the oldest unambiguous example being the *Shepherd of Hermas* (see especially *Sim.* IX.xvi.4). It is noteworthy that to receive and possess the seal is closely associated or even identified with to "wear" (φορέω) the Name (see *ibid* IX:xvi.3; xvii.4). The latter expression might then be synonymous of "being baptized"; see F.J. Dölger, *Sphragis* (SGKA, 5), Paderborn, 1911, pp. 109 f.; cp.

the initiand's forehead with water which is performed right after the immersion[66]. When the priest strokes the forehead of the believer from the right to the left, he speaks the Divine Name "over" (על) him[67]. Through the sealing, the believer receives the Divine Name, as can be seen from the fact that "seal" and "Name" are interchangeable terms: "[...] on my head, the seal is established" (*Left Ginza* 86.17); "On my head, I took my Name [...]" (*Qol.* XC); "For the Name of the First One is established on their heads" (*Right Ginza* 18.12). In a text from the *Commentary on the Marriage Ceremony of the Great Shishlam,* which reveals a spiritualization of the possession of the seal or sign of the Name, "sign" and "Name" are in parallelism: "The sign (אתא) of the Great Life I set upon their minds, and I placed My Name upon them."[68] The liturgical passage just quoted, "On my head, I took my Name," continues: "In my heart, I took my seal."

In the *Odes of Solomon*, too, the sign of the Name is set upon the face of the believers. In *Ode* viii, we read that God has set a "seal" (ܐܬܡܐ) upon the face of the elect before they even existed (see *v.* 13), and this seal seems to be identical with the "Name" of the saviour which is said to be with them and protect them forever (see *vv.* 19, 22). This "seal" (*ṭbʿt*) of the Name apparently is identical with the sign of the Name in xxxix.7 f. Unequivocal evidence that the sign or seal of the Name was placed upon the face of the believers is provided by xlii.20, where the saviour says that he has set his Name upon the face of the elect.

The practice of setting a seal or sign of the Name upon the forehead of the elect is witnessed already in the Bible. In *Ez.* ix.4, we read that God caused a mark to be set upon the forehead of the righteous; this sign was the *Tau* (ת), the last letter of the Hebrew alphabet originally written in the form of a cross (+ or x), which marked its bearer as YHWH's property and protegée. This sign was used at a later time by those who conceived of themselves as belonging to the eschatological community (see *Ps. Sol.* xv.6 ff.; *CD* xix.11 ff.).

Daniélou, *Theology*, pp. 152 f. But, as G. Fitzer rightly points out, this usage of the term "seal" for baptism is "metaphorical and attenuated" (Art. σφραγίς κτλ., in *TDNT*, VII, 1971, reprinted 1975, p. 952). In *Sim.* VIII.ii.2 ff., the seal is a complement to the baptismal clothing and appears to have been received *after* the latter.

66 See Segelberg, pp. 53ff.; Rudolph, pp. 82, 156f. See further below, p. 104, n. 82.
67 According to Rudolph, pp. 82, 200, 345 f., the basic baptismal or sealing formula contains "the Name of the Life and the Name of Manda d'Hayye". However, there are many places where we learn that the baptism is performed in the name of the highest God only, or in the name of Manda d'Hayye only. Segelberg, p. 57, cites examples from *Ginza*, and other Mandean books can match *Ginza* in this respect (see, *e.g., Qol.* LI; *Book of John* ch. 30). There is, of course, only one Divine "Name", *i.e.*, nature; "God and the redeemer belong together" (Rudolph, p. 195). Cp. below, p. 102, n. 74 and n. 80.
68 Drower, *Šarh ḏ-Qabin ḏ-Šišlam-Rba*, p. 23 in the text and pp. 81f. in the translation.

In the *Revelation*, the "seal of the living God" put upon the forehead of the believers (see vii.2 ff.; ix.4) is expressly said to be the Name of God (see xiv.1; xxii.4), either the Tetragrammaton or its symbol in the form of a cross[69]. Commenting upon *Od. Sol.* viii.13, G.W.H. Lampe states: "There appears to be a reference to the use of the sign of the Cross in the baptismal ritual, and this sign set upon the newly baptised is related to the conception we have noted in the Apocalypse of the elect being visibly marked with the stamp of divine ownership on their forehead."[70]

But since xxxix.7 f. apparently refers to the same "use of the sign of the Cross in the baptismal ritual", the sign cannot have been put upon the "newly baptised", as was the practice in Western Christianity, where there was a post-baptismal *signatio crucis* of the forehead associated with an unction and performed with or without oil[71]. In the Syriac-speaking Church, however, the unction came before baptism, and, in this remote part of Christendom, whose roots are to be sought in Palestinian Jewish Christianity[72], the seal or sign of the cross was not — as in the West — a symbol of the name Χριστός or the cross upon which he died, but had retained its significance as an emblem of the Divine Name. This is brought out clearly in the liturgical homilies of Narsai, the Nestorian Church Father who lived in Edessa in the 5th century. In Homily 22, Narsai says that the priest in anointing the believers "signs the flock with the sign of the Lord, and seals upon it His Hidden Name by the outward look."[73] Here, we meet again the concept of the Hidden Name, which was known also to the Valentinians and obviously goes back to the

---

69 On the above, see especially E. Dinkler, "Jesu Wort vom Kreuztragen", in *Neutesta-mentliche Studien für R. Bultmann* (BZNW, 21), Berlin, 1954, pp. 110 ff.; cp. J.L. Teicher, "The Christian Interpretation of the Sign X in the Isaiah Scroll", *VT*, 5, 1955, pp. 189 ff. Additional references are found in the survey by J. Schneider, Art. σταυρός κτλ., in *TDNT*, VII, pp. 578 f.

70 *Op. cit.*, p. 113.

71 Moreover, already in the oldest witnesses, the interpretation of the sign as an emblem of the Divine Name has disappeared. The *Apostolic Tradition* says that it is "a sign of his [*i.e.*, Jesus'] passion" (ch. 37). Tertullian (*Adv. Marc.* III.xxii. 5 f.) identifies the sign with the Greek Tau-mark of *Ez.* ix.4 and says that it will be on the forehead of the righteous in the new Jerusalem, but he does not equate it with the Name of God and associates it with Jesus' passion.

72 See already F.C. Burkitt, *Early Eastern Christianity*, London, 1904. More recently, R. Murray has laid down that Syrian Christianity contains "some features which can only be accounted for by an origin in a thoroughly Jewish form of Christianity" (*Symbols of Church and Kingdom*, Cambridge, 1975, p. 7). For a summary of the arguments in favour of the theory of the Jewish Christian derivation of Syrian Christianity, see G. Quispel, "The Gospel of Thomas Revisited", in B. Barc, ed., *Colloque international sur les textes de Nag Hammadi* (Québec, 22-25 août 1978) (BCNH, Section "Études", 1), Québec & Louvain, 1981, pp. 245 ff.

73 Connolly, p. 40.

Jewish *Shem ha-Mephorash*[74]. That this Name was signed or sealed upon the forehead in the form of a cross is made quite plain: "The Name of the Divinity looks out from the sign on the forehead [...]."[75]

Narsai obviously does not represent a novel development. Already in the *Acts of Thomas*, a source from about the same time and provenance as the *Odes of Solomon*[76], we find this liturgical teaching. The unction is called a "sealing" and communicates the "seal" (*rushma, sphragis*) (see especially chs. 26 f.)[77]. That this "seal" is the seal of the Name is apparent, for the apostle Thomas invokes the Name while anointing. Furthermore, being invoked, the Name (the Spirit) comes to inhabit the oil: "[...] Jesus, let [your] victorious Power come, and let it settle in this oil [...] and let it dwell in this oil, over which we name your holy Name!" (ch. 157). The "Power" is identical with the Name; this is seen clearly in the epicleses of the Name in ch. 27 and 132, where the Divine Name summoned at the unction is called "Power of the Most High" and "Power established in Christ". Two centuries later, Narsai said that the priest, holding the oil in his hand, "shows to the eyes of the bodily senses the Secret Power that is hidden in the visible sign."[78] The "Secret Power" which is contained in the oil is the Hidden Name: "The Name of the Divinity he mixes in his hands with the oil [...]."[79] Through the anointing, the believer receives the Name: "With the Name hidden in it [*i.e.*, the oil], he signs the visible body, and the sharp power of the Name enters even into the soul."[80]

---

74 At the laying-on of hands following the coronation of the believer before his ascent from the water, the Mandean priest invokes several "Hidden Names" (שומההאאתא כאסיאאתא) upon him; see Segelberg, p. 62; Rudolph, *Mandäer*, II, pp. 83, 195. A parallel expression is "Hidden Seals" (*rushume*); see Rudolph, p. 158. There is also an epiclesis of "Hidden Names" upon the oil connected with the *impositio manus* and "sealing" of the forehead of the believer after the ascent from the water; see Rudolph, p. 84, n. 5, and p. 163.

75 Connolly, p. 45.

76 For the origin of the *Odes* in the beginning of the 3rd century in Edessa, see H.J.W. Drijvers, "Die Oden Salomos und die Polemik mit den Markioniten im syrischen Christentum", *OrChrA*, 205 (Symposium Syriacum 1976), 1978, pp. 39 ff.

77 For the concept of the seal in the *Acts*, see Dölger, pp. 95 ff. The *Acts* do not state expressly that the "sealing" was done *in modo crucis*, but this was obviously done from the very beginning in the East as well as in the West, where the word *signaculum*, which was used to denote the sign of the cross upon the forehead of the novice, translated *sphragis*; see *ibid.*, pp. 174 f. The *Acts of Thomas* do say that the oil used in "sealing" the baptizand is a "hidden mystery" revealing the cross (see ch. 121). It is explicitly said that the cross is marked upon the eucharist bread, upon which the Name has been invoked (see ch. 50; cp. ch. 133).

78 Connolly, p. 40.

79 *Ibid.*, p. 44.

80 *Ibid.*, p. 42. There is no difference between the Three-Fold Name and the Hidden Name, for the preceding sentence says: "The Three Names he casts upon the oil and

The same teaching is present already in the *Acts of Thomas*. The apostle prays that the "Power", that is, the Name, in the oil shall be "established upon" the one who is anointed (see ch. 121). A woman prays: "[...] that I may receive the seal and become a holy temple and he dwell in me" (ch. 87). The apostle answers: "[...] that the Word of God may settle upon all and tabernacle in you" (ch. 88). Since the Name is identical with the person, the reception of the "seal", *i.e.*, the anointment containing the "Name" or the "Power", is equivalent to become a habitat of the Son or the Spirit[81].

It seems plausible to conclude that the sign or seal of the Name put upon the heads of the elect in the *Odes of Solomon* denotes the cruciform sign made with oil at the unction before the immersion. That the reception of this seal could be seen as an "investiture" is corroborated by the following passage: "For who vests himself with Your grace and falls into disfavour? Your seal (ﺣﺘﻢ) is known and Your creatures are known to it; and Your hosts have it in possession, and the elect archangels are vested with it (ﻟﺒﺴﻮﻥ)" (iv.6 ff.). The text does not speak explicitly about the seal of the *Name*, but *ḥtm* − "seal" or "sign" − apparently is synonymous with the "seal" (*ṭbʿt*) of the Name in *Ode* viii and the "sign" of the Name in xxxix.7 f. In Syrian Christian texts, this word often occurs as a synonym of *rushma*, which is the usual term for the sign of the cross performed with oil on the forehead of the baptizand at the unction[82].

---

consecrates it [...]." Narsai also says: "To them [*i.e.*, the priests] He gave the signet of the Name of the Incomprehensible Deity, that they might be stamping men with the Holy Name. The stamp of this Name they lay upon the flock continually, and with the Trinity men are signing men" (*ibid.*, p. 41). One is reminded of the two Names in the Mandean sealing formula and of the many Hidden Names invoked at various moments during the Mandean baptismal ritual; see above, p. 100, n. 67, and p. 102, n. 74.

81 In view of the fact that the Name also is invoked upon the eucharist bread, it is interesting to note the following passage from *Didache*: "But, after you are satisfied with food [*i.e.*, the victuals of the eucharist], give thanks thus: "We give thanks to you, O holy Father, for Your holy Name that You made to tabernacle in our hearts, and for the knowledge, faith, and immortality that You made known to us through Jesus Your child. To You be glory for ever! You, Lord Almighty, created all things for the sake of Your Name, and gave food and drink to men for their enjoyment, that they might give thanks to You, but You have blessed us with spiritual food and drink, and eternal light through Your child [...]" (x.1 ff.). E. Peterson, "Didachè cap. 9 e 10", *EL*, 58, 1944, pp. 4 ff., suggests that the "Name" in this passage indicates Christ. The idea of the Name tabernacling in the heart of the believer (οὗ κατεσκήνωσας ἐν ταῖς καρδίαις ἡμῶν) is reminiscent of *John* i.14, where it is said that "the Logos became flesh and tabernacled among us (ἐσκήνωσεν ἐν ἡμῖν)." The latter text is possibly based upon an older form in which the *Name* "tabernacled among us"; see below, p. 256, n. 32.

82 See Segelberg, p. 136, note continued from the preceding page. It is not surprising that רושומא also occurs as the term for the post-baptismal anointing of the Man-

There is also evidence that the ritual symbol of the "investiture" with the
Name was kept more in congruity with the literal meaning of the term[83].
This is found in a Jewish text from the Geonic period named ספר המלבוש,
whose purport is to give magical power. The initiand is told to make himself a
garment modelled on the high priest's ephod and inscribe it with the names of
God. After seven days on a strict, vegetarian diet, he should be "inwardly
clean and fit to vest himself with the Name." The text goes on to say:

> Then go down into the water up to your loins and vest yourself with the Venerable
> and Terrible Name in the water[84]

G. Scholem notes: "The Hebrew phrase לבוש את השם corresponds to the
Syriac one, Odes of Solomon XXXIX,7 לבשו שמה דמרימא."[85] It is to be
added that the rife Samaritan phrase that Moses "vested" himself with the
Name of God is another example of this usage of לבש.

That it is the high priest who here appears as the model of the initiand is
not so strange, for the high priest took over many of the paraphernalia and
functions of the king, whose heavenly enthronement provided the mythical
pattern for the "democratized" coronation ritual. In the *Testaments of the
Twelve Patriarchs*, the description of the installation of Levi as a heavenly

---

deans, for this is generally agreed to be a secondary doublet of the genuinely Mandean water signation; see now Segelberg, pp. 130 ff.; Rudolph, *Mandäer*, II, pp.
159, 165, 174, 351, 354. Even האתאאמתא is an occasional term for the unction of
the Mandeans (see, *e.g.*, *Qol.* XXIV, at the end). In the *Baptism of Hibil Ziwa*, the
water signation (*rushma*) is understood as the act of vesting, even as an investiture
with the Name: " [...] the sign of the right belongs to the Father, so that he is
vested with the Name" (Drower, p. 53). Segelberg, p. 123, note continued from the
preceding page, thinks that this is a secondary explanation of the notion of the investiture, similar to its interpretation as the immersion into water.

83 But note also that the sealing of the forehead with oil was followed by the unction of
the *entire* body (see *Act. Thom.* ch. 157; *Did. Apost.* ch. 16; Cyril of Jerusalem,
Myst. Cat. II.2 f.; *Ap. Const.* III.xvi.2 f.; John Chrysostom, *Bapt. Cat.* ii.22 f.; *et al.*).
For Western evidence for the association of the *signatio* with the unction of the
whole body, see *Ap. Trad.* xxi.19 f.; Tert., *De bapt.* ch. 7. This practice may have
Jewish origin, for *II Enoch* relates that the patriarch Enoch – after having ascended
to heaven – was undressed by the archangel Michael and anointed with an oil whose
appearance was "more than a great light" (ch. 9). By this unction, Enoch was made
"like one of the glorious ones [*i.e.*, the angels], and there was no difference in appearance" (*ibid.*). It is interesting to compare this description with the Samaritan representation of Moses' heavenly investiture with "light", an interchangeable term of
which is the "Name". Compare that the Ophians (Ophites) taught that the reception
of the "seal" was an anointing with "bright" (λευκός) oil (see Orig., *Contra Cels.* VI.
27).

84 Ms. British Museum, Margoliouth 752, fol. 93. For a description of the ritual, see
Scholem, *On the Kabbalah*, pp. 136 f.

85 *Major Trends in Jewish Mysticism*, 3rd ed., New York, 1954, reprinted as Schocken
paperback edition 1961 and subsequently, p. 368, n. 131.

high priest — which no doubt goes back to a royal myth and ritual pattern — probably serves as a paradigm of a Jewish Christian baptismal initiation (see *Test. Levi* ch. viii)[86]. In this connection, we may note that Clement of Alexandria — inspired by the Gnostic Theodotus — sees the entry of the high priest, having "the Name engraved upon his heart," into the holy of holies as an allegory of the entry of the soul into the intelligible world. Clement says that the high priest by removing the golden plate inscribed with the Name of God "indicates the laying aside of the body, which, like the golden plate, has become pure and light through the purification of the soul, [of that body] on which was engraved the lustre of piety, as a result of which he was known to the principalities and the powers as being clothed with the Name (τὸ Ὄνομα περικείμενος)" (*Exc. ex Theod.* xxvii.1).

The golden plate on the high priest's turban is here the symbol of the body, which must be put off when entering into the divine world. The body of the perfect is said to have become "pure and light", resembling the golden plate, and is seen as the Name vesting the soul, in accordance with the fact that the Tetragrammaton was decorating the golden plate on the high priest's turban (cp. Philo, *De vita Mos.* II.114; 132; Joseph., *Ant.* III.331). Clement would here seem to presuppose the notion of the conferment of the Name upon the body, but reinterprets this ritual investiture as an effectuation by "the purification of the soul". Moreover, the investiture of the body with the Name is only a symbol of the spiritual possession of the Divine "Name", for the high priest did not relinquish the Name by taking off his turban — he had "the Name engraved upon his heart," just like it must be assumed that the soul enters into heaven with the "Name" in its possession.

To conclude this discussion of the investiture with the Name, we first note that the concept pertains to a myth and ritual pattern of initiation. Further, since to be "vested with the Name" is a thoroughly Semitic phrase, there is no reason to think that it is a secondary element in the Samaritan representations of Moses' heavenly installation, which reveals a more or less disintegrated royal pattern of mythical enthronement, the archetype of all

---

86 For derivation of the description of Levi's installation from a royal myth and ritual pattern, see H. Ludin Jansen, "The Consecration in the Eighth Chapter of Testamentum Levi", in *La regalità sacra* (SHR: Suppl. *Numen,* IV), Leiden, 1959, pp. 356 ff.; G. Widengren, "Royal Ideology and the Testaments of the Twelve Patriarchs", in F.F. Bruce, ed., *Promise and Fulfilment* (Essays Presented to Professor S.H. Hooke), Edinburgh, 1963, pp. 202 ff. For the theory that *Test. Levi* ch. viii is a symbolical description of a baptismal initiation, see T.W. Manson, "Miscellanea apocalyptica III", *JTS*, 48, 1947, pp. 59 ff.; M. de Jonge, *The Testaments of the Twelve Patriarchs*, Assen, 1953, p. 128. For the baptismal initiation as a democratized royal ritual, see G. Widengren, *Religionsphänomenologie*, trans. by R. Elgnowski, Berlin, 1969, pp. 226 f., 230 ff.

democratized initiations in the Near East. Although it cannot be proved that the Valentinian description of Jesus being "vested with" the Name is directly dependent upon Samaritan Moses traditions, it can be concluded that Samaritanism is at least part of the mould out of which Gnosticism came.

The Hypostasized Name

But Jesus in Valentinianism is not only said to have been "clothed" with the Name; he is even styled the Divine Name. I set forth the complete text of the long and elaborate meditation upon the Son as the Name in the *Gospel of Truth* from Codex I of the Nag Hammadi library:

> Now the Name of the Father is the Son. It is He [*viz.*, the Father] who first gave a name to the one who came forth from Him (what he indeed did)[87] and whom He begot as a Son. He gave him His Name which He possessed, since He — the Father — is the One to whom belong all things existing around Him: He has the Name; He has the Son. It is possible to see him [*viz.*, the Son, hardly the Father]; but the Name is invisible, because it is the very mystery of the Invisible which reaches to ears that are all filled with it. For, indeed, the Name of the Father is not pronounced, but it is revealed in the Son. Great, therefore, is the Name! Who, then, is there who would be able to pronounce a Name for Him, even the Great Name, except him [*i.e.*, the Son] to whom the Name belongs and the sons of the Name in whom the Name of the Father rested, and who in turn rested in His Name? Since the Father is without beginning, it is He alone who brought him forth as a Name for Himself before He produced the aeons, in order that the Name of the Father should be over their head as a Lord, — the Authentic Name, which through His command is firm in perfect power, because the Name is not from words or from appellations, but is invisible. He gave a Name to him alone,[88] he being the only one able to see Him, and He having the power of bestowing a Name upon him. For he who does not exist has no Name. For what name is given to him who does not exist? But he who does exist exists also with His Name, and he knows it; and to give him the Name was the Father alone. The Son is His Name; thus, He did not hide Himself[89] in concealment,[90] but he existed, [namely] the Son.[91] To him alone He gave the Name. The Name therefore, is that of the Father, just as the Name of the Father is the Son, even Mercy. Where, indeed, would he find a Name except with the Father? But, undoubtedly, some will say to his neighbour: "Who is it that will give a Name to Him before whom there was

---

87 ЄNTAϤ   ρω   ΠЄ does not have to be taken as a Christological statement (*e.g.*, "who was Himself"), for ρω may refer to "come forth".

88 Instead of "to him alone", we could translate "Himself". All the following pronouns before the period would then also refer to the Father. The same interpretation is possible in 39.18 f., which I have translated: "and to give him the Name was the Father alpne." Here, we could read: "and to give himself a name is [the prerogative of] the Father." The meaning would then seem to be that the Father's self-denomination is identical with the birth of the Son.

89 It is grammatically possible to translate "him".

90 Emending ⳒωϤ to ⳒωΠ.

91 If the Son is the subject, the obligatory N6I is omitted. If the Father is the subject, "the Son" must be connected with the continuation: "To the Son alone ... ."

none, as if offspring did not receive name from those who begot them?"[92] First of all, then, it is fitting for us to consider the case: What is the Name? It is the Authentic Name. It is therefore not the Name *from* the Father [*i.e.,* derived in the same way as others obtain their name], for it is the *proper Name.* Therefore, he did not receive the Name on loan, like others, in the way as each one is provided with it. But this is the *proper Name;* there is no one else who has given it to Him. But He was unnameable, ineffable, until the moment when he who is perfect spoke it; and it is he who has the power to speak His Name and to see Him. When, therefore, it pleased Him that His Name should become His beloved Son,[93] and when He had given him the Name, he who proceeded from the Depth spoke of secrets about Him, knowing that the Father would not be angry [literally, "is without evil"].[94]

(38.7 - 40.29)

It is not in every case easy to determine whether it is the Father, the Son, or the Name that is referred to by the 3rd person singular pronoun; my interpretation may very well be wrong in some places. But some general remarks regarding this text are quite sound and will suffice in this connection.

The passage is of utmost importance for the theory that Gnosticism has essential roots in Judaism and Samaritanism, for the enormous significance which here is attached to the Name of God can be parallelled only by Jewish and Samaritan sources. The phrase ⲭⲁⲉⲓⲥ ⲛ̄ⲣⲉⲛ (40.8 f., 14), which is translated "proper Name", undoubtedly renders κύριον ὄνομα , behind which we discern שֵׁם המיוחד, the Hebrew expression denoting God's *own* Name. In accordance with Jewish and Samaritan custom, the Name being the "mystery of the Invisible" is not pronounced (see 38.22); it is itself "invisible" (38.16 f.). Thus, the Valentinian "gospel" links the concept of the *agnōstos theos,* so familiar to students of Gnosticism, with the Jewish and Samaritan idea of the incomprehensibility of the Name of God, *i.e.,* the divine nature or mode of being.

Although God himself is unknown and unknowable, he reveals himself through his Son, who is the only one who can comprehend God's Name. The Son therefore is said to have been given the Name, as is also the teaching in the *Gospel of Philip.* Moreover, the *Gospel of Truth* also teaches that the Son, being born from the Father, even *is* the proper Name of God. It is in accordance with the theology of the Old Testament that the "Name" denotes God as he reveals himself, but the "gospel" goes beyond the Old Testament in representing the Name as a distinctly personified entity, even the Son of God. Since the Son is the Name, there is no distinction in nature or mode of being between the Father and the Son. We have here the doctrine of the consub-

---

92 This appears to be a fictitious objection to the discourse; the author may suspect that some people would argue that the highest God is nameless.

93 The text in 40.24 f. seems to be corrupt; it is actually the Name which is loved by God. In any event, the text is meaningful, since the Son and the Name are identical.

94 The nominal sentence must have futuristic sense, as is often the case in Coptic.

stantiality of God and Christ expressed about two hundred years before the
production of the Nicene Creed by means of the Semitic concept of the
"Name", which, however, primarily is ontic, while the Greek concept of
"nature" (οὐσία, *substantia*) used in the Creed is ontological.

The question is where the background of this paradoxical Christology of
the Name can be found. G. Quispel has asserted that it goes back "ultimately
to more, or less heterodox Jewish conceptions, which were taken over into
Gnosis as early as the beginning of the second century."[95] He points to the
Jewish idea of an intermediary called by the Name of God, Yaho, and to the
doctrine of the Name being the instrument of God or even the divine hypostasis responsible for the creation[96]. These notions are important for the
thesis of the present work and will be dealt with in the Part reserved for the
discussion of the Jewish evidence; but they are not of immediate relevance to
the interpretation of the Christology of the Name in the *Gospel of Truth*,
since the Son is not called by the name of Yaho (or by its rendering *Kyrios*)
or ascribed with a cosmogonic function[97].

S. Arai has discerned that the quoted text shows a resemblance to the idea
of revelation in *John* i.1 f., 18, and he has made a list of parallels in thought
amounting to a structural agreement between the passage from the *Gospel of*

---

95 "The Jung Codex and Its Significance", in H.-Ch. Puech, G. Quispel & W.C. van
Unnik, *The Jung Codex*, trans. by F. Cross, London, 1955, p. 72.
96 See "De Joodse achtergrond van de Logos-Christologie", *VoxTheol*, 25, 1954, pp.
48 ff.; Christliche Gnosis und jüdische Heterodoxie", *ET*, 14, 1954, pp. 481 ff.;
"The Jung Codex", pp. 62 ff.; "Het Johannesevangelie en de Gnosis", *NTT*, 11, 1957,
pp. 173 ff.; "L'Évangile de Jean et la Gnose", in F.-M. Braun, ed., *L'Évangile de Jean*,
(RB, III), Bruges, 1958, pp. 197 ff.
97 J.-E. Ménard, "Les élucubrations de l'Evangelium Veritatis sur le "Nom"", *SMR*,
6, 1963, who seems to have simply summarized Bietenhard's paragraphs on the
Divine Name (but without any acknowledgment!), concludes that the Christology
of the Name in the *Gospel of Truth* is inspired by "a thought which is Semitic,
more specifically Jewish and Biblical," and that the Name "takes the form of a
hypostasis in our *Gospel of Truth*, as is the case in certain passages of *Dt.* and in
the rabbinic and apocalyptical texts" (p. 214). I fail to find evidence for the concept
of the hypostasized Name in "rabbinic and apocalyptical texts". Ménard, p. 203 and
p. 204, also says that the rabbinic testimony to the practice of using the Divine
Name in magic has played a rôle in the formation of the meditation upon the Name
in the *Gospel of Truth*; in substantiation, he cites 39.4 ff.: "For the Name is not
from words or from appellations, but is invisible [...]." What is magic in this? I cannot detect any magical connotations in the sublime Christology of the Name in the
Valentinian "gospel". Ménard, pp. 192 f., also points to the magical papyri as showing a resemblance to the theology of the Name in the *Gospel of Truth*, and this is
pertinent inasmuch as the Name appears as a hypostasized entity in certain papyri;
cp. below, p. 285. In addition to the evidence from the magical papyri and the
Bible, chiefly *Deuteronomy*, Ménard, p. 201, cites the conception of the Name in the
Book of Jubilees as being a parallel to the hypostatization of the Name in the Gnostic
"gospel". Cp. below, p. 255.

Truth and the prologue to the *Gospel of John*[98]. The link is supposed to be found in Egyptian Christianity: the Gnostic Theodotus reveals a terminology similar to that of the author of the *Gospel of Truth* and calls Jesus both "Logos" (see Clem. Alex., *Exc. ex Theod.* xxi.3) and "Name" (see *ibid.* xxvi.1; xxxi.3 f.; xliii.4), and Clement of Alexandria too calls the Son the "Name" (see *Strom.* V.xxxviii.6; *Exc. ex Theod.* xxvii.1) and equates Logos and Name in his exposition of the prologue to the Fourth Gospel (see *ibid.* ch. xx)[99]. Theodotus and Clement manifestly do know the *Gospel of John*, but there is no clear quotation from this canonical Gospel in the *Gospel of Truth*. Rather than theorizing that the author of the Valentinian "gospel" is expounding the prologue to the *Gospel of John*, and has transformed the Logos Christology into a Christology of the Name by help of Christian speculations which equated λόγος and ὄνομα, it would seem right to seek for the common tradition which the *Gospel of Truth* apparently shares with the Fourth Gospel[100]. After all, as Arai himself notes, already Philo equates *Logos* and *Onoma*, saying that they both are among the designations of the many-named intermediary (see *De conf. ling.* 146)[101]. The Alexandrian Christians who identified *Logos* and *Onoma* obviously had Jewish forerunners.

J. Daniélou thinks that the Christology of the Name in the *Gospel of Truth* reached the author "through the medium of an earlier Jewish Christian elaboration"[102]. It is true that there was a Christology of the Name in the primitive community in Jerusalem[103], and this Christology was continued by the Fourth Gospel and the Apostolic Fathers[104]. The name Κύριος, which is the LXX's translation or paraphrase of the name YHWH, was transferred to Jesus very early. Thus, for instance, *Joel* iii.5, "Everyone who calls upon the Name of the Lord will be saved," is quoted by Paul as the basis for the statement that Christ "is the same *kyrios* of all and is rich unto all who call upon him" (*Rom.* x.12). Paul was not the author of this usage; as will be made clear below, it was obviously based on the Jewish Christian conception that Jesus on his ascension to heaven received the Divine Name[105].

---

98 See *Die Christologie des Evangelium Veritatis*, Leiden, 1964, pp. 69 f.
99 See *ibid.*, pp. 71 f. Cp. already the notes by M. Malinine, H.-Ch. Puech & G. Quispel, ed. & trans., *Evangelium Veritatis* (SCGJ-I, VI), Zürich, 1956, p. 58. See also Daniélou, *Theology*, pp. 153, 161 ff.
100 Cp. now G.W. MacRae, "Nag Hammadi and the New Testament", in *Gnosis*, pp. 155 f., with references.
101 See p. 71. See below, p. 269, for quotation of the text.
102 *Theology*, p. 157. Cp. the concession by Quispel, "Qumran, John and Jewish Christianity", pp. 154 f.; "The Origins of the Gnostic Demiurge", p. 272.
103 See L. Cerfaux, "La première communauté chrétienne", *ETL*, 16, 1939, pp. 24 ff. (= *Recueil*, II, pp. 147 ff.).
104 See below, pp. 125 ff., and above, p. 81.
105 See below, pp. 293 ff.

But also Philo knows the transference of the name *Kyrios* in the LXX to the Logos, the intermediary. Since it is impossible to see God and live (see Ex. xxxiii.20), the "Lord" who revealed himself to Moses and the elders was the Logos (see *De fug. et invent.* 164 f.; *De mut. nom.* 8 ff.). The "Lord" whom Jacob saw on the heavenly ladder (see *Gen.* xxviii.13) was the "archangel", *i.e.*, the Logos, in whose form God reveals himself (see *De somn.* I.157; cp. *De mut.* 87, 126; *De migr. Abr.* 168; *Leg. all.* III.177; *Quis rer. div. her. sit* 205)[106]. The Logos is identified by Philo with the Angel of the Lord of *Ex.* xxiii.20 f., who has been given the Name of God and in whose form God reveals himself (see *De migr. Abr.* 174; *De agr.* 51)[107]. Philo cannot possibly have been the source of the distinction between God himself and the Tetragrammaton, since — as we shall see in Chapter VI — other traditions showing no acquaintance with Philo are also referring the Tetragrammaton to God's principal angel. It would thus seem that the Jewish Christians and Philo have a common source.

In Jewish Christian tradition, the "Name" also was used absolutely as a designation of Christ. In *James* ii.7, we read: "Do not they blaspheme the good Name called upon you?" The "Name" here does not stand for Christ only, but he obviously partakes of it (cp. Matt. xxviii.19)[108]. But since there is only one Divine Name, the word could also be used of Christ alone. Thus, *Acts* tells that the Christians were rejoicing because "they were counted worthy to suffer for the Name (ὑπὲρ τοῦ ὀνόματος)" (v.41; cp. *III John* 7). The absolute usage of ὄνομα is taken by K. Lake and H.J. Cadbury to be "Christian Greek rather than translated Aramaic"[109], but the usage of השם as a periphrasis of the proper Name of God is well attested[110], and *Onoma* used of Christ must reflect the transference of the Semitic term from God to Jesus. However, as has been stated, Philo knows the "Name" as a designation of the divine intermediary, and, if the Christology of the Name as found in the *Gospel of Truth* really is based upon Jewish Christian theology, the Jewish Christians would appear to have been the heirs of Jews in this respect as in so many others.

As mentioned above, Quispel has cited Jewish texts where the hypostasis of the Name is the demiurgic agent, but the personal character of the Name is not apparent in these texts. Moreover, there actually do not seem to exist Jewish texts where the hypostasized Name appears as the mediator of revelation. The Samaritan tradition, however, shows points of contact with the

106 See A.F. Segal, *Two Powers in Heaven* (SJLA, XXV), Leiden, 1977, pp. 162, 170.
107 Cp. below, pp. 314f.
108 Cp. above, p. 100, n. 67.
109 *The Acts of the Apostles* (BC, I), IV (English Translation and Commentary), London, 1933, p. 63, col. a.
110 See Marmorstein, *Doctrine*, p. 105; Bietenhard, pp. 268 f.

Christology of the Name in the *Gospel of Truth*. The quintessence of the revelation, embodied in the Law, is nothing else than the Name of God. Out of several texts, we can select the following hymn by Marqa:

> At the time when He proclaimed His Name, the world trembled — at the time when He proclaimed and said: "Thou shalt have no gods" [cp. *Ex.* xx.3]. Powers [*i.e.*, angels] and mortals were gathered together. God, who has no equal, descended in order to reveal His Name. [...] The Name of God is [inscribed] on their two sides [*i.e.*, on the two sides of the tablets of the Law]: YHWH — the like of whom there is none, neither in the hidden nor in the seen [world].
>
> (Cowley, 23.16 f., 30)

The uniqueness of the revelation imparted to Moses consists of the communication of the Divine Name as well as of the decrees of God. It is in this light that we must understand the following word which Marqa has God speak to Moses: "Were it not for your prophethood, I would not have revealed Myself [...]" (*Memar Marqa* I.9).

Enormous importance is thus attached to Moses' prophethood[111], and it is significant that it is described as a bestowment in the terms of that of the Name. In his commemoration of Moses, Marqa says: "The prophethood with which he was vested, of which he was worthy, has been hidden away, and no man will ever again be vested with it" (*ibid*. V.4). Amram Dara says that Moses had prophecy as his crown: "Prophecy belonged to him, a crown from the days of covenant; [it was] the glory of Moses, who was worthy to be vested with it" (Cowley, 32.14 f.)[112]. The intimate connection between the reception of prophethood and the reception of the Name is succinctly brought out by Marqa in the following statement to the effect that God promises Moses that he "would be vested with prophethood and the Divine Name" (*Memar Marqa* I.1)[113].

Thus, we see that Moses' office of being the prophet or revealer of God is associated with his possession of the Divine Name. Because he is the possessor of the Name of God, he is able to reveal God. Furthermore, since Moses the Law-giver possesses God's own Name, the pith of Law, he becomes the object as well as the subject of the revelation which he imparts; this aspect is brought out in Marqa's following characterization of the Law, the vehicle of revelation:

> A shining sun which is not extinguishable, the Name of God and the prophet (שם

---

111 For Moses' prophethood, see Meeks, *Prophet-King*, pp. 220 ff., 236 ff.; cp. Macdonald, *Theology*, pp. 204 ff. They both quote this text as an epitome.

112 Although בריתה can be translated "creation", as is done by Macdonald, "Hymns", p. 69, the context shows clearly that here it means "covenant"; see Meeks, *Prophet-King*, p. 236, n. 3.

113 Cp. the text from *Memar Marqa* VI.6 quoted above, p. 87.

(אלה ונביא); therein is written: "YHWH, the victor in the battles" [cp. *Ex.* xv.3, Samaritan version].[114]

(Cowley, 50.1)

Since Moses had been "vested" and "crowned" with the Divine Name, he possesses a share in God's nature or mode of being and thus is a legitimate revealer of God. Moreover, by revealing God's Name or nature, he also reveals his own being. By a paraphrase from Christology, we can say that Moses in Samaritanism is the *hypostasis* and *prosōpon* of the divine *ousia*.

This Samaritan teaching of Moses as the personified Divine Name and the revealer of God furnishes a parallel to the Christology of the Name set forth in the *Gospel of Truth*. If the Valentinians really drew upon Jewish Christian Christology, the Jewish Christians in their turn must have been dependent upon certain conceptions of the redeemer figure which were shared by the Samaritans.

Simon Magus as the Eschatological Prophet like Moses

Since Moses, according to the Samaritans, was the personified Name of God, it is to be expected that the eschatological prophet like Moses also would be portrayed as the possessor of the Name. This inference offers a key to a couple of legends about Simon Magus, who apparently availed himself (or was availed by his followers) of certain traditions belonging to a Samaritan Moses pattern[115]. In the *Acts of Peter* (the *Actus Vercellenses*) from the end of the 2nd century, it is narrated that Simon once lodged with a certain woman called Eubula, and — upon leaving — stole all her money.

> But Eubula, discovering this crime, began to torture her household, saying: "You took advantage of [the visit of] this Man of God and have robbed me, because you saw him coming in to me in order to do honour to a simple woman; his name, however, is the Name of the Lord (*cui nomen est autem nomen domini*)."[116]

(Ch. 17)

A leaf ends before *autem*, and one has suspected that words have fallen out of the original, but there is no gap in the ms., and the title rendered *nomen domini* is perfectly understandable in view of Simon's Samaritan background. The author of the apocryphal *Acts* represents Eubula as a type of the people who were deceived by Simon and took him to be a "Man of God".

---

114 Szuster translates: "A shining sun which is not extinguishable; the Name of God and the Prophet is written in it — "God, the victor in the battles"" (p. 27). Brown translates: "A sun never extinguished, shedding light upon the name of God and the prophet, therein is written, Yahwe is victorious in battle" (p. 271).

115 Cp. above, pp. 62 ff.

116 C.H. Turner, "The Latin Acts of Peter", *JTS,* 32, 1931, pp. 126 f., reads *numen domini* in the passage quoted, and thinks this is a translation of ἡ (μεγάλη) δύναμις τοῦ θεοῦ. But this well-known title of Simon occurs in ch. 4 as *virtus magna dei*.

This appellation perhaps is to be explained in the light of the fact that one of Moses' titles in Samaritanism is (האלהים) איש, the "Man (of God)". Already in *Deut.* xxxiii.1, Moses is called by this name, and it recurs throughout *Memar Marqa*. Mostly, Marqa writes only "Moses the Man", but he has "the Man of God" at least in one place, namely, in the address to Moses by the people when they hear that he is about to die: "Far be it [death?] from you, O Man of God!" (VI.3). In another paragraph of the same book where Marqa is explaining several of Moses' epithets, this name is expounded thus:

> And "Man": the possessor of His power, since His power was manifest in all his actions.
>
> (VI.6)

The title of the Man (of God) designates Moses in his capacity of doing mighty works reserved for God. This description of Moses fits Simon the magician being known as the Great Power of God.

That Simon Magus was known as the possessor of the Name of God can also be inferred from a couple of passages in the Pseudo-Clementine literature. In this literature, there is to be found a strange legend about Simon creating a *homunculus* from the air, which he condensed by certain θεῖαι τροπαί. The text of the *Homilies* runs:

> First, he [*i.e.*, Simon] says, the human *pneuma* transformed itself into warm nature and sucked up the surrounding air like a cupping glass. Then, he transformed this air that had taken form within the *pneuma* into water, then into blood [...]; and, from the blood, he made flesh. When the flesh had become firm, he had produced a man, not from earth but from air, so convincing himself that he could make a new man. He also claimed that he had returned him to the air by undoing the transformations.
>
> (II.26)

G. Scholem has compared this text to the Jewish legends about the sages creating a living being, a so-called *golem*, by means of the letter magic taught in *Sefer Yeṣira*, the "Book of Creation": "What here is accomplished by transformations of the air, the Jewish adept does by bringing about magical transformations of the earth through the influx of the 'alphabet' of the *Book Yetsirah* ... . The 'divine transformations' in the operation of Simon Magus remind one very much of the creative 'transformations' (*temuroth*) of the letters in the *Book Yetsirah*."[117] Now, *Sefer Yeṣira* teaches that the whole alphabet, the instrument of the creation, is based upon the Name of God, and that the Name therefore is the real effective principle of the creation[118]. Thus, as shall be dealt with at some length in Chapter V, the magician who creates a *homunculus* through combinations and permutations of the letters

---

117 *On the Kabbalah*, p. 173.
118 See *ibid.*, p. 168, *et passim.*

of the alphabet in actual fact is availing himself of the Divine Name, the first principle of the creative potency inherent in the alphabet[119]. That Simon the magician claimed to have created a man would seem to imply that he was the possessor of the Name of God.

There is another text in the Clementine romance which is of great importance for the theory that Simon availed himself (or was availed) of certain traditions about the Prophet like Moses, who was the possessor of the Name of God. This is the pericope which represents Simon as prevailing over Dositheus in a contest where both use their magical power. The pericope starts by relating that Simon was a pseudo-Messiah who had been the most esteemed among the thirty disciples of John the Baptist. The way in which Simon succeeded John is said to have been as follows:

> When Simon was away in Egypt to learn the practice of magic, John was killed; and a certain Dositheus, who desired the leadership of John, falsely announced that Simon was dead and succeeded to the leadership of the sect. Not long afterwards, Simon returned and strongly laid claim to the position as him own, although, when he met with Dositheus, he did not demand the place, since he knew that a man who has attained power irregularly cannot be removed. Therefore, pretending friendship, he places himself temporarily in the second place, under Dositheus. After a few days, however, while taking his place among the thirty fellow-disciples, he began to slander Dositheus as not having transmitted the doctrines correctly. And he said that Dositheus did not do so because of unwillingness but because of ignorance. And, on one occasion, Dositheus, perceiving that this tricky accusation of Simon was destroying his reputation in the eyes of the majority, so that they did not think that he was the Standing One, came in a rage to the usual meeting-place and, finding Simon, began to hit him with a staff. But it seemed to pass through Simon's body as if it were smoke. Thereupon, Dositheus, in amazement, says to him: "If you are the Standing One, I too will worship you." When Simon said: "I am", Dositheus, knowing that he himself was not the Standing One, fell down and worshipped; and, associating himself with the twenty-nine chiefs, he placed Simon in his own seat of honour. Then, not long afterwards, while Simon stood, Dositheus fell down and died.
>
> *(Hom.* II.24)

The representation by the *Homilies* of the heresiarchs Simon and Dositheus as disciples of John the Baptist is due to the hostility of the literary bases of the Pseudo-Clementines to the Baptist's disciples, who held their master to be a kind of messianic figure (see *Rec.* I.54, 60; Orig., *In Luc. hom.* 25; cp. *Luke* iii.15). The *Kerygmata Petrou*, a source incorporated into the *Pseudo-Clementines*, and the basic writing of the *Homilies* and the *Recognitions* teach that every manifestation of the "true Prophet" is "male" and has a "female" antagonist, and that Jesus was opposed by John the Baptist[120]. While the

---

119 See pp. 241 ff.

120 For the evidence of the existence of John's sect and the hostility of the *Kerygmata Petrou* and the basic writing against John and his disciples, see O. Cullmann, *Le problème littéraire et historique du roman Pseudo-Clémentin* (EHPR, 23), Paris,

Homilist has retained this representation, the author of the *Recognitions* has preserved the orthodox reputation of John by certain alterations of the original. Thus, John is said to be dead when Dositheus and Simon enter the scene and contend for the leadership of the sect, which is not set off by opposition to the Jesus group[121].

However, it may be asked whether there was a warrant for associating the Samaritan heretics with the Baptist[122]. Christian tradition, which is at least as old as the 4th century, locates John's grave in Sebaste, the capital of Samaria[123]; and the *Gospel of John* says that John went and baptized in "Ainon, near Salim" (iii.23), which is about three miles east of Shechem, the old religious centre in the North. If we can trust that the Baptist had Samaritan connections, we may wonder whether the messianic office which he claimed (or which was claimed for him) was that of the Prophet like Moses, the eschatological figure awaited especially by the Samaritans in the first century C.E., and that this furnished a warrant for associating him with Dositheus and Simon, who were known to have laid claim to the same office. In *Luke* ch. i (*vv*. 5 ff.), which includes pre-Christian legendary material seeing John as the forerunner of God himself and not of the Messiah (see *vv*. 15 f., 76 ff.)[124],

---

1930, pp. 234 ff. The Mandeans have preserved the tradition of an antagonism between Jesus and John, see Rudolph, *Mandäer*, I, pp. 66 ff., especially p. 75.

121 For the alterations of the original by the author of the *Recognitions*, see B. Rehm, "Zur Entstehung der pseudoclementinischen Schriften", *ZNW*, 37, 1938, pp. 135 ff.; G. Strecker, *Das Judenchristentum in den Pseudoklementinen* (TU, LXX), Berlin, 1958, pp. 46, 236 f., 242 f.; cp. Cullmann, p. 73, p. 89, n. 1.

122 A connection between John and Simon is assumed by several scholars; see B.W. Bacon, "New and Old in Jesus' Relation to John", *JBL*, 48, 1929, pp. 40 ff.; E. Lohmeyer, *Das Urchristentum*, I (Johannes der Täufer), Göttingen, 1932, pp. 38 f.; E. Stauffer, "Probleme der Priestertradition", *TLZ*, 81, 1956, pp. 135 ff.; M. Smith, "The Account of Simon Magus in Acts 8", in *H.A. Wolfson Jubilee Volume*, II, Jerusalem, 1965, pp. 735 ff.; P. Pokorný, "Gnosis als Weltreligion und Häresie", *Numen*, 16, 1969, p. 58. E.S. Drower, *The Secret Adam*, Oxford, 1960, pp. 89, 90, and F.H. Borsch, *The Son of Man in Myth and History* (NTL), London, 1967, p. 203 (obviously merely copying Lady Drower), state that also Hippolytus and Eusebius describe Simon as a baptist and the successor of John, but I fail to find any evidence for this. Cyprian (*De rebaptismate* 16), however, seems to say that Simon offered a baptism, but the evidence is too late and isolated to be considered trustworthy. However, it ought to be noted that both Dositheus and Menander, the latter being Simon's successor, had a baptismal rite. The baptism of the Dositheans was performed frequently, while the Christian evidence tells that John's (and Menander's ?) baptism was once and for all. In *Ps.-Clem. Hom.* II.23, however, John is called a Hemerobaptist, and this may be explained from the fact that his followers in the 3rd century practised daily immersions.

123 See J.W. Crowfoot, K.M. Kenyon & E.L. Sukenik, *The Buildings at Samaria* (Samaria-Sebaste, 1), London, 1942, reprinted 1966, pp. 37 ff.; A. Parrot, *Samaria*, London, 1958, pp. 122 ff.

124 See Ph. Vielhauer, "Das Benedictus des Zacharias", *ZTK*, 49, 1952, pp. 259 f., 262 ff.

great importance is attached to John's priestly descent. Moses was of priestly
descent, and the Moses *redivivus* or the eschatological prophet who was
to be like him would also have to be of priestly lineage. Thus, the Teacher of
Righteousness, the Moses-like Prophet of the Qumranians, was of priestly
descent (see 4 Qp *Ps.* 37, ii.15) and appears to have been expected to return
as the priestly Messiah[125].

John baptized in the desert, and it was in fact believed that Moses had
conferred a baptism upon the desert generation (see *I Cor.* x.1 f.). The place
of the Baptist's ministry, *viz.*, the wilderness east of Jordan, is also significant, for this was the last earthly residence of Moses (see *Deut.* xxxiv.1 ff.),
who in fact was believed by some not to have died but to have been translated. The Syriac form of *Ps.-Clem. Rec.* I.54 says that the Baptist's disciples
asserted that their master was not really dead but hidden in concealment,
and this fits the tradition that Moses' grave is unknown and Moses really is
alive all the time[126].

(=*Aufsätze zum Neuen Testament* (TB, 31), Munich, 1965, pp. 32 f., 36 ff.); P.
Winter, "The Main Literary Problem of the Lucan Infancy Story", *ATR*, 40, 1958,
pp. 257 ff., listing previous works on p. 260, n. 6.

125 Although the Teacher is never explicitly identified with the eschatological Prophet
like Moses (see 1 Q S ix.11; 4 Q *test* 1 ff.), he at least "functioned as *a* prophet like
Moses" (Meeks, *Prophet-King*, p. 170). Furthermore, that the Qumranians expected
the return of the Teacher or at least the coming of one who would hold the same
office as the Teacher seems certain. In the expression "the One Teaching the Righteousness at the end of days" (*CD* vi.11), הצדק יורה is synonymous or closely
related to הצדק מורה. Other texts speak of the expectation of a certain "Inter-
preter of the Law" alongside the Davidic Messiah (see *CD* vii.18 ff.; 4 Q *Flor* i.11),
and the Teacher was an expositor of the Law (see *CD* vi.2 ff.). This personage thus
seems to be identical with the priestly Messiah who elsewhere appears in the company of the kingly Messiah (see 1 Q *M* ii.1 ; 1 Q *Sa* ii.11 ff.; 1 Q *S* ix.11, granted that
the plural reading can be maintained).

126 In Christian tradition, John the Baptist is Elijah *redivivus* in the latter's function of
being the forerunner of the Messiah, but both Jesus' disciples – among whom there
apparently were former Baptist disciples (see *John* i.35 ff.) – and the Jews in general do not seem to have associated John with Elijah (see *Matt.* xviii.10 ff.; *Mark*
vi.14 f.; viii.28). On the other hand, if *Luke* i.17 comes from circles which venerated
the Baptist, it would seem that at least some of John's followers at some stage identified him with Elijah in the latter's fundamental rôle of preparing the way of God
himself (see *Mal.* iii.1; iv.5; *Sir.* xlviii.10). Now, there was an old tradition which
described Elijah after a Moses pattern (see *I Kings* ch. xix; *Meg.* 19b; *et al.*; cp.
Mark ix.4; *Rev.* ch. xi), and Elijah *redivivus* and the Prophet like Moses could also
have been associated or even identified by some nonconformist group. Like the
Prophet like Moses, Elijah *redivivus* was held to expound the Law; see the passages
cited by L. Ginzberg, *Eine unbekannte Sekte*, New York, 1922, p. 304, n. 1, who
thought that the Teacher of Righteousness was Elijah, who actually is characterized
as צדק יורה in later sources. Elijah could also be seen as the eschatological high

Whether or not the Baptist had any Samaritan connections and/or claimed (or was claimed) to be the Prophet like Moses, the story of the conflict between the two Samaritan heresiarchs — which belongs to the basic writing, written in Syria-Palestine in the 3rd century[127] — apparently is focused upon the right to be recognized as the Moses-like redeemer. It is not at all improbable that the *Pseudo-Clementines*, which originated in a Jewish-Christian sphere, can have imbibed Samaritan traditions, whereas it would remain incomprehensible why the Christians simply would have invented such a legend[128]. The story of the contest between Simon and Dositheus, occurring in an anti-Simonian context, is not at all anti-Simonian, but anti-Dosithean and pro-Simonian. Although the contest as such obviously is unhistorical, it probably reflects the Simonians' way of describing their master's superiority over Dositheus, who was venerated by other Samaritan sectarians.

As was seen in the previous Chapter, Dositheus claimed or was claimed to be the Prophet like Moses, and the Pseudo-Clementine romance is one of the sources which testify to this claim[129]. Any legend about Dositheus being replaced thus would appear to indicate that he was dispossessed of the office of the Prophet like Moses.

S.J. Isser plausibly has suggested that the staff with which Dositheus tries to bring Simon down is the wonder-working rod of Moses known from *Exodus*[130]. The rod was turned into a snake in order to show the credentials of its owner (see iv.2 f., 17, 20; vii.8 ff.). Moses' raising of his hand holding

---

priest; see J. Jeremias, Art. Ἠλ(ε)ίας, in *TDNT*, II, 1964 and reprints, pp. 932 f.; G. Molin, "Elijahu der Prophet und sein Weiterleben in den Hoffnungen des Judentums und der Christenheit", *Judaica*, 8, 1952, pp. 65 ff.; N. Wieder, "The Doctrine of the Two Messiahs among the Karaites", *JJS*, 6, 1955, pp. 14 ff. In *John* vi.14, the Galileans say that Jesus is "the Prophet coming into the world," and, although they do compare the food supplied by Jesus to the manna given by Moses (see *v.* 31), ἐρχόμενος is a term which was used to describe Elijah (see *Matt.* xi. 14). For the association of Moses and Elijah and the possible background of the Baptist in such a tradition, see T. F. Glasson, *Moses in the Fourth Gospel* (SBT, 40), London, 1963, pp. 27ff.

John vi.15 tells that the Galileans even wanted to make Jesus "king", and it is perhaps noteworthy that the association of the Messiah, Elijah, and the Prophet (like Moses) is also found in the Jews' inquiry about the identity claimed by the Baptist (see i.19 ff.). G. Richter, "Bist du Elias? (John 1,21)", *BZ*, 6, 1962, pp. 79 ff., 238 ff., and 7, 1963, pp. 63 ff., thinks that the emphasis in *John* i.20 f. that the Baptist is not Elijah or the Prophet is rooted in Johannine apologetics against Baptist sectaries. For the association of the concepts of kingship and prophethood in the description of Moses, see Meeks, *Prophet-King*.

127 See Rehm, "Entstehung", p. 157; Strecker, pp. 259 f., 267.
128 Cp. Rudolph, "Simon — Magus oder Gnosticus?", p. 312.
129 See above, p. 48.
130 See *op. cit.*, p. 134.

the rod made the waters of the sea divide so that the Israelites could cross on dry ground, and the second raising of the staff caused the waters to return and engulf the Egyptians chasing them (see xiv.16, 21 ff.). Beating the rock with his staff, Moses made water spring forth (see xvii.5 f.). Finally, standing with the rod in his outstretched arm when the Israelites fought the Amalekites, Moses ensured that Israel would prevail (see xvii.8 ff.).

There is extensive material — both Jewish and Samaritan — concerning the rod of Moses in later sources, and some of it is of immediate relevance to this discussion. The Samaritans believe that the rod was placed in the tabernacle, where it will remain until the tent and its precious contents will be revealed[131], and it is a Samaritan belief that the eschatological saviour will bring the rod. Thus, we read in the *Malef*:

> The rod is preserved in the tabernacle until the Taheb comes. It will be one of the signs which he will bring with him.
>
> (11a)

As has been pointed out in the previous Chapter, the figure of the Taheb is a late accretion to Samaritan eschatology; about the beginning of our era, the Samaritans expected the returning Moses and/or the Prophet like Moses, that is, a new Law-giver or -interpreter[132]. Isser quotes a text from the *Asatir*, a midrashic chronicle-work:

> 'A prince will arise who will write the Law in truth, the rod of miracles being in his hand. There will be light and no darkness.
>
> (xiii.24)

Although the *Asatir* is a Medieval writing, there is no reason to doubt that this tradition existed already in the first century. We have already taken notice of Josephus' report that quite a stir was created among the Samaritans by an enthusiast who promised to recover the sacred contents of the tabernacle. Further, Abu'l Fath relates that the Dosithean sub-sects of the *Qatitay* (or *Qilatay*) and the followers of Shalih went up to Mt. Gerizim waiting for God to reveal the tabernacle[133]

Isser does not note that the staff of Moses was believed to be inscribed with the Name of God, and that this has a bearing upon the Clementine legend. In *Petirath Moshe*, God declares that Moses' staff is an image of "one of the many scepters upon which is engraved the Ineffable Name, one that I employed in the creation of the world."[134] There is, however, no evidence that Dositheus used his staff to attempt an act of creation, the greatest feat to

---

131 See Macdonald, *Theology*, p. 319; cp. J. Bowman, "Early Samaritan Eschatology", *JJS*, 6, 1955, pp. 63 ff.
132 See p. 62, n. 117.
133 See above, pp. 64f.
134 *BH*, I, p. 121.

which the magician aspired; instead, he tried to kill Simon with the staff. The Name of God could also be used for destructive purposes. In *Pesikta Rabbati*, God speaks: " "I am the Lord (YHWH), which even is My Name" (*Is.* xlii.8). Even as I create and destroy worlds, so My Name creates and destroys worlds" (104a). If the Name could destroy entire worlds, it certainly could kill a man. A Jewish legend relates that Moses slew the Egyptian (see *Ex.* ii.11) simply by speaking God's Name (see *Ex. R.* i.29)[135]. A Babylonian rabbi told that he saw a Persian die immediately upon being cursed with the Name of God (see Jer. *Yoma* iii.40d; cp. *Eccl. R.* III.xi.3).

In a long praise of the rod spoken by God in Marqa's midrashic work, we read:

> This [*i.e.*, the rod] will be a wonder to you [*i.e.*, Moses] – no one shall stand (קעם) before you while it is in your hand.
>
> (I.2)

The rod of Moses will bring about the fall, the death, of anyone opposing the one standing and holding it. This is exactly what Dositheus tries to do with his staff. While claiming to be "the Standing One", he strikes Simon with the staff in order to make him fall, that is, die.

In another paragraph of the same book of *Memar Marqa*, God strengthens the heart of Moses when he is about to return to Egypt after his sojourn in Midiam:

> Receive authority from Me and set it in your heart, for all your enemies will fall before you. Do not fear them, for they are in your power. With the rod I gave you, you will subdue them. Who will be able to stand (קעם) before you, when My Great Name is with you? Verily, every foe will fall before you as suddenly as evening falls.
>
> (I.3)

We see the explicit association of the rod and the Name: Moses will subdue his enemies with the rod; the Great Name of God, which is the possession of Moses, will cause every foe to fall, die. It is in reality the Name inscribed upon the rod which effects the downfall, the death, of Moses' enemies.

It is significant to note that the struggle between Dositheus and Simon is put into the form of a contest of magic. The most potent means of magic was the Divine Name, which the Samaritans believed was the possession of Moses, the greatest of all magicians; and the pro-Simonian legend incorporated into the *Pseudo-Clementines* evidently mocks the Dositheans' belief that their hero was carrying the wonder-working rod of Moses, which had the Name inscribed upon it. According to the legend, Simon is the greater magician,

---

135 Clement of Alexandria says that "those being initiated" assert that Moses killed the Egyptian μόνῳ λόγῳ (*Strom.* I.xxiii.154). Does this presuppose the tradition that Jesus, the Logos, was the Name of God?

enabling Dositheus' stick to pass through his body as if it were smoke. It would seem that the legend conceives of Simon as the true Moses-like figure.

However, the legend does not represent Dositheus and Simon as rivalling over the right to the title of the Prophet like Moses, but as contending for the title "the Standing One". As was pointed out in the previous Chapter, this is not to be explained as a philosophical concept[136]. In Philo's philosophy, for instance, God is named ὁ ἑστώς because he is immutable and unchangeable; and the true philosopher who approaches him also must be a "Standing One", that is, keeping his mind under control and being unaffected by the changing conditions of the material world. Thus, Philo can describe Abraham and Moses as prototypes of the wise who "stands" before God (see *De post. Caini* 27 ff.)[137].

In Samaritanism, however, the participle קעים is employed in a different sense, and it is here that we find the pattern for the use of the title "the Standing One" in the *Pseudo-Clementines*. Already A. Ritschl showed good intuition when he took Simon to be a pseudo-Messiah and explained his title ὁ ἑστώς in the light of the idea of "the prophet ὃν ἀναστήσει κύριος" in *Deut.* xviii.15, 18[138]. In the Clementine romance, it actually is said that Simon "intimates that he is the Messiah by calling himself the Standing One" (*Hom.* II.22; cp. *Rec.* II.7). That Simon's title "the Standing One" was a Samaritan Messianic title has been repeated by Th. Zahn and G. Quispel[139]. G. Kretschmar, however, has criticized Quispel on this account and maintained that Simon applied an appellation of God to himself, since it has been known for a long time that God is designated as "the Standing One" in Samaritan texts[140]. Thus, for instance, Marqa in a hymn says:

---

136 See pp. 56 ff.

137 Cp. below, p. 140.

138 See *Die Entstehung der altkatholischen Kirche*, 2nd ed., Bonn, 1857, p. 228, n. 1 (continued on the next page).

139 See Zahn, *Die Apostelgeschichte*, I (KNT, V), 2nd ed., Leipzig, 1919, pp. 308 f.; Quispel, *Gnosis als Weltreligion*, Zürich, 1951, p. 56.

140 See "Zur religionsgeschichtlichen Einordnung der Gnosis", *ET*, 13, 1953, p. 359, n. 18 (= *GG*, p. 433, n. 18). Cp. C. Colpe, Art. ὁ υἱὸς τοῦ ἀνθρώπου, in *TDNT*, VIII, 1972 and reprints, pp. 462 f. Kretschmar and Colpe cite Heidenheim, *Liturgie*, p. XXXVII. Kippenberg, *Garizim*, p. 347, n. 1 (continued on pp. 348 f.), even tries to derive the triadically developed concept of the divine "standing" in the *Megale Apophasis* (ὁ ἑστώς – στάς – στησόμενος) from the Samaritan realm. K. Rudolph says that Simon's title derives from the "Samaritan-Jewish tradition" (*Die Gnosis*, Göttingen, 1978, p. 316), where the term was a "circumlocution for the existence of man as determined by God" (*ibid.*, p. 314). It is true that קעימין is used about men in a couple of places in *Memar Marqa*, but only with the meaning that they are living beings and not as an indication of their potential or realized state of perfection, as is the case with the divine "standing" in the *Megale Apophasis*, which teaches that the divine power is found in men as the one who "stood below in the chaos of waters

He [*i.e.,* God] is standing (קָעִים) for ever; He exists unto eternity. Standing Ones (קָעִימִין) [*i.e.*, angels] and mortals [literally, "dead"] are under His rule.

(Cowley, 27.18)

In contrast to men, God and his angels are imperishable; this is what is expressed by the participle קָעִים. It is a long time since A.E. Cowley noted in his glossary of Samaritan Aramaic: "ptcp. קָעִים (קָעוּם) *living* (God, angels)"[141]. This is exactly the same sense which the term ὁ ἑστώς carries in the *Pseudo-Clementines*. After it has been stated that Simon intimated that he was the Messiah by calling himself "the Standing One", it is said:

He employs this title to indicate that he shall always stand, and that there is no cause of corruption which can make his body fall.

(*Hom.* II.22)

Thus, when Simon had been vindicated as "the Standing One", Dositheus, who had failed in this respect, fell down and died. We see that the term "the Standing One" in the *Clementina* means "the Eternal One", "the Living One", and must be explained against the background of the Samaritan evidence. The epithet as used in Hellenistic philosophy has another connotation than in the *Pseudo-Clementines*.

It is interesting to note that the conception of God's "standing" as found in Samaritan texts recurs in the *Three Steles of Seth* from Codex VII of the Nag Hammadi library, which is put under the protection of the name of Dositheus and thus apparently reflects some relationship between the Samaritan heresiarch and later Gnosticism. The work opens with the following words:

The revelation of Dositheus about the three steles of Seth, the father of the living and untrembling race which he [*i.e.*, Dositheus] saw and understood.

(119.10 f.)

"Dositheus" communicates a "stele", a hymn to God, in which God is characterized as "the Standing One":

Great is the good Self-Begotten who stood, the God who was the first to stand.

(119.15 ff.)

What is meant by this "standing" of God is explained in an address to God a few lines above in the same hymn:

You have stood, being unceasing (ⲁⲧⲱⲭⲛ̄).

(119.4)

[*i.e.*, the material world], begotten in the image [cp. *Gen.* i.26]," but "shall stand on high [again] with the infinite Power when his image is fully formed" (Hipp., VI. xvii.1).

141 *Op. cit.*, p. lxviii, col. b. This is also the meaning of קִים in Judaism; see above, p. 58 with n. 103.

Thus, we see that the conception of God's "standing" is employed by the author of the Gnostic writing in the same way as it is used in Samaritan texts: it denotes the everlastingness of God. It is tempting to conjecture that the *Three Steles of Seth* has a Samaritan background and that the name "Dositheus" indicates the well-known Samaritan heresiarch.

Regardless of whether or not this is true, it would be bizarre if Simon and Dositheus actually vied over the right to be looked upon as God Almighty. R.M. Grant, noting that Dositheus, Simon's rival, claimed to be the Prophet like Moses, wonders whether Simon, too, is to be understood as the Moses-like prophet[142], and it is a fact that the term קעים could be used also with reference to Moses. In *Ex.* xxxiii.21, God says to Moses:

> Here is a place by Me – stand on the rock.

This text is of interest for the present discussion, for the Samaritan Targum reads ותתקומם, that is, uses a form of the verb קום, in this place. But Grant cites a text which is more important. Right after God has promised Moses that he some time in the future will "raise up", קום, a prophet like Moses, he says:

> And, as for you, stand here by Me; and I shall teach you all the commandments, statutes, and laws which you shall teach them.
>
> (*Deut.* v.31)

The Samaritan Targum again uses the verb קום, reading ואתה הכה [...] קום עמי[143]. This text is quoted by Marqa in a long praise of Moses:

> No prophet like Moses has arisen (קום) or will ever arise (יקום). He was exalted above the whole human race and progressed until he joined with the angels, as was said of him: "And I will join you" (Targ. *Ex.* xxv.22). Where is there anyone like Moses who trod the fire? Where is there anyone like Moses to whom his Lord said: "Stand by Me now"? Where is there a Prophet like Moses, whom God addressed mouth to mouth? Where is there a prophet like Moses, who fasted forty days and forty nights, neither eating nor drinking? And he descended carrying two stone tablets inscribed by the finger of God.
>
> (*Memar Marqa* IV.12)

H.G. Kippenberg asserts that Marqa's denial of the possibility of the appearance of a prophet like Moses and his rhetorical questions are aimed at the Dositheans, who claimed that their hero was the Prophet like Moses. It is noteworthy that *Memar Marqa* and the *Defter* do not attach any "messianic" significance whatsoever to *Deut.* xviii.15, 18, while the Targum underlines that this prophecy was fulfilled by Joshua and that no prophet like Moses

---

142 See *Gnosticism and Early Christianity*, New York, 1959, pp. 91 f.

143 As was shown above, pp. 61 f., the Samaritans combine the prophecy of the advent of the Prophet like Moses in *Deut.* xviii.18-22 and the text of *Deut.* v.28-31, and add this unification to the decalogue.

would arise after his time[144]. S.J. Isser, however, has modified Kippenberg's affirmation that the material emphasizing the uniqueness of Moses must be understood as anti-Dosithean. "Dosithean traditions were based on the model of Moses as the eschatological Prophet", and "much of the Samaritan material which emphasizes Moses must have been prior to the Dosithean traditions."[145] As regards the idea of Moses' "standing" by God, Isser's assertion appears to be right. The claiming of the title of "the Standing One" by Dositheus and Simon obviously is based upon this tradition.

Grant and Kippenberg take the title "the Standing One" to imply that the Prophet like Moses is standing by God and receiving the divine revelation[146], while Isser, basing himself upon a text from *Memar Marqa* V.2 where Moses is "standing" before God pleading for the Israelites, says that "Moses' standing designates him as the supplicator *par excellence*."[147] Both these explanations miss that aspect of Moses' "standing" which agrees with the use of the word as found both elsewhere in the Samaritan literature and in the *Clementina*: Moses' ascension of Mt. Sinai and "standing" by God involve the idea of an apotheosis. The text just quoted says that Moses, when ascending to God in order to "stand" by him and receive the Law, "was exalted above the whole human race and progressed until he joined with the angels." Moses on Mt. Sinai, that is, in heaven, was assimilated to the angels, who were described as "Standing Ones". Another text from *Memar Marqa* reads:

> He received with his hand the autograph of God, and it was a treasure-store of all knowledge. His body mingled with the angels above; and he dwelt with them, being worthy to do so.
>
> (VI.3)

Moses not only was assimilated to the angels; it is stated that he actually attained angelic nature or mode of being:

> When he went up to Him and the cloud covered him for six days, his body become holy; and his holiness increased [thereby]. He ascended from human status (מיתוביח) to the status of the angels.
>
> (*Ibid*. V.3)

It is obviously this angelic status of Moses which is indicated when Marqa explicitly characterizes the prophet as a "Standing One":

> Mighty is the great prophet, who clad himself in the Name of the Godhead and

---

144 See *Garizim*, pp. 313 ff.
145 *Op. cit.*, p. 137.
146 See Grant, *loc. cit.*; Kippenberg, *Garizim*, p. 319, n. 72 (without citing Grant). But see also Kippenberg, *ibid.*, p. 131, n. 199, for the contemplation of an interpretation which is similar to the one I am to give. Cp. also pp. 348 f., n. 136, continued from p. 347.
147 *Op. cit.*, p. 139.

received the five books. And he was standing (קָעֵם) between the two assemblies, between the Standing Ones (קְעִימִין) and the mortals.

(Cowley, 54.31 f.)

When Moses ascended to heaven in order to receive the Law, he was "vested with" the Divine Name, which signifies the nature of the divine, and made into a divine or angelic being. When the Torah was given, "the assembly of the Standing Ones above and the assembly of the mortal ones below were gathered" (*ibid.*, 53.27 f.), and Moses was "standing" as an intermediary between the angels and the people. In *Memar Marqa*, it is said that Moses "dwelt among the Standing Ones" (IV.6). This position of Moses no doubt images him as the chief among the angels, God's messengers[148]. The hymn goes on to describe Moses as "the Elohim who is from mankind" (55.5). The divine names "Standing One" and "Elohim" were shared by the angels[149]; and, since Moses is given the self-same names, he obviously is elevated to the position of an angelic being, even the principal angel of God. The title of the Standing One as used in the Pseudo-Clementine account of Simon thus fits a Moses pattern.

It also may be queried if Simon's assertion Ἐγώ εἰμι when being asked whether he is "the Standing One" hints at the fact that he is the true Prophet like Moses and thus the possessor of the Name of God, for the Tetragrammaton is explained as meaning אהיה, "I am", already in *Ex.* iii.13 f. When God

---

148 The Samaritan conception of Moses "standing" by God in heaven may have had influence upon Stephen's vision of "the Son of Man standing (ἑστῶτα) at the right hand of God" in heaven (*Acts* vii.56). Elsewhere, the Son of Man is *sitting* at the right hand of God (see *Mark* xiv.62; Euseb., *Hist. eccl.* II.xxiii.13; cp. *Ps.* cx. 1). O. Bauernfeind, *Die Apostelgeschichte* (THNT, V), Leipzig, 1939, p. 120, says that the peculiar description of the Son of Man *standing* at the right side of God vouches for the authenticity of the tradition. Colpe offers arguments to the effect "that Luke found v. 56 in the tradition and introduced it in his own words in v. 55" (Art. ὁ υἱὸς τοῦ ἀνθρώπου, p. 462). Some scholars see characteristically Samaritan elements in Stephen's speech, and Abu'l Fatḥ (Vilmar, p. 159) actually says that Stephen was a Samaritan. We should note in this connection that Stephen quotes *Deut.* xviii.15 and obviously envisages Jesus as the Prophet like Moses. Stephen's assertion that Jesus would come and (destroy the Jerusalem temple and) change the customs (ἔθη) which derived from Moses (see vi.13 f.) agrees with the evidence about the eschatological Prophet like Moses, who was expected to introduce the Law in final form.

In the *Ascension of Isaiah*, the visionary sees "the Lord and the second angel, and they were standing" (ix.35). Christ, "the Lord", apparently is the *first* angel. The visionary describes him thus: "And I saw One Standing whose glory surpassed all" (*v.* 27). This designation does not simply mean that Christ, being an angel, (cannot or is not allowed to sit, and) stands to minister before God, for Christ is said to have "sat down on the right hand of that Great Glory [...]" (xi.32).

149 For "Elohim" as a designation of the angels in Samaritanism, see above, p. 93 with n. 45.

revealed his Name to Moses, he interpreted it as meaning אהיה אשר אהיה,
"I am who I am", and bid Moses to go to the Israelites and say "I am (אהיה)
sent me to you." The LXX supplies the predicate ὁ ὤν for Ἐγώ εἰμι at this
place, thus stressing the eternal self-existence of God. We also have seen
above in this Chapter that the Jewish Targums take the divine name
אהיה אשר אהיה to signify God's eternal existence with the world. In
Samaritan texts, אהיה frequently occurs as a divine name in this sense. Thus,
for instance, Marqa says:

> He [*i.e.*, God] is the Ancient One who has no beginning. He is the One who existed
> above the abyss of the primeval silence. He it is who created when He willed. He is I
> AM: He is the One who is after the world; and just as He was in the first, so He will
> be in the last.
>
> (*Memar Marqa* IV.4)

> He is eternal in His oneness, I AM in divinity, everlasting in awesomeness.
>
> (*Ibid.* IV.5)

The Samaritans took the divine name אהיה, "I am", from *Ex.* iii.14 to
signify God's everlastingness. In accordance with this understanding of the
phrase interpreting the Tetragrammaton, the Arabic rendering of YHWH is
"Eternal"[150]. Since "I am" is a divine name and carries exactly the same
meaning as "the Standing One" in Samaritanism, one might wonder whether
Simon's assertion of being the Standing One by pronouncing "I am" implies
that he was the possessor of the Name of God.

It commonly is accepted that Jesus in some passages in the *Gospel of John*
employs the phrase ἐγώ εἰμι in order to indicate that he is the possessor of
the Name of God; this would seem certain at least in the cases where the
phrase is used in an absolute sense (*viz.*, in viii.24, 28, 58; xiii.19), for "I am"
without a predicate is meaningless in Greek[151]. It is true that a predicate of

---

150 See Macdonald, *Theology*, pp. 71 f., 95 f.
151 Most scholars think that *John* alludes to the use of ἐγώ εἰμι in *Deutero-Isaiah*
(xli.4; xliii.10, 13; xlvi.4; xlviii.12), where the phrase renders אני הוא, "I am He," a
divine self-style which means "I am (for ever) the same" and apparently refers to the
interpretation of the Tetragrammaton in *Ex.* iii.14 ff.; see especially J.H. Bernard,
The Gospel according to St. John (ICC), I, Edinburgh, 1928, reprinted 1962, pp.
cxx f.; II, Edinburgh, 1928, reprinted 1963, pp. 300 f., 303, 322, 468; H. Zimmermann, "Das absolute *'Egō eimi'* als die neutestamentliche Offenbarungsformel",
BZ, 4, 1960, pp. 54ff., 266ff.; R.E. Brown, *The Gospel according to John* (AB,
29), New York, 1966, pp. 536f.; C.K. Barrett, *The Gospel according to St. John*,
2nd ed., London, 1978, p. 342. It even seems that the LXX considers אני הוא to
be a divine name in some passages (see *Is.* xliii.25; li.6, 12). Moreover, it seems to be
taken as an equivalent of the Tetragrammaton, for *Is.* xlv. 18 renders "I am YHWH"
by ἐγώ εἰμι, and the next verse translates the same expression by ἐγώ εἰμι ἐγώ
εἰμι κύριος. From the 2nd century C.E., there is some rabbinic evidence to the
effect that אני הוא was seen as a divine name. G. Klein, *Der älteste christliche*

'Εγώ εἰμι in the Simonian legend incorporated into the *Pseudo-Clementines* is supplied by Dositheus' question, "Are you the Standing One?," but a deeper meaning nevertheless may be present. There are some borderline cases of 'Εγώ εἰμι in the Fourth Gospel where we cannot be sure whether a divine name is meant even though a predicate can be supplied from the context. R.A. Brown thinks that one such case is vi.20, where Jesus speaks to the disciples being frightened when they see him walking towards them on the water: "'Εγώ εἰμι, be not afraid!" (cp. *Matt.* xiv.27; *Mark* vi.50). Perhaps the meaning here is simply: "It is I, that is, someone you know, and not a ghost." But the statement 'Εγώ εἰμι on the lips of Jesus in this situation makes us think of the awful theophanies in the Old Testament, where God presents himself to men with a directive not to fear (see, *e.g.*, *Gen.* xxvi.24). Thus, *John* may be playing on both the ordinary and sacral use of "I am" here[152].

Katechismus, Berlin, 1909, pp. 44 ff., thought that *John* also knew the rabbinic אני והוא, "I and he", a divine name denoting the intimate association of God with his people. See now C.H. Dodd, *The Interpretation of the Fourth Gospel*, Cambridge, 1953 and reprints, pp. 94 ff.; E. Stauffer, *Jesus, Gestalt und Geschichte*, Bern, 1957, pp. 130 ff. While *Deutero-Isaiah* (especially xliii.10) furnishes the background for viii.24, 28 and xiii.19, it is probably the אהיה (אהיה אשר) of *Ex.* iii.14 which is indicated in viii.58; see K. Zickendraht, "ΕΓΩ ΕΙΜΙ", *TSK*, 94, 1922, p. 163; H. Odeberg, *The Fourth Gospel*, Uppsala, 1929, reprinted Amsterdam, 1968, pp. 309 f.; R. Schnackenburg, *Das Johannesevangelium* (HTKNT, IV), II, Freiburg – Basel – Vienna, 1971, pp. 64 f., 300 f.

Jesus' assertion πρὶν 'Αβραὰμ γενέσθαι ἐγώ εἰμι (*John* viii.58) causes the Jews to take up stones and throw at him. This is only logical, for stoning was the penalty for blasphemy, which required the mention of God's Name (see *Lev.* xxiv.16; *Sanh.* vii.5). In x.31 ff., the Jews again try to stone Jesus; they say that they do it "for blasphemy, because you, a man, make yourself God" (*v.* 33). This refers to Jesus' saying in *v.* 30, "I and the Father are one." Jesus in *John* apparently expresses his unity with God through the claim to possess the Divine Name. That Jesus has been *given* the Name is taught in xvii.11 f. (cp. *v.* 6), and a collocation of xii.23 and 28 would seem to evidence that the Son even *is* the Name of God; see Odeberg, p. 334; Grether, p. 182; Dodd, p. 95.

152 See *op. cit.* (AB, 29), pp. 254 f., 533 f. Brown in commenting upon the ἐγώ εἰμι in iv.26 says that it is "not impossible that this use is intended in the style of divinity" (*ibid.*, p. 172). Already Bernard said: "The phrase ἐγω εἰμι αὐτὸς ὁ λαλῶν is placed in the mouth of Yahweh at Isa. 52[6], and it may be that Jn here intends ἐγώ εἰμι to indicate the style of Deity, as at other points" (*John*, I, p. 291). J. Marsh is rather confident: "The Greek can be literally rendered thus: 'I am he; the one who is speaking to thee.' 'I am'. This phrase is of the highest importance in the fourth gospel, and indeed throughout the Bible. It is the name of Yahweh himself (Exod. 3[14]) ..." (*The Gospel of John* (PNTC), Harmondsworth, 1968 and reprints, p. 219).

If this is the right interpretation, it is perhaps not insignificant that the statement is an assertion to be the deliverer awaited by the Samaritans. Jesus in claiming the Divine Name does not affirm to be God but to be the redeemer figure awaited by the Samaritan woman. The name of the Messiah on the lips of the Samaritan woman has

But xviii.4 ff. is the Johannine pericope being of most relevance to the discussion about the Simonian legend in the *Pseudo-Clementines*. When Judas and the men of the chief priests and the Pharisees arrive in order to arrest Jesus, he asks them: "Whom do you seek?" The narrative continues: "They answered him: "Jesus of Nazareth". Jesus said to them: "Ἐγώ εἰμι." ... As soon as he had said Ἐγώ εἰμι, they stepped backwards and fell to the ground" (*vv.* 5 f.). True, the pronoun "he (of whom you are speaking)" may be supplied from the context, but the reaction to the answer Ἐγώ εἰμι suggests that a deeper meaning must be present[153]. Jews did not fall to the ground for a mere man. The mention of the Divine Name, however, made people drop. The Jewish apologist Artapanus, who lived about 100 B.C.E., relates that Pharaoh fell as if dead when he heard Moses uttered the Name of God (quoted by Euseb., *Praep. evang.* IX.xxvii.25 f.). When the high priest spoke the Name in the special ritual of the Day of Atonement, the priests standing near him fell on their faces (see *Qidd.* 71a; Jer. *Yoma* iii.40d, at the end; *Eccl. R.* III.xi.3). It seems plausible that *John* xviii.5 f. alludes to Jesus speaking the Name of God and the Jews falling to the ground when hearing it.

In a like vein, Dositheus, hearing the words "I am" from the mouth of Simon and becoming convinced that he was the Moses-like redeemer, the Standing One, fell down and worshipped. Simon obviously possessed the Name of God, which was the prerogative of Moses making him a partaker in the eternal life of the divine. Thus, while Simon persisted, Dositheus one day fell down never to rise again.

The Synoptics would seem to offer evidence that first century rivals of Jesus designated themselves with the Name of God. In his discourse on what will come to pass in the last days, Jesus says: "Many will come in my name, saying: "I am" " (*Mark* xiii.6; *Luke* xxi.8). On the ground of the phrase "in

---

no sense, for the Samaritans of the first century did not call the eschatological redeemer by that name but expected the Moses *redivivus* or the Prophet like Moses. It should be noted that the pericope seems to presuppose knowledge of the Samaritan decalogue, where emphasis on Mt. Gerizim as the true place of worship and the expectation of the Prophet like Moses are additions made to the tenth commandment, for the dialogue between Jesus and the woman passes from the subject of Mt. Gerizim *versus* Sion to that of the coming of the saviour; see J. Bowman, "Samaritan Studies", *BJRL*, 40, 1958, pp. 299 f., 310 f. The teaching function ascribed to the redeemer ("he will tell us all things") by the Samaritan woman also fits the office of the Prophet like Moses. The woman's admitting that Jesus is "a prophet" (*v.* 19) must mean that she acknowledges him as the Prophet like Moses, for the Samaritans did not reckon with the appearance of any other kind of prophet. As we have seen, Moses was the possessor of the Divine Name, and the eschatological prophet who was going to be like him would also be the owner of the Name.

153 For the interpretation, I am indebted to S. Bartina, " 'Yo soy Yahweh' – Nota exegética a Jn. 18.4-8", in *SBE*, 18, 1959, p. 393.

my name", some commentators think that the people who are aimed at are men within the Church claiming to be Jesus incarnated anew[154]. That the meaning is that the false teachers assert that Jesus had returned but was concealed for the time being and/or that the *parousia* was imminent cannot be the purport[155], for the phrase "I am" must be the *speaker's* affirmation.

Matthew (xxiv.5) adds "the Messiah", and many commentators think that "in my name" alludes to the Messiah title, and that the people in question were non-Christian Messiah-pretenders arrogating to themselves Jesus' rightful title and authority[156]. Whether the false prophets appeared within or outside the Christian community, it is possibly not insignificant that the context does not clearly suggest a predicate of Ἐγώ εἰμι. Furthermore, the juxtaposition of "my name" and "I am" would seem to imply some special significance. J. Bernard compared the absolute use of the "I am" statement to the same use of ἐγώ εἰμι in the *Gospel of John* and suggested that the people in question arose appropriating the Name of God[157]. If this is right, we would be justified in including Simon Magus among them, for Simon was said to possess and even embody the Name of God. The author of *Mark* would have perfect opportunity to have knowledge of the Samaritan heresiarch.

It may be denied or doubted that prophets such as Simon are alluded to on the ground that the phrase "in my name" then would be used in a very strained way. This objection can be met by citing the doctrine of the Simonians that their hero —

> taught that he himself was the one who had appeared to the Jews as the Son, descended in Samaria as Father, and come to the other nations as the Holy Spirit.
>
> (Iren., I.xxiii.1)

Moreover, Irenaeus goes on to report that the Simonians taught that

---

154 See, of late, R. Pesch, *Das Markusevangelium* (HTKNT, II), II, Freiburg-Basel-Vienna, 1977, p. 279.

155 This is the thesis of W. Manson, "The ΕΓΩ EIMI of the Messianic Presence in the New Testament", *JTS*, 48, 1947, p. 139.

156 For this passage, see the survey of interpretations by V. Howard, *Das Ego Jesu in den synoptischen Evangelien* (MTS, 14), Marburg, 1975, pp. 117 ff.

157 See *John*, I, pp. cxx f. See further the exegetes referred to by Howard, p. 118, n. 1, under "ἐγώ εἰμι b". See also W. Lane, *The Gospel according to Mark* (NIC), Grand Rapids, 1974, p. 457. Some of the commentators listed by Howard, *loc. cit.*, under "ἐγώ εἰμι a", as thinking that "the Messiah" has to be supplied, consider that this claim to messiahship included pretensions about divine authority on the basis of *Ex.* iii.14 and certain passages from *Deutero-Isaiah*; see, *e.g.*, C.E.B. Cranfield, *The Gospel according to Saint Mark* (CGTC), 3rd ed., Cambridge, 1966, p. 395. W. Grundmann, *Das Evangelium nach Markus* (THNT), 2nd ed., Berlin, 1977, p. 353, also thinks that the Divine Name is alluded to, but — as opposed to the exegetes cited in this note — he asserts that the people who claimed it appeared within the Christian community and contended to be manifestations of Jesus.

Simon came in the guise of a man, although he was not a real man, and that "he was thought to have suffered in Judea, although he did not suffer" (I.xxiii. 3). These two examples are the only recognitions of Christianity attributed to Simon by Irenaeus, and it is clear that they are not primary in Simonian Gnosticism. While the representation of Simon as a docetic Christ may be due to Irenaeus' attempt to represent Simonianism after the model of Basilidean Gnosticism[158], the proclamation that Simon was revealing himself as the Trinitarian God in a modalist fashion is totally unparallelled in Gnosticism and a palpable instance of how the Simonians wanted to make pointed that their religion superseded Christianity[159]. Since the Simonians claimed that Simon previously had been incarnated as Jesus, it is only logical that the Christians would refer to his allegedly new and greater manifestation as an imposition "in the name of" Jesus.

The Ascension of the Prophet like Moses

According to the Dositheans, Dositheus — whom they held to be the Prophet like Moses — would have been the owner of the Name of God and the Standing One, and thus the possessor of immortality. Origen in fact gives the following report:

From the Samaritans, one Dositheus arose and asserted that he was the prophesied

---

158 Cerfaux, "La gnose simonienne", pp. 496 ff. (= *Recueil*, I, pp. 191 ff.), found a "plagiarism" of Basilidean Gnosticism in the account of Simonianism in Iren., I.xxiii. 3 f. See now G. Lüdemann, *Untersuchungen zur simonianischen Gnosis* (GTA, 1), Göttingen, 1975, pp. 81 ff.

159 This statement is not made in a context modelled upon any Gnostic system, but in a section where Irenaeus jumbles together material from different sources; see Lüdemann, *Untersuchungen*, pp. 83 f. with n. 13 on pp. 138 f. Beyschlag, pp. 164 ff., notes that the trinitarian formula Son-Father-Spirit occurs in Christian sources and that it even can be used in a modalist fashion as indicating the same person; but, even if we have to do with an original Christian formula, the use of this configuration to explain Simon's superiority over Jesus must be the work of the Simonians and not the invention of Irenaeus. In Christian sources, it is nowhere spoken of a successive revelation of the Son, the Father, and the Spirit. The *earthly appearance* of the Father *after* that of the Son cannot be a Christian idea.

Quispel, *Gnosis*, p. 57, thinks that the Simonian trinitarianism is described falsely, but it actually makes good sense. Quispel thinks that Cyril of Jerusalem (*Cat.* VI.14) gives the correct Simonian trinitarianism when saying that Simon appeared on Mt. Sinai as the Father and later in Judea as the Son, Jesus; but this obviously is a later conformation to orthodox Christian teaching. That Simon appeared in Samaria as the Father after he had appeared in Judea as the Son must have been the original doctrine of the Samaritan Gnostics; cp. Lüdemann, p. 138, n. 13 (continued on the next page). Quispel connects the idea of Simon as the trinitarian God with the conception of the ἐστώς - στάς - στησόμενος in the *Megale Apophasis,* but it is only the first term of this formula which denotes an *earthly appearance* of the divine principle.

> Messiah. There are Dositheans to this day who originate from him; they both preserve
> books by Dositheus and certain myths about him to the effect that he did not taste
> death, but still is alive somewhere.

(Comm. in Joh. XIII.27, ad iv.25)

That Dositheus claimed to be the Messiah is an error; the Samaritans did
not adopt this designation of the saviour before the Middle Ages, and conceived of the coming redeemer after a Moses pattern. Since Dositheus was a
Moses-like figure, he composed books, which are said to have contained
alterations of the text of the Pentateuch. Being a kind of a new Moses, he
possessed the authority to do so; Moses wrote the first Law, while the eschatological Prophet like Moses would have to bring the new Law.

Furthermore, Origen tells that the Dositheans believed that their hero did
not die but still was alive. This tradition too appears to have been based upon
a Moses pattern. It is true that the Bible tells that Moses died, but his death
and burial in the cave at Mt. Nebo are cloaked in mystery: God himself
buried him, and it is said that "to this day, no one knows his grave" (*Deut.*
xxxiv.6). Marqa in his midrashic work is somewhat ambiguous: on the one
hand, he sticks to the Biblical view that Moses died like all men; on the other,
he pictures Moses' ascent of Mt. Nebo as an assumption closely analogous to
the depiction of Moses' ascent to the summit of Mt. Sinai, that is, heaven,
where Moses was "standing" by God and attained angelhood, immortality[160].
I give two excerpts from the section of *Memar Marqa* which deals with Moses'
end:

> The great prophet Moses ascended Mt. Nebo with great majesty, crowned with light;
> and all the hosts of the heavenly angels gathered to meet him.

(V.3)

> How great the hour at which the great prophet Moses stood on the top of Mt. Nebo,
> and all the heavenly angels were doing him honour there [...]. Great was the joy
> which abode in Moses' heart when he saw the angels standing around him, on his
> right and on his left, before him and behind him. The Great Glory took him by the
> right hand, embracing him and walking before him.

(*Ibid.*)

That Moses did not die but was translated to heaven is an idea found in
Jewish sources. In version A of *Aboth de R. Nathan*, a tractate whose composition was not made much later than in the 3rd or 4th century C.E., God
is said to have spoken the following to Moses:

---

160 On the analogy between the two ascents, see Macdonald, *Theology*, pp. 219 ff.;
Meeks, p. 245. The passage from *Memar Marqa* IV.12 quoted by Meeks, p. 244,
as being a description of Moses' final ascension actually refers to the ascent of Mt.
Sinai. Meeks apparently has been misled by the translation of Macdonald, *Memar
Marqah*, II, p. 186, who says that the Samaritan Targum to *Deut.* xxxii.50 is cited,
whereas Marqa actually quotes Targum *Ex.* xxv.22. Cp. Kippenberg, *Garizim*, p. 319,
n. 67. See above, p. 122, for the quotation of the passage.

"Moses, you have had enough of this world, for – lo! – the world to come awaits you. For your place has been ready since the six days of Creation." As it is said: "And the Lord said: "Behold a place by Me: you shall stand on the rock" " (*Ex.* xxxiii.21).

(ch. 12)

The text goes on to say that God took the soul of Moses and put it in safekeeping under the Throne of Glory. Thus, the text speaks only of the immortality of Moses' soul, but this has all the appearance of being a later conception. It is important to note that God's words to Moses right before the latter dies are interpreted by a citation of *Ex.* xxxiii.21, where Moses is bid by God to "stand" by him on Mt. Sinai, for we have seen that the Samaritans interpreted the "standing" of Moses on Mt. Sinai as a transformation into an angelic being taking place in heaven.

In version B of *Aboth de R. Nathan,* we actually read:

Moses our teacher was like a man, but thenceforth he is not, but is like the ministering angels.[161]

That the angels are ministering to God in heaven is a well-known idea, and the teaching of *Aboth de R. Nathan* is that Moses upon dying became like them. This is found also in an allegedly tannaitic source cited in *Midrash ha-Gadol*:

Three men ascended to heaven to perform service: they are Enoch, Moses, and Elijah.

(I.123)

The Bible tells explicitly that Enoch and Elijah did not die, but were taken up to heaven by God; and later tradition said that Moses, too, did not die, but was translated. Enoch, Moses, and Elijah became like the ministering angels.

A text in *Yalqut Shimoni* which preserves a statement from the older *Yelammedenu* commentary reads that God said to Moses:

All creatures descend to Sheol, as it is said: "All who descend to silence" (*Ps.* cxv.17), but you are to ascend, as it is said: "Go up to this mountain of Abarim" (*Num.* xxvii.12).

(III.958)

On Abarim, a hilly region in which Mt. Nebo, the scene of Moses' death, was located, Moses was shown the land which God gave to Israel. The midrash interprets this ascent by Moses at the end of his life as being opposite to ordinary men's descent to the realm of the dead.

There is yet another rabbinic passage bearing witness to the belief that Moses did not die; this is a baraita found in several sources:

Others declare that Moses never died. It is written here: "So Moses died there"

---

161 Schechter, p. 157.

(*Deut.* xxxiv.5). But, elsewhere, it is written: "And he was there with the Lord" (*Ex.* xxxiv.28). As in the latter passage it means standing and serving, so also in the former it means standing and serving.

(*Sifre Deut.* 357, *ad* xxxiv.5; *Sota* 13b; *et al.*)

As in version A of *Aboth de R. Nathan*, Moses' ascension at the end of his earthly life is interpreted by a passage relating to his ascension of Mt. Sinai. Apparently, the ascension of Mt. Sinai was seen as a model and rehearsal of the final ascension, and the guardians of this tradition tried to find clues to their view in the Biblical text. Here, the connection is made through the word שם, "there", which is common to *Ex.* xxxiv.28, where it is referring to Mt. Sinai, and *Deut.* xxxiv.5, where it is referring to Mt. Nebo. The word at the first place is taken to mean "standing and serving", an interpretation which tallies with the Samaritan idea that Moses became like the angels when being with God on Mt. Sinai; and "there" in *Deut.* xxxiv.5 then is explained in the light of this understanding of the word in *Ex.* xxxiv.28. Thus, the text is at one with version B of *Aboth de R. Nathan* and *Midrash ha-Gadol* in teaching that Moses became like the ministering angels upon leaving this world.

This tradition is quite old. Philo compares the "protoprophet" Moses to Enoch and Elijah, saying that "the end of worthy and holy men is not death but translation (μετάθεσις, μεταβολή) and approaching (τὸ ἐγγίζειν) another place" (*Quaest. in Gen.* I.86). To Philo, however, this is not a bodily rapture:

> Afterwards, the time came when he had to make his pilgrimage from earth to heaven, and leave this mortal life to be made immortal (ἀπαθανατίζεσθαι), summoned thither by the Father who resolved his twofold nature of soul and body into a single unity, transforming his whole being into *nous*, pure as sunlight.

(*De vita Mos.* II.288)

The text goes on to tell that "when he already was being exalted and stood at the very barrier, ready at the signal to direct his flight to heaven" (291), he prophesied what would happen after his translation[162].

---

162 Moses even describes his own burial by the supernatural powers, and L. Ginzberg, *The Legends of the Jews*, VI (Notes to Volumes III and IV: From Moses in the Wilderness to Esther), Philadelphia, 1928 and reprints, p. 162, note continued from the preceding page, takes this to mean that Philo insisted on the literal meaning of the Biblical text. But, in view of the whole context, Philo can only be speaking of the burial of Moses' *body*. Also in a fragment of the *Assumption of Moses*, Moses' body is buried, while Joshua sees the soul of Moses carried aloft by the angels (see Clem.Alex., *Strom.* VI.xv.22; Orig., *Hom. in Jos.* ii.1; Euod., *Epist. ad Aug.* 259). J.D. Purvis, "Samaritan Traditions on the Death of Moses", in G.W.E. Nickelsburg, Jr., ed., *Studies on the Testament of Moses* (SBL: SCS, 4), Cambridge, Mass., 1973, p. 114, note continued from the preceding page, wants to contrast this doctrine with that found in *De vita Mos.* II.288, since this text says that Moses' body and soul were united into a single unity of "mind". But Philo does speak about the burial of

This scene is also described in *De virtutibus*. When Moses had finished his song, he began to be changed —

> from mortal existence into immortal life (εἰς ἀθάνατον βίον), and noticed that he was gradually being disengaged from the elements with which he had been mixed. He shed his body which grew around him like the shell of an oyster, while his soul which was thus laid bare desired its migration thence.

(76)

Philo, of course, teaches the ascension of Moses' *soul*, not his body, as does version A of *Aboth de R. Nathan*; but this apparently is a refinement of the tradition that Moses, like Enoch and Elijah, was taken up to God in the body and became a ministering angel. W.A. Meeks has shown that the description of the final ascent of Moses in Philo's corpus, as well as in other Jewish works and in Samaritan literature, is based upon traditions of Moses' ascent of Mt. Sinai[163]. Now Moses was certainly in the body when he ascended to God in order to receive the Law, but Philo conceives of this ascent, too, as a divinization of Moses' soul (see, *e.g., Quaest. in Gen.* II.29, 40). It would seem that Philo has spiritualized Moses' final ascension to heaven as well as the first one.

This conclusion is corroborated by the high age of the curious affirmation that Moses really died. A polemic against the idea of the bodily rapture of the prophet is perhaps to be discerned in *Petirath Moshe*, where Moses' plea to be left alive is met with a very vigorous rejection on God's part[164]. The same motive probably underlies the tradition which emphasizes that Moses was buried in broad daylight and full public (see *Ass. Mos.* i.15; Ps.-Philo, *Ant.* xix.12, 16), which stands in clear contradiction to the Biblical text and diverges from the main stream tradition in Judaism. Josephus is quite openly polemical when stating:

> A cloud suddenly stood over him, and he disappeared in a valley, but he has written in the sacred books that he died in order that, on the ground of his outstanding virtues, it should not be said that he went back up to the Deity.

(Ant. IV.326)

This apparently alludes to the notion of a bodily ascension. Moreover, the polemic must presuppose the practice; there were obviously people who taught that Moses did not die on Mt. Nebo but ascended to heaven.

Moses, and this unity of *nous* cannot have been what was buried. In *De virt.* 76, to be quoted forthwith, Moses leaves his body upon dying. Philo apparently thought that some material form (or a docetic body?) of Moses was left to be buried, while the great prophet soared aloft as pure *nous*.

163 See *Prophet-King*, pp. 124 f., 140 f., 158 f., 209 ff. Pseudo-Philo (*Ant.* xix.10) states that, just before Moses died, the great prophet entered into heaven and was vouchsafed cosmological secrets.
164 See *BH*, I, p. 118.

In view of the fact that there are so few rabbinic witnesses to this tradition, it would seem that its origin must be sought outside main stream Judaism. It is certainly interesting to note that the rabbinic testimonies say that Moses became a ministering angel, for – as we shall see below – the Samaritans teach that Moses serves in the heavenly tabernacle[165]. Furthermore, Philo connects Moses' heavenly translation at the end of his life with *Deut.* v.31, which – as we have seen – was cited by the Samaritans in the context of the description that Moses attained angelic or divine status when ascending to heaven[166]. Some men, Philo says, do not perish when leaving this life but draw near to God.

> Such is Moses, to whom He says: "Stand here with Me." And so when Moses was about to die, we do not hear of him "leaving" or "being added" like those others. [...] But through the Word of the Supreme Cause, he is translated (μετανίσταται) [cp. *Deut.* xxxiv.5].
>
> *(De sacr. Ab. et Caini 8)*

This text is also interesting in that it cites *Deut.* xxxiv.5, which – as we have seen – was taken by the baraita as proof that Moses ascended to heaven in order to perform service before God. It must be concluded that already Philo assumes a nonconformist tradition to the effect that Moses did not die but ascended to heaven and became a ministering angel.

The origin of this tradition may have been in Samaria. It has already been stated that, although Marqa represents Moses' last ascension with colours from the portrait of the ascension of Mt. Sinai, where Moses attained angel-hood, his teaching is that Moses died (see *Memar Marqa* V.3). But Marqa also says:

> The mouth of the cave has been closed by the Divinity and will not be opened or known *until the Day of Vengeance.*
>
> *(Ibid.* V.4)

This statement, given as a midrash on *Deut.* xxxiv.6, "But no man knows the place of his burial to this day," is strange; we may ask *why* the grave will be opened on the last day. Will Moses then be resurrected and come forth? This would be quite peculiar, because Marqa does not seem to teach a general resurrection from the dead[167]. Is Moses really alive all the time? It is well known that Jesus' grave is shown in Jerusalem, but no Christian would say that Jesus is dead and not in heaven with God. The saviour's grave is his last earthly station and the place of his future manifestation. Let it also be noted in this connection that the *Asatir* (ii.38 f.) points out the locality of the grave of Enoch, who is told not to have died but to have been translated to heaven

---

165 See p. 141.
166 See the passage from *Memar Marqa* IV.12 quoted above, p. 122.
167 See above, p. 38, n. 30.

(see *Gen.* v.24). In the passage quoted above, Marqa tentatively may approach a heterodox view of Moses.

That this is a plausible surmise is shown by later evidence. In the Samaritan *Death of Moses*, an Aramaic work which is difficult to date, it is related that Moses' "holy spirit" departed with his breath and was taken up to heaven by the angels[168]. In the Samaritan chronicle known as the *Book of Joshua*, an Arabic work based on various Hebrew sources and incorporating old traditions, there is no mention of an assumption of the soul of Moses but a general reference to his translation:

> His allotted period of life had reached its limit, and the term of his existence among men – peace be upon him! And now his dealings were with his Lord and His angels.
>
> (ch. 6)

Moses' death was no real death but the beginning of his time among the angels. In keeping with the idea of Moses' translation, the *Book of Joshua* makes no mention of his grave and burial.

A.D. Crown has suggested that the *Book of Joshua* originated in Dosithean circles[169], and, although this cannot be correct, the doctrine of the assumption of Moses at least seems to be a Dosithean doctrine. It does not occur in the earlier writings, which come from the priestly circles, and the representation of Moses as the principal angel and high priest in heaven is not to be found ·in texts written before the 14th century, when there was effected a rather successful synthesis of priestly and lay, Dosithean, doctrines[170]. In the post-14th century liturgy, the view is that Moses did not die but ascended on high. Thus, Abisha ben Phinehas in a dream sees "the great prophet glori-

---

168 See Gaster, *Asatir*, p. 57.
169 See "Some Traces of Heterodox Theology in the Samaritan Book of Joshua", *BJRL*, 50, 1967, pp. 178 ff. Lowy, on the other hand, says that "no single doctrine of the Book shows Dosithean features, and its details and general outlook cannot at any point be identified with Dosithean teachings" (p. 265). As regards the doctrine of Moses' assumption, however, Lowy is palpably wrong, for this doctrine is not found in earlier Samaritan literature, which comes from the priestly circles. On the other hand, Crown's ascription of the pro-Joshua features of this chronicle to the Dositheans cannot be correct. The *Book of Joshua*, like the *Death of Moses*, underlines strongly that Joshua succeeded to Moses' office; and this feature, like the identification of Joshua as the Prophet like Moses in the Targum, must be *anti-Dosithean*. Cp. Kippenberg, p. 270, n. 92, and p. 323, n. 96. I suggest that the enhancement of the position of Joshua in the *Book of Joshua* and the *Death of Moses* is a way of checking an identification of Dositheus as the returning Moses, a possibility which was opened up by the adoption of the lay doctrine that Moses was still alive. The Dositheans apparently did not distinguish between Moses returning and the Prophet like Moses. For the basis of Crown's mistake, see above, p. 48, n. 67.
170 For the dialectics between priestly and lay Samaritanism, see also below, pp. 192f., 228ff.

fied, sitting on the throne, there to judge and live for ever" (Cowley, 379.17).
We have seen that Marqa knows the idea of Moses being enthroned in heaven,
but he does not say that this was more than a temporary installation. In the
literature written after the 14th century, when the lay doctrines were adopted to a greater extent than what was the case in the 4th century, Moses is said
to have been translated to heaven and to have resumed his position as God's
vice-regent. This picture of Moses, then, apparently is due to lay teachings[171].

This doctrine of Moses explains Origen's information that the Dositheans
believed that Dositheus, the Prophet like Moses, still was alive. We also have
seen that the Dosithean sect of the Saduqay maintained that the righteous
would be resurrected, or even had been resurrected, because Dositheus was
not really dead[172]. Finally, it also should be recalled that the main body of
the Dositheans taught that, "as soon as a dead man is buried, he arises from
the grave and goes to Paradise."[173] This, of course, would apply also to
Dositheus, the head of the sect.

Epiphanius and Abu'l Fath, however, contradict Origen's report by saying
that Dositheus died after having withdrawn into a cave. Abu'l Fath says that
he died of hunger, while Epiphanius asserts that he caused his own death by
persisting in an arduous fast. They both admit that his body vanished, but
ascribe this to its being devoured by animals. S.J. Isser has offered a solution
to this dilemma: both Epiphanius and Abu'l Fath give an anti-Dosithean version of the career of Dositheus, while Origen simply reports what the Dositheans said[174]. Moses had ended his earthly career by disappearing into a
cave, and so did also Dositheus, the Prophet like Moses, end his mission. The
Dositheans claimed that his body was not recovered because he had been
translated, but the opponents retorted that this had to be explained on the
ground that it had been devoured by beasts[175].

This argument between the Dositheans and the orthodox Samaritans,
whose position is reflected by Epiphanius, furnishes the key to a couple of

---

171 Cp. Purvis, "Samaritan Traditions", pp. 109 ff. Purvis, pp. 112 f., however, is not so
    sure that these "heterodox" people can be identified as Dositheans, and thinks that
    the pro-Joshua traditions as well as the doctrine of Moses' translation were proffered
    by the lay circles in opposition to "orthodox", priestly, Samaritanism. But Purvis
    does not realize that the pro-Joshua traditions in effect are anti-Dosithean.
172 See above, p. 54.
173 Vilmar, p. 157.
174 See *op. cit.*, pp. 32, 46, 98, 137, 139.
175 Compare the allegation that the disciples had removed Jesus' body from the grave in
    order to assert that he had been resurrected (see *Matt*. xxvii.63 ff.). Isser, p. 137, also
    notes that Moses fasted forty days and nights (see *Memar Marqa* IV.12), but his fast
    is connected with his ascent of Mt. Sinai, not with his ascent of Mt. Nebo and his
    egress from this life, However, Moses in Samaritanism was known as the greatest in
    fasting, and Dositheus naturally would try to emulate him.

traditions about Simon Magus, the rival of Dositheus and allegedly the first Gnostic. Hippolytus narrates that Peter's opposition caused the Samaritan magician a lot of worry:

> Finally... he sat down under a plane-tree and taught. And, when at last he was near being refuted because of the passing of time, he said that, if he were buried alive, he would rise again on the third day. Ordering a grave to be dug, he bid his disciples to heap earth upon him. They did as he commanded, but he remained [in the grave] until this day, for he was not the Messiah.
>
> (VI.xx.3)

This quite peculiar tradition has been taken as a Christian invention, a travesty in which Simon appears as an anti-Christ, an *antimimon pneuma* of the works of Jesus[176]; but this explanation is not wholly satisfying because of the fact that Simon is said to have disappeared from the surface of the earth *while still alive*. Jesus, on the other hand, died and rose again. Actually, the motif of the "disappearing shaman who vanishes for a long period into a sacred cave" is quite widespread[177]. For instance, the Thracian Zalmoxis preached to his followers that neither he nor they and their descendants would die; and in order to prove this dictum, he withdrew into an underground room for the period of three years and then suddenly emerged in order to show that he was immortal (see Herodotus, IV.94 ff.). Zalmoxis not only claimed but also did what Simon only claimed to be able of doing.

However, it is not necessary to seek so far for a pattern for Simon, for the Moses doctrine prevailing in some Jewish and Samaritan quarters tallies with this religio-historical theme. It would seem that Simon (or his followers) as well as Dositheus (or the Dositheans) had recourse to traditions about the end of Moses, believed to have disappeared into a cave but not to have died there. The Christians then would have converted the Simonian belief into a parody of the death and resurrection of Jesus.

Moses was believed to have ascended to heaven; and so was in all probability also Dositheus, for the Dositheans taught that their hero was alive and that the righteous would be resurrected and go to Paradise immediately after leaving this world. From the Christian polemics against Simon, we may infer that there were Simonian traditions of his ascension which were complementary to the account that Simon asserted to disappear into a hollow of the earth and then come back. In the *Acts of Peter*, Simon announces his leaving of the world in the following manner:

> Men of Rome, you now think that Peter has prevailed over me, as having greater

---

176 See Beyschlag, pp. 19 f., 21, with n. 28; Lüdemann, *Untersuchungen*, p. 91.

177 E.R. Doods, *The Greeks and the Irrational* (SCL, 25), Berkeley & Los Angeles, 1951, reprinted 1973, p. 166, note continued from the preceding page. Cp. Isser, p. 97, note continued from the preceding page, relating the theme to Dositheus' withdrawal into a cave.

power, and you pay more attention to him. But you are deceived; for tomorrow I shall leave you, who are godless and impious, and fly up to God, whose Power I am, although enfeebled. While you, then, have fallen, behold, I am the Standing One. And I am going up to my Father and shall say to him: "Even me, Your son who is the Standing One, they desired to bring down, but I did not consent to them and am returned to myself."

                                                            (Ch. 2 of the Greek text)

The narrative goes on to tell that Simon was raised in the air, but then brought crashing down to earth when Peter invoked Christ. After a while, the magician died.

Again, the story has been taken as a Christian invention, a travesty of the ascension of Christ, and it is true that the words "I am going up to my Father" are reminiscent of Jesus' words in *John* xx.17[178]. But this interpretation is not entirely adequate. Already G. Ficker pointed out that the author of the apocryphal Acts mistook Simon's attempt to ascend to heaven for an unsuccessful magical flight through the air[179]: he represents Simon's attempt to ascend to God as a magical feat intending to prove that he is a greater magician than Peter, and the continuation of the narrative speaks of Simon flying "all over the city of Rome, being carried over its temples and its hills," comparing this to the flight which he (seemingly) performed when landing in Rome from the East (cp. ch. 4). The narrative part uses verbs as "fly" (πετάομαι) and "lift up and/or carry" (αἴρω), which stand in contrast to the words in Simon's dictum, ἀναπτήξομαι and ἀνέρχομαι. The last verb occurs also twice in a statement by Simon quoted in the following chapter, right before he starts his ascension: "Peter, now of all times, when I am making my ascent [...]. For by ascending, I will show to all this crowd what kind of being I am."

Thus, the author of the *Acts of Peter* does not represent Simon as performing an unsuccessful ascension but as performing an unsuccessful *flight through the air*, while *Simon himself* claims to be able to ascend to heaven. It is not impossible that the story contains genuine words of Simon (or words put into his mouth by his followers), claiming that he would ascend to God, and that this tradition was muddled by the Christians, representing his statements as relating to a magical flight.

It is, of course, also possible that the author of the *Acts of Peter* has misunderstood an already existing *Christian* tradition representing Simon as

---

178 See L. Vouaux, ed. & trans., *Les Actes de Pierre*, Paris, 1922, p. 407; J.M.A. Salles-Dabadie, *Recherches sur Simon le Mage*, I (L'"Apophasis megale") (CRB, 10), Paris, 1969, p. 135; Lüdemann, *Untersuchungen*, p. 90.

179 See *Die Petrusakten*, Leipzig, 1903, p. 93. Salles-Dabadie, pp. 135 f., finds words in the statement by Simon which also occur in the *Megale Apophasis*, and thinks that this fact vouches for the existence of genuinely Simonian traditions in the text. But his thesis that the "Great Announcement" is the work of Simon himself is fantastic.

attempting an ascension to heaven in the manner of Christ[180], for if Simon's words really reveal New Testament influence and are to be ascribed to a Christian author, it is obvious that also his failure of emulating Christ would have been narrated. But would such a tradition have been created if the Simonians did not claim that their hero actually had ascended to God? The story of Simon's unsuccessful ascension or flight is recorded in so many Christian sources that it is difficult to resist the impression that the reason for this is to refute a Simonian claim[181]. Arnobius, a rhetorician living in the latter part of the 3rd century, even acknowledges in one of his books against the pagans that Simon ascended in a fiery chariot (see *Adv. nat.* II.12); and this does not have the appearance of being a Christian addition to the tradition, for the possession of a fiery chariot, being a very numinous object to people basing their religion upon the Bible, hardly would have been attributed to the arch-heresiarch by Christians.

Furthermore, it must be noted that Simon's mode of speech clearly goes beyond Christian phraseology. Simon emphatically connects his ascension project with the claim of being the Standing One, which was a designation of Moses, who actually was believed to have ascended to heaven and attained this status, and who presumably would repeat this ascension when leaving the earth at the end of his career. Jesus died and rose from the dead before ascending to God, while the assumption of Moses agrees with the "traditions about shamans who were carried away still living from the earth to the sky."[182] The (unsuccessful) ascent of Simon also is to be put into the latter category, and we see that it is a Moses pattern, and not a Jesus pattern, which fits the tradition of the ascension of the magician.

Like the Thracian shaman Zalmoxis, Simon also promised immortality to his followers. After having enumerated all the different feats of magic which he had accomplished, Simon is reported to have said:

> Not only have I done these things, but even now I am able to do them, so that I by facts can prove to all that I am the Son of God standing to eternity (*filius dei stans in aeternum*), and that I can make those who believe in me stand in like manner for ever (*similiter stare in perpetuum*).
>
> (*Ps.-Clem.Rec.* III.47)

Simon promises attainment of the status of being a "Standing One" to people on the condition that they become convinced by his magical powers

---

180 R. Reitzenstein, *Hellenistische Wundererzählungen*, Leipzig, 1906, reprinted Darmstadt, 1963, p. 125, n. 3, goes too far when he denies every resemblance to the Christian ascension theme.

181 For a collection of the sources, see R.A. Lipsius, *Die Quellen der römischen Petrussage*, Kiel, 1872, pp. 85 ff.

182 M.A. Czaplicka, *Aboriginal Siberia: A Study in Social Anthropology*, Oxford, 1914, p. 176; quoted by Dodds, *loc. cit.*

that he is the everliving Son of God[183]. We note that the concept of "the Standing One" is used in the same way as in the Samaritan literature.

Clement of Alexandria also relates that the Simonians strove to equal Simon the Standing One:

> Reason, the governing principle, remaining unmoved and guiding the soul, is called its pilot; for access to the Immutable is obtained by a truly immutable means. Thus, Abraham was standing before the Lord, and, approaching, he spoke. And, to Moses, it is said: "And you, stand by Me" (*Deut.* v.31). And the followers of Simon wish to be assimilated in manners to the Standing One whom they worship.
>
> (Strom. II.xi.52)

Clement is here dependent upon Philo, living in the same city a century before him and taking Abraham and Moses as prototypes of the philosopher whose mind is immutable and thus is allowed to approach and "stand" by God, *the* Standing One, that is, the Immutable One. Clement says that the Simonians endeavoured to attain this immutable state of mind by emulating "the Standing One whom they worship," but this meaning of "standing" is quite another than that of the *Pseudo-Clementines* and the *Acts of Peter*, where the concept means "living for ever" and is contrasted with "falling", that is, "dying". It is, of course, possible that Simonians living in Alexandria in the 2nd century could have transformed the original meaning of their idea of "standing" after the pattern of its use in philosophical terminology, but it is just as likely that it is Clement who is responsible for this new connotation of "the Standing One" in the accounts of Simonianism. Immediately before, he compares the one who is not guided by reason to a leaf which falls, and thus witnesses the same counterposition of "standing" and "falling" as that known from the *Clementina* and the *Acts of Peter*[184]. Thus, it would seem

---

183 The depiction of the relationship between God and Simon as a Father/Son relationship probably is to be ascribed to Christian influence. However, in Samaritanism, Moses is the "Son of the house (of God)", an epithet which characterizes him as belonging to the angelic dynasty of the heavenly world; see Kippenberg, p. 318, with note continued from the preceding page. Origen (*Contra Cels.* VI.11) relates that also Dositheus claimed to be the "Son of God", and it is not impossible that the Samaritan heresiarchs asserting to be the Moses-like redeemer referred to themselves as "Son" in order to indicate their angelic status. Compare that "son(s) of God" is a synonym of "angel(s)" in the Hebrew Bible; see G. Fohrer, par. B, "Old Testament", in Art. υἱὸς κτλ., in *TDNT*, VIII, 1972 and reprints, pp. 347 f.

184 Lüdemann, *Untersuchungen*, pp. 97 f., tries to derive the conception of the Standing One in Simonianism from the use of the idea of the ἑστώς - στάς - στησόμενος in the *Megale Apophasis*, but has to admit that this cannot be carried out in the cases of *Strom.* II.xi.2, *Acts of Peter* ch. 31, and *Ps.-Clem. Rec.* III.47. Moreover, since the concept of the Standing One throughout the *Clementina* and in the *Acts of Peter* is not used in a philosophical sense, but has palpable roots in the Samaritan religion, the theory of an influx from the "Great Announcement" must be dismissed. The

that Clement knew something about the theology of "the Standing One" in Simonianism, but — either because of lack of substantial knowledge or for some other reason — represented it in a Philonic dress. In any case, the Simonians in emulating their hero originally desired to become immortal, not to achieve a Stoic-like ideal of mind.

The Simonians' imitation of their hero appears to have a precedent in a Samaritan *imitatio Mosis* doctrine. Marqa says:

> Let us keep His commandments. He who follows in the footsteps of Moses the faithful prophet will not go astray, nor be guilty of sin, but will serve in both worlds.
>
> *(Memar Marqa* IV.9)

Here, Moses is viewed as a hierophant, having prepared the way which the Law-obedient Samaritan can follow. The way leads from earth to heaven, for the reward of keeping the Law is "to serve in both worlds," just as Moses was conceived of as a high priest in the earthly tabernacle and also as one among the angels, the Standing Ones, in the heavenly sanctuary. Marqa says:

> Where is there the like of Moses, and who can compete with Moses, the Servant of God, the Faithful one of His House, who dwelt among the Standing Ones in the sanctuary of the unseen? They all honoured him when he abode with them. He was supplied from their provisions, being satisfied by them. He was brought right in among them. He was made holy priest in two sanctuaries.
>
> *(Ibid.* IV.6)

It is an idea common to Judaism and Samaritanism that the angels minister to God in heaven, and we have seen above that there also was a Jewish teaching to the effect that Moses became like the ministering angels upon leaving this world[185]. Moreover, the Samaritans reckoned with the possibility that the true believers also could be made heavenly servants, that is, angels[186]. The

---

author of the basic writing probably did not know this Simonian work. Cp. Beyschlag, pp. 49 f., 62.

185 See pp. 131f. In my unpublished paper, "Reminisenser", I have collected several Samaritan texts where it is said that Moses was made priest in heaven as well as on earth. The words "will serve in both worlds" in the text from *Memar Marqa* IV.9 literally read: "will serve אנה ושם," *i.e.,* "will serve here and there." Macdonald notes that "אנה does not mean 'here' in Sam., nor is שם normal in an Aram. passage," and suggests that we have to do with a "mystical idiom reflecting a divine name" (*Memar Marqah*, II, p. 170, n. 191). Meeks adds: "It may not be mere coincidence that שם in Ex. 34.28 and Dt. 34.5 is interpreted in *Sifre Dt.*, par. 357, *Yalkut Šimʻoni* on Dt., par. 962, 965 (pp. 686 f.), and Talm. B. *Sota* 13b to mean "standing and serving" on high" (p. 244, n. 1). In *Test. Levi* ii.10, it is spoken to Levi, the heavenly high priest: "You shall stand next to God and shall be His minister."

186 The continuation of the text in *Midrash ha-Gadol* I.123, saying that Enoch, Moses, and Elijah ascended to perform service, states that all pious are transformed into angels after their death. This is probably a late addition to the tannaitic source, but

same prospect would be open to the followers of the Prophet like Moses, and this appears to be the explanation of the tradition that the disciples of Simon strove to equal their master and become Standing Ones, angels.

In this connection, we should cite the reports by Justin and Irenaeus about Menander, Simon's heir, who promised his disciples that they would not die. Justin writes:

> Concerning one Menander, likewise a Samaritan, from the village of Kapparetaia, a disciple of Simon, who also obtained power from the demons, we know that he came to Antioch and deceived many through magical arts, and that he alleged to his disciples that they would not die. And even now there are some of them who assert this.

> *(I Apol.* xxvi.4)

Irenaeus, writing later in the same century, gives a fuller report on Menander inclusive of an extension of the immortality doctrine of this Samaritan Gnostic:

> His [*i.e.,* Simon's] successor was Menander, a Samaritan by race, who also attained the pinnacle of magic. He said that the First Power was unknown to all, and that he himself was the one who was sent by the Invisible Ones as a saviour for the redemption of men. The world was made by angels, who – according to him as well as according to Simon – were brought forth by Ennoia. He added that he gave knowledge about how to overcome the angels who created the world through magic taught by him. His disciples receive resurrection through their baptism into him, and they can no longer die but remain immortal without growing old.

> (I.xxiii.5)

Is Irenaeus right that the immortality which Menander promised his disciples was endless life "without growing old"? It is possible that Justin too understood Menander's teaching on this subject in the same way, for he apparently expresses his astonishment that some Menandrians "even now" accept the immortality doctrine propounded by Menander. R. Haardt is confident that this is a misunderstanding of Menander's teaching of "the immortality of the Spirit-Self"[187], but there is no trace of the classical Gnostic anthropology and its correlative soteriology in the systems of the Samaritan Gnostics. Menander's anthropogonic and anthropological teachings are not reported, but Simon is said to have taught that the end was impending and that men's salvation or doom depended upon whether or not they would put their trust in him. Thus, the immortality doctrine of Samaritan Gnosticism may be connected with eschatological notions.

W. Foerster accepts the heresiological account and cites the fact that mem-

---

the idea of the assimilation of the righteous to angels after death is quite old; see *Wisd.* v.5; *I En.* civ.2, 4, 6; *Matt.* xxii.30.

187 *Gnosis*, trans. by J.F. Hendry, Leiden, 1971, p. 40, note continued from the preceding page.

bers of the German *Jugendbewegung* after the First World War alleged that they would not die[188]. It is not necessary to reach so far for a parallel, for the history of early Christianity shows that the conviction of living at the very eve of the Golden Age and belonging to the elect leads to the enthusiastic view that the Day actually *has* dawned in some way and that the righteous being alive therefore will not taste death (see *II Thess.* ii.2; cp. *I Thess.* iv.15; *I Cor.* xv.51 f.)[189]. We have seen in the preceding Chapter that there were sectarians among the Samaritans who asserted that they already were living in the period of the divine favour; this conviction may have been connected with an enthusiastic eschatology.

However, the resurrection doctrine of Menander is not brought into connection with eschatology but with the baptismal rite which he offered his disciples. It then lies nearer at hand to compare his immortality doctrine to the radical realized eschatology which developed Paul's teaching that the believer was resurrected in the baptism (see *Rom.* vi.1 ff.; cp. *John* xi.25 f.) to the point that the futuristic aspect of the eschatology was denied totally (see *II Tim.* ii.18)[190]. Samaritan sectarianism seems to have been characterized by a *baptismus*, and it is possible that the realized eschatology subsisting among some of the Dosithean sub-sects was connected with a baptismal piety. Furthermore, a realized eschatology with no interest in cosmic events is easily welded with a doctrine of a spiritual resurrection occurring immediately after death, and we know that the main body of the Dositheans, who were baptizers, cherished such a spiritual resurrection tenet and apparently founded it upon the belief that Dositheus did not die but was translated. In this connection, it should be noted that Moses actually was believed to have been baptized when he ascended Mt. Gerizim, that is, to heaven, where he obtained immortality by being assimilated to the angels. Marqa says that Moses "immersed himself in their [*i.e.*, the angels'] basin (בכיורון צבע) and was given

---

188 See "Die "ersten Gnostiker" Simon und Menander", in *OG*, p. 194 with n. 7.
189 Paul's opponents in Thessalonica apparently did not spiritualize or internalize the Last Day, for the Apostle does not have to make pointed that the events of the Day *had to be cosmic*, as though his adversaries denied this. He only states that there still are certain events which would have to take place *before* the arrival of the Day; see the discussion by E. Best, *A Commentary on the First and Second Epistles to the Thessalonians* (BNTC), London, 1972, pp. 275 ff. Did the heretics among the Corinthians, too, share the view that the Day (not necessarily a twenty-four hours period) already had dawned in some way and that that they therefore would not taste dead? Paul, then, would have misunderstood their position to include the idea that the dead would not rise. His opponents in Thessalonica would seem to have taught this.
190 Assuming that Paul has not misunderstood his opponents, this does not seem to have been the position of the Corinthians (see *I Cor.* xv.19, 32), although iv.8 by itself might be taken to imply this idea. The people opposed in *Phil.* iii.12 ff., however, would seem to be among the deniers of a futuristic aspect of the resurrection; cp. Pol., *Phil.* vii.1.

a place in their tabernacle" (*Memar Marqa* IV.6). If this is the background of
Menander's teaching about the resurrection, it would seem that it is based
upon a Moses pattern which has been misunderstood by (Justin and) Irenaeus.

The Apostle of God

If also Menander claimed to be the Prophet like Moses, the strange report
that he promised his followers that they would not die can be explained in
the light of the idea that the followers of the Moses-like Prophet, like the disciples of Moses himself, had angelic status as their reward. That Menander
asserted to have been "sent" by God (*se autem eum esse, qui missus sit ab
invisibilibus*) may indicate this, for the description of having been "sent" by
God and being God's "Sent One" was a common way of representing Moses
in Samaritanism. Already in the Old Testament, Moses is described as being
"sent" by God. Moses is bid by God to go and say to the Israelites: "The
God of your fathers has sent me (שלחני) to you" (*Ex.* iii.13; cp. *v.* 15;
iv.28). G. Widengren has shown that the description of God's agent as being
"sent" goes back to a Near Eastern royal pattern, according to which the king
was commissioned and "sent" by the high god for the salvation of the people.
He has also tracked this conception into the Old Testament, where not only
Moses but also prophets as Isaiah, Ezekiel, and Jeremiah are portrayed by an
imagery taken from the scene of the royal investiture and said to have been
"sent" by God (see *Is.* vi.8; lxi.1; *Ez.* ii.3; *Jer.* i.7)[191].

When it comes to tracing this idea in later Jewish religion, however,
Widengren is not so successful. He says that "Jewish tradition expressly gives
him [*i.e.*, Moses] the term שליח," but, in way of reference, he limits himself to
the paragraph on ἀπόστολος by K.H. Rengstorf in Kittel's *Wörterbuch*, where
we only find the citation that Moses was God's שליח by virtue of striking the
rock so that water issued from it (see *Baba Bathra* 86b), that is, doing a miracle, the performance of which was otherwise reserved for God[192]. But now
J.-A. Bühner has surveyed several rabbinic texts where Moses is designated as
God's שליח[193]. This usage is determined by the profane institution of the
שליח, the principle of which is laid down as follows: "The one sent by a man
is as the man himself" (*Ber.* v.5; *et al.*). Thus, in the sphere of private transac-
tion, for instance, it was possible to become engaged to a woman through the
agency of a *shaliah*. In communal life, the name "'sent one" could be applied

---

191 See *Ascension*, pp. 31 ff. For the "sending" of prophets, see also *Judg.* vi.8; *Hag.*
    i.12; *Zech.* ii.12. In *Judg.* vi.19, Gideon is "sent" as judge to Israel.
192 See Widengren, p. 47, citing Rengstorf, Art. ἀποστέλλω κτλ., in *TDNT*, I, 1964
    and reprints, p. 419.
193 See *Der Gesandte und sein Weg im 4. Evangelium* (WUNT, 2. Reihe, 2), Tübingen,
    1977, pp. 285 ff.

to the person praying on behalf of the community in the synagogue, or to the rabbis who were sent out into the diaspora by the Sanhedrin in order to regulate the calendar, *etc.* The judicial principle of this idea of agency is that the person(s) being sent has (have) to be treated *as if he (they) were* the person(s) being represented.

The Samaritan tradition, too, designates Moses as God's *shaliah*, "Sent One", "Messenger", "Apostle"[194]. It is often spoken of Moses' "apostleship" (שליחותה). When the people are about to break up from Egypt, God addresses Moses in the following way:

> This day is a memorial to your prophethood, just as this deed is a commemoration of the deliverance; for, through you, they [*i.e.*, the people] are saved and rest from fatigue. They have become great through you and are glorified by your apostleship.
>
> *(Memar Marqa* I.9)

In the next book of his great midrashic work, Marqa also mentions Moses' apostleship:

> When Moses recounted the records of the ancestors before the children who succeeded them, they believed the Truth [*i.e.*, God] and knew that the apostleship of Moses was true.
>
> *(Ibid.* II.9)

The apostleship of Moses indicates not only that he is the leader of the desert generation and the organizer of the community of Israel and its life; it also implies that he has knowledge of the heavenly secrets:

> O great prophet Moses, whom God chose especially for apostleship! He [*i.e.*, God] opened before you [*i.e.*, Moses] the gateway to the unseen world.
>
> *(Ibid.* VI.7)

Moses is called the "Apostle" (שליח). When he is about to depart from this life, the people beg him:

> By your life, O Apostle of God, remain with us a little longer!
> By your life, O Seal of the prophets, stop with us a little longer!
>
> *(Ibid.* V.3)

Moses' epithet "apostle" also occurs in passages where his names are enumerated:

> Where is there anyone like Moses, the Apostle of the Truth [*i.e.*, of God], Faithful One of the house of God, and His Servant?
>
> *(Ibid.* VI.3)

The two last quotations show that "Apostle" is a formal title of Moses, comparable to "Seal of the prophets", "Faithful One of the house of God", "Servant", *etc.*[195] This appears to go beyond its usage in Judaism.

---

194 This was noted by Meeks, *Prophet-King*, pp. 226 f. See also Bühner, pp. 302 ff.
195 In *Memar Marqa* I.4, Moses and Aaron are called שלחין מן מרה דכל. In the

The verb לאך, which has the same meaning as שלח, is also used to describe Moses' office of being "sent" by and from God. In one passage of *Memar Marqa,* the verb לאך is closely associated with the title *shaliah*; God says to Moses:

> Take the rod in your hand and go to Egypt, that they may know that you are an Apostle sent by Me (שליח מדילי)!

(I.2)

Ex. ch. iv, however, does not use the verb לאך, which yields the nominal construction מלאך, and it may be wondered whether Marqa by saying that Moses was "sent" by and from God really intends to represent the prophet as God's *mal'ak* as well as his *shaliah*. In the Old Testament, it is impossible to say whether the *mal'ak YHWH* is a heavenly or an earthly being, but it is apparent that he has an ordinarily human form[196]. In the period with which we are concerned, it was generally assumed that the *mal'akim*, that is, the angels, were heavenly beings[197], but we have seen that the Samaritans conceived of Moses as having attained angelic nature upon his ascension to heaven. Furthermore, the old equivalence of the concept of *shaliah* and that of *mal'ak* was maintained, so that the former could be used to gloss or even parallel the latter[198].

But the non-exegetic and formal usage of the term *shaliah* as a synonym of the heavenly *mal'ak* seems to be a Samaritan rather than a Jewish characteristic[199]. Thus, the former term even occurs as a substitute for the Angel of the Lord in the Samaritan Targum, where the important passage of *Ex.* xxiii. 20 ff. is rendered in the following way:

> Behold! I send My Apostle (משלח שלחי) before you in order to keep you and protect you on the way, and to bring you into the place which I have prepared. Give heed to him and obey his voice. Do not rebel against him, because he will not pardon

---

younger part of the Liturgy, Moses is frequently called "Apostle" (see Cowley, 81.15; 82.28; 216.6; 349.25; 368.9; 707.26; *et al.*).

196 See B.J. Bamberger, par. "Bible", in Art. "Angels and Angelology", in *EJ*, 1, col. 957.

197 See Bühner, pp. 317 ff., 323 f.

198 See *ibid.*, pp. 281 f., 323 f., 326 ff.

199 In the evidence given by Bühner, pp. 324, 326 ff., the former word never occurs simply as a substitute for the latter, but is always used as a parallel or as an explanatory term. The Samaritan usage is illustrated by the following example: "Apostles (שלחין) of Your mercy to the bases of our patriarchs – do send (שלח) for our salvation and to the destroyers of our enemies!" (Cowley, 31.17).

A special problem is connected with the eschatological *nuntius* in *Ass. Mos.* x.2. Since his hands are said to "be filled", which is an old expression of being installed as priest (see *Ex.* xxviii.41; *et al.*), Stauffer, col. 142, argues that the *nuntius* is an eschatological high priest like the Messiah of Aaron in the Qumran texts. But his function of being Israel's avenger does not fit this office. The angel Michael, however, is both Israel's guardian angel and a heavenly high priest, and *nuntii* apparently is a translation of ἀγγέλου.

your transgressions; for My Name is in him. But if you hearken attentively to his voice and do all that I say, then I will be an enemy to your enemies and an adversary to your adversaries. For My Apostle (שלחי) shall go before you [...].[200]

The substitution of "Apostle" for "Angel" is also made by the Samaritans in their Targumic version of *Ex.* xxxii.34 and xxxiii.2, where God also speaks about the Angel of the Lord: "[...] Behold! My Apostle (שלחי) shall go before you [...]. And I will send an Apostle (שליח) [...]." Thus, since Moses in Samaritanism not only is given the Name of God but also called God's "Apostle", he obviously is conceived of as a substitute for, or at least as an alternative of, the Angel of the Lord, who possesses the Name of God and is called the Apostle of God in the Samaritan Targum.

There is also a possibility that the figure of the Apostle in the Samaritan Targum as well as in *Memar Marqa* and the later liturgical texts denotes Moses. In the Jewish Passover Aggada, we read: " "And the Lord brought us out of Egypt" (*Deut.* xxvi.8): not by means of an angel (מלאך), and not by means of a seraph (שרף), and not by means of the Apostle (השליח)."[201] Since only the last term is determined by the article, the Apostle obviously is a special agent of God. That this name should distinguish the Angel of the Lord from the ordinary angels and the other heavenly beings like the seraphs is possible, but this would appear to be the only instance where the Angel of the Lord was called "*the* Apostle". In Judaism, as in Samaritanism, it is Moses who is the Apostle *par excellence*.

There is in fact evidence at hand which shows that the "Apostle" in this formula could be regarded as Moses. Interpreting *Sifre Deut.* 42, *ad* xi.14, "... then I will give: I — not by means of an angel and not by means of an apostle," J. Goldin has collated the passages where this formula occurs[202], and a midrash on *Lev.* xxvi.46 appears to be most interesting for the interpretation of the quotation from the Passover Aggada. In version B of *Aboth de R. Nathan,* it is said: "Moses received the Law from Sinai — not from the mouth of an angel and not from the mouth of a seraph, but from the mouth of the King of kings over kings, the Holy One, blessed be He, as it is said: "These are the statutes, and ordinances, and laws" (*Lev.* xxvi.46a)."[203] How the Scriptural verse is understood to bear out the statement in *Aboth de R. Nathan* B is shown by version A, which says: "The Law, which the Holy One, blessed be He, gave to Israel was given by none save by the hand of

---

200 Whereas the Masoretic text has מלאך in *v.* 20, the Samaritan Pentateuch reads "*My Angel*", hence the Targumic "My Apostle".

201 Goldschmidt, p. 122. In *Num.R.* i.1, the "angel" who in *Num.* xx.16 is said to have brought the people out of Egypt is understood to be Moses, but the commentary underlines that the term is here used as a name of the prophets.

202 See "Not by Means of an Angel and not by Means of a Messenger", in *RA*, pp. 412 ff.

203 Schechter, p. 2.

Moses, as it is written: "[which the Lord made] between Him and the children of Israel [in Mt. Sinai by the hand of Moses]" (*Lev.* xxvi.46b). He considered Moses to be Apostle (שליח) between the children of Israel and God" (ch.1).[204] The words "between Him and the children of Israel" are taken to mean that Moses was made God's Apostle, his Messenger to Israel. There is also a variant which reads: "Moses was found worthy of being the middleman (בינוני) between the children of Israel and God."[205]. The Apostle of God or God's middleman in the communication of the Law must receive the statutes and so on directly from the mouth of God.

Since Moses in this midrash merited being the Apostle of God, the third link in the formula was impossible. Thus, although the figure of the Apostle in the formula apparently did not always denote Moses, it certainly had this connotation. In *Sifre Deut.* 42, it actually seems to be Moses who is referred to by the words "not by means of an angel and not by means of an apostle". Since "which I command you" in *Deut.* xi.13 would seem to be spoken by Moses, it appears that it is also Moses who is the "I" in *vv.* 14 f. that gives rain and grass; the rabbis therefore had to underline that this "I" referred to God and not to an angel or an apostle[206]. Considering that the Samaritans entitled Moses the "Apostle" and substituted this term for the Angel of the Lord in the exodus traditions, it is not unreasonable to assume that the formula in the Jewish Passover Aggada is directed against a Samaritan claim for Moses.

The Christian apologist Justin Martyr may provide interesting evidence pertaining to the theory that the Samaritans could see Moses the Apostle of God as the personification of the Angel of the Lord. Justin says that Christ is called both "Angel" and "Apostle":

> Now, the Logos of God is His Son, as we have said before. And he is called "Angel" and "Apostle", for he declares what we ought to know and is sent forth in order to declare whatever is revealed. As our Lord himself says: "He who hears me hears Him who has sent me" [cp. *Luke* x.16].
>
> (*I Apol.* lxiii.5)

Already in the Old Testament, the prophets are called "angels" (see *II Chron.* xxxvi.15 f.; *Is.* xliv.26; *Hag.* i.12 f.), and Jewish tradition explained this use of the term through the concept of apostle[207]. Justin actually says: "Now Isaiah shows that those prophets who are sent to publish tidings from God are called His "angels" and "apostles", for Isaiah says in a certain verse: "Send me (ἀπόστειλόν με)" (vi.8). And that the Prophet whose name was

---

204 See Goldin, p. 420.
205 Cp. S. Lieberman, *Hellenism in Jewish Palestine*, New York, 1962, pp. 81 f.
206 See Goldin, pp. 423 f.
207 See Bühner, pp. 281 ff., 341 ff.

changed [see *Num.* xiii.16], Jesus, was strong and great, is manifest to all" (*Dial.* ch. 75). But the source for Justin's designation of the Son as "Angel" does not seem to be Jewish prophetology, which in fact endeavoured to restrict the use of the term for description of the heavenly messengers, for Christ as Angel in Justin's writings is the Angel of the Lord in the Old Testament (see *Dial.* ch. 56; 61). In *Dial.* ch. 75, Justin discerns his presence in the Angel of the Lord in *Ex.* xxiii.20 f., whom he equates with Joshua. That the function of the Angel was to preach the divine truth is explained by Justin from the fact that the word "angel" means one who "brings messages" (*Dial.* ch. 56). Since Justin obviously sees no difference between "Angel" and "Apostle", the latter term as used of the Son would also seem to designate him as a heavenly being. Thus, Justin apparently reflects two different views of the concept of angel-apostle: on the one hand, the Jewish notion of the prophets as "angels", as explained by the term of apostle, and, on the other hand, the idea of a special Prophet who really is the Angel of the Lord, that is, a heavenly being, and is called God's "Apostle".

In early Christian literature, we often come across a tradition to the effect that the apostle has a higher status than the prophet. In the *Acts of Thomas*, it even is said about Thomas, the "twin brother" of Christ: "This is either God or the Apostle of God" (ch. 9). The alternative of being God himself descended to earth is to be his "Apostle". Thomas is a revealer of divine secrets like Christ (see ch. 31; 39; *et al.*) and is therefore called "the Apostle of God". This is similar to the idea of the Son as the Apostle of God in Justin's works and would seem to depend upon an archaic usage.

Moreover, Justin says that the Son actually is *called* "Apostle", so he must have a certain form of divine manifestation in mind. It is true that Jesus is called "Apostle" in *Heb.* iii.1, but this passage does not use the word in the sense which Justin does. D. Plooij, accepting the theory of the existence of a pre-canonical collection of messianic proof-texts from the Old Testament, argues that both *Hebrews* and Justin were dependent upon a "Testimony-Book" presenting proof from Scripture that Jesus had fulfilled the messianic rôle, which included being God's "Angle", an equivalent of which was "Apostle"[208]. Whether such "testimonies" ever existed as a written collection or were produced sporadically and incompletely by an oral method, we must try to find the source of the tradition describing God's agent as "Apostle". Now we have seen that the Samaritans in their Targum exchange the Angel of the Lord for the "Apostle", which is a frequent Samaritan term for the office held by Moses. Justin actually came from Samaria, and it does not seem pre-

208 See D. Plooij, *Studies in the Testimony-Book* (VKAWA, Afd. Letterkunde, XXXII/2), Amsterdam, 1932, pp. 45 ff.

carious to assume that he describes Christ by aid of Samaritan interpretations of Scripture.

As remarked, the *Epistle to the Hebrews* is the only source from the first century calling Jesus "Apostle". After having stated that Jesus is able to help men being tempted because of the fact that he himself was tempted, the author goes on:

> Whence, holy brothers, sharers of a heavenly calling, consider the Apostle and High Priest of our confession, Jesus, who is faithful to the One making him, as was also Moses in all His house. For this one has been counted worthy of more glory than Moses, inasmuch as the one having prepared it has more honour than the house. For every house is made by someone, but the one having made all things is God. And, on the one hand, Moses was faithful as a servant in all His house, for a testimony of the things being spoken [in the future]; Christ, on the other, [was faithful] as a Son over His house, whose house we are if we hold fast firmly the confidence and the rejoicing of the hope until the end.

(iii.1–6)

This is the beginning of a pericope running to iv.13 and emphasizing the superiority of Jesus over Moses. Some sort of Moses veneration obviously is opposed. Now, the quoted passage contains several epithets being the property of Moses in Samaritanism. Thus, as we have seen, Moses is called "the Faithful One of the house of God" and God's "Servant" in the same context[209]. Moreover, Moses in Samaritanism is also the "Apostle" of God, God's "High Priest", and "the Son of the house of God", but *Hebrews* assigns these titles to Jesus in an attempt to range the latter higher than the former[210]. In Samaritanism, however, there apparently is no distinction in meaning of being the "Son", the "Faithful One", or the "Servant" in God's "house". In a couple of texts, the "Son of the house of God" and the "Faithful One of God" are connected terms:

> Where is there a true prophet like the Faithful One of God? God spoke with the Son of His house mouth to mouth; He revealed wonderful things to him, things revealed to no other.

(Cowley, 32.12 ff.)

> Where is there anyone like Moses, and who can compare with Moses, who was glorified in the unseen things even more than in the revealed things, – the Son of His house, the Faithful One of God, to whom God revealed himself, with whom God spoke?

(*Memar Marqa* IV.1)

---

209 See above, p. 141 and p. 145. These texts, from *Memar Marqa* IV.6 and VI.3, are quoted anew immediately below.

210 R.J.F. Trotter, *Did the Samaritans of the Fourth Century Know the Epistle to the Hebrews*? (LUOS Monograph Series, 1), Leeds, 1961, pp. 9 f., thinks that *Heb.* iii.1 ff. was paradigmatical for the Samaritans, but Kippenberg, p. 317, n. 60, rightly points out that *Hebrews* splits what is connected in Samaritanism.

In another text, the "Son of the house of God" is mentioned together with the "Servant of God":

> Where is there anyone like Moses. Apostle of the Truth [*i.e.*, of God], Faithful One of God, the Son of the house of God?
>
> (*Ibid.*)

Moreover, God's "Faithful One" and "Servant" not only is the "Son of the house" but also God's "Apostle":

> Where is there anyone like Moses, Apostle of the Truth [*i.e.*, of God], Faithful One of the house of God, and His Servant?
>
> (*Memar Marqa* VI.3)

The one being the "Son", the "Faithful One", and the "Servant" in God's "house" is the "Apostle", Moses.

According to *Hebrews*, the "house" in which Moses the "Servant" and Jesus the "Son" are "faithful" is the community (see *v.* 6); but, in Samaritanism, the "house" is the heavenly temple where the angels dwell[211]. Moses is the high priest of this "house":

> Where is there the like of Moses, and who can compare with Moses, the Faithful One of His house, who dwelt with the angels in the Sanctuary of the unseen [...]. He was holy priest in two sanctuaries.
>
> (*Memar Marqa* IV.6)

Moses, the "Servant" and "Faithful One" in God's "house", was high priest in the earthly tabernacle and also among the angels in the heavenly sanctuary. In *Hebrews*, however, Jesus is the heavenly high priest, just as he is the "faithful" "Son" of God's "house".

Moreover, in iv. 14–x.18, the pericope following upon the one emphasizing Jesus' superiority over Moses, Jesus' high priestly office in heaven is contrasted with the function of the Aaronic priesthood. The Samaritans, of course, placed enormous importance upon their possession of an Aaronic priesthood and viewed their high priest as the successor of Moses[212]. J. Macdonald writes: "The affinities of the Epistle to the Hebrews with the Samaritan teachings are in some respects so close, that it is not an irresponsible act to suggest that the Epistle was written to Samaritan Christians."[213] As far as I

---

211 See the text from *Memar Marqa* IV.6 quoted above, p. 141, and p. 140, n. 183. Compare the statement by R. Yose ben Halafta of the 2nd century: "God calls Moses faithful in all His house; thereby he ranks higher than the ministering angels" (*Sifre* 110, on *Num.* xii.7). "Servant", too, is based on *Num.* xii.7. Justin (*Dial.* ch. 56; 130) speaks of Moses as the "faithful servant", but with no reference to *Num.* xii.7.

212 See Macdonald, *Theology*, pp. 310 ff.

213 *Theology*, p. 421; cp. p. 440. In other places, he reckons with the possibility that *Hebrews* has influenced the Samaritans; see pp. 167, 212, 445, 450. Compare the thesis of Trotter.

know, no commentator on *Hebrews* has advocated such a theory, but this brief survey of the first verses of ch. iii at least has shown that the author was acquainted with a portrayal of Moses which also was known to the Samaritans, who do not use the name "Israelites" but actually refer to themselves as "Hebrews".

It would also seem that a Samaritan background or relation can be discerned in the *Gospel of John* [214], where statements to the effect that the Father has "sent" the Son and the Son has been "sent" by the Father occur some forty-five times. W.A. Meeks wonders whether *John*'s conception of Jesus as the one having been sent by God is based in part upon a Moses pattern and is to be explained from the identification of Jesus as the Prophet like Moses, because "the elements of his [*i.e.,* Jesus'] "sending" and "commissioning" overlap with the characteristics of the true prophet" of *Deut.* xviii.18 ff.[215] Thus, just like Jesus does not speak his own words but the words of the one who has sent him (see vii.16, 18; viii.26; xii.49; xiv.24), the characteristic of the Prophet like Moses is that he speaks God's words and not his own.[216] Meeks notes that the Samaritans emphasizes Moses' apostleship[217], and J.-A. Bühner has recently concluded that the Samaritan "doctrine of apostleship in the sense of representation and power of attorney" offers "an important religio-historical parallel to the Apostle-Christology of the 4th Gospel"[218].

---

214 A connection between Samaritanism and *John* has been theorized. Odeberg, *Gospel*, pp. 171 ff., especially pp. 185 f., speculated whether the Fourth Gospel was intended for Samaritan circles. Bowman, "Samaritan Studies", pp. 298 ff., has noted many similarities between *John* and Samaritanism leading to the impression that *John* "sets out the teaching of Jesus in a way that would make it more attractive to the Samaritans [than to the Jews]" (p. 308). See also *Problem*, pp. 59 ff. Bowman now has modified his thesis to the effect that he connects *John* with the Dositheans alone; see *ibid.*, p. 142, n. 57. G.W. Buchanan, "The Samaritan Origin of the Gospel of John", in *RA*, pp. 149 ff., asserts that *John* was written by a Samaritan Christian. See also E.D. Freed, "Samaritan Influence in the Gospel of John", *CBQ*, 30, 1968, pp. 580 ff.; cp. W.H. Brownlee, "Whence the Gospel According to John?", in Charlesworth, ed., *John and Qumran*, pp. 179, 183. I have not seen J.D. Purvis' paper, "The Fourth Gospel and the Samaritans", read at the *SBL* Annual Meeting in Washington, D.C., October, 1974. K. Haacker, *Die Stiftung des Heils* (AT, 1), Stuttgart, 1972, finds "structural" agreements between the theology of *John* and that of the Samaritans, particularly in the conception of the "founder" (*Stifter*); see especially pp. 18 ff.

215 *Prophet-King*, p. 302.

216 See *ibid.*, pp. 45 f. Cp. above, pp. 61 f.

217 See *Prophet-King*, pp. 226 f.

218 *Op. cit.*, p. 306. Both Meeks, pp. 238 f., and Bühner, pp. 302 f., compare the Samaritan demand of *belief* in Moses to the doctrine in the Fourth Gospel that belief in the Son is really belief in the one who has sent him, for the Samaritans actually teach that belief in Moses includes belief in God. Already Bowman emphasized the concept of faith in Samaritan thought, and stated that "the Samaritan connotation

There is also a polemic against a Moses-centered piety in *John*. Meeks has pointed out that the motif of Jesus being the only one who is able to "see" God is associated with a polemic against such a claim for Moses in i.17 f. and v.37 (cp. vi.32 and 46)[219]. This polemic would strike against the Samaritans, who actually taught that Moses had faced God when he ascended to receive the Law[220].

The polemic of the first half of iii.13 would also strike against the Samaritans: "And no one has gone up into heaven, but the one has come down from heaven, the Son of Man."[221] The first half of the verse says that "no *man* has gone up into heaven to learn heavenly secrets,"[222] and H. Odeberg has rightly seen the force of this statement in a reference to the claim made for heroes of the past[223]. The Samaritans claimed that Moses had ascended to heaven and learnt "heavenly things" (*v.* 12), and the Dositheans obviously made the same claim for the one they believed to have fulfilled the rôle as the Prophet like Moses.

We may now profitably return to the teaching of the Samaritan Gnostic Menander, the figure of whom inaugurated the discussion of this section. It

---

of faith can be understood as not unlike that given to faith in the Fourth Gospel, where $\pi\iota\sigma\tau\iota\varsigma$ and $\gamma\nu\tilde{\omega}\sigma\iota\varsigma$ have much in common" ("Samaritan Studies", p. 313). This is correct and can even be seen in passages dealing with Moses' apostleship; thus, Marqa says that the people "believed the Truth [*i.e.*, God] and knew that the apostleship of Moses was true "(*Memar Marqa* II.9). It is interesting to compare this statement to a couple of passages from *John* ch. xvii: "... know You, the only true God, and Jesus Christ, whom You have sent" (*v.* 3); "... they knew truly that I [*i.e.*, Jesus] came forth from You, and they believed that You sent me" (*v.* 8).

219 See *Prophet-King*, pp. 298 ff.

220 See below, p. 228.

221 The conjunction $\kappa\alpha\iota$ links the statement firmly with what has gone before; thus the force of the verse is that no one can speak with authority of the "heavenly things" (*v.* 12) except the Son of Man who has come down from heaven. Most translations, however, drop the introductory conjunction and thereby convey the impression that the verse takes up a new theme, *viz.*, the descent and ascent of the Son of Man. But it is not plausible that *v.* 13a refers to Jesus' ascent. The Evangelist goes on to speak in future tense about the exaltation of the Son of Man through death and resurrection, whereas *v.* 13a uses perfect tense. R. Bultmann suggests that it is "a perf. of the kind used in general statements or fictitious examples" (*The Gospel of John*, trans. by G.R. Beasley-Murray, *et al.*, Oxford, 1971, p. 151, n. 2), but this would be a very awkward anticipation of what is to follow and also a placement of the cart before the horse on account of the fact that *v.* 13b speaks about the *descent* of the Son of Man.

222 Bernard, I, p. 111. The exception involved in $\epsilon\iota$ $\mu\acute{\eta}$, here having the sense of $\dot{\alpha}\lambda\lambda\acute{\alpha}$, refers to the impossibility of man's revelation of "heavenly things" as a result of having ascended to heaven.

223 See *op. cit.*, pp. 72, 88 f., 94 f., 97 f. For a full discussion of the verse, see F.J. Moloney, *The Johannine Son of Man* (BSR, 14), Rome, 1976, pp. 53 ff., 60.

is a correspondence to the teaching of Jesus according to *John* when Menander says that God is "unknown to all" (*incognitam ait omnibus*), and that he was "sent by the Invisible as a saviour for the redemption of men (*missus sit ab invisibilibus salvatorem pro salute hominum*)." In the *Gospel of John*, the statements that only the Son has "seen" the Father and therefore can speak about him are parallelled by the assertations that men do not "know" God but can obtain such knowledge through the one who has been "sent" from God (see vii.28 f.; viii.55; xiv.6 ff.; xvii.25; cp. x.15). Menander apparently considered himself to be the one having been "sent" to men with the saving knowledge of God. This claim of Menander would seem to indicate that he was the Prophet like Moses being God's fully commissioned Apostle and representative. The Greek parallel passage in Eusebius (*Hist. eccl.* III.xxvi.1) has ἀπεσταλμένος, which obviously corresponds to the Aramaic שליח, which is a title of Moses in Samaritanism. The eschatological Moses-like prophet was also God's Apostle.

We should note also that *John*'s idea that the Son was "sent" in order to "save "the world" (see iii.17; cp. iv.42; xii.47) is matched by the notion of Menander's sending "for the salvation of men". This, too, can find a precendent in Samaritan Moses traditions. W. A. Meeks has noted that, in Samaritanism, there is "a universal strain in the traditions about Moses' prophetic office"[224]. Thus, for instance, Marqa calls Moses "the illuminator of the whole house of Adam" (*Memar Marqa* I.2). The message of this idea was developed by the claimants to the office of the Prophet like Moses. While Dositheus would seem to have appealed only to Samaritans, Simon and Menander manifestly designed a broader horizon for their apostleship. The fervid missionary activity of Manicheism, the last and greatest of the Gnostic schools of Antiquity, is the logical outcome of the universal scope of the Gnostic religion. Gnosticism is in essence a world religion, but its roots are clearly detectable in the national religion of the Samaritans and the Jews.

Furthermore, Justin and Irenaeus tell that Menander was a magician. This, of course, is a stock characteristic used of heretics, but it may be that Menander – like Simon – actually claimed to be a great miracle worker. In the Christian polemic, then, Menander's miracle becomes magic. In Samaritanism, Moses was the wonder worker *par excellence*. Already the Bible tells that Moses was "sent" by God with "signs" (σημεῖα) so that the people should "believe" that he was God's commissioned agent (see *Ex.* iii.12 ff.; iv.1 ff., especially *v.* 8). The Prophet like Moses would also have to be a worker of miracles[225]. According to the *Gospel of John*, the "signs" (σημεῖα) of Jesus bear witness to his status as being "sent" by God (see v.36). In vi.29 ff., the

---

224 *Prophet-King*, p. 225. Cp. Macdonald, *Theology*, pp. 204 ff.
225 See above, pp. 117 ff.

crowd asks Jesus for "a sign" so that they can "believe" that he is "sent" by God, and they go on to refer to the manna brought down from heaven by Moses. The Galileans acclaim Jesus as the Prophet like Moses after he has worked a "sign" resembling Moses' bringing down bread from heaven (see vi.17)[226]. Since we do not hear about the miracles performed by Menander, we cannot for sure know whether they were meant to prove his status as the eschatological Mosaic prophet, but this remains at least a very good possibility in view of the fact that he claimed to be "sent" from God.

It has been suggested above that the baptism of resurrection which Menander offered his disciples should be connected with the baptismal rites of the Samaritan sectarians, and that these rituals possibly were intended to effect an ascent to heaven and attainment of immortality similar to the apotheosis of Moses, who even was baptized in heaven. Since there was a Samaritan teaching to the effect that Moses' followers could attain heavenly status, the same would hold true with regard to the disciples of the Prophet like Moses. It is especially interesting to note the phrase that Menander's followers were said to receive the baptism of resurrection to eternal life "in him" (*in eum*), for this is a wording strongly reminding of *John's* saying that the believer may have eternal life "in" the Son of Man through baptism (see iii.15). Paul taught a uniting with Christ in the rite of baptism (see *Rom.* vi.1 ff.), and R. M. Grant says that Menander's "interpretation of baptism looks like a distortion of the Pauline teaching about dying and rising with Christ."[227] But neither Menander nor *John* speaks of a *dying* in baptism, and Grant in fact had hit upon a better parallel from Christianity in an earlier work, where he compares Menander's baptism to "the Eucharist as described by Ignatius of Antioch," who called it a "drug of immortality, an antidote for death" (*Eph.* xx.2)[228]. It is not impossible that Menander and *John* in their respective ways have adapted some Samaritan idea of obtaining eternal life by baptism "in" Moses, who was believed to have ascended to heaven and attained this goal.

There is no reason why not the author of *John*, who wrote by the end of the first century, could have availed himself of Samaritan Moses traditions, for the emergence of a Moses pattern in the reports on the Samaritan heretics Dositheus, Simon, and Menander — the last of whom cannot have been in activity later than around 70 C.E. — shows that the Samaritan Moses traditions were in existence quite early. In any event, the observations on the first Gnostics have demonstrated that there is a connection between Samaritanism and Gnosticism.

---

226 For a correlation between Moses and Jesus as God's "Apostle", see Meeks, pp. 301 ff.
227 *Gnosticism. An Anthology*, London, 1961, p. 30.
228 Quoted in *Gnosticism and Early Christianity*, pp. 93 f. Antioch was the city where Menander had worked (see Just., *I Apol.* xxvi.4); see above, p. 142.

Samaritanism and "Iranian" Gnosticism

In the Gnostic religion of the Mandeans, we also find the term "Apostle" used as a designation of the saviour who is sent to earth. The redeemer speaks thus:

> I am the Apostle of Light (שליהא אנא דנהורא) whom the Great One has sent into this world. I am the true Apostle (שליהא אנא כושטאנא) with whom there is no lie.
>
> *(Right Ginza 64.20 ff.)*

As pointed out in the previous Chapter, G. Widengren has compared the term "the true Apostle" in Mandeism to the Samaritan and Ebionite appellation "the true Prophet"[229]. But Widengren has not seen that also "Apostle" occurs as a pregnant title of Moses in Samaritanism. Correspondingly, "prophet" is a synonym of "apostle" in Mandeism; the Jewish prophets are said to "call themselves prophets and say: "We are apostles"" (*ibid.* 46.19).

Widengren also has noted that the Mandeans speak not only of "the true Apostle" but also of "the Apostle of the Truth", שליהא דכושטא[230]. Thus, we read in a prayer:

> Preserver of the souls, keep us from everything which is abominable! Sender of the Apostles of the Truth (שליהיא דכושטא), remove the wrath from Your friends!
>
> *(Ibid.* 63.9 ff.)

If Widengren had read *Memar Marqa*, and not only Marqa's hymns, he would have seen that Moses actually is called the "Apostle of the Truth", שליח קשטה . It will be remembered that this title occurs in a rhetorical question enumerating some of Moses' appellations:

> Where is there anyone like Moses, the Apostle of the Truth, the Faithful One of the house of God, and His Servant?
>
> *(Memar Marqa VI.3)*

In Samaritanism, *Qušṭa* is a name of God, while *Kušta* in Mandeism is not primarily a name of a mythological person, although the saving truth often is personified (for instance, in a variant in *Right Ginza* 64.21, we read *'ana Kušta*). There can be no doubt, however, that the Samaritan and the Mandean term are related[231].

---

229 See p. 59.

230 A corresponding term is "prophet of the Truth". The Jewish prophets "set themselves up as prophets of the Truth" (*ibid.* 25.5).

231 The concept of "Truth" is also important in other Gnostic systems than that of the Mandeans; see the "Index of Gnostic Concepts", *s.v.* "Truth", in *Gnosis*, II, p. 342, col. b. In some systems, it is conceived of as a heavenly entity, a personal being. The Marcosians used the term to designate their "Mother of all", that is, Wisdom (see Iren., I.xviii.1; xxi.3). The latter name, by the way, was used also by the Simonians, Samaritan Gnostics, to describe Wisdom (see *ibid.* I.xxiii.2; *Ps.-Clem.Hom.* II.25).

In both religions, "(the) Life" is used as a name of God, and Widengren also has pointed out that even expressions as "(the) Word of Life" and "(the) Treasure of Life" occur both in Samaritan and Mandean literature. The Samaritan ממלל חיים corresponds to the Mandean מאלאלא דהייא and similar expressions, apparently being merely "indications of various layers and geographical-cultural influences"[232], while סימתה (שומיה) or אוצר (or הוצר) and (דחיים) כרי חיים in Samaritanism correspond to סימאת הייא or סימתא דהייא and האי עוצאר or עוצאר הייא in Mandeism. In both religions, the first-mentioned term is, of course, a designation of the revelation, and this "Word" of revelation often is personified as one of the saviour figures in Mandeism and identified with Moses in later Samaritan theology.

It is not "the same idea" which is expressed by the various forms of the latter term. In Samaritanism, "(the) Treasure" can be used as a name of God, but "(the) Treasure" as well as "(the) Life" can also be transferred to the Law. In Mandeism, סימאת הייא is a female divinity, and עוצאר האי is one of the male saviour deities, while the less frequent terms of סימתא דהייא and עוצאר הייא are used to designate the individual soul or the entire assemblage of souls, for which גינזא דהייא is more common.

K. Rudolph, who endorses Widengren's attempt to demonstrate a connection between Samaritanism and Gnosticism, especially Mandeism, has added to the table of comparisons that the Mandeans use קאיים of God and thus provide a parallel to the use of קעים in Samaritanism. Thus, a frequent and obviously old Mandean formulary runs:

> The Life stands fast and upright in His שכינא; the Life is victorious in all things.
>   (*e.g., Right Ginza* 274.6)[233]

The Marcosian baptismal formula of "Hebrew words" transmitted by Irenaeus (I.xxi.3) shows that the Aramaic term was קורשטא, that is, the same form as found in Samaritan literature, for ῥουαδὰ κουστὰ in the Marcosian formulary apparently goes back to רוחה דקושטא.

232 *Ascension*, p. 57.
233 See Rudolph, *Mandäer*, I, p. 173, n. 4 (continued on the next page), who also notes that קאיים in Mandeism mostly is used in connection with the baptism. Through baptism, man comes to participate in the divine life. In Samaritanism, קעים can be used to describe people as being "raised up" by God at the end of time.
  Rudolph, "Randerscheinungen", p. 117 (= *GG*, p. 789), has singled out additional terms and ideas occurring in both Samaritanism and Mandeism, but these additions seem rather to belong to the common religious vocabulary of the Near East (*e.g.*, "Tree of Life", "Living Water") or at least being shared also by the Jews (and Christians) (*e.g.*, glorification of Adam, titles and descriptions of the saviour). Rudolph also notes that water and fire are cosmogonic elements in both Samaritanism and Mandeism, but this does not have to mean that the one (in Rudolph's opinion, Samaritanism) has influenced the other; it might also be that the two religions independently have adopted non-Semitic cosmogonic speculations current in the Hellenistic world. The same would hold true with regard to the concept of the

There is one piece of evidence in particular which shows that the Mandeans have appropriated Samaritan traditions. This is the older name of their cult hut, מאשכנא, a word which also is discernable in the name *Mašknāyê*, "Tabernacle people", which Theodore bar Konai in *Book of Scholia* XI gives as an alternate of *Mandāyê* (*manda* being a younger designation of the Mandean cult hut)[234]. M. Lidzbarski noted that the religious vocabulary of the Mandeans usually contains images drawn from the agricultural life, and wrote: "This usage seems to me to be borrowed from a Jewish circle in which the "tabernacle" in the desert was regarded as an ideal and perhaps even copied. Orthodox Judaism has not used this word of its sanctuaries."[235] G. Widengren speculates whether this "Jewish circle" could have been constituted by Essenes[236], but it is A. Adam who is on the right track when suggesting a derivation from "Northern Israelite-Samaritan" traditions centered about the tabernacle and the festival of booths[237]. We have seen that the Samaritan tradition tells that the משכן, the desert sanctuary, was erected on Mt. Gerizim but hidden by God when Eli disrupted the cult at Shechem and moved to Shilo, the place of worship before Jerusalem. Ever since the temple which later was built on Mt. Gerizim was destroyed by John Hyrcanus, the Samaritans have awaited eagerly the recovery of the tabernacle. Enthusiasts promised to retrieve it, and eschatological movements even made prefigurations of it[238]. It is ostensibly from some Dosithean circle that the name of the Israelite desert sanctuary was taken over by the Mandeans.

Since it is generally agreed that Mandeism has roots in the baptismal movement which existed in Palestine at the turn of our era, it is not so surprising that Samaritan terms and concepts are found in the religion of the Mandeans.

"Root", עקר, which is used as a designation of the first being in cosmogonic contexts in both religions, for this appears to have been a popular philosophical term. Since the *Megale Apophasis* actually cites ῥίζα τῶν ὅλων as a name of the primal principle (see Hipp., VI.ix.4; xii.1 f.), Weiss, pp. 136 ff., thinks that this concept came to Samaritanism via Simonianism; but there is nothing which indicates that Simonianism in Samaria was philosophically orientated and knew the philosophy of the "Great Announcement". See also Kippenberg, p. 347, n. 136.

234 See Pognon, p. 154.

235 *Das Johannesbuch der Mandäer*, Giessen, 1915, pp. XX f.

236 See Art. "Die Mandäer", in B. Spuler, ed., *HO* (Erste Abteilung: Der nahe und der mittlere Osten), VIII (Religion)/2 (Religionsgeschichte des Orients in der Zeit der Weltreligionen), 1961, p. 108.

237 See *Die Psalmen des Thomas und das Perlenlied als Zeugnisse vorchristlicher Gnosis* (BZNW, 24), Berlin, 1959, p. 79.

238 See above, pp. 64 f. The Mandeans also call their cult hut שכינתא, which corresponds to the Hebrew שכינה. The Jews taught that the "Presence" of God was to be found especially in the temple and on Mt. Sion; see G.F. Moore, *Judaism*, I, Schocken paperback edition, New York, 1971, p. 369. The Samaritans, however, use השכינה even as a name of the sanctuary itself (see *Malef* 88a).

Furthermore, similarities between the Mandeans and the Elchasaites have induced many scholars to theorize that the Jewish Christian sect of the Elchasaites has contributed to Mandean beginnings[239], and we have seen above that the Elchasaites had Samaritan connections[240]. We now know that the Elchasaites spread into southern Babylonia, where they may have been absorbed by a Jewish Gnostic sect of proto-Mandeans[241], and this might account for the presence of Samaritan terms and ideas in Mandeism.

We may expect to find Samaritan vestiges in Manicheism, too, for the newly discovered Cologne Mani Codex in Greek has confirmed Ibn al-Nadim's report that the father of Mani joined an ascetic baptizing sect founded by a certain *al-Ḥasiḥ*, which obviously is the Arabic form of Elchasai's name (see *Fihrist* IX.1)[242]. The Greek Mani Codex narrates that Mani was brought up and lived until he was twenty-five years old in a Jewish Christian community of Elchasaites in southern Babylonia[243].

---

239 See the survey by Rudolph, *Mandäer*, I, pp. 233 ff.

240 See pp. 65 ff.

241 See G. Quispel, "Jewish Gnosis and Mandaean Gnosticism", in J.-E. Menard, ed., *Les textes de Nag Hammadi* (Colloque du Centre d'Histoire des Religions, Strassbourg 23-25 octobre 1974) (NHS, VII), Leiden, 1975, pp. 112 ff. Quispel, p. 113, cites an allegedly Jewish Christian source written in Syriac in the 5th or 6th century in Haran, and incorporated into a book of Abd al-Jabbar in the 10th century, which says that the Jewish Christians before the destruction of the temple fled as far as Mosul, which is close to the site of the old city of Ninive on the Tigris in northern Mesopotamia; see S. Pines, *The Jewish Christians of the Early Centuries of Christianity according to a New Source* (PIASH, II/13), Jerusalem, 1966, p. 15. Now Theodore says that the Mandeans or Mashknaeans came from Adiabene, which is a district in the upper Tigris region, and that they were called *Nāṣrāyê* in the district of Kufa, just south of the old city of Babylon. The Mandean legendary work known as *Haran Gawaita* tells that the נאצוראייא, another name of the Mandeans, fled from persecution in Jerusalem and took refuge in Haran and the Median hills before travelling south and settling in southern Mesopotamia. It is true that first Christians called themselves Naṣoreans, but this name is not attested for the Jewish Christian sect of the Elchasaites, and we have also seen that Samaritan groups applied this name to themselves; see above, p. 66, n. 128. Moreover, Theodore opens his account of this sect by naming it the sect of the *Dūstayê*, and gives "Followers of Dostai", *i.e.*, Dositheus, as an alternate term of "Naṣoreans" in the district of Kufa. It seems that these people were not called Mandeans before they ultimately settled in Mesene, the district of Basra by the Persian gulf. This may imply that they were not Gnostic before they merged with a Jewish Gnostic group in southern Babylonia (the West Syriac מאנדא is equivalent to *gnōsis*). The Babylonian Jews actually accused the Jews in Mesene of being very outlandish and even mixing with the Samaritans. For these Jews, see H. Graetz, *Das Königreich Mesene und seine jüdische Bevölkerung* (JSF), Breslau, 1897.

242 Al-Nadim relates that Elchasai had a pupil by the name of *Šamʿûn*, which apparently is equivalent to the name of Simon Magus and hints at some kind of connection between Samaritan sectarianism and Jewish Christianity.

243 See A. Henrichs & L. Koenen, "Ein griechischer Mani-Codex", *ZPE*, 5, 1970, pp. 97

Since Mani wrote his works in Aramaic[244], M. Lidzbarski surmised that Manicheism was constituted not only of Iranian elements but also would contain traces of the religion of the Arameans in Babylonia. He cited particularly Mani's assertion in an Iranian hymn that he had stood at "the Gate of the Truth" (M 4, p. 2), an expression which goes back to the Aramaic באבא דקושטא[245]. Since the "Truth" is not known as a name of God in Iranian religion, Lidzbarski asked whether it was an Aramean name of God. As far as I know, this has not been evidenced, but we have seen that it is a very common *Samaritan* divine name[246]. Furthermore, the expression "stand at the gates" of God is very common in Samaritanism; it is used of standing in prayer on Mt. Gerizim, a name of which is the "Gate of Heaven"[247].

According to al-Biruni, Mani even called himself "the Apostle of the God of the Truth"[248], an appellation which is contiguous with Moses' title "the Apostle of God". Mani's standard title "Apostle" apparently points to a Samaritan source, for the Samaritans often designate Moses as God's Apostle.

According to Arabic authors, Mani even referred to himself as "the Seal of the prophets" (*xātimu-n-nabīyīn*)[249], and this is — as we have seen — a name of Moses in Samaritanism. When Moses is about to leave this life, the people beg him:

> By your life, O Apostle of God, remain with us a little longer! By your life, O Seal of the prophets, stop with us a little longer!
>
> (*Memar Marqa* V.3)

We have seen that Elchasai appeared as the eschatological Prophet like Moses on a Samaritan sectarian model: he introduced changes in the

---

ff., with additions in 8, 1971, pp. 243 ff.; *iidem*, ed. & trans. "Der Kölner Mani-Kodex", *ZPE*, 19, 1975, pp. 1 ff.; *iidem*, ed. & trans., "Der Kölner Mani-Kodex", *ibid.*, 32, 1978, pp. 87 ff. Serveral scholars have paid duly heed to this new evidence; see F. Decret, *Mani* (MS, 40), Paris, 1974, pp. 37 ff., 48 ff.; K. Rudolph, "Die Bedeutung des Kölner Mani-Codex für die Manichäismusforschung", in *MP*, pp. 271 ff., especially pp. 482 f.; Quispel, "Jewish Gnosis", pp. 108 ff., 112. But it is not even mentioned in the latest survey of research by G. Widengren, who only says: "Mani grew up in a southern Babylonian baptismal movement which *earlier* was regarded as identical with the Mandean movement" ("Der Manichäismus", in *Gnosis*, p. 309; italics mine).

244 The exception being the *Šābuhragān* dedicated to the Persian king Shahpuhr I and therefore written in Pehlevi.

245 Müller, p. 51. See Lidzbarski, "Warum schrieb Mani aramäisch?", *OLZ*, 30, 1927, col. 916 (= G. Widengren, ed., *Der Manichäismus* (WF, CLXVIII), Darmstadt, 1977, p. 253).

246 See above, p. 145.

247 See, *e.g.*, Macdonald, *Theology*, p. 331.

248 Sachau, p. 207, line 18.

249 See Shahrastani, in Cureton, p. 192, line 15; Abu'Ma'ali, in Schefer, p. 145, line 22; Ibn al-Murtada, in Kessler, p. 349, line 13.

Law[250]. That this picture of Elchasai as a new law-giver or -interpreter persisted in the community in which Mani grew up is seen from the fact that Mani in the Cologne Codex refers to Elchasai as ὁ ἀρχηγὸς τοῦ νόμου, "the founder of the law", of the community (94.10)[251]. Mani, too, ostensibly availed himself of the traditions about the eschatological Mosaic figure who was awaited to come and introduce the Law in its correctness. Thus, Mani declares in the Coptic *Homilies*:

> This work has been completed by the Apostle of Light in the land of ... Babylon [...]. Everything I have written and decided, and admonished my children to do accordingly. In every age, they will fulfil my commandment, both small and great, as it is written.[252]

When Mani committed his revelations to writings, he showed his indebtedness to the Semitic tradition, where the revealed word is the written word, as contrasted with Indo-Iranian religion, where the revelation primarily is transmitted orally and the fixation of the canon in literary form happened late[253]. In this text, Mani actually is describing himself as a law-giver, a new Moses. Since Moses was believed to have written the Pentateuch, it was only natural that the prophet who was going to be like him would write down the new revelation including the changes in the old Law. Thus, while Elchasai is told to have supported his authority to change the Law on a book of revelation that had been vouchsafed to him, Dositheus is reported to have written books dealing with questions of the Law as well as to have made alterations in the Pentateuch. If we are to believe the *Pseudo-Clementines,* Simon cherished the Torah but had supplementary writings produced by himself. One of Mani's writings actually was named the "Treasure of Life", which, as we have seen, is a name of the Law among the Samaritans.

Mani can be viewed as an eschatological Moses-like prophet, for he saw himself as the final prophet of a succession which included Adam, Seth, Enosh, Noah, Shem, and Abraham[254], who occur as predecessors of Moses and the Prophet like Moses in older Jewish Christian and Samaritan thought[255]. Like the Mandeans, Mani repudiated Moses, but it seems that his claim of being the last "Apostle" and the "Seal of the prophets" actually is indebted to a Samaritan sectarian doctrine of the Prophet like Moses.

---

250 See above, pp. 66f.
251 Henrichs & Koenen, *ZPE*, 32, p. 178.
252 Polotsky, p. 29, lines 8 ff.
253 See G. Widengren, *Religionsphänomenologie*, Berlin, 1969, pp. 321 ff.
254 The list of the prophets varies somewhat in the sources; see H.-Ch. Puech, *Le manichéisme* (MG, Bibliotheque de diffusion, LVI), Paris 1949, p. 144, n. 241 (continued on pp. 145 f.). The inclusion of Buddha, Zarathustra, and Jesus (and Paul, the apostle of the gentiles) obviously is meant to underscore the universality of the religion.
255 See above, p. 67, n. 130, and p. 94, n. 48.

Furthermore, a vestige of Samaritan Mosaic traditions seems to be present when Mani in his last prayer, transmitted in the Coptic *Homilies*, says:

> I found myself when ... I gave myself Your Great Name (ⲣ̄ ⲡⲉ ⲛ ⲁⲣⲁⲓ ϩⲙ̄ⲡⲉⲕⲛⲁⲥ ⲛ̄ⲡⲉⲛ).256

Just like Moses in Samaritanism, Mani obtains the Name of God. If Mani availed himself of traditions concerning the Prophet like Moses, this is only logical, for the prophet who is going to be like Moses must be the carrier of the Divine Name. In this respect, the personage of Mani can be compared to Dositheus and Simon, both of whom claimed to be profited by the Name of God.

Like Simon, Mani even was regarded as the hypostasized Name. A hymn in Middle Persian contains the following declaration:

> You have come with blessing, most beautiful and loved Name.257

The "most beautiful and loved Name" is a designation which, of course, must apply to God; thus, when it is used about Mani, it indicates that Mani represents the divine nature or mode of being, the "Name".

Simon Magus as "the Great Power (of God)"

W. Foerster has stressed the peculiar fact that also Simon Magus, the first notable individual in the history of Gnosticism, claimed divine honours[258]. In the case of Simon, this pretension is indicated not only by the title "the Standing One", which is adduced by Foerster, but also by the name "the Great Power (of God)". The latter name is found already in the earliest account of the Samaritan heresiarch:

> Going down to the city of Samaria, Philip proclaimed the Messiah to them. And the crowd with one accord gave heed to the things being spoken by Philip, as they heard and saw the miracles which he was doing: for many had unclean spirits that cried in a loud voice when they came out, and many having been paralyzed and lame were healed; and there was much joy in that city. And a certain man by the name of Simon was already in the city practising sorcery and astonishing the people of Samaria, saying himself to be someone great. And all – from small to great – gave heed to him, saying: "This one is the Power of God called the Great." And they gave heed to him because he had astonished them by his sorceries for a considerable time. But when they believed Philip preaching about the Kingdom of God and the name of Jesus the Messiah, they were baptized, both men and women. And Simon also believed; and having been baptized, attached himself to Philip. And beholding the signs and the great powerful deeds that were happening, he was amazed.
>
> (*Acts* viii.5-13)

---

256 Polotsky, p. 54, lines 3 f.
257 Menasce, p. 305.
258 See "Die "ersten Gnostiker" Simon und Menander", pp. 193 ff.

The story goes on to tell that the apostles in Jerusalem, upon hearing about Philip's mission, sent Peter and John to Samaria in order to put their hands upon the newly converted and give them the Spirit.

> And Simon, seeing that the Spirit was given by the laying on of the hands of the apostles, offered them money, saying: "Give me also the authority that whomever I lay hands on may receive the Spirit."
>
> (*vv.* 18 f.)

Peter then rebukes Simon and threathens him, and Simon answers humbly and asks Peter to pray to God for him. Then, Simon disappears from the New Testament scene.

When Philip came to Samaria in order to preach the Gospel, he found the movement of Simon in full blossom. Which city is intended by τὴν πόλιν τῆς Σαμαρείας cannot be known for sure. H. Conzelmann thinks that the phrase suggests that Luke thought that the province of Samaria had only one city, "the one of the same name"[259]. But the capital was never known by the old name after its restoration by Herod the Great. Still, "the city of Samaria" may be the capital, now called Sebaste, as is argued by some[260]. Others maintain that this cannot have been the case, since Sebaste had a pure pagan population[261]. This appears to be correct, since Luke relates that the Gospel was preached in Samaria before the Apostolic Council of Jerusalem decided that it should be proclaimed to the pagan world, and that even Peter was not opposed to the evangelization of Samaria (see *Acts* i.8; viii.14, 25; ix.31; xv.3). Furthermore, as we shall see, Simon obviously was a Samaritan and therefore would try to bring round primarily his own people. Thus, the people said to have been converted must have been circumcised Samaritans and not Samarians.

Some commentators think that any insignificant town can be meant, and some mss. which leave out the article can be taken to support this[262]. This suggestion often is coupled with the conjecture that the city in question is Gitta (situated some 18 kilometres south-east of Caesarea Philippi), from where Simon came (see Just., *I Apol.* xxvi.2)[263]. Another way of interpreting the absence of the article is to take πόλιν as hinting at an underlying *status constructus* and being a mistranslation of an Aramaic מדינת־, coming from מדינא and meaning "province of" (cp. *Matt.* x.5 f., εἰς πόλιν Σαμαριτῶν,

---

259 *Die Apostelgeschichte* (HNT, 7), Tübingen, 1963, p. 40.
260 See already H.H. Wendt, *Die Apostelgeschichte* (MKKNT, 3), 4th ed., Göttingen, 1913, p. 154.
261 See already J. Wellhausen, *Kritische Analyse der Apostelgeschichte* (AKGWG, phil.-hist. Kl., XV/2), Berlin, 1914, p. 14.
262 See O. Bauernfeind, *Die Apostelgeschichte* (THNT, V), Leipzig, 1939, p. 122.
263 See, for instance, F.F. Bruce, *The Acts of the Apostles*, 2nd ed., London, 1952 and reprints, p. 183.

which we must translate "into the province of Samaria")²⁶⁴. In the mss., πόλις, "city", and χώρα, "province" are interchanged in viii.8. However, C.C. Torrey, who contemplated whether "city" in viii.5 is a mistranslation of מדינא (or Hebrew מדינה), felt that *v.* 8 is best understood as speaking of a city²⁶⁵. Moreover, as J. Jeremias admits, the *status constructus* can come from מדינתא, meaning a (definite) city.

Deciding that "city" is the right translation, it remains to settle which city is intended. G. Staehlin pertinently points out that Philip later worked in Caesarea, the residence of the procurator (see viii.40; xxi.8)²⁶⁶, and takes this as an indication that the first missionary to the Samaritans followed the same working principle as Paul and began his activity in the main cities²⁶⁷. But Staehlin's repetition of the assertion by J. Wellhausen and several other authors that Philip began preaching in Shechem needs emendation, for Shechem was destroyed by John Hyrcanus in 129/8 B.C.E. and ceased to exist before the end of the 2nd century B.C.E. However, Philip can have started his mission among the Samaritans in Sychar (the present day Askar) at the foot of Mt. Ebal in the Shechem valley, for this city — from where Mt. Gerizim easily could be seen and in whose vicinity the well of Jacob (cp. *John* iv.5) and Joseph's grave were located — became the centre of the Samaritans after the destruction of Shechem²⁶⁸.

That Simon really was converted to Christianity is unthinkable, but it is not impossible that he actually was baptized; for, in the Hellenistic world, it was not uncustomary to be initiated into several mysteries in order to secure the utmost of supernatural power. Why Simon was excluded from the imparting of the Spirit is not stated; it is only said that he tried to obtain the Spirit because he believed that the possession of the Spirit supplied miracle-working powers. In fact, Simon's former amount of success among his countrymen — in all likelihood exaggerated by the author (see *v.* 10a) — is said to have been due to magical activities (see *vv.* 9, 11). G. Quispel states: "The Samaritan Magus is a parallel appearance to the Jewish sorcerer. If we want to understand Simon, we must regard him from the viewpoint of the Jewish sorcery system."²⁶⁹ In northern Israel, the figure of the magician

264 See J. Jeremias, *Jesu Verheissung für die Völker* (FDV, 1953), 2nd ed., Stuttgart, 1959, p. 17; cp. Art. Σαμάρεια κτλ., in *TDNT*, VII, p. 92, n. 29.
265 See *The Composition and Date of Acts* (HTS), Cambridge, Mass., 1916, p. 18, n. 2. M. Wilcox, *The Semitisms of Acts*, Oxford, 1965, pp. 142 f., however, thinks that χώρα is more natural than πόλις.
266 In this city, Greek and Samaritan culture mingled; see Kippenberg, pp. 155 f.
267 See *Die Apostelgeschichte* (NTD, 5), 3rd ed., Göttingen, 1970, pp. 118 f.
268 See H.-M. Schenke, "Jacobsbrunnen – Josephusgrab – Sychar", *ZDPV*, 84, 1968, pp. 159 ff.
269 *Gnosis*, p. 53.

actually had very deep roots in the prophetic fraternities: "It is interesting to see how the position of the leader, surrounded by his circle of faithful and obedient disciples, has created an atmosphere of a special kind. As the head of such fraternity, the prophetic leader was both revered and feared, though by outsiders mocked at and called a "madman", $m^e\check{s}ugga^\varsigma$ (II Kings 9,11). But the dominating factor is respect, yea, awe, for this man is in possession of Yahweh's spirit. He is also capable of aquiring this Spirit by external means, chiefly by music. Elisha could transfer himself into the exstatic state, filled with the spirit of Yahweh, by listening to a harp-player (II Kings 3,15). We remember the scenes in I Sam. 10,5 or 19,18-24. This possession of the Spirit was demonstrated by the prophet's power of exercising acts, falling within the department of parapsychic faculties. These actions, illustrated in the Books of Kings, include the following categories: visions and auditions, far-hearing and far-seeing, rain-making, production of food, neutralizing of poison, far-range acting, healing of sickness, causing of sickness, raising from the dead, occasioning death or its prediction, sudden disappearing, walking on water, flying in the air."[270]

It is right that the accusation of practising magic is common in polemics warding off heretics and rivals of the true religion, but E. Haenchen and — following him — G. Lüdemann are not justified in asserting that the author of *Acts* simply has degraded Simon to a mere magician[271]. Rather, the description of Simon as a miracle-worker fits into our picture of the religious leader in northern Palestine. Also, as we have seen, there is the portrayal of Simon as a successful magician in the *Clementina* which is not at all anti-Simonian and appears to go back to an original Simonian tradition.

But Simon would be more than a miracle-worker; above, it has been demonstrated that he availed himself of Samaritan traditions about the Prophet like Moses. Can this be borne out by the narration in *Acts* ch. viii? That Moses was the miracle-worker *par excellence* to the Samaritans is clear. Luke, of course, would explain the miracles through which Simon claimed a Mosaic status as magic. Simon is reported to have been "saying himself that he was someone great" (*v.* 9b), and many scholars following A. Ritschl and seeing Simon as a pseudo-Messiah have taken this to imply that he claimed some sort of messianic status (cp. v.36, where Theudas is said to have alleged εἶναί τινα ἑαυτόν). But the continuation of the narrative would seem to be a setback to this interpretation, for the acclamation by the Samaritans that Simon was ἡ δύναμις τοῦ θεοῦ ἡ καλουμένη μεγάλη (*v.* 10b) has been felt

---

270 G. Widengren, Art. "Israelite-Jewish Religion", in *HR*, I, p. 269.
271 See Haenchen, "Gab es eine vorchristliche Gnosis?", *ZTK*, 49, 1952, pp. 316 ff. (= Haenchen, *Gott und Mensch*, Tübingen, 1965, pp. 265 ff.); cp. *Die Apostelgeschichte* (MKKNT, 3), 6th ed., Göttingen, 1968, pp. 253, 257 f.; "Simon Magus in der Apostelgeschichte", in *GNT*, p. 275; Lüdemann, p. 41.

to indicate something more than a mere messianic status. Some authors think that, while *v.* 9b says that Simon *himself* claimed a messianic status, *v.* 10b says that the *people* took him to be some kind of incarnation of God[272]. But it is unlikely that Luke is imparting such precise historical knowledge, and it is impossible to identify older sources in viii.4-25. However, it is not implausible that "the Great Power (of God)", a name in which the genitive quite early was taken to be secondary, is a title of Simon reflecting the later Simonians' deification of their hero, who originally was a magician and/or a "Messiah" pretender[273]. There is no indication that *v.* 10 has been inserted at a later date, but there does exist the definite possibility that Simon himself did not claim the title said to have been given to him (obviously not by "all, from small to great", of the Samaritans), because *Acts* was written at least about forty years after Simon was active in Samaria. O. Bauernfeind and others have judged that the οὗτός ἐστιν answers to a spoken ἐγώ εἰμι, but G. Lüdemann is right that the latter might be an invention by the early community that venerated Simon.

E. Haenchen, however, is confident that Simon claimed to be the "Great Power", which designates the highest godhead being identified with Simon himself in the heresiological reports[274]. But, even if the historical Simon claimed to be "the Great Power", it does not follow that he was not at all a magician, and still less that the concept occurring in *Acts* has to be seen in a Gnostic context such as that found in the sources from the subsequent cen-

---

272 See already J. Weiss, *Das Urchristentum*, II, Göttingen, 1917, p. 589; cp. now, for instance, Staehlin, p. 120; W. Neil, *The Acts of the Apostles* (NCB), London, 1973, p. 121.

There is no foundation for the theory of A. Klostermann, *Probleme im Aposteltext*, Gotha, 1883, pp. 15 ff. – which was endorsed by Zahn, pp. 282 ff., and recently revived by Salles-Dabadie, pp. 128 f. – that *megalē* is a transliteration of מגלא or מגלי, a participial form of the verb to "lay open", "reveal", and that Simon was known to be "the Revealer" of God. Wilcox, p. 156, suggests that *dynamis* is a mistranslation reading גבורא, "power", in the place of גברא, "man". If "the Great Power (of God)" in *Acts* viii.10 were a mistranslation from the Aramaic, the subsequent reports on Simon simply would build on Luke when citing Simon's title and consequently have to be mistrusted in everything.

273 See F. Chr. Baur, *Die Christliche Gnosis*, Tübingen, 1835, reprinted Darmstadt, 1967, p. 304; W. Möller, Art. "Simon Magus", in *RE*, XIII, 1860, p. 398; W. Waitz, "Simon Magus", pp. 121 f., 134; "Die Quelle der Philippusgeschichten in der Apostelgeschichte", *ZNW*, 7, 1906, p. 341; "Simon der Magier", in *RE*, XVIII, 3rd ed., 1906, pp. 358f.; W. Bousset, *Hauptprobleme der Gnosis* (FRLANT, 10), Göttingen, 1907, pp. 261 ff.

274 W. Ullmann maintains that the occurrence of "the Great Power" and similar terms as divine epithets in Gnostic writings makes it "impossible not to see the δύναμις μεγάλη in Acts 8, 10 in connection with the broadly articulated Gnostic concept of God in later sources" ("Die Gottesvorstellung der Gnosis als Herausforderung an Theologie und Verkündigung", in *GNT*, p. 396).

turies. A substantial period has elapsed between *hē megalē dynamis* in *Acts*
and the *sublissima virtus* in Irenaeus' account[275]. Already J. Grimm in dissert-
ing upon Simon Magus had cited the martyrdom of James the Just as quoted
by Hegesippus saying that the Son of Man was sitting "in heaven by the right
of the Great Power (ἐκ δεξιῶν τῆς μεγάλης δυνάμεως)" (*apud* Euseb., *Hist.
eccl.* II. xxiii.13)[276], and M. Heidenheim in his incomplete edition of Marqa's
Memar had noted that רבה חילה occurred as a name of God in Samaritanism[277]. A couple of years before Haenchen gave his contribution to the study
of Simonian Gnosticism, G. Widengren had made a rather insubstantial attempt to derive the Simonian concept of the Great Power from Samaritanism
with the help of comparable evidence from Mandeism and Syrian Christian-

---

275 While Baur, *Gnosis*, p. 307, n. 74 (continued on pp. 308 ff.), thought that Simon in
the Christian accounts was a projection screen for the image of the sun god, Möller,
Waitz, and Bousset thought that the Simonians *themselves* identified their hero with
the Phoenician-Samaritan sun god. Möller and Bousset seem to mean that the idea
that this god had descended to earth amounted to Gnosticism, whereas Baur and
Waitz reckon with yet a third stage at which Simon and his female consort, Helena,
were identified (by the Christians according to Baur, and by the Simonians according
to Waitz) with the two main personages of Gnostic mythology. Cerfaux, "La gnose",
pp. 270 ff. (= *Recueil*, I, pp. 228 ff.), who – in contrast to Baur and Waitz – took
Helena to be a real person, reckoned with only two stages, one at which Simon was a
θεῖος ἀνήρ, an incarnation of *Helios*, and Helena an embodiment of Lady *Luna*, and
one at which the Simonians identified them with the main characters of the Gnostic
drama. The general orientation of these scholars has recently been repeated by
Beyschlag, who operates with only two stages of development, but does not think
that Simon was *Sol* at either of them or that Helena was a historical person. That
Simon was not identified with the sun god is right; this was simply inferred from the
fact that Helena is said to have been present in Helen of Troy – who has lunar
associations – and is even called *Luna* in the *Pseudo-Clementine Recognitions*.
Moreover, this is a secondary identification of Helena in Simonianism; see the forthcoming article on Helena in *RAC* by Professor Gilles Quispel and the present author.
276 See *Die Samariter und ihre Stellung in der Weltgeschichte*, Munich, 1854, pp. 131 ff.
Grimm's work is an attempt to defend the literal representation in the records of
Simon against the theory of the *Tübinger Schule* that Simon was a cloak for Paul.
For the growth and decline of this theory, which holds good only for some parts of
the *Pseudo-Clementines*, see Lüdemann, pp. 9 ff.
277 See *Der Commentar Marqa's des Samaritaners* (Bibliotheca samaritana, III),
Weimar, 1896, p. XXV. Already J.H. Hottinger, *De translationibus Bibliorum in
varias linguas vernaculas* (Dissertationum theologico-philologicarum fasciculus III),
Zürich, 1660, p. 266, had noted that חירל, probably some participial form, was
used as a divine name in Samaritanism. Cowley wrote in his "Glossary of the Aramaic
Texts" in his edition of the Liturgy: "חילה *power*, variant for אלה" (p. lvi,
col. a). Montgomery compared the frequent Samaritan practice of referring to
God as "the Power" to "Mk. 14, 62; *Vita Adami* 28; Acts 8, 10, where Simon
Magus uses it of himself" (p. 215, inset). But Simon is called "the *Great* Power",
whereas *Mark* has only "the Power". In two of the mss. of *Vita Adae et Evae*, we find
the expression *incomprehensibilis magnitudinis virtus*, and there is one ms. which

ity, and concluded that the claim of being the Great Power was a claim to be
"the incarnate Spirit of God"[278].

About ten years after Widengren and Haenchen had written on Simonianism, M. Black stated: "In the lengthy and learned discussions about pre-
Christian Jewish Gnosticism, too little weight, it seems to me, has been given
to the importance of Acts viii.10 ... . The type of sectarian belief behind Acts
viii.10 (its early date here guaranteed) appears to be some form of Gnosticism."[279] Black noted that the Hebrew and Aramaic word for "Power" was
used as a name of God in Samaritanism as well as in Judaism, and inferred
that the claim of being the Great Power "amounted, in effect, to the claim
to be divine or a divine being."[280] But just how this by itself should amount
to a Gnostic characteristic is not explained by Black any more than had
been done by former scholars. On the contrary, the appearance of a divine
being, even God himself, upon earth seems impossible to the sharp dualistic
system of classical Gnosticism. This very fact, however, shows the primitive
character of Simonianism, whose specially Gnostic nature must be ascertained
on the basis of other kind of evidence.

H.G. Kippenberg, the only one who has undertaken to follow up Widengren's program of deriving Gnostic *topoi* from Samaritanism, has made it
apparent that the Simonian concept of "the Great Power" is rooted in Samaritanism[281]. Kippenberg has made a form critical analysis of the Aramaic
Samaritan texts and shown that חילה is praised as רב in the community's
eulogies responding to the reading from Scripture about God's powerful

---

reads *magna*. The oldest group of mss., however, reads *matutine*. For "the Power" as
a Christian name of God, see also *Gospel of Peter* v.19. In Judaism, גבורה (or
גבורתא) is known as a name of God; see now A.M. Goldberg, "Sitzend zur Rechten der Kraft", *BZ*, 8, 1964, pp. 284 ff.; E.E. Urbach, *The Sages*, trans. by I. Abrahams (PPF), Jerusalem, 1975, pp. 80 ff. Wilcox, p. 156, n. 5, assures that חיל as a
divine name also can be found in Jewish sources, but he does not give any references.
Already G. Dalman, *Die Worte Jesu*, I (Einleitung und wichtige Begriffe), Leipzig,
1898, p. 164, on the ground of the rabbinic evidence, thought that Simon or his followers asserted that he was God, and that τοῦ θεοῦ was a misleading addition by
Luke. Observing the occurrence of "the Power" as a divine name in Jewish texts,
Lake and Cadbury thought that the declaration about Simon in *Acts* viii.10 implied
that he was acknowledged as God of "the monotheistic Samaritan or Jewish religion"
(*Acts*, IV, p. 91). But, again, outside of the Samaritan realm, "the *Great* Power"
is found only in the account of the martyrdom of James. E. Lohmeyer, *Galiläa und
Jerusalem* (FRLANT, 52), Göttingen, 1936, p. 70, sought the origin of this unique
Christian designation of God in Galilee. The northerly orientation is not wrong, since
the province of Samaria separated Judea from James' native land.

278 *Ascension*, p. 55. See above, pp. 58f.
279 *Op. cit.*, p. 63.
280 *Ibid.*, p. 65.
281 See *Gerizim*, pp. 328 ff.

deeds, primarily the rescue of the people out of Egypt and the giving of the Law. From this custom, Kippenberg attempts to understand the people's statement οὗτός ἐστιν ἡ δύναμις (τοῦ θεοῦ) ἡ καλουμένη μεγάλη, taking the participle to mean that an already existing and well-known title was transferred to Simon. According to Kippenberg, the participle expresses that "the Power" was called "great" in a certain usage, namely, in the laudations of the congregation[282].

However, the explanation by Kippenberg is weakened considerably by the fact that Luke usually adds καλούμενος, -η, -ον, to the name of a person, place, or thing; thus the omission of the participle in some of the mss. may be considered an amelioration. Furthermore, not only "the Power" but also "the Great Power" (חילה רבה) appears as a name of God and even is praised as being "great" in Samaritan literature. Thus, older exegesis obviously was correct in taking the participle to be a Lucan addition meant to indicate that "the Great Power" was a name[283]. Still, Kippenberg's essay is very valuable in that he has demonstrated that this name is found in abundance in Samaritan literature and apparently has a fixed *Sitz im Leben* in the doxologies of the community of the Samaritans.

The relevance of the Samaritan material has been denied on the ground that the Samaritan sources are younger than *Acts*, and the scholars who use this trial of chronology add that a concept as "the Standing One" in Simonianism must not be regarded as derived from Samaritanism but rather from the Alexandrian realm[284]. As we have seen, however, this concept in Hellenistic philosophy has quite another meaning than in Simonianism, where it is used in exactly the same sense as in Samaritanism[285]. As for the concept of the Great Power, the martyrdom of James as told by Hegesippus is the only text apart from the Samaritan sources where it is found. James, however, was a Galilean and apparently in touch with the religious traditions of Samaria, the province separating his native land from Judea.

K. Rudolph pertinently points out that Simon is cited as a heretic also in Samaritan sources and that his Samaritan working-field would indicate an employment of native traditions[286]. The story about Simon as a Samaritan

---

282 See *ibid.*, p. 345. See also already "Ein Gebetbuch für den samaritanischen Synagogengottesdienst aus dem 2. Jh. n. Chr.", *ZDPV*, 85, 1969, p. 103.

283 See, for instance, Dalman, *loc. cit.*; Lake & Cadbury, *loc. cit.* For criticism of Kippenberg at this point, see Beyschlag, p. 104; Lüdemann, p. 41.

284 See Beyschlag, pp. 93 f.; Bergmeier, pp. 124 ff., 133 ff., 152; Lüdemann, pp. 45 f. The reference to Waitz, "Simon Magus", pp. 139 f., in respect to the derivation of the Simonian concept of the Standing One from Philo is actually very ineffectual, for Waitz admits that the *Clementina* use the concept in another way than the Alexandrian philosopher; see above, p. 57.

285 See above, pp. 120f.

286 See "Simon", pp. 324, 351; cp. already "Gnosis und Gnostizismus", pp. 323 f., 338 ff.

heresiarch is given by Abu'l Fatḥ, who has inserted it between the account of Dusis and the report on the first Dosithean sub-sect, the Ba'unai[287]; thus, Simon obviously is a heretic belonging to the Dosithean movement. The story starts by recounting that a slave girl whose romantic advances were repulsed by her fancy man, the son of the high priest, got Simon to believe that the high priest wanted him to kill his son. When Simon was made a fool of in front of the high priest, he fled to Rome. This part of the story shows that Simon was in conflict with priestly Samaritanism and thus belonged to the laicising movement.

Abu'l Fatḥ is possibly dependent upon Christian sources when he goes on to state that Simon was the greatest of all magicians. Some dependence upon Christian sources is also apparent in the account that Simon went to Alexandria and asked Philo for help in destroying the sect of Jesus, for Philo is said to have answered with words similar to those used by Gamaliel in *Acts* v.38 f. But the first part of the account by Abu'l Fatḥ is not drawn from any Christian source. The last part of the story, too, is evidencing a peculiar Samaritan tradition, for Abu'l Fatḥ relates that Simon went back to his home town 'Alin, where he died and was buried in the valley opposite the house of Stephen, the first Christian martyr.

The theory that Simon belonged to and addressed the pagan population of Samaria thus does not seem likely. Haenchen says that Simon's claim of being the highest God having become man suggests that he appeared with his message among the pagan population, and he goes on: "... the name Simon, which is purely Greek, does not contradict this. The earliest form of the Simonian teaching certainly contains nothing which leads one to think of a derivation from Judaism."[288] But the genuinely Greek name Σίμων is found very frequently among Jews and even often substituted for Συμεών, the usual and indeclensible form of the Semitic שמעון (see, for instance, the forms of the name of the apostle Peter in *Matt.* iv.18 and *Acts* xv.15). Since we must assume that all converts to Christianity before Cornelius (see *Acts* ch. x) were circumcised, we must regard Simon as a Samaritan.

G. Lüdemann argues that the oldest traditions show that Simon was ven-

---

Rudolph knows only the latter part of the account of Simon as it is translated by Bowman, *Samaritanische Probleme*, p. 54, n. 9 (continued on the next page). A translation of the whole account is now afforded by Bowman, *Documents*, pp. 168 f.

287 See Vilmar, pp. 157 f.

288 *Apostelgeschichte*, p. 257. Already R.P. Casey said that "nothing in the Simonians' theology suggests a connexion with the worship at Gerizim" (Note XIII, "Simon Magus", in K. Lake & H.J. Cadbury, ed., *The Acts of the Apostles* (BC, I), V (Additional Notes), London, 1933, p. 152). For the view that Simonian Gnosticism is of pagan origin, see also G. van Groningen, *First Century Gnosticism*, Leiden, 1967, pp. 135 ff.

erated as Zeus, to whom the temple on Mt. Gerizim was dedicated under Antiochus Epiphanes[289]. Irenaeus (I.xxiii.4) does tell that Simon and his Helena, who had leapt forth from him in the beginning, were worshipped in images of Zeus and Athena, who had vaulted out of her father's head; and Justin Martyr (*I Apol.* xxvi.3), the first to mention Helena, says that she was called Simon's "First Thought", which was a common name of the intelligible world (*nous*), as which Athena was allegorized in contemporary philosophy[290]. It is thus possible that some Samaritans who were attracted to the Gerizim cult of Zeus Hypsistos, being an amalgamation of Zeus and YHWH, were responsible for the identification of Simon and Helena as Zeus and Athena respectively[291], but the genuinely Samaritan components in Simonianism must not be underrated. The divine name of the Great Power, which appears in the oldest account of Simon, is no name of Zeus but a Samaritan name of YHWH. It is true that the epithet "great" was frequently applied to gods in Hellenistic times, and that also the "power" of the gods was praised as "great"[292], but "the Great Power" is an authentically Samari-

---

289 See *op. cit.*, pp. 49 ff. Already Casey declared that "it is evident ... that the Simonian conception of God was a mixture of Zeus and Jehovah" (pp. 153 f.), a statement which in actual fact contradicts his assertion quoted in the previous note.

290 See Lüdemann, pp. 55 f. Justin (*I Apol.* xxvi.2) reports that Simon was venerated as a god in Rome and had a statue with the inscription *Simoni deo sancto* erected to his honour on the island of Tiber, but the inscription, which was turned up in 1574, actually reads *Semoni Sanco deo* and is inscribed to the honour of the old Sabine god Semo Sancus. Casey, p. 154, and Lüdemann, pp. 50 f., think that the Simonians in Rome recognized their hero in the stele, because Semo was often identified with Zeus Horkios or Zeus Pistios in Roman times. Casey also remarks that such an identification could have been facilitated by the similarity of the names Simon and Semo. But Justin's account is really difficult to make out; see Rudolph, "Simon", pp. 324 f. So is his continuation that "almost all Samaritans" recognized Simon as "the supreme God". A.H. Goldfahn, "Justinus Martyr und die Agada", *MGWJ*, 22, 1873, p. 195, suggested that Justin mistook שמה, the substitution for the Tetragrammaton among the Samaritans, for the name of Simon; but Justin – who actually came from Samaria – should have been better informed about Samaritanism as well as Simonianism. Is the statement somehow implying that Simon was regarded as the hypostasis of the Divine Name?

291 In a *Defter* hymn, we read: "The children of Your [*i.e.*, God's] loved ones have established impurity upon the top of the holy place, and all the great holiness is departed from them by reason of wickedness" (Cowley, 39.24 f.). This may refer to the approval on the part of some of the Samaritans of the cult of Zeus Hypsistos, to whom Hadrian in the beginning of the 2nd century C.E. erected a temple at the site of the ruined shrine of the Samaritans. This temple stood to the latter part of the 5th century. For the history of the connection of Zeus with Mt. Gerizim, see Kippenberg, *Garizim*, pp. 74 ff., 96 ff.

292 Thus, a Lydian inscription reads: "One is God in heaven: great [is] the heavenly Men; great [is] the power of the immortal God (μεγάλη δύναμις τοῦ ἀθανάτου θεοῦ)" (J. Keil & A. von Premerstein, *Bericht über eine zweite Reise in Lydien*

tan divine name, and the encomium of "the Power" or even "the Great Power" as "great" is a Samaritan characteristic.

(DKAW, phil.-hist. Kl., 54), Vienna, 1911, p. 109). This was taken as an elucidation of *Acts* viii.10 already by W.M. Ramsey, *The Bearing of Recent Discovery on the Trustworthiness of the New Testament*, London, 1914, p. 117. Already A. Deissmann, *Bibelstudien*, Marburg, 1895, p. 19, n. 6, had quoted a text from a magical papyrus invoking "the greatest power (τὴν μεγίστην δύναμιν), set in heaven by the Lord God" (*PGM*, IV.1275 f.), as a comparison to the phraseology of *Acts* viii.10. Several scholars have adduced these two texts together in order to explain Simon's title; see already O. Schmitz, "Der Begriff δύναμις bei Paulus", in *Festgabe für A. Deissmann zum 60. Geburtstag*, Tübingen, 1927, p. 153, and H. Lietzmann, Art. "Simon Magus", *PW*, 2nd Series (R-Z), III, 1927, col. 181. However, as had been shown by E. Peterson, ΕΙΣ ΘΕΟΣ (FRLANT, 41), Göttingen, 1926, pp. 196 ff., 268 f., the Lydian inscription is an acclamation formulary praising the power of Men in answer to a miracle. There is no question of any hypostatization or incarnation of the power of Men, whereas "the Great Power" is a *name* of Simon. An analogue to the magical invocation of the divine power, which is no entity being incarnated, cannot be obtained in Simonianism, where the magician himself *is* the Great Power. W. Grundmann states: "The analogies break down materially because they do not illustrate actual identity between a concrete person and the concept" (Art. δύναμαι/δύναμις, in *TDNT*, II, 1964 and reprints, p. 305). On the other hand, Grundmann does maintain: "The analogies are most interesting linguistically, esp. in respect of the adjectives, and show us to what circles the Magus belonged" (*ibid.*). "The phrase μεγάλη δύναμις' belongs to the context of the μέγας θεός," Grundmann writes (Art. μέγας κτλ., in *TDNT*, IV, p. 540). But he also notes: "On Palestinian soil it is also found for the divine name" (*ibid.*). Thus: "When Simon Magus is called ἡ δύναμις τοῦ θεοῦ ἡ καλουμένη μεγάλη, this form of expression is part of the world of Hellenistic magic piety which had made its way into Palestine and combined with popular Jewish ideas" (*ibid.*, p. 541). Grundmann thus feels justified to state that Simon was called the Great Power of God "because of his magical feats, in which power became visible" (*Der Begriff der Kraft in der neutestamentliche Gedankenwelt* (BWANT, IV/8), Stuttgart, 1932, p. 76, n. 27); Simon was "supposed to be divine as an incarnation of divine power" (Art. δύναμαι, pp. 304 f.); the phrase in *Acts* viii.10 "characterises Simon as a θεῖος ἄνθρωπος, a mediator of revelation, an incarnation of the μεγάλη δύναμις τοῦ θεοῦ" (Art. μέγας κτλ., p. 541). This way of speaking seems to lead to misunderstandings. Lake and Cadbury do not comprehend the nature of the "power" in the magical texts, since – after having interpreted Simon's title as a claim to be God of "the monotheistic Samaritan or Jewish religion" – they cite the two texts as examples of a "similar use of "great power" in pagan religion and magic" (*Acts*, IV, p. 91). Quispel wrongly says that "the magus is the carrier of a power, even a divine power, which makes him quite great and powerful ..." (*Gnosis*, p. 53). Simon *is* the Great Power and no "carrier" of it, and there is no need of a conjuration which "fetches down the power-deity and effects that the magus himself becomes the greatest power" (*ibid.*, p. 54). Grant, p. 72, speaks in the same terms as Quispel. Conzelmann, *Apostelgeschichte*, p. 53, and Staehlin, p. 120, even take the power in the magical texts to be a subordinate deity who could appear on earth. Cp. already Cerfaux, "La gnose", p. 491 (= *Recueil*, I, p. 248). For criticism of this line of interpretation, see also Kippenberg, *Garizim*, pp. 344, 346; Lüdemann, p. 43.

That Simon really claimed to be God himself traversing the earth may be found difficult to believe, and F.F. Bruce states that the theory "that Simon claimed to be the Grand Vizier (*Ba'al Zebul*) of the Lord of heaven (*Ba'al Shamain*) is most probable ... , certainly more probable than G.H. Dalman's view that he claimed to be God Almighty (Heb. *ha-gebhurah*) Himself ... ."[293] On the other hand, there is some evidence which seems to bear out the statement of H. Conzelmann that Simon's title of the Great Power implies that he gave himself out to be "the Most High God himself or the revelation of God, and thus the Son; at that time the two were not necessarily mutually exclusive."[294] The pagan philosopher Celsus gives the following report on Palestinian and Syrian prophets in the 2nd century C.E.:

> There are many who prophesy at the slightest excuse for some trivial cause both inside and outside temples. And there are some who wander about begging and roaming around cities and military camps, and they pretend to be moved as if giving some oracular utterance. It is an ordinary and common custom for each one to say: "I am God, or God's Son, or a Divine Spirit. And I have come. The world is already [in the process of] being destroyed; and you, O men, shall perish because of your unrighteousness. But I wish to save you. And you shall see me returning with heavenly power. Blessed is he who worships me now! But I will bring eternal fire upon the rest, both upon cities and countries. The men who do not know their punishment shall repent in vain and groan, but I will preserve for ever those who follow me."
>
> (*Apud* Orig., *Contra Cels.* VII.9)

The way in which these prophets spoke often has been compared to the assertions made by Simon. We have seen above that Simon, too, declared that the end was near and stated that the destiny of men depended upon their response to the revelation which now was given them[295]. In particular, the "I am" statement of these prophets can be compared to Simon's declaration "I am the Great Power," which obviously is presupposed by the people's acclamation in *Acts* viii.10, "This one is the Great Power (of God)."[296] Fur-

---

293 *The Books of Acts* (NIC), London & Edinburgh, 1954, p. 179, n. 27, referring to the following statement of J. de Zwaan: "That the deity of Heaven, the great Lord of Heavens (בעל־שמין) should count in his court among other δυνάμεις also a "Grand Vizir", a "Lord of the Palace" (בעלזבול), called the "Great One", is what should be expected. Why should not the Samaritans have their Michael as well as the Jews ... ?" ("The Use of the Greek Language in Acts", in F.J. Foakes Jackson & K. Lake, ed., *The Acts of the Apostles* (BC, I), II (Prolegomena II. Criticism), London, 1922, p. 58). Already A. Merx proffered a similar interpretation; see above, p. 58, n. 104. Merx was probably relying on an erroneous statement of M. Heidenheim; see below, p. 238, n. 89.

294 *History of Primitive Christianity*, trans. by J.E. Steeley, Nashville & New York, 1973, p. 126.

295 See p. 65.

296 For the various "I am" formulas, see Bultmann, p. 226, n. 3 (continued on the next page). The formula of the Palestinian-Syrian prophets is either an identification

ther, Celsus' registration of the variations in the self-predication of the Syrian and Palestinian prophets can be likened to the different accounts of how Simon spoke of himself. Thus, while Justin and the following heresiologists say that Simon claimed to be the highest God and was venerated in statues of Zeus, Irenaeus *also* tells that the Samaritan Gnostic taught that he had descended in Judea as the Son and come to the other nations as the Holy Spirit[297]. We also have seen that Simon in the *Acts of Peter* speaks of God as his father[298]. In the *Pseudo-Clementines*, both perspectives are recorded:

> [...] he wished to be regarded as a certain highest Power, even above the god who made the universe. Sometimes, he intimates that he is Christ by calling himself "the Standing One".

(Hom. II.22)

W. Bauer correctly remarks in reference to the claim of the Syrian-Palestinian prophets to be "God, God's Son, or a Divine Spirit" that there "hardly was a difference between these designations."[299] Thus we also must understand the different names of Simon: the claim to be God amounted to a profession to be the form of the divine manifestation, that is, the Messiah, the Son, or the Spirit.

The titles probably show assimilation of Christian terminology, but it would not be apt to think that the revealer's claim to be God as well as his agent is dependent upon a modalistic Christian teaching. The *Book of Jubilees*, which stems from the Maccabean period and has come down to us in four Ethiopic versions and some Latin fragments, but goes back — by way of a Greek version — to a Hebrew original, provides us with a Jewish and pre-Christian parallel to this way of representing God's proxy. It is told that Pharaoh recognizes that Joseph possesses the Spirit of God and is the wisest in all Egypt, and that he then makes the Israelite his second by attiring him as the royal vizir and appointing him over all his house. Pharaoh says to Joseph: "I am not greater than you, except on the throne" (xl.7). When Joseph rides in his chariot, which occupies a lower status only to that of Pharaoh, one cries out before him: *'El 'El wa-'Abîrer!* This is probably a corruption of אל אל, ואביר אל, "God, God, and the Mighty One of God", a designation

---

formula, in which the speaker identifies himself with another person or object, or a presentation formula, which replies to the question: "Who are you?" Beyschlag, p. 103, argues that Simon used an identification formula, whereas Rudolph, "Simon", p. 315, thinks it is possible that he employed a recognition formula, which was used as a revelation formula in which the speaker revealed himself as the one people were waiting for, looking for, *etc.*

297 See above, p. 128.
298 See p. 138. In *Ps.-Clem. Rec.* III.47, Simon designates himself as "the Son of God"; see above, p. 139.
299 *Das Johannesevangelium* (HNT, 6), 2nd ed., Tübingen, 1925, p. 79.

which R.H. Charles pertinently compared to Simon's appellation in *Acts* viii.10[300].

I wish to emphasize that אביר originally is a name of God (see *Gen.* xlix. 24; *Is.* i.24; xlix.26; lx.16; *Ps.* cxxxii.2, 5), though it here is transferred to his lieutenant. The same is the case with Simon's title "the Great Power". The author of *Jubilees* has driven home that Joseph was not God himself but his assignee by the addition of the genitive "of God", and Luke's reason for adding τοῦ θεοῦ in *Acts* viii.10 apparently was the similar intention of representing Simon as the agent of God. Also, we see that the author of *Jubilees* does not find it illogical to call God's vicegerent "God" as well as "the Mighty One of God". Similarly, Simon was designated as God as well as by names indicating his office of being the revealer.

We must also bear in mind that the usage of the term "the (Great) Power" was not restricted to that of representing a divine name. Primarily, it denotes a divine attribute, the characteristic of the will of the personal God who has created the world and guides personal life and history[301]. But here we must remember that "even if for us the name, the power, or the qualities of a person are abstractions it is not so to the primitive mind, for which qualities and actions are entities relatively independent of the subject."[302] In *Jeremiah*, God's "great power" (כח הגדול) appears in parallelism to his "outstretched arm" as a means wherewith God effected the creation (see xxvii.5; xxxii. 17). In Targum *Is.* xlviii.13, the "power" stands in parallelism to the "word" of God: "By My word, I have established the earth; and by My power, I have suspended the heavens."

God also used his "power" to save his people. In a verse from a Psalm which has been quoted above, the "power" of God is parallel to the "Name": "God, help me by Your Name and save me by Your power (בגבורתך)!" (liv.3). In *Deut.* iv.37, it is said that God brought the people out of Egypt "by His face and by His great power" (בכחו הגדל). This parallelism is particulary interesting, for the "face" of God could be used to replace the figure of the Angel of the Lord as the guide of the people through the wilderness (see *Ex.* xxxiii.14; cp. *vv.*2 ff.)[303]. Moreover, the Samaritan Pentateuch reads

---

300 See "The Book of Jubilees", in *APOT*, II, p. 71, n. *ad loc.* The Latin reads *habirel.* In *Joseph and Asenath* (iii.4; xviii.1), "the Mighty One of God" is a title of Joseph.

301 See Grundmann, Art. δύναμαι/δύναμις, pp. 290 ff.

302 S. Mowinckel, Art. "Hypostasen", in *RGG*, II, 2nd ed., 1928, col. 2065, as translated in E. Jacob, *The Theology of the Old Testament*, trans. by A.W. Heathcote & P. J. Allcock, London, 1958, reprinted 1974, p. 84.

303 See Jacob, p. 78. In Punic texts, the goddess Tinnit — a form of the great West-Semitic mother goddess — is regularly called *pn Bʿl*, an epithet which apparently designates her as the "manifestation" of Baʿal.

חילה רבה in *Deut.* iv.37, thus associating the name of the divine instrument or manifestation claimed by Simon with the figure of the Angel of the Lord.

The same usage of the concept of the divine "power" is found in Samaritanism. In the hymns of Marqa, we often are told that the faithful rely on "Your [*i.e.*, God's] (Great) Power", *etc.* One text may be cited: "By Your goodness, the world came into being, and by Your power, it was ordered. By Your mercy, we live in the midst of Your possessions. Your great power has compassion over us. The seen and the unseen world are great by reason of Your goodness" (Cowley, 18.25 ff.)[304]. It is probably to go too far to assert that the "goodness" and the "power", which also are used as names of God, appear as hypostases in this text, but their instrumental suggestion shows the tendency that "different aspects of the divinity, which represent the fullness and richness of the divine nature, are depicted as independent entities and separated from the divinity as more or less distinctive beings, and even seen as individual divinities."[305]

We are already familiar with the Jewish and Samaritan idea that the hypostasis of the Divine Name fills the whole universe[306]. In the *Letter of Aristeas*, it is the Power of God which is assigned with this function: it "is revealed in everything in so far as every place is filled by His Power" (132); the entire creation "is being sustained as well as having been created by the Power of God" (157). This fits in with the general power philosophy of the time. Thus, the pseudo-Aristotelian writing *About Cosmos*, which stems from the first century C.E., pictures God enthroned in "the height of heaven, from where He effects everything in the universe through His Power" (ch. 6). God himself, of course, cannot be active in the world. In Samaritanism, too, the Power can be described in this way: "His Power is in the heavens above and at the earth below; there is no place outside His control" (*Memar Marqa* VI.1).

We have also seen above that, according to the Deuteronomistic history-work, the hypostasis of the Divine Name is localized in the earthly temple, while God himself resides in heaven. The Power of God could be described in much the same way. In the *II Book of the Maccabees*, it is said of Jerusalem: "[...] in that place, there rules in truth a Divine Power (θεοῦ δύναμις). He who has His abode in heaven is the protector and defender of the place, and He strikes with destruction those who come thereto with evil in their minds" (iii.38 f.). God himself remains in heaven, while his Power is some sort of custodian genius of God's own city on earth.

The concept of God's power was also disintegrated and the term used in the plural as a synonym of "angels". Thus, we have seen above that Marqa in

---

304 "Power, in many passages, is the activating principle, bringing into being the ordered conception of the will ... " (Macdonald, *Theology*, p. 124).

305 Ringgren, col. 504.

306 See above, p. 81, and p. 86.

a hymn says that, when God gave the Law, "powers", that is, angels, and people were gathered on Mt. Sinai[307]. That "power" is a synonym of "angel" should come as no surprise, for we have seen above that the hypostasis formation tends towards individualization and personification. The relation between hypostases and angels has been described concisely by W. Bousset: "The hypostases as well as the angels are intermediaries between God and the world, making the execution of his will in the world possible. They are only more abstract, shadowy, and more difficult to comprehend than the substantial and distinct figures of popular angelology."[308] When all the angelic powers are concentrated into one being, there emerges the concept of the personified Power of God. For evidence of this idea, Jewish mystical texts are most interesting, for the "Power" was used as a name of the Glory, the man-like figure upon the heavenly throne-chariot who could be seen in ecstasy by the Merkaba mystics. The prophet Ezekiel, from whom the visionaries took their departure-point, once had a revelation of what seemed to be a throne, —

and upon the likeness of the throne was a likeness as the appearance of a man (דמות כמראה אדם).

(i.26)

Ezekiel describes this man-like figure as being of some sort of radiant lithic substance from the hips upwards and of a fiery kind from the hips down. He also says that the figure was surrounded by light. Then the prophet states:

This was the appearance of the likeness of the Kabod of YHWH (הוא מראה דמות כבוד יהוה).

(v. 28)

The Kabod, then, according to Ezekiel, is the human form of God. As such, it can be compared to the Angel of the Lord, God's human form of manifestation appearing on earth according to the Pentateuch and Judges (ii.1 ff.). As is well known, often it is impossible "to differentiate between the מ' י and Yahweh Himself. The One who speaks or acts, i.e., Yahweh or the מ' י , is obviously one and the same person."[309] The relation between God and the Glory is set forth in a similar way by Ezekiel. Thus, in ix.3, the Glory of the Lord rises from the throne carried by the cherubs and addresses the angel with "a scribe's inkhorn on his side", whereas the next verse reads: "And

---

307 See above, p. 111. For חילן as angels in Samaritanism, see Macdonald, *Theology*, p. 78. A. Broadie, *A Samaritan Philosophy* (SP-B, XXXI), Leiden, 1981, pp. 54 ff., discusses the concept of the power(s) of God solely from a philosophical perspective and does not take into consideration that the "powers" also are the angels. He suggests that Marqa was indebted to a power philosophy like that of Philo. Philo, however, could also identify the powers of God with angels; see below, p. 200.

308 *Die Religion des Judentums im späthellenistischen Zeitalter* (HNT, 21), 3rd ed. by H. Gressmann, Tübingen, 1926, pp. 342 f.

309 G. von Rad, par. B, " מלאך in the OT", in Art. ἄγγελος κτλ., in *TDNT*, I, p. 77.

YHWH spoke to him ... ." As God's human form of manifestation, the Glory is identical with God.

There are also other Biblical texts which use the *kabod* when narrating that men are vouchsafed a theophany, but the word in these places merely suggests a splendour of light by which God is both revealed and concealed. In the Targums, יקרא, an Aramaic equivalent of the Kabod, is not only used where the Hebrew text has the latter but substituted when Scripture speaks of men's seeing God or God's manifesting himself to men. In rabbinism, however, the Kabod is retained and used of the divine and heavenly mode of being, but occasionally also employed as an interchangeable term for the common Shekina, the divine "Presence" or "Indwelling", which is also found in the Targums (as Shekinta) and used when describing God as coming to a place, abiding at a place, or departing from a place. Yeqara and Shekina are described as light phenomena in conformity with the Biblical precedent of the Kabod, and they do not denote entities different from God; they are reverential ways of speaking about God manifesting himself[310].

In Jewish mysticism, however, the mode of God's manifestation was conceived of differently. The mystics developed Ezekiel's idea of the Kabod in human form being God's form of appearance. Moreover, whatever we may think of the Glory in *Ezekiel*, the later mystics certainly hypostasized the Kabod, for their teaching about this figure "does not imply that God Himself possesses a physical form, but only that a form of this kind may be ascribed to "the Glory", which in some passages is called *guf ha-Shekhinah* ("the body of the Divine Presence")."[311] Since it was a dogma that God himself does not

---

310 See G.F. Moore, "Intermediaries in Jewish Theology", *HTR*, 15, 1922, pp. 41 ff. For a different perspective, see G.H. Box, "The Idea of Intermediation in Jewish Theology", *JQR*, 23, 1932/33, pp. 103 ff. There is at least one text, a comment upon *Gen.* xxxi.8 incorporated in *Midrash ha-Gadol*, where the Shekina is identified with the Angel of the Lord; see A.M. Goldberg, *Untersuchungen über die Vorstellung von der Schekinah in der frühen rabbinischen Literatur* (SJ, V), Leiden, 1969, pp. 339 f. In Mandeism and Manicheism, the term is used in the plural to denote the aeons. In Kabbalism, the Shekina is hypostazised and welded with the figure of Wisdom; see Scholem, *On the Kabbalah*, pp. 104 ff. Since the term שכינה is formed from the verb שכן, it is interesting to note that already the apocrypha and pseudepigrapha state that Wisdom "tabernacled" among men (see *Sir.* xxiv.8; *I En.* xlii.2), and that Philo (*Leg. all.* III.46) equates the tabernacle, the σκηνή, with Wisdom. Moreover, *Sir.* xxiv.4 and *Wisd.* x.17 present Wisdom as being veiled in, or even identified with, the Pillar of Cloud and Fire, in which the rabbis found the Shekina or Kabod (see already *Ex.* xvi.10). In the received text of *Ex.* xiv.19, however, the Pillar is identified with the Angel of the Lord, and Philo (*De vita Mos.* I.166) considers it possible that the Angel is veiled in the Pillar (cp. *Quis rer. div. her. sit* 203 f.). For the many-named intermediary in Hellenistic Judaism, see below, pp. 314ff. Cp. also below, p. 256, n. 32.

311 G. Scholem, *Kabbalah* (LJK, 4), Jerusalem, 1974, p. 17. That the mystics did not see

possess a material form which could be seen, it is obvious that it is his Glory that was seen by the mystics. In the *Visions of Ezekiel*, a Palestinian source from the 4th century C.E. and thus from the same provenance and period as the oldest Samaritan texts, it is said:

> Thus Ezekiel stood by the river Chebar and was looking at the water, and the seven heavens were opened to him, and he beheld the ho[ly] Glory (כבוד הקו[ד]ש).[312]

After God has shown Ezekiel the Merkaba carrying the Glory and being surrounded by myriads of different classes of heavenly beings, he says:

> Son of man, this is My Glory (זהו ככודי).[313]

The "Power" was an alternate name of the Glory. In the *Visions of Ezekiel*, the following passage is found a few lines above the passage already quoted:

> While Ezekiel was looking, the Holy One, blessed be He, opened to him the seven heavens, and he beheld the Power (וראה את הגבורה).[314]

In *Maʿase Merkaba,* which has been edited by G. Scholem, R. Aqiba — one of the pillars of orthodoxy who was ascribed with Merkaba doctrines — says:

> When I ascended and beheld the Power (וצפיתי בגבורה), I saw all the creatures that are to be found in the pathways of heaven.
>
> (§2)[315]

The name "the *Great* Power" does not occur in the representations of the figure upon the throne of the chariot, but the parallel name of הכבוד הגדול or ἡ μεγάλη δόξα is found very frequently; thus, it is used as a name of the figure upon the heavenly throne in the very early version of heavenly journey in *I Enoch* ch. xiv, which clearly recalls *Ezek.* ch. i. In the

---

the essential godhead but his Glory has now been doubted by I. Chernus, "Visions of God in Merkabah Mysticism", *JSJ*, 13, 1983, pp. 144 f., but he has mixed up n. 92 and n. 93 in Scholem's *Major Trends*, p. 365, which give the original texts of the quotations made on p. 66. The "passage which Scholem cites as a crucial piece of evidence" does *not* contain the term שבח, which Chernus does not take to mean "glory". The "crucial piece of evidence" uses the term כבוד and comes from היכלות זוטרתי, our oldest Merkaba text, from the 2nd or 3rd century C.E. It is quoted below, p. 180.

312 *BM*, II, p. 129.
313 Friedmann, ed., סדר אליהו רבה, p. 34; cp. Scholem, *Jewish Gnosticism*, p. 68, n. 11.
314 The work purports to describe the event "when Ezekiel saw the Power" (p. 127).
315 Scholem, *Jewish Gnosticism*, p. 67, asserts that even *Matt.* xxvi.64 and *Mark* xiv.62, "You shall see the Son of Man seated at the right hand of the Power," allude to a vision of the Glory. This is certainly the interpretation in the *Ascension of Isaiah*, where the visionary says that he "saw him [*i.e.*, Christ] sit down at the right hand of that Great Glory" (xi.32). James the Just said that Jesus was sitting at the right side of "the Great Power" (according to Hegesippus, *apud* Euseb., *Hist. eccl.* II.xxiii.13). See further below, p. 191.

mystical texts, its Aramaic counterpart, זיוא רבא, occurs as a name of Metatron, the chief angel[316]. The name of the Great Power obviously was evolved on the analogy of that of the Great Glory.

There is evidence that the Glory or Power of God could be assumed to appear on earth, like the Angel of the Lord in the Old Testament. Epiphanius, giving the name of the Jewish Christian prophet Elchasai as "Elxai", writes:

> They [*i.e.*, the Elchasaites] hold illusory ideas, calling him [*i.e.*, Elxai or Elchasai] "Hidden Power" (δύναμιν ἀποκεκαλυμμένην), since ἤλ means "power" and ξαΐ "hidden".
>
> (*Pan.* XIX.ii.2)

Thus, the Semitic original of the prophet's title would have been חיל כסי or חילא כסיא. This term occurs also in the teaching of Simon Magus as set forth in the *Pseudo-Clementines*, where it denotes the highest God who is incomprehensible to all (see *Rec.* II.50 f.). This idea is permeating Merkaba mysticism as well as Gnosticism, but the paradox of Jewish mysticism is that the adept is able to behold the hidden godhead: "God who is beyond the sight of His creatures and hidden to the angels who serve him has revealed Himself to R. Aqiba in the vision of the Merkaba."[317] It is, of course, not God himself who appears in the vision, but his Hidden Glory, who possesses a human form: "He is like us, as it were, but greater than everything, and this is His Glory that is hidden from us (כבודו שנסתר מפנינו)."[318]

In Jewish Christianity, the Son was regarded as the Glory of God, and Elchasai apparently gave himself out to be the final incarnation of Christ, whose enormous body he had seen in a vision and described in a manner reminiscent of the Merkaba mystics' detailed descriptions of שעור קומה, the "Measurement of the Body", *i.e.*, the immense body of the divine Glory[319]. As a matter of fact, "the (Great) Power" appears as a name of the Son in Jewish Christian tradition. In an address to Christ in the Syriac version of the *Acts of Thomas*, a source which is generally taken to reveal a substantial amount of Jewish Christian ideas, it is said:

> You are the Great Power (ܚܝܠܐ ܪܒܐ), and the Wisdom, and the Knowledge, and the Will, and the Rest of your Father, through Whom you are hidden in glory and revealed in your acts.
>
> (ch. 12)[320]

---

316 See, for instance, *Alphabet of R. Aqiba*, long recension, in *BH*, II, p. 354.

317 היכלות זוטרתי, Ms. Oxford 1531, 45b; quoted by Scholem, *Major Trends*, p. 364, n. 80. Cp. the divine name *incomprehensibilis* (*magnitudinis*) *virtus* in *Life of Adam and Eve* ch. 28.

318 *Ibid*. 40b; quoted by Scholem, *Major Trends*, p. 365, n. 92.

319 See Fossum, "Christology", pp. 260 ff., 273 ff.

320 Bedjan, p. 11. Wright, p. 179, has only "the Power". The Greek version does not contain this passage. In the epiclesis in ch. 132, we even find the term "Hidden Power", but this is a name of the Spirit. However, the *Acts* show a tendency to fuse the Spirit with the Son; see above, p. 103.

Pointing out a parallel to this passage in the *Teachings of Silvanus* from the Nag Hammadi library, a writing saturated with Jewish Christian terms and concepts, J. Zandee cites the following passage: "For he [*i.e.*, the Son] is Wisdom. He is also the Word. He is the Life, the Power (δύναμις), and the Door. He is the Light, the Angel, and the Good Shepherd" (106.21 ff.)[321]. But another passage, which is not quoted by Zandee, is even more important in this connection; this passage shows that the "(Great) Power" is a parallel to the "(Great) Glory":

> A Great Power and Great Glory (ογΝΟϬ   ΝΔΜΔϨΤΕ   ΜΝ   ΟΥΝΟϬ   ΝΕϬΟΥ) has revealed the cosmos.
>
> (112.8 ff.)

Since the name of the Jewish Christian sect-leader Elchasai (Elxai), who appeared as the Prophet like Moses, signified the "Hidden Power", it apparently meant to designate him as the final manifestation of Christ. Elchasai thus is a parallel figure to Simon Magus, who also appeared as the eschatological Moses-like prophet and was hailed as "the Great Power" and a divine manifestation superseding his former incarnation in Jesus[322].

The pattern of describing Christ by the names of all the divine attributes and modes of manifestation, which we have found in the *Acts of Thomas* and the *Teachings of Silvanus*, is especially prominent in the works of Justin Martyr. Among the names of the Son known to Justin, we again find that of the Power of God:

> It is, therefore, wrong to understand the Spirit and the Power of God (δύναμιν θεοῦ) as anything else than the Logos, who is also the Firstborn of God, as the foresaid prophet Moses declared.
>
> (*I Apol.* xxxiii.6)

It has been observed that Justin shows influence from a type of Judaism like that of Philo — though less philosophical — when arguing that the Old Testament witnesses the existence of a many-named intermediary[323]. Among the names of this intermediary, that of the Glory as well as that of the Power is in evidence:

> God has begotten as Beginning (ἀρχή) before all His creatures a kind of rational (λογική) Power from Himself, that is also called by the Holy Spirit "the Glory of the Lord" (δόξα κυρίου) and sometimes "Son", and sometimes "Wisdom", or "Angel", or "God", and "Lord" and "Word".
>
> (*Dial.* lxi.1)

---

321 See " "The Teachings of Silvanus" (NHC VII,4) and Jewish Christianity", in *Studies*, p. 552.

322 See above, pp. 65 ff., and pp. 128 f.

323 See E.R. Goodenough, *The Theology of Justin Martyr*, Jena, 1923, pp. 141 ff., 168 ff. For Justin's Christological interpretation of the theophanies and angelophanies, see D.C. Trakatellis, *The Pre-Existence of Christ in Justin Martyr* (HTR: HDR, 6), Missoula, 1976, pp. 53 ff.

Since God is absolutely transcendent, it is also the intermediary who is meant in those passages where it is told that "God" or "the Lord" appeared to men. That the intermediary who also was the Power and the Glory could appear on earth was also taught by Justin's predecessors; the apologist himself states that —

> some wish to anticipate these remarks and proclaim that the Power (τὴν δύναμιν) sent from the Father of all and appearing to Moses, or to Abraham, or to Jacob, is called "Angel" when he comes to men, because the messages of the Father are announced to men through him, and that he is called "Glory" (δόξαν), because he sometimes appears in a vision that cannot be borne, and that he is called ἄνδρα and ἄνθρωπον because he appears arrayed in such forms if it pleases the Father.
>
> (*Ibid.* cxxviii.2)[324]

There obviously were Jews who welded the Glory of God with the Angel

---

[324] Justin goes on to say that his predecessors assert "that this Power never can be cut off or separated from the Father, just like — as they say — the light of the sun on earth cannot be cut off or separated from the sun, although it is in heaven; and, so, when the sun sinks, the light sinks with it. Thus, they assert, the Father makes, whenever He wills, His Power to spring forward, and, when He wills, He draws it back again into Himself. They also teach that He makes angels in this way" (cxxviii.3). H.A. Wolfson, *The Philosophy of the Church Fathers*, 3rd ed., London & Cambridge, Mass., 1976, pp. 581 f., thinks that the people in question are Christians of the modalistic wing of the Monarchians. But the modalistic doctrine that the same divine being was "nominally called Father and Son according to the change of times [...]" (Hipp., IX.x.11) obviously cannot be suggested by the notion that a "power" emanated from God had appeared to certain men under the old dispensation and was called by various names. Furthermore, the modalists did not begin to make their appearance before half a century after Justin's time.

A. Adam, *Lehrbuch der Dogmengeschichte*, I (Die Zeit der alten Kirche), Gütersloh, 1965, p. 157, thinks that Justin refers to the Jewish Christian doctrine of the repeated appearances of the revealer; see above, p. 67, nn. 129 f. But the Old Testament theophanies and angelophanies do not seem to have concerned the Ebionites and the Elchasaites. Furthermore, although it would seem that some of the "seven pillars of the world" were seen as receivers of the revelation brought to them by the Son (see *Ps.-Clem. Hom.* XVIII.13 f.), it is possible that Moses as well as Adam was held to be a real incarnation of the "True Prophet", cp. H.-J. Schoeps, *Theologie und Geschichte des Judenchristentums*, Tübingen, 1949, pp. 106 f.

Goldfahn, pp. 104 f., thinks that Justin refers to the mystical tradition that God every day created a company of angels that uttered a song before him and then returned to the fiery stream under his throne from which they had been created (see *Ḥag.* 14a; *et al.*). Justin's assertion that his precursors taught that also the angels were temporary existents from God's own substance may be a misunderstanding of some such idea, but the notion of the emanation, earthly appearance, and reabsorption of God's "Power" must have another derivation. The people who taught this may have been identical with the Jewish sect of the Meristae mentioned by Justin in *Dial.* lxxx.4, for this name may be an abusive term indicating that they "divided" the godhead (from μερίζω, to "divide"). For a discussion, see D. Gershenson & G. Quispel, "Meristae", *VigChr*, 12, 1958, pp. 19 ff.

of the Lord and used "the Power" as a name especially for the earthly form of manifestation of this figure.

There is further Jewish evidence for the recognition of the Glory or Power of God in an earthly being. Hippolytus says that the Melchizedekians, who were active in Rome from the eve of the 2nd century, taught that —

> Melchizedek is the Greatest Power (δύναμιν μεγίστην), and this one is greater than the Christ, in whose image, they say, the Christ happens to be.
>
> (VII.xxxvi.1)

Later reports on the Melchizedekians repeat the title of Melchizedek with slight variations of the adjective, as in the records of Simon's title, or with no adjective at all. Thus, for instance, Theodore bar Konai, the last witness, says that, according to this sect, "Melchizedek was the *Great* Power and no mere man."[325]

The Melchizedekians made a schism in the sect of the Theodotians, being adoptianist or dynamic Monarchians "having branched off from the school of the Gnostics Cerinthus and Ebion," who taught that the Spirit or Christ descended upon the man Jesus and worked through him. While the Son worked for the salvation of men, Melchizedek interceded for the angels. As it seems to me, the function assigned to Melchizedek by the so-called Melchizedekians is presupposed already in the *Epistle to the Hebrews*. In this writing, the high priest Melchizedek is represented as the earthly and past type of Jesus, who is a heavenly high priest. At the same time, in the pericope starting with iv.14, Jesus is contrasted with a non-human high priest:

> For *we* have not a high priest who is not able to suffer with our infirmities, but was tempted in all respects like us, yet was apart from sin.
>
> (iv.15)

Here, Jesus is compared to — and not contrasted with — the Aaronite high priest. Like Aaron, Jesus is called from among men (see v.1,4 f.). Like the Aaronite high priest, being a man and dealing "gently with the ignorant and erring" (v.2), Jesus is a true man and thus sympathizes with our weakness (see iv.15; v.7 ff.). The thread from ii.16 ff., the first passage in which Christ is called a high priest, is taken up: Jesus did not take upon himself angelic nature, because he then could not be able to help man.

In view of the teaching of the Melchizedekians, it is tempting to speculate that the elevation of Jesus over Melchizedek and his being contrasted with an angelic high priest are setting right the idea that Melchizedek is a heavenly high priest. The predication about Melchizedek in vii.3a, saying that he was without father, mother or descent, and having no origin or end, is very remarkable and is judged by several scholars to reveal a pre-Christian speculation.

---

325 Pognon, p. 122, line 9.

The proto-Melchizedekians, then, would have heeded the teaching of *Hebrews* that men had to have a human high priest, but did retain the supra-human position of Melchizedek and logically took him to be the intercessor for the angels only.

F. Horton, Jr., who has written the latest monograph on the figure of Melchizedek, asserts that the Melchizedekians were fictitious as a sect and simply were adoptianists who kicked Melchizedek upstairs in order to empha-size the saving work of Christ[326]. This is not convincing. According to the typology of *Hebrews*, Melchizedek is nothing but a figure foreshadowing the Son (see v.6, 10; vi.20; ch. vii). Granted that his rôle in the divine scheme could be misunderstood (see Epiphan., *Pan.* ch. LV), his position immediately under God in the system of the Melchizedekians must have *preceded* the introduction of Christ, for no Christian would place Melchizedek above Christ. Furthermore, the main concern of the adoptianists was to combat the Logos Christology and safeguard the *monarchia* of God, and this concern actually is imperilled by the position of Melchizedek between God and Christ. Thus, the Melchizedekians known to Marcus Eremita in the 5th century denied "that Melchizedek was a man and not Christ himself," and argued the absurdity of the teaching of *Hebrews* vii.3b that Melchizedek was likened to Christ (*De Melch.* ch.4). According to these people, Melchizedek actually was divine, φύσει θεός, and even the λόγος θεός (see *ibid.* ch. 2).

As Horton himself knows, there were substantially non-Christian teachings about Melchizedek as a heavenly power showing no dependence on *Hebrews*. In *Pistis Sophia*, Zorokothra·Melchizedek is an aeon who installs the souls in "the Treasure of Light". In *II Jeu*, Melchizedek imparts the heavenly baptism. In the writing entitled *Melchizedek* from Codex IX of the Nag Hammadi library, Melchizedek receives revelations by heavenly messengers, who discourse on his future rôle as a heavenly high priest being identified with Christ having suffered and then triumphed over death. This rôle of Melchizedek is not unlike that assigned to him by the later Melchizedekians, and there is thus no ground for doubting the actual existence of such people. Their identification of Melchizedek and Christ must be due to a Christianiza-tion of the sect, which first placed Christ below Melchizedek[327].

---

326 See *The Melchizedek Tradition* (SNT, Monograph Series, 30), Cambridge, 1976, pp. 87 ff., especially p. 100.

327 John of Apamea, who lived in the 6th century, is said by Theodore bar Konai (Pog-non, p. 137) to have gone to Alexandria and devised a system according to which the seven primordial sons of the Father of Greatness had produced Melchizedek, who acted as an intercessor, praying to the Father that he should send grace to Abraham, one of the primordial sons who had sinned and fallen. In Islamic Gnosticism, Melchi-zedek is the judge and final revealer coming from heaven at the resurrection; see G. Vajda, "Melchisédech dans la mythologie ismaélienne", *JA*, 234, 1943-45, pp. 173

As was discerned already by M. Friedländer, the Melchizedekians would have been an essentially Jewish sect[328]. In *II Enoch* ch. 23, which is part of what appears to be a later addition to the short recension of the book, it is related that Melchizedek was conceived and born miraculously, and later taken up to Paradise during the Flood. Already when coming out of his mother's womb, he was fully developed and had on his chest the glorious seal of the priesthood, probably containing the Tetragrammaton. In the long recension, which admittedly is late (6th or 7th century?), Melchizedek is even called "God's Word and Power".

A. Vaillant argues that *II Enoch* is of Christian origin, and adduces the parallel between the birth of Melchizedek and that of Jesus as one of his principal arguments[329]; but I cannot see that this proves anything else than a certain dependence upon the Gospel tradition. Would a *Christian* ascribe virginal birth to a figure of the old dispensation? There is no prophecy of Jesus at all in the chapter, and God's promise that Melchizedek is going to be priest for him unto eternity and the priest of the new generation runs counter to the teachings of *Hebrews* (vi.20; vii.17, 21), where it is Christ who possesses this honour.

In later Judaism, Melchizedek was identified with Michael, the angelic high priest in the heavenly tabernacle[330], and this identification obviously had an old basis. Origen reports the view that Melchizedek was considered an

---

ff. For Ismaili Gnosticism, see now H. Halm, *Kosmologie und Heilslehre der frühen Ismāʿīlīya* (AKM, XLIV/1), Wiesbaden, 1978. It goes back to Jewish sources; see the review by G. Quispel, in *IJMES*, 12, 1980, pp. 111 f.

328 See "La secte de Melchisédec et l'epitre aux Hébreux", *REJ*, 5, 1882, pp. 1 ff., 188 ff.; 6, 1883, pp. 187 ff.; *Der vorchristliche jüdische Gnosticismus*, Göttingen, 1898, pp. 28 ff.; cp. B.A. Pearson, "Friedländer Revisted. Alexandrian Judaism and Gnostic Origins", *SPh*, 2, 1973, p. 34.

329 See *Le livre des secrets d'Hénoch* (TIES, IV), 2nd ed., Paris, 1952, reprinted 1976, p. 75, n. 17; cp. H. Sahlin, *Der Messias und das Gottesvolk* (ASNU, 12), Uppsala, 1945, pp. 370 ff.

330 See M. Lueken, *Michael*, Göttingen, 1898, p. 31. In this connection, it may be mentioned that a fragment of the *Gospel of the Hebrews* preserved in a discourse by Cyril of Jerusalem in Coptic translation reads: "When Christ wished to come upon earth to men, the good Father summoned a mighty power in heaven that was called Michael, and entrusted Christ to the care of him. And the power came into the world and was called Mary. And Christ was in her womb for seven months" (Wallis Budge, *Texts*, p. 60). In the fragments of this gospel preserved by Origen and Jerome, however, it is the Holy Spirit that is Jesus' metaphysical mother. Is Michael identical with the Spirit of God? It has been noted above, p. 180, n. 320, that the "Power" is a name of the Spirit-Mother in Syrian Christianity. Note further that it is not impossible that the Melchizedekians actually meant that Melchizedek, who was called "the Great(est) Power", was identical with the Spirit that descended upon Jesus; see A. von Harnack, *Lehrbuch der Dogmengeschichte*, I (Die Entstehung des kirchlichen Dogmas) (STL, I), 4th ed., Tübingen, 1909, pp. 714 f.

angel (quoted by Jerome, *Epist. ad Evang.* lxxiii.2). Philo witnesses Melchizedek speculations when allegorizing Melchizedek as a type of the Logos, one of
whose phases is that of a philosophical-cosmological variant of God's principal angel. At the same time, however, Philo warns against imputing plurality
to God:

> For he is priest, even Logos, having as his portion Him that is, and all his thoughts
> of God are high, and vast, and sublime; for he is priest of the Most High (*Gen.* xiv.18).
> Not that there is any other who is not Most High – for God being one "is in heaven
> above and on earth below, and there is none beside him" (*Deut.* iv.39) – but it be-
> hoves to conceive of God not in low earthbound ways but in lofty terms [...].
>
> *(Leg.all.* III.81 f.)

Already in the Qumran literature, Melchizedek and Michael, or "the Prince
of Light", probably are identical, since they both are described as holders of
th same eschatological office (see 11 Q *Melch* and 1 Q *M* xiii.9 f.; xvii.6 ff.;
1 Q *S* iii.18 ff.; *CD* v.15). At any rate, the Qumranians' picture of Melchizedek merits attention. He is described as the eschatological saviour who brings
back the exiles at the end of days, announcing the expiation of their sins and
liberation. He is then passing judgment on Belial and the evil angels in the
time of the last Jubilee:

> ... for He [*i.e.* God] had decided the year of acceptance of Melchizedek ... God's
> holy ones to the reign of judgment, as is written concerning him in the hymns of
> David, who says: "Elohim stands in the congregation of God (El); among the heaven-
> ly ones (elohim), he judges" (*Ps.* lxxxii.1).
>
> (11 Q *Melch* 9-10)

Melchizedek then is described as being helped by the good angels in
subduing Belial and his company.

A.S. van der Woude, who published the fragment, propounded the thesis
that Melchizedek is a heavenly figure, even identical with Michael, and the
"Elohim" of the Psalm being quoted[331]. The thesis was accepted by some
scholars, but was vehemently opposed by J. Carmignac, who sees Melchizedek as a symbolic or etymological figure and thinks that the subject of *Ps.*
lxxxii.1 is God in 11 Q *Melch* as well as in the Old Testament[332]. However,
further research has vindicated the interpretation by van der Woude[333]. It is
probably also Melchizedek who is intended with the quotation of *Is.* lii.7,

---

331 See "Melchizedek als himmlische Erlösergestalt in den neugefundenen eschatologi-
    schen Midraschim aus Qumran Höhle XI", in P.A.H. Boer, ed., *OS*, XIV, 1965, pp.
    354 ff.

332 See M. de Jonge & A.S. van der Woude, "11 Q Melchizedek and the New Testament",
    NTS, 12, 1965/66, pp. 301 ff.; Y. Yadin, "A Note on Melchizedek and Qumran",
    IEJ, 15, 1965, pp. 152 ff.; J.A. Fitzmyer, "Further Light on Melchizedek from
    Qumran Cave 11", *JBL*, 86, 1967, pp. 25 ff. (= *Essays on the Semitic Background
    of the New Testament*, London, 1971, pp. 152 ff.); Carmignac, "Le Document de
    Qumran sur Melchisédeq", *RQ*, 7, 1970, pp. 343 ff.

"Your god (אלוהיך) is king" (16; 24). Thus, the Kingdom of God is identical with that of his plenipotentiary. According to J.T. Milik's reconstruction of the text, the fragment even says:

> And "your god": that means [Melchizedek, who will deliver] them [from] the hand of Belial.

The bestowal of the name of Elohim on the principal angel by the Qumranians is one of the signs of their relationship with the later Merkaba mystics, in whose literature the divine names are used confusingly of both God and the angels[334]. The Samaritans also fit into this picture, for we have seen that they bestow on Moses the name "Elohim" and even the Tetragrammaton. The Gnostics were heirs to this practice, for the divine names known from the Old Testament appear as the property of the salvic intermediaries in the Gnostic systems; thus, as has been pointed out above, Elohim is the vizir of the highest God in the system of Justin[335]. We can be sure that also the name "the Great Power" used of Melchizedek is rooted in a Jewish tradition.

The evidence concerning Melchizedek as "the Great Power" and "Elohim" illustrates that God's agent possessing the divine names could be discerned in a being who was known to have appeared on earth. Both in Judaism and Samaritanism, Melchizedek even was welded with Shem, the son of Noah[336]; and Targum Neofiti and the Palestinian Fragmentary Targum call Melchizedek "the Great Shem". Since "Shem" apparently means "name", it may be wondered whether this contains an allusion to the idea that Shem-Melchizedek even is the hypostasized "Great Name", the Tetragrammaton. That Shem was regarded as the possessor of the proper Name of God is confirmed by an

---

333 See M. Delcor, "Melchizedek from Genesis to the Qumran Texts and the Epistle to the Hebrews", *JSJ*, 2, 1971, pp. 115 ff., especially pp. 133 f.; F. du Toit Laubscher, "God's Angel of Truth and Melchizedek. A Note on 11 Q Melch 13b", *JSJ*, 3, 1972, pp. 46 ff.; J.T. Milik, "Milkî-ṣedeq et Milkî-reša' dans les anciens écrits juifs et chrétiens", *JJS*, 23, 1972, pp. 95 ff., especially p. 125; "4 Q Visions de 'Amran et une citation d'Origène", *RB*, 79, 1972, pp. 77 ff.; Horton, pp. 64 ff.

334 See Scholem, *Jewish Gnosticism*, p. 71, *et passim; Kabbalah*, p. 19. Merkaba speculation is found in Qumran, for a liturgical fragment says that the angels bless "the image of the Throne-Chariot above the firmament" (4 Q *Serek Širôt 'Olat Haššabāt*). I. Gruenwald, *Apocalyptic and Merkavah Mysticism* (AGAJU, XIV), Leiden, 1980, p. 41, reports that Professor John Strugnell, who published the fragments of the so-called *Angelic Liturgy*, is preparing additional material of this kind for publication. Gruenwald, pp. 155 f., warns against taking the Qumran apocalyptics as Merkaba mystics, since the former did not have the vision of the Glory of God as one of their aims.

335 See p. 8, and further below, pp. 216, 305.

336 I have not seen this identification being made in Samaritan sources, but Jerom (*ad Evagrium, Epist.* 26) and Epiphanius (*Pan.* LV.6) assert that the Samaritans propounded it.

anonymous aggada which obviously alludes to *Gen.* ix.26, where **YHWH** is
called the God of Shem:

> Shem, Ham, and Japheth. Surely Japheth was the eldest? [Shem, however, is
> written] first because he was [more] righteous [than the others]. Also, because he was
> born circumcised, the Holy One, blessed be He, set His Name particularly upon him
> [...].
>
> (*Gen.R.* xxvi.3)

It appears that Shem was regarded by some people as having been especially associated with God by virtue of possessing the Divine Name. As shall be
seen below, Abraham, another patriarch, was accorded the same honour by
some rabbis[337]. Jews obviously had no demur in conceiving of a human
being given the Name of God. There is, however, no direct evidence that
Melchizedek was recognized under the Tetragrammaton, although the divine
names of Elohim and the Great Power were given to him.

Terminating the search for the title of the Great Power as the name of
God's principal angel appearing in human form, reference shall be made to a
fragment of the *Prayer of Joseph* — a Jewish apocryphal work from the 2nd
or even the first century C.E. — which has been transmitted in Origen's
In Johannem Commentarius (II.31). In this fragment, a heavenly being called
Israel, who has come down to earth and been incarnated in the patriarch
Jacob, describes himself thus:

> [... Am I not] Israel, the Archangel of the Power of the Lord (ἀρχάγγελος δυνάμεως
> κυρίου) and the archistrategos among the sons of God? Am I not Israel, the first of
> those who serve before the face of the Lord? And I have called upon my God by His
> Eternal Name.[338]

What is especially interesting in this connection is Israel-Jacob's appellation "the Archangel of the Power of the Lord". J. Daniélou writes: "... the
fact that this title is parallel in construction to the title 'angel of the Holy
Spirit' in the *Ascension* [*of Isaiah* (iii.15; *et passim*)], and that the latter is
used to designate God the Holy Spirit in person, suggests that this expression
too may in effect be equivalent in meaning to 'the power of the Lord'."[339]
This would seem to be a right interpretation. In an identification formula in

---

337 See pp. 246.

338 For the context, see below, p. 314.

339 *Theology*, p. 134. It is interesting that there is at hand an amulet with the inscription
"Jacob the likeness (עקובתא) of YHWH, His son"; see H.C. Youtie, "A Gnostic
Amulet with an Aramaic Inscription", *JAOS*, 50, 1930, pp. 214 ff. Does this mean
that Jacob was seen as the Kabod? The Targumic versions of *Gen.* xxviii.12 relate that
Jacob's "image" (איקונין) is engraved upon the throne of glory (cp. *Hull.* 91b;
Gen.R. lxviii.18). For this term, see below, p. 277, n. 57. In Jewish mysticism, the
name of Akatriel Yah is said to be engraved upon the throne; see Scholem, *Jewish
Gnosticism*, pp. 53 f. Akatriel Yah, however, is a name of the Glory of God; see
below, p. 276.

a Coptic magical papyrus, Jesus says: "I am Israel-El, the Power of Iao
Sabaoth, the Great Power of Barbaraoth (ⲀⲚⲞⲔ ⲠⲈ ⲒⲎⲖ : ⲎⲖ ⲦⲒⲀⲨⲚⲀⲘⲒ̄Ⲥ
ⲚⲦⲈ ⲒⲀⲱ : ⲤⲀⲂⲀⲱⲐ ⲦⲚⲞϬ ⲚϬⲞⲘ ⲚⲦⲈ ⲂⲀⲣⲂⲀⲣⲀⲱⲐ)."[340] Jesus
or Israel-El is here the principal angel of God, YHWH Sabaoth or Barbaraoth[341]. A few lines above, it is said that "the Great Power of Barbaraoth"
is "the Power (δύναμις) that stands before the face of the Father." Jesus-
Israel(-El), "the (Great) Power" of God, is here represented in the same
way as Jacob-Israel, "the Power of the Lord", who is said to be "the first of
those who serve before the face of the Lord." The angel called "Israel"
could obviously be seen as שר הפנים, a name which was usually given to
Michael or Metatron in the office of being the high priest who serves in the
heavenly temple[342]. Furthermore, as we shall see below, this angel was often
regarded as the Angel of the Lord who had been given the Name of God[343],
and Israel-Jacob's declaration that he had called upon God by the ὀνόματι
ἀσβέστῳ apparently means that he is the possessor of the Name of God and
thus the Angel of the Lord.

The association or even identification of the divine Glory with the Angel
of the Lord is also found in Samaritanism. Not possessing the *Book of Ezekiel*,
the Samaritans did not picture the Kabod on the heavenly throne; they found
the Scriptural basis for their teaching in the exodus traditions. While the Elohist writer says that the Angel of the Lord led the Israelites out of Egypt, the
Yahwist and the priestly writer present the Pillar of Cloud and of Fire as the
guide of the people, and the last source adds the peculiarity that the Kabod
of God was veiled in the Pillar. By looking at these traditions, the Samaritans
somehow came to regard the Angel of the Lord and the Glory of God as
one[344].

Since the Glory in Samaritanism is identical with the Angel of the Lord,
God's earthly form of manifestation, it is no wonder that the Glory is described as descending to earth. The descent of the Glory was the same as the descent of the Great Power, as is shown in a hymn by Marqa:

> The Great Power was shaken and the Glory descended in the midst [of the angels
> and the people gathered on Mt. Sinai][345] and made the voice of the trumpet be heard
> from the interior of the burning fire [...]. The Goodness (טובה) [*i.e.*, God] was
> shaken and descended; Mt. Sinai trembled before Him; His children gathered together

---

340 Kropp, I, p. 48.
341 Βαρβαραωθ is also a name of the highest God in the Greek magical papyri (see
   PGM, IV.1008 ff.).
342 Cp. below, pp. 312, 321.
343 See below, pp. 307 ff.
344 See below, pp. 223 ff.
345 ונחת לגו כבודה can be interpreted differently. Szuster renders: "and descended
   in its glory" (p. 30). Kippenberg translates: "and his glory descended in him" (*Garizim*, p. 126). Brown does not have this text.

to hear the voice of God [...]. The Glory was shaken and descended; Mt. Sinai trembled before him; he made the trumpet be heard before Him [...]. The inner of heaven was opened and the Eternal King descended [...].

(Cowley, 54.1 ff.)

The hymn alternates between describing the descent to Mt. Sinai as that of God and that of the Glory, *i.e.*, the Angel of the Lord, and the picture which emerges from this description is similar to the representation of the relation between God and the Angel of the Lord or the Glory in the Old Testament. Although God himself descends to earth, it is by the Angel of the Lord or the Glory that men are approached, for "no man can see Me [*i.e.*, God] and live" (*Ex.* xxxiii.20). Thus, Moses did not see God himself but his Kabod, and only from behind (see *v.* 22). This is the version of the Elohist, who has softened the Yahwist's representation of the close contact between God and Moses (see xxxiii.21; xxxiv.2 ff.). The Elohist traditions were continued by the Samaritans[346], especially by the Dositheans, who were responsible for the development of Samaritan angelology, where even *Ex.* xxiv.10, "And they *saw* אלהי ישראל," and *Num.* xii.8, "And he *saw* תמנת יהוה," were referred to the angels[347]. When Simon Magus claimed to be "the Great Power" (or others claimed this on his behalf), this apparently was a claim to the office of being the Glory of God or the Angel of the Lord[348].

This interpretation offers an explanation of the genitive τοῦ θεοῦ in *Acts* viii.10 (and also in *Luke* xxii.69, where it is said that the Son of Man will be "sitting at the right of the Power of God"), for the scholars who

---

346 See above, p. 42.

347 See Bowman, *Problem*, p. 54 with n. 74 on p. 134, and further below, pp. 225f. In *Ex.* xxiv.10, Targum Onkelos and Pseudo-Jonathan read "יקר (איקר) of the God of Israel", while the Fragmentary Targum (Paris ms.) and Neofiti 1 have איקר שכינתיה (שכינתה). Onkelos and Pseudo-Jonathan also depict this figure as sitting upon a throne, and the latter text even calls him "Lord of the world" (מרי עלמא). Marqa, referring explicitly to the floor of sapphire stone under the feet of the "God of Israel" in *Ex.* xxiv.10, speaks about "the throne for His [*i.e.*, God's] Glory (לכבודה)" (Cowley, 25.15). Cp. Targ. *I Chron.* xxviii.2. LXX *Num.* xii.8 reads δόξαν κυρίου. Onkelos has "likeness of the Glory of the Lord" (דמות יקרא דיוי), while Pseudo-Jonathan reads "likeness of My Shekina" (דמו דבתר שכינתי). The speaker in Pseudo-Jonathan is "the Glory of the Lord" (יקרא דה') (*v.* 5); cp. "the Glory of the Lord's Shekina"(איקר שכינתא דה') in v. 9.

348 This interpretation must not be taken to conflict with the theory that Simon appeared as the Prophet like Moses, for we have seen above, pp. 146ff., that Moses in Samaritanism could appropriate epithets and functions of the Angel of the Lord. It has also been seen, p. 136, that Moses in Samaritanism was pictured as sitting on a throne in heaven, and this representation has a parallel in the Jewish idea that Enoch upon his ascension was enthroned as the Son of Man, who is really a form of the Kabod, or as Metatron, a name of the Angel of the Lord; see below, pp. 292ff. In Abisha's poem, Moses actually is called "the Glory"; see Macdonald, *Theology*, p. 175.

consider that "the (Great) Power" simply denotes God have to admit that the addition of the genitive is "misleading"[349]. K. Beyschlag has pointed out that the phrase τὴν θύραν τοῦ ἱεροῦ τὴν λεγομένην ὡραίαν, "the gate of the temple called "the Beautiful"" (*Acts* iii.2), is the only text of Luke-Acts corresponding completely with ἡ δύναμις τοῦ θεοῦ ἡ καλουμένη μεγάλη in grammatical structure and position of the parts of speech[350]. In the former phrase, of course, the genitive has been added to the name "the beautiful gate" so that readers who did not know so much about the temple should understand that the gate in question belonged to the temple. On this analogy, Beyschlag agrees with earlier exegesis in deducing that τοῦ θεοῦ as well as the participle in viii.10 is an addition, but he does not see that the analogy indicates further that the genitive in the latter place shows that "the Power" in question is *of* God and thus not God himself. It seems that Luke has added the genitive "of God" to "the Power" in *Acts* viii.10 (as well as in *Luke* xxii.69) in order to convey the impression that God's bodily form of appearance, that was called "the Power" as well as "the Glory" or "the Angel of the Lord", was to be distinguished from God himself. If Luke really wanted to elucidate that "the Power" was God himself, the interpretament would only distort his intent.

This Chapter, though starting out from the concept of the divine Name as the agent of creation, has concentered on the figure of the reveler of God. In the next Chapter, the focus will be placed on the figure of the demiurge.

In this connection, we may also direct attention to the drama about the exodus written by a certain Ezekiel in the 2nd century B.C.E. and partly preserved in Eusebius' excerpts from Alexander Polyhistor's works about the Jews (see *Praep. ev.* IX.xxviii.2 ff.; xxix.5 ff.). In this drama, Moses narrates that he had a vision of a throne on Mt. Sinai upon which was seated "a noble Man" (φώς γενναῖος) with a diadem on his head and a sceptre in his left hand (see *vv.* 68 ff.). The author apparently was influenced by the anthropomorphic representation of God on Mt. Sinai in *Ex.* ch. xxiv, where the Samaritans as well as some Jews discerned the form of a hypostasis. The author relates that the Man handed Moses his sceptre and summoned him to sit upon the throne, and then placed the diadem upon his head and "descended from the throne" (*v.* 76). Thus, Moses obviously is enthroned as the ruler and judge of the world in the place of the Glory of God or the Angel of the Lord (see *v.* 86). K. Kuiper, "Le poète juif Ezéchiel", *REJ*, 46, 1903, pp. 174 ff., thought that Ezekiel was a Samaritan, and I hope to reinforce this theory in a later study. For the present, see P.W. van der Horst, "Moses' Throne Vision in Ezekiel the Dramatist", *JJS*, 34, 1983, pp. 21 ff.

349 See, *e.g.*, Dalman, p. 164; Haenchen, *Apostelgeschichte*, p. 253. The suggestion of Torrey, pp. 18 ff., that the phrase in in *Acts* viii.10 goes back to the Aramaic דין חילה די אלהא די מתקרא רב, in which the adjective qualified אלהא, but was taken by the translator to go with חילה, must be rejected on the ground that the participle must be seen as Luke's addition; see above, p. 169. See also the objection against Klostermann and Wilcox raised above, p. 166, n. 272.

350 See op. cit., p. 104.

CHAPTER FOUR

The Angel of The Lord

Angel Cult and Polemics against Demiurgic Notions

A paradox connected with the subject of Samaritan angelology is the fact that there is a tradition which says that the Samaritans do not believe in angels. I do not know who was the first to assert that the Samaritans rejected the belief in angels, but, in the 17th century, the Dutch archeologist H. Reland still kept to that opinion[1]. However, the Samaritans, of course, do believe in angels. In reply to the 18th/19th century French Arabist S. de Sacy's question whether they believed in angels, the laconic answer of the Samaritans was: "We believe in the holy angels who are in the heavens."[2] This belief obviously is age-old. J. Macdonald writes: "From the most ancient literature available it is clear that the Samaritans have believed in angels since the earliest times, indeed from the time of the northern document of the Pentateuch at least, which means that they have held to the belief for about 2,700 years!"[3]

The explanation of the tradition that the Samaritans rejected the belief in angels must be that it is based on testimonies coming from the old priestly party. It has been pointed out that the angelology was a subject of concern

---

1 See *De Samaritanis, Dissertatio* VII with separate pagination, in his *Dissertationes miscellaneae*, Utrecht, 1706, pp. 7, 9. Montgomery, p. 216, n. 39, says that Epiphanius testifies to the Samaritans' denial of the belief in angels, and this is repeated by Bowman, *Problem*, p. 134, n. 74. They refer to *Pan.* ch. IX, where Epiphanius discusses the Samaritans, but does *not* say that they reject the belief in angels. In XIV.2, he states that the Samaritans, as opposed to the Sadducees, *accept* the belief that angels exist.

2 "Correspondance des Samaritains de Naplouse pendant les années 1808 et suivant", *NEMBR*, XII/1, 1829, p. 106; quoted by Montgomery, p. 217.

3 *Theology*, p. 136. Macdonald even asserts that no "near eastern religion is more abundant than that of the Samaritans in reference to angels and to their place in the affairs of the world" (p. 397). The opposite perspective is found in Bowman, *Problem*, p. 54. It is at least true, as stated by Montgomery, that "an account of Samaritan angelology might make a considerable chapter" (p. 216). The present Chapter is not to be regarded as such an essay; its object is to focus on the idea of the principal

to the laicising circles, the Dositheans[4]. During the times when the Dositheans were regarded in a favourable light, their views were admitted into the literature, whereas they could be vehemently debarred at the times when the conservative priestly traditions were prevailing. The priestly party of course could not deny the belief in angels, since it is spelled out in the Bible; but it obviously refrained from discoursing on the angels and endeavoured to render all glory to God. Thus, in the Samaritan version of *Gen.* xlviii.16, "angel" (מלאך) has been changed into "King" (מלך), so that the blessing of Jacob should not be understood to ascribe saving properties to the Angel of the Lord.

In paying regard to the angels as intermediaries between God and men, the Dositheans were in accord with a spirit which also animated Judaism. In the *Preaching of Peter*, the surviving fragments of which allow us to date it to the beginning of the 2nd century, there is a warning against worshipping God in the manner of the Jews,

> for they also, who think that they alone know God, do not understand, and worship angels and archangels, the months and the moon.
>
> (Clem.Alex., *Strom.* VI.v.41)[5]

The philosopher Celsus corroborates this statement when he says that the Jews "worship the angels" (*apud* Orig., *Contra Cels.* I.26; V.6, 8)[6]. That the angels bring the prayers of men before God, an idea which is found frequently (see, *e.g., Tob.* xii.12, 15; *I Enoch* ix.1, 3; cp. already *Job* v.1; *Zech.* i.12)[7], set on foot a veritable angel cult. The rabbis therefore were not approving of the idea of the intercession of angels. While the Talmud advances the principle that prayers must be said only in Hebrew because of the fact that the angels are monolingual, men nevertheless are admonished not to cry to Michael and Gabriel, but to address God directly (see Jer. *Ber* 13a). That the usage assumed dangerous proportions is seen from the fact that worship of the angels had to be forbidden (see *Mekilta, Baḥodesh* ch. 6, *ad Ex.* xx.2 f.) and offerings to Michael denounced (see *Ab.Zar.* 42b)[8].

---

angel as the intermediator between God and the creation. For Samaritan angelology, see Montgomery, pp. 215 ff.; Macdonald, *Theology*, pp. 397 ff.

4 See above, p. 190, and further below, pp. 228 ff.

5 The text is also transmitted by Heracleon in his commentary on the *Gospel of John* (*apud* Orig., *In Joh.* XIII.17); see Dobschütz, No. IVa and No. IIIb.

6 It is possible that already the *Epistle to the Colossians* can be cited as evidence for Jewish angel cult (see ii.8,16,18), because the false teachers in Colossae were Judaizers. Aristides (*Apol.* xiv.14) also says that the religious activity of the Jews in Roman times was directed to the angels rather than to God, but it is generally assumed that this writer relies on the *Preaching of Peter*.

7 For the notion of Michael as Israel's guardian angel and intercessor, see below, p. 327 with nn. 184 ff.

8 Cp. W. Lueken, *Michael*, Göttingen, 1898, p. 6.

The angels not only communicate men's prayers to God, but also convey God's messages to men and even execute the will of God in the whole universe. Angelic ministration was inferred frequently in Biblical narratives not mentioning it, thus expanding the idea of angels as intermediaries between God and man. Thus, the angels were said to have appeared on Mt. Sinai and taken part in the giving of the Law (see LXX *Deut.* xxxiii.2; *Sifre Num.* 102, *ad* xii.5; *Mekilta, Baḥodesh* ch. 9, *ad Ex.* xx.18; *Pes.R.* 21, 104a; Joseph., *Ant.* XV.136; *Acts* vii.38; *Gal.* iii.19; *Heb.* ii.2)[9]. This, of course, is in clear contradiction to the Biblical account (see *Ex.* xxxiii.11; *Num.* xii.8), and some of the rabbis again tried to check the rôle assigned to the angels by maintaining that the revelation of the Law to Moses on Sinai was one of God's actions in behalf of Israel which were accomplished "not by an angel and not by a seraph"[10].

There apparently were people who posited one or more angelic intermediators of the creation as well as of the giving of the Law. The rabbis actually tried to guard against this:

> All [*viz.*, the rabbis] agree that none [of the angels] were created on the first day, lest you should say: "Michael stretched [the world] in the south of the firmament, and Gabriel in the north, while the Holy One, blessed be He, measured it in the middle." [It is said:] "I am the Lord, who makes all things, who stretched forth the heavens alone, who spread the earth all by Myself"(*Is.* xliv.24). It is written מי אתי: [that is,] "who was with Me" as a partner in the creation of the world?
>
> (*Gen.R.* i.3)[11]

This text, which we shall have occasion to cite more than once[12], changes מאתי, which usually is understood to mean "by Myself", to מי אתי, "Who was with Me?" The question is rhetorical, but the polemic of the text must presuppose the practice of maintaining that the principal angels were created on the first day and helped God in the work of creation. The rabbis, although differing between themselves as to the day on which the angels were created, all agreed that it was not on the first day for the purpose of checking the heretical speculations.

That the angels were created on the first day of the first week actually was the older notion (see *Jub.* ii.2), and the Samaritans, being conservative in this as in other respects, kept to the old doctrine and maintained that the angels were created "in the beginning" (Cowley, 32.24)[13]. At the same time, we also

---

9 For the various instances and interpretations of the tradition, see Str.-Bill., III, 1926 and reprints pp. 554 ff.

10 See J. Goldin, "Not by Means of an Angel and not by Means of a Messenger", in *RA*, pp. 412 ff.

11 The tradition is repeated *ibid.* iii.8. See also *Midrash Tanḥ.* B i.12.

12 See below, pp. 236, 265.

13 Cp. Macdonald, *Theology*, p. 406.

find polemics in Samaritan literature against the idea that God had help when he created the world. The following list of quotations from the earliest literature is far from exhaustive:

O Sole, You have no associate, no second, no partner: powerful, eternal, fearsome, great, mighty, awesome. You do not resemble the one who is like You; You are beyond the one who seeks You. Without an associate You brought into being; without a second You created!

(Cowley, 29.11 ff.)

You are our Maker, who was without anyone. You created the world and all it contains without any help.

(*Ibid.* 30.24)

God, our God, who existed before all created things, made, began and ended the world all by Himself!

(*Ibid.* 32.23)

You shall have no other gods besides Me. I am He who has created the world; it is from Me and not from another.

(*Ibid.* 55.6 f.)

Praise be to the Maker who perfected the creation and had no other god with Him. Any that is apart from Him is alien and false, and has no part in the Divinity. He created without a helper; He made without an associate; He [also] formed without using any model. He is one in His Divinity, peerless in His original state! He has no associate, and He formed without using any model in anything He made. Let us understand all this in great faith, and testify and say: "There is only one God!"

(*Memar Marqa* IV.7)

Thanks be to the God of gods, Owner of Divinity, Possessor of Eternity, persisting in Sovereignty, Lord of undividedness, [being] one, unequalled, powerful, awesome, faithful, Creator [and] Orderer of all things by His command, without help, without an associate, without a second, without a companion, without anyone being connected with Him!

(*Ibid.* VI.1)

That the Samaritans emphatically denied that God had help in the creation obviously had a polemical purpose, and the prevailing opinion is that the texts show a contest with Christianity. This was already the explanation by W. Gesenius, who referred to the mediate agency of the Son set forth in *John* i.3, 10 ("All things were made through him, and without him nothing that has been made was made ... and the world was made by him ..."), *Heb.* i.10 ("And you, Lord, laid the foundation of the world in the beginning, and the heavens are the works of your hands")[14], and *Col.* i.16 f. ("For in him were created all things in the heavens and upon the earth, the visible and the invisible, whether thrones or lordships, or rulers or authorities: all things have

---

14 Cp. i.2f. for the idea of the Son as the agent of the creation and sustenance of the world.

been created through him and for him, and he is before all things and all things consisted in him")[15].

It cannot be ruled out that there can be found polemics against Christianity in Samaritan literature. We know that the bishop of Sebaste was present at the council of Nicea, where the co-equality of the divinity of Christ with that of the Father was established formally. Contention with Christianity may be present in the following words of Marqa: "The liers say: "There is one god besides Him, one who is like Him" "(*Memar Marqa* IV.7). But the Samaritans' altercation with Christianity must not be exaggerated. A. von Harnack judged that Palestinian Christianity before the 4th century was not very forcible and confined almost entirely to the big cities, where the population mostly was Greek[16]. Further, the recrudescence of Samaritanism in the 4th century under Baba Rabba, within whose scheme Amram Dara and Marqa worked, was aided by the internal strifes occupying the Christian Church and by the tolerant attitude of the emperors of the century[17]. This was a period prior to the time when Christianity presented any great threat to the Samaritans, and the Samaritan authors would not have any reason for attacking Christian doctrines on such a large scale.

Moreover, the Christian doctrine of the mediate agency of the Son in the work of creation does not fit as the target of the polemic. The Father has created *through* the Son, yes; but God and Christ are not represented as *co-workers* in the creation by the New Testament or the creeds. We can also rule out the possibility that the Samaritan authors attack Gnosticism, where the demiurge creates alone (or in company with his angels) in ignorance of God. However, when Marqa says that God "formed without using any model," he probably polemizes against a Platonic idea. A. Broadie, who has seen this,

---

15 See *De Samaritanorum theologia ex fontibus ineditis commentatio*, Halle, 1823, § 1, pp. 1 ff.; cp. Montgomery, p. 208; Macdonald, *Theology*, p. 65 ff. Heidenheim, *Commentar*, pp. XVII f., however, thought that the passages had to be seen against a background of Alexandrian ideas, which had penetrated Samaria and influenced liberal Samaritans; cp. above, p. 57, n. 100, and p. 55.

16 See *Die Mission und Ausbreitung des Christentums in den ersten drei Jahrhunderten*, II, 4th ed., Leipzig, 1924, pp. 630 ff. That Christianity ever influenced Samaritanism was doubted also by M. Gaster, "Popular Judaism at the Time of the Second Temple in the Light of Samaritan Traditions", Paper Read Before the Congress of the History of Religions, Oxford, September 17, 1908, and printed in his *Studies and Texts*, II, London, 1927, pp. 726 f. On the other front, we find Macdonald, one of whose objects "is the demonstration from quoted sources of the Samaritan absorption of Christian concepts" (*Theology*, p. 53). N.H. Snaith, in his recension of Macdonald's *Theology*, in *SJT*, 18, 1965, p. 103, was sceptical to the thesis of Macdonald that Samaritanism is indebted to Christianity, especially to the Christology. See also Kippenberg, *Garizim*, p. 24, n. 137. Recently, Lowy, pp. 88 f., *et passim*, has reacted strongly against it.

17 See Montgomery, pp. 99 ff.

states: "Indeed, Marqah's persistence on this matter strongly suggests that the doctrine was a live option for at least some of Marqah's Samaritan contemporaries. It is tempting to see in Marqah's words a veiled reference to a heretical Samaritan sect."[18] But the notion that God had help in the creation is no Platonic idea, for the demiurge in Platonic tradition does not work in cooperation with the highest God. Like many of the rabbinic refutations of the tenet of "two powers in heaven", Marqa and Amram Dara obviously subsume a variety of associated doctrines. Their focus, however, undoubtedly is the teaching that God had a partner in his work of creation. Since the two Samaritan authors had as their main concern to mediate between various groups within their own community, it is logical to inquire whether such a doctrine subsisted in Samaritanism.

In this investigation, as in the previous Chapter, extra-Samaritan evidence will play a considerable part, for, as it appears, the idea that God had angelic assistance when he created was at one time shared by different groups within the wider spectrum of Judaism. In the rabbinic refutations of the "two powers" heresy, opposition against the notion that the heretics asserted that God was not alone in the creation begins to appear in the 3rd century[19], but A.F. Segal has suggested that this idea must be earlier[20]. Already A. Geiger pointed out that the Samaritans are preservers of halakhic traditions which were once in vogue also among the Jews[21], and it appears that they also have preserved ancient aggadic material which the Jews decided to abdicate because it led to heresy.

The Evidence of Philo

Philo of Alexandria, although trained in the philosophies of the time and being influenced by the piety of the mystery religions, had as his main concern to demonstrate the truth of the Jewish Bible. It has been known for a long time that Philo's major works dealing with the book of *Genesis*, namely, *De opificio mundi* and *Legum allegoriae* I-III, are no scientific treatises but

18 *Op. cit.*, p. 150. Broadie goes on: "But I shall not seek here to identify Marqah's likely target."
19 See A.F. Segal, *Two Powers in Heaven* (SJLA, XXV), Leiden, 1977, pp. 122 ff.; cp. p. 27.
20 See *ibid.*, pp. 112 f.; 176 f.; cp. p. 129 and pp. 74 ff.
21 For a convenient presentation of Geiger's view, see S. Poznanski, "Geschichte der Sekten und der Halacha", in L. Geiger, ed., *Abraham Geiger*, Berlin, 1910, pp. 352 ff. Recently, Lowy, pp. 5 ff., has criticized Geiger's general theory that there once was a single halakha prevailing everywhere, and that the rabbinic halakha must be understood as a series of changes meant to nullify the ancient customs. Still, Lowy, pp. 9, 19, *et passim*, must admit that the Samaritans in numerous cases do represent an ancient halakha. Geiger, *Urschrift*, pp. 197 ff., even suggests that there once was a common aggada.

homiletical expositions of the Biblical text having their *"Sitz im Leben"* in the preaching being held on the Sabbath in connection with the reading of the Torah in the synagogue[22].

In the vein of Platonism, Philo strongly underlines that God is the cause of good only:

> There are some whose definition of reverence is that it consists in saying that all things were made by God, both beautiful things and their opposites. We would say to these: One part of your opinion is praiseworthy; the other part, however, is faulty. It is praiseworthy that you regard with wonder and reverence that which is alone worthy of honour; on the other hand, you are to blame for doing so without clear-cut distinctions. You never ought to have mixed and confused the matter by representing Him as the author of all things indiscriminately, but to have drawn a sharp line and owned Him author of good things only.
>
> *(De agr.* 128 f.)[23]

God is by nature such that he cannot do anything evil to men; he cannot even punish:

> For it is unbecoming to God to punish, seeing that He is the original and perfect Law-giver. He punishes not by His own hands but by those of others who act as His ministers (ὑπηρετούντων). Boons, gifts, and benefits it is fitting that He should extend, since He is by nature good and bountiful, but punishments by the agency of others who are ready to perform such services, though not without His command given in virtue of His sovereignty.
>
> *(De fuga et invent.* 66)

According to the Jewish philosopher, God employed agents also when he was creating man:

> [...] Moses, when treating in his lessons of wisdom of the creation of the world, after having said of all other things that they were made by God, described man alone as having been fashioned with the co-operation of others. His words are: "God said: "Let us make man after our image"" (*Gen.* i.26). "Let us make" indicates more than one. So the Father of all things is holding parley with His powers (δυνάμεσιν), whom He allowed to fashion the mortal portion of our soul by imitating the skill shown by Him when He was forming that in us which is rational. He deemed it right that by the Sovereign should be wrought the sovereign faculty in the soul, the subject part being wrought by subjects. And He employed the powers that are associated with Him not only for the reason mentioned, but because — alone among created beings — the soul of man was to be suspectible to conceptions of evil things and good things,

---

22 This was first pointed out by Z. Frankel, *Über die palästinensische und alexandrinische Schriftforschung* (PBS), Breslau, 1854, p. 33. See now H. Thyen, *Der Stil der jüdisch-hellenistischen Homilie* (FRLANT, 47), Göttingen, 1956, p. 7. The third work on *Genesis* by Philo, namely, *Quaestiones in Genesim*, has the character of a treatise.

23 See also below, pp. 200f. with n. 26. The doctrine that God is the author of good only is attributed to the sect of the Essenes by Philo (see *Quod omn. prob. liber sit* 84). The doctrine goes back to Plato (see *Republic* 379 A - 380 C).

and to use one sort or the other, since it is impossible for him to use both [at the same time]. Therefore, God deemed it necessary to assign the creation of evil things to other makers (δημιουργοῖς), reserving that of good things to Himself alone.

(Ibid. 68-70)

Since Philo observes the bipartite division of the soul into one rational and good part and one irrational and evil part (cp., *e.g., Leg. all.* II.6; *De spec. leg.* I.333), he has to assign the creation of the latter to beings inferior to God, who cannot do anything else than what is good. This teaching is set forth most fully in *De opificio mundi*:

> One may not unfittingly raise the question of what reason there could be for his [*i.e.*, Moses'] ascribing of the creation in the case of man only not to one Creator, as in the case of the rest, but, as the words would suggest, to several. For he represents the Father of the universe as speaking thus: "Let us make man after our image and likeness" (*Gen.* i.26). Can it be, I would ask, that He to whom all things are subject, is in need of anyone whatever? Or can it be that, when He made the heaven and the earth and the seas, He required no one to be His fellow-worker (συνεργήσοντος), yet was unable apart from the co-operation of others by His own unaided power to fashion a creature so puŋy and perishable as man? The full truth about the cause of this it must needs be that God alone knows, but the cause which by probable conjecture seems plausible and reasonable we must not conceal. It is this: Among existences, some partake neither of virtue nor of vice, like plants and animals devoid of reason: the one sort because they are without animal life and furnished with a nature incapable of consciously receiving impressions; the other sort because from them mind and reason have been eliminated, since mind and reason are – as it were – the dwelling-place of vice and virtue, which are by nature constituted to make their abode in them. Others, again, have partnership with virtue only, and have no part or lot in vice. Such are the heavenly bodies, for these are said to be not only living creatures endowed with mind, or, rather, each of them being a mind in itself, excellent through and through, and unsuspectible of any evil. Others are of mixed nature, as man, who is liable to contraries, wisdom and folly, self-mastery and licentiousness, courage and cowardice, justice and injustice, and – in a word – to good things and evil, fair and foul, to virtue and vice. Now, it was most proper to God the universal Father to make those excellent things by Himself alone, because of their kinship to Him. To make those which are neither good nor bad was not strange to Him, since those too are free from vice, which is hateful to Him. To make those of mixed nature was in one respect proper to Him, in another not so: proper in so far as the better principle which forms an ingredient in them is concerned; alien, in virtue of the contrary and worse principle. So we see why it is only in the instance of man's creation that we are told by Moses that God said "Let us make man," an expression plainly showing the taking with Him of others as fellow-workers (συνεργῶν). It is to the end that, when man orders his course right, when his thoughts and deeds are blameless, God the universal Ruler may be owned as their source, while others from the number of subordinates (ὑπηκόων) are held responsible for thoughts and deeds of a contrary sort. For it could not be that the Father should be the cause of an evil thing to His offspring, and vice and vicious activities are an evil thing.

(72-75)

Philo apparently is impressed by the anthropogony of *Timaeus,* where the demiurge assigns the gods, who are his productions, with the work of creating the two mortal "souls" as well as the body of man, while he supplies the immortal soul (see 41C ff.; 69C ff.). To Philo, of course, God's co-creators are not the Olympians. In the quotation from *De fuga et inventione*, he calls them "powers", which we have seen is a synonym of "angels"[24]. That Philo presupposes this equation is brought out clearly in a passage from *De confusione linguarum*, where the idea that God is not the immediate agent of punishing and the idea that he is not the creator of evil are associated. God's auxiliaries here are called "innumerable powers being helpers and saviours of all created existences" and "unbodied souls, commonly called "angels" in the inspired writings, who attend to these heavenly powers" (174). In other places, too, Philo identifies the souls that are not incarnated with angels (see *De gig.* 16; *De sacr. Ab. et Caini* 5; *De Somn.* I.147). In some passages, the "powers" — who are said to be served by the angels in *De conf. ling.* 174 — are limited to five or six (see *De fuga* 94ff.; *De prov.* 18; *Quaest. in Ex.* II 68). The chief of the "powers" is the Logos (see also *De agr.* 51; *De fuga et invent.* 101), that also is identified with the principal angel, the highest of the archangels (see *De conf. ling.* 146; *De migr. Abr.* 174; *Quis rer. div. her. sit* 205 f.). The "powers" that helped God in the creation of man obviously are the archangels[25].

After having identified God's agents as "powers", that is, archangels, and "unbodied souls", that is, angels, Philo goes on to say that "the King converses with His powers and employs them as His servants for the performance of such duties which are not appropriate for God Himself" (*De conf. ling.* 175). In order to indicate what kind of matters God cannot allow himself to deal with directly, Philo makes the now well-known point that man is capable of both good and evil, and states:

> Thus, it was meet and right that when man was formed, God should assign a share in the work to His lieutenants (ὑπάρχοις), as He does with the words "Let us make man," that so man's right actions might be attributed to God, but the sins to others. For it seems to be unfitting to God the All-Ruler that the road to wickedness within the reasonable soul should be of His making, and therefore He delegated this part to His inferiors. So much for this point. But it is well also to have considered the truth that God is the cause of good things only and of nothing that is bad at all, since He Himself was the most ancient of beings and the good in its most perfect form. And it best becomes Him that the work of His hands should be akin to His nature, surpass-

---

24 See above, p. 177.

25 The number of archangels in Judaism was said to be four, six, or seven. For sources having six archangels, see J. Michl, Art. "Engel II (jüdisch)", *RAC*, V, 1962, cols. 77, 90. For Philo's identification of the Logos (logoi) and angel(s), see further *Leg. all.* III.177; *De conf. ling.* 28; *De somn.* I.239; *De cher.* 3; 35; *De mut. nom.* 87; *De post. Caini* 91. He also could construe the incorporeal souls as logoi; see H.A. Wolfson, *Philo*, I, 2nd ed., Cambridge, Mass., 1948, pp. 376 f. As has been pointed out, the souls are identified with angels.

ing in excellence even as He surpasses, but that the chastisement of the wicked should be assured through His underlings. My thoughts are attested also by the words of him who was made perfect through practice: "the God who nourishes me from my youth, the angel who saves me from all my evils" (*Gen.* xlviii.15 f.)[26]. For, he, too, hereby confesses that the truly good gifts, which nourish virtue-loving souls, are referred to God alone as their cause; but, on the other hand, the province of evil things has been committed to angels (ἀγγέλοις) — though they have not full and absolute power of punishment — in order that nothing which tends to destruction should have its origin in Him whose nature is to save. Therefore, He says: "Come and let us go down and confound them" (*Gen.* xi.7). The impious indeed deserve to have it as their punishment, that God's beneficial and merciful and bountiful powers should be brought into association with works of vengeance; yet, though knowing that punishment was salutary for the human race, He decreed that it should be executed by others. It was meet that, while mankind was judged to deserve correction, the fountains of God's ever-flowing gifts of grace should be kept free not only from all that is, but also from all that is deemed to be evil.

(179-182)

In this text, the "powers" that helped God in the creation and are employed by him in the carrying out of punishments are identified expressly as "angels". Philo takes the divine plurals in Scripture to include the angels and uses these passages in order to drive home the point that God is the author of good only[27].

In the plural of God's words in *Gen.* i.26, Philo found a warrant for the view that the evil part of man's psychical constitution had other makers, *viz.*, the angels. But Philo does not say that the angels also created the body of man, although he takes no lofty view of the material world. In order to explain why God stated that no one should kill Cain (see *Gen.* iv.15), Philo allegorizes the Biblical account as holding the meaning that the evil Cain

---

26 This passage also is quoted in other writings in support of the thesis that God is the bestower of good alone (see *De fuga et invent.* 67; *Leg. all.* III.177).

27 In *De mut. nom.* 30 f., too, *Gen.* i.26 is cited as proof that inferior beings made the soul being inclined to evil as well as having the possibility to do what is good. This text also speaks of "the soul of the bad", but it does not say by whom it was made. Plato teaches that — in addition to the good world soul — there is an evil soul in the universe (see *Laws* 896 E - 897 D; *Epinomis* 988 D-E). In the first century, the concept of an evil or at least ambivalent world soul was taught by Plutarch; see J. Dillon, *The Middle Platonists* (CLL), London, 1977, pp. 199 ff. In the next century, Numenius of Apamea in Syria taught that — corresponding to the two souls in the universe — there were two souls in man, one good and one evil (see Calc., *Comm. in Tim.* 300; Iamblichus, in Stob., *Eclog.* I.49, 25a). In *Quod det. pot. ins. soleat* 80 ff., Philo reckons with a lower, animal soul situated in the blood. In *Quaest. in Gen.* ii.59, this soul is identified as an irrational and sense-perceptive soul which is in opposition to the rational soul. Does Philo in *De mut. nom.* 30 f. mean that some men possess only this soul? In that case, they would not be destined for immortality. Philo (*Quaest. in Gen.* i.16; iii.11) actually seems to reckon with the existence of some utterly evil men who cannot achieve immortality.

soul never would pass away: "[...] impiety is an evil that cannot come to an end" (*De fuga et invent.* 61; cp. *Quod det. pot. ins. soleat* 177). For this pessimistic view, Philo leans on Plato, citing from *Theaetetus*:

> Evils can never pass away, for there must always remain something that is antagon-istic to good. Having no place among gods in heaven, they of necessity hover around the mortal nature and this earthly sphere, wherefore we ought to fly away from earth to heaven as quickly as we can. And to fly away is to become like God, as far as this is possible; and to become like Him is to become holy, just and wise.
>
> (*De fuga et invent.* 63, citing *Theaet.* 176A-B)

Since the material world is the sphere of evil and thus despicable[28], it would not seem logical that it has been made directly by God. In an exposi-tion of *Ex.* xv.17, which says that God leads his people into his holy abode that he has made by himself, Philo exclaims:

> For, of good and holy things only, You are, O Master, the Maker, as from the creation come things evil and profane.
>
> (*De plant.* 53)

Here, it actually seems that evil derives from the material creation itself,

---

28 According to Josephus, the Essenes taught that the soul was imprisoned in the body, from which it was liberated upon death (see *Bell.* II.154 f.). A similar sentiment seems to have penetrated even rabbinic circles. An exposition of *Gen.* i.31, "And God saw everything that He had made, and – behold! – it was very good," refers the last statement to the evil desire as well as to the good desire, because – as runs the argu-ment – without the evil desire there would be no ambitious force driving man to excel and keeping the world going (see *Gen.R.* ix.7). Thus, the assertion in *Gen.* i.31 is defended on the ground that even the evils in the world are good *sub specie aeternitatis.*
  But another interpretation of *Gen.* i.31 is even more interesting, since it changes מאד, "very", to מות, "death" (see *Gen.R.* ix.5). Death was usually regarded as having come into the world through Adam's fall and being the enemy of man, but here it viewed as *the* good thing in God's creation and as a means of escaping an evil or at least repugnant world.
  The first interpretation is ascribed to R. Samuel, a late 3rd century Palestinian amora, and the second exposition is attributed to R. Meir, a 2nd century tanna, and it is perhaps worth noting that both of these rabbis are said to have been occupied with mystical studies. Moreover, R. Meir encouraged contact with the non-Jewish world and was particularly friendly with the pagan philosopher Oenomaus of Gadara of the school of the younger Cynics, who defined his cynicism as "a sort of despair, a life not human but brutish, a disposition of the soul that reckons with nothing noble, or virtuous, or good" (*apud* Julian, *Or.* VII, 209). But probably even more important than the impulses which R. Meir received from Oenomaus are the influences which must have reached him from Elisha ben Abuya, one of his teachers. As is well known, the latter was the arch-heretic who believed that there were "two powers in heaven"; see below, pp. 308ff. It is worthy of note that R. Meir was the only tanna who had rela-tions with Elisha after the latter's apostasy, for this may be taken to show that a negative world view and the idea of an angelic intermediary, ruler of this world, agreed with each other.

and that the latter cannot have been made by God, who is the author of good only. But Philo does not pursue the subject[29]. In commenting upon *Gen.* ii.7, however, where man is said to have been composed of the Spirit of God and a material body, Philo reckons with an inferior demiurge of the latter:

> It says, however, that the formation of the individual man, the object of sense, is a composite one made up of earthly substance and Divine Breath (ἔκ τε γεώδους οὐσίας καὶ πνεύματος θείου), for it says that the body was made by the artificer (χοῦν τοῦ τεχνίτου), taking clay and moulding out of it a human form, while the soul was originated from nothing whatsoever, but from the Father and Ruler of all. For that which He breathed in was nothing else than a Divine Breath that migrated hither from that blissful and happy existence for the benefit of our race, to the end that – even if it is mortal in respect of its visible part – it may in respect of the part that is invisible be rendered immortal.

> *(De op. mundi* 135)

Here, there is no discourse upon man being apportioned a base and material soul and a good and spiritual one; the subject matter is the basic division between the material and mortal body and the immaterial and immortal spirit. The term *technitēs* in Philo's writings is used of both God and the Logos; here, it obviously is set off by opposition to "the Father and Ruler of all", that is, God, who supplies man with the "Divine Breath", the Spirit. The body, on the other hand, is made by "the artificer".

When Philo's disquisitions on man receiving his base and material soul from God's agents are disrobed of their Platonic dress and transferred to a

---

29 That matter in itself was evil could be derived from Plato (see *Statesman* 273 B-C; cp. *Timaeus* 30 A). Although matter is neutral in the philosophy of Aristotle, the great critic of Plato could speak of the κακοποιόν of matter (see *Phys.* I.19, 192a; *Met.* Λ 9, 1051a). Matter is mostly neutral also in Plutarch, but he, too, could regard it as evil (see *Obsolescence of Oracles* 9, *Moralia* 414 D). The same idea is at least implied by his teacher, Ammonius, since he taught that "[...] there is nothing in nature (physis) which has permanence or even existence" (*apud* Plut., *E at Delphi* 19, *Moralia* 393 A). In the following century, Numenius taught that matter was evil (see Calc., *Comm. in Tim.* 297). Furthermore, by the end of the 2nd century, Atticus, too, agreed with Plato in teaching the concept of the inherently chaotic matter as well as the idea of an evil world soul; see Dillon, pp. 252 ff.
   In the Dead Sea Scrolls, there are some remarkable passages where man is depreciated and his *bodily* nature closely associated with sinfulness (see 1 Q S xi.9 ff.; 1 Q H i.21 ff.); for a discussion, see K.G. Kuhn, "New Light on Temptation, Sin and Flesh in the New Testament", in K. Stendahl, ed., *The Scrolls and the New Testament*, New York, 1957, pp. 94 ff.; W.D. Davies, "Paul and the Dead Sea Scrolls: Flesh and Spirit", *ibid.*, pp. 157 ff. The idea that the senses and passions are the source of error and moral evil is the concomitant of the notion that the physical organism, as material, is evil *per se*, and the Essenes are reported to have lived very ascetically (see Philo, *Quod omn. prob. liber sit* 76 f.; *Hyp.* xi.11; Joseph., *Bell.* II.120 ff.), even banning marriage as well as sexual life in general (see Philo, *Quod omn. prob. liber sit* 84; *Hyp.* xi.14; Pliny, *Nat. hist.* V.xv.73; Joseph., *Ant.* XVIII.21). Cp. below, p. 331, n. 193.

Jewish setting, it becomes clear that they are midrashim saying that the angels were the creators of the body of man. Jews in Palestine assented to the view that the world of matter was an evil place and that God's will in the universe was executed by intermediators, but they did not accept the sophisticated Platonic psychology. For the Jews, the demarcation line ran between matter and the soul or spirit. From *Gen.* i.26, they deduced that God had co-creators, the angels; from *Gen.* ii.7, they inferred that the angels created the body of man, while God supplied the spirit.

Rabbinic Evidence

The rabbis regarded *Gen.* i.26 as a dangerous text. A tradition ascribed to R. Jonathan, who flourished in Sepphoris in the beginning of the 3rd century C.E., reads:

> When Moses was engaged in writing the Law, he had to write the works of each day. When he came to the verse "And God said: "Let us make man," " he said: "Sovereign of all, why do You provide the heretics with an argument?" God replied: "Write! Whoever wishes to err, let him err!"
>
> (*Gen.R.* viii.8)

That it was the plural "Let us make" which supplied the "heretics" (*minim*) with an argument is clearly set forth in a saying by R. Yoḥanan, who lived in the latter part of the century:

> In all the passages which the heretics have taken as proofs, their refutation is near at hand. Thus: "Let us make man in our image"; "And God created man in His own image" (*Gen.* i.27). "Come, let us go down and confound their language!" (*Gen.* xi.7); "And the Lord came down" (*Gen.* xi.5).
>
> (*Sanh.* 38b).

The continuation gives some additional verses as heretical proofs and rabbinical counter-proofs. R. Yoḥanan takes a contextual verb in the singular as proof that God alone is the subject, even if God gives the exhortation to act by using a plural form.

In other versions of this teaching, R. Simlai, the student and colleague of R. Yoḥanan, is cited as its author. In either case, the 3rd century attribution of the tradition remains unaffected. R. Simlai, however, although being credited with having refuted the *minim*, is said to have left his pupils discontented:

> When they [*i.e.*, the heretics] went out, his disciples said to him: "You have dismissed them with a mere makeshift, but how will you answer us?" He said to them: "In the past, Adam was created from the dust, and Eve was created from Adam, but henceforth it shall be "in our image, after our likeness": neither man without woman nor woman without man, and neither of them without the Shekina."
>
> (*Gen.R.* viii.9)[30]

---

30 The context of the parallels in Jer. *Ber.* 12d-13a and *Deut.R.* ii.13 contains many

R. Simlai first refers to the anthropogony in *Gen.* ch. ii, and then interprets the words "in our image, after our likeness" to be a sanctification of the institution of marriage, thus giving them general application instead of connecting them with the creation of the first man. Whether the rabbi was as successful in silencing his pupils as he was in silencing the heretics need not occupy us; the point to be noted is that some of the rabbis tried to detach the plurals in *Gen.* i.26 from the subject of that verse.

By the end of the 3rd century, we find rabbinic interpretations to the effect that God's exhortation "Let us make man" was addressed to the "works of heaven and earth", the "works of each day", or his "heart", *i.e.*, himself[31]; but before the middle of the century, the common exposition was that the address was directed to the angels. Thus, about 240, R. Ḥanina taught:

> When He came to the creation of Adam, He took counsel with the ministering angels, saying to them: "Let us make man."
>
> (*Gen.R.* viii.4)

The angels then ask what the character of man will be like, and the rest of R. Ḥanina's discourse deals with this question, dropping the subject of the making of Adam.

R. Judah is reported to have spoken as follows in the name of Rab, the famous rabbi who came to Palestine from Babylonia in the beginning of the 3rd century:

> When the Holy One, blessed be He, wished to create man, He [first] created a company of ministering angels and said to them: "Is it your desire that we make man in our image?" They answered: "Sovereign of all, what will his deeds be?" He replied that such and such would be his deeds. Thereupon, they exclaimed: "What is man that You are mindful of him, and the son of man that You think of him?" (*Ps.* viii.5). Thereupon, He stretched out His little finger among them and consumed them with fire. The same thing happened with the second company. The third company said to Him: "Sovereign of the universe, what did it avail the former [companies of angels] that they spoke to You [as they did]? The whole world is Yours, and whatever You wish to do therein You do."
>
> (*Sanh.* 38b)

It is tempting to argue that "the angels share in the creation of man in this story,"[32] for the third company of angels does consent to God's will, expressed by the question "Is it your desire that we make man in our image?" But the plural may simply be *pluralis majestatis*, and the angels may merely be considered God's counsellors. The tradition — occurring in an anthology of amoraic Adam legends — has no continuation.

---

texts as proofs and counter-proofs.

31 See *Gen.R.* viii.3; cp. xxvii.4. But already Justin (*Dial.* ch. 62) says that these interpretations were made by Jewish "teachers".

32 Segal, *Two Powers*, p. 113, n. 11.

The Pseudo-Jonathan Targum, which probably dates from the 2nd century C.E., also finds an address to the angels in *Gen.* i.26:

> The Lord spoke to the angels who were serving Him and who were created on the second day of the creation of the world: "We will create man after our image and likeness."

As we have seen above, it was denied that the angels were created on the first day, for in that case some could argue that they helped God to make the firmament[33]. But did the angels help God to make man? This is not the teaching of Pseudo-Jonathan, for *Gen.* i.27 reads: "And the Lord created man in His likeness [...]."

It was the idea that God spoke to the angels which was found dangerous by R. Jonathan and R. Yoḥanan and/or R. Simlai. R. Jonathan explains the plural in *Gen.* i.26 by saying that God "took counsel with the ministering angels" in order that no great man should ever say that he did not have to ask permission for a proposed action from one of lesser importance. The "erring" of the *minim* apparently consists in the idea that the angels were summoned as God's co-creators, whereas R. Jonathan asserts that the address to the angels only has moral significance.

R. Yoḥanan explains the divine plurals in Scripture as necessary on the ground that God "does nothing without consulting his heavenly court, for it is written: "The matter is by the decree of the watchers, and the sentence by the word of the holy ones" (*Dan.* iv.14)." The heretical position supported by the "proofs" of divine plurals obviously is that God employed his heavenly court in carrying out actions.

The tradition that God spoke to the angels in *Gen.* i.26 was continued after the time of R. Yoḥanan and R. Simlai, but now it was elaborated in a censorious way. Thus, R. Ḥuna of Sepphoris, who flourished about 300, gives the following exposition:

> While the ministering angels were arguing with each other and disputing with each other, the Holy One, blessed be He, created him [*i.e.*, Adam]. He [*i.e.*, God] said to them: "What can you avail? Man is already made!"

>   (*Gen.R.* viii.5)

This is preceded by an aggada which begins by relating that, when God "came to create Adam, the ministering angels formed themselves into groups and parties, some of them saying: "Let him be created!", whilst others urged: "Let him not be created." " R. Ḥuna asserts that this was a vain contention, for God did not depend upon the angels in any way when creating man. The words in *Gen.* i.26a certainly were addressed to the angels, but the verb should read *neʿesah*, "is made", not *naʿaseh*, "Let us make" or "We will

---

33 See p. 194.

make". Thus, the verse contains no exhortation to the angels. The polemical
gist is obvious.

Other expositions retained the reading *na῾aseh* and explained it as meaning
that God took counsel with the angels. R. Aha, a 4th century Palestinian
amora, developed the notion that the angels responded to God's plan of making Adam by asking what man would be like. According to R. Aha, God
answered that Adam would be wiser than they were, and proved this by
bringing beasts before Adam in order that he could give them names, which
the angels were unable to find out (see *Gen.R.* xvii.4). It is not related how
Adam was created; he suddenly appears on the scene as already created.

An anonymous tradition found in different sources relates that the angels
responded to God's words in *Gen.* i.26a by quoting the words of *Ps.* viii.5,
a verse which already Rab had cited as the angelic response to God's idea of
creating man. God then created man all by himself and brought the beasts
before him[34].

Our supposition that the rabbinic polemics are directed against a widespread and old tradition, which was adapted by Philo, is corroborated by
many rabbinic texts reporting that *Gen.* i.26 was among the verses where the
Greek translation changed the Masoretic text. The *Mekilta of R. Ishmael*
is the earliest source which contains a passage to this effect:

> "The time of the staying of the children of Israel in Egypt, the land of Canaan,
> and the land of Gosen was 430 years" [cp. *Ex.* xii.40]. This is one of the things that
> was written for King Ptolemy. They also wrote for him: "God created in the begin-
> ning [cp. *Gen.* i.1]; "אעשה אדם בצלם ובדמות" [cp. *Gen.* i.26]; "The man and
> his נקובין He created them" [cp. *Gen.* i.27]; "And He completed on the sixth
> day and rested on the seventh" [cp. *Gen.* ii.2].

> *(Pisha xiv.64 ff.)*

King Ptolemy, of course, is Ptolemy II Philadelphus, at whose request the
LXX is said to have been written. We need not be detained with the problem
that, out of more than the thirteen alterations said to have been made, only
four appear in surviving mss.[35]; it is sufficient for our purpose to note that the
rabbis insisted on a certain understanding of these verses, obviously because
the Masoretic text provoked heretical deductions. Whether the rabbinic concern really dates back to the 2nd century school of R. Ishmael is not so
important[36]; the important point is that the rabbis assumed that the heretical

---

34 See *Pesikta R.* ch. 4, 34a; *Num.R.* xix.3; *Midrash Tehillim ad Ps.* viii, ch. 2, *ad v.* 2;
   Tanh. Behokoth ch. 4, 224b; cp. *Eccl.R.* VII.xxiii.1 (where it is not said that God
   created Adam, but that he answered the angels by stating: "The man whom I propose
   to make will have wisdom exceeding yours"). *Midrash Tehillim* attributes this tradition to Rab.
35 Some more attestations appear in African versions. The five passages quoted above
   are not attested.
36 The rendering of *Gen.* i.1 shows that it was the word בראשית which provoked

explanation of these verses went back to the 3rd century B.C.E.

That the rendering of *Gen.* i.26 aimed at checking the notion that God had co-workers is evident, for it changes the verb form from the plural to the singular and omits the pronominal suffix in בצלמנו and בדמותנו. If we collate the rabbinic reports on the changes made in the LXX with the interpretation of these places by Philo[37], it would seem that the rabbis had Hellenistic Jews or proselytes as targets. But Hellenistic Jews were obviously not the authors and only supporters of the idea that God spoke to the angels and created man in cooperation with them. We have seen that the rabbis maintained that God spoke to the angels[38] — an explanation which does not harmonize with the reports on the change of this verse in the LXX. The interpre-

---

heretical inferences, and we know that teachings predating the 2nd post-Christian century construed ראשית as Wisdom and explained the preposition as *Beth instrumentalis*; see below, pp. 316 f. The construction אלהים ברא בראשית blocks the interpretation that *Reshith* is Wisdom, a personal being, through whom God made the world. The Mekilta rendering of *Gen.* i.27c is probably directed against the idea that the first man was an androgynous being, and this idea is also to be recognized before the 2nd century C.E.; see next note.

37 Philo took *Gen.* i.27c as evidence that the *genos* of man was androgynous (see, for instance, *Leg. all.* II.13). That *v.* 27b has an object in the singular ("in the image of God, He created him"), while *v.* 27c has an object in the plural ("man and woman He created them"), obviously was a problem for Jewish exegetes. Substituting נקובין for נקבה, the pronominal object in the plural could be retained, while at the same time the problem of *v.* 27b-c was solved, for the substitution obviously implied that only the male was created. The Pseudo-Jonathan Targum and a couple of other sources change the pronominal suffix in the singular into plural. Both changes prevent the conception that the first man was a hermaphrodite. There are also outspoken polemics against this idea in other texts (see, *e.g.*, *Berak.* 61a). Later, however, the rabbis admitted the idea (see Gen.R. viii.1; *et al.*). The change of the pronominal object in *Gen.* i.27c into the singular was probably meant to signify the androgynous character of the first man (see, for instance, *Meg.* 9a; cp. *Ps.-Clem. Hom.* III.54).

38 They also maintained that man was created in the image of the angels (see *Gen.R.* viii.11; *Ex.R.* xxx.16; *et al.*). This interpretation easily would allow that God not only spoke to the angels in *Gen.* i.26, but also that the angels actually helped in the creation of Adam. Significantly, however, the idea that man was created in the image of the angels is nowhere proffered as an exposition of *Gen.* i.27b-c in conjunction with the reference of נעשה in *v.* 26 to the angels; it is associated mostly with *Gen.* iii.22. But Targum Onkelos *Gen.* i.27b as well as *Gen.* v.1 and ix.6 would seem to teach that man was created in the image of the angels, since "Elohim" is not paraphrased, as is usually the case in Onkelos; the name of Elohim would here seem to denote the angels. The Samaritan Targum *Gen.* ix.6 reads: "Have I not created man in the image of the angels?" But Onkelos does not follow Pseudo-Jonathan in taking נעשה to be addressed to the angels, because it then would be really difficult to avoid the impression that they actually assisted in the creation of man. There was also opposition to the view that man was created in the image of the angels (see *Mekilta, Bashalah* vii.73 ff.).

tation obviously had a well-established status in the Jewish community; it must stem from a time when the line between orthodoxy and heterodoxy was not yet drawn. Since the aggada more often than not includes polemics against the idea that the angels acted as God's co-creators, it is not likely that it originally implied no more than the notion that God took counsel with the angels. In Judaism, too, orthodoxy did not always precede the heresy, and it apparently was a certain development of the aggada which caused the rabbis to drop the logical conclusion that the angels acted as God's co-creators.

Still, all traces of the idea that God had helpers when making man have not disappeared from rabbinism. In a tradition given by R. Joshua of Siknin in the name of R. Levi (whose aggada R. Joshua often transmitted) or R. Simeon, we find the concept of several יוצרים:

> God took counsel with the souls of the righteous in creating the universe, since we read: "These were the formers (היוצרים) and those that dwelt among plantations and hedges; there they were with the King in His work" (*I Chron.* iv.23). "These were the formers": They are termed thus on account of the verse "Then YHWH Elohim formed (וייצר) man" (*Gen.* ii.7). "And those that dwelt among plantations" corresponds to "And the Lord planted a Garden in the east" (*Gen.* ii.8). "And hedges" corresponds to "I have placed the sand for the bound of the sea" (*Jer.* v.22). "There they were with the King in His work": With the Supreme King of kings, the Holy One, blessed be He, sat the souls of the righteous, with whom He took counsel before creating the world.
>
> (*Gen.R.* viii.7)

This midrash, ascribed to the 3rd century, is given as a commentary on God's words in *Gen.* i.26a, "Let us make man."[39] The interpretation says that God took counsel with the pre-existing souls of the righteous; in fact, it says that God took counsel with them before he created the *world*[40]. The support of this opinion is found in *I Chron.* iv.23, which is supposed by the author of the tradition to be referring to the pre-existing souls of the righteous. Then, this verse is expounded by three passages which all describe God's creative activity in primal times. The "makers" of *I Chron.* iv.23 are first recognized in *Gen.* ii.7, because the latter verse refers to the anthropogonic activity of YHWH Elohim by using a verb form from the same root as that of the word "makers" in the former verse.

Further, since *I Chron.* iv.23 says that the pre-existing souls "dwelt among plantations," they are supposed to have been present when God "planted a Garden" (*Gen.* ii.8). Because *I Chron.* iv.23 says that the souls dwelt among "hedges" as well as among plantations, they are held to have been present

---

39 The parallel in *Midrash Ruth* ii.3 expounds *I Chron.* iv.23 itself.

40 It is possible to argue that the pre-existent souls are angels; see above, p. 200. However, it is also possible that the tradition tries to make manifest that men are more important than angels. This might have been the reason for the tolerance of the interpretation.

when God made "the bound of the sea" (*Jer.* v.22). Finally, since it says that the souls "were with the King in His work," God's words "Let us make" were addressed to them.

The midrash agrees with the rabbinic tradition that God in *Gen.* i.26 "took counsel" with his agents. But it goes further than the expositions examined above in that it explicitly calls God's agents "makers", "formers", with reference to *Gen.* ii.7. Thus, the agents of God could be recognized in the grammatical subject of the first part of *Gen.* ii.7, where it is related that YHWH Elohim "made", "formed", man.

It will be remembered that Philo discerned that *Gen.* ii.7 as well as *Gen.* i.26 allowed the conclusion that man was not created by God alone, and this tradition can be followed over the teacher of R. Joshua of Siknin to a Spanish aggada manuscript, the sister manuscript of the so-called Golden Aggada from the 14th century. In this work, the creation of Adam as told in *Gen.* ii.7 is elucidated by a picture showing three beings with wings effecting the creation of man, while a fourth personage – a juvenile-looking figure without wings – is standing by. One of the winged beings is kneeling beside Adam and palpably moulding his limbs; the second is standing behind the first and touching Adam's head with his right hand; and the third is standing to the right of the other two and facing Adam with his right hand raised in a gestus of speech. The figure without wings is standing further to the right. U. Schubert has seen that the acts of the winged beings illustrate respectively the creation of the body of Adam, his endowment with the spirit, and his reception of the soul, a personification of which is found in the young personage without wings[41]. The illustration of *Gen.* ii.7 obviously presupposes that the plural in *Gen.* i.26 includes the angels.

The manuscript includes a duplication of the representation of the four figures on the other side of Adam, but the copyist depicting the figures to the left of Adam has reversed the order of the figure with the raised hand and the youth, and also made them face each other instead of Adam. This shows that the copyist did not understand that the illustration shows a trichotomic anthropology, and that the paradigm of the portrayal of the creation of Adam derives from Hellenistic times, when the trichotomic anthropology was current. As Schubert points out, the idea that man was composed of matter, spirit, and soul was adopted by Hellenistic Jews. In the synagogue of Dura Europos, there is a pictoral representation of the revivification of the dead as told by *Ez.* ch. xxxvii founded upon this particular anthropology. Josephus even renders *Gen.* ii.7 in the following way: "And God fashioned

---

41 See "Die Erschaffung Adams in einer spanischen Haggadah-Handschrift des 14. Jahrhunderts (Br. Mus. Or. 2884) und ihre spätantike jüdische Bildvorlage", *Kairos*, 18, 1977, pp. 213 ff.

man by taking soil from earth, and sent spirit and soul into him" (*Ant.* I.34). Thus, the anthropogony conveyed by the illustration of *Gen.* ii.7 must not be dismissed as a late innovation; rather, the evidence of the illustration corroborates the theory that there was a "preservation of a Hellenistic Jewish illustrated Bible as far as the thirteenth century."[42]

It is perfectly natural that a graphic representation of *Gen.* ii.7 pictures the creation of man as a work done by angels alone, for God could not be depicted. However, as submitted above, the angelic assistance originally was restricted to the production of the material body. This is in fact what was taught by the Samaritans, who found that God had help when creating man in the text of *Gen.* ii.7 as well as in *Gen.* i.26.

Extraneous Evidence for Angelic Assistance in Creation

Before probing the Samaritan material, it would be apt to adduce some extraneous evidence supporting the conclusion that Jews in the first century C.E. could teach that the body of man was a fabrication of the angels. Furthermore, we shall see that this teaching was exploited to illustrate the ontological and theological dualism of Gnosticism.

The author of the *Tripartite Tractate* from Codex I of the Nag Hammadi library shows better learning than many modern scholars when he says that Judaism has given birth to –

> many heresies, which have existed to the present among the Jews. Some say that God is one, who has spoken in the ancient scriptures. Others, however, say that He actually is many. Some say that God is singular and individual in His nature. Others, however, say that His activity is double and linked up with the origin of good and evil. Some say that He is the creator of everything that has come into being. Others, however. sav that He has created through His angels (ⲇⲉ ⲁⲛ ⲉⲩϫⲱ ⲙ̄ⲙⲟ[ⲥ] ϫⲉ ⲁⲃⲁⲗ [ϩⲓ]ⲧⲛ̄ ⲛⲉ[ϥⲁ]ⲅⲅⲉⲗⲟⲥ ⲡⲉⲧⲁϥⲣ̄ ϩⲱⲃ).
>
> (112.19-113.1)

This passage apparently refers to the fact that some Jews tried to conceive a theodicée. After all, the Old Testament contains many sayings by God which are difficult to imagine as having been spoken by the good Lord described in other passages. By attributing the passages revealing the malign character of God to other beings, it was possible to maintain the notion of the goodness of God. If not, it would be most consistent to assert that the only God was author of both good and evil. As we have seen above, Philo, for one, was a Jew who denied that God was the author of evil.

That some also claimed that God had created through his angels is also a solution to the problem of how the notion of the good God can be harmonized with the hard facts of life. God thus became detached from the material

---

42 B. Narkiss, *The Golden Haggadah*, London, 1970, p. 63.

world, in which evil resided according to the philosophy of the time. Philo, as we have seen, supported his theodicée by citing *Gen.* i.26 as proof that God had co-creators who were responsible for the evil inclination in man. Moreover, by ascribing the work of creation to the angels, the Jews also endeavoured to solve the problem of the anthropomorphisms in Scripture, for *Genesis* represents the creator as having made the universe by manual occupation, an anthropomorphic feature.

In the 2nd century, the Christian apologist Justin wrote in his dialogue with the Jew Trypho:

> For I would not say that the dogma of that heresy which is said to be among you is true, or that the teachers of it can prove that [God] spoke to angels, or that the human frame was the workmanship of angels (ὅτι ἀγγέλοις ἔλεγεν, ἤ ὅτι ἀγγέλων ποίημα ἦν τὸ σῶμα τὸ ἀνθρώπειον).
>
> (*Dial.* lxii.3)[43]

Justin in the context treats of divine plurals in the Old Testament, in particular that of *Gen.* i.26. He argues that God when speaking in plural does not use a plural of majesty or address the elements or the angels. The two former interpretations are well attested in Jewish literature, and there is no reason to doubt that there were Jews who taught that the angels not only were addressed by God, but also acted as the creators of the body of man. In the 2nd century, the notion that God had used the angels as helpers when making man apparently was not yet censured. Justin, who came from Neapolis in Samaria, would have had good opportunity to learn to know Jewish as well as Samaritan expositions of the Bible. In fact, his own interpretation, namely, that God spoke to Wisdom, *i.e.*, the Son, and that the latter was God's helper in the creation of man, obviously is derived from a Jewish interpretation of *Gen.* i.26[44].

In the century before Justin, the Jewish historian Josephus, who belonged to the aristocratic and conservative priesthood, spoke thus of the creation of the natural phenomena:

> These God made, not with hands, not with toil, not with assistants (συνεργασομένων), of whom He had no need.
>
> (*Contra Ap.* II.192)

The theme that God had used helpers in the creation obviously was propounded in Palestine in the first century, for Josephus' denial of this notion must presuppose its assertion by others. It is probably no coincidence that Philo in *De op. mundi* 72 and 75 uses terms closely related to *synergasomenos* when writing that God had help when he created man. It may be that this is a

---

43 See also Basil, *Hom. in Hex.* IX.6.
44 See below, p. 317 with n. 158.

translation of שותף, which — as we shall see when discussing the Samaritan evidence — appears to have been a title of God's co-creator.

Comparing the evidence surveyed in this section with the Philonic and rabbinic evidence, some conclusions press for acceptance. There was a teaching that God acted and had created through or together with assistants. This was inferred especially from divine plurals in Scripture, chiefly *Gen.* i.26, and the anthropogony thus came into focus. The rabbis and Josephus denied the doctrine, but Philo and extraneous sources confirm its protestation among Jews. The idea was not peculiar to Hellenistic Judaism, for some of the rabbis retained the first part of the aggada, saying that God's words in *Gen.* i.26 were addressed to the angels. That the angels created the bad part of man's psychical constitution, as was taught by Philo, obviously is a Platonized version of the aggada; Justin says that the angels created the body of man. The doctrine must have originated at least as early as in the first century C.E., but was censured about 200. It was very vital, however, for it crops up in a 14th century aggadic ms.

The Development of Gnostic Dualism

Irenaeus, the first heresiologist to give us the Gnostic myth proffered by Simon Magus, does not report any anthropogonic teaching of the Samaritan who is said to have been the first Gnostic. For the anthropogony of Simon or his followers, we must turn to the source material incorporated in the *Pseudo-Clementines*. Like the heretics opposed by R. Yoḥanan and /or R. Simlai, Simon in this literature takes the plural in *Gen.* i.26 as proof that God was not alone when he created man. In the *Homilies*, he is quoted as having said:

> For there are evidently two who created, since Scripture says: "And God said: "Let us make man in our image, after our likeness." " Now, "Let us make" implies two or more, certainly not one only.
>
> (XVI.11)

In the *Recognitions*, Simon argues:

> [...] it is manifest that there were many gods engaged in the making of man. Also, whereas at the first God said to the other gods: "Let us make man after our image and likeness."
>
> (II.39)

In substantiation of his thesis that there are many gods, Simon cites other texts too, and *Gen.* i.26 is not the only verse which reappears in the rabbinic enumerations of the alleged changes in the LXX and among the proof-texts of the heretics combatted by R. Yoḥanan and/or R. Simlai. But Simon and his followers obviously were not the authors of the idea that the divine plurals in Scripture suggest that several beings were involved in the actions referred to, for already Philo — apparently attesting to a widespread tradition — could use the same verses as Simon and the opponents of the rabbis in order to prove that God was the cause of good only. Thus, in *Rec.* II.39, Simon also cites, *inter alia, Gen.* xi.7 as proof that there are many "gods" (cp. *Hom.* III.39, where *Gen.* xi.7 is conflated with xviii.21 as evidence of anthropomorphism showing that the god of the Old Testament cannot be the highest God). As we have seen above, Philo (*De conf. ling.* 179 ff.) quotes *Gen.* xi.7 as well as i.26 as proof that God works through angels, and R. Yoḥanan opposes the heretical opinion that *Gen.* xi.7 as well as i.26 implies that God works together with the angels. Furthermore, the rabbis could take *Gen.* xi.7, "Come let us go down," as "one of the things that they altered for King Ptolemy, [changing it to] "Come, I will go down" " (*Gen.R.* xxxviii.10). Simon thus is heir to a Jewish heresy.

In the immediate context of the quotation from the *Homilies*, Simon does not give a reason for the existence of "many gods". Later, however, in order to prove that the framer of the world is not the highest God, he cites the words of Jesus in *Matt.* xi.27 ("No one knew the Father except the Son, as no one knows even the Son except the Father, and those to whom the Son may wish to reveal Him") and argues that the highest God was unknown under the old dispensation (see XVI.21; XVII.4; XVIII.4). In the context of the quotation from the *Recognitions*, Simon says that the highest God is "incomprehensible and unknown to all" (II.38; cp. II.47, 49). As we shall see in Chapter VI, the pre-Christian sect of the Magharians taught the same, and Simon appears to reveal a sentiment similar to these people, who referred the descriptions of God in the Bible to the principal angel, who was even the demiurge, "for otherwise it would not be possible to describe God at all."[45]

In the wider context of the quotation from the *Homilies*, however, Simon also maintains that the god of the old dispensation is not good and therefore cannot be the highest God (see XVII.4 f.; XVIII.1 ff.; cp. III.38 ff.; *Rec.* III.37 f.); thus, Simon's motive for arguing the existence of "many gods" under God would also seem to be that of freeing God from the blame for the evil in the world. This would bring Simon in accord with Philo and some of the Jews known to the author of the *Tripartite Tractate*. We must also keep in mind that, as in fact is evidenced by some chapters of the *Clementina* (*viz., Hom.* III.38 f.; *Rec.* II.53), the view that God is the author of good only, and that another cause must be assumed for the evil in the world, easily concurs with the idea that God is highly exalted above the world and beyond anthropomorphisms, and that the work of creation and the divine dealings with the world must be attributed to one or more intermediaries. In any case, Simon clearly is heir to a Jewish heresy.

The "other gods" obviously are the angels. According to both Jewish and Samaritan usage, "Elohim", the name of God in *Gen.* i.26, could designate

---

45 Shahrastani, in Cureton, p. 169, and Haarbrücker, p. 257. See below, pp. 329 ff.

the angels. In the *Homilies*, Simon in fact regards the demiurge as an angel. Peter opposes Simon's teaching by saying:

> We, Simon, do not say that, from the Great Power, that is also called the Dominant Power, two angels were sent forth – the one to create the world, the other to give the Law – nor that each one, when he came, proclaimed himself on account of what he had done as the sole creator [...].

(XVIII.12)

It is worthy of note that the demiurgic angel is not in opposition to God from the beginning; he is sent out by God. In the *Recognitions*, too, Simon says that the demiurge originally was the agent of the highest God, but later deviated from him:

> He [*i.e.*, the highest God] sent out god the creator to make the world, and he – when he had made it – gave himself out to be God.

(II.57)

It is well known that Simon Magus in the *Pseudo-Clementines* often is a cloak for Paul, the Apostle of the Gentiles, but this cannot be the case in the passages given above. Nor can Simon be a mask for some radical Paulinist like Marcion or Apelles, for these people did not teach that the demiurge was the agent of the unknown God and that the Old Testament evidences that God works through angels. On the other hand, there do exist differences between the teaching of Simon in the *Clementina* and the Simonian myth as given by Irenaeus. According to the heresiologist, Simon taught that the world was made by "angels and powers", while Simon in the Clementine romance posits a single angelic demiurge of the world. But this is in reality an insignificant dissimilarity, corresponding to the vacillation in the *Pseudo-Clementines* as to whether Simon taught that God employed only the principal angel or several angels when he created man. There obviously were differences of opinion within the Simonian school.

We must not overlook a very significant correspondence between the teaching of Simon in the *Clementina* and in the system transmitted by Irenaeus. The heresiologist reports that Wisdom (Ennoia) brought forth the angels who created the world because she knew "what her Father willed" (I.xxiii.2). The sin of the angels consists in their detainment of Wisdom and in their bad rule of the world. Their creation of the world is no sin, but the will of God. This agrees with the teaching of Simon in the Clementine literature, where God himself sends out his angel to create the world, but afterwards is deserted by him. That the creation took place by the will and at the command of God is a very peculiar idea in the history of Gnosticism; that the rebellion of the demiurge did not occur until *after* the world had been made indicates that we are on the border between Jewish and Samaritan heresy and Gnosticism.

There are other teachers who testify to this borderline case. Cerinthus, a Jewish Christian whose acitivity fell in the period of the Apostle or Presbyter John (see *Iren.*, III.iii.4), taught that the world was not made by the First God, but by a power that was widely separated and remote from the Power that is above all, and not knowing the Supreme God.

(*Iren.*, I.xxvi.1)

Irenaeus goes on to tell that Cerinthus proffered an adoptionist Christology, and later authors add that he also taught an eschatology of an earthly millennium and practised circumcision and observed the Sabbath[46]. All this shows that he was a Jewish Christian; and, since the doctrine that the world was created by an angelic being ("power" being a well-known synonym of "angel") is not Jewish-Christian, it would seem to be a heritage from Judaism.

Cerinthus asserts that the angel who created the world did so without any knowledge about God, but he has nothing to say about any maliciousness of the demiurge. That the demiurge was not evil and did not oppose God was also the teaching of Justin the Gnostic, whose system is mainly an adaptation of Old Testament material. Here, Elohim is said to have "established and formed the world out of mutual good pleasure" (Hipp., V.xxvi.14), and the angels of Elohim are asserted to have moulded man from the earth (see *ibid.*, V.xxvi.7). Furthermore, Justin agrees with Cerinthus that the demiurge did not know the highest God. He tells that Elohim and his angels ascended to heaven in order to "see whether anything was defective in the creation," and that Elohim beheld the light coming from the heaven of the highest God. The latter let Elohim into his realm and placed him on a throne by his side (see *ibid.*, V.xxvi.14 ff.). From his place in the highest heaven, Elohim emits saviours into the world of men (see *ibid.*, V.xxvi.21 ff.). The demiurge, then, is the first to be saved and the author of the salvation of men. The mediator has not yet been split up into a good saviour and an evil demiurge.

It is not known when Justin lived, but it may have been very early, for it is noteworthy that his system does not contain any distortions of the basic gist of the Biblical accounts. Thus, for instance, the eating from the Tree of Knowledge still is regarded as a transgression, and the serpent is not taken to be a manifestation of the saviour, but still is conceived of as guilty of misdeed. At any rate, the absence of any maliciousness of the demiurge is matched by a powerfully Jewish tenor.

The teaching that the breach between God and the demiurgic angel(s) was manifested already in the creation was not proffered before the time of Satornil, who followed Menander, Simon's successor. Contrary to Simon and Menander, Satornil did not speak about Wisdom, but asserted that there was "one Father unknown to all, who made angels, archangels, powers, and principalities" (Iren., I.xxiv.1). Further, Satornil is reported to have taught:

The world and everything in it came into being from certain seven angels, and man

---

46 See above, p. 16.

is also a creation of the angels. When a shining image appeared from above, from the highest Power, which they were not able to detain, he [*i.e.*, Satornil] says, because it immediately returned aloft, they exhorted each other, saying: "Let us make a man after the image and likeness." When this was done, he says, and their product could not stand erect because of the powerlessness of the angels, but crawled around like a worm, the Power above took pity on him because he had been made in His likeness, and sent forth a spark of life, which raised man up, equipped him with limbs, and made him alive.

(Ibid.)

Now the *angels* address each other with the words of *Gen.* i.26, saying: "*Faciamus hominem ad imaginem et similitudinem.*" The name of God in *Gen.* i.26, "Elohim", is construed as "angels". Simon, however, taught: "[...] *dicit Deus ad ceteros deos:* "*Faciamus hominem ad imaginem et similitudinem nostram.*"" Satornil has preserved the idea that the angels made the body of man, while God gave him the spirit, but he does not conceive of this as a cooperation. In the system of Satornil, the angels who create the body of man are no longer God's agents, although the notion that they have a divine origin has been retained.

"The god of the Jews, he [*i.e.*, Satornil] says, was one of the angels" (*ibid.*, I.xxiv.2), and we apparently are right when inferring that "the god of the Jews" is no one else than Michael, the guardian angel of Israel. Already in the *War Scroll* from Qumran, we read that God "has exalted among the gods the ministry of Michael, and the dominion of Israel over all flesh" (1*QM* xvii.7 f.). The "gods" apparently are the angels of the nations, who are going to be subordinate to Michael, just like the nations are going to be subordinate to Israel. Satornil says that Satan "acted against the world-creators, and especially against the god of the Jews" (*Iren.*, I.xxiv.2), and it is well known that Michael is the adversary of Satan in Jewish tradition. In Satornil's system, then, the head of the demiurgic angels is Michael, as is also the case in the system of the Ophians (Ophites) known to Origen (see *Contra Cels.* VI.30)[47].

Simon included the angel of the Jews in the plurality of the "many gods" in God's service, saying that one of them "was chosen by lot, that he might be the god of the Jews" (*Rec.* II.39). Already in Simon's teaching, we see that the angel of the Jews is identified with "the framer of the world, who also created Adam," and revealed himself in the Old Testament (*Hom.* XVIII. 4; cp. III.38 f.; XVI.21; XVII.4 f.; *Rec.* II.53). It is not improbable that the Samaritan Gnostics would teach this in their altercation with Jews and Christians. Peter, the voice of the Jewish-Christians in the *Clementina*, admits that "angels are called "gods" by Scripture" (*Hom.* XVI.14), but upholds against Simon the *monarchia* of the God of the Jews, the creator (see, *e.g.*,

---

47 For Michael as Satan's opponent in Jewish tradition and the demiurge of the Ophites, see below, pp. 326 ff.

Rec. II.40). The Samaritan heretics assented that the god of the Jews was the creator, but added that he could not be the highest God, since the latter was unknown. According to the first Gnostics, the Jews and the Christians mistook the guardian angel of the Jews for God.

However, the Jewish Christians could also teach that God "gave to His Son, who is also called "Lord", and who brought into being heaven and earth, the Hebrews as his portion, and appointed him to be god of gods, that is, of the gods who received the rest of the nations as their portions" (*Hom.* XVIII. 4; cp. *Rec.* II.42). Thus, the Jewish Christians could in fact deny that the highest God was the creator and accept the view that he created through the principal angel, the guardian angel of the Jews. This is no doubt a teaching of Jewish origin. The Jewish Christians identified the angel as Christ, the Son of God, while the Gnostics exploited the idea in another way and developed a dualism of opposition.

In the system of the Ophites, who must have preceded Valentinus, we perceive that the demiurge is no longer only an angel; now he is also a travesty of the God of the Old Testament. Irenaeus says that the Ophites taught that the demiurge

> Jaldabaoth said: "Come, let us make a man in the image" literally, *imaginem nostram*, but "our" is unitelligible. When the six powers heard, [...] they came together and made a man [...].

(I.xxx.6)

The creator of the world, Jaldabaoth by name, is not one among the creators of the body of man. He begets a son, who in his turn produces a son, and so on, until Jaldabaoth all in all has six descendants (see *ibid.*, I.xxx.4). Moreover, he does not take part in the creation of the body of man; "the six powers" effect this work by themselves. However, Sophia manages to get Jaldabaoth to breathe into man the breath of life, thus unwittingly emptying himself of power, which he had obtained from his mother, Sophia. Then man could stand erect.

In the system of the Ophites, then, the demiurge is a grotesque imitation of the God of the Old Testament. He is clearly superior to the angels, the creators of the body of man, and is allured into giving man the spirit, which he unfortunately possesses. Still, he has not yet become identical with the devil, for it is Jaldabaoth, who really is Michael in Ophite tradition, who is said to have cast Samael down into the world below (see I.xxx.8).

In the *Hypostasis of the Archons* from Codex II of the Nag Hammadi Library, the teaching of the Ophites is developed further[48]. We read:

---

48 There are points of connection between the two systems: the serpent is an instructor; Norea is Eve's daughter; the names of Seth and Samael occur.

The archons held a council. They said: "Come, let us make a man from the dust of the earth." They fashioned their creature as one wholly of dust.

(87.23-27)

The creator of the world, who is called "this archon" in 94.34, is perhaps among "the archons" in this passage. In *On the Origin of the World*, which is clearly related to the *Hypostasis of the Archons*, Jaldabaoth creates the body of man together with his fellow-rulers (see NHC II, 114.29-115.3). In the *Tripartite Tractate*, the demiurge "took counsel with his archons" (105.3), whom he had created, before making the material man in cooperation with "his angelic servants" (105.1).

Whether or not the demiurge is among the archons whose creation of the material man is described with reference to *Gen.* i.26 and ii.7a, he is said explicitly to have breathed into the face of man so that he became psychic (see 88.3 f.; cp. *Apoc. Adam* 66.19 ff.). This is how *Gen.* ii.7b is expounded. But man is unable to get up on his feet until he receives the spirit from above; then, as is said with reference to *Gen.* ii.7c, man "became a living soul" (88.15).

In this system, the creator of the world is no longer a *primus inter pares*, as he still was in some way in the Ophite system. According to the Ophites, Jaldabaoth was the first of the seven archons, but the demiurge in the *Hypostasis of the Archons* is the creator of the seven archons and stands above them. Furthermore, the demiurge in the latter system is not opposing the devil, as did the demiurge of the Ophites; in fact, the demiurge in the *Hypostasis of the Archons* is the devil, bearing the name of Samael (see 87.3). The God of the Old Testament and the devil are welded into one being.

Finally in this section, let us note another work, *viz.*, the *Apocryphon of John*, which shows us the last step in the development of Gnostic dualism. In the short recension, it is told that the seven powers created by Jaldabaoth —

said to one another: "Let us make man after the image of God and his likeness."
(*BG* 48.10 ff.)

In the long recension, however, the chief archon — called by the names of Jaldabaoth, Saklas, and Samael (see NHC II, 11.17f.) — is portrayed as having —

said to the principalities which attend him: "Come, let us make a man after the image of God and according to our likeness [...].
(15.1 ff.)

Whereas it is uncertain whether the demiurge in the *Hypostasis of the Archons* takes part in the creation of the body of man, the case is clear in the *Apocryphon of John*: neither in the short nor in the long recension does the creator of the world take part in the creation of the body (which actually is a psychic body); the seven powers effect this work by themselves. Then the *Apocryphon of John* gives the story about how the demiurge was lured by the powers of light and "blew into his face the spirit which is the power of his mother" (NHC II, 19.25 ff.; cp. *BG* 51.15-52.1)[49].

Thus, Jaldabaoth in the Apocryphon of John is a clear travesty of the God of the Jews, who breathes his spirit into the body which was made by his seven archangels. The creator of the world is also the devil, having no evil power opposing him. The Gnostic dualism is complete.

When Gnostic dualism unfolded in the 2nd century C.E., the rabbis had to censure the part of the aggada on *Gen.* i.26 which said that the body of man was the creation of the angels, since this idea was exploited to support the theological as well as the ontological dualism of Gnosticism. Still, the rabbis retained part of the aggada by admitting that God did speak to the angels[50]. A picture in an aggada manuscript stemming from Hellenistic times shows the active part played by the angels. Here, the angels even convey the non-material part of the human constitution, but the basic idea apparently was that the spirit was given by as well as from God. In the 2nd century, this is assumed by Justin who says that there were Jews who taught that God spoke to angels and that the angels made the body of man. In the first century, the notion is presupposed by Philo, who used it to teach that the evil part of man's soul was not made by God, but by his assistants, even the angels. However, Philo also testifies to the idea that the material body was made by a lower demiurge, while the spirit was given by God. As we shall see in the following section, this was also the teaching of the Samaritans, who identified the demiurge as the Angel of the Lord. The vacillation between the idea that God used a single helper and the notion that he had several assistants is seen in Simon Magus' system, where we can observe the transition from Jewish-Samaritan heresy to Gnosticism.

The Angel of the Lord in Samaritanism

The question of H. Jonas whether there are "Hebrew writings" teaching a dualism between God and the demiurge like that of the *Apocryphon of John* obviously must be answered negatively[51]. But when it is realized that this sort

---

49 R. van den Broek, "The Creation of Adam's Psychic Body in the Apocryphon of John", in *Studies*, pp. 38 ff., has shown that the creation of the psychic body of Adam in the *Apocryphon* corresponds to that of the material body in *Timaeus*. Van den Broek, p. 57, suggests that the author has given a Gnostic twist to the Alexandrian Jewish idea that *Gen.* i.26 f. describes the creation of a heavenly man, while *Gen.* ii.7 refers to the creation of the material man. Irenaeus (I.xxix) used a source similar to that of the *Apocryphon of John* when describing the doctrines of the Barbelo-Gnostics, but he did not relate the anthropogony of these people, and we do not know whether there was a devil in their system.

50 And they also retained the idea that man was created in the image of the angels; see above, p. 208, n. 38.

51 See "Response", p. 290; cp. above, p. 19.

of dualism is secondary, the question loses its relevance as a test of the theory that Gnosticism has a Jewish origin. There certainly is both Hebrew and Aramaic evidence that God had a commissioned demiurge. This evidence comes from the Samaritans.

We have seen above that Amram Dara and Marqa polemize against the notion that God had help in the creation, and that the people who upheld this view probably constituted a group within the Samaritan community[52]. Can they be identified? There have been made attempts to identify the target of Marqa's polemics in a text which refers to a related doctrine. In an answer to Pharaoh's suggestion in *Ex.* viii.25 that the Israelites might sacrifice within the borders of Egypt, Moses and Aaron underline the differences between the two peoples:

> You say that there are two gods in the universe, one in heaven and another upon the earth; but we say that there is only one God, who has acquired heaven and earth for himself [cp. *Gen.* xiv.19, 22]. You say that spirits are shared among the animals and men, but we speak of soul and spirit, referring the soul to the body and the spirit to men. The governing of living human beings is by means of both soul and spirit; the governing of animals is sufficiently done by the soul. You say that the eating of flesh is not permissible; we want to slaughter and sacrifice cattle. You worship animal forms, but we sacrifice animal flesh to our God.
>
> *(Memar Marqa* I.8)

The text then continues with citations from *Ex.* viii.26 ff., and it is obvious that the digression quoted above does not refer to differences between the Egyptians — who did not know only two gods or were vegetarians — and the Hebrews, but to discords between main line Samaritans and heretics within the community. H.G. Kippenberg thinks that Marqa refers to the Simonian teaching that the world was created by several lower $\delta \upsilon \nu \acute{\alpha} \mu \epsilon \iota \varsigma$[53], but this form of Simonianism cannot be under attack, because the text speaks of only *one* god over this world. R.F.J. Trotter states that the passage seems to contain a "reference either to the teaching of Cerinthus or of Marcion"[54]. Now there is little probability that the teachings of these two men represented threats to the Samaritan community[55], but it is still possible to regard them as representative of a respectively mild and extreme Gnosticism[56]. However, there is no indication that the heretics spurned the god over this world and the

---

52 See pp. 195 ff.

53 See *Garizim*, p. 340.

54 *Gnosticism and Memar Marqah*, p. 8.

55 Cerinthus taught in Asia Minor by the end of the first century (see Iren., I.xxvi.1), and the Marcionite church, although it spread as far east as Mesopotamia, does not seem to have had special influence in Samaria.

56 Whether or not Marcion should be reckoned to the Gnostics is a matter of dispute. By regarding him as a type of radical Gnosticism, his theological and cosmological dualism is in view.

material creation, as did the extreme Gnostics. As we have seen, Cerinthus did
not teach any baseness on the part of the demiurge or a depreciation of the
world, but he did maintain that the demiurge was ignorant of the highest
God. The god over this world in the teaching rejected by Marqa, however,
would rather seem to be the lieutenant of God in heaven. It would seem that
the heretics are identical with those who taught that God had a partner in
the work of creation, and that the god who is set over this world is identical
with the lower creator. This is all the more probable inasmuch as קנה means
to "create" as well as to "acquire" and to "possess". Marqa thus underlines
that God is the sole creator as well as the only ruler of the entire universe. If
Cerinthus should be reckoned to the Gnostics, we must go back to the pre-
history of Gnosticism in order to be able to identify the heretics.

The following disputation, which actually is neither quoted nor discussed
by Trotter and Kippenberg, may be helpful in identifying the heretics. A.
Broadie despairs of giving an explanation of the trichotomic anthropology
propounded by Marqa, but this seems to have been caused by his acceptance
of the translation of J. Macdonald, who renders "the dead" instead of "the
animals" (שתיקיה, literally, "the dumb") and "the living" instead of "men"
(ממלליה, literally, "the speaking")[57]. In addition to being the "breath of
life", spirit in *Memar Marqa* is often related to feelings, emotions, and cogni-
tions[58]. Marqa denies that animals have this kind of spirit. He admits that
they have "soul" (נפשה), which we obviously must understand as the principle of physical life. The heretics, however, are ascribed with the view that
also animals have spirit. Thus, their reason for not killing animals and eating
flesh may be that they had adopted the Greek idea of metempsychosis. But
it can also be that the view that animals have the same kind of spirit as men is
a fabrication by Marqa, who wants to present a (ridiculous) justification for
the heretics' abstinence from meat and the sacrificial cult. That the heretics
are said to "*worship* animal forms" undoubtedly has to be accounted for by
Marqa, wanting to ridicule their abstention from eating meat and slaughtering animals; he thus also effects that the representation of the heretics merges
into the image of the Egyptians, who were known to have many gods in sub-
human form.

Abu'l Fath ascribes ascetic traits to several of the Dosithean branches, and
Epiphanius (*Pan*. ch. XIII) relates that Dosithean asceticism included abstention from the consumption of meat. As a matter of fact, Abu'l Fath reports
that Dositheus himself did not eat meat for a period of two years, and his assertion of the discontinuation of this abstention is obviously not to be trust-
ed[59]. Moreover, the Dositheans were opposed to the cult on Mt. Gerizim and

57 See *op. cit.*, pp. 195 f.
58 See *ibid.*, p. 196.
59 See Vilmar, p. 151. Cp. above, p. 66, n. 128.

thus to the ritual slaughtering and sacrifices. It thus appears that the people who taught that God had an agent who was responsible for the creation of matter and was set over this world were Dositheans.

However, as we already have seen, the doctrines of the Dositheans were also assimilated to a certain degree under Baba Rabba, to whom Marqa and Amram Dara owned their allegiance. Can there be found an approach to a creation doctrine which would appeal to the dissidents? M. Heidenheim, in his incomplete edition and translation of *Memar Marqa*, wrote that the Samaritans had a "Logos doctrine" according to which both God and the Kabod were instrumental in the creation of Adam[60]. As proof, Heidenheim cites a passage where the context deals with the imparting of the Law to Moses:

> The Divinity (אלהותה) appeared and established the Covenent; and the Glory (כבודה) appeared and magnified what was good; and the angels (מלאכיה) came to magnify what was glorious, and they were all assembled for Adam. The Divinity formed him, and the breath of life was breathed into him; and the Glory made him complete with a great spirit: the two of them were clad in two crowns of great light. The Divinity put into him a perfect mind; and the Glory gave him powerful illumination. The Divinity also glorified him with speech; and the Glory glorified him with perfect knowledge. The angels were witnesses to Him of what he would do, and they all are gathered in every place where God is mentioned in truth.
>
> (VI.3)

Marqa now turns to a kabbalistic inquiry into the nature of the seven letters which are not found in the decalogue.

Since the Samaritans do not have the prophetical canon, they did not advert to *Ezekiel* for the figure of the Glory, but found the Glory in the *exodus* traditions of the Pentateuch. According to the *E* tradition, the Angel of the Lord led the Israelites out of Egypt (see *Ex.* xiv.19a; xxiii.20; xxxii.34; *Num.* xx.16), whereas the *J* source represents YHWH himself as leading the Israelites by going before them "by day, in a pillar of cloud" and "by night, in a pillar of fire" (see *Ex.* xiii.21; xiv.19b; *Num.* xiv.14). *E* too knows the Pillar of Cloud, but only as an indication of the presence of God at a particular place, *viz.*, at the door of the tent (see *Ex.* xxxiii.7 ff.; *Num.* xi.25; xii.5, 10; *Deut.* xxxi.15). The Priestly Code combines *E* and *J*: the Cloud that covered the tabernacle (see *Ex.* xl.34 ff.; cp. *Num.* xvii.7) had at night the appearance of fire, "and the Israelites could see it at every stage of their journey" (*Ex.* xl.38; cp. *Num.* ix.15 ff.). Thus, *P* agrees with *E* in associating the Cloud with the tent of meeting, and with *J* in regarding it as a guiding Cloud.

P also introduces the concept of the כבוד, the "Glory". God says that he will meet the people "at the entrance of the Tent of Meeting" (*Ex.* xxix.42), and declares: " ... it shall be hallowed by My Glory" (*ibid.* xxix.43b). The Glory, then, is obviously akin to the Pillar of Cloud that descended and "stood

---

60 See *Commentar*, pp. XX f.

at the door of the Tent" according to the *E* source (*Ex*. xxxiii.9). *P* actually
associates the Pillar of Cloud and Fire with the Glory: "The Glory of YHWH
rested upon Mt. Sinai, and the Cloud covered it ... . The Glory of YHWH
looked in the sight of the people of Israel like a devouring flame on the
top of the mountain" (*Ex*. xxiv.16 f.); " ... the Glory of YHWH appeared
in the Cloud" (*ibid*. xvi.10b); "then, the Cloud covered the Tent of Meeting,
and the Glory of YHWH filled the Tabernacle" (*Ex*. xl.34); "... the Cloud
covered it [*i.e.*, the Tent], and the Glory of YHWH manifested itself" (*Num*.
xvii.7).

In the treatise on the subject of angels in Abu'l Hasan al-Suri's *Kitab al-
Tabaḥ*, a priestly work of the 11th century, *Ex*. xxiv.17 is cited as proof that
some angels have a fiery nature:

> They are formed out of fire and air, as the noble Book indicated when it said:
> "Now the appearance of the Glory of YHWH was like devouring fire on the top of
> the mountain in the sight of the people of Israel." This is the fiery kind.[61]

The Glory, then, is identified as an angel. But the Samaritans did not follow *P*'s close association of the Glory with the Pillar. Marqa says:

> The Pillar of Cloud and of Fire and the Glory were the guides of the Israelites when
> they crossed the Red Sea, both before and behind them, until they had gone out
> safely.

> *(Memar Marqa* II.11)

This text apparently alludes to *Ex*. xiv.19, where both the Angel of the
Lord and the Pillar move from the front to the rear of the army of the Israelites when they cross the sea[62]; Marqa, however, would seem to keep one of
them at the front. In any event, he clearly detaches the Glory from the Pillar.
In II.6, we read that only the Glory went before Moses and the Israelites
when they crossed the sea. Furthermore, just some lines below the statement
just quoted, we read that God saved his people "as they followed His Glory
(כבודו)." Here, the Pillar has disappeared. Finally, at the very end of the
same chapter, the Glory even appears as an associate of Moses, both being
attributed with the work of bringing the people out safely.

The Glory in Samaritan thought obviously was welded with the Angel
of the Lord, who is the guide of the people of Israel in the *E* document, an
ancient northern source. In chapter 5 of Book III of Marqa's *Memar*, the
Glory speaks up and applies to himself God's publication about the Angel of
the Lord as found in *Ex*. xxiii.20 f.:

> The Glory said: "The Great Name (שמה רבה) is within me, and I do not shun him

61 Bowman, *Documents*, p. 248.
62 U. Cassuto, a modern Jewish exegete who does not accept the source-critical approach, takes them to be the same figure; see *Commentary on the Exodus* (PPI),
   Jerusalem, 1967, p. 166. This is an old construal; see above, p. 178, n. 310.

who is rebellious in action. When a man deviates, I forfeit him; and thus it is said of me: "For he will not pardon your transgression, since My Name is in him" (*Ex.* xxiii.21)."

The Glory is the Angel of the Lord, who is the carrier of the Name of God and therefore acts as if he were God himself.

Another name of the Angel of the Lord in Marqa's *Memar* is שלטן, "regent". This term is substituted for that of "the Destroyer", who apparently is the Angel of the Lord (cp. *I Chron.* xxi.16 and *Wisd.* xviii.15 f.). The identification is brought out in an earlier chapter, where God gives instructions for the eating of the Passover meal and then says:

> After that [*i.e.,* after the eating of the meal], My regent will descend and kill the firstborn of the Egyptians.
>
> (I.9)

In the three so-called Levitical mss. of *Memar Marqa*, כבודה is substituted for שלטן. The Glory, the Angel of the Lord, is God's vice-regent.

In another place in the same chapter, God says:

> [...] about midnight, My Glory (כבודי) will descend and slay all the firstborn in the land of Egypt.

This text, which continues with a quotation of *Ex.* xi.5b-6, is a paraphrase of *Ex.* xi.4c-5a and xii.12a, where YHWH says that he will go through Egypt and kill all the firstborn. Marqa has substituted the Glory, that is, the Angel of the Lord, for the divine "I".

In *Ex.* ch. xii, God – after having given the instructions concerning the slaughtering and eating of the Passover lamb, and said that the blood must be smeared on the doorpost and the lintel of the house – declares: "That night, I will go through the land of Egypt and strike down all the firstborn in the land of Egypt, man and beast alike; and I shall deal out punishment to all the gods of Egypt – I am YHWH!" (*v.* 12). When Moses repeats the admonitions to the people, however, he says: "Then, when YHWH goes through Egypt to strike it, and sees the blood on the lintel and on the two doorposts, he will pass over the door and not allow the Destroyer to enter into your house and strike" (*v.* 23). The substitution of the Destroyer for YHWH is due to the *E* document, the insertion of which starts with *v.* 21. Marqa is at one with the northern sentiment in ascribing the killing of the firstborn to the Destroyer:

> The Destroyer descended at midnight and slew all the firstborn – they did not know what was happening! Every firstborn in the land of Egypt was destroyed that night, including Pharaoh's god, along with his firstborn and even the very guards who surrounded him. When the hour arrived, the Destroyer descended, felled the gods and slew the firstborn. They looked afterwards for the firstborn of Pharaoh and found him slain – his blood still inside him! Their souls were shattered and their hearts anguished when they saw him slain and his god felled.
>
> (I.9)

Marqa obviously takes the Destroyer to be the same as God's regent, the Glory, that is, the Angel of the Lord. The Biblical text, however, which comes from the *J* source, ascribes the killing of the firstborn to YHWH: "Then it happened at midnight that YHWH killed all the firstborn in the land of Egypt ... " (*Ex*. xii.29). Since the Angel of the Lord carries "the Great Name", Marqa's midrash, which substitutes the Destroyer for YHWH, is well-founded. The Samaritan theologian even feels justified in using "the Destroyer" and "YHWH" interchangeably, for he continues his exposition:

> At midnight, YHWH slew unclean firstborn and towering gods. At midnight, YHWH destroyed the trees which were planted at Sheba. At midnight, YHWH destroyed the slingers who did their slinging among unfruitful trees. At midnight, YHWH destroyed firstborn who were offered to the destroyers. At midnight, YHWH destroyed lofty gods and their vain worshippers. At midnight, YHWH destroyed all the firstborn of Egypt, while Israel drew near and called to the Lord.
>
> (I.9)

The "Destroyer", who is the Regent or Glory, that is, the Angel of the Lord, is identical with YHWH in the midrash.

That the Tetragrammaton signified an angel, even the Angel of the Lord, was also known to Abu'l Hasan. Thus, the saying of *Num*. xii.8 that Moses saw "the form of YHWH" is taken to mean that he saw an angelic form. The angels do have material form; *Ex*. xviii.20 f. is exploited thus:

> So many learned people hold that they are spirits without bodies. But as for us, we go back in describing them to what the noble Book has informed us about their corporeal description, regarding their standing up and their mobility, and ability to talk and the organs of speech and hearing and the organs of seeing and (having) two hands and two feet according to what He has said regarding the Angel who talked to Abraham, viz. His saying: "And YHWH said; 'Because the outcry against Sodom and Gomorrah is great and because their sin is very grave"; etc ... down to His saying: 'I will go down now and see (whether they have done altogether) according to the outcry, which has come to Me' ". So he established in this section five parts, (lit. Divisions) viz; mobility, articulation, the organs of speech, hearing and sight.[63]

We have seen above that the Samaritans, in particular the Dositheans, asserted that God himself had no material form and did not descend to earth[64]; thus, when it is said that YHWH descended as a man to Sodom and Gomorrah, this was interpreted as the descent of the Angel of the Lord. The Samaritans thus contrived to avoid anthropomorphisms in the description of God and bringing him into contingence with the material world.

The divine descents to Egypt and to Sodom and Gomorrah were punitive expeditions, and the Samaritans obviously ascribed also the judging and punishing aspect of God to his vicegerent. We have seen that Philo asserted that

---

63 Bowman, *Documents*, pp. 248 f.
64 See above, p. 190.

God had delegated the punishing office to the angels[65]; in fact, the Alexandrian Jewish philosopher even teaches that *theos*, the equivalent of Elohim, represents the beneficent power of God, while *kyrios*, the translation of the Tetragrammaton, stands for the punishing power[66]. N.A. Dahl and A.F. Segal have shown that Philo in this respect testifies to a tradition which later appears in the rabbinic refusals of the heresy of "two powers in heaven"[67]. The earliest denials of the heresy – found in different versions of the Mekiltoth – are aiming to show that the God who appeared as a "man of war" at the Red Sea (*Ex.* xv.3) is the same as the God who appeared "like an old man full of mercy" on Mt. Sinai (see *Mekilta de R. Simeon ben Yoḥai, Bashalaḥ* ch. xv; *Mekilta de R. Ishmael, Baḥodesh* ch. v; *Shirta* ch. iv). While the tradition in the Mekilta of R. Simeon says that the name YHWH is repeated twice in *Ex.* xv.3 ("YHWH is a man of war; YHWH is His name") in order to make clear that it is the same God, even YHWH, who is appearing in both places, the Mekilta of R. Ishmael defines the dangerous doctrine as the idea that YHWH the man of war and the Elohim of *Ex.* xxiv.10 ("And they saw the Elohim of Israel") were two different divine manifestations, one just and one merciful. The two texts obviously are variations of the same underlying tradition, which must have been an exegesis of the two divine names, YHWH and Elohim. The latter text is a comment on *Ex.* xx.2 ("I am YHWH, your Elohim"), which is used to show that both names belong to the same God. The rabbinic doctrine of the two *middoth* or "measures" of God is an implicit aspect of this text. Although the received rabbinic doctrine used the Tetragrammaton to denote the merciful aspect of God and "Elohim" to denote God in his aspect of a righteous judge, the concurrence of the Philonic evidence and the description of the heresy in the Mekiltoth shows that there was an old and widespread tradition to the opposite effect. Whether or not the rabbis originally affirmed the latter idea, the deeper issue in their polemics was whether the divine names stood for complimentary attributes of God or referred to two divine manifestations. The latter tradition seems to have developed around the description of YHWH as a "man of war" in *Ex.* xv.3[68].

The reason for touching upon the subject of "the two powers in heaven" here is that the heretics who found the second divine manifestation in *Ex.* xv. 3 may have been Samaritans. In *Memar Marqa*, we read:

---

65 See above, pp. 198, 201.

66 Philo can also connect the two names with God and the Logos respectively; cp. above, p. 110. In some places, an ambiguity results from his special elaborations, modifications, and harmonizations of older traditions (see *De op. mundi* 20 f.; *De conf. ling.* 137). In other places, the Logos is placed above the other powers of God; see above, p. 200. Cp. below, 335 f.

67 See Dahl & Segal, "Philo and the Rabbis on the Names of God", *JSJ*, 9, 1978, pp. 1 ff.; Segal, *Two Powers*, pp. 159 ff.

68 There is some evidence that Philo knew this tradition; see Dahl & Segal, pp. 7 f.

The Glory too seemed to be saying: "O congregation, keep yourself from me, for is there not before me a mighty deed? I slew, I oppressed, I destroyed, I made alive; and, with you, I did all this when I was at the sea and showed you every wonder and made you cross with great marvels by the mighty power of God."

(III.5)

The Glory, that is, the Angel of the Lord, the possessor of the Divine Name, goes on to say that he will punish the Israelites if they deviate from the good life. The Angel of the Lord here describes himself as the one who killed the Egyptians at the Red Sea, though the Bible ascribes this act to YHWH (see *Ex.* xiv.24 f.; xv.1 ff.). When the Bible narrates that YHWH has annihilated and punished evil-doers, the Samaritans ascribed the actions to the Angel of the Lord. That it was the Angel of the Lord who destroyed the Egyptians obviously is an old interpretation, for *Wisd.* x.15, 17 ff. attributes this work to Sophia, the figure of whom has assimilated that of the principal angel.

The label "two powers in heaven" was used to cover a variety of binitarian doctrines; thus, Christianity may have been a target already in the oldest texts, since they cite *Dan.* vii.9, speaking about two heavenly thrones, one for the Ancient of Days and one for the Son of Man. Although this passage is brought forth as a proof-text against the heresy, it does not fit well as a demonstration of the thesis that there is only one God manifesting himself in different ways, and it really may have been a *locus* of the heresy[69]. The figure of the Son of Man was extremely important to the Christians, while the Samaritans did not possess the *Book of Daniel* and did not speak about this eschatological personage. On the other hand, there is no Christological interpretation of *Ex.* xv.3, so already the earliest texts dealing with the "two powers" heresy may have several binitarian groups in mind. One of them seems to be the Samaritan community.

At any rate, Samaritanism must have been one of the religious currents opposed by the rabbis who maintained that some of God's acts in behalf of Israel were performed "not by an angel and not by an apostle", for the deliverance of the people out of Egypt was one of these acts[70]. Other prominent acts were the punishment of Israel and the revelation of the Law to Moses. The Samaritan Liturgy from the 14th century, when there was a rather successful realization of the striving to unify priestly and laicising Samaritanism, reads that Moses received the Law from the hand of an angel, while the liturgists of the previous centuries stress that Moses spoke with God face to face and that "no third was between them."[71] A millennium before the 14th cen-

---

69 This holds good for *Ex.* xxiv.10 too; see Segal, *Two Powers*, p. 40 with n. 10, pp. 50 f., and above, p. 190, nn. 347 f.

70 See above, p. 147.

71 See Macdonald, *Theology*, pp. 180 ff., 286 f., 403. Due to lack of knowledge of the

tury, when the reformer Baba Rabba for the first time tried to bring the orthodox party and the Dosithean circles together, we find that Marqa actually
represents the Angel of the Lord as an intermediator between God and Moses.
The Samaritan theologian says that the Glory appeared on Mt. Sinai and proclaimed the Ten Commandments to Moses:

> A question now. Give ear and apply your mind! Listen to it! When God wrote the
> Ten Words [of Commandments] (עסרתי מליה), He first of all wrote twenty-two
> letters which are the basic elements of the words of the Law. When the Kabod pro-
> claimed the Ten Words [of Commandments] before him [*viz.*, Moses], which He [*viz.*,
> God, or Moses?] magnified, He proclaimed first [...]. When the Truth (קשטה)
> proclaimed the first Ten before him [*i.e.*, before Moses], the Glory repeated them
> before him. He [*viz.*, Moses] responded and also proclaimed ten. When the Truth
> proclaimed, he was not permitted to proclaim; but when the Glory proclaimed, he
> was permitted to do so.
>
> (*Memar Marqa* VI.3)

The interstice within square brackets is put in the place of a quotation of
Ex. xxxiv.6b-7, "YHWH, God of tenderness and compassion – slow to anger,
rich in kindness and faithfulness, maintaining for thousands His kindness –
forgives faults, transgression, sin, yet letting nothing pass unchecked, punishing the father's fault on the children and on the grandsons to the third and
fourth generation." This saying embodies the "Words of Mercy" (מלי רחמיה)
requested by Moses at the very end of the previous paragraph. The "first
Ten" proclaimed by the Truth, that is, God, and then by the Glory are in the
sequel explained as referring to *Ex.* xxxiv.6b (from "YHWH" to "faithfulness"), and the "ten" proclaimed by Moses are said to start with "YHWH,
slow to anger" and end with "fourth generation". But, while the words
proclaimed by the Truth and then by the Glory do amount to ten in number,
the number of words proclaimed by Moses amounts to far more than ten; and
the maintenance upon the number ten obviously is due to a desire to correlate the "Words of Mercy" spoken by Moses as well as by God and the Angel
of the Lord with the "Ten Words of Commandments" written by God and
spoken by the Angel of the Lord before Moses.

Thus, the Angel of the Lord appears as an intermediator between God and
Moses. God has written the Law and given the Commandments, but the
Glory has to utter them in front of Moses. God also proclaims the "Words of
Mercy", and the Angel of the Lord repeats the first ten of these Words before

---

dialectical process going on in the history of the Samaritan community, former
authors put forward contradictory statements. Nutt, p. 69, said that an angel acted as
the intermediary between God and Moses on Mt. Sinai, while Montgomery, p. 220,
inset, asserted that the Samaritans insist upon the direct transference of the Law to
Moses. Both propositions are right: they reflect the different views of two bodies
within the Samaritan community, and both views are represented in the literature of
the Samaritans.

Moses, who then is allowed to proclaim the last "ten". In keeping with his tentative approach to the lay doctrines, Marqa does not say outright that the Angel of the Lord handed over the Law, but that he had to recite the revelation of God before Moses[72]. Yet, in the subsequent centuries, the idea of the Angel of the Lord appearing on Mt. Sinai between God and Moses was censured, and it does not crop up again before in the 14th century. In this century, when the Dosithean doctrines were incorporated *en masse* in the Liturgy, the notion that the Angel of the Lord handed Moses the Law was adopted.

As we shall see forthwith, there is also a Samaritan doctrine stating that the Angel of the Lord was instrumental in creating the body of man. But the text brought up by M. Heidenheim would not seem to be teaching this. If Heidenheim's interpretation were right, the Glory would be a allotted a position superior to that of God: while God forms man, breathes the life into his nose, puts a perfect mind into him, and glorifies him with speech, the Glory makes man complete with a a great spirit, gives him powerful illumination, and glorifies him with perfect knowledge. The passage evidently is not to be understood in this way, but as a collocation of the creation of Adam by God and the conveyance of a superior insight to Moses by the Glory. On this interpretation, we must take the phrase that "the two of them were clad in two crowns of great light" to mean that both Adam and Moses received a crown, the former when he was created and the latter on Mt. Sinai[73]. The passage thus attests that the Angel of the Lord had a revealing function when the law was given.

In the unpublished Samaritan catechism known as the *Malef* and translated from Arabic into Hebrew, we read:

> Question: How did the creation of our father Adam come to pass?
> Answer: The Angel of the Lord formed him from the dust of the earth and made
> him in our image and likeness (יצר אתו מלאך יהוה עפר מן האדמה
> ועשה אתו בצלמנו וכדמותנו). The Name, that is to be praised, breathed the
> breath of life into him, and he became a soul, gifted with speech and perfect in form.
>
> (Section 16; 3a-b)

This is a midrash combining *Gen.* i.27 and ii.7. However, while *Gen.* ii.7 ascribes both the making of the body of man and the conferring of the spirit to God, the *Malef* assigns the two acts to the Angel of the Lord and God

---

72 That the Glory acts as an intermediator between God and Moses was seen already by H. Baneth, ed. & trans., *Des Samaritaners Marqah an die 22 Buchstaben, den Grundstock der hebräischen Sprache anknüpfende Abhandlung*, Halle, 1888, notes on pp. 50 ff.

73 See above, p. 91. Heidenheim, however, translates: "and both (the Godhead and the Kabodah) furnished him [*i.e.*, Adam] with two crowns" (*Commentar*, p. XX). Baneth translates: "and both gave him two crowns each" (p. 55).

respectively. "The Name", הֵשֵׁם, is here, of course, a circumlocution for the proper Name of God. The anthropogony of the *Malef* corresponds to that of the Gnostics, according to whom the demiurge (and his angels) made man and God supplied the spirit, so that man came alive and could stand upright. It is true that the creation of the body of man according to the Gnostics did not take place with the consent of God, but we have seen that there is good reason to see this as a secondary development in their anthropogonic myth, which is based upon a certain midrashic exposition of the Biblical account. The Samaritan catechism affords us with a *"Hebrew* text" indicating that this construction is sound.

The *Malef* is a late literary composition, but J. Bowman feels that "there is no reason to see this as a late innovation."[74] Since the work is a catechism for the instruction of children, no one would write such a book "unless there were enough children needing instruction to make the proposition a reasonable one";[75] and this would compel us to date the book to a time before 1671, when the bishop of of Raphoe paid a visit to Nablus and counted only thirty Samaritan families[76]. This number was reduced further during the subsequent years until the Samaritans actually were on the verge of extinction in the 19th century[77].

---

74 "Samaritan Studies", p. 303, note continued from p. 302. Cp. the following statement: "There exists for the instruction of children a Samaritan manual which they must learn that they may be sound on the doctrines of their religion and the facts of their history. There is no reason to see this as a late innovation" (*ibid.*, p. 309). The *terminus ad quem* is determined by the colophonic statement of the book itself that it was translated in 1917.

75 E.C. Baguley, ed. & trans., *A Critical Edition, with Translation, of the Hebrew Text of the Malef*, Diss., Leeds, 1962, p. clxxiv, referring to M. Gaster, *The Samaritan Oral Law and Ancient Traditions*, I (Eschatology), New York, 1932, p. 124; *Asatir*. p. 140.

76 See Nutt, p. 24, cited by Baguley, pp. clxxiv f. Baguley says that the *Hilluk*, a Samaritan work presumably from the 17th century, "is one of the works on which the author of M. *seems* to be dependent" (p. clxxiv; italics mine). But there is no clear quotation from the *Hilluk*, and "the doctrines and practices set forth in the *Hilluk* are indeed old" (Bowman, *Documents*, p. 298). Baguley himself is willing to date the *Malef* to a period before the 17th century; see p. clxxv.

77 A small community in Gaza came to an end about this time. The Samaritans who had taken refuge in islands in the Red Sea after the Arab invasion of Egypt, and still were found there in the 12th century, must have died out much earlier. In the 12th century, there were also Samaritans in Caesarea, Ascalon, and Damascus, but they gradually were reduced in number and power. A tiny community in Jaffa died out long before the 19th century. The community in Egypt, once powerful, was reduced severely, and its members finally joined the community in Shechem, in the beginning of the 18th century. In 1909, eight years before the *Malef* was translated into Hebrew, P. Kahle counted 173 Samaritans in Nablus. For the statistics of the Samaritans throughout their history, see Tsedaka, par. "Statistics", cols. 736 ff.

The *terminus post quem* for the date of the *Malef* is determined by internal evidence, since it refers to *Kitab al-Tabaḥ* of Abu'l Hasan, who lived in the 11th century (see Answer 148; 37a). It would seem plausible to date the *Malef* to the 14th century, when the Samaritans made a great effort to consolidate their faith and resist the pressure to convert to Islam. Bowman, having shown that the Samaritan religion has developed through a dialectical process in which the orthodox party and the Dosithean lay circles were working upon each other, has pointed out that the revival of Samaritanism in the 14th century was in effect a rather successful realization of a synthesis of the two groups and their respective doctrines[78]. In this century, many of the lay tenets were incorporated into the literature. Since the lay movement among the Samaritans began with the destruction of their temple in the 2nd century B.C.E.[79], an incident which gave rise to the formation of new religious and social associations around the institution of the synagogue, it is to be allowed for that notions turning up in the 14th century literary monuments may be quite old.

It has been mentioned repeatedly that the angelology was a subject of concern especially to the Dositheans, and it is in the liturgical pieces from the 14th century that we begin to learn about individual angel names. The Medieval literature, on the other hand, is remarkably reticent on the subject of angels, and even Abu'l Hasan, who devoted a part of his book to the angels, mentions only the Glory by name. However, as we shall see below, the Angel of the Lord possibly had a personal name even before the time of Marqa, just like the Jews called the principal angel Michael, Gabriel, or Raphael. Similarly, the notion of the demiurgic function of the Angel of the Lord apparently was no Medieval innovation.

Even if it cannot be known for sure that the *Malef* is a work from the 14th century, the anthropogony of the catechism certainly is the property of the laicising people, for it does not occur in earlier writings which set forth the priestly view. Moreover, as we have seen, Marqa and Amram Dara actually combat the idea that God had a partner in the work of creation. They wrote under the unification scheme of Baba Rabba, who tried for the first time to bring the orthodox party and the laicising circles together, but did not go as far as his successors a millennium later. Still, as has been seen, Marqa had to make some concessions to the lay teachings, and there can in fact be found an approach to the anthropogony of the Dositheans in *Memar Marqa*. This overture is found in an interpretation of the Song of Moses in Deut.

---

78 Bowman has set forth his view in many works; see now *Problem*, which is a translation of his *Samaritanische Probleme* with a new introduction and a bibliography of his works.

79 See above, pp. 45 ff.

ch. xxxii, in which Marqa by means of his midrashic technique detects deep mysteries. The beginning of this Song, *Deut.* xxxii.3a, כי בשם יהוה אקרא, "For in the Name YHWH I will proclaim,"[80] is made to correspond with *Gen.* i.1, בראשית ברא אלהים, "In the beginning Elohim created," and even with the whole creation narrative, since *Gen.* i.1 is taken as a summary of the whole of this story[81]. Some of the correlations made by Marqa may seem obscure[82], but the following passage can be deciphered with some ease:

> Note the greatness of his [*i.e.*, Moses'] knowledge. What he [or, "He", *i.e.*, God?] did בשם is a mystery; he [or, "it"] established (אקים) the glory with which his Lord vested him. YHWH is the word referring to the form of Adam, for it was established by him (יהוה אמרה על צורתה דאדם כי בו הוקמת). And by Elohim it was perfected (הכללת). "Then YHWH Elohim formed man" (*Gen.* ii.7).[83]
>
> (IV.2)

It is apparently Moses' knowledge, manifested through the allegory ingrained in his Song, which is to be noted. A couple of lines below, it is said: "Moses was magnified mightily in knowledge, wholly of faith." The text perhaps means that Moses, by speaking כי בשם *etc.*, in a mysterious way pointed to "the glory with which his Lord vested him." But it is also possible that it is *God* who is said to have acted בשם and thus effected the "establishment" of "the glory" with which Moses was "vested". In any event, Marqa

---

80 While the Masoretic text has only "the Name", the Samaritan Pentateuch reads "in the Name".

81 See the quotation and discussion of the text from *Memar Marqa* IV.2 on p. 83 above, After this passage, Marqa begins to interpret *Deut.* xxxii.3.

82 In my article "Samaritan Demiurgical Traditions and the Alleged Dove Cult of the Samaritans", in *Studies*, p. 159, I declared that בשם יהוה corresponded to בראשית (and also that the latter was interpreted by the former, so that "the Name YHWH" was seen as the creative instrument). But it actually seems that בראשית is represented by כי alone, and that (ב)שם primarily is interpreted as the Elohim in *Gen.* i.1 and ii.2; cp. the translation of Macdonald, *Memar Marqah*, II, p. 139. However, the passage to be quoted forthwith apparently regards (ב)שם as belonging to יהוה and considers the latter as the word to be interpreted by the text from *Gen.* ii.7.

83 Macdonald gives the following translation: "The Lord said it of the form of Adam, for by it it was established, and by God it was perfected" (*Memar Marqa*, II, p. 139). This is grammatically possible and implies that Adam was created by two agents, but there is no clue in the context as to what would be meant by "it". Professor Simeon Lowy, Leeds, writes to me: "The present translation is utterly meaningless unless we presume that Marqah occupied himself with idle tautologies." Professor Lowy offers the following translation: "The tetragrammaton was said about the form of Adam, for by it he was established, and by Elohim he was perfected." If אמרה were a verb, the translation is wrong, but Lowy does bring out the right meaning. Cp. the translation by Heidenheim: "He spoke YHWH over the form of man, for by it he was established and by Elohim perfected" (*Commentar*, p. 91). This is also grammatically impossible, but brings out the point that the "form" of Adam was "established" by YHWH.

refers to the idea that Moses was "vested" with the glorious image which Adam had possessed but lost. He says that the Name was effective in the "establishment" of this image.

Since the creation narrative of the priestly source does not contain the name YHWH, Marqa has to seek the correspondence of the Tetragrammaton in *Deut.* xxxii.3a in the creation story of the Yahwist. Significantly, he does not cite *Gen.* ii.4 or ii.5, which are the first verses where the Tetragrammaton occurs, but ii.7, which speaks about the creation of man. The Biblical account speaks about two phases in this work: first, the material body was formed, and then the spirit of God was breathed into this body. Marqa has retained the two-parted anthropogony, but – in contrast to the Biblical text, which ascribes both parts in the creation of Adam to YHWH Elohim – the Samaritan theologian allots the "establishment" of the body to YHWH and the "perfection" of this material creation to Elohim. Just like the image of Moses was "established" by the שם, so the "form" of Adam was "established" by YHWH. This is perfectly logical, for the image was to be found in the "form", that is, the body[84]. As proof that YHWH in *Deut.* xxxii.3a refers to the צורתה of Adam, Marqa cites *Gen.* ii.7, where we read that YHWH Elohim יצר, "formed", Adam's body from the dust of the earth.

By the "perfection" of Adam's body by Elohim, the communication of the spirit must be indicated. In another passage in *Memar Marqa*, we read: "The body of Adam was created by God and perfected with a holy spirit and a living soul (והכללת ברוח קדשה ונפשה ממללה)" (II.10).

Although Marqa and Amram Dara denied that God had a partner in the creation of the world, Marqa approached his opponents when he admitted that a figure possessing the proper Name of God had a rôle in the creation of man. The dialectic apparently was directed to the Dositheans, for the priestly works from the succeeding centuries, when the coalition policy of Baba Rabba had abated, do not acknowledge 'the demiurgic traditions discussed in the 4th century literature. In the 14th century, however, when the allowance of lay doctrines was much more marked than in the 4th century, the Angel of the Lord appeared as the creator of the body of man in Samaritan literature. That Marqa in his *Memar* IV.2 implies that the creator of the body of man is the Angel of YHWH seems probable, for – as we know – the Bible says that the proper Name of God is the possession of Angel of the Lord.

That the Dositheans actually held that God's helper in the work of creation was the Angel of the Lord is also to be inferred from the Samaritan texts cited in the first section of this Chapter, for the term שותף, "associate", used to designate God's helper – whose existence is denied by Amram Dara

---

84 See above, pp. 93 ff.

and Marqa — appears to be a *terminus technicus* denoting a figure sharing
divine honours by means of possessing the Name of God[85]. In rabbinic texts,
we read that it is forbidden to "associate" (שִׁתֵּף) the Name of God with
another person or a material object, since that would amount to a belief in
two gods. Thus, we read:

> The sages said that [Israel, adverting to the golden calf,] said: "'This is your god
> (זֶה אֱלֹהֶיךָ)" (*Neh.* ix.18), who redeemed us!" R. Haggai ben Eleazar said: "It
> does not say: "This is your god," but "These are your gods (אֵלֶּה אֱלֹהֶיךָ)" (*Ex.*
> xxxii.4). For they associated Him with the calf and said: "God and the calf redeemed
> us." [God therefore speaks:] "Seeing that they have spoken falsehoods about Me,
> how can I redeem them?'"
>
> (*Ex.R.* xliii.3)

R. Haggai opposes the common opinion that the Israelites regarded the
golden calf as the god who had saved them out of Egyptian bondage, for,
although *Neh.* ix.18 has the demonstrative pronoun in the singular, *Ex.*
xxxii.4 has it in the plural, the formally correct correlate to אֱלֹהֶיךָ, which is
the *nomen pluralis* אֱלֹהִים plus the personal suffix. Thus, according to R.
Haggai, the Israelites regarded both God and the calf as redeeming divinities.
But the "association" of an object or a person with God is equal to polytheism, for it implies that the Name of God, *i.e.*, the divine nature, is shared
by that object or person.

In a Talmudic tract, in a context dealing with the grounds for being
uprooted from the world, we read:

> R. Jonathan said: "If not for the letter *waw* in הֶעֱלוּךָ ("they have brought you
> up") (*Ex.* xxxii.4), the wicked of Israel would have deserved uprooting." The sages
> [were disputing this]: Many were saying that, were it not for the letter *waw* in
> הֶעֱלוּךָ, the wicked of Israel would have deserved uprooting. R. Simeon ben Yoḥai,
> however, said: "The one who associates (הַמְשַׁתֵּף) the Name of God with another
> object will be uprooted from the world, for it is said: "Save the Lord alone" (*Deut.*
> xxxii.12). But הֶעֱלוּךָ means that they had taken to other gods."
>
> (*Sanh.* 63a)

In this passage, too, there is a difference of opinion among the rabbis. By
the insertion of the letter *waw*, the verb under discussion changes from the
singular to the plural. R. Jonathan's opinion is that Israel was saved because
the people after all included God in the saving act and did not ascribe the
redemption to the calf alone. R. Simeon, however, agrees with R. Haggai
that the people deserved uprooting because they associated God's Name with
another object. According to R. Simeon, the verb form הֶעֱלוּךָ means that
they had elapsed into polytheism.

In another Talmudic tractate, in a comment upon a part of the ritual of

---

85 See Segal, *Two Powers*, pp. 111 f., p. 137 with n. 6, p. 141 with n. 15.

the festival of booths, we find an explanation of the following words of the Mishna: "When they departed [*viz.*, from the altar, after having made seven circumambiences], what did they say? "Homage to you, O altar! Homage to you, O altar!" R. Eliezer says: "To Yah and to you, O altar! To Yah and to you, O altar!"" (*Succa* iv.5). Some mss. omit this passage entirely, and the Gemara makes it perfectly clear why the passage was regarded as perilous:

> When they departed, what did they say? One associated (משתתף) the Name of God with another object, although it is taught: The one who associates (המשתתף) the Name of God with another object will be uprooted from the world, because it is stated: "Save the Lord alone." This is the meaning: God we thank, you [*i.e.*, the altar] we praise! God we thank, you we glorify!

(45b)

It is certainly interesting that Marqa, in the context of his refusal of the notion that God had an "associate" in the work of creation, quotes *Deut.* xxxii.12 (see IV.7), which the rabbis had brought forward against those who "associated" the Name of God with another being. This shows that he uses a standardized means of defense against those who maintained that God had an "associate". Moreover, this implies that his opponents held that God's partner in the creation shared the Divine Name.

That the demiurge would have to possess the Name of God can also be corroborated by the rabbinic renunciation of the view that the angels were created on the first day; we have seen that the rabbis thus tried to ward off the opinion that the angels had helped God in making the world, quoting *Is.* xliv.24, where God says that he was alone when the world was made[86]. God's words are paraphrased thus: מי היה שותף עמי בבריית העולם. The rhetorical question apparently is aimed at people who taught that God received demiurgic help from one or more angelic "associates" sharing his Name.

Furthermore, as we shall see, there were also *minim* who held Adam to have been created before the sixth day and acted as God's שותף in the creation[87]. It obviously was by virtue of possessing the Divine Name that Adam was regarded as a demiurgic being, for there were traditions relating that he had been given the Name of God. Finally, as we also shall see, there is evidence to the effect that another hero of the past, namely, Abraham, was regarded as the possessor of the Divine Name and, by virtue of this, as though he had been "associated" with God in the creation[88].

It apparently is because the helper in the creation possessed the Name of God that the Samaritan authors emphasize God's *monarchia* at the same time as they deny that God had a partner in the creation, for the Divine Name

---

86 See above, p. 194.
87 See below, pp. 264f.
88 See below, pp. 246f.

signified God's very nature. As a matter of fact, Marqa time and again feels it necessary to urge his co-religionists in the following manner:

> Let us bow down before Him and say with great reverence and great faith: "There is only one God!"
>
> (*Memar Marqa* IV.12)

There apparently were people among the Samaritans who distinguished between Elohim and YHWH, thus believing in two gods according to the orthodox judgment. Marqa must have had these people in mind when he said that Moses, in citing the song in *Deut.* ch. xxxii,

> sought to combine the two names as one – Elohim and YHWH.
>
> (*Ibid.* IV.7)

This song uses the two divine names interchangeably, declaring that Israel has only one God, and Marqa elaborates on this theme, maintaining that the one God also is the creator and had no "associate" when he created the world. In this context, he cites *v.* 12, which was adduced by the rabbis asserting that God had no שותף sharing his Name.

That the Angel of the Lord was a demiurgic being should not be dismissed as a late innovation, for the laicising movement among the Samaritans originated in the 2nd century B.C.E. I do not argue that the Samaritans were the authors of this idea or that the rabbis opposed Samaritans; apparently, several groups – *e.g.*, laicising Samaritans and Hellenistic Jews such as Philo – maintained the same tenet, which stems from a time when the borderlines between the various divisions within the wider phenomenon of Judaism were vague. While *Gen.* i.26 could be taken to imply that the body of man was the production of (certain) angels, *Gen.* ii.7 lent itself to the view that Adam's body was produced by the principal angel, the Angel of YHWH. In commenting upon *Gen.* ii.7, Philo says that "the artificer" made the body of Adam, while God gave him the spirit. This is also what the laicising Samaritans taught, ascribing this work to the Angel of the Lord, whom they recognized under the Tetragrammaton in *Gen.* ii.7. In the system of Simon Magus, the pupil of Dositheus, who was the head of laicising Samaritanism in the first century C.E., we retrieve the idea that God used angelic help when he created man. Moreover, Simon also taught that God had assistance when he created the world, but this was a Dosithean teaching which Marqa and Amram Dara refused[89].

---

89 Macdonald states: "In the fourteenth century a few writers, who often express variant concepts, gave the credit for the creation of man to the angel Kebala" (*Theology*, p. 141). This statement seems to be unsupportable (not even an epistolary communication with Professor Macdonald has led to a solution). There can be no doubt, however, that Kebala is the Angel of the Lord. He is said to be "the Secret of the Name" (Cowley, 511.23), which we apparently must understand to mean that he is even an embodiment of the Divine Name. His name probably is derived

from *Num.* iv.20; cp. J.H. Petermann, *Reisen im Orient,* I, 2nd ed., Leipzig, 1865, p. 283. This passage gives the prohibition with regard to certain officials of the sanctuary that "they shall not enter lest they see כבלע את הקדש ומתו." Gaster writes: "The Samaritans translate את as 'within or with', and therefore translate the verse: 'lest they see Kebalaᶜ within the sanctuary and die.' The word Kebalaᶜ is a hapax legomenon and was misunderstood by them; thus a new angel was created" (*Samaritans*, p. 78). In a letter to me, Professor Lowy, Leeds, endorses this explanation and adds that Prohibition 208 of the *613 Commandments and Prohibitions* of the Samaritans "could also mean that they were prevented to enter the sanctuary where they could meet this angel. Consequences of such desecration would be death." It is well known that the Jews knew the idea that an angel guarded the temple but left it upon its destruction; see M. de Jonge, *The Testaments of the Twelve Patriarchs,* Assen, 1953, p. 124; Daniélou, *Theology,* pp. 145 f. This does not have to be a late idea in Samaritanism, for Marqa paraphrases *Ex.* xl.34 as follows: "Then the Cloud covered the Tent of Meeting, and the Glory of YHWH dwelt within the veil (ושרא כבוד יהוה מלגו פרכתה)" (*Memar Marqa* V.3). The Bible, however, says: "... and the Glory of YHWH filled the Tabernacle (וכבוד יהוה מלא את־המשכן)." In several places, Marqa says that Mt. Gerizim is כבודה, משרוי, "the dwelling-place of His [*i.e.,* God's] Glory", and it is interesting to note that the Samaritan Targum substitutes the root שרי for שכן, which is used in *Deuteronomy* to describe the "dwelling" of the Name of God at the holy site. In one passage, Marqa characterizes Mt. Gerizim as "the House of Elohim and the dwelling-place of His Glory", and then admonishes the people to seek this divine לשכין by a quotation from *Deut.* xii.5, where it is said that the Israelites shall seek God at the place where his Name dwells (see II.10). Since the Glory is the Angel of the Lord, who possesses or even embodies the Name, the substitution is logical. See also Fossum, "Samaritan Demiurgical Traditions", attempting to explain the Jewish charge that the Samaritans worshipped the image of a dove – which can be shown to be the symbol of a goddess with some such name as (א)שימא – as an exploitation of the Samaritan notion of the dwelling of the Name (שמה) on Mt. Gerizim.

Heidenheim, *Commentar*, p. XXV, and Montgomery, p. 219, inset, cite that Kebala also appears as the minister of God in the ninth heaven, like Michael or Metatron in Judaism. Heidenheim surmised that "the Great Power" denoted the Angel of the Lord and was an epithet of Kebala, but he added that it appears as a divine name in *Memar Marqa*. Montgomery misunderstood Heidenheim to say that Kebala appears as identical with God in the *Memar.*

Part Three

The Jewish Evidence

CHAPTER FIVE

The Name of God

The Golem Legend and the Demiurgic Rôle of the Alphabet

Since Samaritanism must be viewed within the wider phenomenon of the Jewish religion, it will be pertinent to present material from Judaism proper which is corroborative to the thesis of the present work. In this Chapter, the idea about the agency of the Name of God in the creation process will be expounded; then, in the next Chapter, the various traditions about the Angel of the Lord which are relevant to this topic will be set forth.

An apt introduction to the Jewish teaching about the Divine Name as the instrument of the creation is the so-called *golem* legend. It is not too well known that the greatest feat to which the Jewish magician aspired actually was that of duplicating God's making of man, the crown of the creation. In the Middle Ages, Jewish esotericism developed a great cycle of *golem* legends, according to which the able magician was believed to be successful in creating a גלם (גולם)[1]. But the word as well as the concept is far older. Rabbinic sources call Adam a *golem* before he is given the soul:

> In the first hour [of the sixth day], his dust was gathered; in the second, it was kneaded into a *golem*; in the third, his limbs were shaped; in the fourth, a soul was infused into him; in the fifth, he arose and stood on his feet [...].
>
> (*Sanh.* 38b)

In 1615, Zalman Ṣevi of Aufenhausen published his reply (*Jüdischer Theriak*) to the animadversions of the apostate Samuel Friedrich Brenz (in his book *Schlangenbalg*) against the Jews. In his response, Zalman Ṣevi wrote *inter alia*:

> The renegade said that there are those among the Jews who take a lump of clay, fashion it into the figure of a man, and whisper incantations and spells, whereupon the figure lives and moves. [...] he writes that we call such an image *ḥomer golem*,

---

1 On the golem, see B. Rosenfeld, *Die Golemsage*, Breslau, 1934; G. Scholem, *On the Kabbalah and Its Symbolism*, trans. by R. Manheim, New York, 1965, Schocken paperback edition, New York, 1969 and reprints, pp. 158 ff. (chapter based on "Die Vorstellung vom Golem in ihren tellurgischen und magischen Beziehungen", *E-J*, XXII (1953), 1954, pp. 235 ff.).

i.e., an unshaped mass of material [...]. I myself have never seen such a performance, but some of the Talmudic sages possessed the power to do this, by means of the Book of Creation [...]. We German Jews have lost this mystical tradition; but in Palestine, there are still to be found some men who can perform great miracles through the Kabbalah.[2]

The response by Zalman Ṣevi no doubt expresses the general attitude of the Jewish folk religion on the subject of the *golem*: the creation of a man-like being is quite possible for the sage who utilizes the correct means, namely, the *Book of Creation*, that is, *Sefer Yeṣira*.

But the notion of the creation of a *golem* by means of the *Book of Creation* is not confined to a late stage in the history of Judaism. In fact, the legend about the *golem* is rooted firmly in the Talmud:

> Raba said: "If the righteous desired it, they could be creators; for it is written: "But your iniquities have distinguished between you and your God" (*Is.* lix.2)."[3] Raba created a man and sent him to R. Zera. The latter spoke to him but received no answer. Thereupon he said to him: "You are a creation by the magicians – return to your dust!"
>
> R. Ḥanina and R. Hoshayah spent every Sabbath eve studying *Sefer Yeṣira*, by means of which they created a three year old calf, which they ate.[4]

(Sanh. 65b)

Raba (R. Abba ben Joseph ben Ḥama) was a leading Babylonian amora who died in the middle of the 4th century, while the associates R. Ḥanina (Hananiah) and R. Hoshayah were Palestinian amoraim of the end of the 3rd and the beginning of the 4th century. As shall be seen forthwith, however, the mystical doctrine of creation as found in the *Book of Creation* is of an even older date than the generation of R. Ḥanina and R. Hoshayah.

But, first of all, let us note that the magician was not able to endow his *homunculus* with speech, for the faculty of speech is a token of the soul or spirit of man. *Targum Onkelos* on *Gen.* ii.7, " ... and man became a living spirit," reads: " ... and man became a speaking spirit." God's infusion of his spirit into man was at the same time an endowment of the faculty of speech. It will be immediately clear that the Jewish magician creating a *golem* bears likeness to the Gnostic demiurge: he is able to create a corporeal man, but he cannot give his creation spiritual life[5]. The Jewish *golem* legend presents us

---

2 Quoted by M. Grünbaum, ed., *Jüdischdeutsche Chrestomatie*, Leipzig, 1882, p. 566.

3 Raba apparently insists on the freedom from sin as a prerequisite for the work of creation.

4 According to a variant reading, the means utilized for the magical act of creation is called *Hilkoth Yeṣira,* and this is also the name of the work in question in old mss. However, there is the possibility that the reference in the Talmud is to an early version of the book or to some prototypal traditions; see Scholem, *On the Kabbalah*, p. 167; *Kabbalah* (LJK), Jerusalem, 1974, p. 26.

5 Compare that the Gnostics taught that Adam, when he received the spirit from God,

with the same dichotomic anthropogony as does Gnosticism: the body is
made by an inferior being, whereas the soul or spirit can only be supplied by
God. G. Scholem accurately states: " ... a man who creates a golem is in some
sense competing with God's creation of Adam; in such an act the creative
power of man enters into a relationship, whether of emulation or antagonism,
with the creative power of God."[6] This description fits the Gnostic demiurge
just as well as it fits the Jewish magician.

Although some sources actually represent God as a great magician who
creates the universe by means of *Sefer Yesira*[7], the teaching of the book itself
is that God made the world "through the thirty-two secret paths of Wisdom",
that is, the ten *Sefiroth, i.e.*, the four elements of the cosmos (the Spirit of
God, ether, water, and fire) and the six dimensions (*kesaboth*, literally, "extremities") of space, added to the twenty-two letters of the Hebrew alphabet.
In ch.i, it is described that the first four *Sefiroth* emanate from each other;
and, while nothing specific is said about the manner of creation of the last six
Sefiroth, it is stated that God created the twenty-two letters from the ether,
the chaos from the water, and the Throne of Glory and the host of the angels
from the primal fire[8]. The remaining five chapters of the book, however, have
nothing whatsoever to say about the *Sefiroth* and deal exclusively with the
mystical part played by the letters in the creation of the universe. The whole
work of creation was enacted through the combinations of the Hebrew
consonants. The existence of every single thing in the universe depends upon
the exact combination of letters that lies hidden in it:

> By means of the twenty-two letters, by giving them a form and a shape, by mixing
> them in different ways, God made the soul of all that which has been made and of all
> that which will be.

(ii.2)

That *Sefer Yesira* is not meant to be solely a theoretical discourse on
cosmogony but also has a practical design, as indeed is implied in the narratives about its use for magical creation acts, is confirmed by the fact that the
earliest mss. are accompanied by introductory chapters emphasizing magical
practices which are to be performed on the completion of the study of the
book[9]. A further proof of the practical-magical aim of the *Book of Creation*
is found at the very end of the book itself, where its contents are ascribed to
a revelation to Abraham. Here, it is stated:

---

immediately began to speak and praise God (see Iren., I.xxx.6, on the Ophites;
Right Ginza 104.4 ff.).

6 *On the Kabbalah*, p. 159.

7 See, *e.g., Pesikta Hadatha*, in *BH*, VI, p. 36.

8 The nature of this second act of creation is obscure, since the verbs used, חקק and
חצב, do not mean "create", but "engrave" and "hew out" respectively.

9 See Scholem, *Kabbalah, loc. cit.;* cp. *On the Kabbalah*, pp. 169 ff.

When our father Abraham came, he contemplated, meditated, and saw; he search-
ed, understood, outlined, and dug; and he *combined* and *created* – and he was successful!

Abraham is here more than a sage possessing divine wisdom; he is a great
magician knowing how to make the combinations of the letters constituting
the creative power.

That Abraham could perform magical acts of creation is a tradition to be
supplied from various sources. The German Kabbalists held that *Gen.* xii.5,
which says that Abram and Sarah "acquired" (עשׂו) people (הנפשׁ) in Haran, indicated a magical act of creation performed by Abraham. They took the
verb עשׂה in the sense "make", "fabricate", which is also one of its meanings.
As G. Scholem has observed, this mystical exegesis may be quite ancient, for
it seems to be under attack in an aggada dating from the 2nd century C.E.:
"R. Eleazar observed in the name of R. Jose ben Zimra: "Are we to believe
that Abraham could make נפשׁ? If all the nations assembled in order to
make one insect, they could not endow it with life; and yet you say: "and the
נפשׁ that they had made"! It refers to [nothing else than] the proselytes [that
they had acquired]. So let it be read: "that they had converted" " (*Gen. R.*
xxxix.14). A couple of texts to be furnished below support the theory that
Abraham already in the 2nd century C.E. was regarded as the prototype of
the magician who fashions a *golem* through word and letter magic.

The teaching about the *Sefiroth*, a novel term coined by the author to
signify "numbers", probably derives from Neopythagorean sources, while the
part dealing with the letters is to be explained against the background of Jewish mystical doctrines. The Babylonian amora Rab (Abba ben Aibu), who is
said to have come to Palestine in the beginning of the 3rd century, declared
that Beṣalel, the chief architect of the tabernacle, knew "how to combine the
letters by which the heavens and the earth were created" (*Ber.* 55a). The explanation of this statement is found in the more or less universal idea about
the sanctuary being a microcosmic representation of the universe. In *Midrash
Rabba,* there is to be found an anonymous exposition of the import of the
tabernacle which brings God's various works on the successive days of the
creation into close parallelism to the description of the construction of the
tabernacle (see *Num. R.* xii.13)[10]. It is stated plainly in *Midrash Tadshe*:
"The Tabernacle was constructed corresponding to the creation" (ch. 2).

Thus, just like Abraham, Beṣalel was believed to have possessed the faculty
of making the combinations of letters that constitute the creative power.
Since the conveyor of this tradition is said to be Rab, the mystical doctrine

10 J.B. Schaller, *Gen. 1.2 im antiken Judentum*, Diss., Göttingen, 1961, pp. 121 ff.
with notes on pp. 224 ff., has mustered evidence concerning the collation of the
sequence of the creation to the construction of the tabernacle.

of the creation through the letters of the alphabet presents itself as a good deal older than the composition of *Sefer Yeṣira*, which is dated to the time between the 3rd and the 6th century C.E. by G. Scholem[11].

The idea that the letters of the alphabet are the basis of the work of creation recurs throughout later Jewish mystical literature[12]. I confine myself to quote a passage from *III Enoch* (also known as the *Hebrew Book of Enoch* or the *Book of the Hekaloth*), a Merkaba writing probably belonging to the 5th or 6th century C.E. but containing much material from a far older age. This book purports to be revelations given to R. Ishmael by the patriarch Enoch, who was taken up to heaven and translated into the figure of Metatron, the prince of the angels. R. Ishmael relates that Enoch-Metatron announced to him that he was in possession of a crown upon which God had inscribed the letters by which the whole universe was created:

> R. Ishmael said: "Metatron, the Angel, the Prince of the Presence, the Glory of all Heavens, said to me:
> "Because of the great love and mercy with which the Holy One, blessed be He, loved and cherished me more than all the children of heaven, He wrote with His finger with a flaming style upon the crown on my head the letters by which were created heaven and earth, the seas and rivers, the mountains and hills, the planets and constellations, the lightnings, winds, earthquakes and voices [*i.e.*, thunders], the snow and hail, the storm-wind and the tempest – the letters by which were created all the needs of the world and all the orders of Creation." "[13]

(xiii.1)

Summing up the discussion of the present Chapter so far, we see that there was a Jewish teaching to the effect that the world was created by means of the letters of the alphabet or rather by certain combinations of them, and that it was rumored that gifted persons could learn the creative manipulation of the letters and thus emulate the divine act of creation. By the end of the 3rd century C.E., outstanding rabbis exercised this magical faculty according to the tradition. Their prototype was Abraham, the belief in whose creative powers has been traced back into the 2nd century C.E.

The "Sealing" of the Creation with the Divine Name

But what kind of combinations of letters effected the creative acts? The 10th century exegete Solomon ben Isaac Rashi of Troyes gives the following comment upon the Talmudic story about R. Ḥanina and R. Hoshayah creating a calf through the agency of *Sefer Yeṣira*:

---

11 He inclines toward the earlier dating; see *On the Kabbalah*, p. 167, n. 3.
12 For references to texts, see L. Ginzberg, *The Legends of the Jews*, V (Notes to Volumes I and II), Philadelphia, 1925 and reprints, p. 5, n. 10.
13 There is a parallel passage in ch. xli, where the letters are said to be engraved upon the throne of glory.

They used to combine the letters of the Name, by which the universe was created. This is not to be considered forbidden magic, for the works of God were brought into being through His holy Name.[14]

In *Sanh.* 67b, the tradition about the two amoraim creating a calf by means of *Sefer Yeṣira* is related as an example of what kind of magic is permitted, and Rashi upholds this by explaining that the rabbis were penetrating into the mysteries of the Name of God and the practical consequences. The magical acts said to be performed by means of this esoteric book ultimately turned upon the Divine Name. The Talmudic sages thus effected their creations through combinations and permutations of the letters of the Name. Raba, who was said to have created a golem, had clear affinities with an esotericism concerning the Name of God: on one occasion, he even wished to discourse in the *beth midrash* upon the mystery of the Tetragrammaton, but was stopped by a certain old man, probably representing the *sensus communis* of the rabbis (see *Pes.* 50a).

Similarly, the "Great" *Yalqut Reubeni*, one of the two published parts of the anthology of Kabbalistic lore complied by Reuben Hoeshke ben Hoeshke Katz of Prague in the 17th century, interprets the combination of the creative letters known to Beṣalel as the name אהיה or a construction of twelve letters derived from it. It is said that "Beṣalel, by the name of אהיה, constructed twelve letters by which the heaven and earth were created," and that "Beṣalel, by the name of אהיה, constructed the tabernacle."[15]

Since *Sefer Yeṣira* imparts that Abraham actually succeeded in his efforts to create by manipulating the letters of the alphabet, this would imply that the patriarch possessed the power of the Divine Name, which was the real means by which everything came into being. A couple of details to the effect that Abraham possessed the creative Name of God can in fact be obtained. In *Midrash Rabba*, we read:

> "And I [– it is God who is speaking to Abram –] will make your name great" (*Gen.* xii.2). This means: "I will add the letter *He* to your name." R. Abbahu commented on this: "It is not written: "Look now השמים," but: "Look now השמימה" (*Gen.* xv.5). [God said:] "With this *He*, I made the world. And – behold! – I will add it to your name, and then you will be fruitful and multiply." "

> (*Gen. R.* xxxix.11)

R. Abbahu, a Palestinian amora who flourished about 300 C.E., gives a very peculiar interpretation (quite casually bringing in *Gen.* xv.5) of God's changing of the name Abram to Abraham: the letter ה that was added to the old name was the letter with which God made the world. The letter *He*, however,

---

14 *Talmud Babli. Tractate Sanhedrin with Rashi, Tosafot ... according to the Venice Text,* Jerusalem, no date, *ad loc.*

15 See Ch. Kaplan, "The Hidden Name", *JSOR*, 13, 1929, p. 182.

was regarded as an equivalent or abbreviation of the proper Name of God, the real creative instrument. Thus, when Abram receives the letter *He*, with which God created the universe, this implies that he actually gets the Divine Name conjoined to his own. Abraham's name became "great", that is, he was fruitful and multiplied, because he possessed the Great Name, the means of the creation.

Another passage runs thus:

> "And he [*viz.*, Melchizedek] blessed him [*viz.*, Abram] and said: "Blessed be Abram by God the Most High, Creator of heaven and earth (קנה שמים וארץ)!"
> "(*Gen.* xiv.19). From whom did he acquire them? R. Abba said: "As one says: so-and-so has beautiful eyes and hair." R. Isaac said: "Abraham used to entertain wayfarers; and, after they had eaten, he would say to them: "Say a blessing!" They would ask: "What shall we say?" He replied: "[Say:] Blessed be the God of the universe of whose bounty we have eaten!" Then, the Holy One, blessed be He, said to him: "My Name was not known among My creatures, and you have made it known among them. I will regard you as though you were associated with Me in the creation of the world." Hence it is written: "And he blessed him and said: "Blessed be Abram by God the Most High, who has created heaven and earth!" " " "
>
> (*Ibid.* xliii.7)

In the Biblical text, קנה שמים וארץ obviously refers to God, but R. Isaac takes it as referring to Abraham (Abram). קנה can mean to "acquire" and also to "possess", and R. Abba takes the verb in an attributive sense, apparently indicating God's possessing of the universe. R. Isaac, however, obviously chooses another meaning of the verb, namely, to "create", and maintains that the words about the creating of heaven and earth in *Gen.* xiv.19 refer to Abraham. R. Isaac, a tanna of the mid-2nd century known to have engaged in mystical studies (see *Ḥag.* 13a), evidently reckons that it was because Abraham knew the Name that God elevated him to the position of being regarded as an associate in the process of the creation. The explanation of this apparently is that the Name of God is the instrument by which the creation was effected: since Abraham knew the creative medium, God raised him to the position of being regarded as a partner in the creation of heaven and earth. The two last-quoted texts allow us to conclude that, in the 2nd century C.E., there were circles that associated Abraham with creative activity by virtue of his possessing the proper Name of God.

Here is the place to return to the teaching of *Sefer Yeṣira* that the letters of the alphabet were the means of the creation. Actually, the author of the book knows that the creative letters are based upon the Name of God:

> How did he [*i.e.*, God] combine, weigh, and exchange them [*i.e.*, the letters]? *Aleph* with all, and all with *Aleph*; *Beth* with all, and all with *Beth*; *Gimel* with all, and all with *Gimel*; and all of them return circlewise back to the starting-point through 231 gates, the number of the pairs that can be formed from the twenty-two [letters]; and that is why *everything which is created and everything which is spoken proceed from one Name*.
>
> (ii.5)

Everything in the universe depends upon fixed interconnections of the
letters of the alphabet according to certain gematrical permutations. At every
"gate" in the circle formed by the letters of the alphabet, there is a combination of two letters through which the creative powers enter into the universe.
What is of importance in this connection, however, is to note that the author
obviously holds the opinion that the whole alphabet is based upon a mystical
name. The idea that the alphabet is founded upon a secret name can be corroborated by Greek and Latin sources[16]. That the author of *Sefer Yeṣira* has
in mind the proper Name of God, the most efficacious of all names, appears
certain. The author undoubtedly regards God's Name as the foundation of
the whole creation, for, in another passage, he states that the six extremities
of the world are "sealed", that is, kept together, by the six different permutations of "the Great Name יהו " (i.3).

That the stability of the world is dependent upon God's "sealing" the
creation with his own Name is a teaching which occurs in several writings
dealing with mystical lore. In *Hekaloth Rabbati*, a Merkaba writing probably
edited in the 6th century but containing considerably older strata, we read
about "the sealing of the order of the creation" by the Divine Name (ch. 23).
In *Yalqut Reubeni*, there are several passages saying that אהיה or some
name derived from it is the "seal" of heaven and earth[17].

The passages from *Sefer Yeṣira* and *Hekaloth Rabbati* are among those
texts repeatedly cited by G. Quispel as evidence for the view of the Jewish
origin of the Gnostics' reflections upon the Name of God and of their concept of the demiurge. Admittedly, these two esoteric books are younger than
the Gnostic sources, but we shall see that the notion of the Name of God as
the *agens* of the creation has very deep roots. As a matter of fact, the sealing
of the six extremities of the world with the name *Yaho* seems to be a ramifi-
cation of the same basic idea as that adapted in ch. 136 of *Pistis Sophia*,
where Jesus turns towards the four corners of the world and cries out: ιαω,
ιαω, ιαω. The crying out of "Iao" in all the four directions of the world apparently signifies that this word is the name of the lord who is over the whole
cosmos. Since *Pistis Sophia* probably stems from the 3rd or 4th century, we
can conclude that the notion of the sealing of the extremes of the universe
with the name *Yaho* in *Sefer Yeṣira* is at least as old as the *terminus post
quem* of the Gnostic book.

That this cosmological notion of the name Yaho (Iao), a variation of the
Tetragrammaton, is of Jewish origin appears to be certain. We discern the
Jewish origin of the cosmological function of the name Iao in a magical

---

16 See F. Dornseiff, *Das Alphabet in Mystik und Magie*, 2nd ed., Leipzig, 1925, pp. 69
   ff.; cited by G. Scholem, *Ursprung und Anfänge der Kabbalah* (SJ, III), Berlin,
   1962, p. 25, n. 44.
17 See Kaplan, pp. 181 f.

papyrus where it is related that the dragon of chaos moved and rocked the creation, whereupon God brought it to rest and made the world stable again by exclaiming: ῎Ιαω![18] This is a turn of the ancient myth of God's conquering the dragon of chaos and creating the world; in the Old Testament, we find several reminiscences of a cosmogonic myth telling that God has conquered the Deep (Tehom) or the Sea (Yam), often described as a great aquatic monster (and called by the name of Leviathan, Rahab, or simply Tannin, the "Dragon"), thereby making the creation of the world possible[19]. In *Psalm* civ, God combats the Waters by his powerful Word: "At Your rebuke, they fled; at the sound of Your thunder, they took to flight" (*v.* 7). The account of the creation in *Psalm* civ stands in a halfway position between the mythological-dramatical versions and the sober priestly creation narrative of *Genesis* ch. i, where God solemnly creates and orders the universe by his Word of Command (cp. *Ps.* xxxiii.6, 9). The magical papyrus obviously interprets God's Word as the Name of God. In this respect, the papyrus can be likened to the eulogy of the Creator in the opening stanzas of the Jewish apocryphon known as the *Prayer of Manasseh*:

> Lord, Sovereign of all! You, God of our fathers, of Abraham, Isaac, and Jacob, and of their righteous seed. You who have made the heaven and the earth with all their beauty; You who have prisoned the Sea by Your Word of Command, who have closed the Abyss and sealed it by Your terrible and glorious Name [...].
>
> (1-3)

The prisoning of the Sea through the Word of God is here brought into close parallelism to the closing and sealing of the Abyss with God's Name. "Sea" (θάλασσα) and "Abyss" (ἄβυσσος) are obviously regarded as identical, since ἄβυσσος is the LXX rendering of *Tehom*, the meaning of which oscillates between that of a surging flood and a subterranean locality. The Word of God, the means wherewith the cosmos was established, is here interpreted as the Name of God: through God's Word, the Sea was prisoned; through God's Name, the Abyss was closed and sealed.

The *Prayer of Manasseh* is also related to the passages from the mystical texts discussed above in that it knows the idea of the "sealing" with the Di-

---

18 *PGM*, XIII.539. Scholem, *Ursprung*, p. 27, also compares this text to the Valentinian idea that "Iao" was the name by which Horos, literally, the "Limit", turned back Sophia-Achamoth from entering Pleroma again (see Iren., I.iv.1; cp. Epiphan., *Pan.* XXXI.xxxv.4). Scholem poses the question whether the notion of the "sealing" of the entremes of the universe with the name Yaho is a monotheistic and anti-dualistic polemic against the Gnostic myth. However that may be, the "sealing" of the foundations of the cosmos with the Name of God is much older than the Valentinian myth.

19 For a more recent discussion of the myth, see O. Kaiser, *Die mythische Bedeutung des Meeres* (BZAW, 78), wnd ed., Berlin, 1962.

vine Name in a cosmogonic context. The apocryphon, however, does not tell
about the sealing of the universe, but states that the primeval sea was sealed by
the Name. In this respect, we can compare it to a passage from the *Pseudo-
Jonathan Targum* where it is said:

> The Name is distinctly engraved upon the Shetiya Stone, with which God sealed up
> the mouth of the Tehom.[20]

(Ex. xxviii.30)

The Shetiya Stone (אבן השתיה, or אבן שתיה, אבן שתיא), whose surface was breaking through in the temple on Sion, was the centre of a great
cycle of myths[21]; in this connection, it suffices to note that it carried the inscription of the Name of God (see also, *e.g.*, Targ. *Eccl.* iii.11), and that it was
the first part of the earth to have been raised above the primeval waters and
therefore the place from where the creation began (see *Midrash Tanḥ.* B *Eccl.*
ii.5). When David was digging the pits (שיתין) of the temple, he was breaking
open the Tehom — for the temple stood over the Tehom (see *Par.* iii.3) — and
a potshard upon which the Divine Name was engraved was cast into the pits
in order to suppress the uprushing Sea (see *Succa* 53b; *Makk.* 11a). This
aggada in the Babylonian Talmud obviously presupposes the cosmogonic
myth about the *Eben ha-Shetiya*; David is in a way copying the first cosmogonic act, the suppressing of chaos[22].

---

20 That the mouth of the Deep had been sealed by God obviously was an old Near
Eastern *mythologoumenon*; an Ugaritic text seems to read that El has "sealed the
mouth of the Tehom (וייצ[מ]ר[ד את גיף התהום)" (H.L. Ginzberg, ed., כתבי
אוגרית, Jerusalem, 1963, p. 80).

21 See D. Feuchtwang, "Das Wasseropfer und die damit verbundenen Zeremonien",
MGWJ, 54, 1910, pp. 546 f., 720 ff.; 55, 1911, pp. 43 ff.; J. Jeremias, *Golgotha*
(Ἄγγελος, Beiheft I), Leipzig, 1926; cp. Ginzberg, *Legends*, V, p. 15, n. 39. For the
wider cosmological pattern, see E. Burrows, "Some Cosmological Patterns in Babylonian Religion", in S.H. Hooke, ed., *The Labyrinth*, London, 1935, pp. 45 ff.

22 The Scriptural support for writing the Name upon a shard and casting it into the
Deep was found in *Num.* v.23, "The priest shall write these curses [*viz.*, those cited in
vv. 21 f.] on a scroll and cast them into water." Since the curse in question contains
the name of YHWH, the erasing of which was forbidden (see *Deut.* xii.3 f.; *Sheb.* 35a-
b), the aggada finds the exceptional enjoinment of God to blot out his Name at this
place: "[...] the Torah said: "Let My Name which was solemnly inscribed be blotted
out by water" [...] ." "The Torah is here identified with the Lord, whose words it
reveals" (M.E. Lazarus, trans., "Makkoth", in Epstein, *Talmud*, Seder Nezikin VIII,
1935, p. 74, n. 5). We know that there was a tradition according to which the
Torah was regarded as a mystical composition of God's names, as can be seen from
Shimmush Torah and *Shimmush Tehillim*, which date from Geonic times, and
from the later *Sefer Gematriaoth*; see J. Trachtenberg, *Jewish Magic and Superstition* (JPSA), New York, 1939, Atheneum paperback edition (TB, 15), New York,
1970, pp. 108 ff.; Scholem, *On the Kabbalah*, pp. 37 f. Perhaps, as Scholem per-
pends, this tradition is premised already in the comment by R. Eleazer in *Midrash
Tehillim ad Ps.* iii, ch. 2, *ad v*.1, "Man does not know its [*i.e.*, Wisdom's] order,"

The Palestinian Talmud, however, records a version according to which David did not cast the shard into the pits, but unexpectedly came upon it when he was digging the foundations (תימליוסים : θεμελίωσις) of the temple. The shard told him that it had been placed there at the time when God revealed himself on Mt. Sinai: "Then, the earth shuddered and began to subside, and I am placed here in order to suppress the Tehom" (*Sanh.* 29a).

Again, the version of the Palestinian Talmud is repeated in *Midrash Samuel*, a rather late Palestinian work, only with the notable exception that it is maintained that the potsherd was placed over the Tehom at the time of the creation (see ch. 26). This rendering is also to be found in the "Great" *Yalqut Reubeni*, where it is narrated that, when the Ten Commandments were given, the voice of God caused the foundations of the earth to shake, but the slate placed over the Tehom prevented the subterranean waters from engulfing the world (see 210b). It must be assumed that the slate is to be understood to have been put in its place at the time of the creation. It ought to be apparent that the agreement between *Midrash Samuel* and *Yalqut Reubeni* represents the original notion over against the conflicting opinions of the two Talmuds.

The version of the Palestinian Talmud makes no explicit mention of the Name of God being inscribed upon the sherd, but *Midrash Samuel* states that

---

which this 3rd century rabbi took to mean that the real order of the Law had to be hidden from men in order that they should not utilize it in magic. The Kabbalists of the later Middle Ages speculated that the Law is not only made up of the various divine names but is as a whole based on or derived from the Tetragrammaton. Moreover, they made the outright identification of the Torah with the Name of God and thus with God himself; the whole issue is summed up in the following statement by Joseph Gikatilla in his work on the mystical foundations of the Commandments: "His Torah is in Him, and that is what the Kabbalists say, namely, that the Holy One, blessed by He, is in His Name and His Name is in Him, and that His Name is His Torah" (MS Jerusalem, 8° 597, 21b; quoted by Scholem, *On the Kabbalah*, p. 44). Scholem thinks that the Spanish Kabbalists were the first who taught that the Law "is as a whole the one great Name of God" (*ibid.*, p. 39), but the aggada cited above shows that the foundation of this idea was at least as old as the 3rd century C.E., which is the age of the rabbis to which the tradition is assigned. Another instance of a non-Kabbalistic text interpreting the Name of God as the Law is found in *Deut.R.* vii.3, where "the Name" of the Lover in *Song of Songs* i.3 is interpreted as "the words of the Torah".

It is obviously because the Torah could be interpreted as the Name of God that an ancient midrash teaches that the means wherewith God sealed the primeval ocean was the Torah: "And by it [*i.e.*, the Law as identified with Wisdom] He has sealed the Great Sea, so that it might not well up and wash away the world[...]. And by it He sealed the Deep, so that it might not overcome the world" (*Midrash Tanḥ. Gen.* i.1). Certain linguistic and stylistic traits suggest that the midrash is dependent upon the *Prayer of Manasseh*; thus, התהום [...] אוקיינוס ים can be compared to θάλλασσαν [...] ἄβυσσον, and התהום את חתם to ὁ κλείσας τὴν ἄββυσσον καί φραγισάμενος. The midrash has substituted the Torah for the Name.

the slate had the "seventy-two letter Name engraved upon it." The Divine
Name of seventy-two letters, mentioned in an oft-repeated passage in *Midrash
Rabba* (*Gen. R.* xliv.19; *et passim*), was, of course, regarded as a derivative of
the original Name of God[23]. *Yalqut Reubeni* also knows that the slate con-
tains the inscription of the Name[24]. The potshard or slate suppressing the
Deep apparently is a representation of the *Eben ha-Shetiya*, upon which
God's Name was inscribed.

In the Babylonian Talmud, the tradition is cited in the name of Rab or in
the name of R. Yoḥanan. Both these rabbis belong to the 3rd century, but
the myth about God shutting or sealing up the Tehom with the Shetiya Stone
must be earlier. The *Prayer of Manasseh* is witnessed in the *Didascalia*, a Syrian
Christian work from the beginning of the 3rd century, and the Jewish apocryphon thus has a safe *terminus ante quem* in the end of the 2nd century
C.E.[25] But we may work further back. An apocalyptic amendment of the
cosmogonic myth is discernible in the last book of the New Testament:
"And I saw an angel coming down from heaven, having the key of the Abyss
and a great chain in his hand. And he laid hold of the Dragon, the old Serpent,
who is the Devil and Satan, and bound him for thousand years, and cast him
into the Abyss and shut him up and set a seal upon him ..." (*Rev.* xx.1-3).

In the *Revelation*, which was probably written during the persecutions
under Domitian (d. 96 C.E.), there is no explicit mention of the "seal" containing God's Name; but it is only a logical inference that it was understood
to do so. The apocalyptic vision is related to the strange Talmudic legend
that Ashmedai, the "prince of the demons", was caught and fettered by
means of a chain, upon which the Divine Name was engraved, and the ring of
Solomon, whose seal contained the Name of God (see *Gitt.* 68a). In the so-
called *Alphabet of R. Aqiba*, we read that the heaven and the earth "are sealed
with the ring [containing the Name] אהיה אשר אהיה."[26] It would seem
evident that the *Revelation of John* as well as the aggada reflects a cosmogonic *mythologoumenon*. When it is said that God "sealed up" his work of
creation or the underworld with his Name, the meaning of the phrase is that
the powers of evil cannot prevail, and this notion of "sealing" obviously
could be transferred to other contexts[27]. Since the most effective "seal" of

---

23 For the divine name of twelve, twenty-two, forty-two, and seventy-two letters, see
   Trachtenberg, pp. 90 ff. with notes on pp. 289 ff.
24 See Kaplan, p. 182.
25 Many scholars, however, even want to assign a pre-Christian date to the *Prayer of
   Manasseh*; see, for instance, O.F. Fritzsche, *Kurzgefasstes exegetisches Handbuch zu
   den Apokryphen des Alten Testaments*, I, Leipzig, 1851, p. 158; O. Zöckler, *Die
   Apokryphen des Alten Testaments* (KKSANT: Altes Testament, 9), Munich, 1891,
   p. 236; V. Ryssel, trans., "Das Gebet Manasses", in *APAT*, I, p. 167.
26 *BH*, III, p. 25.
27 Cp. above, pp. 98 ff., for the seal of the Name set upon the believer.

all is that of the Name of God, it cannot be doubted that *Rev.* xx.1 ff., re-flecting a cosmogonic myth, suggests the seal of the Divine Name.

The Creation through the Name

As we have seen already, the Name of God was not only regarded as the "seal" of the creation; it was even understood as the instrument through which the world came into being. It is possible that this notion was assumed already by R. Isaac; about 300 C.E., R. Abbahu certainly professes it when stating that the *He* added to the name of Abram was the creative instrument of God. Other rabbis found abbreviations of the Tetragrammaton and thus the creative instrument in other words of the Old Testament. Thus, in a dis-cussion in *Midrash Rabba,* the word בהבראם, "When they [*viz.*, "the gen-erations of the heavens and the earth"] were created" (*Gen.* ii.4), is read as בה' בראם, "By *He* He created them," "He created them with *He*." The first passage to be examined reads:

> בהבראם: R. Berekiah said in the name of R. Judah bar R. Simeon: "Not with labour or wearying toil did the Holy One, blessed be He, create the world, but: "By the Word of the Lord, and the heavens were already made" (*Ps.* xxxiii.6). בהבראם: By means of *He*, He created them."

> (*Gen.R.* xii.10)

R. Berekiah was a 4th century Palestinian amora, and R. Judah bar Simeon was a late 3rd and early 4th century aggadist. What does the latter mean by the statement that God created without exertion? In the same paragraph of *Midrash Rabba*, we read:

> R. Abbahu said in R. Yoḥanan's name: "He created them [*viz.*, the heavens and the earth] with the letter *He*. All letters take a hold on the tongue, but the *He* demands no effort. Similarly, not with labour or wearying toil did the Holy One, blessed be He, create His world, but: "By the Word of the Lord, and the heavens were already made" (*Ps.* xxxiii.4)."

> (*Ibid.*)

R. Abbahu, as we already know, was a Palestinian amora who flourished about 300 C.E.; he was the disciple of R. Yoḥanan ben Nappaḥa, who used to call him "Abbahu, my son". R. Yoḥanan was a Palestinian amora who died at an old age in 279 C.E. Instead of reading בהבראם, both R. Yoḥanan and R. Abbahu read בה' בראם, "He created them with *He*," splitting the word in two. The letter *He*, ה, occurring twice in the Tetragrammaton, is here obvious-ly representing the full Name of God. The letter *He*, being an aspirate, requires no effort to be pronounced; and this is the explanation of the phrase that God created the universe without any exertion. The Word of God, which is the instrument of the creation according to such Biblical texts as *Genesis* ch. i and *Psalm* xxxiii, is really nothing else than the letter *He*, a representative of the original Name of God.

In the self-same paragraph of *Midrash Rabba* from which the two last passages are culled, the following exposition of *Is.* xxvi.4 is being made during a discussion between R. Judah II and R. Samuel ben Naḥman:

> The verse "Trust in YHWH forever, for *be-Yah* YHWH is an everlasting rock" (*Is.* xxvi.4) means: By these two letters, the Lord created His worlds. Now, we do not know whether this world was created with a *He* or the next with a *Yod*; but, from what R. Abbahu said in R. Yoḥanan's name, namely, "בהבראם means: By *He*, He created them," it follows that this world was created by means of *He*.
>
> (*Ibid.*)

R. Abbahu refers to a saying in the name of R. Yoḥanan which is recorded in the Palestinian Talmud (*Ḥag.* ch. 2, 77c). Here, it is said: "The two worlds are created by two letters, this world and the future world, one by ה, the other by י." As proof, *Is.* xxvi.4 is adduced. The saying כי ביה יהוה צור עולמים is interpreted as meaning: "For with *Yod-He* the Lord created the worlds." In the Biblical text, יהוה· is probably apposite to יה, which is also a form of the Divine Name[28], while the *Beth* is ב *essentiae*[29]. In the rabbinic exposition, however, the letter Beth is taken as ב *instrumentalis*, and the verse expounded as meaning that it is through the agency of *Yod* and *He* that God is the "rock", that is, the creator and sustainer, of both this world and the future world. Besides constituting the Divine Name יה, these two letters occur in both יהוה and אהיה, the two great names of God. R. Abbahu says that he is not certain which letter was responsible for which world, but, on account of the reading בה׳ בראם in *Gen.* ii.4, he guesses that this world was created with the *He* and the future world with the *Yod*[30].

In the Babylonian Talmud (*Men.* 29b), these interpretations are reported by R. Ammi in the name of Judah bar Ilai, a tanna of the mid-2nd century C.E. When having the choice between two authors of a rabbinic tradition, we should perhaps incline towards the youngest authority, but there can be no doubt that the sophisticated rabbinic discussions about which letter representing the Tetragrammaton that was responsible for the creation of the two worlds must have been preceded by the simpler notion that the full Name of God was the creative instrument.

Up to now, the Name has been found to be an instrument used by God when he was engaged in the creation of the world. But there were also traditions according to which it was a hypostasis. In the *Book of Jubilees*, a

---

28 Cp. *Ps.* lxviii.5: ביה שמו , "His Name is [none other than] *Yah*!"

29 There are other ways of explaining the phrase in *Is.* xxvi.4 (and the one in *Ps.* lxviii.5), but the different explanations do not affect the interpretation of the rabbinic understanding of the Biblical passage.

30 In "Great" *Yalqut Reubeni* I.8b, the other alternative seems to be preferred. See also *Alphabet of R. Aqiba*, in *BH*, III, pp. 23, 24, 53, 55, 66; *Yalqut Reubeni* I.4a; *Masseketh Hekaloth* ch. 7.

midrashic work on the period from the creation to the giving of the Law, we find the following passage in which Isaac admonishes his sons to swear an oath with the Divine Name:

> And now I shall make you swear a great oath — no oath being greater than it by the Name, glorious and honoured, and great and splendid, and wonderful and mighty, that created the heavens and the earth, and all things together — that you will fear and worship him [...].
>
> (xxxvi.7)

This highly eulogized Name, which is the creative potency, obviously is the Tetragrammaton. It is significant to note that *Jubilees* continues the ideology of the concept of the Divine Name as found in *Deuteronomy* and the historical books inspired by it. In the so-called Deuteronomistic history-work, we are told that, while God himself remains in heaven, the Name of God dwells in the temple[31]. Similarly, in *Jubilees*, the temple is the abode of God's Name (see xxxii.10; xlix.20 f.). As was pointed out in Chapter III, the Deuteronomic concept of the Divine Name comes very close to the idea of the hypostasis of the Name, and the Name in *Jub.* xxxvi.7 is "the power which creates and sustains the cosmos, a hypostasis."[32] Here, then, the crea-

---

31 See above, pp. 86f.

32 H. Bietenhard, Art. ὄνομα κτλ., in *TDNT*, V, 1967 and reprints, p. 267. It is interesting to note that the Logos in the prologue to the Fourth Gospel is also ascribed with cosmogonic function and residency on earth. J. Jeremias argues that the concept of the Logos had a pre-history before it was used in the prologue, and he cites *Wisd.* xviii.15 f. in substantiation of the thesis that the Logos originally was a "designation of the returning Lord" ("Zum Logosproblem", *ZNW*, 59, 1968, p. 85). In *Is.* xxx.27, however, the *Name* is described in the same manner as the Logos in *Wisd.* xviii.15 f.; see above, p. 85. In the *Revelation*, it is said that the returning lord has "a Name inscribed which no one knows but himself ... and the name by which he is called is the Word of God" (xix.12 f.). Thus, we would perhaps be right to seek the Divine Name behind the "Word". M. McNamara, *The New Testament and the Palestinian Targum to the Pentateuch* (AB, 27), Rome, 1966, pp. 97 ff., points out the probability that the author of the *Revelation* drew upon Targumic interpretations of the Name in *Ex.* iii.14 for his version of the Name of Jesus as related in i.8, " "I am the Beginning and the End," says the lord, "who is, and who was, and who is to come." " Cp. above, pp. 79 f.

C.T.R. Hayward, "The Holy Name of the God of Moses and the Prologue of St. John's Gospel", *NTS*, 25, 1978, pp. 16 ff., argues that Memra in the Targums is an exegetical term standing for the Divine Name revealed to Moses in the Bush, and that this Targumic concept may have been influential in the formation of the figure of the Logos in the prologue to the Fourth Gospel. In *John*, however, the Word is a hypostasis; but it would not seem impossible that the teaching about the Logos in the prologue is based upon a Jewish Christian Christology of the Name: "In the begin-

tive Name is not merely an instrument used by God but a hypostasized power. In the *Book of Jubilees*, we have a pre-Christian testimony to the idea of the cosmogonic Name as an individual agent.

---

ning was the Name, and the Name was with God, and the Name was God. It was in the beginning with God. Everything has been made by it ... . The Name became flesh and tabernacled among us ... ." *Pirke de R. Eliezer* says: "Before the world, God and His Name were alone" (ch. 3). Ps.-Philo (*Bibl. Ant.* lx.2) says that the Name was created right after the light had come into being. It truly can be said of the Name that it is God, for the Name is an expression of God's being. Already Zickendraht, p. 167, cited the idea of the creative potency of the Name with reference to the Logos concept in the prologue to *John*. The Name was present in the Angel of the Lord, the human appearance of God. Moreover, the "tabernacling", σκηνοῦν, of the Name on earth is the teaching of the Deuteronomistic history-work, using the root שׁכן to express this dwelling of the Name and localizing it in the temple (see *Deut.* xii.5, 11). The LXX, however, does not have the verb σκηνόω in these places, though the word σκηνή in the LXX translates מִשׁכָן, the "tabernacle", the forerunner of the temple. But κατασκηνόω, a compound of σκηνόω, is used causatively in some important places. God according to *Jer.* vii.12 says: "Go to My place which is in Silo, where I caused My Name to tabernacle (κατεσκήνωσα τὸ ὄνομά μου) before ... ." *Ez.* xliii.7 contains the following oracle by God: "... My Name shall tabernacle (κατασκηνώσει τὸ ὄνομά μου) in the midst of the house [*i.e.*, the temple] of Israel for ever ... ." *Neh.* i.9 has also a word by God containing the promise of gathering the people and bringing them "into the place which I have chosen to cause My Name to tabernacle there (κατασκηνῶσαι τὸ ὄνομά μου ἐκεῖ)." Cp. *Ps. Sol.* vii.6: "When Your Name tabernacles (κατασκηνοῦν τὸ ὄνομά) in our midst, we shall find mercy." Cp. further *Did.* x.2; see above, p. 103, n. 81. See also above, p. 178, n. 310.

CHAPTER SIX

The Angel of the Lord

The Demiurgic Oath and Name of Michael

There is another ostensibly pre-Christian text which teaches that the universe was created as well as made stable by the Name. In a section of *I Enoch* (also called the *Ethiopic Book of Enoch*) termed by modern scholars the "Parables (or, Similitudes) of Enoch" (chs. xxxvii-lxxi), which, according to R.H. Charles and others, belongs to the first pre-Christian century[1], there is to be found a long excursus on a mysterious oath which contains "the Hidden Name", by which the universe is created and sustained:

> And this is the task of Kâsbeêl, the chief of the oath which he showed to the holy ones when he dwelt high above in glory, and its name is Bîqâ. This [angel] requested Michael to show him the Hidden Name, that he might enunciate it in the oath, so that those might quake before that name and oath who revealed all that was secret to the children òf men. And this is the power of this oath, for it is powerful and strong, and he placed this oath Akâe in the hand of Michael.
> And these are the secrets of this oath ...
> And they are strong through this oath:
> And the heaven was suspended before the world was created,
> And for ever.
> And through it the earth was founded upon water,
> And from the secret recesses of the mountains come beautiful waters,
> From the creation of the world and unto eternity.

---

1 See Charles, trans., "The Book of Enoch", in *APOT*, II, p. 171. The "Parables of Enoch" are the only part of *I Enoch* not found among the fragments of the book at Qumran, but this "argument from silence" cannot be considered conclusive in disproving a pre-Christian date. For a pre-Christian dating, see also E. Sjöberg, *Der Menschensohn im äthiopischen Henochbuch*, Lund, 1946, pp. 1 ff. J. Milik, ed. & trans. (in collaboration with M. Black), *The Books of Enoch. Aramaic Fragments of Qumran Cave 4*, Oxford, 1976, pp. 91 ff., compares the "Parables" to the Christian Sibylline literature and dates this part of *I Enoch* to the latter part of the 3rd century C.E. I am not convinced by his argument, especially because the saviour designations the "Son of Man" and the "Elect One" in *I Enoch* do not occur in the pericopes recalling the New Testament. See now M.A. Knibb, "The Date of the Parables of Enoch", *NTS*, 25, 1979, pp. 343 ff.

And through that oath the sea was created,
And as its foundation He set for it the sand against the time of [its] anger,
And it dare not pass beyond it from the creation of the world unto eternity.
And through that oath are the depths made fast,
And abide and stir not from their place from eternity to eternity.
And through that oath the sun and the moon complete their course,
And deviate not from their ordinance from eternity to eternity,
And through that oath the stars complete their course,
And He calls them by their names,
And they answer Him from eternity to eternity.
(And in like manner the spirits of the water, and of the winds, and of all zephyrs, and
[their] paths from all the quarters of the winds. And there are preserved the voices of
the thunder and the light of the lightnings: and there are preserved the chambers of
the hail and the chambers of the hoarfrost, and the chambers of the mist, and the
chambers of the rain and the dew. And all these believe and give thanks before the
Lord of the Spirits, and glorify [Him] with all their power,
and their food is in every act of thanksgiving: they thank and glorify
and extol the Name of the Lord of the Spirits for ever and ever.)
And this oath is mighty over them,
And through it (they are preserved and) their paths are preserved,
And their course is not destroyed[2]

                                                          (lxix.13-25)

The opening of this meditation on the Oath and the Name is very obscure;
Charles states that he cannot interpret it. Immediately preceding the passage
quoted, the names and the functions of the fallen angels are given; and the
pericope is obviously one of the fragments of the confused Shemyaza cycle of
myths[3]. Perhaps Kasbeel, who once had "dwelt high above in glory," is a
name of Shemyaza, the ringleader of the fallen angels[4]. In the original myth,
then, Shemyaza, whose name may mean "He sees the Name" (שמיחזה), can
have been described as successful in his attempt at capturing "the Hidden
Name" from Michael. It is significant that Kasbeel is said to be in possession
of the great Oath, which is called "Biqa" and "Akae", two names that probably are to be explained according to certain gematrical permutations with
the letters of the Divine Name[5].

However all this may be, what is of foremost importance to note is the

---

2 Translation by Charles, p. 234. The words within brackets are reckoned as interpola-
   tions.

3 For this myth cycle, see Charles, "The Book of Enoch", p. 191, n. *ad* chs. vi-xi.

4 Cp. A. Caquot & P. Geoltrain, "Notes sur le texte éthiopien des "Paraboles"
   d' Hénoch", *Semitica*, 13, 1963, p. 52.

5 For an attempt at explaining these two designations of the oath, see Kaplan, pp.
   181 ff. It is possible that two different oaths are involved: the oath Biqa sworn by
   the angels (cp. vi.4 f.) in *vv.* 13 f., and the oath Akae containing the Name being
   given to Michael in *vv.* 15 ff.; see M.A. Knibb, ed. & trans. (in consultation with
   E. Ullendorff), *The Ethiopic Book of Enoch*, 2 (Introduction, Translation and
   Commentary), Oxford, 1978, pp. 162 ff.

fact that the archangel Michael is presented as being entrusted with the formula containing the Hidden Name, the instrument of the creation. It is obviously God who "placed this oath Akae in the hand of Michael." That the Hidden Name is the proper Name of God, the *Shem ha-Mephorash*, is evident. Also in the *Testament of Solomon*, Michael appears to be entrusted with the Name of God: it is the angel Michael who is sent down from heaven bringing Solomon the ring with the seal which wards off all demons (see i.6 f.)[6]. Apparently, being the principal angel, the Angel of the Lord, Michael is the possessor of the Name of God. And, since there is ample evidence to show that the Name is the cosmogonic instrument, it is only legitimate to ask whether Michael ever is described as holding a demiurgical office.

The angels Michael, מיכאל, "Who is like God"(!), and Gabriel, גבריאל, the "Man of God"(?)[7], are named already in the *Book of Daniel*[8]; and the two continue to be the most popular of the angels. It will be recalled that the rabbis warned against a teaching according to which these two archangels were God's co-workers in the creation[9]. When a configuration of archangels appears, Michael or Gabriel is often designated as the principal one[10]. Although it is maintained that Michael is greater than Gabriel (see *Ber.* 4b)[11], there are indications that Gabriel has been ousted from the highest position by Michael[12]. We will therefore first consider Gabriel.

The Angel and Apostle Gabriel

In the *Pseudo-Clementine Homilies*, Peter opposes a teaching according to which God acts through angels:

> We, Simon, do not assert that, from the Great Power, that is also called the Dominant Power, two angels were sent forth – the one to create the world, the other to give the Law [...].

(XVIII.12)

The teaching refused here seems to represent a primitive Jewish Gnosticism. As has been pointed out in Chapter IV, it is a well attested Jewish doc-

---

6 Concerning this ring, see also above, p. 252.
7 The name Gabriel may also be interpreted as the "Power of God" or "God has shown Himself mighty"; see M. Noth, *Die israelitischen Personennamen im Rahmen der gemeinsemitischen Namengebung* (BWANT, 3/10), Stuttgart, 1928, p. 190.
8 Michael: x.13, 20; xii.1; Gabriel: viii.16; ix.21.
9 See above, pp. 194, 236, and further below, p. 265.
10 For a survey of the teachings about these two angels and references to the literature bearing upon them, see J. Michl, Arts. "Engel VI (Gabriel)" and "Engel VII (Michael)", *RAC*, V, 1962, cols. 239 ff. and 243 ff. respectively.
11 For the predominance of Michael over Gabriel and the other angels, see W. Lueken, *Michael*, Göttingen, 1898, pp. 32 ff.
12 See Bousset, *Religion*, p. 328. Cp. also below, p. 279, n. 61.

trine that the Law was communicated through the agency of the angels[13]. Apparently, there were circles that held the Law to have been delivered by Michael in particular. According to the *Book of Jubilees*, when Moses ascended to the top of Mt. Sinai, God commanded the Angel of the Presence: "Write for Moses from the beginning of the creation until My sanctuary has been built among them for all eternity [...]" (i.27). Although the Angel of the Presence does not write the Torah but imparts the secret revelation of the *Jubilees* (cp. ii.1), it is of significance that he has a part in the revelation vouchsafed to Moses on Sinai.

That the Angel of the Presence is to be identified as Michael can be inferred from other sources[14]. In the introduction to the so-called *Apocalypse of Moses*, a Greek writing belonging to the Adamic literature, it is stated that the book contains a teaching given to Moses by Michael the archangel. As is imparted by some of the versions, this teaching was an esoteric revelation accompanying the communication of the Law[15]. In *Petirath Moshe*, Michael declines to fetch Moses' soul and says: "I am his [*viz.*, Moses'] teacher; he has been my pupil".[16] Finally, let us note Similitude VIII of the *Shepherd of Hermas*, a book drawing upon Jewish sources in many respects. Here, the Angel of the Lord is giving out branches from a great willow-tree to those who are "called by the Name of the Lord" and are assembled under the cover of the tree (i.1 f.). According to the interpretation, "this great tree, which covers plains and mountains and all earth, is the Law of God [...]. And the great and glorious angel is Michael [...]" (iii.2 f.). In view of the references given above, it ought to be clear that this teaching of *Hermas* is of Jewish origin[17]. It can then be asked whether the Jewish doctrine of Michael as the bestower of the Law was coupled with the notion of Gabriel as the creator of the heaven and the earth.

G. Quispel states that he is of the opinion that even the "learned Gnostics, Basilides, Valentinus, Marcion, and Apelles must have been familiar with some form of the vulgar Gnosis...."[18] This appears to be correct, for Apelles, who, according to Hippolytus, was an apostate pupil of Marcion, seems to have retreated to the primitive Jewish teaching about the mediation at the creation and the giving of the Law. Between God and the devil, Apelles posited the "creator of all things" *and* "he who spoke to Moses," calling them

---

13 See p. 194.
14 In *I En.* ch. xl, Michael is the foremost of the four "angels of the Presence".
15 See C. Fuchs, trans., "Das Leben Adams und Evas", in *APAT*, II, p. 514, n. a.
16 *BH*, VI, p. 75. Cp. further *Jude* 9, where Michael vies with Satan for Moses' body. Is the angel in *Acts* vii.38 Michael?
17 See M. Dibelius, *Die apostolischen Väter*, IV (Der Hirt des Hermas) (HNT, Ergänzungs-Band), Tübingen, 1923, pp. 586 ff.
18 "Origins", p. 276.

both angels (Hipp., VII.xxxviii.1). This squares with the Simonian teaching opposed by Peter in the *Pseudo-Clementine Homilies*. It is indeed possible that Apelles had access to Simonian sources, for Irenaeus tells us that Cerdo, Marcion's teacher, "took his start from the Simonians" (I.xxvii.1). That there were Jews who cherished the teaching combatted in *Ps.-Clem. Hom.* XVIII.12 and endorsed by Apelles seems plausible by now. The definition of הכופר בעיקר, that is, one who denies the essence of faith, as one who denies his Creator and the Giver of the Law (*Tos. Shabb.* iii.7) may be designed for Jews who asserted that both the creation and the communication of the Law were effected by the two principal angels.

There is definite evidence that the archangel Gabriel was regarded as the creator of the world. G. Quispel has noted that the demiurge of the Mandeans is named Gabriel[19]. There is no unified version of the cosmogony in the Mandean corpus, and different conceptions overlap; but mostly the demiurge is known as Ptahil[20], the secret name of whom, however, is said to be Gabriel. In the third book of the *Right Ginza*, which provides the most detailed information on the cosmogony, Bhaq-Ziwa, another name of Abathur, the "Third Life" of the Mandean pantheon and the father of Ptahil, figures as the inaugurator of the creation:

> He called Ptahil-Uthra, embraced him, and kissed him like a mighty one. He bestowed names on him which are hidden and protected in their place. He gave him the name Gabriel the Apostle; and he called him, gave command, and spoke to him: "Arise, go, and descend to the place where there are no shekinas or worlds. Call forth and create a world for yourself, just like the sons of perfection, whom you saw. Set up and establish a world, establish a world for yourself and make uthras in it [...] ."

(93.19 ff.)

Here, Bhaq-Ziwa, *i.e.*, Abathur, endows his son Ptahil-Gabriel with "Hidden Names", שומהאתא דכסעיא, and sends him out in order to create the world. Although the text speaks of "Hidden Names", that is, uses a plural form, the passage obviously is to be compared to *I Enoch* lxix.14 ff., where Michael is said to have been entrusted with "the Hidden Name", which is used in the Oath through which the whole cosmos is created and sustained. As suggested in Chapter III, the Mandean concept of the "Hidden Names" goes back to the Jewish doctrine of the unutterable Name of God, the *Shem ha-Mephorash*[21]. The Divine Name(s) is (are) an essential apparatus for the demiurge, the Angel of the Lord.

---

19 See "Jewish Gnosis", p. 119.
20 The name of Ptahil is differently explained; see Rudolph, *Mandäer*, I, p. 81, n. 4. Possibly, it preserves a West-Aramaic amalgamation of the Egyptian creator god Ptah and El, the high god of the Canaanites.
21 See p. 102, n. 74.

Several other Mandean texts name the demiurge Gabriel. In the thirteenth book of the *Right Ginza*, we find the following wording:

> Ptahil, the Apostle, whose name is Gabriel [...] who spanned out the sky without supports and solidified the earth without solidification through the strength of the Life and the word of his Father. [By him,] stars were fashioned in the sky; and fruits, grape-clusters, and trees were given to the earth. [From him,] radiance was brought to the sun, and brightness to the moon [...].

> (286.10 ff.)

The expression "Ptahil, whose name is Gabriel" occurs also in the *Baptism of Hibil-Ziwa*[22]. Behind the name of the demiurge Ptahil, we must discern the name of the angel Gabriel[23].

But not only Ptahil is said to carry the name Gabriel; the same is also said of Hibil-Ziwa, who is one of the messengers of light and figures as the demiurge in some texts. Thus, in a passage found in two recensions in the *Right Ginza*, we come across the identification of Hibil the demiurge with Gabriel:

> An uthra was called forth from the side of that Lord of Greatness and was sent out, whose name is Hibil-Ziwa and who is called Gabriel the Apostle [...]. He [*i.e.*, "the

---

22 Drower, line 56 in the text and p. 34 in the translation.

23 In a standard prayer formulary enumerating the prime deities of the Mandean pantheon, a figure called Yophin-Yophaphin (ירופין יורפאפין) occupies the place otherwise held by Ptahil, the "Fourth Life": "[...] to the First Life, the Second Life, the Third Life; to Yophin-Yophaphin; to Sam; to the well-preserved Mana; and the Vine that is wholly Life; and the Great Tree that is all healings [...]." Since this formula occurs several times both in the two parts of the Ginza and in the liturgical texts, Lidzbarski, *Ginza*, p. 191, n. 1, holds it to be very old. The texts where the formula is found are cited by K. Rudolph, *Theogonie, Kosmogonie und Anthropogonie in den mandäischen Schriften* (FRLANT, 88), Göttingen, 1965, pp. 57 ff. Yophin-Yophaphin is always associated with salvific figures or carrying out redemptory functions. In *Qol.* XXII, Yophin and another celestial being called Nbat appear side by side as emanations from the Life. For Nbat, see Rudolph, *Theogonie*, pp. 71 ff. Now, this Nbat is at least once described as the son of Ptahil; see E.S. Drower, ed. & trans., *Diwan Abatur* (ST, 151), the Vatican, 1950, p. 25. In another text, however, Nbat is represented as the son of Yophin (see *Right Ginza* 71.1). It is thus probable that Yophin(-Yophaphin) was regarded by some as still another secret name of Ptah the demiurge.

As the basic element of the name Yophin(-Yophaphin), namely, יו, shows, the name is to be explained against the background of Jewish theology. Lidzbarski, *Johannesbuch*, p. XXVII, suggests that the name is to be derived from the Jewish angel names Yophiel (ירפיאל) and Yophiphyah (יפיפיה). For these angels, see the references given by J. Michl, Art. "Engel V (Engelnamen)", *RAC*, V, col. 217 and col. 218. In *III En.* xlvii[d].1, "Yophiel" is said to be one of the secret names of Metatron. The connection with Metatron certainly is interesting, since the figure of Metatron has absorbed the names and functions of the Angel of the Lord as he appears in earlier traditions; see below, pp. 307 ff. Perhaps, then, Yophiel or the like, a name which actually contains the Name of God, was regarded as a cognomen of the Angel of the Lord, in whom God's Name dwelt.

Sublime King of Light"] said to him: "Go, trample down the darkness and the mysteries [Recen. B: "its inhabitants"] which were fashioned from it. Solidify the earth, span out the firmament and make stars in it. Give radiance to the sun, brightness to the moon and lustre to all the stars. Give the water a pleasant taste and radiance to fire. Call forth fruits, grapes and trees which look fine in the world. Let domestic animals, fishes and birds come into being, of every kind, male and female, and let them render service to Adam and his whole generation [...]. Let the four winds of the house [*i.e.*, the world] and the air, which blows over them, be called into being. May fire come into being and spread over the whole world [...]. Gabriel the Apostle [Recen. B: "Ptahil"] came, hoisted up the sky, spanned it out, and solidified the earth. [Recen. B: "He called forth the angels of fire, gave radiance to the sun, brightness to the moon, lustre to the stars, and he raised them to the heavenly sphere. Wind, fire, and water were planted. He also made domestic and wild animals of every kind from the dust..."] And he established it [*i.e.*, the earth] together with the whole world by the might of the Sublime King of Light.

(Recen. A: Book I, 12.14 ff.; Recen. B: Book II, 32.20 ff.)

Thus, whether the demiurge is called Ptahil or Hibil, his real name is Gabriel. Therefore the demiurge can also be known simply by the name of Gabriel. In a passage from the third book of the *Right Ginza*, the following speech is made by one of the messengers of light to Ur, the Lord of Darkness:

The wonderful living fire shall be established, and Gabriel the Apostle shall be called forth. He shall be called forth and commissioned; he will be sent hither. He shall be called forth and commissioned; he will call forth the earth. He shall come and perform solidification, and call forth the earth skilfully. He shall call forth the earth skilfully and stop the springs of turbid waters.

(7.9 ff.)

K. Rudolph avers that the idea about the creation performed by an angel commissioned by one of the highest divinities belongs to a later stage in the history of the Mandean religion. Over against this "monistic" version of the cosmogony, there is a "dualistic" version according to which the world is the work of Ptahil and the forces of chaos, who act contrary to the will of God. Rudolph holds the dualistic version to be the oldest one[24]. This may be right, but it does not follow that the doctrine of the creation of the world by the angel Gabriel is an innovation made by the Mandeans at a late stage in their history. The Mandeans may well have adopted this doctrine from a circle of Jewish Gnostics.

That the figure of Gabriel in Mandeism is derived from Islam, as Rudolph – following S.A. Pallis – asserts, seems improbable[25]. In Islam, the angel Gabriel is the bringer of the revelation to the Prophet; he is not a demiurgic figure. Rudolph tries to substantiate his thesis by equating the title שליהא, "Apostle", which is given to Gabriel in the Mandean texts, with the well-

---

24 See *Theogonie*, pp. 97 ff.
25 See *ibid.*, pp. 199 f.

known Islamic term *rasul*. This is most untenable; the term שליהא cannot
have been derived from another source than Judaism. As we have seen above,
in Judaism, שליח was used to designate a person having the power of attorney of another, and the angels could be seen as God's "apostles"[26].

Some rabbis even regarded the שליח as the שותף, "associate", of the
person he represented (see *Bab. Kamm.* 70a). It will be recalled that the
rabbis polemized against the notion that the Name of God was "associated"
with another object or person[27], and that the earliest parts of the theological
and liturgical literature of the Samaritans contain many polemics against a
teaching to the effect that God had an "associate" or "second" in the creation
and government of the universe[28]. There are Jewish analogues to these
polemics. In *Midrash Rabba*, we read:

> "There is one that is alone, and he has no second" (*Eccl.* iv.8). "There is One":
> that is the Holy One, blessed be He, of whom it is said: "The Lord our God, the Lord
> is One" (*Deut.* vi.4). "And He has no second": He has no associate in the universe.
> Yea, "He has neither son nor brother" (*Eccl.* iv.8): since He has no אח, whence
> should He have a son?
>
> (*Eccl.R.* iv.8)

The traditional interpretation of the passage is that אח is not to be construed as "brother" but as "consort", and the meaning of the phrase would
then be that God could not possibly have a son because he has no consort.
This denial seems to be best understood as a response to Christianity. However, in another version of the saying, appearing in *Deut.R.* ii.33, the terminating question is lacking; and, by itself, the denial that God is one of two
brothers might be taken as a refusal of some Zurvanite inspired doctrine,
where the good and evil principles were conceived of as twin brothers. Thus,
it is possible that the passage aims at discomfiting various heresies of binitarian, ditheistic, and dualistic nature. This agrees with the fact that the saying seems to belong to a late date, for, in *Deuteronomy Rabba*, it is attributed
to R. Aha, a Palestinian amora of the 4th century.

What is of importance in this connection, however, is the term used
to describe the second deity: שותף. The text does not speak expressly of the
work of creation, and the second deity seems to be regarded as the "associate" of God in the government of the universe. It was probably the heretics
themselves who designated the second deity as God's שותף; at least, this
seems to be implied in another passage:

> Our rabbis taught: "Adam was created on the eve of the Sabbath [*i.e.*, at the last
> moment of the sixth day]." And why? Lest the *minim* should say: "The Holy One,

---

26 See pp. 144f., 146.
27 See above, pp. 235f.
28 See above, pp. 194ff.

blessed be He, had an associate in His work of creation."
(Tos. Sanh. viii.7; Sanh. 38a)

In the Talmud, this saying appears in an amoraic anthology of Adam traditions, but its occurrence in the Tosefta evidences that it is quite old. The import of the saying is that Adam was created last of all beings, so that he could not be held to have assisted God in the work of creation. The designation used for the helper of God in the creative work is שותף, and it is used by the heretics (instead of reading "Sadducees", we ought to follow the manifold early versions which have *minim*; the former word has probably been inserted by the censors, who thought that *minim* always referred to the Christians). The locution שותף appears to be a technical description used by the heretics to designate God's agent in the creation and government of the universe. From the discussion of the Samaritan evidence, it will be known that the term שותף could be used technically to denote the sharing of divine status by means of God's Name. We ought to take especial note of the tradition that God regarded Abraham as having been "associated" with him in the creation because of the patriarch's knowledge of the Divine Name[29]. The second deity evidently was held to be God's "associate" in the work of creation in virtue of his sharing the Divine Name, the instrument of the creation.

It is helpful to review the rabbinic declaration denying that the angels were created on the first day:

> R. Luliana ben Tabri said in the name of R. Isaac: "Whether we accept the view of R. Ḥanina or of R. Yoḥanan, all agree that none [of the angels] were created on the first day, lest you should say: "Michael stretched forth in the south of the firmament, and Gabriel in the north, while the Holy One, blessed be He, measured it in the middle." "But I am the Lord who makes all things, who stretched forth the heavens alone, who spread abroad the earth מאתי" (*Is.* xliv.24). It is written מי אתי : "Who was associated with Me in the creation of the world?""
>
> (Gen. R. i.3; iii.8)

R. Isaac refers to a discussion between R. Ḥanina and R. Yoḥanan (the latter was R. Isaac's teacher) about the day on which the angels were created. However the opinions differ, the rabbis agree that the angels were not created on the first day, so as not to give an occasion to assert that the two principal angels were God's assistants in the work of creation taking place on the five following days. R. Isaac finds a scriptural support for the orthodox position in *Is.* xliv.24: he sides with the LXX, the *Kethib*, some thirty mss., and lQ *Isa* in reading *mî ʾittî*, "Who was with Me?," over against some of the best of the mss. and the *Qere*, which have "from with Me", usually taken to mean "by Myself". Thus, R. Isaac derives a rhetorical question from the passage. The Hebrew text runs: מי היה שותף עמי בבריית העולם . The rhetorical

---

29 See above, p. 247.

question apparently is aimed at people who actually claimed that the principal angels were God's שותפים, "associates", in the work of creation.

After this discussion of the terms שליח and שותף in Jewish religion, it seems justified to conclude that the Mandean concept of the demiurge Gabriel שליהא derives from a Jewish teaching about the angel Gabriel being God's שליח and שותף, "apostle" and "associate", in creation by virtue of his possession of the Divine Name[30].

The Heavenly Man

In this section, we shall follow up the problem posed by the text implying that there were heretics who held that Adam had acted as God's "associate" in the creation. The rabbis retorted against these people that the Bible tells that Adam was made after the rest of the creation was completed[31]. That there

---

30 Already W. Brandt, *Die Mandäer* (VKAWA, 16/3), Amsterdam, 1915, p. 25, passed the correct judgment that the figure of Gabriel in Mandeism could only belong to a layer of tradition which derives from a period in which the Jewish element was dominating. Quispel, "Jewish Gnosis", pp. 117 ff., has drawn attention to the fact that the demiurge in Mandean writings often is called *sakla*, "fool". *Saklas* is also a name of the demiurge in several primitive Gnostic systems with a marked Jewish tinge (*e.g.*, the *Apocryphon of John* and the *Apocalypse of Adam*). The creator of the world is called a fool because he does not know that there is a higher God above him: he boasts that he is the only god, quoting or paraphrasing *Deut*. xxxii.39 and *Is*. xliv.6 (and/or xlvi.9). That the demiurge is called "Fool" with a name from Aramaic is perfectly understandable in a Jewish milieu, for Scripture states that the man who says in his heart that there is no God must be considered a "fool" (*Ps*. xiv.1); cp. Quispel, "Origins", pp. 275 f. Thus, naming the demiurge *sakla* also evidences the Jewish origin of Mandeism, though the idea of the angelic demiurge as a "fool" derives from a later stage in the development of Gnosticism.

We can note also that the Manicheans called the demiurge a fool. Augustine reports that the archon that was responsible for the creation of man was named Saklas (see *De haer. ad Quod.* xlvi.4). Theodore bar Konai (*Book of Scholia* ch. 11), quoting from one of Mani's own writings, gives the name of the archon as *Ashaklun*, which is obviously the same word.

31 Another polemic against the idea that Adam had acted as a demiurge seems to be present in *Gen.R.* xix.4, where the serpent's words in *Gen.* iii.5, "... you will be as Elohim, knowing good and evil," are said to have implied the false promise that man would be able to create new worlds if he would eat from the Tree of Knowledge. R. Tanhuma reports that he in Antioch had to silence some people by arguing that the plural verb form in ידעי אלהים does not refer to "Elohim", but to "you will be," thus safeguarding the monotheistic dogma. In *Ps.-Clem. Hom.* XVI.6, this Scriptural verse is actually said to have been used by Simon Magus as proof that there are more than one God. Since *Gen.* iii.5 obviously was used as a polytheistic argument, the rabbis found even the notion that Adam was God's "fellow craftsman" to be implied in the words of the serpent, for the idea that God had a co-creator connoted the tenet that the latter shared God's own Name, *i.e.*, the divine nature or mode of being.

was a heavenly Man who preceded Adam, whose creation is narrated in *Gen.* i.26 f., is a teaching found in many Gnostic systems, but there is very slight evidence that the Gnostics ascribed demiurgic functions to the heavenly Man. In the fragmentary texts of the *Gospel of the Egyptians* from the Nag Hammadi library, Adamas, "[a light] which radiated [from the light] ," is "the first Man, he through whom and to whom everything became, and without whom nothing became" (Codex IV, 61.8 ff., and Codex III, 49.10 ff.). In the so-called "Naassene Homily", summarized by Hippolytus, the celestial Adamas is said to have brought the chaotic matter to rest in primordial times (see VI.viii.22). Furthermore, it is he who constantly rotates the universe in a circle (see VI.viii.34). Finally, he emits the world ocean which is surrounding the universe (see VI.viii.20). In *Poimandres,* the first tractate of *Corpus Hermeticum,* Anthropos, the heavenly Man, is said to have "wished himself to create, and was permitted by the Father" (13). "But here the world is already created, and it is difficult to see what the Man either in collaboration or in competition with the Demiurge has still left for him to do. Nor does the subsequent narrative provide an answer to this question ... . These inconsistencies suggest that we have here an adapted form of the Anthropos myth, with some traces of an original cosmogonic function of the figure faintly preserved."[32]

Poimandres 4 ff. is some sort of exposition of *Gen.* ch. i[33]; Anthropos is brought forth after the irrational beasts have been produced by earth (cp. *Gen.* i.20 ff.), and his origin is described with clear reference to *Gen.* i.27 f.: "Now the Nous, Father of all, being Life and Light, brought forth Man, who was like him, whom He loved as His own child, for he was very beautiful and wore his Father's image. Indeed, even God loved his own form and delivered over to him all his creatures" (12). Furthermore, it is said that Anthropos "was androgynous, having issued from the androgynous Father [...]" (15), and there was in fact an interpretation which deduced from *Gen.* i.27 that the first man was a hermaphrodite[34].

In spite of the fact that *Poimandres* is wholly free from specially Christian features but replete with Jewish elements, it is perhaps wise not to consider it a Jewish document[35]. However, among the many agreements between *Poi-*

---

32 Jonas, *Gnostic Religion*, pp. 155 f.

33 This was pointed out by E. Meyer, *Ursprung und Anfänge des Christentums*, II, Stuttgart & Berlin, 1921, pp. 375 f., and has been amply demonstrated by C.H. Dodd, *The Bible and the Greeks*, London, 1935, pp. 99 ff. However, E. Haenchen, "Aufbau und Theologie des 'Poimandres'", *ZTK*, 53, 1956, pp. 149 ff., has modified Dodd's interpretation by demonstrating that the author has used a number of sources.

34 See above, p. 208, n. 37.

35 B.A. Pearson, although demonstrating the Jewish apocalyptic structure of *Poimandres* as a whole and the Jewish influence in chs. 27 ff., concludes that "we are not,

mandres and Philo, we find the tenet that *Gen.* i.27 describes the creation of a heavenly Man, so this would not have to be considered a pagan interpretation. As is well known, Philo could find the creation of the heavenly Man described in *Gen.* i.26 f., while he took *Gen.* ii.7 to refer to the creation of the earthly man (see *De op. mundi* 134; *Leg. all.* I.31; 53 ff.; 88 ff.; II.4; *Quaest. in Gen.* I.4; II.56). The heavenly Man is therefore called ὁ κατ᾽ εἰκόνα ἄνθρωπος and said to have been created κατ᾽ εἰκόνα θεοῦ.

In other passages, however, Philo takes *Gen.* i.26 f. to refer to the creation of the earthly man, and interprets the "image (and likeness)" of God after which man was created as pertaining to the Logos. He says: "Why does it say, as if [speaking] of another god: "in the image of god He made man" and not "in His own image"? " (*Quaest. in Gen.* II.62). Philo answers the question himself: "It is because nothing can be made in the likeness of God but only "in that of the second god (πρὸς τὸν δεύτερον θεόν), who is His Logos."[36]

This prepares us for passages in which the heavenly Man is identified with the Logos. Philo gives the following comment on *Gen.* xlii.11 ("We are all sons of one man; we are peaceful"): "How should you not hate war and love peace, you who have enrolled yourselves as children of one and the same

---

after all, dealing with a Jewish text, but with a "Hermetic" one," and that the work is a "curious mixture of Jewish piety and Hermetic paganism" ("Jewish Elements in *Corpus Hermeticum* I (*Poimandres*)", in *Studies*, p. 346 and p. 347). The ground for his judgement is that the "creed" of *Poimandres* is that *gnosis* comes by means of self-knowledge through the guidance of Hermes Trismegistus. On the other hand, H. Ludin Jansen, "Die Frage nach Tendenz und Verfasserschaft im Poimandres", in G. Widengren & D. Hellholm, ed., *Proceedings of the International Colloquium on Gnosticism, Stockholm, August 20-25, 1973* (KVHAH, Filol.-filos. ser. 17), Stockholm, 1977, pp. 157 ff., sees the author as a Jew who has lived through the mystical experiences described in chs. 1 ff., 27 ff., and thus the document itself as a Jewish Gnostic writing. But if the author really was a Jew by upbringing, he has stepped far outside his tradition when choosing a non-Jewish καθοδηγός.

36 Philo goes on to say that the rational part of man was formed on the model of the Logos. This he also states in *De op. mundi* 69, where he interprets the Logos as the "image and likeness" in *Gen.* i.26 f. However, in other passages where the same interpretation is found, the "image (and likeness)" is (are) not said to relate specifically to the mind (see *Leg. all.* III.96; *Quis rer. her.* 230 f.; *De op. mundi* 25; 139). (In *Quaest. in Gen.* I.4, "the Man made in accordance with [God's] form (εἶδος)" is a *copy* of the Logos and the incorporeal model of the earthly man whose creation is narrated in *Gen.* ii.7.)

That the image after which Adam was created had an independent existence is an idea which also crops up in rabbinism. Thus, God is said to be blessed because "He made man in His image, in the image of the likeness of His form (יצר את האדם בצלמו בצלם דמות תבניתו)" (*Keth.* 8a). This means that "Adam was created after the image of a God-created type (תבנית)" (L. Ginzberg, Art. "Adam Kadmon", in *JE*, I, 1901 and reprints, p. 183, col. a). Cp. the usage of דיוקן in *Ps.-Jon. Targ. Gen.* v.1, 3 and *Moed Qatan* 15b. See also below, p. 277, n. 57.

father, who is not mortal but immortal, God's Man (ἄνθρωπον θεοῦ), who, being the Logos of the Eternal (τοῦ ἀιδίου λόγος), must needs himself be imperishable?" (*De conf. ling.* 41). A little further on, Philo says:

> But, if there be any as yet unfit to be called son of God, let him press to take his place under God's Firstborn (πρωτόγονος), the Logos, who holds the eldership among the angels, their ruler as it were. And many names are his, for he is called "Beginning", and "the Name of God", and His "Logos", and "Man after His image" (ὁ κατ᾽ εἰκόνα ἄνθρωπος), and "He that sees", that is, Israel.
>
> (146)

Philo goes on to state: "And, therefore, I was moved a few pages above to praise the virtues of those who say that "we are all sons of one man," for – if we have not yet become fit to be thought of as sons of God, still we may be sons of His invisible Image, the most holy Logos, since the Logos is the eldest-born Image of God."[37]

Summing up the Philonic evidence surveyed above, we note an inner inconsistency: on the one hand, the heavenly Man, even the Logos, is said to have been created *after* the image and likeness of God; on the other hand, the Man-Logos *is* that Image, after which the earthly man was created. There can be little doubt that the former interpretation is absurd and secondary.

The latter notion is found in several Gnostic sources. Thus, the "Naassene Homily" says that Adam, the first earthly man, was "an image (εἰκόνα) of that celestial being praised in song, the Man Adamas" (Hipp., V.vii.6). In *On the Origin of the World* from Codex II of the Nag Hammadi Library, a "likeness (ЄΙΝЄ) of Man" (108.8) called "Light-Adam" (108.21) is the model of the earthly man, whom the demiurge urges his angels to create "[...] according to the likeness (ЄΙΝЄ) of that one [...]" (112.35-113.1).

Although *Poimandres* refers *Gen.* i.27 to the heavenly Man, it does teach that the earthly man was made after the image of the heavenly Man. The latter, as we have seen, "wore his Father's image (εἰκόνα)" and even *was* his "form" (μορφή). This "form" was reflected and became hypostasized in matter, and Anthropos fell in love with it and "came to inhabit the irrational form (μορφήν)" (14). Thus arose the primal man. Later, it is told that "Matter produced bodies after the form (εἶδος) of Anthropos" (17).

The term μορφή simply is interchangeable and synonymous with צלם/εἰκών and דמות/ὁμοίωσις, which are used in *Gen.* i.26 f. Like *Poimandres*, the *Sibylline Oracles* use εἰκών and μορφή together with allusion to *Gen.* i.26 f.: "Men, you who possess μορφήν created by God in [His] εἰκόνι [...]" (III.8; cp. 27; VIII.265 ff.; 440). Here, μορφή seems to have replaced ὁμοίωσις

---

37 The Logos is said to be God's "image" in several passages (see, for instance, *De fuga* 101; *De somn.* I.239; II.45). In *De conf. ling.* 62 f., the heavenly Man, without being explicitly identified with the Logos, is called the "image" of God; see below, p. 287.

(דמות). Conversely, the Peshitta version of *Phil.* ii.6 uses the Syriac form of דמות in the translation of the μορφὴ θεοῦ in which Christ is said to have been. On the other hand, LXX *Dan.* iii.19 uses μορφή to translate צלם, which is usually rendered by εἰκών. Furthermore, many Church Fathers saw the μορφὴ θεοῦ in *Phil.* ii.6 as a parallel to the Christological title εἰκὼν τοῦ θεοῦ in *II Cor.* iv.4 and *Col.* i.15[38]. That μορφή could equal צלם / εἰκών as well as דמות/ὁμοίωσις is perfectly logical[39], for these two pair of concepts — whatever be their original meaning and their respective nuances — were used interchangeably and synonymously[40]. Thus, Gnostics such as those responsible for *On the Origin of the World* and *Poimandres* as well as Philo testify to a tradition which hypostasizes the "image and likeness" of God in *Gen.* i.26 f. as a heavenly Man.

R. Reitzenstein and W. Bousset asserted that Philo's heavenly Man, that is, the Logos, was an echo of the Gnostic Anthropos[41], but it is extremely complicated to maintain the thesis of the existence of a pre-Christian Gnosticism. Moreover, E. Bréhier and H. Leisegang have shown conclusively that the metaphysical Man in Philo's works can be satisfactorily explained as having evolved from a Platonic exegesis of *Genesis*[42]. However, it would not be right to follow E. Meyer and W. Scott, who simply reverse the Reitzenstein-Bousset hypothesis and explain the origin of the Gnostic Anthropos as a development from the heavenly Man in Philo[43]. The celestial Man in Philo's system is first and foremost a philosophical concept, whereas the Gnostic Anthropos is a figure of mythological plasticity and vitality. Even if we doubt that *mythos* in every case precedes *logos*, we would have to ask the following question: *Why* did Philo develop the teaching about a heavenly Man? Obviously, we cannot simply assume that a mixture of *Genesis* and Plato would have produced the Man teaching of Philo. *Genesis* is certainly not encouraging a glorification of Adam, and Plato's philosophy places no special emphasis upon the idea of man.

---

38 See J. Jervell, *Imago Dei* (FRLANT, 76), Göttingen, 1960, pp. 203 f.

39 Jervell, pp. 167 f., 204, also points out that דמות stands for both εἰκών and μορφή in Mandean texts.

40 S. Kim, *The Origin of Paul's Gospel* (WUNT, 2. Reihe, 4), Tübingen, 1981, pp. 200 ff., gives a convenient survey citing all the relevant literature.

41 See Reitzenstein, *Poimandres*, Leipzig, 1904, p. 110; Bousset, *Hauptprobleme*, pp. 194 ff.

42 See Bréhier, *Les idées philosophiques et religieuses du Philon d'Alexandrie*, Paris, 1907, pp. 121 ff.; Leisegang, *Pneuma Hagion* (VFVRUL, 4), Leipzig, 1922, pp. 102 ff.; cp. p. 78, n. 5.

43 See Meyer, pp. 371 ff.; Scott, ed. & trans., *Hermetica*, II (Notes on the Corpus Hermeticum), Oxford, 1925, reprinted London, 1968, pp. 4 f. Bousset, *Religion*, 3rd ed. by Gressman, p. 353, correctly points out that Philo is not simply evidencing an *exegesis* of the Biblical text.

Furthermore, if Philo merely read *Genesis* through Platonic glasses, how could he possibly develop a celebration not only of the heavenly Man but also of the *first earthly* man? It is palpable that Philo assigned enormous import to the first man. Thus, he says:

> That first man, born of earth, ancestor of our whole race, was made – as I gather – most excellent in each part of his being, in both soul and body, and greatly excelling those who came after him in the transcendent qualities of both alike; for this man was the one truly beautiful and good.
>
> > *(De op. mundi* 136)

The text of *Genesis* certainly does not offer a warrant for this extolment of the first man. Now it is true that, according to Philo, Adam is made in the likeness and imitation of God's Logos, and that "the copy of an especially beautiful model must by necessity itself be very beautiful" (*ibid.* 139), but Philo apparently was also dependent upon a certain tradition. A little further on, we read:

> Quite excellently, Moses ascribes the bestowal of names also to the first man; for this is the undertaking of wisdom and royalty, and the first man was wise through a wisdom learned and taught by Wisdom's own lips; for he was made by divine hands. He was, moreover, a king; and it befits a ruler to bestow titles on his several subordinates. And we may guess that the sovereignty with which that first man was invested was a most lofty one, seeing that God has fashioned him with utmost care and deemed him worthy of the second place, making His own viceroy and lord of all others.
>
> > (148)

That Adam was made God's vice-king over the creation is an old and widespread tradition which is elaborated upon particularly in the so-called Adam literature[44]. Thus, in the Syrian *Cave of Treasure*, a Christian work from the 6th century, it is said:

> When the angels saw his [*viz.*, Adam's] splendid appearance, they were moved by the fairness of his countenance. And God gave him the dominion over all creatures, and over all the wild animals and the cattle, and all the birds. And they all came before Adam, and he gave them names. And they bowed their heads before him and

---

44 The term "Adam (or, "Adamic") literature" is applied to a group of accounts of the lives and vicissitudes of Adam and the Adamites. These writings have come down to us in Greek, Latin, Syriac, Ethiopic, Armenian, and Slavonic. In all of them, there are to be discovered Christian elements, but there is general agreement that the Adam literature has grown out of Jewish midrashic occupation with the first chapters of *Genesis*. In the *Apocalypse of Adam* from Codex V of the Nag Hammadi library, we have now a non-Christian Gnostic adaptation of the sort of material found in the Adam literature.

worshipped him, and all their natures worshipped him and served him. And the angels and the powers heard the voice of God, who said to him: "O Adam, behold! I have made you king, priest, prophet, ruler, head, and guide of all creatures. They shall serve you and belong to you. And I have given you dominion over all I have created." And when the angels heard this word, they all bent their knees and worshipped him.[45]

In a Coptic discourse on the Angel of Death, Abbaton by name, delivered by Timothy, patriarch of Alexandria in the 4th century, we also find the idea of Adam being installed in heaven as the viceroy of God. The discourse on Abbaton is attributed to a revelation by Christ himself. After the narration about the creation of Adam, Christ goes on to tell:

> Thereupon, my Father set him upon a great throne, and he placed upon his head a crown of glory, and he put a royal sceptre [in his hand]. And my Father bade every order [of angels] in the heavens to come and worship him, whether angel or archangel. And all the hosts of heaven worshipped God at first, and then they worshipped Adam, saying: "Hail, you image and likeness of God!" And He intended that the order of the angels who were fashioned [before Adam] should worship him; and my Father said to him, that is, to their chief: "Come, you, too, shall worship My image and likeness!"
>
> (13a)

Timothy states that he has transcribed the discourse from an ancient volume which he has found in the library in Jerusalem, and which "had been made by our holy fathers, the apostles" (1b). Of course, we cannot trust this information, but it does seem that the myth about Adam being installed as God's vice-king goes back to old sources. Since it is testified to already by Philo, the myth must be of Jewish origin. As a matter of fact, there are several Jewish witnesses to this tradition about Adam. Thus, R. Tanḥuma bar Abba, a Palestinian amora of the 2nd half of the 4th century, taught the following:

> God intended to make him [i.e., Adam] the ruler of this world and the king over all His creation. God said: "I am king in the upper worlds (מלך בעליונים); let Adam be king in the nether worlds (מלך בתחתונים).
>
> (Pesikta Rabbati xlviii.2)

R. Tanḥuma goes on to relate that God brought Adam into the Garden of Eden and made him king there. He supports this by quoting Gen. ii.8b: "And there he set man." As proofs the rabbi quotes Deut. xvii.15, "You shall in any wise set him king over you," and I Kings ii.19, "And the King ... caused a throne to be set for the king's mother."

A. Altmann thinks that the lofty position assigned to the first man in the Adamic literature and reflected in certain rabbinic traditions (some of them of a polemical nature) is rooted in the Gnostic doctrine of the glorious primal

---

45 Bezold, p. 5.

man[46], but scattered references in the apocrypha and the pseudepigrapha as well as in Philo's works evidence that the relationship is to be explained the other way round. In *II Enoch* (also known as the *Slavonic Book of Enoch* or the *Book of the Secrets of Enoch*), God says of Adam:

> I placed him upon earth, a second angel, honourable, great and glorious; and I appointed him as a ruler to rule the earth and to have My wisdom; and there was none like him on earth of all My existing creatures.
>
> (xxx.11 ff.)

Here, it is expressly stated that Adam is God's principal angel. He is a very glorious being, endowed with the wisdom of God and installed as God's vicegerent over the whole world. The next chapter relates that God created the Garden of Eden and that Adam abided there. The Garden is in the third heaven (see ch. viii; cp. *II Cor.* xii.3 f.), from where Adam could clearly see the angels before the throne of God (see xxxi.2). Abiding continuously in Paradise, he was "lord on earth, ruling and controlling it" (xxxi.3).

II Enoch is extant in two versions which are dated differently. The citations made here are not found in the short recension, which is the older one and stems from the first century B.C.E., but apocryphal literature matches Philo as pre-Christian evidence for the notion of Adam being God's vicegerent and king in Paradise. In the *Book of Sirach*, it is said: "Above every living thing in the creation is Adam" (xlix.16). This declaration follows immediately upon the great praises of Enoch, Joseph, Shem, and Seth, and is the culmination of the strange part known as "the Praise of the Fathers" (xliv.1–xlix. 16). This allusion to the elevated state of Adam is evidently the reflection of a larger mythological picture. In the *Book of Wisdom*, we find two cognate statements about Adam. In ch. ix, God is addressed the following way:

> You, God of my fathers, merciful Lord, who have created all things by Your Word, and through Your Wisdom equipped man so that he should have dominion over the creatures which were made by You, and rule the world in holiness and righteousness, and execute judgment in rightfulness.
>
> (*vv.* 2 f.)

That "man" in this statement does not intend the generic idea of man but

---

46 See "The Gnostic Background of the Rabbinic Adam Legends", *JQR*, 25, 1945, pp. 371 ff. There are several texts relating that the angels and the creatures who wanted to worship Adam were set right – either by God or by Adam himslf (see, for instance, *Gen.R.* viii.10; *Pirke de R. Eliezer* ch. 11). A genuinely Jewish aggada narrating that God commanded the angels to worship Adam is found in the *Midrash Rabbati* which was fathered on R. Moses ha-Darshan of Narbonne, who lived in the 11th century. This story is also quoted by Raymundus Martinus, *Pugio fidei*, p. 563, where it is told that Satan was cast down when he refused to pay honour to Adam. This is perhaps a later addition, since it is not found in the extant ms. of *Midrash Rabbati*. However, the story is very old; see below, p. 274, n. 48.

the individual first man, Adam, is shown by the parallel in ch. x. Here, it is said that Wisdom guarded Adam and gave him "strength to get dominion over all things" (*vv*.1 f)[47].

The authors who glorified Adam obviously felt discomfortable when they had to account the fall and its aftermath. The Adamic literature underlines strongly that it was Eve, and not Adam, who transgressed God's command (see, for instance, *Life of Adam and Eve* ch. 18; cp. ch. 16; *II En.* xxxi.6; *I Tim.* ii.4). In Jewish apocryphal and pseudepigraphic literature, there is a clear tendency to shift the blame for the present degraded state of man from Adam to others (see *Wisd.* x.3; *I En.* ch. vi; *Jub.* v.1 ff.). Some taught that Adam repented and was reinstated in Paradise (see *Wisd.* x.1 f.; *Epist. Apost.* ch. 39; Tert., *De paen.* xii.9, quoting from a lost apocryphon), while the Jewish Christian group responsible for the *Pseudo-Clementines* even denied that he sinned (see *Hom.* III.17; 21; cp. II.52).

In the Adamic literature, it is claimed that Adam will be reinstated at the end of days; then Adam will be re-installed in the position intended for him. When Adam is buried in Paradise, God declares:

> Your sorrow I will turn to joy, and I will install you again in your power upon the throne of your seducer; but he shall be cast down, so that he can see you be enthroned above himself. Then he and they who obeyed him shall be condemned, and they shall grieve and cry, when they see you sit on his precious throne.
>
> *(Apoc. Mos.* xxxix.3 ff.)

In *Life of Adam and Eve* ch. 47, God delivers the body of Adam over to the archangel Michael with these words:

> He shall be in your custody until the day of avengement in punishment until the last years, when I will turn his sorrow to delight. Then, he shall be placed upon the throne of him who seduced him.

Throughout the Adam literature, it is related that Adam was created to take the place of Satan, who was the prince of all the angels and the ruler of this world[48]. Satan, however, managed to cause Adam to sin and usurped the rule over the world, which he now conducted perversely. But Adam is prom-

---

47 For the context, see below, p. 285.

48 Satan was cast down from heaven because he refused to worship Adam (see *Life of Adam and Eve* chs. 13 ff.; *Discourse on Abbaton* 13b-14a; *Cave of Treasure*, in Bezold, p. 5). There are several references to this myth in the Quran (see ii.27 ff.; vii.10 ff.; xv.26 ff.; xvii.62 ff.; xx.114 ff.; xxxviii.71 ff.). In the Armenian Adam literature, which goes back to a Greek source (possibly by way of a Semitic translation) and is dated to the 5th century, Satan is thrown down *before* the creation of Adam because he tried to "raise his throne to the equal elevation of the throne of God" (Preuschen, p. 27). In *Life of Adam and Eve* ch. 15, however, Satan threatens to do this if God becomes angry with him because of his refusal to worship Adam.

ised to regain his position as God's lieutenant and be seated upon the throne
of the ruler of this world at the end of times[49].

In order to account for the glorious picture of Adam in Jewish tradition,
scholars have postulated an influence from various *Urmensch* figures in Iranian and Semitic religion[50]. However, Jewish tradition had for centuries
cherished the notion of a figure of the "likeness as the appearance of Adam"
being seated on a heavenly throne, and it would seem that the picture of
Adam in the texts surveyed above is due to a *rapprochement* between the
Kabod, the heavenly Man, and the first earthly man. Unequivocal evidence
for this is furnished by the *Testament of Abraham*, a Jewish writing which
has been dated to the first century C.E. Here, it is related that Abraham was
taken up to heaven, where he saw two gates, one leading to Paradise and the
other to hell. Outside the two gates, he saw an "all-marvellous Man" (ὁ ἀνὴρ

---

49 In the Armenian literature, Adam is seated upon the *divine* throne; see Preuschen,
p. 25. The expectation in the Dead Sea Scrolls of a restoration of כבוד אדם to the
community (see 1 Q S iv.23; *CD* iii.20; 1 Q H xvii.15; cp. 4 Q p Ps. 37 iii.1 f.; 1 Q H
viii.4 ff.) must probably also be taken to reflect traditions like those examined above.
It is totally anachronistic to state that this Adam figure is not only "the Biblical
Adam, the Lord of creation; but also, no doubt, mythical Man, the Anthropos of
Gnostic speculation" (A. Dupont-Sommer, trans., *The Essene Writings*, trans. by
G. Vermes, Oxford, 1961, p. 82, n. 3).

50 This postulation is a corollary of the hypothesis that the figure of the Son of Man
and the Gnostic Anthropos have a common root in an Oriental *Urmensch* figure.
This hypothesis is now relinquished, but it is still possible that the picture of the
glorious Adam in Jewish traditions owes to reflections on the portrait of some
Oriental *Urmensch* figure. Since the great master of the *religionsgeschichtliche
Schule,* Richard Reitzenstein, pointed to Gayomart, a primal man figure in Iranian religion, as the basis for the development of the Gnostic Anthropos, his associates and
followers have seen a more or less Gnosticized form of Gayomart as the model upon
which the novel Adam image was formed; see, for instance, C.H. Kraeling, *Anthropos
and Son of Man* (CUOS, XXV), New York, 1927, reprinted 1966, pp. 158 ff. But the
sources from which we can reconstruct a Gayomart mythology are mainly the late Pehlevi texts, and a more interesting personage from Iranian religion would seem to be
Yima, the first man and king of paradise who became the ruler of the realm of the
blessed dead; see H. Gressmann, *Der Ursprung der israelitisch-jüdischen Eschatologie*
(FRLANT, 6), Göttingen, 1905, pp. 272 ff., 362 ff., who held the untenable hypothesis that Yima was the ancestor of the Son of Man. However, the links between
Iran and Palestine are tenuous, and Iranian elements are elusive in Mesopotamia from
the time of the Arsacides, *i.e.*, from 250 B.C.E. onwards, until the first century B.C.E.,
when the Iranian elements gradually begin to reassert themselves. We must also note
that several scholars have argued that the ancient Semites held the first man to be the
first king and thus the present king as the representative of the former. F.H. Borsch,
The Son of Man in Myth and History (NTL), London, 1967, pp. 75 ff., 89 ff.,
surveys both the Iranian and Semitic material and emphasizes the interrelationship
of various *Urmensch* figures and even the archetypal nature of the idea in question;
see especially pp. 84 ff., with reservation regarding Iranian influence.

ὁ πανθαύμαστος) "sitting on a golden throne" and watching the godly entering into Paradise and the wicked going to hell (ch. 11). It is said that "the
appearance of the Man (ἡ ἰδέα τοῦ ἀνθρώπου) was fearsome, like unto that
of the Lord." There can be no doubt that this description of the Man alludes
to LXX *Ez.* i.26, where the Kabod upon the heavenly throne is described as
ὁμοίωμα ὡς εἶδος ἀνθρώπου[51]. Upon inquiring about the identity of the
Man, however, Abraham learns that it is "the protoplast Adam". Thus, Adam
is enthroned in heaven as the Glory at the end of times.

It might be objected that the Kabod does not sit at the gate of heaven, but
has his seat in the innermost of the heavenly world, and that Adam in *Test.
Abr.* ch. 11 therefore occupies a position inferior to the divine Glory. However, there were obviously different traditions regarding the place of the
throne of God's vicegerent. In the *Mystery of Sandalphon*, Elisha ben Abuya
says: "When I ascended to Paradise, I beheld Akatriel YHWH, the Lord of the
hosts, who is sitting at the entrance of Paradise (פתח פרדס), and 120
myriads of ministering angels surrounded him."[52] Neither the personal name
of the second power in heaven nor the site of his throne agrees with the traditional form of the story of the four sages who entered Paradise[53], but the
salient point – *i.e.*, that he is viewed as a divine hypostasis through his possession of the Name of God – is retained. Apparently, God's vicegerent, depicted as the Angel of the Lord or the Glory, could be recognized under different
names and seen enthroned in various places in the heavenly world. In *Test.
Abr.* ch. 11, Adam occupies the position of the Glory on his throne at the
gate of Paradise.

The *Testament of Abraham* leaves no doubt that it adopts and adapts
traditions about the Kabod, for it goes on to depict a "wondrous Man (ἀνήρ)
shining like the sun", who sits on a fiery crystal throne and judges the souls
of men (ch. 13). This vision has pertinently been compared to that of the
Great Glory in the very early version of heavenly journey in *I En.* ch. xiv,
which – in turn – clearly recalls *Ez.* ch. i[54]. In *I En.* xiv.20, the Great Glory

---

51 God is repeatedly called "fearsome" (δεσπότης) in chs. 13 f.; thus, the Man is his
    delegate.
52 MS. Oxford 1531, 60a; quoted by Scholem, *Jewish Gnosticism*, p. 53. R. Ishmael
    is reported to have seen Akatriel Yah seated on a throne in the Holy of Holies in
    the Jerusalem temple (see *Ber.* 7a). On the idea of an angel abiding in the temple,
    see above, p. 238, n. 89. According to *Ezekiel* (ix.3; x.1, 4), the Glory sits on the
    cherubim throne in the Holy of Holies.
53 For the Talmudical form of the story, where the name of the figure is "Metatron",
    see below, pp. 308f. In *III Enoch* (or, the *Hebrew Book of Enoch*), Metatron is said
    to sit on his throne outside the hall of God (see x.2; xlviii [c].8); see below, p. 298.
    See also "Great" *Yalqut Reubeni* II.66b.
54 See G.H. McCurdy, "Platonic Orphism in the Testament of Abraham", *JBL*, 61,
    1942, p. 224.

is said to wear clothes more radiant than the sun and whiter than the snow, and to sit on a crystal throne surrounded by fire.

The Man in *Test. Abr.* ch. 13, however, is no longer Adam, but Abel, "the son of Adam, the protoplast", but it is on account of his father that he holds his lofty position: "For every man has sprung from Adam the protoplast, and therefore here first by his son all are judged."[55] The glory ascribed to Adam apparently has passed over to his son[56].

In the Adamic literature, there is still another characteristic of Adam which shows that he has assimilated features belonging to the Glory. As we have seen above, the *Discourse on Abbaton* says that Adam was the "image and likeness" of God. This is not a late accretion to the tradition glorifying Adam, for already the *Life of Adam and Eve* relates that Michael summoned all the angels, commanding them: "Worship the image of God the Lord, as the Lord has commanded!" (ch. 14)[57]. Thus, Adam is no longer made in or

---

55 The references to the *Testament of Abraham* are to the long recension. In ch. 10 of the short recension, the Man is described as being of exceedingly great stature and wearing three golden crowns. The ascription of immense stature to the Man apparently must be seen in the light of the Merkaba mystics' descriptions of שָׁעוּר קוֹמָה, the "Measurement of the Body", *i.e.*, the body of the divine Glory, which was of enormous size; cp. above, p. 180. The attribution of three crowns to the Man is reminiscent of the relation in the *Pseudo-Clementines* that Adam wore the crowns of kingship, priesthood, and prophethood (see *Rec.* I.46). The *Clementina* actually hold Adam to be an incarnation of Christ, whom the Jewish Christians regarded as the Glory of God; see Fossum, "Christology", pp. 267, 269.

56 We might here remember that Enoch, who is the seventh son and thus the true representative of Adam, is elevated to the position and rôle of the Son of Man in *I En.* lxxi.14 ff., for the figure of the Son of Man clearly denotes the Glory; see below, p. 279. We may also note that Adam and all the subsequent bearers of the revelation in the *Pseudo-Clementines* are given the title of the Son of Man (see *Hom.* II.17; III.22; 26). F. Schmidt, ed. & trans., *Le Testament d'Abraham*, Diss., I, Strassbourg, 1971, pp. 64 f., suggests that the Greek translator of the Semitic original of the *Testament of Abraham* misunderstood *ben adam* to mean "son of Adam", thus Abel, whereas it should have been translated "Son of Man".

57 See also *Apoc. Mos.* ch. 33; 35. Adam is also called the image of God in *Ps.-Clem. Hom.* III.17; cp. above n. 55. There are some statements to the same effect even in rabbinic literature. Thus, it is told that, when R. Banaah, after having seen the grave of Abraham, came to the grave of Adam, he was told by a *bath qol*: "You have seen the likeness of My image (בדמות דיוקני); My image itself (בדיוקני עצמה) you are not allowed to see" (*Baba Bathra* 58a). (איקונין) דיוקן is, of course, a loan-word denoting εἰκών and thus synonymous with צלם (and דמות); see the survey by Kim, pp. 203 f. Jervell, pp. 97 ff., suggests that the distinction between *Urbild* and *Abbild* in rabbinism reflects the traditions which we have found in Philo and Gnosticism. That Adam as the very דיוקן of God is regarded as far more than the first man created afte the image of God is suggested by the prohibition to look upon his body. Originally, however, the second-grade likeness to God pertained to Adam himself. Cp. above, p. 268, n. 36.

after the image and likeness of God; he even *is* the divine image and likeness. As we have seen above, this is also how Philo and the Gnostics portrayed the heavenly Man. Since Ezekiel's representation of the Glory as the "likeness as the appearance of man (ʾadam)" seems to describe the reverse side of the statement that Adam was made in the "image and likeness" of God[58], the heavenly Man was in the course of time identified with the divine image and likeness in which the earthly man was created. Like so much of ancient Jewish imagery and speculation, this identification was revived in Kabbalism, where the "figure of the Man upon the throne personifies this highest *Urbild*, in whose image (*Ebenbild*) man was created."[59] When the earthly Adam is glorified and called the divine "image", he obviously is described like the heavenly Man, the Glory.

The heavenly Man would of course have come into being long before his earthly copy. In *I Enoch* (or, the *Ethiopic Book of Enoch*), the Son of Man, *i.e.*, the Man, is a pre-existent being: "Before the sun and the signs were created, before the stars of the heaven were made, – his name was named before the Lord of the spirits" (xlviii.3). This does not seem to imply only ideal pre-existence, for the text goes on to say: "[...] he has been chosen and

58 See O. Procksch, "Die Berufungsvision Hesekiels", in *Karl Budde zum siebzigsten Geburtstag* (BZAW, 34), Giessen, 1920, p. 148; E. Feuillet, "Le Fils de l'Homme de Daniel et la tradition biblique", *RB*, 60, 1953, p. 190. Cp. G. von Rad, *Old Testament Theology*, I, London, 1975, p. 146; J. Barr, "Theophany and Anthropomorphism in the Old Testament", in *Congress Volume, Oxford, 1959* (Suppl. VT, VII), Leiden, 1960, p. 38.

59 G. Scholem, *Von der mystischen Gestalt der Gottheit*, Zürich, 1962, p. 21. See also Ginzberg, Art. "Adam Kadmon", p. 181, col. a, and p. 183, col. a; G. Scholem, Art. "Adam Kadmon", in *EJ*, 1, col.248. The term *Adam ha-Kadmoni* occurs in *Num.R.* x.2, but here it designates the first man on earth, whereas it is used of the heavenly Man in Kabbalistic texts from the 13th century onwards. But the latter usage appears to be old. In Mandeism, we find the figure of "Adam Qadmaia, the 'First Adam', Adam Kasia, the Mystic or Secret Adam who preceded the human Adam called *Adam pagria* (physical man) by many myriads of years ..." (E.S. Drower, *The Secret Adam*, Oxford, 1961, pp. 21 f.). In Manicheism, the heavenly Man who is sent forth to fight against the powers of darkness is called *Nasha Qadmaia* in Theodore bar Konai's summary in Part XI of his *Book of Scholia*. In the Nag Hammadi texts, we occasionally come across the name *Geradamas*, which A. Böhlig, "Zum "Pluralismus" in den Schriften von Nag Hammadi", in M. Krause, ed., *Essays on the Nag Hammadi Texts in Honour of Pahor Labib* (NHS, VI), Leiden, 1975, p. 26, has deciphered as "Old Adam", deriving the prefix ger- from the Greek γέρων, "old man". Thus, for instance, in the writing called *Melchizedek* from Codex IX, we hear about "the Man of Light, immortal aeon ΠΙΓΕΡΑΔΑΜΑC " (6.5 f.). G. Quispel has suggested that this name has the same meaning as Adam Kadmon (Qadmaia) and denotes the Glory; see "Hermetism and the New Testament, especially Paul", in W. Haase, ed., *ANRW*, II.22 (Gnostizismus und Verwandtes), appearing – it is hoped – in the foreseeable future; "Ezekiel 1:26 in Jewish Mysticism and Gnosis", *VigChr*, 34, 1981, pp. 3 f.

hidden before Him before the creation of the world and for evermore" (*v.* 6). Moreover, we read in lxii.7: "For from the beginning, the Son of Man was hidden, and the Most High preserved him in the presence of His might [...]." There can be no doubt that the Son of Man, who is seated upon a heavenly throne which can be identified as God's own throne[60], is the Glory, for he is introduced in the book as a being "whose countenance had the appearance of a man" (xlvi.1), a phrase which clearly alludes to *Ez.* i.26[61].

Some of the Gnostics, however, preserved a tradition according to which

---

60 According to li.3, the Elect One will sit on God's throne at the end of times (another reading, however, identifies the throne as that of the Elect One himself). In lxi.8, it is said that God will place the Elect One on the "throne of glory", and lxii.2 says that God sat down on the "throne of glory". In view of lxi.8, however, the last passage would make better sense if it is taken to say that God placed "him", *i.e.*, the Elect One, on the throne of glory.

61 Procksch thought that the Glory in *Ez.* ch. i is the ancestor of the one "like a son of man" in *Dan.* ch. vii, a chapter which is clearly alluded to in the judgement scene in *I En.* ch. xlvi. J. Bowman, "The Background of the Term "Son of Man" ", *ExT*, 59, 1948, p. 285, noted the influence of both *Ez.* ch. i and *Dan.* ch. vii on the "Similitudes of Enoch" and later Merkaba mysticism. For a development of Procksch' thesis, see Feuillet, pp. 180 ff.; H.R. Balz, *Methodische Probleme der neutestamentlichen Christologie* (WMANT, 25), Neukirchen, 1967, pp. 80 ff.; M. Black, "The Throne-Theophany Prophetic Commission and the Son of Man", in R.G. Hamerton-Kelly & R. Scroggs, ed., *Jews, Greeks and Christians* (Essays in Honor of William David Davies) (SJLA, XXI), Leiden, 1976, pp. 56 ff.

Much ink has been spilled over the question whether the one "like a son of man" in *Dan.* ch. vii is a heavenly figure or merely a symbol of the saints of the Most High. The latter interpretation no doubt holds good for *vv.* 15-27, which expound the preceding vision, but the vision itself, *vv.* 2-14, is best understood to represent the one "like a son of man" as an individual who has a throne by the side of God (see *v.* 9). Apparently, the latter notion was later seen as dangerous and caused the allegorization in *vv.* 15 ff.

The one who is "like a son of man" (כבר אנש) would seem to be no one else than the archangel Gabriel, who is said to have the "appearance of a man" (כמראה גבר) (viii.15 ff.) and is even called "the man (האיש) Gabriel" (ix.21). Gabriel apparently is identical with the angel who is called איש in x.5 ff. and xii.6 ff., as can be seen by comparing the functions of the "man" with those of Gabriel in chs. viii f. In x.16, the angelic figure is described as כדמות בן אדם (or, בני אדם). In x.18, he is said to be כמראה אדם. The association to דמות כמראה אדם in *Ez.* i.26 is palpable. Note also that the vision of the angel in *Dan.* x.4 ff. alludes to the vision in *Ez.* ch.i.

If the correct translation in *Rev.* xiv.15 is "another angel" and not "another, an angel", the Son of Man in *v.* 14 would seem to be viewed as an angel (cp. *v.* 6, which may look back to the Lamb in *v.* 1). If *vv.* 15-17 constitute an interpolation, it would seem that even the original document taught that the Son of Man is an angel. In order to avoid this conclusion, we would have to translate "another, an angel" in *v.* 18 and regard "the angel" in *v.* 19 as another interpolation. Note also that *I Enoch* says that the Son of Man, that is, the Glory, looked "like one of the holy angels" (xlvi.2).

the heavenly Man was brought into being on the first day of creation. In *On the Origin of the World*, the "likeness of Man" called "Light-Adam" is said to have come into being with the light which shone forth on the first day according to the myth in *Gen.* ch. i: "When this light appeared, a likeness of Man, which was marvellous, revealed itself in it" (108.7 ff.). The heavenly Man is here said to be encompassed by light in a way reminiscent of Ezekiel's description of the fire-like body of the Glory of God: "... brilliant light surrounded him. Like the appearance of a rainbow in the clouds on a rainy day, so was the radiance around him" (i.28a).

The non-Christian *Letter of Eugnostos* from Codex III of the Nag Hammadi library has adopted the same myth of the origination of the heavenly Man:

> In the beginning, He [*i.e.*, God] decided to let His likeness ($ϵ\text{!}ℵϵ$) come into being as a Great Power ($ΟΥ$ ℵΟϬ $ℕϬΟΜ$). Immediately, the ἀρχή of that light was manifested as an immortal, androgynous Man.
>
> (76.19 ff.)

This Man, who is later named "Adam of the Light" (81.12), obviously is the light which, according to the *Genesis* myth, was brought into being on the first day. That he is the Glory of God is made clear by his being described as the "likeness" of God and a "Great Power", the latter epithet having been shown to be a parallel to the "Great Glory"[62].

G. Quispel has argued that the myth of the origination of the heavenly Man as the primordial light presupposes a pun on *phōs*, meaning both "man" (φώς) and "light" (φῶς): "And God said: "Let *phōs* come into being!" And *phōs* came into being" (*Gen.* i.3)[63]. In the teaching of the Gnostic alchemist Zosimus, it is said that the spiritual Man's "common name is φώς, which is φῶς."[64] *Phōs* actually was used as a name of the heavenly Man in Jewish tradition. This is shown by an early document, the drama on exodus written by the playwright Ezekiel in the 2nd century B.C.E. In this play, Moses relates that he in a dream has seen a "noble Man" (φώς γενναῖος) with a diadem on his head and a sceptre in his hand being seated on a great throne on Mt. Sinai (see *vv.* 68 ff.)[65]. As is quite palpable, this is the throne of God's

---

62 See above, pp. 179f.

63 See "Hermetism"; "Ezekiel", p. 6.

64 Reitzenstein, *Poimandres*, p. 104.

65 G. Quispel, "Gnosis", in M. J. Vermaseren, ed., *Die orientalischen Religionen im Römerreich* (EPRO, 93), Leiden, 1981, p. 417, argues that this vision alludes to Ezekiel's vision of the Glory, and that the text is an important bridge between the figure of the Glory in *Ezekiel* and the heavenly Man in Gnosticism. Certain elaborations upon the theophany in *Ex.* xxiv.10 were apparently also important antecedents of the throne in Ezekiel the Dramatist; see above, p. 190, nn. 347f.

vicegerent charged with superintendence over the world and the office of being the judge of men at the end of times (see *vv.* 85 ff.).

In the light of the foregoing, we can infer that when the rabbis had to maintain that Adam was created on the eve of the Sabbath, they were contending against a doctrine of a heavenly Man who was pre-existent or had been brought into being on the first day of creation. This doctrine was of Jewish origin and lived on in Gnosticism. The reason for the rabbis' insistence upon the Biblical text is said to be that they would not accept that the heavenly Man was regarded God's "associate" in the creation, and we would now have to ask whether this idea was part of the Jewish doctrine of the heavenly Man.

As a matter of fact, the Merkaba mystics designated the Glory on the heavenly throne as יוצר בראשית, the "creator in the beginning". G. Scholem thinks that this reveals an adaptation of the concept of the demiurge in dualistic Gnosticism[66]. But why should Jews feel the need to mitigate Gnostic dualism? It is far more probable that Jewish mysticism in this respect reflects the kind of dualism of subordination which was the matrix of Gnostic dualism.

The Jewish mystical texts do not ante-date the rise of Gnosticism, but there is in fact quite early Jewish evidence for the ascription of demiurgic activity to the heavenly Man. We first turn to a couple of prayers in the Greek magical papyri, admirably analyzed by E. Peterson, who was able to demonstrate that they rest upon an archaic form of Jewish Adam mysticism which "goes back to even the first periods of Hellenism."[67] From the terms of the prayers in the papyri, we learn that man longs to escape from Fate and return to the spiritual state from which he has fallen. The celebrant reciting these incantations obviously regards himself as being mystically identified with the primal man, Adam: he characterizes himself as "man, the most beautiful creation of God who is in heaven, made of spirit, of dew, and of earth" (IV. 1177 f.)[68]. This must refer to the first man being composed of the elements[69].

The identification of the celebrant of magical incantations with Adam is also found in other texts. Thus, in the so-called *Mithraic Liturgy*, the cele-

---

66 See *Major Trends*, pp. 65 f. In *Von der mystischen Gestalt*, p. 27, however, Scholem asks whether the idea of the Glory as the "creator in the beginning" preceded that of the anti-divine demiurge of Gnosticism. He then states that the historical sequence may also have been the opposite, and leaves the question open.

67 "Die Befreiung Adams aus der 'Ανάγκη", in *Frühkirche, Judentum und Gnosis*, Rome – Freiburg – Vienna, 1959, p. 122.

68 The magical papyri are referred to by number of papyrus and line(s) in *PGM*.

69 In *II En.* XXX.8 (long recension), man's blood is said to have been made from the dew.

brant refers to himself as the first man, being created with a "perfect body" by the right hand of God (see IV.494 f.). Lamenting over his miserable state, he expresses hope of being restored to his spiritual nature when Fate is abolished. There are clear correspondences between the modes of speech in our two prayers and the *Mithraic Liturgy*. We may also cite the *Paris Magical Papyrus*, the Jewish affiliations of which are recognizable throughout; here, the celebrant describes himself as the "creature that God formed in His holy Paradise" (IV.3026 ff.). He begs to be freed from the demonic sway over this world.

Our two prayers are not addressed to God. The older of the two texts begins thus:

> The prayer of salvation to the first-manifested and first-born deity ([π]ρωτοφυοῦς θεοῦ καὶ πρωτογε[ν]οῦς) runs thus: "You I call upon, lord! Hear me, O holy deity, who rests among the holy ones, at whose side there are venerable spirits! You I call upon, first father (προπάτωρ), and I beg you, eternal αἰών, strong lord, eternal lord of the pole (αἰωνοπολοκράτωρ), you who are resting upon the ἑπταμερ[ί]ου [there follows a long magical formula], you who are holding the root (ῥίζωμα) fast for ever and ever, you who possess the powerful Name (τὸ ἰσχυρὸν ὄνομα), which is adored by all the angels. Hear me, you who have created mighty ministers and archangels, who are standing beside innumerable myriads of angels. You have been transported through the heavens (κατ᾽ οὐρανὸν), and the Lord [*i.e.*, God] has brought testimony to your wisdom and praised your power, and acceded that you should have power after His likeness (καθ᾽ ὁμοιότητα αὐτοῦ), just like He has power Himself."
>
> (I.195 ff.)

Peterson's hypothesis "that the text refers to the heavenly ascension of the προπάτωρ Adam, who is πρωτοφυής and πρωτογενὴς θεός,"[70] seems to have been accepted by the scholars[71]. The testimony which God is said to have brought concerning his wisdom may refer to *Gen.* iii.22, "Adam is become as one of us to know good and evil." We have seen above that there was a tradition to the effect that Adam repented and was reinstated in Paradise, and this repentance and reinstatement were actually connected with God's words in *Gen.* iii.22. Thus, R. Aqiba expounded the verse in the following way: "It means that the Holy One, blessed be He, set up two ways before him, and he chose the other path" (*Mekilta, Besh.* vii.73 f.)[72]. The rabbi takes ממני as 3rd singular, "of himself", and not as meaning "of us", thus interpreting the verse: Adam has become one who knows and chooses good and evil "of himself", of his own free will. This undoubtedly refers to *Sir.* xv. 14 ff.: "It was He who created man in the beginning, but then left him to his

---

70 Peterson, p. 118.

71 See E. Brandenburger, *Adam und Christus* (WMANT, 7), Neukirchen, 1962, pp. 77 ff.; Colpe, Art. ὁ υἱὸς τοῦ ἀνθρώπου, p. 411, n. 69; Conzelmann, *Korinther*, pp. 339 f.

72 The tradition is also found in *Gen.R.* xxi. 5.

own free will. If you desire so, you can keep the commandments, and if you want to show trustfulness, it depends on your own free choice. He has set fire and water before you, and you can stretch out your hand after what you like." R. Aqiba followed the Biblical narrative and maintained that Adam chose the wrong path, but others apparently took the verse to mean that Adam chose the right path and became "as one of" the heavenly beings[73]. Thus, the *Epistula Apostolorum*, a Christian work from the early (?) 2nd century, says:

> Adam was given the power that he might choose what he wanted from the two, and he chose the light and stretched out his hand and took it, and left the darkness and withdrew from it.
>
> (ch. 39)

Whereas the first man in the Adamic literature has to wait until the end of times for his restoration to Paradise, Adam in the magical text is ceded a restitution already during his lifetime. Obviously, Adam in the magical text is adapted to the concept of the heavenly Man, the divine Glory, as is also the figure of the primal man in the Adamic literature. This becomes still clearer when we study the beginning of the other magical prayer:

> You, the only one and blessed one among the aions, and father of the world (πατέρα κόσμου), I call upon with cosmic prayers. Draw near to me, you who breathed animation into the whole world, you who have put the fire on the ocean of heaven and separated the earth from the water. Hearken Μορφή and Spirit, and earth and sea, to the words of the wise one of the divine necessity, and attend to my prayer like reeds of fire.
>
> (IV.1167 ff.)

It is of utmost interest that the "Adam" who is enslaved under the laws of Fate invokes first Μορφή and Πνεῦμα, and then "earth and sea"; "Μορφή and Πνεῦμα are mentioned before the earth and the sea no doubt because they were created before the earth and the sea."[74] Peterson compares the Μορφή in this text with the σῶμα τέλειον which the celebrant in the *Mithraic Liturgy* conjures the deity to get back. "The Μορφή is there of course the μορφή which Adam originally had possessed in Paradise, and the Πνεῦμα is the πνεῦμα which animated this μορφή."[75] Since this Μορφή preceded the

---

73 R. Aqiba offers his interpretation as a corrective of R. Pappias' opinion that the verse means that Adam became "like one of the ministering angels". It may be that the issue at stake is only the plural form used of God, and that the status of Adam is not intended at all, but in *Cant.R.* I.ix.2, it is R. Aqiba who says that man became like the angels, while R. Pappias asserts that Adam became like God himself. That *Gen.* iii.22 meant that Adam had angelic or even divine status is argued in several rabbinic texts, which thus may reflect a heretical exposition (see *Gen.R.* xxi.1; 5).

74 Peterson, p. 113.

75 *Ibid.* Cp. p. 119, n. 41.

earth and the sea, it must be pre-existent or have come into being on the first (or at least not later than on the second) day of the creation. Since Adam *salvandus* "cannot be completely differentiated conceptually or substantially"[76] from Adam *salvator*, who has experienced the restoration which the former begs to receive, the Μορφή (and Πνεῦμα) which is (are) invoked must denote the heavenly Man, the Glory. As we have seen, *Poimandres* calls the heavenly Man the Μορφή of God and teaches that this Man came down to earth and settled in the "irrational" replica of his μορφή in matter.

Moreover, μορφή is used interchangeably with δόξα, the Greek translation of כבוד, in Old Testament theophanies. In *Job* iv.16, the תמונה, "form", "appearance", of the divine spirit (רוח) which revealed itself to Eliphas is rendered by μορφή in the LXX. In *Num.* xii.8, however, the LXX translates God's תמונה, which is beheld by Moses, with δόξα. Similarly, *Psalm* xvi.15 renders the divine תמונה, which the Psalmist expects to be revealed unto salvation, by δόξα. We also ought to note that, in the Christologically important text of *Is.* lii.14, the תאר, "form", "shape", of the Servant is translated with μορφή by Aquila, but with δόξα by the LXX[77]. Thus, the heavenly Adam who is invoked as Μωρφή in the Jewish magical text apparently is the Glory of God, as is Anthropos in *Poimandres*[78].

In the two magical texts, the heavenly Adam is ascribed with cosmological functions and is even described as a demiurge. That he is the "lord of the pole" dwelling in the zenith of heaven is reminiscent of the way in which the "Naassene Homily" describes Adamas as "ἀειπόλος, that is, "he who always turns round" (ὁ ἀεὶ πολῶν), and turns and rotates the whole universe in a circle. For "turning" means turning and altering things. For this reason, [...] the two centres of the heavens are always called "poles" (πόλους)" (Hipp., VI.viii.34 f.).

In the older of the two magical prayers, the heavenly Man is said to have "created mighty ministers and archangels," while the more elaborate text even says that he has "breathed animation into the whole world" and "separated the earth from the water." The latter cosmogonic activity clearly refers to *Gen.* i.9, while the former is reminiscent of God's infusion of his spirit into Adam (see *Gen.* ii.7).

In the first text, Adam is said to "possess the powerful Name, which is venerated by all the angels," and by the end of the prayer, the celebrant says:

---

76 Colpe, *loc. cit.*

77 On the above, see Jervell, pp. 45, 100 ff., 168.

78 If Peterson, p. 114, is right that the obscure word ἐπταμέριον (I.201) denotes the constellation of the Chariot, this would be a further indication that the heavenly Adam is the Glory, for this astronomical location of the Man would carry the allusion to the throne chariot of the Glory.

"In truth, O lord, I call upon your Hidden Name (τὸ κρυ[π]τὸν ὄνομα), which reaches from the firmament to the earth" (I.219 ff.). The Name possessed by the heavenly Man is here represented as a cosmological power holding the universe together. As we have seen in the preceding Chapters, this function is ascribed to the Name of God in Jewish, Samaritan, and Christian texts[79]. There can be no doubt that the "Hidden Name" in Adam's possession is the שם המפרש, the Name peculiar to God which was generally kept secret.

Moreover, we have seen above that the Name could be hypostasized and personified. This is also the case in the second of the magical texts, where the celebrant says:

> I call upon you by your Name! [A magical formula follows]. You who alone possess the root [of all], you are the holy and powerful Name (σὺ εἶ τὸ ὄνομα τὸ ἅγιον καὶ τὸ ἰσχυρόν), which is adored by all the angels! Protect me, N.N., from all accidents wrought by non-earthly power and all arrogance! Yea, do that, lord, deity of deities [there follows a long magical formula, ending with], creator of the world, creator of all (κόσμου κτίστα, τὰ πάντα κτίστα), lord, deity of deities (κύριε, θεὲ θεῶν) [a new magical formula, ending with] Ἰάω!
>
> (IV.1181 ff.)

The Name is here personified as the heavenly Man who is ascribed with demiurgic activity. Further, it is designated as Ἰάω, the Greek form of the Tetragrammaton. By the end of the prayer, the celestial Adam is even invoked as κύριε Ἰάω (IV.1218)[80]. Thus, Adam is the hypostasized Tetragrammaton.

All this fits very well as the target of the rabbinic rebuttal maintaining that Adam was created at the eve of the Sabbath lest certain heretics should assert that he was God's "associate" in the creation. Since the magical texts hold Adam to be the demiurge, they necessarily imply that he had pre-mundane existence. Moreover, since he is said to have shared God's own Name, he is rightly to be described as the "associate" of God, for this term – as we have seen – was used to denote participation in the Name, the divine nature or mode of being.

A passage from the *Book of Wisdom*, which already has been referred to, reflects elements of the same myth as that assumed in the magical texts[81]. The passage reads:

> She [*viz.*, Wisdom] guarded to the end the first-formed father of the world (πρωτό-πλαστον πατέρα κόσμου) who was created alone, and delivered him out of his transgression and gave him power to get dominion over all things.
>
> (x.1 f.)

---

79 See pp. 81, 248 ff., 257 f.
80 However, the end of the prayer seems to be a later addition; see Peterson, p. 119.
81 See *ibid.*, pp. 122 ff.

The "first-formed father of the world who was created alone" can only be Adam[82]. In the first of the magical texts which were quoted, the deity is called "the first-manifested and first-born". More importantly, while the first of the texts calls the deity προπάτωρ, the second actually contains the same name as the *Book of Wisdom*, that is, "the father of the world". While Adam in the magical texts is raised to heaven and praised by God because of his σοφία and δύναμις (see I.209 f.; IV.1205 f.), the *Book of Wisdom* has it that Sophia, a veritable hypostasis, delivered Adam out of his transgression and consorted with him[83]. While the magical texts describe Adam as the ruler over the cosmos, the *Book of Wisdom* states that he was given dominion over all things. There can be no doubt that both the magical texts and the *Book of Wisdom* allude to the same myth about Adam being elevated to heaven and installed as God's viceroy.

The magical texts also describe Adam as the demiurge, and this is a notion which actually is presupposed in the passage from the *Book of Wisdom*. In a study written more than forty years ago, A. Dupont-Sommer pointed out that the designation "Father of the world" was a well-known name of the creator of the world in the Hellenistic age[84]. Thus, for instance, in *Corpus Hermeticum,* God is said to be the Father of the world (πατὴρ μὲν οὖν ὁ θεὸς τοῦ κόσμου), while the world is called God's son (καὶ ὁ μὲν κόσμος υἱὸς τοῦ θεοῦ) (see IX.8). These terms of relationship are also found in the works of Philo, who attributes the title πατὴρ κόσμου to the Logos (see *De dec.* 134; cp. *De op. mundi* 146) as well as to God (see *De vita Mos.* II.134; II.238; *Quis rer. div. her.* 98).

Dupont-Sommer hypothesized that *Wisd.* x.1 f. shows Gnostic influence, but there is no evidence for the existence of Gnosticism at the time of the composition of the *Book of Wisdom*. Moreover, as has been pointed out above, there are very few traces of a cosmogonic function of the heavenly Man in Gnosticism. We must conclude that there were Jews who conceived the idea that the heavenly Man, who was regarded as pre-existent or as having come into being on the first day, had performed demiurgic activities. Since Adam took over traits from the heavenly Man, we come across even the bizarre notion that the first man had acted as the demiurge.

Evidence for the demiurgic function of the heavenly Man might be provid-

---

82 That Adam "was created alone (μόνον κτισθέντα)" is a statement which may be taken to imply a denial of the Scriptural relation that Adam was created together with Eve on the sixth day.

83 Peterson, p. 117, sees σοφία in IV.1205 f. as Αἰών and thus as a personified being, but ὅ ἐστιν Αἰών would rather seem to refer to the Kyrios who is said to have brought testimony to Adam's σοφία.

84 See "Adam. 'Pere du Monde' dans la Sagesse de Solomon (10, 1.2)", *RHR*, 119, 1939, pp. 182 ff.

ed by Philo. In a comment upon *Zech.* vi.12, ἰδοῦ ἄνθρωπος ᾧ ὄνομα ἀνατολή, Philo states:

> A strange appellation, if you think that the reference is to the man composed of body and soul; but if it refers to the incorporeal Man, who is no other than the divine image, you will admit that the name Ἀνατολή has been given him most appropriately, for the Father of all caused him to spring forth (ἀνέτειλε) as His eldest (πρεσβύτατον) son, whom he elsewhere calls "first-born" (πρωτόγονον); and the begotten one, imitating his Father's ways, looked to the archetypal models and shaped the forms.
>
> *(De Conf. ling.* 62 f.)

Here, the heavenly Man and divine "image" is said to be God's "eldest son" and "first-born", and is ascribed with the work of creation. But elsewhere, the eldest son and first-born of God is said to be the Logos[85], and the creation is the function of the Logos (see *Leg. all.* III.96; *De cher.* 125; 127; *De migr. Abr.* 6; *De spec.* leg. I.81; *De sacr. Ab. et Caini* 8; *Quod Deus immut. sit* 57; *De op. mundi* 20; *De fuga* 94). Philo's Logos concept is highly complex, and the attribution of cosmogonic activity to the Logos cannot be explained by simply referring to some Man doctrine. Similarly, the ascription of cosmogonic activity to the Logos in the aspect of God's metaphysical Man in the text above does not have to be derived from a Jewish teaching about the heavenly Man.

There is, however, another supposedly Alexandrian Jewish source which may be seen to offer evidence for the creative activity of the celestial Man. In the short and oldest recension of *II Enoch*[86], we read:

> When I [– it is God who is speaking –] had envisaged to make a foundation in order to fashion the visible creation, I commanded in the lowest part that one of the invisible things should come forth [and become] manifest. And Adoil went forth, being very great; and I looked at him, and – behold! – he had in his belly the great aeon [the long version: "the great light"]. And I told him: "Bring forth, Adoil, and let that which is born from you be visible!" And he brought forth; and the great aeon was born from him, and thus [the light] from it, which carries the whole creation which I wanted to make. And I saw that it was good. And I established a throne for Myself, and sat on it. And I said to the light: "Ascend on high and be firm, and be the foundation of the higher elements!" And there is nothing that is higher than the light.
>
> (ch. 11)

This is obviously a comment on *Gen.* i.3-5. But the creation of the light has now become the result of its origination from an angelic being, whose stomach issues the light.

---

85 See above, p. 269, and below, p. 315.
86 R.H. Charles, in the introduction to the translation in *APOT*, II, pp. 426, 429, points out that this work contains many ideas which also occur in Hellenistic Judaism, and suggests that it was written in Alexandria.

R.H. Charles suggests that the name of this being comes from יד אל,
"Hand of God"[87]. It was a Jewish doctrine that God had created the world
and man with his very hand(s)[88], and the creative Hand of God even seems to
have been hypostasized. Thus, in the *Book of Wisdom*, Sophia is represented
as a demiurge (see vii.22; viii.1, 5 f.) or as God's agent and associate in the
creation (see ix.1 f., 9; cp. viii.4), and, in one passage, we even read about
"Your [*i.e.*, God's] all-powerful Hand, which created the world out of form-
less matter" (xi.17). When, with this in mind, we note that it is said that
Wisdom "formed" man (see ix.2), it lies near at hand to identify Wisdom
with the creative Hand of God. In *Ps.-Clem. Hom.* XVI.12, Wisdom is compared to the extended Hand of God which created the universe[89], and the
Teachings of Silvanus states outright: "Only the Hand of the Lord has created
all these things. For the Hand of the Father is Christ, and it forms all. Through
it, all has come into being, since it has become the mother of all" (115.3 ff.).
In *Silvanus*, the Son is identified with Sophia (see 106.23; 107.9 ff.; 112.
33 ff.; 113.15), and "the mother of all" is in fact a name of Wisdom (see
Philo, *Quod det. pot. insid. soleat* 115 f.; *Leg. all.* II.49; *De ebriet.* 30 f.; cp.
Quod det. pot. insid. soleat. 54)[90]. It would thus seem that the "Hand of
God" was a name of Wisdom in her demiurgic capacity, and it is not unthinkable that this epithet could be transferred to other figures who were ascribed
with demiurgic function[91].

The concept of the creative Hand of God, however, carries associations
to manual operation, and it thus does not fit as a clue to the meaning of the
name of Adoil as he appears in *II En.* ch. 11. A. Vaillant suggests that the
name derives from עד, "eternity", with suffix and the termination -*el* (cp.
the Jewish angelic names: Michael, Gabriel, *etc.*)[92]. If this is right, we would
have to regard the name of Adoil as similar to the Greek Αἰών, which is a
name given to the heavenly Adam in the older of the two magical texts discussed above.

A third and very interesting etymology of the name of Adoil has been
suggested by G. Quispel, who derives it from *Adonai-el,* where the first ele-

---

87 See *ibid.*, p. 445, n. *ad* xxv.1 (long recension).

88 See L. Ginzberg, *The Legends of the Jews*, V (Notes to Volumes I and II), Philadelphia, 1925 and reprints, p. 63, n. 3 (continued on p. 64).

89 In *Rec.* VI.7 this image is applied to the Spirit, which is identical with Wisdom in
   Hom. XVI.22.

90 It recurs as a name of Wisdom in Gnosticism; see above, p. 156, n. 231.

91 On the Jewish Christian "Hand Christology", see Zandee, pp. 570 ff. Irenaeus (V.vi.1)
   identifies the "hands" of God which created Adam with Christ and the Spirit. In a
   Coptic magical papyrus, Christ is hailed as "Hand that made our father Adam"
   (Kropp, II, p. 130).

92 See *op. cit.*, p. XI.

ment is the well-known circumlocution for the Tetragrammaton[93]. If this be the right explanation, the name of the cosmogonic agent would be equal to that of *Yaho-el*, who appears as the Angel of the Lord and the Glory of God in the *Apocalypse of Abraham*[94].

Whatever is the right interpretation of the name of Adoil, *II En.* ch. 11 furnishes clear evidence that the *phōs* that was brought into being on the first day of creation was seen as an angelic being who had a function in the cosmogony. The light which is emitted from Adoil becomes "the foundation of the higher elements" and is even said to be carrying "the whole creation"[95]. Adoil is thus the prime cosmogonic agent[96]. Since he is the primordial *phōs*,

---

93 See "Hermetism".

94 See below, pp. 318ff.

95 Charles, p. 445, nn. *ad* xxv.2 f. (long recension), points out that this cosmogonic myth is a modification of the ancient Egyptian notion that the universe originated in an egg, from which the god of light, Re, came forth and created the world. Charles also refers to the presence of this myth in the *Pseudo-Clementine Homilies* (VI.3 ff., for which Charles gives a false reference). The Jewish Christian source quotes a version of the Orphic cosmogony according to which Phanes, the "Shining One", was born from the cosmic egg, and then created the world and ascended to the summit of heaven. Quispel, "The Demiurge in the Apocryphon of John", pp. 6 ff., has shown that some of the Gnostics adapted this myth; cp. above, p. 13. As is shown by *II En.* ch. 11, already their Jewish ancestors did that; cp. Quispel, "Hermetism". The fact that *II En.* ch. 11 as well as the Gnostic Basilides (see Hipp., VII.xx.1 ff.) represented the demiurge as Aion is explicable from the identification of Phanes with the young Aion of the Mithraic mysteries; see G. Quispel, "Herman Hesse and Gnosis", in *Gnosis*, pp. 504 ff. There is also something to be said for Quispel's explanation of the name of Adoil from the fact that Phanes, with whom the heavenly Man is welded in *II En.* ch. 11, could be given the names of Iao and Adonai; see M.J. Vermaseren, "A Magical Time God", in *MS*, p. 446.

96 The continuation relates that another being, Arukhaz (for which there are variants), came forth. Charles, p. 445, n. *ad* xxvi.1 (long recension), suggests that this name is from רקיע, the Hebrew word for the firmament which was created on the second day (see *Gen.* i.6-8), or from ἀρχή. Vaillant, p. 31, n. 13, thinks that it is a transposition of ἀρχάς, a word which I cannot find in the dictionaries. Does he mean ἀρχαῖος, which can be used of that which has existed from the beginning? If Charles is right about the Hebrew derivation, it is tempting to connect Arukhaz with the "spirit of the firmament" in *IV Ezra* vi.40, where it is said: "On the second day, You created the spirit of the firmament (*creasti spiritum firmamenti*) and commanded him to set a barrier between the waters, so one part ascended and the other remained below." But Arukhaz, who is "very great and black" and is commanded to come forth with "that which is solid", becomes the "foundation of the lower things". This apparently refers to the creation of the earth on the third day (see *Gen.* i.9-13). As can be seen from the continuation, the creation narrative in *II Enoch* does not follow that in *Gen.* ch. i slavishly, and Charles apparently is right that the "great aeon" which came out of Adoil refers to "the world of the heavens". The term "great aeon" is also used of the future world (see ch. 15; 17), which easily is merged with the heavenly world. As far as I know, no one has seen *II En.* ch. 11 in relation to R. Aqiba's statement

or – rather – the archetypal *phōs*, which means "man" as well as "light", *II En.* ch. 11 apparently bears witness to the notion of the demiurgic function of the celestial Man.

That the primordial light and the heavens issued from the body of the celestial Man is a notion which recurs in the Jewish mystical texts. Mostly, however, it is said that it was the robe (חלוק) of the Glory which emitted the light and the heavens. Thus, when R. Simeon asked to be told "whence the light was created," R. Samuel answered: "The Holy One, blessed be He, wrapped Himself in a white garment, and the splendour of His glory shone forth from one end of the world to the other" (*Gen.R.* iii.4; *et al.*). Similarly, *Pirke de R. Eliezer* says: "Whence were the heavens created? From the light of the garment with which He was robed: He took and stretched it like a garment" (ch. 3)[97].

Now, "the vision of the garment [of the Glory] apparently arouses the same numinous qualities as are aroused by the vision of the mystical "body of the glory" itself"[98]; thus, although it is repeatedly stated that it cannot be seen, it is paradoxically admitted that the one who looks at the garment is transformed into a being of fiery nature (see, for example, *Hekaloth Rabbati* iii.4)[99]. It is therefore not surprising that *Hekaloth Rabbati* says: "From his glory (הדר), the depths were enkindled, and from his form (תאר), the heavens are sparkling. His form sends out the lofty [...]" (xxiv.3)[100]. In this hymn, it is said that the foundations of the world as well as the heavens were created – and, as it seems, continuously are being recreated – from

---

that את, the *nota accusativi*, in *Gen.* i.1, בראשית ברא אלהים את השמים ואת הארץ, was necessary, lest heaven and earth should be seen as divine beings, even demiurgic deities, the words being regarded as nominatives and additional subjects of the verb, or – perhaps – as appositions to "Elohim" (see *Gen.R.* i. 14; *Ḥag.* 12a; *et al.*). Since the rabbinic discussion whether or not את signifies an inclusion in the meaning of the text is attached to a variety of Biblical verses, Segal, *Two Powers*, pp. 74 ff., plausibly argues that an exegetical controversy has been transferred to a context where it could carry polemical intent. Segal suggests that a redactor wanted to defeat a variety of cosmogonic teachings, but none of the doctrines he refers to fits as well as the teaching in *II En.* ch. 11, where heaven and earth, or their procreators, are two independent figures being active in the creation.

97 Scholem, *Jewish Gnosticism*, pp. 57 ff., has shown that these texts cannot be understood save in the light of mystical traditions.

98 *Ibid.*, p. 60.

99 In the *Pseudo-Clementines*, it is said that "the incorporeal Μορφή of the Father or the Son" cannot be seen, because "it is illuminated by exceedingly great light," but then it is paradoxically admitted that this Form may be seen if one's "flesh be changed into the nature of light, so that it can see light" (*Hom.* XVII.16). For the Pseudo-Clementine idea that the Son is the "Form", and thus the Glory, of God, see Fossum, "Christology", pp. 267 ff.; cp. above, p. 277, n. 55.

100 Quoted by Scholem, *Jewish Mysticism*, pp. 61 f.

the light shining forth from the body of the Glory. This is not unlike the idea in *II En.* ch. 11 that the light which shone forth from the body of Adoil "carries the whole creation" and is "the foundation of the higher elements", which apparently denote the stars and constellations of the firmament.

Summing up the evidence in this section, we begin by recalling that both Philo and certain Gnostic works testify to a tradition according to which the divine image after which man was created is a heavenly Man, a hypostasis of God[101]. Neither Philo nor the Gnostics invented this figure; he is originally the Glory of the "likeness as the appearance of a man" (*Ez.* i.26). In Jewish tradition, the Glory was conceived of as pre-existent or as having come into being as the *phōs*, "man", "light", which shone forth on the first day of creation, and the Gnostics adopted the latter as well as the former notion. There is also Jewish evidence that the celestial Man acted as a demiurge, and some faint traces of this function of the Man are preserved in Gnostic texts. In later mystical texts, the Glory is described as יוצר בראשית, the "creator in the beginning", and the peculiar idea that the primordial light and the heavens issued from his body is anticipated in the pre-Christian *II Enoch*. The rabbis who maintained that Adam was created on the eve of the Sabbath, lest the *minim* should say that he had acted as God's "associate" in the creation, apparently opposed a heresy developed within their own fold.

We have also seen that there developed a *rapprochement* between the heavenly Man and the first man on earth, and that many texts attribute traits of the former to the latter[102]. In the next section, we will turn to some traditions which elevated other religious heroes from the human stock to the position and rôle of God's vicegerent in heaven.

---

101 H.-M. Schenke, *Der Gott "Mensch" in der Gnosis*, Göttingen, 1962, thinks that the concept of Anthropos was developed through an allegorical exegesis of *Gen.* i.26 f., where it is said that man was created after the image and likeness of God. However, as has been pointed out by several scholars, a mythological figure is hardly the product of exegesis; the idea of a celestial Man must already have been in existence and then read *into* the text.

102 This merger explains why some scholars have tried to derive the Gnostic Anthropos from the Jewish Adam figure. Dodd, discussing primarily the figure of Anthropos in *Poimandres*, which describes the origination of the celestial Man with clear reference to *Gen.* i.26 f., stated: "The Ἄνθρωπος doctrine in its familiar Hellenistic forms owes much to direct reflection by Jewish thinkers and others influenced by them, upon the mysterious story of man's origin as told in Genesis, and possibly to more fantastic forms of that story handed down in Jewish tradition" (*Bible*, p. 147). This cue was worked out by G. Quispel, "Der gnostische Anthropos und die jüdische Tradition", *E-J*, XXII (1953), 1954, pp. 195 ff., who set forth an impressive argument to the effect that a cosmological Sophia myth, which had adapted the Orphic allegorization of the myth of the severance of Dionysos as the dispersion of the cosmic soul, was exchanged for an anthropological myth about Adam, who was known to have incorporated all mankind and to have fallen from his lofty place in a heavenly

The Ascension to Heaven and Reception of the Name

We have seen that there was a tradition to the effect that Adam was reinstated in Paradise, which was thought of as situated in heaven. Furthermore, it is well known that *I En.* ch. lxxi teaches that the patriarch Enoch was taken up to heaven and installed in the position and rôle of the Son of Man, who can be identified as the Glory[103]. According to another tradition, however, Enoch was believed to have been translated to heaven and enthroned as Metatron, which was a special name of the Angel of the Lord, "whose name is like the Name of his Master."

In the New Testament, it is Jesus who is the one being translated to heaven, and both traditions used to describe Enoch's heavenly status recur in the picture of Jesus. Without entering into the debate whether Jesus designated himself as the Son of Man (and, in case he did, what he would have meant by it), A.F. Segal recently has drawn attention to the fact that the representation of Jesus as the Son of Man with reference to *Dan.* vii.13 was linked to *Ps.* cx (LXX cix).1, "The Lord said to my lord (Εἶπεν ὁ κύριος τῷ κυρίῳ μου): "Sit at My right side until I make your enemies your footstool." " This is the Old Testament passage which is most quoted in the New Testament and the Scriptural proof for Jesus' ascension and heavenly enthronement, and Segal intriguingly asks: "Might it be that the connection between the earthly Jesus and the son of man was made because Jesus was believed to have ascended to the throne in heaven – thus identifying him with the manlike figure (BRNŠ̌ "son of man") who fought against the unjust, and who was seated on His divine throne?"[104]

---

realm. For the hypothesis that the Gnostic Anthropos derived from the Jewish Adam figure, cp. W. Staerk, *Die Erlöserwartung in den östlichen Religionen* (Soter II), Stuttgart & Berlin, 1938, pp. 7 ff. Already B. Murmelstein, "Adam, ein Beitrag zur Messiaslehre", *WZKM,* 35, 1928, pp. 242 ff., and 36, 1929, pp. 51 ff., had seen the Jewish Messiah as a second Adam.

103 Sjöberg, pp. 154 ff., conclusively rejects any textual alteration made out of embarrassment over the question of how two figures can become one. The exact meaning of the identification of Enoch, a human being, with the heavenly Son of Man is a problem which has taxed the scholars' minds and brought forth some subtle considerations, none of which we need to discuss. Also, whether or not ch. lxxi is a later addition is a question which does not have to be discussed. Another question which has not been entirely settled is whether or not the three Ethiopic expressions in *I Enoch* which are rendered by the phrase "Son of Man" reproduces a pregnant title or describes a heavenly being as man-like. Above, I have chosen the former alternative, but it is equally possible that the figure in question should be understood like the one "like a son of man", *etc.*, in the *Book of Daniel.*

104 *Op. cit.,* p. 207. Very strangely, Segal gives the following references as examples of the combination of *Ps.* cx.1 and *Dan.* vii.13: "Mk. 2:32 f., 8:56 f., 13:26, 14:62" (p. 206, n. 68). The first two passages do not exist at all, and the third cites only the

That the representation of Jesus as the Son of Man of *Dan.* ch. vii is linked to his identification with the second lord of *Ps.* cx.1, taken to depict Jesus' ascension and heavenly enthronement, is well worth noting, for the designation of Jesus with the same name as that used of God actually identifies him as the Angel of the Lord, the possessor of the Name of God. The word *kyrios* was used with reference to God by Greek speaking Jews; it was used as a translation of the Biblical *Adonai*, "(my) Lord", as well as of YHWH, which was replaced in pronunication by the former word. In quoting *Ps.* cx(cix).1, Aramaic speaking Jews would have said *Adon* twice (although the Hebrew consonant text runs לאדני   יהוה   נאם), just as Greek speaking Jews would have said *kyrios* twice. That Jesus was given the Divine Name when having ascended to heaven is in fact part of a primitive Christology predating Paul and appearing in the hymn in *Phil.* ch. ii, which describes Jesus as the one —

who, being (ὑπάρχων) in a form (μορφῇ) of God, did not regard equality with God as a thing to be grasped (ἀρπαγμὸν), but (ἀλλὰ) emptied himself. Having taken a servant's form (μορφὴν), having become (γενόμενος) in a likeness of a man (ἐν ὁμοιώματι ἀνθρώπου), and, having been found (εὑρεθεὶς) in a fashion as a man (σχήματι ὡς ἄνθρωπος), he humbled himself, having become (γενόμενος) obedient unto death, even the death upon a cross. Therefore, God highly exalted (ὑπερύψωσεν) him and gave him the Name above every name (τὸ ὄνομα τὸ ὑπὲρ πᾶν ὄνομα), in order that, at the Name of Jesus, every knee should bend, in heaven and upon earth and under the earth, and every tongue should confess that Jesus Christ is Lord (κύριος Ἰησοῦς Χριστὸς) to the glory of God the Father.

(*vv.* 6-11)

I have given a rather literal translation, rendering the aorist participles by English perfect participles in order to make manifest the rule that the action of the aorist participles precedes the action of the main verb[105]. I have not tried to arrange the verses in a poetic or hymnic form[106]; rather, interest is

---

Daniel passage. In addition to the fourth, Segal should have referred to *Acts* vii.55f. Note also that *Mark* xii.35-40 combines *Ps.* cx.1 with the eschatological judgement, which is the theme in *Dan.* vii.9 ff. In *Rev.* i.5 ff., the return of Jesus as the judging Son of Man is connected with his death and heavenly kingship.

The one "like a son of man" in *Dan.* ch. vii actually seems to have a throne of his own (see *v.* 9). For the idea of the sharing of God's throne, see above, p. 279, n. 60 (cp. *Wisd.* ix.4, 10). Cp. also p. 275, n. 49.

105 Cp. Borsch, p. 250. I have followed Papyrus 46 and several early witnesses reading ἀνθρώπου in lieu of "of men" in *v.* 7.

106 See the survey of the study of the literary form of the hymn by R.P. Martin, *Philippians* (NCB), London, 1976, pp. 109 ff. There is no reason for recasting the wording. To what extent Paul has made additions to the original version is difficult to decide; it depends upon how the structure of the hymn is arranged. My punctuation is unusual, but it is not essential for the interpretation.

to be focused upon the sources on which the passage is dependent and the categories of the ideas used[107].

There is a general agreement that the hymn describes Jesus' pre-existent state, his descent from the heavenly abode and his incarnation, suffering and death, and his raising and reinstallation in heaven by God[108]. Scholars who have taken a liking to the hypothesis of the existence of a pre-Christian Gnostic myth of the descent and ascent of the redeemer claim that the myth has a Gnostic model; but, rather than the use of a Gnostic myth that is unattested for the pre-Christian period, a far better tool for interpretation is the Adam mythology that has been discussed above. That Jesus is said to have been in a "form" ($\mu o \rho \varphi \acute{\eta}$) of God (*v.* 6a) is a clear reference to the concept of the first man having been made in the "image and likeness" of God (*Gen.* i.26 f.). As has been noted above, the Greek word $\mu o \rho \varphi \acute{\eta}$ is translated by דמות, the word used of Adam's "likeness" (דמות/$\acute{o}\mu o\acute{\iota}\omega\sigma\iota\varsigma$) to God, in the Peshitta version of *Phil.* ii.6, and $\mu o \rho \varphi \acute{\eta}$ is in fact interchangeable and synonymous with צלם/$\epsilon\acute{\iota}\kappa\acute{\omega}\nu$ as well as with דמות/ $\acute{o}\mu o\acute{\iota}\omega\sigma\iota\varsigma$[109].

There is no need to turn away from traditions about Adam to, say, Hellenistic Jewish Sophia traditions in order to explain the representation of Jesus having a heavenly existence; for, as has been seen above, there were Jewish traditions which had it that the Paradise in which Adam dwelled was a supraterrestrial realm. Adam fell from his blessed situation because he transgressed God's command and ate of the Tree in order to become like God (see *Gen.* iii.4 f.), while Jesus, the second Adam (cp. *Rom.* v.12 ff.; *I Cor.* xv.22, 45), "did not regard equality with God as a thing to be grasped ($\acute{a}\rho\pi\alpha\gamma\mu\acute{o}\nu$)." The meaning of the word *harpagmos* is much debated, but the conjunction $\acute{a}\lambda\lambda\acute{a}$, introducing the next clause, which states what Christ actually did do, would seem to show that the former sentence describes what was a temptation to Christ but was disowned by him in favor of his "emptying" himself. The older view that *v.* 6b says that Christ "did not hold [his] equality with God as a booty" does not make sense in view of the conjunction emphasizing a choice between two things[110].

---

107 Cp. Martin, *Philippians*, pp. 90 ff., 113 ff., for a valuation of the various interpretations. See also his earlier *Carmen Christi* (SNTS: Monograph Series, 4), Cambridge, 1967.

108 A few writers, however, take *vv.* 6-8 to speak solely about Jesus' earthly existence; see the references in J. Behm, Art. $\mu o\rho\varphi\acute{\eta}$ $\kappa\tau\lambda.$, in *TDNT*, IV, 1967, reprinted 1975, p. 750, n. 48. See further the attempts by Borsch, pp. 250 ff.; C.H. Talbert, "Preexistence in Philippians 2:6-11", *JBL*, 86, 1967, pp. 141 ff.; H.-W. Bartsch, *Die konkrete Wahrheit und die Lüge der Spekulation* (TW, 1), Bern, 1974.

109 For the theory of allusions to Adam in *v.* 6, see the references in Martin, *Philippians*, p. 95. See further Borsch, p. 251. None of them cites Peterson, "Befreiung", p. 121, who has inspired the present interpretation.

110 See Martin, *Philippians*, pp. 96, 112.

Christ's "having become in a likeness of a man" and "having been found in a fashion as a man" would seem to hint at the incarnation, but we should also take note of the fact that the wordings are strongly reminiscent of the expressions used about the heavenly vicegerent of God, the Glory of *Ezekiel* and the Son of Man of *Daniel* and *I Enoch*[111]. The aorist participles plausibly can be taken to convey the meaning that Jesus possessed the "likeness" and "fashion" of man also *before* his "emptying" and humbling himself. The phrases actually do not say that Christ *became* man; they say that he *was like* a man[112]. Christ is both in the image of God and in the likeness of man; he is both God-like and man-like. He is the mediator between God and man.

---

111 The allusion to a Son of Man Christology in the first expression has been championed by M. Black, "The Son of Man Problem in Recent Research and Debate", *BJRL*, 45, 1963, p. 315. E. Lohmeyer, *Kyrios Jesus* (SHAW, phil.-hist. Kl., IV, 1927/28), 2nd ed., Heidelberg, 1961, p. 42, thought that the Son of Man figure was to be found behind the second phrase. Some exegetes have assumed an Adam/Christ typology in *v.* 8, but yet maintained that its origin lies in the Anthropos part of the Gnostic redeemer myth; see R.H. Fuller, *The Foundations of New Testament Christology* (LL), London, 1965, pp. 211 f.

112 O. Michel, "Zur Exegese von Phil. 2.5-11", in his *Theologie als Glaubenswagnis*, Hamburg, 1954, p. 91, correctly points out that the word "likeness" implies that Jesus is not identified outright as man; he is something different from – but yet resembling – man. For Christ having the "likeness" of man, see also *Rev.* i.13; *Test. Ash.* vii.3; *Test.Benj.* x.7; *Asc.Is.* iii.3.

There are possibly some other New Testament passages where Christ is identified with the Glory. In the *Gospel of John*, Jesus says that the Jews have not heard God's voice or seen his εἶδος (see v.37), obviously alluding to the statement that to hear Jesus' word is to obtain eternal life (see *vv.* 24 f.). Εἶδος is synonymous with μορφή, which, as we have seen above, p. 284, is used interchangeably with δόξα in Old Testament theophanies. We may note especially *Num.* xii.8, where εἶδος stands in parallelism to δόξα; God says concerning Moses: "I will speak to him mouth to mouth ἐν εἴδει καὶ οὐ δι' αἰνιγμάτων, καὶ τὴν δόξαν Κυρίου εἶδεν." Thus, the Son in *John* ch. v probably is the Glory of God. Some scholars think that *John* xii.41 identifies the Son with the Glory with reference to Isaiah's vision of God on the throne (see *Is.* ch. vi). However, since *John* says that Isaiah saw "*his* glory", it would rather seem that the Son is seen as the Kyrios upon the throne. Thus, Targum *Is.* vi.1 reads "יקרא of the Lord". With no apparent difference, *John* speaks of "seeing" the glory of Christ and "seeing" the glory of God (see i.14; xi.40; xvii.24). But in *Is.* vi.5, the Targum has "יקר שכינת of the King of the worlds." Thus, we might wonder whether the Son in *John* xii.41 is regarded as the Shekina. Cp. above, p. 256, n. 32, and see further p. 178, n. 310. In mystical tradition, "Shekina" could be used interchangeably with "Kabod"; thus, *Maᶜase Merkaba* contains the following passage: "[...] I gazed upon the Shekina and saw everything that they do before his throne of glory" (§ 32, at the beginning).

In *James* ii.1, there may be found an identification of Christ as the Glory, for here we perhaps ought to read: "... our Lord Jesus Christ, [who is] the Glory." To be sure, this verse admits of several renderings; see the recent discussion by J.B. Adamson, *The Epistle of James* (NIC), Grand Rapids, 1976, reprinted 1977, pp. 103 f.,

As a matter of fact, neither the pre-existence nor the incarnation of Christ is described so explicitly, although the first part of the hymn obviously does delineate a decline. This fits perfectly with the apocryphal myth of Adam, who fell from his supramundane place into this world but evidently possessed his humanity already before the fall. That *Phil.* ii.6 does not state expressly that Christ existed before the creation and thus seems to reckon only with some sort of limited pre-existence is also homologous with the myth of Adam, who was part of God's creation.

However arbitrary these comparisons to Adam may seem, the second part of the hymn shows unmistakeably the presence of a motif from the Adam mythology that has been examined above: the notion of Christ being elevated to heaven by God and given the lordship over the universe and "the Name above every name" is without parallel in the Sophia myth or in the myth of the Gnostic redeemer[113.] It is possible that the preposition of the verb $\dot{\upsilon}\pi\epsilon\rho\upsilon\psi\acute{o}\omega$ indicates that Christ was exalted to a position higher than the one he had before he humbled himself; and this would seem to be inferred also from *v.* 6a, which intimates that Christ, although he was in God's "form", had the possibility of gaining an even greater status, namely, "equality with God". Because Jesus "emptied" and "humbled" himself, God actually bestowed divinity upon him, for there cannot be any doubt that "the Name above every name" is God's own Name, that is, the nature of the divine. Thus, all creation must confess that Jesus is *kyrios*, which is the Greek translation of the proper Name of God. The apocryphal Adam mythology related that Adam fell as a consequence of trying to become like God, but then

---

who chooses the meaning "the Lord Jesus Christ, our Glory", but does think that "the latent argument" is that "Jesus Christ is the true Glory" (p. 104). For the possible identification of the Son with the Glory in the Pauline *corpus*, Quispel's essay "Hermetism" should be studied carefully. Scholem, *Von der mystischen Gestalt*, p. 276, n. 19, asks whether *Phil.* iii.21 – which speaks of Jesus' $\sigma\hat{\omega}\mu\alpha$ $\tau\hat{\eta}\varsigma$ $\delta\acute{o}\xi\eta\varsigma$ – reflects the tradition of the "body of the Shekina", *i.e.*, the Glory, which we find in the later mystical texts. Cp. above, p. 178. For associations and possible identifications of Christ with the Glory, see further *Luke* ii.32; *Eph.* i.17; *Heb.* i.3; *Tit.* ii.13; *I Pet.* iv.14. For post-Biblical evidence, see Fossum, "Jewish-Christian Christology".

113 Borsch recognizes the connection between *Gen.* i.26 f. and *Phil.* ii.6a, but postulates that the fuller background of the Christ hymn must be sought in some myth of a "king-Man" trying to ascend to heaven and become God's equal, but then humbling himself and winning God's favour. However, in all his pursuits of the "royal Man", Borsch fails to come up with a motif resembling the bestowal of "the Name above all names" upon the exalted Christ. The examples which Borsch, p. 254, n. 4, gives as parallels to *Phil.* ii.9 speak about the exaltation of the king's "name", that is, his royal power and glory, through the great deeds which he effects by God's help; he is not being given a *new* name, *i.e.*, a new nature, which in reality is that of God, but is realizing his own kingly nature.

repented and actually was raised by God and given the Divine Name, while the Jewish Christians presented Jesus as the second Adam, who did not try to grasp divinity and voluntarily came down to earth, and was exalted by God and given the Divine Name because of his "emptying" and "humbling" himself[114].

Admittedly, the magical texts calling Adam by the Name of God do not expressly state that he received this Name upon his exaltation, but this is to be assumed[115]. The tradition about Enoch's ascension corroborates this inference. Enoch is not said to have received the Name of God when having been installed in heaven as the Son of Man[116], but this notion appears in *III Enoch*, where it is related that Enoch was enthroned as Metatron, another name of God's principal angel, "whose name is like the Name of his Master." The doctrine is set forth clearly in two of the first chapters:

> R. Ishmael said: "In that hour, I asked Metatron, the Angel, the Prince of the Presence: "What is your name?" He answered me: "I have Seventy Names, corresponding to the seventy tongues of the world, and all of them are based upon the Name of my King, the Holy One; but my King calls me "Youth" (נער).""
>
> R. Ishmael said: "I asked Metatron and said to him: "Why are you called by the Name of your Creator, by Seventy Names? You are greater than all the princes, higher than all the angels, beloved more than all the servants, honoured above all the mighty ones in kingship, greatness, and glory – why do they call you "Youth" in the high heavens?" He answered and said to me:
>
> "Because I am Enoch, the son of Jared. For, when the generation of the flood sinned and were confounded in their deeds, saying to God: "Depart from us, because we do not desire the knowledge of Your ways" (*Job* xxi.14), then the Holy One,

---

114 Does also the description of Jesus' resurrection and enthronement in the highest heaven by the author of the *Ephesians* allude to the belief that Jesus was given the Ineffable Name? Jesus is here said to have been enthroned "above ... any name named" (i.21). Cp. also *Heb.* i.3 f.

115 Cp. Peterson, "Befreiung", p. 120.

116 Segal says that the Son of Man in *I En.* ch. lxix "learns" the Name by which the world was created (p. 196), and that this creative Name also "becomes the possession" of the Son of Man (p. 197). But there is no evidence for this. However, an Aramaic text from Cave 4 at Qumran, which presumably comes from a *Daniel* apocryphon, contains a very interesting description of God's principal agent: "[...] [He shall be called the Son of] the [G]reat [God], and by His Name shall he be named. He shall be hailed as the Son of God, and they shall call him the Son of the Most High [...]" (J.A. Fitzmyer, "The Contribution of Qumran Aramaic to the Study of the New Testament", *NTS*, 20, 1973/74, pp. 391 ff.). Although the text as a whole is fragmentary and hard to supplement, the wording "and by His Name shall he be named" seems to be certain. If the text really speaks of the Son of Man, we would have evidence that this figure was endowed with the Divine Name; but, although the text appears to be part of a *Daniel* apocryphon, it is far from certain that the figure in question is the Son of Man being represented in *Dan.* ch. vii. However, the text is very interesting in that it offers evidence for a non-Christian redeemer being entrusted with the Name of God.

blessed be He, removed me from their midst to be a witness against them in the high heavens to all the inhabitants of the world, that they may not say: "The Merciful One is cruel [...]." Hence the Holy One, blessed be He, lifted me up in their lifetime before their eyes to be a witness against them to the future world. And the Holy One, blessed be He, assigned me for a prince and a ruler among the ministering angels [...]. And because I am small and a youth among them [*viz.*, the angels] in days, months, and years, they call me "Youth"." "

(chs. iii-iv)

The notion that Enoch-Metatron has "Seventy Names" is connected with the idea of "the seventy tongues of the world". The meaning undoubtedly is that Enoch-Metatron in virtue of possessing the "Seventy Names" is the ruler of the entire world. Elsewhere, *III Enoch* speaks of the "seventy-two princes of kingdoms on high" who are angelic representatives of the kingdoms on earth (xvii.8; ch. xxx). The numbers "seventy" and "seventy-two" are, of course, not to be taken literally; they signify the multitude of the nations of the world. Metatron, who is "a prince and a ruler over all the princes of My kingdoms and over all the children of heaven" (x.3), must by necessity be the ruler over the whole world (cp. xvi.1 f.). While some said that Adam or Jesus was raised to heaven and given the Divine Name and the regency over the universe, the Enoch circle held that the patriarch Enoch had been elevated to heaven and entrusted the "Seventy Names" and the rule over the world. The two notions amount to exactly the same thing, for the "Seventy Names" "are based upon the Name of my King, the Holy One [...]."

That Metatron's "Seventy Names" are based upon the proper Name of God is also stated in other passages. When Enoch-Metatron was enthroned in heaven, God conferred the "Seventy Names" taken from his own Name upon his vicegerent:

[...] I took him, I appointed him, [namely,] Metatron, My Servant, who is the unique one among all the children of heaven. I made him strong in the generation of the first Adam. But, when I beheld the men of the generation of the flood, that they were corrupt, I went and removed My Presence from among them [...]. And I took him, [namely,] Enoch, the son of Jared, from among them [...]. I appointed him over all the treasures and stores that I have in every heaven. And I committed into his hand the keys of every several one. I made him the prince over all the princes and a minister of the Throne of Glory. [There follows an enumeration of Metatron's heavenly functions.] And I put upon him My honour, My majesty, and splendour of My Glory that is upon the Throne of Glory. And I called him "the Lesser YHWH" (יהוה הקטן), "the Prince of the Presence", "the Knower of Secrets"; for every secret I revealed to him as a father, and all the mysteries I declared to him in uprightness. I set up his throne at the door of My hall, in order that he might sit and judge the heavenly household on high. And I placed every prince before him, to receive authority from him and perform his will. Seventy Names I took from [My] Names and called him by them in order to enhance his glory. Seventy princes I gave into his hands, to command unto them the precepts and My words in every language.

(xlviii[c].1 ff., 7b ff.)

Metatron's "Seventy Names", which give him supremacy over the "seventy princes" (obviously equivalent to the "seventy-two princes of kingdoms on high" in the earlier parts of the book), are in fact Names belonging to God himself. In xlviii[d].1, we read:

> Seventy Names has Metatron, which the Holy One, blessed be He, took from His own Name and put upon him [...].

There follows an enumeration of all these Names, which, in actual fact, amount to a larger number than seventy. Some of the appellations are angelic names known from other sources (Yahoel, Yophiel, *etc.*); while others are plays upon the name Metatron (Mitton, Mottron, *etc.*); and others still are permutations of the letters of יהוה and אהיה (WHYH, ʾW, *etc.*). And it is only logical that the Tetragrammaton itself and various abbreviations of it (*e.g.*, Yah) also are among the Names which God bestowed upon Metatron, for the Name of God that is the basis of all the Names of Metatron is nothing else than the *original* Name of God:

> These Seventy Names are a reflection of the Explicit Name upon the Merkaba which are engraved upon the Throne of Glory. For the Holy One took from His Explicit Name and put upon the name of Metatron Seventy Names of His by which the ministering angels call the King of the kings of the kings, blessed be He, in the high heavens, and the twenty-two letters that are upon the ring upon His finger with which are sealed the destinies of the princes of kingdoms on high in greatness and power, and with which are sealed the lots of the Angel of Death and the destinies of every nation and tongue.
>
> (xlviii[d].5)

The passages describing the heavenly enthronement of Enoch provide us with the elucidation of the Mandean text which narrates that Abathur summoned Ptahil-Gabriel and conferred "Hidden Names" upon him before sending him out to create the world[117]. The "Hidden Names" which are bestowed upon Gabriel the demiurge have their counterpart in the "Seventy Names" which Metatron receive. All the manifold Names entrusted to God's vicegerent are Divine Names which are considered to be based upon the proper Name of God.

The "Hidden Names" which are given to the angel Gabriel are no doubt the means wherewith he effects the creation. Attention should once more be drawn to *I En.* lxix.14 ff., where the angel Michael is said to have been entrusted with the oath containing the "Hidden Name", through which the whole universe is created and sustained[118]. In the last quotation from *III Enoch*, the "Seventy Names", which are reflecting the Explicit Name, stand parallel to the "twenty-two letters" of the alphabet: both the Names and the letters are entrusted to the angel Metatron. As was shown in the previous

---

117 See above, p. 261.
118 See above, pp. 257 f.

Chapter, *III Enoch* is among the writings teaching that the letters of the Hebrew alphabet constitute the means by which the universe was created[119]. In xli.4, these letters are said to be inscribed upon the Throne of Glory. Here, however, in xlviii[d].5, the Divine Names are said to be found upon the Throne. Further, in xiii.1, it is stated that God also inscribed the creative letters upon the crown on Metatron's head. Here, Metatron is given the Divine Names. Obviously, then, *III Enoch* knows the idea that the creative letters of the alphabet are based upon the Name of God[120]. Hence, "Names" and "letters" are interchangeable terms[121]. Just like the angels Gabriel and Michael, Metatron is also depicted as being entrusted with the instrument of the creation, the Name(s) of God or the twenty-two letters of the Hebrew alphabet.

It is evidently by virtue of being the Angel of the Lord that Gabriel, Michael, and Metatron are confided the Divine Name. In *III En.* xlviii[c].7b, quoted above, Metatron is called "the Little YHWH". This appellation occurs also in the enumeration of Metatrons's Name in xlviii[d].1; here, the cognomen is expanded into the full phrase "the Little YHWH, after the Name of His Master; "for My Name is in him" (*Ex.* xxiii.21)." The naming of Metatron as "the Little YHWH", with direct reference to the publication about the Angel of the Lord in *Ex.* xxiii.21, is also found in the description of Metatron's heavenly installation in *III En.* ch. xii:

> R. Ishmael said: "Metatron, the Prince of the Presence, said to me: "By reason of the love with which the Holy One, blessed be He, loved me more than all the children of heaven, He made a garment of glory, on which were fixed all kinds of lights, and He clad me in it. And He made me a robe of honour on which were fixed all kinds of beauty, splendour, brilliance, and majesty. And He made me a royal crown, in which were fixed forty-nine costly stones like unto the light of the globe of the sun; for its splendour went forth into the four corners of the 'Araboth Raqia', and into the seven heavens, and to the four corners of the world. And He called me "the Little YHWH" (יהוה הקטן) in the presence of all His household, as it is written: "for My Name is in him" (*Ex.* xxiii.21)." "

The next chapter goes on to relate that God wrote with a flaming style on Metatron's crown all the letters by which the universe was created[122]. Meta-

---

119 See p. 245.
120 For this idea, see above, pp. 246, 247f.
121 Note that *III En.* xlviii[d].5 asserts that the twenty-two letters are found on the seal of God's ring, while the prevailing notion is that the seal of the ring of God contains the Divine Name; see above, pp. 252, 259. Further, note that the idea of the creative letters being inscribed upon the crown of Metatron stands counter to the predominant notion of the Divine Name being inscribed upon the crown of God. For the latter idea, see Scholem, *Jewish Gnosticism*, pp. 54 f. The crown of Metatron, of course, is to be considered as a counterpart of God's own crown, just like Metatron's throne and curtain are counterparts of God's throne and curtain respectively (see x.1).
122 The text is quoted above, p. 245.

tron, then, is described as being installed as the ruler over the whole universe; and it is evident that he holds this office by virtue of being the Angel of the Lord in whom the Divine Name dwells. The name יהוה הקטן is meant to designate Metatron as the Angel of the Lord, who is second only to God. The Angel of the Lord is the "Little" or "Lesser" YHWH, as distinguished from God himself; it is this manifestation of YHWH that is the direct operative divine power in the universe.

Admittedly, although Enoch-Metatron is said to have been entrusted the creative instrument, the Divine Name or the letters of the alphabet, he is not described expressly as the demiurge. Nevertheless, the sifting of the traditions about Enoch's heavenly investiture as Metatron, the Angel of the Lord, and his reception of the Name(s) of God has proved valuable, for it points to the matrix of ideas out of which the Gnostic concept of the demiurge has risen. It is true that *III Enoch* is a rather late literary composition, but we have seen that there were much earlier traditions about Adam and Jesus containing the same motif as that elaborated upon by the circle behind the Enoch literature. Moreover, Gnostic sources predating *III Enoch* witness the appropriation of the Jewish idea of God's agent carrying the Divine Name(s). Before following up the earlier Jewish evidence about the principal angel of God possessing the Divine Name, it would be well to cite these Gnostic texts.

Gnostic Intermediaries

As a matter of fact, the precise term "the Little YHWH", which was given to the Angel of the Lord[123], crops up in Gnostic literature[124]. It is met with in *Pistis Sophia*, a 3rd century work, where Jesus is made to declare:

> And, when I set out for the world, I came to the midst of the archons of the spheres. And I had the form of Gabriel, the angel of the aeons; and the archons of the aeons did not recognize me, but thought I was the angel Gabriel. Now, it happened that, when I had come to the midst of the archons of the aeons, I looked down upon the world of mankind at the command of the First Mystery. I found Elizabeth, the mother of John the Baptist, before she had conceived him; and I sowed into her a power which I had taken from the Little Iao (ⲡⲕⲟⲩⲓ̈ Ⲛ̄Ⲓⲁⲱ̄), the Good one, who was in the middle, that he might be able to proclaim me and prepare my way, and baptize with water of the forgiveness of sins. This power is now to be found in

---

123 The mystical writings abound with statements to the effect that Metatron is "the Little YHWH"; see H. Odeberg, ed. & trans., *3 Enoch*, Cambridge, 1928, reprinted (LBS) New York, 1973, Part I, pp. 33 f. One ms. of *Sefer ha-Qoma*, a work which is an expanded redaction of *Shiur Qoma*, even contains the following statement: "The Explicit Name — that is Metatron, the Youth" (Bodl. ms. Oppenheimer 467, 61b). Here, the Name of God is personified.

124 Odeberg, Part I, p. 82, would seem to think that the concept of Metatron as the Little YHWH "reflects" Gnostic ideas. The relationship, however, must be explained the other way round. See the correct judgement by Odeberg, Part I, p. 192.

the body of John. And, furthermore, instead of the soul of the archons, which he is
destined to receive, I found the soul of the prophet Elijah in the aeons of the sphere;
and I took it with me, and I took his soul and brought it to the Virgin of Light.
And she delivered it to her *Paralemptores*, and they brought it to the sphere of the
archons and threw it into the mother womb of Elizabeth. Thus, the power of the
Little Iao, the one who is in the middle, and the soul of the prophet Elijah are bound
in the body of John the Baptist.

(ch. 7)

The idea that John the Baptist was some sort of reappearance of Elijah is
known from the Gospels, but it is no Christian doctrine that also "the power
of the Little Iao" was enclosed in his body. Although the passage does not
say expressly that "the Little Iao" had been incarnated in previous prophets,
we apparently are dealing with the idea of the cyclic manifestation of the
identical spiritual essence in a series of revealers. Some of the Jewish Christians believed that Adam was identical with Christ, and that the Adamite
Christ had manifested himself on earth several times[125]. It is possible that
some esoteric teaching about Adam is the foundation of the idea of "the
Little Iao" being incarnated in the prophets, for, as we have seen, Adam was
believed to have been given the Divine Name and appointed as God's vicegerent. Adam actually was the Little YHWH or Little *Yaho*, the latter form
being represented in Greek by "Little Iao". In any case, whatever is the
identity of the figure called the Little Yaho, the idea of the appearance of a
figure carrying God's Name in the prophets obviously is of Jewish origin.

To my knowledge, the name "Little Iao" occurs nowhere else in Gnostic
literature. However, *Pistis Sophia* also speaks about "the Little Sabaoth".
This personage is characterized as "the Good One" and "the one in the
middle", as is the Little Iao in ch. 7. In one passage, the Little Sabaoth works
in close relation with Sabaoth, who elsewhere is called "the Great Sabaoth"
and is a redemptory power (see ch. 63). In another context, the Little Sabaoth
appears in connection with "the Great Iao", who is also a salutary power in
the higher realms (see ch. 140). Thus, the name "Little Sabaoth" is obviously
evolved on the analogy of the name "Little Iao". That this distinction between (the Great) Sabaoth or the Great Iao on the one hand and the Little
Sabaoth on the other originated with Jews seems most probable. There apparently were Jews who posited a vicegerent of God carrying the Divine
Names qualified by the adjective "little" in order to be distinguished from
God. An 8th century Christian work in Syriac does in fact speak of the
"disgusting Jewish error" of distinguishing between אדוני גדול and אדוני
קטן [126]. This Jewish doctrine was taken over by Gnosticism, but modified

---

125 Cp. above, p. 67, nn. 129f. For the later idea of the incarnation of Metatron in the
righteous, see Odeberg, Part I, pp. 122 f.
126 The text is quoted by Scholem, *Major Trends*, p. 366, n. 106.

to the effect that the names of God and his vicegerent were applied to two figures in the elaborate divine hierarchy.

Pistis Sophia defines the functions of the Little Sabaoth rather dimly. Throughout the last chapters, he plays a rôle in the judgment of the various classes of the souls of men. He is also identified with Zeus (the planet Jupiter) and thought of as the governor of the revolving sphere (see ch. 137). This is reminiscent of the rôle of Adamas in the "Naassene Homily" and of the celestial Adam in the Jewish magical texts. Once, he is represented as some kind of conveyor of *gnōsis* to the elect (see ch. 147). Thus, in *Pistis Sophia*, the Little Sabaoth is a power carrying out divine offices. Usually, however, in the Gnostic systems, the name of Sabaoth is given to one of the seven archons or even to the chief archon, the demiurge. But, even so, Sabaoth is not always held to be systematically and wholly evil. According to Epiphanius, the so-called Archontics regarded Sabaoth as the archon in the seventh heaven:

> And Sabaoth, they say, is the god of the Jews, and the devil is an evil son of his; and, being from earth, he opposes his own father. And his father is not like him, nor again is he the Incomprehensible God whom they call the Father [...].
>
> *(Pan.* XL.v.1 f.)

In the same manner, Severus, who followed after Marcion's pupil Apelles, viewed Sabaoth as holding a medial position between God and the evil principle:

> He wants to ascribe the creation of our world to authorities and powers. There is, in an unnamed highest heaven and aeon, a good God. The devil, he says, is the son of the great ruler over the host of the powers, whom he now names Jaldabaoth, now Sabaoth. This one who was born from him is a serpent. He was cast down by the power above to the earth [...].
>
> *(Ibid.* XLV.1.3 ff.)

According to both the Archontics and Severus, it is the devil, and not Sabaoth, who is responsible for the evils in the world: to the devil, the origins of the enmity between men – wine, sexual passion, and woman – are ascribed (see *ibid.* XL.v.3 ff.; XLV.i.5 ff., ii.1 ff.). Sabaoth, the chief of the demiurgic powers and the ruler in the seventh heaven, has retained his basic position as God's vicegerent, the *little* Sabaoth, the demiurgic and ruling agent of God, the great Sabaoth.

In two of the writings from the Nag Hammadi library, *On the Origin of the World* (formerly called the *Untitled Writing*) and the *Hypostasis of the Archons*, both found in Codex II, we find a description of Sabaoth being enthroned upon the Merkaba which palpably draws upon Jewish tradition. In these works, Sabaoth is not the demiurge but his son. *On the Origin of the World* relates that Sophia condemned the demiurge, Jaldabaoth, to be cast down into the deep, and Sabaoth "received great power over all the forces of chaos" from Sophia because he realized that the words of his father, who boasted that he was the only god, were untrue (see 103.5 ff.). Jaldabaoth and the powers of chaos envied the glory that was given to Sabaoth, and prepared to wage war against him, but Sophia sent divine messengers to his aid and let him establish his abode in the eighth heaven. Here, Sabaoth created a throne upon a chariot called "Cherubin" with forms of a lion, a bull, a man, and an eagle (cp. *Ez.* i.10; *Rev.* iv.7). He also created myriads of angels, who surround his throne. On his right, Jesus is seated, while "the Virgin of the Holy Spirit" sits on his left. This position of Sabaoth corresponds to that of the "Great Glory" in the *Ascension of Isaiah* (xi.32 f.), where the latter is sitting with Jesus on his right and "the Angel of the Holy Spirit" on his left.

The *Hypostasis of the Archons* narrates the same story. Sophia creates an angel who binds Jaldabaoth and casts him down into the Tartaros. Sabaoth, however, repents and condemns his begetter. Sophia thereupon installs Sabaoth over the seventh heaven, and he is given the name "god of the powers". Then, Sabaoth makes for himself "a great cherubim-chariot, with four faces, and many angels without numbers to serve, and harps and zithers" (95.27 ff.). Sophia places Zoe on his right side and the angel of wrath on his left.

The figure of Sabaoth in these Gnostic writings evidently is modelled upon the concept of the vicegerent of God in Judaism. The Merkaba mystics defined the figure upon the throne described in *Ez.* ch. i as the Glory, but it has been shown that there were traditions about different figures being enthroned in heaven. Sabaoth in *On the Origin of the World* and the *Hypostasis of the Archons* is more or less perfectly equivalent to Adam in some recondite Jewish quarters: both repent and are enthroned by Wisdom in heaven as the ruler over the lower world, while the evil one is cast down. Moreover, although Sabaoth in these Gnostic texts is not the creator of the world, he is described as the creator of the heavenly hosts surrounding him, as is Adam in the magical papyri examined above. We obviously are dealing with a figure whose contours remain consistent although his name changes[127].

It is significant to note that the name of Sabaoth is one of the Biblical names of God, although it is not the proper Name, the Tetragrammaton, which was given to Adam and Enoch-Metatron. The principal agent of God apparently could be endowed with the diverse Divine Names. One recalls the Christian allegation that there were Jews who called God's agent "the Little Adonai". I can find no textual indication of this; but the "Book of Baruch" by Justin the Gnostic offers interesting evidence for the designation of the demiurge and kosmokrator by another Old Testament name of God, namely, Elohim.

---

127 F.T. Fallon says that the figure of Sabaoth has arisen from a conflation of "the God of the Old Testament, the leading angels [*prb 1* angel], and the apocalyptic visionary" (*The Enthronement of Sabaoth* (NHS, X), Leiden, 1978, p. 34). This construction cannot account for important elements in the picture of Sabaoth.

According to the "Book of Baruch", as summarized for us by Hippolytus, the highest God, called "the Good", cannot enter into contact with the material world, and a primal power by the name of Elohim holds the demiurgical office. It is said that, "when Elohim had established and formed the world out of mutual good pleasure, he wished to go up into the lofty parts of heaven and see whether anything was defective in his creation, and he was taking his angels with him" (V.xxvi.14). To his astonishment, Elohim sees that there exists a higher deity than himself in the uppermost spheres. Elohim asks to be let into the highest heaven and is allowed so by the highest God. He is enthroned beside the Good ; and from his throne in heaven, he acts as the *factotum* for the salvation of men.

It must be underlined that Elohim is not the ignorant and arrogant demiurge of classical Gnosticism ; quite on the contrary, he realizes that there is a higher God above him. We find again the motif of the agent of God humbling himself and then being enthroned in heaven. Justin actually cites *Ps.* cx.1 with reference to the enthronement of Elohim beside the Good. However, Elohim is not said to have received the name *kyrios*, the Greek translation of the Tetragrammaton; Elohim is vicegerent of God carrying one of the Divine Names, though not the proper Name.

That the demiurge was the carrier of the diverse Divine Names is an idea which we can catch a glimpse of even in the later and elaborated Gnostic systems. G. Quispel has noted that a certain rehabilitation of the demiurge has taken place in the *Tripartite Tractate* from Codex I of the Nag Hammadi library, possibly written by Heracleon, one of the most important pupils of Valentinus[128]. In this treaty, we read:

> Therefore, he [*viz.*, the demiurge] is embellished with all the Names, which are an image of Him [*viz.*, the highest God], who possesses all the attributes and all the honours[132]

(100.25 ff.)

Origen, in his commentary on the *Gospel of John*, has preserved a comment by Heracleon on *John* iv.46 which seems to vouch that the Valentinians conserved quite clear reminiscences that the demiurge was God's vicegerent:

> Heracleon seems to say that the βασιλικὸς was the demiurge; "for [, he says,] he himself ruled like a king over those under him." "Because his domain is small and transitory, he was called βασιλικὸς," he says, "like a little prince who is set over a small kingdom by the universal king."

(*In Joh.* xiii.60)

Apparently, because he is God's vicegerent, the demiurge is enriched with all the Names of God. It will be recalled that the angel Metatron in esoteric Judaism and the demiurge Gabriel in Mandeism are presented as being endowed with all the Divine Names.

---

128 See "Origins", p. 276.

Surveying the Gnostic texts for traces of the principal agent of God carrying the Divine Name, we must include the figure of Ἰεου in the works from Codex Askewianus and Codex Brucianus. The name Ieu is obviously equivalent to Iao, the Name of God. "The Gnostic figures of Ιαω and Ιευ are doublets, the former reflecting the old southern, the latter the old North-Israelite pronunciation."[129] But Ieu is not the highest God; he is the vicegerent of "the First Mystery". Among his manifold tasks, we note that he has erected the diverse aeons, ordered the heimarmene and the sphere, and installed archons and ministers in the various domains (see *Pistis Sophia* ch. 15; 21; 25; *Fragment of a Gnostic Prayer, passim*). He is called the "king" and "father" of "the Treasure of Light", a region situated beneath the uppermost realms and which the Gnostics attain to after death (see *II Jeu* ch. 50; *et passim*). Ieu also presides over the judgment and tries the souls (see *Pistis Sophia* ch. 130). As regards his appellations, it is of importance to note that he is constantly designated as the "First Man" or the "Great Man", and, since he carries out the same functions as Adam according to Jewish mysticism, it is difficult to escape the conclusion that the Gnostic figure of Ieu shows influence from the Jewish Adam teachings which conceived of the first man as God's vicegerent possessing the Divine Name.

Except *Pistis Sophia*, the name Iao appears usually in the Gnostic sources as the name of one of the archons, but one reference at least contains a positive connotation of the name. Irenaeus reports that the initiate into the mysteries of one of the branches of the Valentinians had to say:

> "I am established; I am redeemed; and I redeem my soul from this age and from all that comes from it, in the name of Iao, who redeemed his soul unto redemption in Christ, the Living One." Then the bystanders add: "Peace be with all upon whom this Name rests."
>
> (I.xxi.3)

It is difficult to determine what this liturgical formula refers to; I cannot find any allusion to a figure called Iao in any other text pertaining to the Valentinians[130]. The formula occurs in a section where Irenaeus cites various Valentinian formularies bearing upon the redemption effected or, at least, symbolized by the Gnostic rites. The heresiologist makes specific mention of the rite of baptism and the sacrament of the bridal chamber. Of the latter, he says: "Some of them prepare a bridal chamber and perform a mystical rite, with certain invocations, for those who are being consecrated; and they claim that what they are effecting is a spiritual marriage, after the image of

---

129 W.F. Albright, *Yahweh and the Gods of Canaan* (SOAS: JL, VII, 1965), London, 1968, p. 228, n. 155.

130 But notice that "Iao" is the efficacious word by which Horos turns Achamoth back from entering the Pleroma again; see above, p. 249, n. 18.

the syzygies above." This sacrament is referred to again and again in the Valentinian *Gospel of Philip* from Codex II of the Nag Hammadi library[131]; and it is said that it is superior to baptism (see *log.* 76). In the bridal chamber, an anointing also takes place (see *log.* 95); and Irenaeus relates that, after the bystanders have prayed for peace upon the one who has got the name Iao upon him, "they anoint the initiate with oil from the balsam tree." The formula, then, may relate to the sacrament of the bridal chamber. This *hieros gamos* sacrament symbolizes the union of the soul with its celestial counterpart, and the rite has a mythical correlative in the union of the fallen Sophia with Christ (cp. also Clem. Alex., *Exc. ex Theod.*lxiv.1). In the Gnostic "gospel" (*log.* 9), Jesus is said to have saved his own soul; and it is thus possible, as argued by G. Quispel, that Iao is a name of Christ who actually redeems his own soul through his redemption of Sophia[132]. Anyway, the Valentinian formulary shows that Iao is the name of a saviour figure and no base being.

This quick tour of Gnosticism has shown that the Old Testament appellatives of God including his proper Name were applied to an intermediary that was far from being an evil figure. The contours of this intermediary are more or less consistent. He can be described as carrying out saving functions and being a regent and judge in a heavenly region, where he also can be conceived of as enthroned upon the Merkaba; and he can also be described as the demiurge, either of some heavenly spheres or of the whole universe. We have every reason to suspect that Jewish traditions about the Glory or the principal angel of God were the formative forces in creating this Gnostic intermediary.

The Angel of the Lord

The Gnostic evidence for the intermediary carrying the Name of God takes us back to the 2nd century C.E., but it is possible to detect the figure in Jewish traditions from an earlier date. The Talmudic traditions about Metatron shall claim our attention first, for the idea that Metatron had a name "like that of his Master" is not confined to the late date of *III Enoch*. The following tradition is ascribed to R. Naḥman:

He who is as skilled in refuting the *minim* as is R. Idi let him do so, but not otherwise. Once a *min* said to R. Idi: "It is written: "And, unto Moses, He [*viz.*, God] said: "Come up to the Lord" " (*Ex.* xxiv.1). But surely it should have been stated:

131 See H.-G. Gaffron, *Studien zum koptischen Philippusevangelium unter besonderer Berücksichtigung der Sakramente*, Diss., Bonn, 1969, pp. 63ff., 185ff. Cp. Rudolph, *Die Gnosis*, pp. 251 f.

132 See "Mandaeërs en Valentinianen", *NTT*, 8, 1954, pp. 144 ff. Cp. also "Gnosis und hellenistische Mysterienreligionen", in U. Mann, ed., *Theologie und Religionswissenschaft,* Darmstadt, 1973, p. 329.

"Come up to Me." " "It was Metatron," he [*viz.*, R. Idi] replied, "whose name is similar to that of his Master, for it is written: "For My Name is in him" (*Ex.* xxiii. 21)." [The *min* said:] "But, if so, we should worship him!" "The same passage," replied R. Idi, "says: "Be not rebellious against him," [that is,] "do not exchange Me for him." [The *min* said:] "But, if so, why is it stated: "He will not pardon your transgression" (*Ex.* xxiii.21)?" He [*viz.*, R. Idi] answered: "We hold the belief that we would not accept him even as a messenger; for it is written: "And he [*viz.*, Moses] said to Him [*viz.*, God]: "If Your Presence does not go, *etc.* " " (*Ex.* xxxiii.15)."[133]

(Sanh. 38b)

R. Nahman was a Babylonian amora of the late 3rd century, and the language of the text is Babylonian Aramaic; thus, the text itself cannot be dated earlier than to the 3rd century. However, R. Nahman relies on R. Idi, whose identity is uncertain but who must have been an older authority.

The passage states that a heretic asserted that one ought to worship Metatron, because R. Idi held Metatron to be the Angel of the Lord spoken of in *Ex.* xxiii.21 and referred to by the Tetragrammaton in *Ex.* xxiv.1. The rabbi counters the argument by saying that *Ex.* xxiii.21 actually contains a warning against confusing the angel and God: R. Idi takes אל תמר בו in *Ex.* xxiii.21 as meaning אל תמירני בו. Obviously, some *minim* ascribed divine properties to the principal angel of God. R. Idi, however, although admitting that the angel carries the Divine Name, strongly emphasizes that he must not be confused with God and worshipped. The rabbi will not even accept the angel as Israel's guide: he interprets *Ex.* xxxiii.15 as Moses' prayer that God himself should always be the guide of Israel. This interpretation is made in answer to the heretic's question why the Bible needed to say that the angel would not pardon Israel. The *min* apparently means that, since the angel is described as not pardoning Israel at this one place, the pardoning is normally offered by that angel, who thus has a share in the divine properties.

But how can Metatron's name be said to be "like that of his Master"? G. Scholem argues that the story rests on an earlier version which actually held that the name of the angel included the Divine Name[134]. The Karaite theologian al-Qirqisani read in his text of the Talmud: "This is Metatron, who is the Little YHWH." This might be the original reading of *Sanh.* 38b. As has been seen above, "the Little YHWH" is a name given to Metatron in the mystical literature. The Karaites viewed the name as a sign of heresy and deviation from monotheism, and attacked the Rabbanites because of its appearance in the literature which they had inherited.

The other important Talmudic tradition mentioning Metatron is the well-known story about the four rabbis who entered Paradise. It is said that R. Aqiba alone departed unhurt, while Ben Azzai died, Ben Zoma "looked

---

133 The passage has been analyzed by Segal, pp. 68 ff.
134 See *Major Trends*, p. 68; *Jewish Gnosticism*, pp. 41, 47, 50 f.; *Kabbalah*, p. 378.

and became demented," and Aḥer "cut the roots." The part of the story relevant for our purposes deals with Aḥer's fortunes:

> Aḥer cut the roots. Of him, Scripture says: "Suffer not your mouth to bring your flesh into guilt" (*Eccl.* v.5). What does this refer to? He saw that permission was granted to Metatron to sit and write down the merits of Israel. He said: "It is taught as a tradition that, on high, there is no sitting and no emulation, no back and no weariness. Perhaps – God forfend! – there are two powers?" Thereupon, they led Metatron forth and punished him with sixty fiery lashes, saying to him: "Why did you not rise before him when you saw him?" Permission was then given to him to strike out the merits of Aḥer. A *bath qol* went forth and said: " "Return all you backsliding children" (*Jer.* iii.22), except Aḥer."[135]

> (*Ḥag.* 15a)

Again, the language is Babylonian Aramaic; hence, the text itself is rather late. But we have good reason to believe that the concept of the mediating angel is quite old. Also, the idea of a heavenly scribe pre-dates the time of Aḥer. Quite early, the office of being the scribe in heaven who records men's deeds was attributed to Enoch (see *Jub.* iv.23), and Enoch – as we have seen – was identified with Metatron in another stream of tradition. In *II En.* chs. xxii ff. (long recension), Enoch sits at God's left hand. There is nothing which compels us to dismiss the story as relating to Elisha ben Abuya, who flourished at the beginning of the 2nd century C.E. and was called Aḥer, that is, "Other", because of his heretical turning. That Jewish mystics undertook journeys to heaven is witnessed already in the first century by Paul (*II Cor.* xii.2 ff.).

---

135 The passage is discussed by Segal, pp. 60 ff. S. Lieberman, "Metatron, the Meaning of His Name and His Functions", Appendix to Gruenwald, pp. 234 ff., has shown that the word *metathronos* is a younger form of *synthronos*, which designates a lesser deity and means "one who shares a throne alongside the major deity". However, as Liebermann says, *synthronos theou* could also denote one who has a throne beside the throne of God. Thus, Metatron probably is understood to sit on a *throne*.

When R. Aqiba interpreted the second throne in *Dan.* vii.9 as the throne of the Messiah, he was set right immediately by R. Yose the Galilean, who said that the two thrones were for the merciful and the judging aspect of God, and R. Eleazar ben Azariah sharply denounced R. Aqiba for dealing with aggadic matters (see *Ḥag.* 14a; cp. *Sanh.* 38b). It is perhaps worthy of note that Aḥer is said to have doubted God's justice (see Jer. *Ḥag.* 77a *et al.*), for his might be taken to mean that he hypostasized the divine justice as the principal angel. In any event, the discussion between R. Aqiba and R. Yose shows that the first part of the 2nd century was a period in which the Jews were occupied with questions about a *synthronos theou*. See also Segal, pp. 47 ff.

The Tosefta version (*Ḥag.* ii.3 f.) of Elisha ben Abuya's defection does not contain the Metatron vision, and Jer. *Ḥag.* 77b and *Cant.R.* i.4 have replaced it by a story about Elisha discouraging students of the Torah, thus probably associating "Paradise" with study activity. *III En.* ch. xvi contains an elaboration of the story in the Babylonian Talmud. In this version, Metatron sits upon the Merkaba.

Aḥer's lapse into heresy ("cutting the roots") was caused by his wondering whether Metatron was a second deity. The Talmud explains that the angel Metatron was allowed to be seated because he was the heavenly scribe, and, in order to prove that Metatron is no deity, the angels punished him. However, as we have seen time and again, it is a constant trait in the traditions about God's vicegerent that he is enthroned in heaven in a way equivalent to God himself. It thus seems that the rabbis are concealing some of the implications of the heresy which they are trying to refute.

Aḥer's exclamation, "Perhaps there are two powers?," presents us anew with the heresy defined as "two powers in heaven". A.F. Segal has shown that the basic form of this heresy consisted in assuming that God had a vicegerent who was enthroned in heaven and possessed the Divine Name. Since this heresy reaches back into the first century of the common era, we would seem to be justified in connecting Aḥer with the "two powers" doctrine. If Metatron – or, rather, his prototype – carried the Name of God, Aḥer's "mistake" becomes comprehensible: he was taking the angel as a second deity because he shared in holding the Divine Name, that is, the divine nature.

W. Bousset, on the basis of some passages in the rabbinic literature, took Metatron to be "the angel to whom God entrusts the creation of the world, that is, the demiurge."[136] Although this is a most questionable assertion, the texts referred to by Bousset are important for the present discussion. In a section of *Genesis Rabba* dealing with God's words in *Gen.* i.9, "Let the waters under the heavens be gathered ... ," we find the following comment:

> The voice of the Lord became Metatron to the waters, as it is written: "The voice of the Lord is over the waters" (*Ps.* xxix.3)

(v.4)

Does this mean that Metatron was regarded by some as the personified creative command of God? It is intriguing that the greatest champions of this tradition are said to have been Ben Azzai and Ben Zoma, both of whom met with a disastrous end when ascending to heaven. Did their vision of the principal angel lead them to the conclusion that he was the Logos of God? Furthermore, that the voice of God is said to have been על־המים is reminiscent of the statement in *Gen.* i.2 that the Spirit of God was על־פני המים, and so we may also ask whether Metatron is identified with the pre-existent Spirit. In Gnosticism, we find the idea that the Spirit in *Gen.* i.2 separates the primeval elements (see *CH* I.5; Iren., I.xxx.1, on the Ophites; Epiphan., *Pan.* XXV.v.1, on certain "Gnostics"; cp. Hipp., V.xix.13 ff., on the Sethians).

---

136 *Hauptprobleme*, p. 200. Trachtenberg says that Metatron is "the demiurge of classical Jewish mysticism" (p. 76), but he does not support this characterization by textual evidence. Arai, p. 71, note continued from the preceding page, and p. 72, n. 2, says that Metatron is described as the demiurge in *III Enoch*. This is not correct.

In view of the rabbinic text, where God's creative command seems to be associated with the Spirit, it is especially interesting to note that *Poimandres* (*CH* I) calls this demiurgic Spirit a "spiritual Word" (πνευματικὸς λόγος).

In the Gnostic sources, the Spirit performs its demiurgic activity through an adhesion to matter; thus, *Poimandres* says that the spiritual Word "came upon" (ἐπέβη) matter. In this connection, we must note that the space between the upper and lower waters in *Gen.* i.6 f. was only a hand-breadth or even two or three fingers' breadth wide, and that the Spirit in *Gen.* i.2 therefore was hovering over the lower waters like a bird right above its nest, "touching and yet not touching" (*Tos. Ḥag.* ii.5; Jer. *Ḥag.* ch. 2, 77b; cp. *Ḥag.* 15a; *Gen.R.* ii.4). H. Odeberg thinks that this suggests that the upper waters have an "engendering function" in relation to the lower waters, but in view of the close "association between Spirit and Water", it would not seem implausible that here the *Spirit* is ascribed with the fructifying powers of the waters above the firmament[137]. It is not impossible that Ben Zoma could have identified the demiurgic Spirit with the principal angel. In the *Shepherd of Hermas*, the pre-existent Holy Spirit, who is attributed with the work of creation (see *Sim.* V.vi.5), is identified with the Son (see *ibid.* IX.i.1), who – in turn – is identical with the "glorious angel" Michael (see *ibid.* VIII.i-iii; IX. xii.7 f.; *et passim*).

Before returning to the text from *Gen.R.* v.4, however, another tradition about Ben Zoma is to be cited. His interpretation of *Gen.* i.7, "And God made (ויעש)," is said to have been one of the expositions with which he "shook the world" (*Gen.R.* iv.6). Unfortunately, the actual interpretation is not reported, but it must have concerned the verb עשׂה, which occurs here for the first time in the creation narrative. The rabbinic text says: "This is a strange thing. Is it not by a word (מאמר) of God?" This cannot have been spoken by Ben Zoma, for such an interpretation of the verb עשׂה cannot be said to have shaken the world; it must have been spoken by the rabbis in opposition to Ben Zoma. The verb עשׂה, as opposed to ברא, which is also found in *Gen.* ch. i, is not used exclusively of God's work, and has a strong connotation of handicraft. Thus, Ben Zoma may have used *Gen.* i.7 as proof

---

137 Odeberg, *Gospel*, p. 53. For discussion of the relationship between Ben Zoma's cosmogonic views and Gnosticism, see Graetz, *Gnosticismus*, pp. 79 f.; Weiss, *Untersuchungen*, pp. 102 ff.; Urbach, pp. 189 f.
   The Samaritan theologian Abu'l Hasan cited *Gen.* i.2 as proof that the angels have wings; see Bowman, *Documents*, p. 249. That the Spirit was welded with the concept of angel is known from Hellenistic Judaism; see below, p. 318, n. 160. Regarding the angel pneumatology of Jewish Christianity, see W.-D. Hauschild, *Gottes Geist und der Mensch* (AET, 38), Munich, 1972, p. 81. Jewish exegesis could claim pre-existence for Adam or the Messiah with reference to *Gen.* i.2 (see *Gen.R.* viii.1; *Pesikta R.* xxxiii.6; *et al.*).

that the world was fabricated by a lower demiurge, or at least that the creation narrative in *Gen.* i.7 ff. assumes another creator than God.

Ben Zoma manifestly was considered to be dissentient in his cosmogonic expositions and may have taught the concept of a demiurge, but this would not seem to be the case in the text from *Gen.R.* v.4, which is one of the three texts referred to by Bousset in substantiation of his statement that Metatron was represented as a demiurge. There are manifold variants for the word "Metatron" in *Gen.R.* v.4, and the most unusual and apparently original word appearing in the mss. is מטטור, which is recognized as the Latin *metator*, "guide", "index". The existence of so many variants in the mss. shows that the original word was unknown to the copyists, who substituted similar-looking words; and the word מטטרון may simply have been picked because of its similarity in characters. If the existence of the name of Metatron in some of the mss. is due to the fact that some really regarded him as an intermediary of the creation, this would appear to be a later explanation.

In the Talmudic tractate *Ḥullin* (60a), "the Prince of the world", שר העולם, is said to have been present when God created the world, praising the creation with the words of *Ps.* civ.31. But the Prince of the world himself is not said to have been allotted a share in the work of creation. In another Talmudic tract, the words of *Ps.* xxxvii.25, "I have been a youth and now I am old," are put into the mouth of the Prince of the world because he has been present during the whole history of the world from its very beginning (see *Yeb.* 16b). But, again, creative functions are not ascribed to him.

The name "the Prince of the world" is given to Metatron in later sources, but the figure's identity is unknown in the two Talmudic passages. As we have seen, Metatron is called "Youth" in *III Enoch*, but this interpretation of Metatron as the Youth has nothing to do with the words of *Ps.* xxxvii.25. G. Scholem thinks that the epithet "Youth", נער, which also means "servant", originally belonged to Michael as the Prince of the world and the cultic "servant" in the heavenly tabernacle, while both *Yeb.* 16b and *III En.* chs. iii-iv represent new explanations of this epithet of God's principal angel[138]. M. Hengel suggests that the title "Youth" was substituted for that of the Son of Man because the latter had taken on a Christological significance and therefore was abandoned by Jews[139]. It is not necessary to enter into this discus-

---

138 See *Jewish Gnosticism*, pp. 44, 48 ff. Scholem opposes Odeberg, Part I, p. 104, who says that the Prince of the world is Metatron. In *Shiur Qoma*, Metatron is the high priest in the heavenly tabernacle, which, in a late text, is called the "tabernacle of the Naʿsar" (see *Num. R.* xii. 12). Originally, this function belonged to Michael; see below, p. 321.

139 See *The Son of God*, trans. by J. Bowden, Philadelphia, 1976, p. 46. Cp. Segal, *Two Powers*, p. 67, n. 24; "Ruler", p. 405, n. 18 (continued on the next page). If the epithet "Youth" is essentially equal to that of the Son of Man, it is worth noting that

sion. What we should take note of, however, is the fact that the appellation
recurs in Gnosticism. Already H. Odeberg pointed out that this epithet of
Metatron recurs in Gnostic sources: in the untitled writing of *Codex Brucianus*, we hear about "the Overseer who is called the Youth (ⲡⲁⲗⲟⲩ)" (ch. 3),
and the Mandean literature contains some passages where a salutary figure is
called ראביא טאליא, "the Youthful Boy"[140]. C.A. Baynes pointed out that
Jesus is called ⲡⲁⲗⲟⲩ in the *Apocryphon of John* (*BG* 34.10), and after the
publication of the Coptic Manichean texts and the Nag Hammadi library, it
has become clear that the epithet also is used in these sources[141].

When the Nag Hammadi corpus became known, it was discovered that the
Gnostics even explained the name of the demiurge Jaldabaoth as the "Youth".
In *On the Origin of the World*, Sophia addresses her son, the demiurge:
"Youth (νεανίσκος), move over (διαπερᾶν) to this place." The author of the
treatise immediately adds: "Whence the product "Jaldabaoth" " (100.12ff.).
Here, then, the name of the demiurge, Jaldabaoth, is expounded as νεανίσκε
διαπέρα, ילדא בעוט. It is of no moment whether or not this etymology is
right[142]; the notable point is that the Gnostics called the demiurge "Youth".
The Gnostics modelled the figure of the demiurge upon the principal angel.
It does not seem impossible that there even were *Jews* who ascribed the
creation to "the Youth".

The figure of Metatron obviously has absorbed many features belonging to
the principal angel in earlier traditions. There is quite early evidence that this
angel possessed the Name of God, which we have learnt to know as being the

LXX *Dan.* vii.13 says that the one "like a son of man" "came *as* the Ancient of
Days," for this verse describes the second power in heaven as both a youth and an old
man, just like the Prince of the world describes himself in *Yeb.* 16b. The term
זקן, which is claimed by the Prince of the world on the basis of *Ps.* xxxvii.25, was
often used with reference to the Ancient of Days in *Dan.* ch. vii. Cp. below, pp. 319f.
140 See Odeberg, Part I, pp. 68 f., 191. Odeberg thinks that the figure in the untitled
writing in *Codex Brucianus* is identical with the "Overseer" who is the second being
in the confusing divine hierarchy in this work. The latter is called, *inter alia*, "demiurge", but it is not clear what his creative activity consists in (see ch. 2). However,
C.A. Baynes, ed. & trans., *A Coptic Gnostic Treatise Contained in the Codex Brucianus*, Cambridge, 1933, pp. 63 ff., is probably right to identify the ⲁⲗⲟⲩ with
Christ. Later on in ch. 3, this being is called μονογενής. According to Baynes, we
should translate ⲁⲗⲟⲩ as "servant", for Christ is described as διάκονος in ch. 8.
His function is to order and consolidate the Pleroma. In the Mandean texts, "the
Youthful Boy" can be identified with Hibil, a salutary power.
141 In *Kephalaia*, Jesus is once called ⲡⲁⲗⲟⲩ (see Polotsky, p. 61, line 27). In the Psalm-Book, the term is ⲗⲓⲗⲟⲩ, which is used of the Primordial Man, the Anthropos. The
word has an Egyptian derivation, but may have been chosen because "Lillu" or
"Lullu" was a name of the primal man in Babylonian religion (see *Enuma Elish* VI).
In the *Three Steles of Seth* from Codex VII of the Nag Hammadi Library, the androgynous aeon being next to the Father is called "divine ⲁⲗⲟⲩ" (123.7).
142 See above, p. 11, n. 45.

creative instrument. In a fragment of the *Prayer of Joseph*, which has been preserved in Origen's commentary on the *Gospel of John* and dates from the 2nd or even the first century C.E., an angel called "Jacob" and "Israel" declares:

> I, Jacob, who am speaking to you, am also Israel, an angel of God and a ruling spirit. Abraham and Isaac were created before any work; but I, Jacob, whom men call Jacob but whose name is Israel, am he whom God called Israel, that is, a man seeing God, because I am the first-born of every living thing to which God gives life [...]. And, when I was coming up from Syrian Mesopotamia, Uriel, the angel of God, came out and said that I had descended to earth and tabernacled among men, and that I had been called by the name of Jacob. He envied me, and fought with me and wrestled with me, saying that his name and the Name of Him who is before every angel were to be above mine. I told him his name and what rank he held among the sons of God: "Are you not Uriel, the eighth after me, and I, Israel, the archangel of the power of the Lord and the chief captain among the sons of God? Am I not Israel, the first minister before the face of God?" And I called upon my God by the Inextinguishable Name [...].

(In Joh. II.31)

Here, then, in a fragment of an apocryphon "in use among the Hebrews", we find a pre-existent angel called "Jacob" and "Israel", who claims superiority over the angel Uriel on the basis of his victory in personal combat where he availed himself of the Divine Name. The angelic name "Israel", explained as אִישׁ רָאָה אֵל, is among the names of the many-named intermediary in Philo's works[143], and, in one of the passages where Philo presents this name as one of the designations of the intermediary, he also says that the "Name of God" is among the appellations of this being[144]. Thus, "Israel" apparently was a name of the Angel of the Lord, the possessor of the Divine Name, in some circles[145]. Justin also testifies to this tradition, for he gives the name "Israel" as one of the names of the Son as he appeared under the old dispensation, and, in one passage, where he identifies the Angel of the Lord in *Ex.* xxiii.20 f. as Jesus, he says that "he was also called "Israel", and he bestowed this name on Jacob" (*Dial.* lxxv.2).

Justin concurs with the *Prayer of Joseph* when he says that the angel Israel is "the first-born of all creatures" (πρωτότοκον τῶν ὅλων κτισμάτων) (*ibid.* cxxv.3). The description of the angel Israel as "first-born" may be implying demiurgic claims. Since Jacob-Israel is an angel, it is remarkable that

---

143 See *Leg. all.* I.43; *De conf. ling.* 146. For a discussion of the *Prayer of Joseph*, see J.Z. Smith, "The Prayer of Joseph", in *RA*, pp. 253 ff.

144 See above, p. 269.

145 That the many-named intermediary, the Logos, in Philo's system is the Angel of the Lord is made quite clear in those passages where he is described with reference to *Ex.* xxiii.20 f. (see *De agr.* 51; *De migr. Abr.* 174).

it is said that he has come into being before all other creatures, for — as we have seen — the rabbis agreed that the angels were *not* created on the first day, lest some should assert that they had acted as God's "associates" in the creation[146]. Philo often calls the many-named intermediary, to whom he attributes demiurgic activity[147], πρωτόγονος[148], and, in one place, he expressly associates this epithet with the creative work of this figure[149]. We have also seen that Adam is called πρωτοφυής and πρωτογενής in a Jewish magical prayer where he is portrayed as the demiurge[150].

Already H. Windisch pointed out that the description of the angel Israel in the *Prayer of Joseph* as πρωτόγονος παντὸς ζῴου ׀ζωουμένου ὑπὸ, θεοῦ is reminiscent of the representation of Christ in the hymn in *Col.* i.15-20[151]:

> He is the image of the invisible God, the first-born of all creation (πρωτότοκος πάσης κτίσεως), for in him, all things were created, in heaven and upon earth, visible and invisible, whether thrones or dominions, or principalities or authorities — all things were created through him and for him. He is before all things, and all things hold together in him; and he is the head of the body (the Church [this is a gloss][152]). He is the beginning, the first-born from the dead ... .
>
> (*vv.* 15-18)

The hymn now changes from speaking of the cosmogonic and cosmological rôle of the Son to celebrating his redemptory work. It is the first part alone which is of interest in this connection.

It is generally agreed that the background of the first part of the hymn is to be sought in Hellenistic Jewish traditions about Sophia[153]. Admittedly,

---

146 See above, pp. 265f.
147 See the references given above, p. 287.
148 In addition to *De conf. ling.* 146, see *ibid.* 62 f.; *De agr.* 51 (where the Logos and "first-born Son" of God is identified with the Angel of the Lord); *De somn.* 1.215.
149 See the quotation from *De conf. ling.* 62f. above, p. 287.
150 See above, p. 282.
151 See "Die göttliche Weisheit der Juden und die paulinische Christologie", in *Neutestamentliche Studien für G. Heinrici* (UNT, 6), Leipzig, 1914, p. 225, n. 1.
152 The reference to "the Church" spoils the parallelism of the lines and the cosmic scope of the hymn; originally, "the body" referred to the universe. The idea that the *pantokrator* was the "head" of the cosmos, which, in turn, was his "body", was common in the ancient world; see E. Lohse, *Die Briefe an die Kolosser und an Philemon* (MKKNT, 9/2), Göttingen, 1968, pp. 93 f.; E. Schweizer, *Der Brief an die Kolosser* (EKK), Zürich, 1976, pp. 53, 60, 62, p. 125, n. 415. Philo represents the Logos as the head of the universe, his body; see Lohse, p. 94.
153 See Lohse, pp. 77 ff.; Schweizer, pp. 50 ff. However, C.F. Burney, "Christ as the ᾿ΑΡΧΗ of the Creation", *JTS*, 27, 1926, pp. 160 ff., has propounded the intriguing theory that the hymn is an elaborate exposition of בראשית in *Gen.* i.1 in the rabbinic manner, which found a clue to the meaning of this word in *Prov.* viii.22, where Wisdom characterizes herself as the ראשית of God's creation. According to

Wisdom is never explicitly called "first-born", but the description of Christ as "the first-born of all creation" undoubtedly alludes to *Prov.* viii.22, where Wisdom says: "The Lord begat me as the beginning (ראשית/ἀρχὴν) of His ways, before all His other works."[154] The beginning of the second part of the Christ hymn, where the Son is named ἀρχή as well as "first-born", clearly refers back to the opening of the hymn, which describes Christ as "the first-born of all creation". Moreover, πρωτότοκος as well as ἀρχή can be seen as a translation of ראשית, one of the meanings of which is "first-fruit". In *Prov.* ch. viii, Wisdom claims pre-mundane existence and asserts that she was by God's side as a "master craftsman" when the world was made (see *v.* 30)[155], and the characterization of Wisdom as the ראשית/ἀρχή of God's creation was often taken as a key to the interpretation of ראשית in *Gen.* i.1, בראשית ברא אלהים, while the preposition was seen as *Beth instrumentalis*. Thus, the Palestinian Fragmentary Targum *Gen.* i.1 reads: "In the beginning: Through Wisdom, the Lord created and perfected the heavens and the

---

this interpretation of בראשית, the preposition ב is explained by three expressions, namely, by the statements that all things were created "*in* him" (*v.* 15), "*through* him" (*v.* 16), and "*for* him" (*v.* 16), while the substantive ראשית is explained by four expressions, namely, by the statements that the Son is "before all things" (*v.* 17), that all things "hold together in him" (*v.* 17, indicating the sum-total connotation of the noun), that he is "the head" (*v.* 18), and that he is "the beginning, the first-born" (*v.* 18). Thus, at the back of the hymn, there may be a rabbinic exposition of בראשית in *Gen.* i.1 understood to describe the instrumentality of Wisdom in creation.

154 The scholars are not agreed on the understanding of the verb קנה. Its most usual meaning is "acquire" and "possess (what is acquired)" (which is the meaning elsewhere in *Proverbs* and given by the Vulgate, the Greek versions of Aquila, Theodotion, and Symmachus, and the Syro-Hexaplar, the Syriac version of Paul of Tella), but it can also mean "create" (as read by the LXX, the Peshitta, and the Targum) as well as "engender" (see *Gen.* iv.1). The continuation, which speaks about Wisdom's birth, vouches for the last rendering; see also W. McKane, *Proverbs* (OTL), London, 1970, pp. 352 f.; B. Lang, *Frau Weisheit*, Düsseldorf, 1975, pp. 90 f. The *Book of Sirach* (xxiv.3) and the *Book of Wisdom* (vii.25) represent Wisdom as being emanated from God, but the former writing (i.4, 9; xxiv.8) can also describe Wisdom as being created. Philo (*De fuga et invent.* 50) says that Sophia is the daughter of God and begotten by him. In *De cher.* 49 f., Wisdom is said to have called upon God as her father.

It is possible that ראשית דרכו should be taken in a temporal sense ("The Lord begat me *at* the beginning ..."); see McKane, p. 354. This is also the understanding of the Peshitta and the Targum. But all the Greek versions and the best ms. of the Vulgate, *viz.*, *Codex Amiatinus*, have only "[as] the beginning".

155 It is possible that the word אמון has the meaning "ward", "darling", in the Hebrew text (so Aquila), but the principal ancient versions (the LXX, the Vulgate, the Peshitta, and the Targum) support the translation above. For discussion of the term, see McKane, pp. 356 ff.; Lang, pp. 93 ff. In the *Book of Wisdom*, Sophia is a demiurgic being; see above, p. 288.

earth."[156] Furthermore, as we have seen above, the *Book of Wisdom* ascribes demiurgic activity to Sophia[157]. Finally, it may be noted that already *II Enoch* knew the idea that Wisdom even created man, for this pre-Christian pseudepigraphon teaches that, after God had made the world and all the animals, he said: "When I had completed all this, I commanded My Wisdom to create man" (ch. 11)[158].

Thus, it is palpable that the name "first-born" has associations to Wisdom, who was regarded as a demiurgic figure. Wisdom originally was a female being, but – as is shown by *Col.* i.15 ff. and other ancient Christian texts – the creative Wisdom was facilely construed as Christ[159]. This identification is related to the Hellenistic Jewish tradition about a many-named intermediary who is Wisdom as well as Son, Logos, Angel, *etc.*[160]. As C.H. Talbert has evidenced, the *Prayer of Joseph* must be seen as part of this tradition, and the

---

156 This is the version of MS. Paris Hebr. 110. MS. Vatican Ebr. 440 leaves out "and perfected". Targum Neofyti I should probably read: "From the beginning, the Memra of the Lord created." See A. Diez Macho, ed. & trans., *Neophyti 1*, I (Génesis) (TE, 7), Madrid & Barcelona, 1968, p. 2, n. 1, and the critical *apparatus* on p. 3.

   In Samaritan literature, there are several texts which construe *Gen.* i.1 in the same way (see Cowley, 36.22 f.; *et al.*); see the forthcoming article on Helena in *RAC* by Professor Gilles Quispel and the present author. The rabbis substituted the Torah for Beginning-Wisdom in order to avoid that Wisdom was conceived of as a goddess, but this substitution opened up for quasi-personifications of the Law (see *Gen.R.* i.1; *Tanh. B Ber.* ch. 5, 2b; *et al.*; cp. *Aboth de R. Nathan* ch. 31).

157 See p. 288.

158 This is from the short recension. The long recension says: "On the sixth day, I commanded My Wisdom to create man" (xxx.8). In *Ps.-Clem. Hom.* XVI.12, Peter argues that God in *Gen.* i.26 spoke to Wisdom, *i.e.*, the Son. Justin (*Dial.* ch. 62) and Theophilus of Antioch (*Ad Autol.* II.18) knew this interpretation of *Gen.* i.26 f. The rabbis again substituted the Torah for Wisdom; thus, *Pirke de R. Eliezer* says: "God spoke to the Law: "We will make man in our image and likeness"" (ch. 11).

159 For ancient recognitions of the Son as Beginning-Wisdom in *Gen.* i.1 and *Prov.* viii. 22, see Daniélou, *Theology*, pp. 166 ff. In *Rev.* iii.14, Christ is called ἀρχὴ τῆς κτίσεως.

   In addition to *Col.* i.15 ff., there are some other New Testament passages which ascribe demiurgic function to the Son and are taken to reveal influence from Sophia speculations (see *John* i.3; *Heb.* i.2c-3b; *I Cor.* viii.6). But see also above, p. 255, n. 32, where it is suggested that there may be a Name theology behind the Logos doctrine in the prologue of the *Gospel of John*. In *Heb.* i.10, where Christ is the direct creative agent and not only the medium through which God has created the world, he is called *Kyrios*, the Greek rendering of the Tetragrammaton, by having *Ps.* cii.25 made to apply to him. In *I Cor.* viii.6, too, the demiurgic Christ is called *Kyrios*. H. Langkammer, "Christus mediator creationis", *VD*, 45, 1967, pp. 201 ff., wants to find the source of the belief in Christ's creative activity in the implication of the Christological interpretation of *Ps.* cx.1 and in the retro-interpretation of the idea of the "new" creation.

160 See Talbert, "The Myth of the Descending-Ascending Redeemer", who refers to the

attribution of the term "first-born" to Jacob-Israel, the Angel of the Lord, at least *associates* this figure with demiurgic activity[161].

Another very interesting angelic figure is Yahoel in the *Apocalypse of Abraham*, which is extant only in a Slavonic version but stems from the first or the beginning of the 2nd century C.E. In this writing, Abraham is said to have been vouchsafed an angelophany by a figure who describes himself in the following manner:

> I am called Yahoel by Him who moves that which exists with me on the seventh expanse on the firmament, a power in virtue of the Ineffable Name which is dwelling in me.

(x.9)

Obviously, this is a reference to the figure of the Angel of the Lord in *Ex.* xxiii.20 f., where God says that he has put his Name into (or, unto) his special angel. It is quite possible that Yahoel even is regarded as a personification of the Divine Name, since his name, יהו אל , is the name of God himself. Some such name as Yahoel seems to have been the original one in the traditions about the angel who is said to be the "Little YHWH" and to have a name "similar to that of his Master"[162].

Jewish collection of liturgical fragments in the *Apostolic Constitutions* (Books VII f.), the *Book of Wisdom*, the works of Philo, and the *Prayer of Joseph*. What Talbert has not noted is that *Sir.* xxiv.4 as well as *Wisd.* x.17 closely associates or even identifies Wisdom with the Pillar of Cloud and Fire, which could be seen as a manifestation of the Angel of the Lord; see above, p. 178, n. 310. Furthermore, the *Book of Sirach* (xxiv.3, 5 f.) also seems to identify Wisdom with the Spirit in *Gen.* i.2; see G.H. Box & W.O. Oesterley, trans., "The Book of Sirach", in *APOT*, I, pp. 396 f., n. *ad* xxiv.3. Thus, we must add to the evidence marshalled by Talbert that *Sirach* knows a divine intermediary identified variously as Wisdom, Angel, and Spirit.

161 The epithet itself apparently derives from *Ex.* iv.22, "Israel is My first-born son," where, however, God refers to the nation and not to the patriarch, who has become a pre-existent angel in the *Prayer of Joseph*. Interestingly, on the basis of this verse, the rabbis made *Ps.* lxxxix.27, "Also I will give him [*i.e.*, the king, the title of] first-born," apply to the Messiah (see *Ex.R.* xix.7). In the Jewish source incorporated into the *Apostolic Constitutions*, one of the names of the many-named redeemer is "Angel of the Great Council", which is a title of the Messiah in LXX *Is.* ix.6. It is probably *Ps.* lxxxix.27 which is alluded to in *Heb.* i.6, which calls the Son πρωτότοκος in a context where he is ascribed with demiurgic function; see O. Michel, *Der Brief an die Hebräer* (MKKNT, 13), 2nd ed., Göttingen, 1949, pp. 52 f.

162 For angel names containing the Divine Name or an element of it, see E. Peterson, "Engel- und Dämonennamen. Nomina barbara", *RM*, 57, 1926, pp. 404 f.; Odeberg, *3 Enoch*, Part II, p. 29, n. *ad* x.3, p. 103, n. *ad* xxix.1, pp. 104 f., n. *ad* xxx.1; J. Michl, Art. "Engel V (Engelnamen)", *RAC*, V, cols. 216 f. In Mandeism, there are several deities having names beginning with *Ya-* or *Yo-* ; see Lidzbarski, *Johannesbuch*, pp. XXII ff.; cp. above, p. 262, n. 23. The figure called "Yoshamin" has demiurgical traits; see Rudolph, *Mandäer*, I, p. 81, n. 4; *Theogonie*, pp. 103 ff., especial-

Furthermore, we must note that Yahoel is the divine Glory as well as the Angel of the Lord, as are also other mediators[163]. Abraham says: "And the angel came, whom He [*i.e.*, God] had sent to me, in the likeness of a man [...]" (x.5). As has been repeatedly seen, the mention of human *likeness* is a constant trait in the representations of the Glory.

In ch. xi, Yahoel is described in the following manner: "[...] the appearance of his body was like sapphire, and the look of his countenance like chrysolite, and the hair of his head like snow, and the turban upon his head like the appearance of a rainbow, and the clothing of his garments like purple, and a golden sceptre was in his right hand" (*v*.2). This description contains adaptations of various portraits of the Glory. The radiant appearance of the body of the Glory is mentioned already in *Ez.* i.27. In the *Book of Daniel*, the angel Gabriel, who is represented as the Glory, is in one place described in the following way: "His body was like beryl, his face like the appearance of lightning, his eyes like flaming torches, his arms and legs like the gleam of burnished bronze ..." (x.6)[164]. In the *Shiur Qoma* texts, there is frequent reference to the shining appearance of the body of the Glory, and chrysolite is even used expressly to describe it: "His body is like chrysolite. His light breaks tremendously from the darkness [...]."[165]

That Yahoel is said to have hair as white as snow is a clear reference to the representation of the Ancient of Days in *Daniel* (vii.9) and *I Enoch* (xlvi.1; lxxi.10), and shows which passages the author had in mind. It is perhaps astonishing that Yahoel in this respect is modelled upon the Ancient of Days and not upon the Son of Man, but already LXX *Dan.* vii.13 reads that the Son of Man "came *as* (ὡς) the Ancient of Days," whereas Theodotion follows the Hebrew text and translates "unto (ἕως) the Ancient of Days". A.F. Segal wonders whether already the LXX text defends against "two powers" heretics[166], but a change from ἕως to ὡς in *Dan.* vii.13 would hardly have constituted a sensible defense against a two powers heresy, and it would rather seem that the LXX version intends to present the Son of Man as God's delegate in much the same way as the Angel of the Lord often is represented as indistinguishable from God himself.

We may here note that the "one like a son of man" in *Rev.* i. 13 ff. is also described as a coalescence of the Ancient of Days and the second power: " ... His head and his hair were white as white wool, white as snow; his eyes

---

ly pp. 119 ff.; cp. p. 170, n. 4. Arai, p. 69, mistakenly says that Yahoel in the *Apocalypse of Abraham* is a demiurge.

163 See above, pp. 179f., 181ff., 188ff., 276. Cp. p. 279, n. 61.

164 Cp. above, p. 279, n. 61.

165 Musajoff, 37a; quoted by Scholem, *Major Trends*, p. 64.

166 See *Two Powers*, pp. 201 f.

were like a flame of fire, his feet were like burnished bronze, refined as in a furnance ... and his face was like the sun shining in full strength." In this description of the mediator, which – like the representation of Yahoel in *Apoc. Abr.* ch. xi – recalls the portraiture of Gabriel in *Dan.* ch. x, the characteristic of the white hair of the Ancient of Days again appears. The Christians, who actually were liable to be characterized as two powers heretics, obviously would not try to reduce the impression that God had a proxy, and the ascription of a trait of God to his delegate apparently is meant to denote the divine status of the latter.

That Yahoel is said to have a turban may be a sign of his high priestly function (cp. *Ex.* xxviii.4, 36 ff.) and suggest that G. Scholem is right that the epithet נער as used of the principal angel indicates that he is God's cultic "servant".[167] The rainbow-like appearance of Yahoel's turban is reminiscent of *Ez.* i.28, which says that "the appearance of the brightness round about" the Glory was "like the appearance of the bow that is in the cloud on the day of rain." Finally, the sceptre which Yahoel has in his right hand recalls the sceptre held by the *phōs* whom Moses saw upon the great throne in the drama of Ezekiel the Tragedian[168].

That Yahoel obviously is the Glory of God as well as the Angel of the Lord may provide a clue to the interpretation of his enigmatic statement that God "moves that which exists with me on the seventh expanse on the firmament." In ch. xviii, we hear that Abraham saw the divine throne on the seventh firmament (cp. xix.5), so we may ask whether "that which exists with" Yahoel is the throne. That God is said to "move" the throne is not so strange, for already *Ez.* ch. i describes the throne of the Glory as being placed upon a chariot, the depiction of whose wheels is meant to indicate its omni-directional mobility (see *vv.* 15 ff.). It is noteworthy that it is not said that Abraham sees any figure upon the throne – possibly, the throne is empty because Yahoel accompanies Abraham. Already in *Ezekiel*, the Glory is not bound to the throne upon the chariot and can appear apart from it. In the second vision of the cherubim throne upon the chariot, the prophet saw that the Glory of YHWH went up from the cherubim to the threshold of the house [*i.e.*, the temple]..." (x.4). In ch. viii, "a likeness as the appearance of a man"(דמות כמראה איש) (*v.*2), which in the continuation of the verse is described like the Glory in i.27, appears to the prophet and transports him from Babylonia to Jerusalem (see *v.* 3). This is not unlike the function of Yahoel in the *Apocalypse of Abraham*, where the patriarch is guided to the divine world by an intermediary who is described as the Angel of the Lord and the Glory of God.

---

167 The commentators point out that the garment of the one "like a son of man" in *Rev.* i.13 is modelled upon that of the high priest as well as upon that of the king.

168 See above, p. 191, n. 348.

It is obvious that Yahoel is the prototype of Metatron, who is said to possess the Name of God and to have been enthroned in heaven. However, other angelic figures, too, merged into Metatron. There is, for instance, firm evidence that Metatron and the archangel Michael were fused. This is found in the *Visions of Ezekiel*, a Palestinian document from the 4th century C.E. In a description of the seven-tiered heaven which is parallel to the account found in both *Ḥag.* 12b and *Aboth de R. Nathan* ch. 37, we read the following about the third heaven, *Zebul*, where Michael stands and makes offerings according to the Talmudic version (which says that *Zebul* actually is the fourth heaven):

> The Prince [apparently, then, Michael] is not dwelling anywhere but in *Zebul*, and he is the very fullness of *Zebul*; and, before him, there are thousands of thousands and myriads of myriads who minister to him. Of them, it is said by Daniel: "I beheld till thrones were placed, *etc.*"; "a fiery stream issued, *etc.*" (vii.9 f.). And what is his name? Kimos is his name. R. Isaac said: "Maṣatah is his name." R. Inyanei bar Sisson said: "Bizbul [*i.e.*, "in *Zebul*"] is his name." R. Tanḥum the Old said: "ʾAtatiyah is his name." Eleazar Nadwadaya said: "Metatron, like the Name of the Power." And those who make theurgical use of the Name say: "Salnas is his name; Kasbak is his name, similar to the Name of the Creator of the world."[169]

Eleazar Nadwadaya says that the secret name of Michael is "Metatron", which is a name similar to that of "the Power", which in this context must denote God. This is a Palestinian parallel to the explanation by R. Idi in the Babylonian Talmud. As we have seen, the meaning is not that the Name of God is like "Metatron", but that the principal angel has a name which includes the Divine Name. This is also made clear by the explanations of the theurgists; it would be meaningless if the Name of the Creator really was "Salnas" or "Kasbak". The phrase that the principal angel had a name that was "like" the Name of God obviously is older than the 4th century and must have been framed at a time when the name of the angel really included the Divine Name. The *Apocalypse of Abraham* offers evidence for this idea. Obviously, other angels, such as Michaël, could also be regarded as the possessor of the Name. Later, the figure of Metatron came to be the *beau idéal* of this angelic intermediary.

That Michael was held to have a name "like" the Name of God offers an opportunity for following up the question put at the beginning of this Chapter: is Michael, who is represented as being entrusted with the Oath containing the demiurgic Name in *I En.* 1xix.13 ff., ever described as a demiurge? In order to probe this problem, we will revert to the Gnostic sources.

Ariel and Michael in Gnosticism

Gnostic texts frequently state that the demiurge Jaldabaoth has the face or

---

169 *BM*, II, pp. 132 f.; quoted by Scholem, *Jewish Gnosticism*, p. 46.

appearance of a lion (see *Hyp. Arch.* 94.17; *Origin* 100.7, 25 f.; *Apocr. Joh.
BG* 37.21 f.; Orig., *Contra Cels.* VI.30 f., on the Ophians)[170]. In *On the Origin of the World*, it is stated that "the perfect call him "Ariael", because he looks like a lion" (100.24 ff.). It also happens that a Gnostic gem has been recovered which has on its obverse side a depiction of a man-like figure with the head of a lion together with the names Aariel and Jaldabaoth inscribed in Greek letters, while the reverse side of the amulet contains the names of the Ophite archons[171]. As C. Bonner points out, Ariel is a Hebrew name and means the "Lion of God". Thus, the name Ariel is simply another appellation of Jaldabaoth, who was believed to be lion-faced or to have the shape of a lion. The accounts of the Ophites found in ch. xxx of the first book of Irenaeus' *Ad-*

---

170 In the *Apocryphon of John* (*BG* 41.18), the first of the archons under Jaldabaoth is also said to be lion-faced. In *Pistis Sophia* and the two *Books of Jeu*, the lion-faced Jaldabaoth is one of the demoniac powers.

171 The gem is described and discussed by C. Bonner, "An Amulet of the Ophitic Gnostics", *Hesperia. Supplement to Vol. VIII*, 1949, pp. 43 ff.; cp. *Studies in Magical Amulets* (UMS, Humanistic Series, XLIX), London, 1950, pp. 135 ff. See also Scholem, *Jewish Gnosticism*, pp. 71 f. The amulet is reproduced also by J. Doresse, *The Secret Books of the Egyptian Gnostics*, London & New York, 1960, reprinted New York, 1970, p. 166.

The first alpha of the name AAPIHΛ, which is read downward at the right edge of the obverse side, is directly over the top of the staff held by the right hand of the figure depicted, and is perhaps actually an ornament belonging to the top of the staff. There is no doubling of the alpha in the other instances in Greek and Coptic where the name occurs; and the Hebrew form of the name does not contain an initial guttural, which might have accounted for the two alphas of the Gnostic gem. However, if the sign commonly taken to be an alpha is no ornament but really the first letter of the name of the archon, the second alpha may be explained as due to lapidary's carelessness or as a deliberate repetition made necessary by the placement of the first alpha too near the tip of the staff.

The names written on the reverse side of the gem are the following from the top: Ia, Iao, Sabaoth, Adonai, Eloai, Oreos, Astapheos. Bonner suggests that the first name, Ia, is another form of Iao, or a mnemonic abbreviation of Jaldabaoth made necessary by the narrow space at the top of the oval amulet. Either of these suggestions would seem to be right, because then we get complete agreement with the lineage of the Ophite archons according to the report by Irenaeus (I.xxx.5, 11). As regards the first four archons, the list of the gem and Irenaeus' report agree further with the enumeration of the archons as found in the Ophite liturgy rendered by Origen. In Origen's account of the passwords for the different archons that the Ophites had to recite on their way to heaven, the password for the fourth archon is lacking; however, when assigning the names of the archons to their respective sources, Origin lists Adonai as one of the archontic names to be derived from the Biblical names of God (see VI.31 f.). Thus, Adonai obviously is the fourth archon also in the source of Origen. As regards the last three archons, Origen has the names of Astaphaeus, Ailoaeus, and Horaeus in this order. Thus, he is rendering the last three archontic names in a succession other than Irenaeus and the designer of the gem.

versus haereses and in ch. VI of *Contra Celsum* by Origen do not mention the name of Ariel; but, from the description of the obscure diagram of the Ophites, which Celsus made use of in his attack on the Christians, we learn that the first archon was said to have the face of a lion (λεοντοειδής). Origen, who obtained a copy of this diagram representing the universe, states:

> And we find in the diagram which we ourselves obtained that the arrangement is exactly as Celsus described it. Celsus said that the first [archon] is having the face of a lion.

> (VI.30)

It is thus evident that the Gnostic who designated the Ophite gem was well aware of the meaning of the Jewish name Ariel. But the name of the demiurge and chief archon in the diagram does not concur with the name given on the gem. While Celsus does not inform us what the head of the archons was named, Origen found out. The Father continues the passage just quoted:

> But he [*viz.*, Celsus] does not tell us what these people, who are really the most blasphemous ones, call it. We, however, have found that the angel of the Creator, who is spoken of with great praise in Holy Scripture, is affirmed by that filthy diagram to be Michael the lion-faced.

> (*Ibid.*)

Thus, according to the Ophite diagram, the lion-faced archon is really the archangel Michael. It appears that Ariel, the "Lion of God", originally was one of Michael's appellations. The figure with a lion's face is, of course, one of the four Living Creatures surrounding the Throne in *Ez.* ch. i; and, in Jewish tradition, Michael is one of the four Angels of the Presence who environ the Throne of God, standing to the right of it[172]. There is also to be found a magical gem which actually represents Michael in the form of a lion and reading the inscription Μιχαὴλ ὕψιστε, Γαβριὴλ κράτιστε[173]. Further, there is another amulet depicting a lion on the one side and reading *Micha X* on the reverse. The spelling undoubtedly is representing the name of the angel Michael, for it occurs in other sources in that sense[174]. Michael, then, is most logically to be identified with the lion shown on the obverse.

In VI.27, Origen cites Celsus as declaring that the Christians hold that there are seven "archontic angels" and that the chief of them, who is called an "accursed god", is the demiurge and the god of Moses. Origen corrects Celsus and says that this applies only to the Ophite sect and not to the body of the orthodox. The "archontic angels" obviously are to be identified with

---

172 See Lueken, pp. 33 ff.; Str.-Bill., III, pp. 806 f. For Ariel as the name of an angel, see Peterson, "Engel- und Dämonennamen", pp. 396 f.

173 See M. Kopp, *Palaeographia critica*, IV, Mannheim, 1829, p. 228 (§ 766).

174 See E.R. Goodenough, *Jewish Symbols in the Greco-Roman Period* (BS, XXXVII), II (The Archeological Evidence from the Diaspora), New York, 1953, p. 260, n. 379.

the seven "archontic demons" mentioned in the report on the diagram, for Origen, in his description of the diagram, says that Celsus "returns to the seven archontic demons which are not mentioned by the Christians, but, which are, I believe, spoken of by the Ophites" (VI.30). Then follows the passage which has just been quoted in two portions. Thus, it is clear that the "accursed god", who is the chief of the seven "archontic angels" and the demiurge, is to be regarded as one with the archangel Michael, the first of the "archontic demons". Obviously, the Ophites retained the Jewish notion that the demiurge was an angel, even the angel Michael, but, in true Gnostic fashion, they viewed him and his band to be *"archontic* angels".

Origen, in his description of the Ophite diagram of the spheres of the universe, goes on to report the shapes and names of the other six archons. The next three are call carrying well-known Jewish angel names, to wit, Suriel, Raphael, and Gabriel. Thus, the first four of the seven "archontic angels" or "archontic demons" are actually the four Angels of the Presence in Jewish tradition. It is not to be denied that the seven archons are representing the demoniac planetary rulers of astrology; however, the nomenclature of the rulers of the universe according to the Ophites as well as the frequent declaration by the Gnostics that the archons are angels leads us to the conclusion that they have solid roots in the Jewish teaching of the seven archangels.

Origen then recites the passwords which the Ophites had to utter when they ascended upwards to the spiritual realm, passing through the successive spheres of the seven archons or angels (see VI.31). Striding past the different aeons, the pneumatic had to address the respective rulers by their other set of names: Jaldabaoth, Iao, Sabaoth, Adonai, Astaphaeus, Ailoaeus, and Horaeus (the name of the fourth, Adonai, has fallen out, but can be supplied from VI.32). This nomenclature of the archons agrees with the names of the rulers of the aeons found in Irenaeus' report on the Ophites and on the gem already described. Further, the names of the Ophite archons are related to the archontic names in the *Apocryphon of John*. Thus, the diagram and the liturgy of the Ophites give different sets of names of the archontic angels or demons. That the archons have double names is a conception also found in the *Apocryphon of John*: in addition to their ordinary names, the archons are said to have "names of glory" revealing their true nature (see 41.1 ff.). When a comparison between the geneaology of the Ophite archons according to Irenaeus and the Ophite gem is made, it appears that Origen's list begins at the top with the name of the archon of the supreme aeon. Origen is actually rendering the Ophite liturgy in reverse order[175]. The first power to be met

---

175 This is generally acknowledged; see, for instance, H. Chadwick, trans., *Origen: Contra Celsum,* Cambridge, 1953, p. 346, n. 3. The reason why the archons are cited in the reverse order, however, is explained differently. W. Anz, *Zur Frage nach dem*

with when ascending would be Horaeus. Concerning the last aeon to be passed, Origen relates:

> Then, as they pass through the one they call Jaldabaoth, they are taught to say:
> "And you, Jaldabaoth, first and seventh, who have arisen to rule with confidence,
> ruling Logos of pure Nous, perfect work of the Son and Father, – I carry a sign mark-
> ed with the imprint of life and have opened to the world the gate which you closed
> for your aeon. As a free man I pass your authority. Let grace be with me Father;
> yes, let it be with me!" And they say that the star Phainon [*i.e.*, Saturn] is in sym-
> pathy with the lion-faced archon.

(VI.31)

That the lion-faced archon is called by the name of Jaldabaoth squares
with the representation on the Ophite amulet, which depicts the chief archon
with the head of a lion and furnishes him with the names Jaldabaoth and
Ariel, the latter of which means the "Lion of God". As we have seen, however, the lion-faced archon was named Michael in the diagram. Thus, according to the Ophites, the angel Michael was considered the same as the demiurge
Jaldabaoth.

That the "archontic demons" named in the diagram (VI.30) are identical
with the archons enumerated in the liturgy (VI.31) is also brought out in a
later passage. Origen cites Celsus as addressing the Christians that it is because
of –

> the miraculous words addressed to the lion, and the animal with double form, and
> the one shaped like an ass, and the other superhuman doorkeepers, whose names you
> poor unfortunates have wretchedly learnt by heart so that terrible madness has taken
> hold of you, ... [lacuna] that you are crucified.

(VII.40)

Origen, of course, retorts that this applies solely to the Ophites, whom
he does not want to regard as Christians at all. Thus, Celsus and Origen agree
that the archontic doorkeepers of the liturgy are identical with the animal-
faced figures of the diagram[176]. According to the diagram, Michael has the
face of a lion and the seventh of the "archontic demons" is ass-headed. The
archon with a "double form" may be the third angel of the diagram, namely,
Raphael, who is said to be an amphibian.

Ursprung des Gnostizismus (TU, XV/4), Leipzig, 1897, pp. 12 f., thought that the
liturgy was not intended to be used by the ascending mystic, but was spoken by the
descending saviour. P. Wendland, *Die hellenistisch-römische Kultur* (HNT, II),
4th ed. by H. Dörrie, Tübingen, 1972, p. 174, n. 4 (continued on p. 175), thinks
that the reason for the rendition of the liturgy in the reverse order is due to the fact
that the seven spheres and their archons were represented graphically in the source:
the seventh archon and his aeon were depicted at the top of the page in accordance
with the ascent ideology, and the copyist rendered the formulae from the top down-
wards when he reproduced them.

176 Cp. Wendland, p. 174; Bonner, *Studies*, p. 138. See also R.M. Grant, *Gnosticism
and Early Christianity*, New York, 1959, p. 48.

That Jaldabaoth, "the lion-faced archon", is said to be related to Saturn is a clear indication that he is the one presiding over the highest sphere, for Saturn is the planet that is most remote. Thus, the lion-faced Jaldabaoth of the Ophite liturgy indisputably is to be identified with Michael of the Ophite diagram, for Michael is also said to have the face of a lion and being the chief of the "archontic demons"[177]. Michael is thus the secret identity of Jaldabaoth, the demiurge of the Ophites. This is a parallel to the Mandean notion that Gabriel was the secret name of Ptahil, the demiurge[178]. The deduction to be made from this is that the demiurge in reality is a Jewish angel: the name of the angel is of less importance; the notable point is that the demiurge is the principal angel, the Angel of the Lord, who is possessing the Name of God.

When we turn to Irenaeus' account of the Ophites, we learn that the demiurge Jaldabaoth was said to have cast down the serpent, that is his own son, from heaven:

> But the serpent, too, because he worked against his father, was cast down into the world below; and he got the angels who are there within his control, and produced six sons, with himself as the seventh, in imitation of the hebdomad surrounding his father.

(I.xxx.8)

This myth has already been met with in the system of Severus[179]. Here, too, the demiurge, called Jaldabaoth and Sabaoth, was said to have cast down his own son, Satan, identified as the serpent. We also come across the motif of the strife between the demiurge and the devil in the system of the Archontics and in Satornil's teaching. It will be remembered that the Archontics taught that the devil was in opposition to his father, the demiurge Sabaoth[180]. Concerning the teaching of Satornil, Irenaeus reports that "Satan, who is himself an angel according to his [*viz.*, Satornil's] doctrine, is the adversary of the world-creators but especially of the god of the Jews" (I.xxiv.2). "The god of the Jews" is said expressly to be "one of the angels" (*ibid.*), and he is obviously thought of as the head of the seven angels that made the world[181].

The theme of the conflict between the highest of the angels and Satan derives from Jewish religion. According to Jewish tradition, it was Michael who threw down the dragon or serpent from heaven:

> And there was a war in heaven: Michael and his angels fought against the dragon. And the dragon and his angels fought, but they did not prevail; and neither was their

---

177 There is also some evidence from Jewish magic that Michael could be connected with Saturn; see Trachtenberg, pp. 250 f.

178 See above, pp. 261 ff.

179 See above, p. 303.

180 See above, *ibid.*

181 For Satornil's view of the creation, see above, pp. 216 f.

place found any more in heaven. And the great dragon was cast out, that old serpent, that is called the devil and Satan, that deceives the whole world; he was cast down to earth, and his angels were cast out with him.

(Rev. xii. 7-9)

This pericope, followed by a song of triumph celebrating the victory over Satan, *vv.* 10-12, is found splitting a section which relates the birth of the Messiah and the persecution of his "mother", that is, the people of God, *vv.* 1-6, 13-17. The relation of the fortunes of the Messiah and his mother is an adaptation of what might be called an international saviour myth, current throughout the ancient world in the day of the seer. Since the tale in the *Apocalypse* is more in tune with Jewish conceptions of the Messiah than with the history of Jesus, many scholars think that the seer has taken this myth from a Jewish source[182]. It is also to be noted that, even in the heavenly song of triumph, a specifically Christian idiom is to be found only in *v.* 11[183]. As regards *vv.* 7-9, a Jewish source is certainly to be reckoned with. R.H. Charles has argued convincingly that the pericope originally was written in Semitic, and W. Bousset has pointed out that the archangel Michael, who emerges only in this place in the whole *Apocalypse*, is intercepting the figure of the Messiah, just as is the case in the *Book of Daniel*, where Michael, the guardian angel of the people of Israel[184], is fighting the angel patrons of the nations in the eschatological battle (see x.13, 21; xii.1 ff.; LXX viii.11)[185]. The Jewish Messiah is an earthly figure, and it is quite natural that the conquest of the evil angels is accomplished by Israel's guardian angel; but to suppose that a Christian could have devised *Rev.* xii.7-9 is not reasonable.

We do not have to enter into the discussion about the place of xii.7-9 in the sequence and time of the seer's apocalyptic scheme; in Jewish tradition, Satan could be thought of as having been cast down from heaven in primal times. In *II En.* xxix.4, Satan is said to have been thrown down on

182 See, for instance, R.H. Charles, *The Revelation of St. John* (ICC), I, Edinburgh, 1920 and reprints, pp. 308 f.; cp. pp. 299 f., 303 ff. (citing predecessors as H. Gunkel and J. Wellhausen on p. 306), 313 f.; G.R. Beasley-Murray, *The Book of Revelation* (NCB), London, 1974, pp. 193 ff. See P. Prigent, *Apocalypse 12* (BGBE, 2), Tübingen, 1959, pp. 110 ff., 128 ff., for a survey of the discussion about the number and nature of the sources employed by the Christian seer.

183 The limit of the author's work in *vv.* 10-12 is difficult to ascertain; see Beasley-Murray, p. 196, n. 1.

184 Cp. *I En.* xx.5; 1 Q *M* xvii.6 ff. See also *II Macc.* xi.6, 8; *I En.* xc.14; *Test. Levi* v.6 f.; *Test. Dan.* vi.2 ff.; 1 Q *M* xiii.10; 1 Q *S* iii.20 ff. For rabbinic evidence that Michael is Israel's angel, see *Yoma* 77a; Targ. *Ps.* cxxxvii.7; *Pesikta R.* xliv.10.

185 See Bousset, *Der Antichrist in der Überlieferung des Judentums, des neuen Testaments und der alten Kirche,* Göttingen, 1895, p. 153. Cp. Prigent, pp. 128 ff., 145 ff. Cp. *I En.* x.20 ff.; 1 Q *M* xvii.6 ff. See also *Test. Dan.* vi.1 ff.; *Ass. Mos.* x.2. For rabbinic evidence that Michael is the eschatological warrior of Israel, see *Ex.R.* xviii.5.

the second day. Throughout the Adamic literature, he is said to have been
hurled down when refusing to adore Adam on the sixth day.

While *II Enoch* has it that God himself threw down Satan, the Adam lore
can ascribe this work to the angels. In Timothy's discourse on the angel of
death, Abbaton by name, God orders "all the armies of heaven" to cast Satan
down (13b). In *Vita Adae et Evae* (ch. 14ff.), an essentially Jewish work,
Michael bids Satan to worship Adam, but Satan refuses, and he and his band
are hurled down. It is not stated expressly that Michael accomplished this
(nor is it made specific in the *Apocalypse*), but it is probably taken for granted. In the *Damascus Document* (v. 17 ff.), the Prince of Light, who undoubtedly is Michael, is opposed to Beliar (cp. 1 Q *S* iii.20f.). In the *Testaments of
the Twelve Patriarchs*, the guardian angel of Israel is said to "rise up against
the kingdom of the Enemy" (*Test. Dan.* vi.2). In rabbinism, Michael is Samael's opponent in heaven: Samael is the accuser of man, while Michael is
man's defender (see *Ex. R.* xviii.5; *Deut. R.* xi.10; cp. *Jude* 9)[186]. This idea
is perhaps presupposed in *Rev.* xii.7 ff., for the verb $\beta\acute{\alpha}\lambda\lambda\omega$, "cast out",
found three times in *v.* 9, has a judicial aspect (cp. ii.10; *Matt.* iii.10; xiii.41 f.;
John xii.31)[187]. In *Pirke de R. Eliezer* (ch. 26), it is said that, when Samael
fell, he tried to take hold of Michael and bring him down with him, but
Michael was saved by God[188].

It should be quite palpable by now that the angel Michael is the exemplar
of the figure of the demiurge in Ophitism. When Irenaeus relates that the serpent in the teaching of the Ophites was called *both* Samael and Michael (I.
xxx.9: "[...] and the objectionable serpent has, they say, two names: Michael
and Samael."), he is obviously confusing their tradition. In the Jewish texts,
the serpent that is opposed by Michael is known as Samael. That the Ophites

---

186 For the notion of Samael accusing Israel or mankind as a whole in heaven, see further the references in Str.-Bill., I, pp. 141 ff. That the seer knew that Satan was
"the accuser of the brothers" is made plain in xii.10 (cp. *I Tim.* iii.6; *I Pet.* v.8).
The idea is rooted in the Old Testament (see *Job* i.6 ff.; ii.1 ff.; *Zech.* iii.1 ff.). In
I. En. xl.7, we hear about *several* Satans accusing the righteous before God. For Michael as Israel's advocate, see also the rabbinic texts referred to above in n. 184.

187 See J. Massyngberde Ford, *Revelation* (AB, 38), New York, 1975, p. 206. G.B.
Caird says that, "although John depicts the battle between Michael and Satan in
military terms, it was essentially a legal battle of opposing counsel, which resulted in
one of them being disbarred" (*A Commentary on the Revelation of St. John the
Divine* (BNTC), London, 1966, p. 155).

188 For the later midrashic ramifications of the idea of Michael throwing down Satan,
see M. McNamara, *The New Testament and the Palestinian Targum to the Pentateuch*
(AB, 27) Rome, 1966, p. 226. Note also the rôle of Michael in *I En.* x.11: he is bid
by God to descend and fetter the angels that came down to earth and defiled themselves with women (cp. *Gen.* ch. vi).

knew that the demiurge, who had cast down the serpent, was Michael is reported – as we have seen – by Origen[189].

The Magharians

In terminating the presentation of evidence for the existence of the concept of a lower demiurge in Judaism, we must discuss the teaching of the Angel of the Lord in the sect of the Magharians. In the 12th century, Shahrastani, the Muslim historian of religion, related that Arius, the Christian heretic of the 4th century, had borrowed his doctrine of the Messiah as the principal angel of God from the Magharians, "who had lived 400 years before Arius and had laid great stress on continence and a simple mode of life." According to the Magharians, this angel was God's vicegerent and acted on behalf of God towards men:

But one sect of the Maqariba claims that God spoke to the prophets – may peace

---

189 In the *Questions of Bartholomew* (iv.56), God commands Michael to bring him the material from which he intends to fashion Adam. This tradition recurs in Timothy's *Discourse on Abbaton*, where, however, the Angel of the Lord, who is said to have "brought" Adam to God (21b), is called "Mouriel" or "Abbaton". This writing relates that Earth refused to yield her dust to the angels who were despatched by God, and that only Mouriel-Abbaton was successful (see 11a-b). The version of this myth as told by the Falashas, the autochthonous Jews of Ethiopia, has the incomprehensible turn that God became angry with the angel Bernael, who at last managed to make away with the dust, and had Michael throw him down to earth; see W. Leslau, trans., *Falasha Anthology,* Schocken paperback, New York, 1969, pp. 3 ff. Leslau, p. 144, n. 34, suggests that the Falashas may have been dependent upon Muslim lore, where it is told that Izrael, the Angel of Death, managed to bring the dust after both Gabriel and Michael had failed. In any event, the Coptic version, where Abbaton is the Angel of Death, precedes the version of the Falashas and the Muslims.

In the Jewish *Yerahmeel Chronicle* (ch. 6), it is narrated that God sent out Gabriel, but Earth refused to give him her dust, so God himself had to collect it. This version apparently checks the notion that the angel(s) played a part in the creation of man, and it would seem that the variant shared by the Falashas and the Muslims also displays a repugnance of this idea. Moreover, these three sources as well as the *Discourse on Abbaton* appear to oppose a tradition to the effect that Earth actively helped in the creation of man. This is found, *e.g.*, in the system of Justin the Gnostic (see Hipp., V.xxvi.7 f.) and in the Marcionite doctrine described by the Armenian theologian Eznik of Kolb in his treatise *Against the Sects*. Justin clearly alludes to *Gen.* i.26 and ii.7, and the peculiar Marcionite teaching reported on by Eznik even has it that God addressed "Matter" with the words in *Gen.* i.26a, and that Matter supplied the earthen material from which Adam was made, while God gave him the soul. This teaching is possibly of Jewish origin. In *Midrash ha-Neʾlam Zohar Hadash* ch. 16, God's words in *Gen.* i.26a are said to have been directed to Earth, and *Gen.* ii.7 is said to mean that Earth moulded the body of man, while God gave him the soul. I have treated of all this more fully in my paper "Gen. 1,26 and 2,7 in Judaism, Samaritanism, and Gnosticism", forthcoming in *JSJ*.

be upon them! – through the agency of an angel, whom He had elected and given prominence over all creatures, and had appointed viceroy over them. They say: "Every description of God in the Law and in the rest of the Books is an account on the authority of this angel; for otherwise it would not be possible to describe God in any way at all." They also say: "Furthermore, he who addressed Moses – may peace be upon him! – is that angel. And God, the Exalted One, is too exalted to address mortal man in a human way."[190]

The angel is obviously the Angel of the Lord, who appeared to Moses in the Burning Bush (see *Ex.* ch. iii). The Magharians regarded the figure of the Angel of the Lord as a defense against bringing God into too close contact with the world as well as a means of explaining the anthropomorphisms in Scripture. The Karaite writer al-Qirqisani, who lived in the first half of the 10th century, tells us something more about this great concern of theirs:

> Their interpretations of some of the passages in the Scriptures are altogether improbable and resemble foolish talk. Daud ibn Marwān al-Muqammis says in one of his books that the Sadducees ascribe corporeality to God and understand all Scriptural ascriptions of Him which imply anthropomorphisms in their literal sense. The Magharians are said to be opposed to this: that is, they do not profess anthropomorphisms; yet, at the same time, they also do not take these descriptions [of God] out of their literal meanings, but assert instead that these descriptions refer to one of the angels, namely, to the one who created the world. This is similar to the view of Benjamin al-Nahawendi which we shall explain below.[191]

Al-Qirqisani, then, knew that the Magharians went as far in their ascription of transcendence to God that they even postulated that the Angel of the Lord was the creator of the material universe.

What are we to make out of these reports on the Magharians? Is the sect a fiction? In view of all the evidence gathered in the present work, there is no reason to doubt that there were Jews as well as Samaritans about the beginning of our era who cherished the doctrines ascribed to the Magharians. Is it possible to identify the Magharians with any known group among the Jewish people? Al-Qirqisani, placing them between the Sadducees and Jesus, agrees with Shahrastani in dating the time of the origination of the Magharians to the first pre-Christian century. Their name, being Arabic, means "men (people) of the cave", and al-Qirqisani explains it from their habit of keeping their sacred writings in caves in the hills of Palestine. At the end of the previous century, A.E. Harkavy tried to identify the Magharians as Essenes[192]. Al-Qirqisani omits the Essenes from his list of Jewish sects, and this would be natural for him if he knew them under the name of the Magharians. The appearance of the sect of the Magharians in pre-Christian times squares with the

---

190 Cureton, p. 169; Haarbrücker, I, p. 257.
191 Nemoy, pp. 363 f.
192 I rely on M. Mansoor, Art. "Sects", in *EJ*, 14, cols. 1088 f.

time of the origination of the sect of the Essenes. Both on archeological and literary evidence, it seems that the branch of the Essenes that constituted the Qumran community originated in the 2nd century B.C.E., but they would probably not have come to the fore-front until a century later. Harkavy explained the name of the Magharians from the simple mode of life of the Essenes; and, although his critics pointed out that the reports on the Essenes say that they lived in towns and villages (see Philo, *Quod omn. prob. liber sit* 76; Joseph., *Bell.* II.124), the excavations of Khirbet Qumran suggest that at least some of the Essenes lived in caves. And what is more: the Qumran-Essenes actually did hide their writings in caves, and this tallies neatly with al-Qirqisani's explanation of the name of the Magharians.

The fact that there is no teaching about an angelic demiurge in the Qumran library cannot be taken as proof that the identification of the Magharians as Essenes is totally unwarranted. Apparently, there were several factions of Essenes, differing from each other in both belief and practice[193]. In this connection, it is profitable to turn to the evidence of the Karaites. There is a rare unanimity among early Medieval writers, both Rabbanite and Karaite, that the movement instigated by Anan, the founder of Karaism, was an off-shoot of the "Sadducees", and that the Karaites used "the writings of the Sadducees" or the books of an ancient heresiarch called Sadoq[194]. This might in actual fact refer to the Qumran-Essenes, who called themselves the "sons of Ṣadoq" and referred to their founder (or leader during their early period) as מורה הצדק, "the Teacher of Righteousness". This might account for the fact that there are so many similarities between Qumranism and Karaism[195]. Moreover, in the strife with the Rabbanites over the issue of the origination of Karaism, some of the later Karaites began to invoke the testimony of ancient sectarian writings found in caves[196]. That there actually have been discoveries of books in Palestinian caves before 1947 is confirmed. In the early Muslim period, the Nestorian patriarch Timothy I of Baghdad (780–823) reported that, in his own time ("ten years ago"), Palestinian Jews had discovered a bulk of ancient writings in a cave in Judea. Essene writings hid in caves in

---

193 Thus, Josephus (*Bell.* II.160) says that some of the Essenes differed from the others in that they married (cp. *CD* iv.21 ff.). At least some of the Essenes would seem to have taught that the body is a prison for the soul, and that evil resides in the material body; see above, p. 202, n. 28, and p. 203, n. 29. Note also that the Essenes are reported to have taught that God is the author of good only; see above, p. 198, n. 23. It thus does not seem improbable that there were some Essenes who taught that the material creation was not the work of God.

194 See S.W. Baron, *A Social and Religious History of the Jews*, V (Religious Controls and Discussions), 2nd ed., New York, 1957, pp. 187 f. and p. 377, n. 50 (continued on the next page).

195 See N. Wieder, *The Judean Scrolls and Karaism*, London, 1962.

196 See Baron, p. 255 and p. 406, n. 54 (continued on the next page).

Palestine may very well have come into the hands of the Karaites. In contrast to the scrolls found at Qumran, these writings could have taught that the Angel of the Lord was the demiurge.

In any case, this was what Benjamin ben Moses al-Nahawendi, who was the outstanding representative of Karaism just before the middle of the 9th century, was teaching. Benjamin sought to remove all taints of anthropomorphism from the conception of God, and taught that all Biblical descriptions of God resembling a human referred to the principal angel. Further, God was so highly exalted above the world that it was to this angel that the creation of the world and the giving of the Law were attributed[197].

Whether or not Benjamin al-Nahawendi was inspired by a doctrine of angelic intermediation as found in an old (Essene) book is not so important; the point of significance is that he was a Jewish theologian. In view of all the evidence presented in this Chapter, there should be no reason to doubt the report of al-Qirqisani that a sect within Benjamin's own people anticipated his teaching by a thousand years.

Wider Scope and Conclusion

By the time when the sect of the Magharians is said to have emerged, reflections upon the philosophical heritage left behind by Plato were obligatory for all intellectual people in the Hellenistic world, and Platonism taught the concept of a demiurge[198]. Whatever Plato himself meant by this figure need not concern us, but it is important to note that "the Demiurge came to be seen as a second God, Intellect (*nous*), the agent or *logos* of the Supreme God ... ."[199] While some Platonists — *e.g.*, Plutarch — dit not make a distinction between two *gods*, but between God and his Logos, merging the latter with the world soul in its rational aspect, others — *e.g.*, Ammonius, Albinus, Apuleius, and Numenius — distinguished between two deities, *i.e.*, the transcendent God and the second god, the latter being conceived of as an acitve demiurgic intellect working upon the world from without. Philo stands in a middle position, for although his Logos is no personal hypostasis, the Jewish philosopher can call it God's "Man", "Angel", "First-Born Son", or even the "second god".

Most of the appellations which Philo uses when describing the Logos are taken from a less sophisticated Jewish tradition about a many-named inter-

---

197 See J. Fürst, *Geschichte des Karäerthums* (SIFIL), I, Leipzig, 1862, pp. 75 f. with notes on pp. 159 f. In view of the Samaritan identification of the Angel of the Lord with the Glory, it is interesting that Benjamin called the principal angel "the Glory". If Benjamin was dependent upon "Essene" sources, these may have come from Samaritan "Essenes". Cp. above, p. 71, n. 144.

198 The *locus classicus* is Plato, *Tim.* 28 A ff.

199 Dillon, p. 7.

mediary[200], but the use of mythological language in representations of the relationship between God and the intermediate power was warranted by Platonic tradition and could even find a precedent in the works of the master himself. Thus, in *Epistle* VI, the author asks his addressee to "swear by the god who is the ruler (θεὸν ἡγεμόνα) of all that is and shall be, and swear by the Lord and Father of the ruler and cause (ἡγεμόνος καὶ αἰτίου πατέρα κύριον) [...]" (323 D)[201]. As we shall see below, Xenocrates, who assumed leadership of the academy in 339 B.C.E. and can be described as the second founder of Platonism, continued the use of mythological language in representations of the transcendent monad and the ruler of our world.

The Jews and Samaritans who posited the Angel of the Lord or the Glory of God as the creator and ruler of the universe were thus in consonance with a well-established philosophical tradition. The portraits of the Angel or the Glory which have been examined in the preceding pages show a figure being apparently distinct from God, as is also the case with the demiurge in Platonism. Yet, and again in agreement with Platonic philosophy, the second power is the lieutenant of the highest being. The idea of the distinction and yet intimate association between God and the second power was in Judaism and Samaritanism expressed through the identification of the latter as the Angel of the Lord, who shared God's own "Name", *i.e.*, nature or mode of being.

This identification made it also possible to maintain that God's vicegerent could appear upon earth, as did the Angel of the Lord according to the Old Testament. Thus, the *Apocalypse of Abraham* relates that Yahoel descended and appeared to the patriarch, and became his guide to the heavenly world. Furthermore, the identification of the lieutenant of God as the Angel of the Lord made it possible for various groups to detect this figure in their respective heroes of the past – Adam, Enoch, Melchizedek, Jacob, Moses, Jesus, or Simon Magus. Whether or not actual pre-existence was claimed for these men, a part of the tradition which identified the mediator with a human being seems to have been that the hero ascended to heaven and demonstrated his identity as God's plenipotentiary through heavenly enthronement.

That the vicegerent of God was seen as the Glory of God as well as the Angel of the Lord also offered a solution to the problem of anthropomorphism. When the visionaries ascended to heaven, they did not see God upon the throne, but the Glory with a "likeness as the appearance of a man". Some even maintained that all anthropomorphic representations of God in Scrip-

---

200 See above, pp. 314f.

201 It is of no significance whether the letter was not written by Plato, for its authenticity was not in doubt. It cannot be known for certain whether the author had in mind the demiurge and the Idea of Good, but this would be a most natural explanation, and it was in fact the interpretation given by Plotinus (*Enn.* VI.1, ch. 8).

ture really referred to his lieutenant. This was only the culmination of a process which had begun already with the redaction of some passages in the Old Testament, where it is seen that the anthropomorphism of the older source has been toned down through the introduction of the figure of the Angel of the Lord, who thus became more or less indistinguishable from God himself.

In descriptions of the creation of man, the intermediation is often effected by a plurality of angels, to whom God speaks: "Let us create man." The angels then make the body of man, and God gives him the spirit. Again, Platonism offered a warrant for this representation, for the demiurge in *Timaeus* entrusts the creation of the two mortal souls and the material body to the younger gods (see 41 D ff.), while his own share in the anthropogony is restricted to the supply of the immortal soul (see 69 C ff.). In the Jewish adaptation of this story, God corresponds to the Platonic demiurge, but the equation of the demiurge and the monad was also occasionally made in Platonic tradition. Thus, Porphyry (*apud* Procl., *In Tim.* I.305.6 ff.) reports that Atticus identified the demiurge with the Good. Philo is clearly influenced by *Timaeus* when he teaches that God assigned the creation of the lower part of the soul to the angels, while he reserved the creation of the good part of the soul for himself[202]. However, the demiurge in *Timaeus*, who creates the universe after the pattern of the world of ideas and is the pilot of his creation, is also seized upon by Philo as the model of his Logos, the medium of intercourse between God and this world[203].

When the reason for the interposition of a mediator between God and the world not only is that God is supremely exalted above the creation, but also that he is the author of good only and that another cause must be assumed for the imperfection of the creation and the evil in the world[204], the intermediary inevitably comes in a dubious position. This is seen clearly in Platonic tradition. Already Xenocrates is reported to have assumed a lower Zeus ruling the earth: "[...] Xenocrates calls Zeus who is among things invariable and identical "Topmost" ($\H{v}\pi\alpha\tau\sigma\nu$), but "Nethermost" ($\nu\acute{\epsilon}\alpha\tau\sigma\nu$) him who is beneath the moon" (Plut., *Platonic Questions* IX.1, *Moralia* 1007 F)[205]. The "Topmost" Zeus obviously is the monad, which Xenocrates calls $\pi\rho\tilde{\omega}\tau\sigma\varsigma$ $\theta\epsilon\acute{o}\varsigma$ and $\nu\sigma\tilde{v}\varsigma$, and describes in mythological language as reigning "in heaven"

---

202 See above, pp. 198 ff. In *De mut. nom.* 29 ff., however, it seems that God's "creative power" is ascribed with the latter work. The "creative power" at least is said to have made the world. For the "creative" and the "sovereign" power of God, see below, pp. 335 f.

203 See above, p. 287.

204 For the idea that God is the author of good only see above, pp. 198 ff., with n. 23 on p. 198. For the notion that the material creation is evil, see above, pp. 202 f., with nn. 28 f. For the Platonic idea of the evil world soul, see above, p. 201, n. 27.

205 Heinze, Fragment 18.

(*apud* Aetius, *De plac.* I. vii.30, 304b, 1 D)[206]. The "Nethermost" Zeus is the chthonian Zeus or Hades, whose domain, however, is not the netherworld, as in popular religion, but the whole sublunar region of the universe (cp. Plut., *Face on the Moon* 27; 28, *Moralia* 942 F; 943 C).

This teaching of the two gods who split the universe horizontally between them was spun out in a dismal way by Ammonius, who was in charge of the academy about the middle of the first century C.E. In Plutarch's dialogue *The E at Delphi*, Ammonius distinguishes sharply between the realm of being and the realm of becoming (see 18, *Moralia* 392 C). There are two distinct gods, presiding over one realm each, and all the changes in the world, which usually are attributed to the supreme being, are really to be referred "to some other god, or, rather, a *daimon*, whose office is concerned with nature (φύσιν) in dissolution and generation" (21, *Moralia* 394 A). This is a sublunar deity who is named Hades or Pluto; he is the "lord of the darkling night and idling sleep" and "of all the gods most hateful to mortals" (*ibid.*; cp. Plut., *Life Unknown* 6, *Moralia* 1130 A)[207].

The teaching of an inferior god who rules the sublunar world is also reflected by Philo. In a remarkable passage, the Jewish philosopher says that the sublunar world of growth and decay is created and ruled by the "sovereign power" (βασιλικὴ δύναμις), while the "creative power" (ποιητικὴ δύναμις) controls the heavenly world, and God is to be found in the intelligible realm (see *Quaest. in Gen.* IV.8). In another work, Philo lays down that the less perfect will not be able to ascend higher than to the sovereign power, while others will make their way to the creative power and some even to God himself (see *De fuga et invent.* 97 ff.). The sovereign power is no evil figure or a rival of God, but his fearsome character is apparent in that he is the one who punishes wrong-doers "through retributive chastisement and banishment [from God]" (*Quaest. in Gen.* IV.8).

Philo finds the regal and punitive power in the divine name Κύριος, the LXX's translation or paraphrase of the Tetragrammaton, while he detects the creative power, which is said to be beneficent and merciful, in the name Θεός, which ist used to render "Elohim" (see *ibid*. II.51; IV.2)[208]. Both powers can be said to proceed from the Logos (see *Quaest. in Ex.* II.68; cp. *De Cher.* 27 ff.), but Philo is also content to let *Kyrios* refer to the Logos and *Theos* to God himself[209]. Furthermore, since Philo can say that the Logos is "filled" with all the powers of God (see *De Somn.* I.62), or — as we

---

206 *Ibid.*, Fragment 15.

207 Quoting a fragment of Adespota and Hom., *Il.* IX.59.

208 For the doctrine of the two powers of God in Philo, see further *De vita Mos.* II.99; *De plant.* 20; 86; *De Abr.* 24; 121; *De migr. Abr.* 182; *et al.*

209 Cp. above, p. 110.

have seen – that the Logos is the head of all the powers, which can be identified with the angels[210], it is clear that the basic scheme is the distinction between God, *Theos*, and the Logos, *Kyrios*. This is corroborated by the fact
that Philo's teaching about the two powers of God symbolized by the two
divine names is an adaptation of a less sophisticated Jewish doctrine which
hypostasized the Tetragrammaton as God's punitive agent[211]. To Philo, the
two powers are no real hypostases, but – as in rabbinism – different aspects
of God's activity in relation to men; but it is significant that he can describe
them as distinct beings and even assign them to the presidency over differently ranked levels of the universe. Apparently, the less sophisticated Jews, too,
adapted the Platonic doctrine of an inferior demiurge and ruler of the lower
world.

Finally, let us also note the teaching of Numenius of Apamea in northern
Syria, although his *floruit* was about the middle of the 2nd century C.E. and
thus at a time when Gnosticism had been in existence for quite some while.
According to this philosopher, who stands on the border between Platonism
and Pythagoreanism, the intermediary power between the πρῶτος θεός
and the ποίημα is the δεύτερος θεός (see, *e.g.,* Euseb., *Praep. ev.* XI.xviii.24)
and ποιητής (see, *e.g.,* Procl., *In Tim.* I.3003.28)[212]. The First God does not
create, he is exempt from all activity and is the father of the creator god (see
Euseb., *Praep. ev.* XI.xviii.6)[213]. The latter is a double god, because "in the
process of coming into contact with matter, which is the dyad, he gives unity
to it, but is himself divided by it, since matter has a character prone to desire
and is in flux. Thus, in virtue of not being in contact with the intelligible –
which would mean being turned in upon himself – by reason of looking towards matter and taking recognition of it, he becomes disregarding (ἀπερίοπτος)
of himself" (*ibid.,* XI.xviii.1 ff.)[214]. The demiurge of Numenius is no evil
being, but he is good only in so far as he participates in the Good[215].

These few glimpses into the history of Platonism have been sufficient to
show that a degradation of the demiurge could develop as the result of a
negative world view. This development was carried through in Gnosticism,
but first the concept of the demiurge had been incorporated by Samaritans
and Jews into a new system of reference. The creator and ruler of the world
was now no longer an ill-defined "craftsman" or a "lower Zeus", but had
become the Angel of the Lord. Accordingly, the Gnostics almost unanimous-

---

210 See p. 200.
211 See above, p. 227.
212 See des Places, Fragment 18; 21.
213 See *ibid.,* Fragment 12.
214 Fragment 11.
215 See Fragment 16; 19; 20.

ly maintained the notion that the demiurge was an angel. If the idea of a collective of creative powers was entertained, this was conceived of as the assembly of archangels. That Gnosticism has open roots in such Samaritan and Jewish doctrines of creation is shown by the fact that "in the reports on the earliest gnostics the demiurgic angel(s) is (are) not opposed to God from the beginning ... ."[216]

A characteristic of Gnosticism is that the revelatory and redemptive properties of the intermediary angel have been transferred to another being than the creator(s) and ruler(s) of this world. Thus, Simon Magus, allegedly the first Gnostic, claimed to be God's agent sent for the salvation of mankind. His appearance was necessary because the angels who had created the world subsequently had turned against God and brought the world to the brink of destruction through their bad government. Menander, another Samaritan Gnostic, conceived of himself in the same way as Simon. In the system of the Jewish Christian Gnostic Cerinthus, who also lived in the first century, it is Jesus who appears as the redeemer and is distinguished from the demiurgic angel, who — although being no evil figure — is "widely separated and remote" from God, whom he thus does not know. Already in the New Testament, however, traditions about God's agent, who shared the divine Name and could be described as the divine Glory, the man-like being ("Son of Man") in heaven, were used to represent Jesus.

The identification of the Angel of the Lord and the Glory of God by means of a personal name, whether that of one of the archangels or that of a human being, was a very significant step. Whereas God's agent formerly was not clearly distinguishable from God himself and had existence only as long as the situation for which he was required lasted, he acquired a distinct personality and permanent existence through a personal name. The rabbis opposed this development because it impinged upon the monotheistic doctrine. The identification of the demiurge with the God of the Jews has been explained as a response to this rabbinic opposition[217]. Yet, even the "unknown God" of the Gnostics has traits which make him identifiable as God of a theology based on Biblical tradition[218].

---

216 Van den Broek, "Present State", p. 60, rightly apprehending a point in my dissertation. Perhaps it would be better to call Simon, Menander, Cerinthus, *et al.*, "proto-Gnostics". This would be a more appropriate usage of the term than that suggested by the *Documento finale* of the Messina Colloquium, which used "proto-Gnosticism" of phenomena in Orphicism, Zoroastrianism, and Indian tradition; see *OG*, p. XXVIII. Cp. Th. P. van Baaren, "Towards a Definition of Gnosticism", *ibid.*, p. 177. Drijvers, "Origins", p. 328 (= *GG*, p. 808), however, is of the opinion that the term should not be used before a definition of Gnosticism is agreed upon. Cp. above, p. 4, n. 6.

217 See above, p. 17.

218 This is correctly emphasized by Rudolph, *Die Gnosis*, pp. 293 f.

It is interesting to note that the portrayal of the demiurge as the God of the Jews occurred concomitantly with an intensification of Gnostic dualism, so that the demiurge became more and more evil at the same time as he was merged into the God of the Old Testament[219]. This appears to be only logical. The demiurge and the world which was created and ruled by him grew more and more evil in the perception of the Gnostics as they continued to experience opposition. Gnosticism was erected upon an "ontological" or "metaphysical" dualism which had made its way into Samaritan and Jewish quarters[220], but the development of the radical dualism and the anti-Jewish sentiment apparently must be accounted for by certain social dynamics[221]. The object of the present work, however, does not include a discussion of this question.

---

219 See above, pp. 218 ff.
220 Cp. Rudolph, *Die Gnosis*, p. 67, from whom the terms are taken.
221 See Segal, "Ruler", especially pp. 259, 262 f., 265.

Bibliography

Primary Sources: Texts and Translations*

Aboth de R. Nathan: Schechter; Goldin
Abu'l Fatḥ, *Annals* (Samaritan Chronicle VI): Vilmar; excerpts in Bowman, *Documents*,
   pp. 114 ff.
Abu'l Hasan, *Kitab al-Tabaḥ*: Excerpts in Bowman, *Documents*, pp. 239 ff.
Abu'l Maʿali, *Kitab Bayan al-Adyan:* Schefer, pp. 131 ff. (The part on Mani.)
The *Acts of Peter*: *AAA*, I, pp. 45 ff.; Vouaux; Schneemelcher
The *Acts of Thomas*: *AAA*, II/2, pp. 99 ff.; Bedjan, pp. 3 ff.; Wright, I, pp. 171 ff. (text),
   146 ff. (translation); Bornkamm; Klijn
E.N. Adler & M. Séligsohn, ed. & trans., "Une nouvelle chronique samaritaine", *REJ*,
   44, 1902, pp. 188 ff.; 45, 1902, pp. 70 ff., 223 ff.; 46, 1903, pp. 123 ff.
Ch. Albeck, ed., ששה סדרי משנה, I-VI, Jerusalem & Tel Aviv, 1957/58
The *Alphabet of R. Aqiba*: *BH*, III, pp. 12 ff.; *BM*, II, pp. 333 ff.
Amram Dara, the hymns of: Cowley, pp. 27 ff., 491 ff.; Secondary Sources, Ben-Hayyim,
   pp. 41 ff. (text); Macdonald
The *Apocalypse of Abraham*: Bonwetsch; Box; Riessler, pp. 13 ff.
The *Apocalypse of Adam*: Böhlig, pp. 86 ff.
The *Apocalypse of Moses*: Nagel; Wells
The Apocrypha of the Old Testament: *APAT*, I; *APOT*, I
The *Apocryphon of John*: Kraūse, pp. 109 ff. (NHC II, 1); Till, pp. 79 ff. (*BG – Bero-
   linensis Gnosticus*)
The *Apostolic Fathers*: Lake
The *Asatir*: Ben-Hayyim; Gaster

F.C. Babbit, ed. & trans., *Plutarch's Moralia* (LCL), V, London & Cambridge, Mass.,
   1936 and reprints
E.C. Baguley, ed. & trans., *A Critical Edition, with Translation, of the Hebrew Text of
   the Malef*, Diss., Leeds, 1962
H. Baneth, ed. & trans., *Des Samaritaners Marqah an die 22 Buchstaben, den Grundstock
   der hebräischen Sprache anknüpfende Abhandlung*, Halle, 1888
The *Baptism of Hibil Ziwa*: Drower, *Haran Gawaita*, pp. 30 ff.
Ch. A. Baynes, ed. & trans., *A Coptic Gnostic Treatise Contained in the Codex Brucianus*, Cambridge, 1933

---

* For texts extant only in mss., see note *ad hoc*. Works marked by "Diss." (*i.e.*, dissertation) are not published. In entries listing both text publications and translations,
   the former are cited first.

P. Bedjan, ed., *Acta Martyrum et Sanctorum*, III, Paris, 1892

Z. Ben-Hayyim, ed. & trans. (Hebrew), ‫אסטיר‬ ‫ספר‬, *Tarbiz*, 14, 1943, pp. 104 ff. (introduction and text), 147 ff. (translation); 15, 1944, pp. 71 ff. (translation continued)

J.H. Bernard, ed. & trans., *The Odes of Solomon* (TS, VIII/3), Cambridge, 1912

C. Bezold, ed. & trans., *Die Schatzhöhle*, I-II, Leipzig, 1883/88

Al-Biruni, *The Dear Memories of Past Generations*: Sachau

C. Blanc, ed. & trans., *Origène, Commentaire sur Saint Jean*, III (SChr, 222), Paris, 1975

D.R. Blumenthal, trans., *Understanding Jewish Mysticism* (LJL, II), New York, 1978

A. Böhlig & P. Labib, ed. & trans., *Die koptisch-gnostische Schrift ohne Titel aus Codex II von Nag Hammadi im Koptischen Museum zu Alt-Kairo* (DAW: Institut für Orientforschung, 58), Berlin, 1962

Idem, ed. & trans., *Koptisch-gnostische Apokalypsen aus Codex V von Nag Hammadi im Koptischen Museum zu Alt-Kairo* (WZUH, Sonderband), Halle, 1963

Idem & F. Wisse, ed. & trans. (in cooperation with P. Labib), *Nag Hammadi Codices III, 2 and IV, 2* (The Gospel of the Egyptians)(NHS, IV), Leiden, 1975

G.N. Bonwetsch, ed. & trans., *Die Apokalypse Abrahams* (SGTK, I/1), Leipzig, 1897, reprinted Aalen, 1972

G. Bornkamm, trans., "The Acts of Thomas", in *NTA*, II, pp. 425 ff. (English by R. McL. Wilson). (Translation of the Greek text.)

J. Bowman, ed., *Transcript of the Original Text of the Samaritan Chronicle Tolidah*, limited lithographic edition by the Department of Semitic Languages, University of Leeds, 1954.(Obtainable from the Yale University Library.)

Idem, trans., *Samaritan Documents* (POT&TS, 2), Pittsburgh, 1977

G.H. Box & J.I. Landsman, trans., *The Apocalypse of Abraham* (TED, I; Palestinian Jewish Texts), London, 1919

Idem, trans., *The Testament of Abraham* (TED, I; Palestinian Jewish Texts), London 1927.

Idem & W.O. Oesterley, trans., "The Book of Sirach", in *APOT*, I, pp. 268ff.

S. Brown, trans., *A Critical Edition and Translation of the Ancient Samaritan Defter (i.e. Liturgy) and a Comparison of it with Early Jewish Liturgy*, Diss., Leeds, 1955

A. Brüll, ed., *Das samaritanische Targum*, I-IV, Frankfurt am Main, 1872-1874, reprinted (in a one-volume edition) Hildesheim & New York, 1971

S. Buber, ed., ‫והישן‬ ‫הקדום‬ ‫תנחומא‬ ‫מדרש‬, Vilna, 1885, reprinted Jerusalem, 1963/64

Idem, ed., ‫שמואל‬ ‫מדרש‬, Lemberg, 1893

E.A. Wallis Budge, ed. & trans., *Coptic Martyrdoms in the Dialect of Upper Egypt*, London, 1914

Idem, ed., & trans., *Miscellaneous Coptic Texts*, London, 1915

R.A. Bullard, ed. & trans., *The Hypostasis of the Archons* (PTS, 10), Berlin, 1970

R.G. Bury, ed. & trans., *Plato* (LCL), IX, London & Cambridge, Mass., 1929 and reprints

The *Cave of Treasure*: Bezold

H. Chadwick, trans., *Origen: Contra Celsum*, Cambridge, 1953

R.H. Charles, ed., *The Ethiopic Version of the Hebrew Book of Jubilees* (AO, Semitic Series, VIII), Oxford, 1895

Idem, trans., "The Book of Jubilees", in *APOT*, II, pp. 1 ff.

Idem, trans., "The Book of Enoch", in *APOT*, II, pp. 163 ff.

J.H. Charlesworth, ed. & trans., *The Odes of Solomon*, Oxford, 1973

H. Cherniss, ed. & trans., *Plutarch's Moralia* (LCL), XIII/1, London & Cambridge, Mass., 1976

Clement of Alexandria, *Excerpta ex Theodoto*: Sagnard

J.M. Cohen, ed. & trans., *A Samaritan Chronicle* (SP-B, XXX), Leiden, 1981

L.H. Colson and G.H. Whitaker, ed. & trans., *Philo* (LCL), I-X, London & Cambridge, Mass., 1929 ff. with reprints

R.H. Connolly, trans., *The Liturgical Homilies of Narsai* (TS, VIII/1), Cambridge, 1909

A.E. Cowley, ed., *The Samaritan Liturgy*, Oxford, 1909. (Two volumes paginated as one.)

Idem, ed. & trans., *Aramaic Papyri of the Fifth Century B.C.*, Oxford, 1923, reprinted Osnabrück, 1967

W. Cureton, ed., *Book of Religious and Philosophical Sects by Muhammed al-Shahrastani*, I, London, 1846, reprinted Leipzig, 1923

O.T. Crane, trans., *The Samaritan Chronicle or the Book of Joshua the Son of Nun*, New York, 1890

H. Danby, trans., *The Mishnah*, Oxford, 1933

The *Death of Moses*, the Samaritan version of: Gaster, *Asatir*, pp. 55 ff. (text) and pp. 303 ff. (translation)

E. von Dobschütz, ed. & trans., *Das Kerygma Petri kritisch untersucht* (TU, XI/1), Berlin, 1893

M. Dods & G. Reith, trans., "Justin Martyr", in *A-NF*, I, reprinted 1979, pp. 159 ff.

E.S. Drower, ed. & trans., *Diwan Abatur or Progress through Purgatories* (ST, 151), The Vatican, 1950

Idem, ed. & trans., *Šarḥ ḏ-Qabin ḏ-Šišlam Rba* (BO, 12), Rome, 1950

Idem, ed. & trans., *The Haran Gawaita and the Baptism of Hibil-Ziwa* (ST, 176), The Vatican, 1953

H. Duensing, trans., "Epistula Apostolorum", in *NTA*, I, pp. 189 ff. (English by E.R. Taylor)

A. Dupont-Sommer, trans., *The Essene Writings from Qumran*, trans. by G. Vermes, Oxford, 1961

I Enoch (the *Ethiopic Book of Enoch*): Knibb; Charles

II Enoch (the *Book of the Secrets of Enoch*, or the *Slavonic Book of Enoch*): Vaillant; Forbes

III Enoch (the *Hebrew Book of Enoch*, or *Sefer Hekaloth*): Odeberg

Epistula Apostolorum: Schmidt, *Gespräche*; Duensing

I. Epstein, translation ed., *The Babylonian Talmud*, 35 volume edition, London, 1935-1952 with reprints

Epiphanius, *Ancoratus; Panarion*: Holl; excerpts in *Gnosis*, I; Grant; Haardt; Klijn & Reinink

J.W. Etheridge, trans., *The Targums on the Pentateuch*, I (Genesis and Exodus), London, 1862

Eulogius, *Decree Proclaimed against the Samaritans*, summary of, *apud* Photius, *Bibl.*, Cod. 230, 285 ff.: Henry, pp. 60 ff.

Eusebius, *Historia ecclesiastica* II-IV: Lake, pp. 102 ff.

Evangelium Veritatis (the *Gospel of Truth*): Malinine

Ezekiel the Dramatist, *Exagoge*, the fragments of, in Alexander Polyhistor, *Peri Ioudaion*, *apud* Euseb., *Praep. ev.* IX.xxviii.2-4; xxix.5-16: Snell, pp. 288 ff.; Riessler, pp. 337 ff.

S. Farid, *et al.*, ed., *The Facsimile Edition of the Nag Hammadi Codices*, III, Leiden, 1976; VII, Leiden, 1972

N. Forbes, trans., "The Book of the Secrets of Enoch", in *APOT*, II, pp. 425 ff. (Both the long and the short version.)

H. Freedman & M. Simon, translation ed., *Midrash Rabbah*, I-X, London, 1939 and reprints

G. Friedländer, trans., *Pirke de R. Eliezer*, London, 1916

M. Friedmann, ed., מדרש פסיקתא רבתי, Vienna, 1880, reprinted Tel Aviv, 1962/63

Idem, ed., סדר אליהו רבה, Vienna, 1902

C. Fuchs, trans., "Das Leben Adams und Evas", in *APAT*, II, pp. 506 ff. (Both *Vita Adae et Evae* and *Apocalypsis Mosis*.)

A.F. von Gall, ed., *Der hebräische Pentateuch der Samaritaner*, Giessen, 1918, reprinted Berlin, 1966

M. Gaster, ed. & trans., *The Asatir* (RAS: OTF, New Series, 26), London, 1927

M. Ginsburger, ed., *Pseudo-Jonathan*, Berlin, 1903, reprinted Hildesheim & New York, 1971

The *Ginza*: Petermann; Lidzbarski; excerpts by Rudolph in *Gnosis*, II, pp. 148 ff.

H.L. Ginzberg, ed. & trans. (Hebrew), כתבי אוגרית, Jerusalem, 1963

J. Goldin, trans., *The Fathers According to R. Nathan*, Schocken paperback edition, New York, 1974. (Version A.)

D. Goldschmidt, ed., אגדה של פסח, Jerusalem, 1960

I. Goldschmidt, ed. & trans., *Der babylonische Talmud*, I-IX, The Hague, 1933/35

E.J. Goodspeed, ed., *Die ältesten Apologeten*, Göttingen, 1914

The *Gospel of the Ebionites*, the fragments of, *apud* Epiphanius, *Pan.* XXX, *passim* (entitling it the "Gospel of the Hebrews"): Holl

The *Gospel of the Egyptians*: Böhlig

The *Gospel of the Hebrews*, a fragment of, in a discourse by Cyril of Jerusalem: Wallis Budge, *Texts*, p. 60 (text) and p. 637 (translation)

The *Gospel of Philip*: Menard

The *Gospel of Truth* (*Evangelium Veritatis*): Malinine

R.M. Grant, trans., *Gnosticism. An Anthology*, London, 1961

M. Grünbaum, ed., *Jüdischdeutsche Chrestomatie*, Leipzig, 1882

L. Grünhut, ed., מדרש שיר השירים, Jerusalem, 1897

L. Gulkowitz, trans., "Der kleine Talmudtraktat über die Samaritaner", ΑΓΓΕΛΟΣ, 1, 1925, pp. 48 ff.

T. Haarbrücker, trans., *Abu'l Fath Muhammed asch-Schahrastani, Religionspartheien und Philosophen-Schulen*, I, Halle, 1850

R. Haardt, trans., *Gnosis. Character and Testimony*, trans. by J.F. Hendry, Leiden, 1971

Haran Gawaita: Drower

M. Heidenheim, ed., *Die samaritanische Liturgie* (Bibliotheca Samaritana, II), Leipzig, 1885

Idem, ed. & trans., *Der Commentar Marqa's des Samaritaners* (Bibliotheca Samaritana, III), Weimar, 1896

Hekaloth Rabbati: BM, I, pp. 63 ff.

A. Henrichs & L. Koenen, ed. & trans., "Der Kölner Mani-Kodex. Edition der Seiten 1-72", *ZPE*, 19, 1975, pp. 1 ff.

Idem, ed. & trans., "Der Kölner Mani-Kodex. Edition der Seiten 72,8-99,9", *ibid.*, 32, 1978, pp. 87 ff.

R. Henry, ed. & trans., *Photius, Bibliothèque*, V (AGB: Collection Byzantine), Paris, 1967

Hippolytus, *Refutatio omnium haeresium* (Philosophumena): Wendland; excerpts in *Gnosis*, I; Grant; Haardt; Klijn & Reinink

K. Holl, ed., *Ancoratus und Panarion*, I-III (GCS, 25/31/37), Leipzig, 1915/22/33
The *Hypostasis of the Archons*: Bullard

Irenaeus, *Adversus haereses*, I: Rousseau; Klebba; Roberts; excerpts in *Gnosis*, I; Grant; Haardt
M.R. James, ed., *The Testament of Abraham* (TS, II/2), Cambridge, 1892
I and *II Jeu*: Schmidt
The Mandean *Book of John*: Lidzbarski; excerpts by Rudolph in *Gnosis*, II, pp. 148 ff.
The *Book of Joshua* (Samaritan Chronicle IV): Juynboll; Crane; excerpts in Bowman, *Documents*, pp. 61 ff.
Josephus, *Antiquitates Judaicae* IV; *Bellum Judaicum* II; *Contra Apionem*: Thackeray, IV, pp. 477 ff.; II, pp. 322 ff.; I, pp. 161 ff.
The *Book of Jubilees*: Charles
Justin Martyr, *I Apology; Dialogue with Trypho*: Goodspeed, pp. 24 ff., 90 ff.; Dods, pp. 163 ff., 194 ff.
T.G.J. Juynboll, ed. & trans. (Latin), *Chronicon Samaritanum*, Leiden, 1848

P. Kahle, trans., "Die zwölf Marka-Hymnen aus dem "Defter" der samaritanischen Liturgie", *OrChr*, 3, 1932, pp. 77ff. (= *Opera Minora*, ed. by M. Black *et al.*, Leiden, 1956, pp. 186 ff.)
R. Kasser, M. Malinine, H.-Ch. Puech, G. Quispel & J. Zandee, ed. & trans., *Tractatus Triparitus*, II et III, Bern, 1975
Kephalaia: Polotsky
O. Kern, ed., *Orphicorum Fragmenta*, Berlin, 1922, reprinted 1963
Kerygma Petrou: von Dobschütz; Schneemelcher
E. Klebba, trans., *Des heiligen Irenäus fünf Bücher gegen die Häresien*, I (BKV, 3), Kempten & Munich, 1912
M.L. Klein, ed. & trans., *The Fragment-Targums of the Pentateuch*, I (Texts, Indices and Introductory Essays)-II (Translation) (AB, 76), Rome, 1980
A.F.J. Klijn, trans., *The Acts of Thomas* (Suppl. *NT*, V), Leiden, 1962. (Translation of the Syriac text.)
Idem & G.J. Reinink, ed. & trans., *Patristic Evidence for Jewish-Christian Sects* (Suppl. *NT*, XXXVI), Leiden, 1973
M.A. Knibb, ed. & trans. (in consultation with E. Ullendorff), *The Ethiopic Book of Enoch*, 1-2, Oxford, 1978
P. Koetschau, ed., *Origenes, Werke*, I-II (GCS, 2/3), Leipzig, 1899

M. Krause & P. Labib, ed. & trans., *Die drei Versionen des Apokryphon des Johannes im Koptischen Museum zu Alt-Kairo* (ADAIK, Koptische Reihe 1), Wiesbaden, 1962
A.M. Kropp, ed. & trans., *Ausgewählte koptische Zaubertexte* (EFERE), I (Text-Publikationen), II (Übersetzüng), III (Einleitüng), Bruxelles, 1930/31

K. Lake, ed. & trans., *The Apostolic Fathers* (LCL), I-II, London & Cambridge, Mass., 1912/13 and reprints
Idem, ed. & trans., *Eusebius, The Ecclesiastical History* (LCL), I, London & Cambridge, Mass., 1926 and reprints
J.E. Lauterbach, ed. & trans., *Mekilta de-Rabbi Ishmael* (SLJC), I, Philadelphia, 1933
M.E. Lazarus, trans. "Makkoth", in Epstein, *Talmud*, Seder Nezikin VIII, 1935. (With separate pagination.)
W. Leslau, trans., *Falasha Anthology*, Schocken paperback edition, New York, 1969

The *Letter of Eugnostos*: Farid, III, pp. 70 ff.

M. Lidzbarski, ed. & trans., *Das Johannesbuch der Mandäer*, Giessen, 1915

Idem, ed. & trans., *Mandäische Liturgien* (AKGWG, phil.-hist. Kl. XVII/1), Berlin, 1920, reprinted Hildsheim, 1962

The *Life of Adam and Eve* (*Vita Adae et Evae*): Meyer; Fuchs; Wells

E. Lohse, ed. & trans., *Die Texte aus Qumran*, Munich, 1964

D. Luria, ed., פרקי דר' אליעזר, Vilna, 1837, reprinted Warsaw, 1852

Maᶜase Merkaba: Secondary Sources, Scholem, *Jewish Gnosticism*, pp. 101 ff. (text)

J. Macdonald, trans., "The Theological Hymns of Amram Darah", in J. Macdonald, ed., *ALUOS*, II, 1961, pp. 54 ff.

Idem, ed. & trans., *Memar Marqah* (BZAW, 84), I (The Text)-II (The Translation), Berlin, 1963

Idem, ed. & trans., *The Samaritan Chronicle No. II* (BZAW, 107), Berlin, 1969

A. Díez Macho, ed. & trans., *Neophyti 1* (Targum palestinense MS de la Bibliotheca Vaticana), I (Génesis) (TE, 7), Madrid & Barcelona, 1968; II (Exodo) (TE, 8), Madrid & Barcelona, 1970

Magical Papyri, the Coptic: Kropp

Magical Papyri, the Greek: *PGM*

The *Malef*: Baguley

M. Malinine, H.-Ch. Puech & G. Quispel, ed. & trans., *Evangelium Veritatis* (SCGJ-I, IV), Zürich, 1956

M. Malinine, H.-Ch. Puech, G. Quispel & W.C. Till, ed. & trans., *De resurrectione* (*Epistula ad Rheginum*), Zürich, 1963

Manichean Homilies, the Coptic: Polotsky

Manichean Hymns, Iranian: Menasce; Müller

Mani Codex, the Greek: Henrichs

R. Marcus, trans., *Philo* (LCL), Two Supplementary Volumes, London & Cambridge, Mass., 1953 and reprints

Marcus Eremita, *De Melchizedech*: Migne, cols. 1118 ff.

Marqa, the hymns of: Cowley, pp. 1-90 ff., *passim*; Brown, *passim*; Secondary Sources, Ben-Hayyim, pp. 133 ff. (text); Kahle; Szuster

Masseketh Kuthim: Gulkowitz; Nutt, pp. 168 ff. (trans.); Secondary Sources, Montgomery, pp. 197 ff. (trans.)

F. Marx, ed., *Philastrius episcopus Brixiensis, Diversarum hereseon liber* (CSEL, 38), Vienna, 1898

Mekilta de R. Ishmael: Lauterbach

Memar Marqa: Macdonald; Baneth (Book V), Heidenheim (books I-V); Rettig (Book IV)

J.É. Ménard, ed. & trans., *L'Evangile selon Philippe*, Paris, 1967

J. de Menasce, ed. & trans., "Fragments manichéens de Paris", in M. Boyce & I. Gershevitch, ed., *W.B. Henning Memorial Volume*, London, 1970, pp. 304 f.

W. Meyer, ed., *Vita Adae et Evae* (AKBAW, philos.-philol. Cl., XIV/3), Munich, 1878

Midrash Bereshith Rabba: Theodor; Aryeh Mirkin, I-IV; Freedman, I-II

Midrash ha-Gadol Sefer Bereshith: Schechter

Midrash Rabba: Aryeh Mirkin; Freedman; Theodor (*Genesis Rabba*)

Midrash Samuel: Buber

Midrash Shir ha-Shirim: Grünhut

מדרש שוחר טוב על תהלים, Jerusalem, 1960. (For translation, see Braude.)

Midrash Tadshe: *BH*, III, pp. 164 ff.

מדרש תנחומא ..., Vilna, 1833

Midrash Tanḥuma B: Buber

J.-P. Migne, ed., *Patrologiae graecae cursus completus*, LXV, Paris, 1858

J. Milik, ed. & trans. (in collaboration with M. Black), *The Books of Enoch. Aramaic Fragments of Qumran Cave 4*, Oxford, 1976

M. Aryeh Mirkin, ed., ... מדרש רבה, I-X, Tel Aviv, 1957-68

The Mishna: Albeck; Danby

F.W.K. Müller, ed. & trans., *Handschriften-Reste in Estrangelo-Schrift aus Turfan, Chinesisch-Turkistan*, II (PAW, Phil. und hist. Abh. II), Berlin, 1904

Ibn al-Murtada, The *Overflowing Sea*: Secondary Sources, Kessler, pp. 346 ff. (text), 349 ff. (translation). (The part on Mani.)

S. Musajoff, ed., מרכבה שלמה, Jerusalem, 1921, reprinted 1971

Ibn al-Nadim, *Fihrist al-ʿUlum*: Secondary Sources, Flügel. (The part on Mani.)

M. Nagel, ed., *La vie grecque d'Adam et Ève* (Apocalypse de Moïse), 1 (Histoire du texte), 2 (Notes sur l'histoire du texte), 3 (Edition du texte avec synopse de toutes les variantes), Oberbronn, 1972, reprinted Lille, 1974

Narsai, the liturgical homilies of: Connolly

L. Nemoy, trans., "Al-Qirqisani's Account of the Jewish Sects and Christianity", *HUCA*, 7, 1930, pp. 317 ff.

A. Neubauer, ed., "Chronique samaritaine", *JA*, 14, 1869, pp. 385 ff. (Reprinted as extract No. 14 of the same series, in 1873.)

A.D. Nock, ed., & A.-J. Festugière, trans., *Corpus Hermeticum*, I (Traites I-XII) (CUF), Paris, 1945, reprinted 1960

Numenius, the fragments of: des Places

J.W. Nutt, ed. & trans., *Fragments of a Samaritan Targum*, London, 1874

H. Odeberg, ed. & trans., *3 Enoch*, Cambridge, 1928, reprinted, with a Prolegomenon by J.C. Greenfield (LBS), New York, 1973

The *Odes of Solomon*: Bernard; Charlesworth

F. Oehler, ed., *Corpus haereseologicum*, I, Berlin, 1856

Oenomaus, a fragment of, *apud* Julian, *Or.* VII, 209: Cave Wright, p. 84

Origen, *Contra Celsum*: Koetschau; Chadwick

Idem, Commentarius in Johannem: Blanc

On the Origin of the World (or, the *Untitled Writing*): Böhlig

The Orphic Fragments: Kern

E. Oswald, trans., "Das Gebet Manasses", in W.G. Kümmel, translation ed., *Jüdische Schriften aus hellenistisch-römischer Zeit*, IV (Poetische Schriften)/1, Gütersloh, 1974, pp. 15 ff.

Pesikta Hadatha: BH, VI, pp. 36 ff.

Pesikta Rabbati: Friedmann; Braude

H. Petermann, ed., *Thesaurus, sive Liber Magnus vulgo "Liber Adami" appellatus, opus Mandaeorum summi ponderis*, I (Text. contin.)-II (Lect. codd. addit. et corr. cont.), Leipzig, 1867

Petirath Moshe: BH, VI, pp. 71 ff.

Philaster, *On the Heresies*: Marx; Oehler, pp. 1 ff.

Philo, the works of: Colson; Marcus

Pirke de R. Eliezer: Luria; Friedlander

Pistis Sophia: Schmidt

The *Pitron*: Gaster, *The Asatir*. (Hebrew translation of the Arabic *Pitron* at the foot of the Aramaic text of the *Asatir*.)

E. des Places, ed. & trans., *Numenius, Fragments* (CUF), Paris, 1973

Plato, *Epistle* VI: Bury, pp. 456 ff.

Plutarch, *The E at Delphi*: Babbit, pp. 194 ff.; *Platonic Questions*: Cherniss, pp. 2 ff.
H. Pognon, ed. & trans., *Inscriptions mandaites des coupes de Khouabir*, Paris, 1898/99. (Three volumes paginated as one.)
Poimandres (Corpus Hermeticum I): Nock, pp. 1 ff.; Secondary Sources, Reitzenstein, *Poimandres*, pp. 328 ff. (text)
H.J. Polotsky, ed. & trans., *Manichäische Homilien* (MHSChB, I), Stuttgart, 1934
Idem & A. Böhlig, ed. & trans., *Kephalaia* (MHSMB, I), 1, Stuttgart, 1940
The *Prayer of Joseph, apud* Origen, *Comm. in Joh.* II.31: Blanc, pp. 334 ff.
The *Prayer of Manasseh*: Oswald; Ryle; Ryssel; Secondary Sources, Zöckler, pp. 236 ff.
E. Preuschen, trans., *Die apokryphen gnostischen Adamschriften aus dem Armenischen*, Giessen, 1900
The *Pseudo-Clementine Homilies* and *Recognitions*: Rehm; Smith
The *Pseudo-Jonathan Targum*: Ginsburger; Etheridge, pp. 157 ff. ("The Targum of Palestine")

Al-Qirqisani, The *Book of Light and Watch-Towers*: Nemoy. (The account of Jewish Sects and Christianity.)
Qolasta (the Mandean Liturgy): Lidzbarski
The Questions of Bartholomew: Scheidweiler
The Qumran Texts: Lohse ; Dupont-Sommer

Solomon ben Isaac Rashi: *Commentary on the Sanhedrin: Talmud babli*
B. Rehm, ed., *Die Pseudoklementinen*, I (Homilien) (GCS, 42), Berlin & Leipzig, 1953; II (Rekognitionen in Rufins Übersetzung) (GCS, 51), Berlin & Leipzig, 1965
D. Rettig, ed. & trans., *Memar Marqa* (BOS, 8), Stuttgart, 1934
P. Riessler, trans., *Altjüdisches Schrifttum ausserhalb der Bibel*, Augsburg, 1928
A. Roberts & W.H. Raumbaut, trans., "Irenaeus", in *A-NF*, I, reprinted 1979, pp. 315 ff.
A. Rousseau & L. Doutreleau, ed. & trans., *Irénée de Lyon, Contre les Hérésies Livre I*, I (Introduction, Notes Justificatives, Tables) (SChr, 263)-II (Texte et Traduction) (SChr, 264), Paris, 1979
K. Rudolph, trans., "Mandean Sources", in *Gnosis*, II, pp. 121 ff. (English by P.W. Coxon)
H.E. Ryle, trans., "The Prayer of Manasseh", in *APOT*, I, pp. 612 ff.
V. Ryssel, trans., "Das Gebet Manasses", in *APAT*, I, pp. 165 ff.

E. Sachau, ed., *Chronologie orientalischer Völker von Alberuni*, Leipzig, 1878, reprinted 1923
Idem, trans., *Chronology of Ancient Nations*, London, 1879
A.I.S. de Sacy, ed. & trans., *Chrestomathie arabe*, I, Paris, 1826
F. Sagnard, ed. & trans., *Clement d'Alexandrine, Extraits de Théodote* (SChr, 23), Paris, 1948
The Samaritan Pentateuch: von Gall
The Samaritan Targum: Brüll; Nutt
S. Schechter, ed., מסכת אבות דרבי נתן בשתי נוסחאות, Vienna, 1887, reprinted New York, 1945. (Both Version A and Version B.)
Idem, ed., מדרש הגדול...ספר בראשית, Cambridge, 1902
Ch. Schefer, ed., *Chrestomathie Persane*, I (PELOV, II/7), Paris, 1883
F. Scheidweiler, trans., "The Questions of Bartholomew", in *NTA*, I, pp. 486 ff. (English by R. McL. Wilson)
C. Schmidt, ed. & trans., *Gespräche Jesu mit seinen Jüngern* (TU, XLIII), Leipzig, 1919, reprinted Hildesheim, 1967
Idem, ed., & V. MacDermot, trans., *The Pistis Sophia* (NHS, IX), Leiden, 1978

C. Schmidt, ed., & V. MacDermot, trans., *The Books of Jeu and the Untitled Text in the Bruce Codex* (NHS, XIII), Leiden, 1978

I. Schmidt, ed. & trans., *Le Testament d'Abraham*, Diss., I, Strassbourg, 1971

W. Schneemelcher, trans., "The Kerygma Petrou" in *NTA*, II, pp. 94 ff. (English by G. Ogg)

Idem, trans., "The Acts of Peter", in *NTA*, II, pp. 259 ff. (Englisch by G.C. Stead)

A. Schollmeyer, ed. & trans., *Sumerisch-babylonische Hymnen und Gebete an Šamaš*, Paderborn, 1912

M. Schwab, trans., *Le Talmud de Jérusalem*, I-XI, Paris, 1871-89

Seder Eliyahu Rabba: Friedmann

ספר יצירה, Jerusalem, 1964. (For translation, see Blumenthal, pp. 13 ff.)

Zalman Ṣevi, *Jüdischer Theriak*: excerpts in Grünbaum, pp. 560 ff.

Ash-Shahrastani, *Book of Religious Sects and Philosophical Schools*: Cureton; Haarbrücker

שעור קומה: Musajoff, 32a ff.

The *Book of Sirach*: Box

Th. Smith, trans., "Recognitions of Clement", in *A-NF*, VIII, reprinted 1978, pp. 75 ff.

Idem, P. Peterson & J. Donaldson, trans., "The Clementine Homilies", *ibid.*, pp. 213 ff.

B. Snell, ed., *Tragicorum graecorum fragmenta*, I (Didascaliae tragicae), Göttingen, 1971

The *Three Steles of Seth*: Farid, VII, pp. 124 ff.

M.E. Stone, trans., *The Testament of Abraham: The Greek Recensions* (SBL: TT, 2; Pseudepigrapha Series, 2), Missoula, 1972. (With a reprint of James' text.)

I. Szuster, trans., *Marqa-Hymnen aus der samaritanischen Liturgie*, Bonn, 1936

Talmud babli. Tractate Sanhedrin with Rashi, Tosafot ... according to the Venice Text, Jerusalem, no date

Talmud, the Babylonian: Goldschmidt; Epstein

תלמוד ירושלמי ..., I-IV, Jerusalem, 1960. (For translation, see Schwab.)

Targum, the Fragmentary: Klein

Targum Neofyti: Diez Macho

The *Teachings of Silvanus*: Farid, VII, pp. 90 ff.

The *Testament of Abraham*: James; Box; Stone

H. St. J. Thackeray, ed. & trans., *Josephus* (LCL), I, II, IV, London & Cambridge, Mass., 1926/27/30, with reprints

J. Theodor & C. Albeck, ed., מדרש בראשית רבה, 2nd printing (corrected), Jerusalem, 1965. (Three volumes paginated as one.)

Theodore bar Konai, *Book of Scholia* XI: Pognon

W.C. Till, ed. & trans., *Die gnostischen Schriften des koptischen Papyrus Berolinensis 8502* (TU, 60), 2nd ed. by H.-M. Schenke, Berlin, 1972

Timothy, patriarch of Alexandria, *Discourse on Abbaton*: Wallis Budge, *Martyrdoms*, pp. 225 ff. (text), 474 ff. (translation)

The *Tolida* (Samaritan Chronicle III): Bowman; Neubauer

The *Tripartite Tractate*: Kasser

A. Vaillant, ed. & trans., *Le livre des secrets d'Hénoch* (TIES, IV), 2nd ed., Paris, 1952, reprinted 1976. (The short version.)

E. Vilmar, ed., *Annales Samaritani Abulfathi*, Gotha, 1865

The *Visions of Ezekiel*: BM, II, pp. 127 ff.

L. Vouaux, ed. & trans., *Les actes de Pierre*, Paris, 1922

L.S.A. Wells, trans., "The Life of Adam and Eve", in *APOT*, II, pp. 123 ff. (Both *Vita Adae et Evae* and *Apocalypsis Mosis*.)

P. Wendland, ed., *Hippolytus, Refutatio omnium haeresium* (Philosophumena) (GCS, 26), Berlin, 1916, reprinted Hildesheim & New York, 1977

W. Cave Wright, ed. & trans., *The Works of the Emperor Julian* (LCL), II, 1913 and reprints

W. Wright, ed. & trans., *The Apocryphal Acts of the Apostles*, I, London, 1871

The *Untitled Writing of the Bruce Codex*: Baynes; Schmidt

Xenocrates, the fragments of: Secondary Sources, Heinze, pp. 157 ff. (text)

ילקוט ראובני, Prague, 1660

ילקוט ראובני על התורה, Wilmersdorf, 1681, reprinted Warsaw, 1901

ילקוט שמעוני, I-II (containing three vols.), Warsaw, 1876/77, reprinted 1925

Secondary Sources

A. Adam, *Die Psalmen des Thomas und das Perlenlied als Zeugnisse vorchristlicher Gnosis* (BZNW, 24), Berlin, 1965

Idem, "Neuere Literatur zur Gnosis", *GGA*, 215, 1963, pp. 31 ff.

Idem, Lehrbuch der Dogmengeschichte, I (Die Zeit der alten Kirche), Gütersloh, 1965

Idem, "Ist die Gnosis in aramäischen Weisheitsschulen entstanden?", in *OG*, pp. 291 ff. (= *Sprache und Dogma*, Gütersloh, 1969, pp. 101 ff.)

J.B. Adamson, *The Epistle of James* (NIC), Grand Rapids, 1976, reprinted 1977

W.F. Albright, *Archaeology and the Religion of Israel* (ALC-RDS, 1941), 2nd ed., Baltimore, 1946

Idem, The Biblical Period from Abraham to Ezra, New York, 1963

Idem, "Simon Magus as "the Great Power of God"", Appendix VII in J. Munck, *The Acts of the Apostles* (AB, 31), revised by W.F. Albright & C.S. Mann, New York, 1967, pp. 305 ff.

Idem, Yahweh and the Gods of Canaan (SOAS: JL, VII, 1965), London, 1968

A. Altmann, "The Gnostic Background of the Rabbinic Adam Legends", *JQR*, 25, 1945, pp. 371 ff.

W. Anz, *Zur Frage nach dem Ursprung des Gnostizismus* (TU, XV/4), Leipzig, 1897

M. Appel, *Quaestiones de rebus Samaritanorum*, Breslau, 1874

S. Arai, *Die Christologie des Evangelium Veritatis*, Leiden, 1964

Th. P. van Baaren, "Towards a Definition of Gnosticism", in *OG*, pp. 174 ff.

H.R. Balz, *Methodische Probleme der neutestamentlichen Christologie* (WMANT, 25), Neukirchen, 1967

B.J. Bamberger, par. "Bible", in Art. "Angels and Angelology", in *EJ*, 1, cols. 957 ff.

S.W. Baron, *A Social and Religious History of the Jews*, V (Religious Controls and Discussions), 2nd ed., New York, 1957

J. Barr, "Theophany and Anthropomorphism in the Old Testament", in *Congress Volume, Oxford, 1959* (Suppl. *VT*, VII), Leiden, 1960, pp. 31 ff.

C.K. Barrett, *The Gospel according to St. John*, 2nd ed., London, 1978

S. Bartina, " 'Yo soy Yahweh' – Nota exegética a Jn. 18.4-8", in *SBE*, XVIII, 1959, pp. 393 ff.

H.-W. Bartsch, *Die konkrete Wahrheit und die Lüge der Spekulation* (TW, 1), Bern, 1974

W. Bauer, *Das Johannesevangelium* (HNT, 6), 2nd ed., Tübingen, 1925

O. Bauernfeind, *Die Apostelgeschichte* (THNT, V), Leipzig, 1939

F. Chr. Baur, *Die christliche Gnosis*, Tübingen, 1835, reprinted Osnabrück, 1967

Idem, Das Christentum und die christliche Kirche der drei ersten Jahrhunderte, 2nd ed., Tübingen, 1860. (Reprint of pp. 175-189 in *GG*, pp. 1 ff.)

G.R. Beasley-Murray, *The Book of Revelation* (NCB), London, 1974

W. Beltz, "Samaritanertum und Gnosis", in *GNT*, pp. 89 ff.

Z. Ben-Hayyim, review of Macdonald, *Memar Marqah*, in *BO*, 23, 1966, cols. 185 ff.

Idem, The Literary and Oral Tradition of Hebrew and Aramaic amongst the Samaritans, III/2 (The Recitation of Prayers and Hymns) (AHL: TS, VI), Jerusalem, 1967. (In Hebrew.)

R. Bergmeier, "Zur Frühdatierung samaritanischer Theologoumena", *JSJ*, 5, 1974, pp. 121 ff.

J.H. Bernard, *A Critical and Exegetical Commentary on the Gospel according to St. John* (ICC), I-II, Edinburgh, 1928, reprinted 1962/63

E. Best, *A Commentary on the First and Second Epistles to the Thessalonians* (BNTC), London, 1972

O. Betz, "Was am Anfang geschah (Das jüdische Erbe in den neugefundenen koptisch-gnostischen Schriften)", in O. Betz, *et al.*, ed., *Abraham unser Vater* (Festschrift für O. Michel) (AGSU, V), Leiden, 1963, pp. 24 ff.

K. Beyschlag, *Simon Magus und die christliche Gnosis* (WUNT, 16), Tübingen, 1974

U. Bianchi, "Le problème des origines du gnosticisme et l'histoire des religions", *Numen*, 12, 1965, pp. 161 ff. (= *GG*, pp. 601 ff.)

Idem, "Perspectives de la recherche sur les origines du gnosticisme", in *OG*, pp. 716 ff. (= *GG*, pp. 707 ff.)

E. Bickermann, "The Historical Foundations of Postbiblical Judaism", in his *From Ezra to the Last of the Maccabees*, New York, 1962, pp. 41 ff.

H. Bietenhard, *Die himmlische Welt im Urchristentum und Spätjudentum* (WUNT, 2), Tübingen, 1951

Idem, Art. ὄνομα κτλ., in *TDNT*, V, 1967 and reprints, pp. 242 ff.

M. Black, *The Scrolls and Christian Origins*, London, 1961

Idem, "The Son of Man Problem in Recent Research and Debate", *BJRL*, 45, 1963, pp. 305 ff.

Idem, "The Throne-Theophany Prophetic Commission and the Son of Man", in R.G. Hamerton-Kelly & R. Scroggs, ed., *Jews, Greeks and Christians* (Essays in Honor of William David Davies) (SJLA, XXI), Leiden, 1976, pp. 56 ff.

A. Böhlig, "Religionsgeschichtliche Probleme aus der Schrift ohne Titel des Codex II von Nag Hammadi", *WZUH*, Ges.-Sprach. Reihe, 10, 1961, pp. 1325 ff. (= *Mysterion und Wahrheit* (AGSU, VI), Leiden, 1968, pp. 119 ff.)

Idem, "Der jüdische und judenchristliche Hintergrund in gnostischen Texten von Nag Hammadi", in *OG*, pp. 109 ff. (= *Mysterion und Wahrheit*, pp. 80 ff.)

Idem, "Zum "Pluralismus" in den Schriften von Nag Hammadi", in M. Krause, ed., *Essays on the Nag Hammadi Texts in Honor of Pahor Labib* (NHS, VI), Leiden, 1975, pp. 19 ff.

C. Bonner, "An Amulet of the Ophitic Gnostics", *Hesperia. Suppl. VIII*, 1949, pp. 43 ff.

Idem, Studies in Magical Amulets (UMS, Humanistic Series, XLIX), Ann Arbor & London, 1950

W. Bousset, *Der Antichrist in der Überlieferung des Judentums, des neuen Testaments und der alten Kirche*, Göttingen, 1895

Idem, Hauptprobleme der Gnosis (FRLANT, 10), Göttingen, 1907, reprinted Darmstadt, 1973

Idem, Die Religion des Judentums im späthellenistischen Zeitalter (HNT, 21), 3rd ed. by H. Gressmann, Tübingen, 1926

J. Bowman, "The Background of the Term "Son of Man" ", *ExT*, 59, 1948, pp. 283 ff.

Idem, "The Exegesis of the Pentateuch among the Samaritans and among the Rabbis", in J.A.H. de Boer, ed., *OS*, VIII, 1950, pp. 220 ff.

Idem, "Early Samaritan Eschatology", *JJS*, 6, 1955, pp. 63 ff.

Idem, "Ezekiel and the Zadokite Priesthood", *TGUOS*, 16, 1955/56, pp. 1 ff.

Idem, "Contact between Samaritan Sects and Qumran?", *VT*, 7, 1957, pp. 184 ff.

Idem, "Samaritan Studies", *BJRL*, 40, 1958, pp. 298 ff.

Idem, "The Importance of Samaritan Researches", in *ALUOS*, I, 1958/59, pp. 43 ff.

Idem, "Is the Samaritan Calendar the Old Zadokite One?", *PEQ*, 91, 1959, pp. 23 ff.

Idem, "Pilgrimage to Mt. Gerizim", *EI*, 7, 1963, pp. 17[+] ff.

Idem, *Samaritanische Probleme* (FDV, 1959), Stuttgart, 1967

Idem, *The Samaritan Problem*, trans. by A.M. Johnson, Jr. (PMTS, 4), Pittsburgh, 1975

G.H. Box, "The Idea of Intermediation in Jewish Theology: A Note on Memra and Shekinah", *JQR*, 23, 1932/33, pp. 103 ff.

E. Brandenburger, *Adam und Christus* (WMANT, 7), Neukirchen 1962

W. Brandt, *Die mandäische Religion*, Leipzig, 1889

Idem, *Elchasai*, Leipzig, 1912

Idem, *Die Mandäer* (VKAWA, XVI/3), Amsterdam, 1915

E. Bréhier, *Les idées philosophiques et religieuses du Philon d'Alexandrie*, Paris, 1907

A. Broadie, *A Samaritan Philosophy* (SP-B, XXI), Leiden, 1981

R. van den Broek, "The Creation of Adam's Psychic Body in the Apocryphon of John", in *Studies*, pp. 38 ff.

Idem, "The Present State of Gnostic Studies", *VigChr*, 37, 1983, pp. 41 ff.

R.A. Brown, *The Gospel according to John* (AB, 29), New York, 1966; *op. cit.* (AB, 29A), New York, 1970

L.E. Browne, "A Jewish Sanctuary in Babylonia", *JTS*, 17, 1916, pp. 400 ff.

Idem, *Early Judaism*, Cambridge, 1929

W.H. Brownlee, "Whence the Gospel according to John?", in J. Charlesworth, ed., *John and Qumran*, London, 1972, pp. 166 ff.

F.F. Bruce, *The Acts of the Apostles*, 2nd ed., London, 1952

Idem, *The Book of Acts* (NIC), London & Edinburgh, 1954

G.W. Buchanan, "The Samaritan Origin of the Gospel of John", in *RA*, pp. 149 ff.

A. Büchler, "La relation du Josèphe concernant Alexandre le Grand", *REJ*, 36, 1898, pp. 1 ff.

J.F. Buddeus, *Introductio ad historiam philosophiae Hebraeorum*, Halle, 1702/21

J.-A. Bühner, *Der Gesandte und sein Weg im vierten Evangelium* (WUNT, 2. Reihe, 2), Tübingen, 1977

R. Bultmann, *The Gospel of John*, translation ed. by G.R. Beasley-Murray, Oxford, 1971

F.C. Burkitt, *Early Eastern Christianity*, London, 1904

C.F. Burney, "Christ as the ʾAPXH of the Creation", *JTS*, 27, 1926, pp. 160 ff.

E. Burrows, "Some Cosmological Patterns in Babylonian Religion", in S.M. Hooke, ed., *The Labyrinth*, London, 1935, pp. 43 ff.

G.B. Caird, *A Commentary on the Revelation of St. John the Divine* (BNTC), London, 1966, reprinted 1971

Th. Caldwell, "Dositheus Samaritanus", *Kairos*, 4, 1962, pp. 105 ff.

J. Campbell, *The Masks of God*, I (Primitive Mythology), 2nd ed., New York, 1969, reprinted London, 1973

A. Caquot & P. Geoltrain, "Notes sur le texte éthiopien des "Paraboles" d'Henoch", *Semitica*, 13, 1963, pp. 52 ff.

J. Carmignac, "Le Document de Qumran sur Melchisédeq", *RQ*, 7, 1970, pp. 343 ff.

R.P. Casey, "Simon Magus", Note XIII in K. Lake & H.J. Cadbury, ed., *The Acts of the*

Apostles (BC, I), V (Additional Notes), London, 1933, pp. 151 ff.

Idem, "The Study of Gnosticism", *JTS*, 36, 1935, pp. 45 ff. (= *GG*, pp. 352 ff.)

U. Cassuto, *Commentary on the Exodus* (PPF), Jerusalem, 1967

L. Cerfaux, "La gnose simonienne", in *RSR*, 15-16, 1925/26 (= *Recueil Lucien Cerfaux* (BETL, VI-VII), I, Gembloux, 1954, pp. 191 ff.)

Idem, "La première communauté chrétienne", *ETL*, 16, 1939, pp. 5 ff. (= *Recueil*, II, Gembloux, 1954, pp. 125 ff.)

R.H. Charles, *The Revelation of St. John* (ICC), I, Edinburgh, 1920 and reprints

I. Cherniss, "Visions of God in Merkabah Mysticism", *JSJ*, 13, 1983, pp. 100 ff.

D. Chwolsohn, *Die Ssabier und der Ssabismus*, I, Petersburg, 1856

R.J. Coggins, *Samaritans and Jews* (GPT), Oxford, 1975

C. Colpe, review of Macdonald, *Memar Marqah*, in *ZDMG*, 115, 1965, pp. 200 ff.

Idem, Art. ὁ υἱὸς τοῦ ἀνθρώπου, in *TDNT*, VIII, 1972 and reprints, pp. 400 ff.

H. Conzelmann, *Die Apostelgeschichte* (HNT, 7), Tübingen, 1963

Idem, Der erste Brief an die Korinther (MKKNT, V), Göttingen, 1969

Idem, History of Primitive Christianity, trans. by J.E. Steeley, Nashville & New York, 1973

C.E.B. Cranfield, *The Gospel according to Saint Mark* (CGTC), 3rd ed., Cambridge, 1966

F.M. Cross, Jr., "The Discovery of the Samaritan Papyri", *BA*, 26, 1963, pp. 110 ff.

Idem, "Aspects of Samaritan and Jewish History in Late Persian and Hellenistic Times", *HTR*, 59, 1966, pp. 201 ff.

J.W. Crowfoot, K.M. Kenyon & E.L. Sukenik, *The Buildings at Samaria* (Samaria-Sebaste, 1), London, 1942, reprinted 1966

A.D. Crown, "Dositheans, Resurrection and a Messianic Joshua", *Antichton*, 1, pp. 70 ff.

Idem, "Some Traces of Heterodox Theology in the Samaritan Book of Joshua", *BJRL*, 50, 1967, pp. 178 ff.

I.P. Culianu, "The Angels of the Nations and the Origins of Gnostic Dualism", in *Studies*, pp. 78 ff.

O. Cullmann, *Le problème littéraire et historique du roman Pseudo-Clémentin* (EHPR, 23), Paris, 1930

F. Cumont, *Textes et monuments figurés relatifs aux mystères de Mithra*, I, Bruxelles, 1899

M.A. Czaplicka, *Aboriginal Siberia: A Study in Social Anthropology*, Oxford, 1914

N.A. Dahl & A.F. Segal, "Philo and the Rabbis on the Names of God", *JSJ*, 9, 1978, pp. 1 ff.

G. Dalman, *Die Worte Jesu*, I (Einleitung und wichtige Begriffe), Leipzig, 1898

J. Daniélou, "Catéchèse pascale et retour au Paradis", *M-D*, 45, 1955, pp. 99 ff.

Idem, "L'étoile de Jacob et la mission chrétienne à Damas", *VigChr*, 11, 1957, pp. 121 ff.

Idem, The Theology of Jewish Christianity (The Development of Christian Doctrine before the Council of Nicaea, I), trans. by J.A. Baker, London, 1964

W.D. Davies, *Torah in the Messianic Age and/or Age to Come* (*JBL*, Monograph Series, 7), Philadelphia, 1952

Idem, "Paul and the Dead Sea Scrolls: Flesh and Spirit", in K. Stendahl, ed., *The Scrolls and the New Testament*, London, 1958, pp. 157 ff.

Idem, The Setting of the Sermon on the Mount, Cambridge, 1964

F. Decret, *Mani* (MS, 40), Paris, 1974

A. Deissmann, *Bibelstudien*, Marburg, 1895

M. Delcor, "Melchizedek from Genesis to the Qumran Texts and the Epistle to the Hebrews", *JSJ*, 2, 1971, pp. 115 ff.

M. Dibelius, *Die apostolischen Väter*, IV (Der Hirt des Hermas) (HNT, Ergänzungsband), Tübingen, 1923

J. Dillon, *The Middle Platonists* (CLL), London, 1977

E. Dinkler, "Jesu Wort vom Kreuztragen", in *Neutestamentliche Studien für R. Bultmann* (BZNW, 21), Berlin, 1954, pp. 110 ff.

C.H. Dodd, *The Bible and the Greeks*, London, 1935

Idem, The Interpretation of the Fourth Gospel, Cambridge, 1953 and reprints

E.R. Dodds, *The Greeks and the Irrational* (SCL, 25), Berkeley & Los Angeles, 1951, reprinted 1973

F.J. Dölger, *Sphragis* (SGKA, 5), Paderborn, 1911

J. Doresse, *The Secret Books of the Egyptian Gnostics*, London & New York, 1960, reprinted New York, 1970

Idem, Art. "Gnosticism", in *HR*, I, pp. 533 ff.

F. Dornseiff, *Das Alphabet in Mystik und Magie*, 2nd ed., Leipzig, 1925

H.J.W. Drijvers, "The Origins of Gnosticism as a Religious and Historical Problem", *NTT*, 22, 1967/68, pp. 321 ff. (= *GG*, pp. 798 ff.)

Idem, "Die Oden Salomos und die Polemik mit den Markioniten im syrischen Christentum", *OrChrA*, 205 (Symposium Syriacum 1976), 1978, pp. 39 ff.

G.R. Driver, *The Judaean Scrolls*, Oxford, 1965

E.S. Drower, *The Secret Adam*, Oxford, 1960

J. Duchesne-Guillemin, *Ormazd et Ahriman* (MR, 31), Paris, 1953

Idem, "Ahriman et le dieu suprême dans les mystères de Mithra", *Numen*, 2, 1955, pp. 190 ff.

A. Dupont-Sommer, "Adam. 'Père du Monde' dans la Sagesse de Solomon (10, 1.2)", *RHR*, 119, 1939, pp. 182 ff.

R. Eisler, *Weltenmantel und Himmelszelt*, I, Munich, 1910

Chr. Elsas, "Das Judentum als philosophische Religion bei Philo von Alexandria", in *AT-F-G*, pp. 195 ff.

I.H. Eybers, "Relations between Jews and Samaritans in the Persian Period", in *Biblical Essays 1966* (Proceedings of the Ninth Meeting of the Oud-Testamentiese Werkgemeenskap in Suid-Afrika), Potchefstroom, 1967, pp. 72 ff.

F.T. Fallon, *The Enthronement of Sabaoth* (NHS, X), Leiden, 1978

D. Feuchtwang, "Das Wasseropfer und die damit verbundenen Zeremonien", in *MGWJ*, 54-55, 1910/11

F. Feuillet, "Le fils de l'homme de Daniel et la tradition biblique", *RB*, 60, 1953, pp. 170 ff., 321 ff.

G. Ficker, *Die Petrusakten*, Leipzig, 1903

G. Fitzer, Art. σφραγίς κτλ., in *TDNT*, VII, 1971, reprinted 1975, pp. 939 ff.

J.A. Fitzmyer, "Further Light on Melchizedek from Qumran Cave 11", *JBL*, 86, 1967, pp. 25 ff. (= *Essays on the Semitic Background of the New Testament*, London, 1971, pp. 152 ff.)

Idem, "The Contribution of Qumran Aramaic to the Study of the New Testament", *NTS*, 20, 1973/74, pp. 391 ff.

G. Flügel, *Mani*, Leipzig, 1862, reprinted Osnabrück, 1969

W. Foerster, "Die "ersten Gnostiker" Simon und Menander", in *OG*, pp. 190 ff.

G. Fohrer, "Die israelitischen Propheten in der samaritanischen Chronik II", in M. Black & G. Fohrer, ed., *In Memoriam Paul Kahle* (BZAW, 103), Berlin, 1968, pp. 129 ff.

Idem, par. B, "The Old Testament", in Art. υἱός κτλ., in *TDNT*, VIII, 1972 and reprints, pp. 340 ff.

J. Massingberd Ford, "Can We exclude Samaritan Influence from Qumran?", *RQ*, 6, 1967, pp. 109 ff.

Idem, Revelation (AB, 38), New York, 1975

J. Fossum, "Samaritan Demiurgical Traditions and the Alleged Dove Cult of the Samaritans", in *Studies*, pp. 143 ff.

Idem, "Jewish-Christian Christology and Jewish Mysticism", *VigChr*, 37, 1983, pp. 260 ff.

Idem, "Gen. 1, 26 and 2, 7 in Judaism, Samaritanism, and Gnosticism", *JSJ*, forthcoming issue

Idem, "Reminisenser av det "konglige mønstret" i samaritanismen", preliminary and unpublished paper

Idem & G. Quispel, Art. "Helena", in *RAC*, forthcoming volume

Z. Frankel, *Über die palästinensische und alexandrinische Schriftforschung* (PBS), Breslau, 1854

E.D. Freed, "Samaritan Influence in the Gospel of John", *CBQ*, 30, 1968, pp. 580 ff.

S. Freud, *Totem and Taboo*, trans. by J. Strachey, Routledge paperback edition, London, 1960 and reprints

M. Friedländer, "La secte de Melchisédeq et l'épître aux Hebreux", *REJ*, 5, 1882, pp. 1 ff., 188 ff.; 6, 1883, pp. 187 ff.

Idem, Der vorchristliche jüdische Gnosticismus, Göttingen, 1898

O.F. Fritzsche, *Kurzgefasstes exegetisches Handbuch zu den Apokryphen des Alten Testaments*, I, Leipzig, 1851

R.H. Fuller, *Foundations of New Testament Christology* (LL), London, 1965

J. Fürst, *Geschichte des Karäerthums* (SIFIL), Leipzig, 1862

H.-G. Gaffron, *Studien zum koptischen Philippusevangelium unter besonderer Berücksichtigung der Sakramente*, Diss., Bonn, 1969

B. Gärtner, *Die rätselhaften Termini Nasoräer und Iskariot* (HS, IV), Uppsala, 1957

Idem, The Theology of the Gospel of Thomas, trans. by E. Sharpe, London, 1961

M. Gaster, *The Samaritans* (SL, 1923), London, 1925

Idem, "Popular Judaism at the Time of the Second Temple in the Light of Samaritan Traditions", in his *Studies and Texts*, II, London, 1927, pp. 725 ff.

Idem, "Das Schiur Komah", *ibid.*, pp. 1330 ff.

Idem, Samaritan Oral Law and Ancient Traditions, I (Eschatology), New York, 1932

A. Geiger, *Urschrift und Übersetzungen der Bibel*, Breslau, 1857

Idem, "Zur Theologie und Schrifterklärung der Samaritaner", *ZDMG*, 12, 1858, pp. 132 ff. (= *Nachgelassene Schriften*, ed. by L. Geiger, III, Breslau, 1876, pp. 255 ff.)

D. Gershenson & G. Quispel, "Meristae", *VigChr*, 12, 1958, pp. 19 ff.

W. Gesenius, *De Samaritanorum theologia ex fontibus ineditis commentatio*, Halle, 1823

L. Ginzberg, Art. "Adam Kadmon", in *JE*, I, 1901 and reprints, pp. 181 ff.

Idem, The Legends of the Jews, V (Notes to Volumes I and II: From the Creation to the Exodus), Philadelphia, 1925 and reprints; VI (Notes to Volumes III and IV: From Moses in the Wilderness to Esther), Philadelphia, 1928 and reprints

T.F. Glasson, *Moses in the Fourth Gospel* (SBT, 40), London, 1963

A.M. Goldberg, "Sitzend zur Rechten der Kraft", *BZ*, 8, 1964, pp. 284 ff.

Idem, Untersuchungen über die Vorstellung von der Schekhinah in der frühen rabbinischen Literatur (SJ, V), Leiden, 1969

A.H. Goldfahn, "Justinus Martyr und die Agada", in *MGWJ*, 22, 1873 (= *Justinus Martyr und die Agada*, Breslau, 1873)

J. Goldin, "Not by Means of an Angel and not by Means of a Messenger", in *RA*, pp. 412 ff.

E.R. Goodenough, *The Theology of Justin Martyr*, Jena, 1923

Idem, Jewish Symbols in the Greco-Roman Period (BS, XXXVII), II (The Archeological Evidence from the Diaspora), Princeton, 1953

R.L. Gordon, "Franz Cumont and the Doctrines of Mithraism", in *MS*, pp. 221 ff.

H. Graetz, *Gnosticismus und Judenthum*, Krotoschin, 1846

Idem, Das Königreich Mesene und seine jüdische Bevölkerung (JSF), Breslau, 1897

R.M. Grant, *Gnosticism and Early Christianity*, New York, 1959

H. Gressmann, *Der Ursprung der israelitisch-jüdischen Eschatologie* (FRLANT, 6), Göttingen, 1906

O. Grether, *Name und Wort Gottes im Alten Testament* (BZAW, 64), Giessen, 1934

J. Grimm, *Die Samariter und ihre Stellung in der Weltgeschichte*, Munich, 1854

G. van Groningen, *First Century Gnosticism*, Leiden, 1967

I. Gruenwald, *Apocalyptic and Merkavah Mysticism* (AGJU, XIV), Leiden, 1980

Idem, "Jewish Merkavah Mysticism and Gnosticism", in J. Dan & F. Talmage, ed., *Studies in Jewish Mysticism* (Proceedings of the Regional Conferences held at the University of California, Los Angeles, and McGill University in April, 1978), Cambridge, Mass., 1982, pp. 41 ff.

W. Grundmann, *Der Begriff der Kraft in der neutestamentlichen Gedankenwelt* (BWANT, 4/8), Stuttgart, 1932

Idem, Art. δύναμαι/δύναμις, in *TDNT*, II, 1964 and reprints, pp. 284 ff.

Idem, Art. μέγας κτλ., in *TDNT*, IV, 1967, reprinted 1975, pp. 529 ff.

Idem, Das Evangelium nach Markus (THNT), 2nd ed., Berlin, 1977

K. Haacker, *Die Stiftung des Heils* (AT, 1), Stuttgart, 1972

R. Haardt, "Schöpfer und Schöpfung in der Gnosis", in *AT-F-G*, pp. 37 ff.

L. Haefeli, *Geschichte der Landschaft Samaria von 722 vor Chr. bis 67 nach Chr.* (ATA, VIII/1-2), Münster, 1922

E. Haenchen, "Gab es eine vorchristliche Gnosis?", *ZTK*, 49, 1952, pp. 316 ff. (= *Gott und Mensch*, Tübingen, 1965, pp. 265 ff.)

Idem, "Aufbau und Theologie des "Poimandres" ", *ZTK*, 53, 1956, pp. 149 ff. (= *Gott und Mensch*, pp. 335 ff.)

Idem, Die Apostelgeschichte (MKKNT, 3), 6th ed., Göttingen, 1968

Idem, "Simon Magus in der Apostelgeschichte", in *GNT*, pp. 267 ff.

A.S. Halkin, "Samaritan Polemics against the Jews", *PAAJR*, 7, 1935/36, pp. 13 ff.

H. Halm, *Kosmologie und Heilslehre der frühen Ismāʿīlīya* (AKM, XLIV/1), Wiesbaden, 1978

A. von Harnack, *Lehrbuch der Dogmengeschichte*, I (Die Entstehung des kirchlichen Dogmas) (STL, I), Freiburg, 1886; 4th ed., Tübingen, 1909

Idem, Die Mission und Ausbreitung des Christentums in den ersten drei Jahrhunderten, II, 4th ed., Leipzig, 1924

W.-D. Hauschild, *Gottes Geist und der Mensch* (AET, 38), Munich, 1972

C.T.R. Hayward, "The Holy Name of the God of Moses and the Prologue of St. John's Gospel", *NTS*, 25, 1978, pp. 16 ff.

R. Heinze, *Xenokrates*, Leipzig, 1892, reprinted Hildesheim, 1965

M. Hengel, *Judentum und Hellenismus* (WUNT, 10), Tübingen, 1969

Idem, The Son of God, trans. by J. Bowden, Philadelphia, 1976

A. Henrichs & L. Koenen, "Ein griechischer Mani-Codex", *ZPE*, 5, 1970, pp. 97 ff., with additions in 8, 1971, pp. 243 ff.

A. Hilgenfeld, *Das Urchristentum in den Hauptwendepuncten seines Entwickelungsganges*, Jena, 1855

Idem, Die Ketzergeschichte des Urchristentums, Leipzig, 1884

Idem, "Der Gnostizismus", *ZWT*, 33, 1890, pp. 1 ff. (= *GG*, pp. 174 ff.)

G. Hölscher, *Palästina in der persischen und hellenistischen Zeit* (QFAGG, V), Berlin, 1903

A. Hönig, *Die Ophiten*, Berlin, 1889

P.W. van der Horst, "Moses' Throne Vision in Ezekiel the Dramatist", *JJS*, 34, 1983, pp. 21 ff.

F. Horton, Jr., *The Melchizedek Tradition* (SNTS, Monograph Series, 30), Cambridge, 1976

J.H. Hottinger, *De translationibus Bibliorum in varias linguas vernaculas* (Dissertationum theologico-philologicarum fasciculus III), Zürich, 1660

V. Howard, *Das Ego Jesu in den synoptischen Evangelien* (MTS, 14), Marburg, 1975

S.J. Isser, *The Dositheans* (SJLA, XVII), Leiden, 1976

E. Jacob, *The Theology of the Old Testament*, trans. by A.W. Heathcote & Ph.J. Allcock, London, 1958, reprinted 1974

E.O. James, *Christian Myth and Ritual*, London, 1933

H. Ludin Jansen, "The Consecration in the Eighth Chapter of Testamentum Levi", in *La regalità sacra* (SHR: Suppl. *Numen*, IV), Leiden, 1959, pp. 356 ff.

Idem, "Die Frage nach Tendenz und Verfasserschaft im Poimandres", in G. Widengren & D. Hellholm, ed., *Proceedings of the International Colloquium on Gnosticism, Stockholm, August 20-25, 1973* (KVHAH, Filol.-filos. ser., 17), Stockholm, 1977, pp. 157 ff.

J. Jeremias, *Golgotha* (ΑΓΓΕΛΟΣ, Beiheft I), Leipzig, 1926

Idem, Jesu Verheissung für die Völker (FDV, 1953), 2nd ed., Stuttgart, 1959

Idem, Art. Ἠλ(ε)ίας, in *TDNT*, II, 1964 and reprints, pp. 928 ff.

Idem, Art. Μωυσῆς, in *TDNT*, IV, 1967, reprinted 1975, pp. 848 ff.

Idem, "Zum Logosproblem", *ZNW*, 59, 1968, pp. 82 ff.

Idem, Art. Σαμάρεια κτλ., in *TDNT*, VII, 1971, reprinted 1975, pp. 88 ff.

J. Jervell, *Imago Dei* (FRLANT, 76), Göttingen, 1960

M. Joël, *Blicke in die Religionsgeschichte zu Anfang des zweiten christlichen Jahrhunderts*, I, Breslau, 1880

H. Jonas, *Gnosis und spätantiker Geist*, I (Die mythologische Gnosis) (FRLANT, 51), 3rd ed. with *Ergänzungsheft*, Göttingen, 1964

Idem, The Gnostic Religion, 2nd ed., Boston, 1963, reprinted 1967

Idem, "Response to G. Quispel's "Gnosticism and the New Testament" ", in J.P. Hyatt, ed., *The Bible in Modern Scholarship* (Papers read at the 100th Meeting of the Society of Biblical Literature, December 28-30, 1964), Nashville & New York, 1965, pp. 287 ff.

Idem, "Delimitation of the Gnostic Phenomenon – Typological and Historical", in *OG*, pp. 90 ff. (= *GG*, pp. 626 ff.)

M. de Jonge, *The Testaments of the Twelve Patriarchs*, Assen, 1953

Idem & A.S. van der Woude, "11 Q Melchizedek and the New Testament", *NTS*, 12, 1965/66, pp. 301 ff.

P. Kahle, review of A. Merx, *Der Messias oder Taʾeb der Samaritaner* (BZAW, 17), Giessen, 1909, in *TLZ*, 36, 1911, cols. 198 ff.

Idem, "Zu den Handschriftrollen in Höhlen beim Toten Meer", *Das Altertum*, 3, 1957, pp. 37 ff.

O. Kaiser, *Die mytische Bedeutung des Meeres* (BZAW, 78), 2nd ed., Berlin, 1962

Ch. Kaplan, "The Hidden Name", *JSOR*, 13, 1929, pp. 180 ff.

J. Keil & A. von Premerstein, *Bericht über eine zweite Reise in Lydien* (DKAW, phil.-hist. Kl., 54), Vienna, 1911

K. Kessler, *Mani*, I (Voruntersuchungen und Quellen), Berlin, 1889

S. Kim, *The Origin of Paul's Gospel* (WUNT, 2. Reihe, 4), Tübingen, 1981

H.G. Kippenberg, "Ein Gebetbuch für den samaritanischen Synagogengottesdienst aus dem 2. Jh. n. Chr.", *ZDPV*, 85, 1969, pp. 76 ff.

Idem, Garizim und Synagoge (RGVV, XXX), Berlin & New York, 1971

G. Kittel, par. E, " כבוד and יקרא in Palestinian Judaism", in Art. δόξα, in *TDNT*, II, 1964 and reprints, pp. 245 ff.

Idem, par. E, "The Divine Likeness in Judaism", in Art. εἰκών, *ibid.*, pp. 392 ff.

G. Klein, *Der älteste christliche Katechismus*, Berlin, 1909

A. Klostermann, *Probleme im Aposteltexte*, Gotha, 1883

M.A. Knibb, "The Date of the Parables of Enoch", *NTS*, 25, 1979, pp. 343 ff.

K. Kohler, "Dositheus, the Samaritan Heresiarch, and His Relations to Jewish and Christian Doctrines and Sects", *AJT*, 15, 1911, pp. 404 ff.

M. Kopp, *Palaeographia critica*, IV, Mannheim, 1829

S. Krauss, "Dosithée et les Dosithéens", *REJ*, 42, 1901, pp. 27 ff.

G. Kretschmar, "Zur religionsgeschichtlichen Einordnung der Gnosis", *ET*, 13, 1953, pp. 354 ff. (= *GG*, pp. 426 ff.)

W. Brede Kristensen, *The Meaning of Religion*, trans. by J.B. Carman, The Hague, 1960 and reprints

K. Kuiper, "Le poète juif Ezéchiel", *REJ*, 46, 1903, pp. 174 ff.

K.G. Kuhn, "New Light on Temptation, Sin and Flesh in the New Testament", in K. Stendahl, ed., *The Scrolls and the New Testament*, New York, 1957, pp. 94 ff.

K. Lake & H.J. Cadbury, *The Acts of the Apostles* (BC, I), IV (English Translation and Commentary), London, 1933

G.W.H. Lampe, *The Seal of the Spirit*, London, 1951

W. Lane, *The Gospel according to Mark* (NIC), Grand Rapids, 1974

B. Lang, *Frau Weisheit*, Düsseldorf, 1975

H. Langkammer, "Christus mediator creationis", *VD*, 45, 1967, pp. 201 ff.

P.W. Lapp, "The Second and Third Campaign at ʿArâq el-ʾEmîr", *BASOR*, 171, 1963, pp. 8 ff.

F. du Toit Laubscher, "God's Angel of Truth and Melchizedek. A Note on 11 Q Melch 13b", *JSJ*, 3, 1972, pp. 46 ff.

J. Legge, "The Lion-Headed God of the Mithraic Mysteries", *PSBA*, 34, 1912, pp. 125 ff.

H. Leisegang, *Pneuma Hagion* (VFVRUL, 4), Leipzig, 1922

Idem, Die Gnosis, 2nd ed., Leipzig, 1936, reprinted 1941 and, as Kröner Taschenbuch, Stuttgart, 1955

J. Levy, *Chaldäisches Wörterbuch über die Targumin und einen grossen Teil des rabbinischen Schrifttums*, II, 3 rd ed., Leipzig, 1881, reprinted Köln, 1959

M. Lidzbarski, "Warum schrieb Mani aramäisch?", *OLZ*, 30, 1927, cols. 913 ff.

S. Liebermann, *Hellenism in Jewish Palestine*, New York, 1962

Idem, "Metatron, the Meaning of His Name and His Functions", Appendix to Gruenwald, *Mysticism*, pp. 234 ff.

H. Lietzmann, Art. "Simon Magus", in *PW*, 2nd Series (R-Z), III, 1927, cols. 180 ff.

K. Lincke, *Samaria und seine Propheten*, Tübingen, 1903

R.A. Lipsius, Art. "Gnostizismus", in *AEWK*, I/71, pp. 223 ff. (Reprint of pp. 223-249, 269 f., and 286-296 in *GG*, pp. 17 ff.)

Idem, Die Quellen der römischen Petrussage, Kiel, 1872

E. Lohmeyer, *Das Urchristentum*, I (Johannes der Täufer), Göttingen, 1932

Idem, Galiläa und Jerusalem (FRLANT, 52), Göttingen, 1936

Idem, Kyrios Jesus (SHAW, phil.-hist. Kl., IV, 1927/28), 3rd ed., Heidelberg, 1961

E. Lohse, *Die Briefe an die Kolosser und Philemon* (MKKNT, 9/2), Göttingen, 1968

S. Lowy, *The Principles of Samaritan Bible Exegesis* (SP-B, XXVIII), Leiden, 1977

G. Lüdemann, *Untersuchungen zur simonianischen Gnosis* (GTA, 1), Göttingen, 1975

M. Lueken, *Michael*, Göttingen, 1898

P. Lundberg, *La typologie baptismale dans l'ancienne église* (ASNU, X), Uppsala, 1942

J. Macdonald, "The Tetragrammaton in Samaritan Liturgical Compositions", *TGUOS*, 17, 1959, pp. 37 ff.

Idem, The Theology of the Samaritans (NTL), London, 1964

Idem, par. "Dating", in Art. "Pentateuch, Samaritan", in *EJ*, 13, col. 267

Idem, par. "History, Until 1300", in Art. "Samaritans", in *EJ*, 14, cols. 728 ff.

M. McNamara, *The New Testament and the Palestinian Targum to the Pentateuch* (AB, 27), Rome, 1966

G.W. MacRae, 'Nag Hammadi and the New Testament", in *Gnosis*, pp. 153 ff.

J. Maier, "Jüdische Faktoren bei der Entstehung der Gnosis?", in *AT-F-G*, pp. 239 ff.

T.W. Manson, "Miscellanea Apocalyptica III", *JTS*, 48, 1947, pp. 59 ff.

W. Manson, "The ΕΓΩ ΕΙΜΙ of the Messianic Presence in the New Testament", *JTS*, 48, 1947, pp. 137 ff.

M. Mansoor, Art. "Sects", in *EJ*, 14, cols. 1087 ff.

R. Marcus, "Alexander the Great and the Jews", Appendix C in Marcus, ed. & trans., *Josephus* (LCL), VI, London & Cambridge, Mass., 1951, pp. 523 ff.

A. Marmorstein, *The Old Rabbinic Doctrine of God*, I (The Names and Attributes of God), London, 1927. (Also in *The Doctrine of Merits in Old Rabbinical Literature and the Old Rabbinic Doctrine of God* (with a prolegomenon by R.J. Zwi Werblowski), New York, 1968, retaining original pagination of the individual works.)

J. Marsh, *The Gospel of John* (PNTC), Harmondsworth, 1968 and reprints

R.P. Martin, *Carmen Christi* (SNT, Monograph Series, 4), Cambridge, 1967

Idem, Philippians (NCB), London, 1976

A.J. Matter, *Histoire critique du gnosticisme*, II, Paris, 1828

H.G. May, "The Ten Lost Tribes", *BA*, 6, 1943, pp. 55 ff.

G.H. McCurdy, "Platonic Orphism in the Testament of Abraham", *JBL*, 61, 1942, pp. 213 ff.

W. McKane, *Proverbs* (OTL), London, 1970

W.A. Meeks, *The Prophet-King* (Suppl. *NT*, XIV), Leiden, 1967

Idem, "Moses as God and King", in *RA*, pp. 354 ff.

J.-E. Ménard, "Les élucubrations de l'Evangelium Veritatis sur le "Nom" ", *SMR*, 6, 1963, pp. 185 ff.

Idem, "Les origines de la gnose", *RSR*, 43, 1968, pp. 24 ff.

A. Merx, *Die vier kanonischen Evangelien*, II/2 (Das Evangelium des Johannes), Berlin, 1911

E. Meyer, *Ursprung und Anfänge des Christentums*, II, Stuttgart & Berlin, 1921

R. Meyer, par. C, "Prophecy and Prophets in the Judaism of the Hellenistic-Roman Period", in Art. προφήτης κτλ., in *TDNT*, VI, 1968 and reprints, pp. 812 ff.

Idem, Art. Σαδδουκαῖος, in *TDNT*, VII, 1971, reprinted 1975, pp. 35 ff.

O. Michel, *Der Brief an die Hebräer* (MKKNT, 13), 2nd ed., Göttingen, 1949

Idem, "Zur Exegese von Phil.2.5-11", in his *Theologie als Glaubenswagnis*, Hamburg, 1954, pp. 77 ff.

J. Michl, Art. "Engel II (jüdisch)", *RAC*, 1962, cols. 60 ff.; Art. "Engel III (gnostisch)", *ibid*., cols. 97 ff.; Art. "Engel V (Engelnamen)", *ibid*., cols. 200 ff.; Art. "Engel VI (Gabriel)", *ibid*., cols. 239 ff.; Art. "Engel VII (Michael)", *ibid*., cols. 243 ff.

J.T. Milik, "Milkî-ṣedeq et Milkî-reša‘ dans les anciens écrits juifs et chrétiens", *JJS*, 23, 1972, pp. 95 ff.

Idem, "4 Q Visions de ‘Amram et une citation d'Origène", *RB*, 79, 1972, pp. 77 ff.

G. Molin, "Elijahu der Prophet und sein Weiterleben in den Hoffnungen des Judentums und der Christenheit", *Judaica*, 8, 1952, pp. 65 ff.

W. Möller, Art. "Simon Magus", *RE*, XIII, 1860, pp. 389 ff.

F.J. Moloney, *The Johannine Son of Man* (BSR, 14), Rome, 1976

J.A. Montgomery, *The Samaritans* (BL, 1906), Philadelphia, 1907, reprinted New York, 1968

G.F. Moore, "Intermediaries in Jewish Theology", *HTR*, 15, 1922, pp. 41 ff.

Idem, Judaism, I, Schocken paperback edition, New York, 1971

J.L. von Mosheim, *Geschichte der Schlangenbrüder* (Versuch einer unpartheiischen und gründlichen Ketzergeschichte, I), Helmstädt, 1746

S. Mowinckel, Art. "Hypostasen", *RGG*, II, 2nd ed., 1928, cols. 2065 ff.

B. Murmelstein, "Adam, ein Beitrag zur Messiaslehre", *WZKM*, 35, 1928, pp. 242 ff.; 36, 1929, pp. 51 ff.

R. Murray, *Symbols of Church and Kingdom*, Cambridge, 1975

B. Narkiss, *The Golden Haggadah*, London, 1970

J.A.W. Neander, *Genetische Entwickelung der vornehmsten gnostischen Systeme*, Berlin, 1818

W. Neil, *The Acts of the Apostles* (NCB), London, 1973

E. Nielsen, *Shechem*, Copenhagen, 1955

M. Noth, *Die israelitischen Personennamen im Rahmen der gemeinsemitischen Namengebung* (BWANT, III/10), Stuttgart, 1928

Idem, The History of Israel, 2nd ed., translation revised by P.R. Ackroyd, London, 1960 and reprints

H. Odeberg, *The Fourth Gospel*, Uppsala, 1929, reprinted Amsterdam, 1968

E. Pagels, "The Demiurge and His Angels – a Gnostic View of the Bishop and Presbyters?", *HTR*, 69, 1976, pp. 301 ff.

A. Parrot, *Samaria*, London, 1958

B.A. Pearson, "Friedländer Revisited. Alexandrian Judaism and Gnostic Origins", *SPh*, 2, 1973, pp. 23 ff.

Idem, "Jewish Elements in *Corpus Hermeticum* I (*Poimandres*)", in *Studies*, pp. 336 ff.

R. Pesch, *Das Markusevangelium* (HTKNT, II), II, Freiburg – Basel – Vienna, 1977

J.H. Petermann, *Reisen im Orient*, I, 2nd ed., Leipzig, 1865

E. Peterson, ΕΙΣ ΘΕΟΣ (FRLANT, 41), Göttingen, 1926

Idem, "Engel- und Dämonennamen. Nomina Barbara", *RM*, 57, 1926, pp. 393 ff.

Idem, "Didachè cap. 9 et 10", *EL*, 58, 1944, pp. 3 ff.

Idem, Art. "Gnosi", in *EC*, VI, 1951, cols. 876 ff.

Idem, "Die Befreiung Adams aus der ’Ανάγκη", in his *Frühkirche, Judentum und Gnosis*, Rome – Freiburg – Vienna, 1959, pp. 107 ff.

S. Pétrement, "Le mythe des sept archontes créateurs peut-il s'expliquer à partir du christianisme?", in *OG*, pp. 460 ff.

J. Piaget, *The Child's Conception of the World*, trans. by J. & A. Tomlinson, New York, 1929, reprinted London, 1971

S. Pines, *The Jewish Christians of the Early Centuries according to a New Source* (PIASH, II/13), Jerusalem, 1966

D. Plooij, *Studies in the Testimony-Book* (VKAWA, Afdeeling Letterkunde, XXXII/2), Amsterdam, 1932

P. Pokorný, "Der Ursprung der Gnosis", *Kairos*, 9, 1967, pp. 94 ff. (= *GG*, pp. 749 ff.)

Idem, "Gnosis als Weltreligion und Häresie", *Numen*, 16, 1969, pp. 51 ff.

J. Ponthot, *Le "Nom" dans la théologie des Pères Apostoliques*, Diss., Louvain, 1950

R. Posner, par. "Halakhic Definitions", in Art. "Jew", in *EJ*, 10, cols. 23 ff.

S. Poznanski, "Geschichte der Sekten und der Halacha", in L. Geiger, ed., *Abraham Geiger*, Berlin, 1910, pp. 352 ff.

P. Prigent, *Apocalypse 12* (BGBE, 2), Tübingen, 1959

O. Procksch, "Die Berufungsvision Hesekiels", in *Karl Budde zum siebzigsten Geburtstag* (BZAW, 34), Giessen, 1920, pp. 141 ff.

H.-Ch. Puech, *Le manichéisme* (MG, Bibliothèque de diffusion, LVI), Paris 1949

Idem, "Une collection de paroles de Jésus récemment retrouvée", *CRAI*, 1957, pp. 146 ff.

J.D. Purvis, *The Samaritan Pentateuch and the Origin of the Samaritan Sect* (HSM, 2), Cambridge, Mass., 1968

Idem, "Samaritan Traditions on the Death of Moses", in G.W.E. Nickelsburg, Jr., ed., *Studies on the Testament of Moses* (SBL: SCS, 4), Cambridge, Mass., 1973, pp. 93 ff.

G. Quispel, *Gnosis als Weltreligion*, Zürich, 1951

Idem, "Mandaeërs en Valentinianen", *NTT*, 8, 1953/54, pp. 144 ff.

Idem, "Der gnostische Anthropos und die jüdische Tradition", *E-J*, XXII (1953), 1954, pp. 195 ff. (= *Gnostic Studies*, I, pp. 173 ff.*)

Idem, "Christliche Gnosis und jüdische Heterodoxie", *ET*, 14, 1954, pp. 474ff.

Idem, "De Joodse achtergrond van de Logos-Christologie", *VoxTheol*, 25, 1954, pp. 48ff.

Idem, "The Jung Codex and its Significance", in H.-Ch. Puech, G. Quispel and W.C. van Unnik, *The Jung Codex*, trans. by F. Cross, London, 1955, pp. 35 ff. (= *Gnostic Studies*, I, pp. 3 ff.).

Idem, "Het Johannesevangelie en de Gnosis", *NTT*, 11, 1956/57, pp. 173 ff.

Idem, "L'Évangile de Jean et la Gnose", in F.M. Braun, ed., *L'Évangile de Jean* (RB, III), Bruges, 1958, pp. 197 ff.

Idem, "Gnosticism and the New Testament", in J. Ph. Hyatt, ed., *The Bible in Modern Scholarship* (Papers read at the 100th Meeting of the Society for Biblical Literature, December 28-30, 1964), Nashville & New York, 1965, pp. 252 ff. (= *VigChr*, 19, 1965, pp. 65 ff., and *Gnostic Studies*, I, pp. 196 ff.).

Idem, review of Grant, *Gnosticism and Early Christianity*, 2nd ed., London, 1966, in *BO*, 26, 1969, p. 276, col. b f.

Idem, "The Origins of the Gnostic Demiurge", in P. Granfield & J.A. Jungmann, ed., *KYRIAKON* (Festschrift Johannes Quaesten), Münster i. Westf., 1970, pp. 271 ff. (= *Gnostic Studies*, I, pp. 213 ff.).

Idem, "John, Qumran and Jewish Christianity", in J.H. Charlesworth, ed., *John and Qumran*, London, 1972, pp. 137 ff. (= "John and Jewish Christianity", in *Gnostic Studies*, II, pp. 210 ff.).

Idem, "Gnosis und hellenistische Mysterienreligionen", in U. Mann, ed., *Theologie und Religionswissenschaft*, Darmstadt, 1973, pp. 318 ff. (= "Gnosis und Religionswissenschaft", in *Gnostic Studies*, II, pp. 259 ff.).

Idem, "From Mythos to Logos", *E-J*, XXXIX (1970), 1973, pp. 323 ff. (= *Gnostic Studies*, I, pp. 158 ff.).

Idem, "Jewish Gnosis and Mandaean Gnosticism", in J.-É. Menard, ed., *Les textes de Nag Hammadi* (Colloque du Centre d'Historie des Religions, Strassbourg 23-25 octobre 1974) (NHS, VII), Leiden, 1975, pp. 82 ff.

Idem, review of Beyschlag, in *BO*, 32, 1975, p. 420, col. b ff.

Idem, review of *GG*, in *VigChr*, 29, 1975, pp. 235 ff.

---

* The references in the notes do not cite Professor Quispel's *Gnostic Studies*, I (UNH-AII, XXXIV/1) – II (UNH-AII, XXXIV/2), Istanbul, 1974/75.

Idem, "The Demiurge in the Apocryphon of John", in R. McL. Wilson, ed., *Nag Hammadi and Gnosis* (Papers read at the First International Congress of Coptology (Cairo, December 1976), (NHS, XIV), Leiden, 1978, pp. 1 ff.

Idem, "Hermann Hesse and Gnosis", in *Gnosis*, pp. 492 ff.

Idem, "Ezekiel 1:26 in Jewish Mysticism and Gnosis", *VigChr*, 34, 1980, pp. 1 ff.

Idem, review of Halm, in *IJMES*, 12, 1980, pp. 111 f.

Idem, "The Gospel of Thomas Revisited", in B. Barc, ed., *Colloque international sur les textes de Nag Hammadi* (Québec, 22-25 août 1978) (BCNH, Section "Études", 1), Québec & Louvain, 1981, pp. 218 ff.

Idem, "Gnosis", in M.J. Vermaseren, ed., *Die orientalischen Religionen im Römerreich* (EPRO, 93), 1981, pp. 413 ff.

Idem, "Hermetism and the New Testament, especially Paul", in W. Haase, ed., *ANRW*, II.22 (Religion: Gnostizismus und Verwandtes), forthcoming

G. von Rad, par. B, " מלאך in the OT", in Art. ἄγγελος, in *TDNT*, I, 1964 and reprints, pp. 76 ff.

Idem, Old Testament Theology, I, London, 1975

W.M. Ramsay, *The Bearing of Recent Discovery on the Trustworthiness of the New Testament*, London, 1914

B. Rehm, "Zur Entstehung der pseudoclementinischen Schriften", *ZNW*, 37, 1938, pp. 77 ff.

B. Reicke, *The New Testament Era*, London, 1969

R. Reitzenstein, *Poimandres*, Leipzig, 1904

Idem, Hellenistische Wundererzählungen, Leipzig, 1906, reprinted Darmstadt, 1963

H. Reland, *De Samaritanis*, Dissertatio VII in *Dissertationes miscellaneae*, Utrecht, 1706

K.H. Rengstorf, Art. ἀποστέλλω, in *TDNT*, I, 1964 and reprints, pp. 398 ff.

G. Richter, "Bist du Elias? (Joh. 1,21)", *BZ*, 6, 1962, pp. 79 ff., 238 ff.; 7, 1963, pp. 63 ff.

H. Ringgren, Art. "Hypostasen", *RGG*, III, 3rd ed., 1959, cols. 504 ff.

A. Ritschl, *Die Entstehung der altkatholischen Kirche*, 2nd ed., Bonn, 1857

B. Rosenfeld, *Die Golemsage*, Breslau, 1934

H.H. Rowley, "Sanballat and the Samaritan Temple", *BJRL*, 38, 1955, pp. 166 ff. (= *Men of God: Studies in Old Testament History and Prophecy*, London, 1963, pp. 246 ff.)

Idem, "The Samaritan Schism in Legend and History", in B.W. Anderson & W. Harrelson, ed., *Israel's Prophetic Heritage: Essays in Honor of James Muilenberg* (PL), New York, 1962, pp. 208 ff.

K. Rudolph, *Die Mandäer*, I (Prolegomena: Das Mandäerproblem) (FRLANT, 74) – II (Die Kult) (FRLANT, 75), Göttingen, 1960/61

Idem, "War der Verfasser der Oden Salomos ein Qumran-Christ? Ein Beitrag zur Diskussion um die Anfänge der Gnosis", *RQ*, 4, 1964, pp. 523 ff.

Idem, Theogonie, Kosmogonie und Anthropogonie in den mandäischen Schriften (FRLANT, 88), Göttingen, 1965

Idem, "Randerscheinungen des Judentums und das Problem der Entstehung des Gnostizismus", *Kairos*, 9, 1967, pp. 105 ff. (= *GG*, pp. 768 ff.)

Idem, "Gnosis und Gnostizismus, ein Forschungsbericht", *TR*, 37, 1972, pp. 289 ff.

Idem, "Die Bedeutung des Kölner Mani-Codex für die Manichäismusforschung", in *MP*, pp. 471 ff.

Idem, Die Gnosis, Göttingen, 1978

Idem, "Simon – Magus oder Gnosticus?", *TR*, 42, 1978, pp. 279 ff.

Idem, "Sophia und Gnosis", in *AT-F-G*, pp. 221 ff.

S. de Sacy, "Correspondance des Samaritains de Naplouse pendant les années 1808 et suivant", *NEMBR*, XII/1, 1829, pp. 1 ff.

H. Sahlin, *Der Messias und das Gottesvolk* (ASNU, 12), Uppsala, 1945

J.M.A. Salles-Dabadie, *Recherches sur Simon le Mage*, I (L'"Apophasis megale") (CRB, 10), Paris, 1969

J.B. Schaller, *Gen. 1.2 im antiken Judentum*, Diss., Göttingen, 1961

H.-M. Schenke, *Der Gott "Mensch" in der Gnosis*, Göttingen, 1962

Idem, "Jakobsbrunnen – Josephusgrab – Sychar", *ZDPV*, 1968, pp. 159 ff.

O. Schmitz, "Der Begriff δύναμις bei Paulus", in *Festgabe für A. Deissmann zum 60. Geburtstag*, Tübingen, 1927, pp. 139 ff.

R. Schnackenburg, *Das Johannesevangelium* (HTKNT, IV), II, Freiburg – Basel – Vienna, 1971

H.-J. Schoeps, *Theologie und Geschichte des Judenchristentums*, Tübingen, 1949.

Idem, "Zur Standortbestimmung der Gnosis", *TLZ*, 81, 1956, cols. 413 ff. (= *Urgemeinde-Judenchristentum-Gnosis*, Tübingen, 1956, pp. 30 ff., and *GG*, pp. 463 ff.)

G. Scholem, *Major Trends in Jewish Mysticism*, 3rd ed., New York, 1954, Schocken paperback edition, New York, 1961 and reprints

Idem, Jewish Gnosticism, Merkabah Mysticism, and Talmudic Tradition (JTSA), New York, 1960

Idem, Von der mystischen Gestalt der Gottheit, Zürich, 1962

Idem, Ursprung und Anfänge der Kabbalah (SJ, III), Berlin, 1962

Idem, On the Kabbalah and Its Symbolism, trans. by R. Manheim, New York, 1965, Schocken paperback edition, New York, 1969 and reprints

Idem, Sabbatai Sevi, trans. by R.J. Zwi Werblowski (BS, XCIII), Princeton, 1973

Idem, "Jaldabaoth Reconsidered", in *MP*, pp. 405 ff.

Idem, Kabbalah (LJK), Jerusalem, 1974

U. Schubert, "Die Erschaffung Adams in einer spanischen Haggadah-Handschrift des 14. Jahrhunderts (BR.MUS.OR. 2884) und ihre spätantike jüdische Bildvorlage", *Kairos*, 18, 1977, pp. 213 ff.

E. Schweizer, *Der Brief an die Kolosser* (EKK), Zürich, 1976

W. Scott, *Hermetica*, II (Notes on the Corpus Hermeticum), Oxford, 1925, reprinted London, 1968

A.F. Segal, *Two Powers in Heaven* (SJLA, XXV), Leiden, 1977

Idem, "Ruler of this World", in E.P. Sanders, ed., *Jewish and Christian Self-Definition*, II (Aspects of Judaism in the Greco-Roman Period), London, 1981, pp. 245 ff.

O.R. Sellers, "Coins of the 1960 Excavation at Shechem", *BA*, 25, 1962, pp. 87 ff.

E. Sjöberg, *Der Menschensohn im äthiopischen Henochbuch*, Lund, 1946

J.Z. Smith, "The Prayer of Joseph", in *RA*, pp. 253 ff.

M. Smith, "The Description of the Essenes in Josephus and the Philosophumena", *HUCA*, 29, 1958, pp. 273 ff.

Idem, "The Image of God", *BJRL*, 40, 1958, pp. 473 ff.

Idem, "The Account of Simon Magus in Acts 8", in *H.A. Wolfson Jubilee Volume*, II, Jerusalem, 1965, pp. 735 ff.

Idem, "The History of the Term Gnostikos", in B. Layton, ed., *The Rediscovery of Gnosticism* (Proceedings of the International Conference on Gnosticism at Yale, New Haven, Connecticut, March 28-31, 1978), II (Sethian Gnosticism) (SHR: Suppl. *Numen*, XLI), Leiden, 1981, pp. 208 ff.

N.H. Snaith, review of Macdonald, *Theology*, in *SJT*, 18, 1965, pp. 102 ff.

A. Spiro, "Samaritans, Tobiads, and the Judahites in Pseudo-Philo", *PAAJR*, 20, 1951, pp. 279 ff.

G. Staehlin, *Die Apostelgeschichte* (NTD, 5), 3rd ed., Göttingen, 1970

E. Stauffer, "Probleme der Priestertradition", *TLZ*, 81, 1956, cols. 135 ff.

Idem, Jesus, Gestalt und Geschichte, Bern, 1957

G. Strecker, *Das Judenchristentum in den Pseudoklementinen* (TU, 70), Berlin, 1958

Idem, Art. "Elkesai", in *RAC*, IV, 1959, cols. 1171 ff.

Idem, "Judenchristentum und Gnosis", in *AT-F-G*, pp. 261 ff.

C.H. Talbert, "Pre-Existence in Philippians 2:6-11", *JBL*, 86, 1967, pp. 141 ff.

Idem, "The Myth of a Descending-Ascending Redeemer in Mediterranean Antiquity", *NTS*, 22, 1976, pp. 418 ff.

V. Tcherikover, *Hellenistic Civilization and the Jews*, Philadelphia, 1961

J.L. Teicher, "Christian Interpretation of the Sign X in the Isaiah Scroll", *VT*, 5, 1955, pp. 189 ff.

H. Thyen, *Der Stil der jüdisch-hellenistischen Homilie* (FRLANT, 47), Göttingen, 1956

C.C. Torrey, *The Composition and Date of Acts* (HTS, I), Cambridge, Mass., 1916

J. Trachtenberg, *Jewish Magic and Superstition* (JPSA), New York, 1939, Atheneum paperback edition (TB, 15), New York, 1970

D.C. Trakatellis, *The Pre-Existence of Christ in Justin Martyr* (HTR: HDR, 6), Missoula, 1976

K.-W. Tröger, "Gnosis und Judentum", in *AT-F-G*, pp. 155 ff.

R.J.F. Trotter, *Did the Samaritans of the Fourth Century Know the Epistle to the Hebrews*? (LUOS, Monograph Series, 1), University of Leeds, 1961

Idem, Gnosticism and Memar Marqah (LUOS, Monograph Series, 4), University of Leeds, 1964

B. Tsedaka, par. "History, 1300-1970", in Art. "Samaritans", in *EJ*, 14, cols. 733ff.; par. "Statistics", *ibid*., cols. 736 ff.

C.H. Turner, "The Latin Acts of Peter", *JTS*, 32, 1931, pp. 119 ff.

W. Ullmann, "Die Gottesvorstellung der Gnosis als Herausforderung an Theologie und Verkündigung", in *GNT*, pp. 383 ff.

W.C. van Unnik, "Die jüdische Komponente in der Entstehung der Gnosis", *VigChr*, 15, 1961, pp. 65 ff. (= *GG*, pp. 476 ff.)

Idem, "Gnosis und Judentum", in *Gnosis*, pp. 65 ff.

E.E. Urbach, *The Sages*, I-II, trans. by I. Abrahams (PPF), Jerusalem, 1975

G. Vajda, "Melchisédech dans la mythologie ismaelienne", *JA*, 234, 1943-45, pp. 173 ff.

R. de Vaux, *Ancient Israel*, 1 (Social Institutions) – 2 (Religious Institutions) (paginated as one volume), translated from the French, London, 1961, McGraw-Hill paperback edition, New York, 1965

M.J. Vermaseren, "A Magical Time God", in *MS*, pp. 446 ff.

Ph. Vielhauer, "Das Benedictus des Zacharias", *ZTK*, 49, 1952, pp. 255 ff. (= *Aufsätze zum Neuen Testament* (TB, 31), Munich, 1965, pp. 28 ff.)

H. Waitz, "Simon Magus in der altchristlichen Literatur", *ZNW*, 5, 1904, pp. 121 ff.

Idem, "Die Quelle der Philippusgeschichten in der Apostelschichte", *ZNW*, 7, 1906, pp. 340 ff.

Idem, Art. "Simon der Magier", in *RE*, XVIII, 3rd ed., 1906, pp. 351 ff.

M. Weinfield, par. "The Tradition Underlying the Sources – Form Criticism", in Art. "Pentateuch", in *EJ*, 13, cols. 257 ff.

H.-F. Weiss, *Untersuchungen zur Kosmologie des hellenistischen und palästinensischen Judentums* (TU, 97), Berlin, 1966

Idem, "Das Gesetz in der Gnosis", in *A-F-G*, pp. 71 ff.

J. Weiss, *Das Urchristentum*, II, Göttingen, 1917

J. Wellhausen, *Kritische Analyse der Apostelgeschichte* (AKGWG, XV/2), Berlin, 1914

P. Wendland, *Die hellenistisch-römische Kultur* (HNT, II), 4th ed. by H. Dörrie, Tübingen, 1972

H.H. Wendt, *Die Apostelgeschichte* (MKKNT, 3), 4th ed., Göttingen, 1913

G. Widengren, "Den himmelska intronisationen och dopet", in *RoB*, V, 1946, pp. 28 ff.

Idem, "Till det sakrala kungadömets historia i Israel", in *Melangés Johs. Pedersen* (HS, I), 3, Uppsala, 1947, pp. 12 ff.

Idem, *The Ascension of the Apostle and the Heavenly Book* (King and Saviour III) (UUÅ, 1950:7), Uppsala & Leipzig, 1950

Idem, "Early Hebrew Myths and their Interpretation", in S.H. Hooke, ed., *Myth, Ritual and Kingship*, Oxford, 1958, pp. 149 ff.

Idem, Art. "Die Mandäer", in B. Spuler, ed., *HO* (Erste Abteilung: Der nahe und der mittlere Osten), VIII (Religion)/2 (Religionsgeschichte des Orients in der Zeit der Weltreligionen), 1961, pp. 83 ff.

Idem, "Royal Ideology and the Testaments of the Twelve Patriarchs", in F.F. Bruce, ed., *Promise and Fulfilment* (Essays Presented to Professor S.H. Hooke), Edinburgh, 1963, pp. 202 ff.

Idem, "Les origines du gnosticisme et l'histoire des religions", in *OG*, pp. 28 ff. (= *GG*, pp. 668 ff.)

Idem, "Israelite-Jewish Religion", in *HR*, I, pp. 223 ff.

Idem, *Religionsphänomenologie*, trans. by R. Elgnowski, Berlin, 1969

Idem, "Der Manichäismus", in *Gnosis*, pp. 278 ff.

N. Wieder, "The Doctrine of the Two Messiahs among the Karaites", *JJS*, 6, 1955, pp. 14 ff.

Idem, *The Judean Scrolls and Karaism*, London, 1962

S.L. Wikander, "Études sur les mystères de Mithras, I", in *VLÅ*, 1950, pp. 5 ff.

U. Wilckens, Art. στολή, in *TDNT*, VII, 1971, reprinted 1975, pp. 687 ff.

M. Wilcox, *The Semitisms of Acts*, Oxford, 1965

H.G.M. Williamson, *Israel in the Book of Chronicles*, Cambridge, 1977

R. McL. Wilson, "Gnostic Origins", *VigChr*, 9, 1955, pp. 199 ff.

Idem, "Simon, Dositheus and the Dead Sea Scrolls", *ZRGG*, 9, 1957, pp. 21 ff.

Idem, *Studies in the Gospel of Thomas*, London, 1960

Idem, *The Gnostic Problem*, 2nd ed., London, 1964

H. Windisch, "Die göttliche Weisheit der Juden und die paulinische Christologie", in *Neutestamentliche Studien für G. Heinrici* (UNT, 6), Leipzig, 1914, pp. 220 ff.

P. Winter, "The Main Literary Problem of the Lucan Infancy Story", *ATR*, 40, 1958, pp. 257 ff.

H.A. Wolfson, *Philo*, I, 2nd ed., Cambridge, Mass., 1948

Idem, *The Philosophy of the Church Fathers*, 3rd ed., London & Cambridge, Mass., 1976

A.S. van der Woude, "Melchizedek als himmlische Erlösergestalt in den neugefundenen eschatologischen Midraschim aus Qumran Höhle XI", in P.A.H. Boer, ed., *OS*, XIV, 1965, pp. 354 ff.

L. Wreschner, *Samaritanische Traditionen*, Halle, 1888

G.E. Wright, "The Samaritans at Shechem", *HTR*, 55, 1962, pp. 357 ff.

Idem, *Shechem*, London, 1965

Y. Yadin, "A Note on Melchizedek and Qumran", *IEJ*, 15, 1965, pp. 152 ff.

H.C. Youtie, "A Gnostic Amulet with an Aramaic Inscription", *JAOS*, 50, 1930, pp. 214 ff.

R.C. Zaehner, *Zurvan*, Oxford, 1955

Idem, The Dawn and Twilight of Zoroastrianism, London, 1961

Th. Zahn, *Die Apostelgeschichte*, I (KNT, V), 2nd ed., Leipzig, 1919

J. Zandee, " "The Teachings of Silvanus" (NHC VII, 4) and Jewish Christianity", in *Studies*, pp. 498 ff.

K. Zickendraht, "ΕΓΩ ΕΙΜΙ", *TSK*, 94, 1922, pp. 162 ff.

H. Zimmermann, "Das absolute '*Egō eimi*' als die neutestamentliche Offenbarüngs-formel", *BZ*, 4, 1960, pp. 54 ff., 266 ff.

O. Zöckler, *Die Apokryphen des Alten Testaments* (KKSANT: Altes Testament, 9), Munich, 1891

J. de Zwaan, "The Use of the Greek Language in Acts", in F.J. Foakes Jackson & K. Lake, ed., *The Acts of the Apostles* (BC, I), II (Prolegomena II: Criticism), London, 1922, pp. 30 ff.

Indexes

Index of Scriptural Citations
Subsuming Passages from the Apocrypha of the Old Testament

Genesis

ch. i	77
i.1	83f., 207, 233, 290 n. 96, 315 n. 153, 316, 317 n. 156 and n. 159
i.2	310f.
i.3	78, 280
i.3–5	287
i.6	78
i.6f.	311
i.6–8	289 n. 96
i.7	311
i.7ff.	312
i.9	284
i.9–13	289 n. 96
i.14	78
i.20ff.	267
i.26	16, 121 n. 140, 198, 199, 201, 204ff., 212ff., 217, 218, 219, 220, 237, 329 n. 189
i.26f.	268, 269, 270, 291 n. 102, 294, 296 n. 113
i.27	204, 206, 207, 208 nn. 36ff., 230, 268, 269
i.27f.	267
i.31	202 n. 28
ch. ii	205
ii.2	83, 207, 233 n. 82
ii.4	234, 253, 254
ii.5	234
ii.7	203, 204, 209, 210f., 219, 230, 233, 234, 237, 242, 268, 284, 329 n. 189
ii.8	209, 272

iii.4f.	294
iii.5	266 n. 31
iii.22	208, 282, 283 n. 73
iv.1	316 n. 154
iv.15	201
v.1	208 n. 38
v.24	135
ch. vi	328 n. 188
ix.6	208
ix.26	188
xi.5	204
xi.7	201, 204, 214
xii.2	246
xii.5	244
xiv.19	247
xiv.19,22	221
xv.5	246
xv.17	202
chs. xviii f.	15
xxvi.24	126
xxviii.10ff.	41 n. 47
xxviii.13	110
ch. xxx	74
xxxv.1ff.	41 n. 47
xxxv.14ff.	41 n. 47
xlii.11	268
xlviii.15f.	201
xlviii.16	193
xlix.24	175

Exodus

ii.4	207
ii.11	119
ch. iii	330
iii.1–iv.17	90
iii.12ff.	154

iii.13	144	xxxii.4	235
iii.13f.	124	xxxii.34	223
iii.14	126 n.152, 255 n.32	xxxiii.2	147
iii.14f.	79	xxxiii.2ff.	175
iii.14ff.	125 n.151	xxxiii.7ff.	223
iii.15	144	xxxiii.9	224
iv.1ff.	154	xxxiii.11	194
iv.2f.	117	xxxiii.14	175
iv.10	90	xxxiii.15	308
iv.17	117	xxxiii.20	110, 190
iv.20	117	xxxiii.21	122, 131, 190
iv.22	318 n.161	xxxiii.22	190
iv.28	144	xxxiv.2ff.	190
vii.1	89	xxxiv.6f.	229
vii.8ff.	117	xxxiv.28	132, 141 n.185
viii.25	221	xl.34	224, 238 n.89
viii.26ff.	221	xl.38	223
xi.4f.	225		
xi.5f.	225	*Leviticus*	
xii.12	225	xviii.6	85
xii.23	225	xxiv.16	126 n.151
xii.29	226	xxvi.46	147f.
xiii.21	223		
xiv.16	118	*Numbers*	
xiv.19	178 n.310, 223, 224	iv.20	238 n.89
xiv.21	118	ix.15ff.	223
xiv.24f.	228	xi.25	223
xv.1ff.	228	xii.5	223
xv.3	227f.	xii.7	151 n.211
xvi.10	178 n.310, 224	xii.8	190, 194, 284, 295
xvii.5ff.	118		n.112
xvii.8ff.	118	xii.10	223
xviii.20f.	226	xiii.16	149
xx.2	227	xiv.14	223
xx.17	37	xvii.7	223, 224
xx.18	61	xx.16	223
xxiii.20	223	ch. xxi	6
xxiii.20f.	86, 110, 146f., 149,	xxiv.17	52 n.80
	224f., 314, 318	xxvii.12	131
xxiii.21	300, 308		
ch. xxiv	191 n.348	*Deuteronomy*	
xxiv.1	307f.	iv.36	86
xxiv.10	190, 227, 228 n.69, 280	iv.37	175, 176
	n.65	iv.39	186
xxiv.15f.	92 n.38	v.18	37
xxiv.16f.	224	v.28b−29	61, 62
xxiv.17	224	v.28b−31	62, 122 n.143
xxviii.4	320	v.30f.	62
xxviii.36ff.	320	v.31	122, 134
xxviii.41	146 n.199	vi.4	264
xxix.42	223	xi.13	148
xxix.43	223	xi.14	147

xi.26ff.	37 n.28
xi.29	37
xii.3f.	250 n.22
xii.5	86, 238 n.89, 256 n.32
xii.11	86, 256 n.32
xiv.23f.	86
xvi.11	86
xvii.15	272
xviii.15, 18	47, 62 n.117, 67 n.130, 120, 122
xviii.18ff.	152
xviii.18–22	62, 122 n.143
xxvi.36	86
xxvii.2ff.	37
xxvii.4f.	37 n.28
xxxi.10ff.	37 n.28
xxxi.15	223
xxxi.30	89
ch. xxxii	237
xxxii.3a	233, 234
xxxii.3b	82
xxxii.6	82f.
xxxii.12	235, 236, 237
xxxii.29	266 n.30
xxxii.36	82
xxxii.39	17
xxxiii.1	113
xxxiii.2	194
xxxiv.1ff.	116
xxxiv.5	132, 134, 141 n.185
xxxiv.6	130

Joshua
viii.30	37 n.28
xxiv.25ff.	37 n.28
xxiv.33	40

Judges
i.22ff.	40
ii.1ff.	177
vi.8	144 n.191
vi.19	144 n.191
vi.34	96
xx.18	40
xx.26ff.	40
xx.27	40
xxi.2ff.	40

I Samuel
iii.3	40
iv.1ff.	40
x.3	40, 41 n.47

x.5	165
vii.16	40
xix.18–24	165
xxv.9	85

II Samuel
vii.13	87

I Kings
ii.19	272
iii.2	87
v.7	87
viii.12ff.	87
ix.3	87
ix.7	87
xii.32	40
xvi.24	30
ch. xix	116 n.126

II Kings
iii.15	165
ix.11	165
xv.19f.	29
ch. xvii	28, 43
xvii.24	30
xvii.24-41	43
xvii.26	28, 30
xvii.28	40
xvii.29	31
xvii.33	28
xvii.41	28
xxi.7	87
xxiii.15	40

I Chronicles
iv.23	209
vi.5ff.	39
xii.18	96
xxi.16	86, 225

II Chronicles
xx.8	87
xxiv.20	96
ch. xxx	29
xxxiv.6	40
xxxiv.9	29
xxxv.18	29
xxxvi.15f.	148

Ezra
ii.28	40
iv.1ff.	30
iv.2, 8ff.	29

Nehemiah

i.9 (LXX)	256 n. 32
vii.32	40
ix.18	235
xii.10f.	32
xii.11	32
xii.22	32
xiii.28	36
xiii.28f.	32

Job

i.6ff.	328 n.186
ii.1ff.	328 n.186
iv.16	284
v.1	193

Psalms

viii.2	86
viii.5	205, 207
viii.10	86
xiv.1	266 n. 30
xx.1	85
xxix.3	310
xxxiii.4	256
xxxiii.6, 9	76 n. 2, 249
xxxvii.25	312, 313 n.139
xliv.6	85
liv.3	85, 175
liv.6f.	85
lxvii.5	254 n. 28
lxxxii.1	186
lxxxiv.7	87
lxxxix.5	85
lxxxix.27	318 n.161
cii.25	317 n.159
civ.7	249
civ.31	312
cx.1	124 n.148, 292, 293, 305, 317 n.159
cxv.17	131
cxviii.10f.	85
cxxxii.2	175
cxxxii.5	175
cxlviii.13	85

Proverbs

viii.22	315 n.153, 316, 317 n.159
viii.30	316
xviii.10	85

Ecclesiastes

iv.8	264
v.5	309

Song of Songs (Canticles)

i.3	251 n.22

Isaiah

	175
i.24	175
vi.8	144, 148
vii.8	29
ix.6 (LXX)	318 n.161
xi.12	29
xxvi.4	254
xxx.27	85, 225 n. 32
xli.4	125 n.151
xlii.8	119
xliii.7	94 n.49
xliii.10	125 n.151
xliii.13	125 n.151
xliii.25	125 n.151
xliv.6	266 n. 30
xliv.24	194, 236, 265
xlvi.4	125 n.151, 266 n. 30
xlvi.9	17
xlviii.12	125 n.151
xlix.26	175
li.6	125 n.151
li.12	125 n.151
lii.14	284
lix.2	242
lx.16	175
lxi.1	144

Jeremiah

i.7	144
iii.22	309
v.22	209, 210
vii.12 (LXX)	256 n. 32
xxiii.5f.	29
xxvii.5	175
xxx.3	29
xxxi.5	29
xxxi.17ff.	29
xxxii.17	175
xli.5	29

Ezekiel

ch.i	179, 279 n.61, 323
i.10	304
i.15ff.	320

i.26	7, 177, 276, 279, 291
i.27	319
i.28	177, 280, 320
ii.3	144
vii.2	320
viii.3	320
ix.3	276 n.52
ix.3f.	177f.
ix.4	100, 101 n.71
x.1	276 n.52
x.4	276 n.52, 320
ch. xxxvii	210
xxxvii.15ff.	29
chs. xl ff.	38
xliii.7	256 n.32

Daniel

iii.19	270
iv.14	206
vi.2ff.	327 n.184
ch. vii	279 n.61, 297 n.116
chs. vii f.	279 n.61
vii.2–14	279 n.61
vii.9	279 n.61, 319
vii.9f.	321
vii.9ff.	293 n.104
vii.13	292
vii.13(LXX)	313 n.139, 319
vii.15–27	279 n.61
viii. 11 (LXX)	327
viii.15ff.	279 n.61
viii.16	259 n.8
ix.21	259 n.8, 279 n.61
ch. x	320
x.4ff.	279 n.61
x.5	279 n.61
x.6	319
x.13	259 n.8, 327
x.16	279 n.61
x.20	259 n.8
x.21	327
xii.1	259 n.8
xii.1ff.	327
xii.6ff.	279 n.61

Joel

ii.26	85
iii.5	109

Amos

ii.7	85
iv.4	41 n.47

Haggai

i.12	144 n.191
i.12f.	148
ii.10ff.	30 n.7

Zechariah

i.12	193
ii.12	144 n.191
iii.1ff.	328 n.186
vi.12	287
vii.2f.	40 n.42
ix.13	29
x.6f.	29

Malachi

i.11	85
iii.1	116 n.126
iv.5	116 n.126

IV Ezra (II Esdras)

vi.40	289 n.96

Tobit

xii.12, 15	193

Wisdom of Solomon

ii.24	74
v.5	142 n.186
vii.22	288
vii.25	316 n.154
viii.1	288
viii.4	288
viii.5f.	288
ix.1	76 n.2
ix.1f.	288
ix.2	288
ix.2f.	273
ix.4	293 n.104
ix.9	288
ix.10	293 n.104
x.1f.	274, 285f.
x.3	274
x.15, 17ff.	228
x.17	178 n.310, 318 n.160
xi.17	288
xviii.15f.	86, 225, 255 n.32

Sirach (Ecclesiasticus)

i.4	316 n.154
i.9	316 n.154
i.26	36
xv.14ff.	282f.

xxiv.3	316 n.154, 318 n.160
xxiv.4	178 n.310, 318 n.160
xxiv.5f.	318 n.160
xxiv.8	· 316 n.154
xlii.15	76 n.2
xlviii.10	116 n.126
xlix.16	273
l.26	30

II Maccabees

iii.38f.	176
v.22f.	30
vi.1ff.	36
xi.6	327 n.184
xi.8	327 n.184

Prayer of Manasseh

1–3	249

Matthew

iii.10	328
iv.18	170
x.5f.	163
xi.14	117 n.126
xi.27	214
xiii.41f.	328
xiv.27	126
xviii.10ff.	116 n.126
xxii.30	142 n.186
xxiv.5	128
xxvi.64	179 n.315
xxvii.63ff.	136 n.175
xxviii.19	110

Mark

i.10	96
vi.14f.	116 n.126
vi.50	126
viii.28	116 n.126
ix.4	116 n.126
xii.35–40	293 n.104
xiii.6	127
xiii.26	292 n.104
xiv.62	124 n.148, 167 n.277, 179 n.315, 292 n.104

Luke

ch. i	115
i.5ff.	115
i.15ff.	115
i.76ff.	115
ii.32	296 n.112

iii.15ff.	114
iv.6	75
x.16	148
xxi.8	127
xxii.69	190, 191

John

i.1f.	108
i.1ff.	76 n.2, 255 n.32
i.3	195, 317 n.159
i.10	195
i.14	103 n.81, 295 n.112
i.17f.	153
i.18	108
i.35ff.	116
iii.12	153
iii.13	153
iii.15	155
iii.17	154
iii.23	115
iv.5	164
iv.20	38
iv.42	154
iv.46	305
v.24f.	295 n.112
v.36	154
v.37	153, 295 n.112
vi.14	117 n.126
vi.17	155
vi.20	126
vi.29ff.	154
vi.31	117 n.126
vi.32	153
vi.46	153
vii.16	152
vii.18	152
vii.28f.	154
viii.24, 28	125
viii.26	152
viii.55	154
viii.58	125, 126 n.151
x.15	154
x.30	126 n.151
x.31ff.	126 n.151
x.33	126 n.151
xi.25f.	143
xi.40	295 n.112
xii.23	126 n.151
xii.28	126 n.151
xii.31	75 n.162, 328
xii.41	295 n.112
xii.47	154

xii.49	152
xiii.19	125
xiv.6ff.	154
xiv.24	152
xiv.30	75 n.162
xvi.11	75 n.162
xvii.3	153 n.218
xvii.6	126 n.151
xvii.8	153 n.218
xvii.11f.	126 n.151
xvii.24	295 n.112
xvii.25	154
xviii.4ff.	127
xx.17	138

Acts

i.8	163
iii.2	191
v.36	166
v.38f.	170
v.41	110
vi.13f.	124 n.148
vii.38	194, 260 n.16
vii.55f.	293 n.104
vii.56	124 n.148
ch. viii	iii
viii.4–25	166
viii.5	164
viii.5–13	162
viii.8	164
viii.9	164
viii.9b	166
viii.10a	164
viii.10	166, 167 n.277, 168, 172 n.292, 175, 190, 191
viii.10b	166
viii.11	164
viii.14	163
viii.18f.	163
viii.25	163
ix.31	163
xv.3	163
xv.15	170

Romans

v.12ff.	294
vi.1ff.	143, 155
x.12	109
xiii.14	96

I Corinthians

viii.6	317 n.159
x.1f.	116
xv.12	55
xv.19	143 n.190
xv.22	294
xv.29	95
xv.32	143 n.190
xv.45	294
xv.51f.	143

II Corinthians

iv.4	75 n.162, 270
xii.2ff.	309
xii.3f.	273

Galatians

iii.19	194
iii.27	96

Ephesians

i.17	296 n.112
i.21	297 n.114
ii.2	75 n.162
vi.12	75 n.162

Philippians

ii.6	270
ii.6–8	294
ii.6–11	293ff.
ii.9	97
ii.9ff.	95
iii.12	143 n.190
iii.21	296 n.112

Colossians

i.15	270, 316 n.153
i.15–20	315ff.
i.16	316 n.153
i.16f.	195
i.17	316 n.153
i.18	316 n.153

I Thessalonians

iv.15	143

II Thessalonians

ii.2	143

I Timothy

ii.4	274
iii.6	328 n.186

II Timothy
ii.18   143

Titus
ii.13   296 n.112

Hebrews
. i.2f.   195 n.14, 317 n.159
i.3   82 n.18, 296 n.112
i.3f.   297 n.114
i.6   318 n.161
i.10   195, 317 n.159
ii.2   194
ii.16ff.   184
iii.1−6   150
iv.14−x.18   151
iv.15   183
v.1   183
v.2   183
v.4f.   183
v.6   184
v.7ff.   183
v.10   184
vi.20   184, 185
ch.vii   184
vii.3b   184
vii.17   184
vii.21   184
xi.3   76 n.2

James
ii.1   295 n.112

I Peter
iv.14   296 n.112
v.8   328 n.186

I John
v.19   75 n.162

III John
7   110

Jude
9   260 n.16, 328

Revelation
i.5ff.   293 n.104
i.8   255 n.32
i.13   295 n.112
iv.7   304
vii.2ff.   101
vii.9   293 n.104
ix.4   101
ch. xi   116 n.126
xii.1−6   327
xii.7ff.   328
xii.7−9   327
xii.9   74f.
xii.10   328 n.186
xii.10−12   327
xii.13−17   327
xiv.1   101, 279 n.61
xiv.6   279 n.61
xiv.14   279 n.61
xiv.15   279 n.61
xiv.15−17   279 n.61
xiv.18   279 n.61
xiv.19   279 n.61
xix.12f.   255 n.32
xx.1−3   252
xx.3   75

Selected Index of Names and Subjects*

Abel, as the Kabod, 276f.

Abisha ben Phinehas, the dream of, 135f., 190 n.348

Abraham, the patriarch, effected a magical act of creation, 243f.; possessor of the Name of God, 246f.

Adam, 333; type of Moses, 90f.; his lost "image" restored by Moses, 93f.; created in the image of the angels, 94 n.45, 208 n.38; androgynity of, 208 n.37; his creation depicted, 210f.; creation of, 230 f., 233f.; said not to have been

---

* The index does not contain references which would be evident from the table of contents.

active in the creation, 264 f., 266 n. 31; created after God's hypostasized Image, 268 n. 36, 269; as represented by Philo, 271; installed as king, 271 f.; worshipped by the angels, 271 f., 273 n. 46; glorification of, 271 ff.; rival of Satan, 273 n. 46; restitution of, 274 f., 282 f., 285 f.; enthroned in heaven, 274 f., 275 f.; and the Son of Man, 275 n. 50; and the Anthropos, 275 n. 50; as the Kabod, 275 f., 277 f., 282 ff.; identical with God's "Image", 272, 277 f.
See also "Anthropogony/Anthropology".
Adamas, 267, 269; his function in the creation, 267, 284
Adam Kadmon, 278 n. 59
Adoil, 287 ff.
Adonai, the "Little", 302, 304
See also "YHWH (Yaho, Iao)".
Agnōstos theos, 107
Aher. See "Elisha ben Abuya".
Ahriman, 13, 14
Aion, 13, 14, 286 n. 83, 289 n. 95; name of the Kabod, 282, 288
Akatriel Yah (YHWH), 188 n. 339, 276
Alexander the Great, and the Samaritan temple, 32, 33 ff.
Alexandria, Dositheans in, 48
Alexandrian Jewish philosophy, 8
Al-Ilfan, 52 n. 80
Ammonius, 335
Angels, demiurgic, 14, 16, 214 f., 216 ff., 337; of the nations, 73, 217; evil, in Elchasaitism, 73; in Simonianism, 74; as "powers", 111, 177, 200; and hypostases, 177; communicated the Law, 194; created on the first day, 194; said not to have been created on the first day and active in the creation, 194, 265; addressed by God in *Gen.* i. 26, 205 ff.; in Simonianism, 214 f.; in Gnosticism, 323 f.
Angel of the Lord, iii, 18, 24, 333 f., 336 f.; created the body of man, 230 f.; by the Magharians, 329 f.
See also "Kabod", "YHWH (Yaho, Iao)".
Angel of the Presence, 323, 324; vouchsafed Moses a revelation, 260
See also "Prince of the Presence".
Angelology, Samaritan, 192 f.; Philonic, 200 f.

Anthropogony/Anthropology, Philonic, 198 ff., 268; Platonic, 199 f.; Jewish, 210 f., 212, 220, 237; Simonian, 213 f.; Gnostic, 217 ff.; Samaritan 222, 230 f., 232 ff.
Anthropomorphism, the problem of, 9 f., 18, 190, 214, 330, 332, 333 f.
Anthropos, 7, 267, 269, 275 n. 50, 291 n. 102; and Philo's heavenly Man, 270
Antinomianism, Jewish and Samaritan, 6, 62; Simonian, 61, 62 f.; Dosithean, 64 f.; Elchasaite, 66 f.
Antiochus IV Epiphanes, 39
Antisemitism, "metaphysical", 3, 4
Apelles, 14, 215
Apocalypticism, and Gnosticism, 13
Apolytrōsis, Valentinian sacrament of, 96 f.
Apostle, in Mandeism, 156; in Manicheism, 160
Aqiba, Rabbi, and the Samaritans, 22
Archons, 322 nn. 170 f., 323 ff.
Archontics, 303, 324
Ark, 40
Arukhaz, 289 n. 96
Ascension, 153; of Moses, 122 ff., 130 ff.; of Simon, 137 ff.; of Adam, 281 ff.; of Jesus, 292 ff.; of Enoch, 292, 297 f.; of visionaries, 179, 308 f.
Ayeh (Asher Ayeh). See "I am (who I am)".

Baal-Kronos, 12
Baba Rabba, 45, 56, 196, 232; opposed by the Subuai, 69 f.
Baptism(al rites)/Baptizers, in Samaritan sectarianism, 21, 69, 115 n. 122; specifically Dosithean, 68; in Samaritanism in general, 68 n. 135, 69, 70 n. 141; Elchasaite, 68 f.; Ebionite, 69; initiation of, 97 ff.
Basilidean Gnosticism, drawn upon by Irenaeus in his description of Simonianism, 129
Ben Zoma, 310 ff.
Bereshith, 315 n. 153, 316 f.
Besalel, mastered the demiurgic letter combination, 244, 246
Bethel, 28, 34, 36, 40 f., 43; name of Mt. Gerizim, 41
Bridal Chamber, Valentinian sacrament of, 306 f.

Calendar, Samaritan disputes concerning, 46 n.62, 63f., 70f.

Carpocrates/Carpocratianism, 14, 16, 20

Cerinthus, 6, 7, 11, 14, 16, 215f., 221f., 337

Christianity, and Judaism, 5, 15f.; and Gnosticism, 15; and Samaritanism, 196 See also "Jewish Christianity".

Chronos, 13, 14

Cleobius, 20, 22, 47

Creed, Samaritan, 37; Nicene, 108

Cuthean(s), 31, 32, 35 n.23

David, suppressing the Tehom by means of the Name of God, 250ff.

Decalogue, Samaritan addition to, 37, 61f.

Defter, 77 n.7

Demiurge, Gnostic, iii, 3, 4, 7ff., 75, 215ff., 303, 313; Platonic, 9, 12, 15, 197, 332f., 334, 336; of the Magharians, 330; of al-Nahawendi, 332

Devil, 74f., 219f.; fettered, 252; opposed his father, Sabaoth, 303 See also "Samael", "Satan".

Dositheans/Dositheism, iii, 20, 21 n.3, 22, 39, 222f.; name of, 46 n.62, 53; asceticism of, 66 n.128, 222; angelology of, 190, 192f.

Dositheus, associated with Simon Magus, iii, 47f.; his rival, 114f., 117, 119f.; possessor of Moses' rod, 117ff.; in the *Three Steles of Seth*, 215f.; said not to have died, 129f., 136; as the Prophet like Moses, 48, 63, 117, 119, 130

Doxa, synonymous with *morphē*, 284; with *toar*, 284; with *eidos*, 295 n.12 See also "Eikōn".

Dualism, Gnostic, 3, 17, 19, 23, 75, 338; Platonic, 12, 202, 203 n.29, 334f., 336; Iranian, 15; Jewish, 19, 211f.; Zurvanite, 26; Philonic, 201ff. See also "Demiurge".

Ebal, Mt., 27

Ebionites/Ebionitism, 20 n.83, 64, 67 nn. 129f.

Egō eimi, spoken by Simon, 114, 124, 125f., 127; spoken by Jesus, 124ff. See also "I am (who I am)".

Eidos, synonymous with *eikōn* and *homoiōsis* in *Gen.* i.26 and identical with the Logos in Philo, 268 n.36; sy-

nonymous with *morphē*, 269, 295 n.112; with *doxa*, 295 n.112

Eikōn (= *şelem*), synonymous with *morphē*, 269f.; with *homoiōsis/demuth*, 270 See also "*Eidos*", "Image", "*Tabenith*".

Elchasai, as the Prophet like Moses, 67, 160f.; as the Kabod and the final manifestation of Christ, 67f., 180, 181

Elchasaitism, 65ff., 72f.; and Manicheism, 72, 159, 161

Eleazar, son of Aaron, 27, 38, 39, 40

Elephantine papyri, 32, 36

Eli, 27, 38, 39

Elijah *redivivus*, 116 n.126

Elisha ben Abuya, 23 n.90, 202 n.28, 276, 309f.

Elohim, denoting the angels, 94 n.45, 208 n.38, 214f., 217; name of Moses, 124; of Melchizedek, 186; in Justin the Gnostic, 216, 305; in Philo, 227, 335f.

Elohist, traditions of, continued in Samaritanism, 42, 190, 225f.

Ennoia, in Simonianism, 215

Enoch, 333; as the Son of Man, 277 n.56, 292; as Metatron, 297f.; possessor of the Name of God, 297ff.; installed as God's viceroy, 298ff.

Ephraim, 27, 43

Essenes, 20, 39, 46 n.62, 52 n.79, 71 n.144; and the Magharians, 330f. See also "Qumran/Qumranians".

Eschatology, Simonian, 65, 74f.; Elchasaite, 67, 73; realized, 143; in Dositheism, 53ff. See also "Resurrection", "Standing One".

Exile, and return, of the Northern tribes, 28f.; of the Judaeans, 29f.

Ezra, 30

Form, divine. See "*Eidos*", "*Morphē*", "*Tabenith*", "*Toar*".

Gabriel, 193, 259; secret name of Ptahil, 261f.; demiurge in Mandeism, 261ff.; secret name of Hibil, 262f.; identical with the one "like a son of man" in *Daniel*, 279 n.61

Gayomart, 275 n.50

Geradamas, 278 n.59

Gerizim, Mt., 27, 30, 37f., 42, 64, 164,

237 n. 89
See also "Temple, Samaritan".
Glory, divine. See *"Doxa"*, "Kabod", *"Yeqara"*.
Gnosticism/Gnostics, 3f., 7f.; origin of, iii, iv, 3, 4, 10f.; pre-/proto-, iv, 9 n. 31, 337 n. 216; definition of, 3 n. 6; and Samaritanism, 55ff.
God, of the Old Testament, of the Jews, 16, 17, 18, 217ff.
Gorathenians (Gorothenians), 20, 21

Hand, divine, hypostasized, 288
Hekaloth mysticism. See "Merkaba/Merkaba mysticism".
Helena, Simon's companion, 61, 167 n. 275, 171
Hemerobaptists, 20, 21; and John the Baptist, 115 n. 122
Heresy/Heretics, Jewish, 23 n. 90
See also "Sects".
Herod the Great, 30
Hibil, demiurge in Mandeism, 262
Homoiōsis (= demuth), synonymous with *eikōn/ṣelem*, 270f.; with *morphē*, 269f.
See also "Image".
Hypostasis, 112; definition of, 262
Hyrcanus, John, 27, 45, 46, 47, 164

"I am (who I am)", divine name, 79 f., 90, 98 n. 59, 125, 246, 248, 252
See also *"Egō eimi"*.
Iao. See "YHWH (Yaho, Iao)".
Ieu, 306
Image, divine, 267, 268; „vested" Adam and Moses, 90, 93f.; hypostasized, 268 n. 33, 269, 277f.; interchangeable with "form" and "likeness", 269f.
Israel, angel, 189, 314
Ithamar, son of Aaron, 27, 38

Jacob, 333; as the Kabod, 188 n. 339
Jacob-Israel, angel, 188f., 314f., 317f.
Jaldabaoth, 11 n. 45, 12, 218, 219f., 303, 304, 313; as a lion, 321f., 324ff.
James the Just, 20 n. 83; speaks of "the Great Power",167, 169, 179 n. 315
Jesus (Christ), 10, 16, 47; "vested" with the Name of God, 95, 97; baptism of, 95f., 97; identical with the Name of God, 96, 106ff.; Logos, 109, 255 n. 32; Kyrios, 109, 292f., 296; Angel, 124

n. 148, 148f., 189, 314; speaking *Egō eimi*, 125ff.; possessing the Name of God, 125ff., 255 n. 32, 293, 296; Apostle, 148ff.; "sent", 152, 154, 154f.; as the Kabod, 180f., 295, 333, 337; active in the creation, 195f., 218, 315ff.; as the Son of Man, 292, 295; ascension of, 292ff.; and Adam, 293f., 296f.; as Wisdom, 288, 315ff.
Jewish Christianity, and Gnosticism, 10f.; and Samaritanism, 65ff.
Jews, and Judaism, and Gnosticism, iii, 3ff.; and Christianity, 5, 15f.; Hellenistic, 9 n. 31; (Judaeans) and Samaritans (Northerners), 22, 37f., 42, 44, 47
John the Baptist, 47, 48; associated with Dositheus and Simon, 114ff.; as a messianic figure, 114ff.; the "power of the Little Iao" incarnated in, 301f.
Joseph, called by divine names, 174f.
Joshua, 27; as the Prophet like Moses, 122, 135 n. 169
Justin the Gnostic, 5, 7, 11, 216, 305

Kabbalism/Kabbalists, Shekina in, 22; the Kabod in, 278
Kabod, hypostasized, 7, 19, 67 n. 131, 87 n. 29, 177ff., 333f., 337; as the creator, 19, 281ff.; and the Angel of the Lord, 177f., 276, 319f.; the "Power", 179f.; earthly appearance of, 180ff., 189f.; identical with the Angel of the Lord in Samaritanism, 223, 224f., 229f., 238 n. 89; in the P source, 223; vicegerent of God, 225f., 228; intermediary at the giving of the Law, 229f.; Adam as, 275f., 277f.; Abel as, 276f.; as the "image" or "likeness of God", 278, 280; identical with the Son of Man, 278f.; as *phōs*, the primordial light, 280, 287, 289f.; possessor of the Name of God, 284f.; radiant body of, 290f., 319; Jesus as, 295
See also *"Phōs"*.
Karaites, 331f.
Kebala, 237 n. 89
Kofer ba-ikkar, 23 n. 90, 261
Kyrios, used of Jesus, 109, 292f., 296; in Philo, 110, 227, 335f.
See also "YHWH (Yaho, Iao)".

Law (Torah), 4, 5, 6, 10; in Simonianism, 60ff.; alterations of, in Samaritan sectarianism, 63ff.; in Elchasaitism, 66f.; in Ebionitism, 67 n.129; associated and even identified with the Name of God, 111, 250 n.22; given through angelic intermediation, 194, 215, 228, 261f.

Leontocephaline, Mithraic, 13f.

Likeness, divine. See "Image".

Logos. See "Jesus (Christ), Logos", "Philo, his Logos".

Lord of the world. See "Ruler of the (this) world".

Magharians, 18, 214

Manasseh, tribe of, 27; priest expelled by Nehemiah, 32, 33ff., 43

Mandeans/Mandeism, 5 n.10, 21 n.84, 156ff., 261ff.

Man (of God), title of Moses, 93 n.42, 113; of Simon Magus, 112f.

Mani/Manicheism, 159ff.; dualism of, 17, 72; Elchasaite connection of, 72, 159, 161

Marcion/Marcionitism, 14, 15, 20, 215, 221

Masbotheans, 20, 21, 47

Melchizedek, "the Great(est) Power", 183; identical with Michael, 185f.; as Elohim, 186; identified with Shem, 187

Melchizedekians, 183ff.

Menander, 14, 15, 16, 20, 55; immortality doctrine of, 142ff.; baptism of, 142, 143, 155; as the Prophet like Moses, 144, 153ff.; "sent", 153f.

Meristae, 21 n.83, 182 n.324

Merkaba/Merkaba mysticism, 6f., 19, 178ff., 187 n.334, 277 n.55, 303f.

Metatron, 262 n.23, 276 n.53, 310, 312; crown of, 245, 300; enthroned, 276 n.53, 298, 309; possessor of the Name of God, 297ff., 308; the "Little YHWH", 298, 300, 308; as the Angel of the Lord, 300, 308

Michael, 173 n.293, 193; identical with Melchizedek, 185f.; Israel's guardian angel, 217, 327; head of the demiurgic angels, 217, 323ff.; brought revelation to Moses, 260; heavenly high priest, 313, 321; fused with Metatron, 321;

possessor of the Name of God, 321; adversary of Satan, 326ff.

Minim, 21, 23 n.90; occupied with *Gen.* i.26, 204, 206

Monarchianism, 182 n.324

Morphē, denotes the heavenly Man, 267, 269, 283f., 290 n.99; synonymous with *eikōn/ṣelem* and *homoiōsis/demuth*, 269f.; with *doxa*, 284; with *eidos*, 295 n.112.
See also *"Tabenith"*, *"Toar"*.

Moses, 333; in Gnosticism, 5, 6; light of, in Samaritanism, 59 n.109; "vested" or "crowned" with the Name of God, 83, 87ff.; with light, 89, 90ff.; role in the creation, 91 n.36; as king, 92f.; "Man (of God)", 93 n.42, 113; "vested" with the image of God, 93f.; revealer of God, 111f.; as the Name of God, 111f.; staff of, 117f.; attained angelic or divine nature, 122, 123f., 131ff.; ascension of, 122ff.; "Standing One", 122ff.; "Elohim", 124; translation of, 130ff.; enthroned, 135f., 190 n.348, 191 n.348; "Son of the house (of God)", 140 n.183, 150f.; heavenly high priest, 141, 151; *imitatio* of, 141; baptism of, 143f.; Apostle, 144ff.; as the Angel of the Lord, 146f.

Naar, 312, 320

Naassenes, 6, 11, 75 n.160

Nablus, 27

Nahawendi, Benjamin ben Moses al-, 332

Name of God, hypostasized, iii, 24, 85ff., 95f., 176f., 285; abbreviation of, seen as the creative instrument, 79, 82f., 253ff.; localized in the sanctuary, 86f.; identical with the Spirit, 96, 102; with the Son, 96, 106ff.; "Hidden", 97, 98, 101f., 257, 258, 259, 261, 285, 299; "Seal" or "Sign" of, conferred upon the initiand, 98ff.; "tabernacling" of, 103 n.81, 255 n.32; possessed by Simon Magus, 112ff., 124ff.; inscribed upon Moses' rod, 118f.; possessed by Jesus, 125ff., 255 n.32, 293, 296; possessed by Mani, 162; basic constituent in letter combinations used in magical creation acts, 245f., 247f., 300; possessed

by the heavenly Man, 284f.; and the Son of Man, 297 n.116
Nasareans, 21 n.83, 66f.
Nazirate/Nazirs, 66 n.128
Neapolis, Flavia, 27
Nehemiah, 30, 32f.
Northern Kingdom/Northerners, 28, 29, 30, 36, 40, 41, 42f.
Numenius, 336

Old Testament, 9, 10, 18
Onias III, 39
Ophites (Ophians), 11f., 75 n.160, 218; the diagram of, 323ff.
Orphicism, the demiurge in, 13f., 289 n.95
Ossenes, 21 n.83, 71 n.144

Pentateuch, Samaritan, 42
Peter, apostle, 163
Phanes, 13, 14, 289 n.95
Philip, apostle, 162f.
Philo, his Logos, demiurgic function of, 8, 286, 287, 334; the "Name", 109, 269; Kyrios, 110, 335f.; identified with the Angel of the Lord, 110, 314 n.145; as a heavenly Man, 268f., 287; as the Image of God, 268 n.36, 269; many names of, 269, 287, 314, 315, 332f.; theodicee in, 198ff. ; angels in, 200f.; "powers" in, 200, 227, 335f.
See also "Adam, as represented by Philo", "Anthropogony/Anthropology, Philonic".
Phinehas, son of Eleazar, 27, 39, 40
Phōs, the heavenly Man, 191 n.348, 280f., 320
See also "Kabod".
Pillars of the world, Ebionite doctrine of, 67 n.130, 182 n.324
Platonism/Platonists, 12, 19, 196f., 198, 199f., 201f., 332ff.
Power, hypostasized, the "Great", 10, 57 n.99, 58f., 67, 113; "Hidden", 67, 180; synonymous with "Glory", 67 n.131, 179f.; synonymous with "angel", 111, 177, 200
See also "Philo, "powers" in".
Priesthood, Samaritan, 27, 38ff.
Prince of the Presence, 189, 321
See also "Angel of the Presence".

Prince of the world. See "Ruler of the (this) world".
Prophet like Moses, 47, 48, 62, 63, 64, 67, 130
Prophet, the "True", 59, 67 nn.29f., 150, 156
Prophetical canon/Prophets, in Simonianism, 61f.; in Samaritanism, 62
Prosōpon, 112
Ptahil, 261f.

Qumran/Qumranians, 21 n.84, 46 n.62, 52 n.79, 331

Religionsgeschichtliche Schule, iii, 3, 275 n.50
Resurrection, 38; Dosithean views of, 48ff., 53ff.
See also "Eschatology", "Standing One".
Ruler of the (this) world, 75, 312

Sabaoth, the "Little", 302; opposed by his son, the devil, 303; enthronement of, 303f.; as the Kabod, 304; and Adam, 304
Sadducees/Sadduceism, 31f., 38, 39
Sadoq/Sadoqites, 31f., 38f.
Sakla(s), 219, 266 n.30
Samael, 219; opposed by Michael, 328
See also "Devil", "Satan".
Samaria, name of, 30; city of, 33, 43
Samaritanism/Samaritans, iii, iv, 6, 20ff.; name of, 30f., 66 n.128; and Gnosticism, 55ff.; and Christianity, 196; preserving an ancient halakha and aggada, 197; polemics against binitarianism in, 195ff., 221f.
Sampseans, 69
Sanballat, 32f., 35, 36
Sar ha-Panim. See "Prince of the Presence".
Satan, 7, 13, 14, 16; adversary of Michael, 217, 326ff.; fettered, 252; cast down from heaven, 303, 326ff.
See also "Devil", "Samael".
Satornil, 14, 15, 16, 20, 216f., 326
Saturn, 12, 326
Seal of the prophets, 160
Sebaste (Augusta), 30
Sebueans, 21, 69ff.
Sects, Jewish, 20f.; Samaritan, 20ff., 47, 52 n.80, 53ff., 63ff., 69ff.
See also "*Minim*".

Seth, 59 n.109, 94 n.48
Sethians, 6, 59 n.109
Severus, 14, 303, 326
Shaliḥ, 54f., 64
Shaman, 137, 139
Shamerim (Shomerim), 31, 66 n.128
Shechem, 27, 29, 30, 33, 34, 36, 41, 42, 43, 164
Shechemites, 34f.
Shekina, 22, 178, 190 n.347, 295 n.112
Shem, 187f.
Shem ha-Mephorash. See "Name, Hidden".
Shem ha-Meyuḥad, 107
Shemyaza, 258
Shetiya Stone, 250
Shiloh, 27, 29, 39, 40
Shiur Qoma, 7, 180, 277 n.55
Shomron, 30
Shutaf, God's "associate" in the creation, 195, 213, 234ff.; and Apostle, 264ff.
Simon Magus/Simonianism, iii, 5, 10, 11, 14, 15, 16, 20, 22, 23, 24, 47, 48, 55, 56, 57, 58, 59, 60ff., 67, 74, 137ff., 159 n.242, 213ff., 333, 337
Son of Man, 124 n.148, 153, 179 n.315, 275 n.50, 277 n.56, 292, 297 n.116, 312, 319f.; identical with the Kabod, 279, 337; an angel, 279 n.61
Sophia. See "Wisdom".
Souls, incorporeal, identified with angels by Philo, 200; pre-existent, active in the creation, 209f.
Spirit, identical with the Name, 96, 102; with the Son, 96; demiurgic, 310f.; as angel, 311, 318 n.160
Standing One, 55, 56ff., 120ff., 138, 139ff., 169
Stephen, the speech of, 124 n.148
Substantia, 108
Subuai (Sabuai), 69f.

Tabenith, hypostasized, 268 n.36
See also "*Morphē*".
Tabernacle, in Samaritanism, 27, 64, 65, 118; in Mandeism, 158
Taheb, 61 n.117, 118
Teacher of Righteousness, 116, 331
Tehom, checked by means of the Name of God, 249ff.

Temple, Samaritan, building of, 32ff., 40ff.; destruction of, 46f.; Judaean, rebuilding of, 29f., 35f.
Ten Words of Creation, 77f.
Tetragrammaton. See "YHWH (Yaho, Iao)".
Thomas, the "twin of Christ", 149
Toar, 284, 290; synonymous with *doxa*, 284; with *morphē*, 284
See also "*Morphē*".
Treasure of Life, 157, 161
Trickster, 16
Two Powers (in heaven), iv, 17, 197, 227f., 310, 319f.

Valentinianism, 6, 15, 17, 95ff., 305, 306f.

Wadi Daliyeh, 33
Wisdom, hypostasized, 7, 15, 22, 156 n.231, 215, 288, 315ff.

Xenocrates, 333, 334f.

Yahoel, 289; the Angel of the Lord, 318; the Kabod, 319f.
Yeqara, 178, 190 n.347
YHWH (Yaho, Iao), distinct from the highest God, 14f., 24, 108, 226f., 233f., 237, 285, 299, 306f.; abbreviation of, seen as the creative instrument, 79, 82f., 253ff.; part of the name of an intermediary, 188 n.339, 262 n.23, 276, 289, 318ff.; its utterance checked the dragon of chaos, 249; the "Little", 298, 300ff., 308, 318
See also "Kyrios", "Name of God".
Yima, 275 n.50
Yophin (-Yophaphin), 262 n.23
Yoṣer Bereshith, 19, 281, 291
Youth, 297f., 312
Yusuf ben Salama, 46

Zalmoxis, 137, 139
Zeus, cult of, on Mt. Gerizim, 171; Simon worshipped in images of, 171; in Xenocrates, 334f.
Zurvan-Chronos, 12, 14